Lecture Notes in Computer Science 9354

Commenced Publication in 1973
Founding and Former Series Editors:
Gerhard Goos, Juris Hartmanis, and Jan van Leeuwen

More information about this series at http://www.springer.com/series/7410

Rajat Subhra Chakraborty · Peter Schwabe
Jon Solworth (Eds.)

Security, Privacy, and Applied Cryptography Engineering

5th International Conference, SPACE 2015
Jaipur, India, October 3–7, 2015
Proceedings

 Springer

Editors
Rajat Subhra Chakraborty
Indian Institute of Technology Kharagpur
Kharagpur
West Bengal
India

Jon Solworth
Department of Computer Science
University of Illinois at Chicago
Chicago
IL, USA

Peter Schwabe
Digital Security Group
Radboud University Nijmegen
Nijmegen, Gelderland
The Netherlands

ISSN 0302-9743   ISSN 1611-3349   (electronic)
Lecture Notes in Computer Science
ISBN 978-3-319-24125-8   ISBN 978-3-319-24126-5   (eBook)
DOI 10.1007/978-3-319-24126-5

Library of Congress Control Number: 2015948708

LNCS Sublibrary: SL4 – Security and Cryptology

Springer Cham Heidelberg New York Dordrecht London

Printed on acid-free paper

Springer International Publishing AG Switzerland is part of Springer Science+Business Media
(www.springer.com)

Preface

It gives us immense pleasure to present the proceedings of the Fifth International Conference on Security, Privacy, and Applied Cryptography Engineering 2015 (SPACE 2015), held during October 3–7, 2015, at the Malaviya National Institute of Technology (MNIT), Jaipur, Rajasthan, India. This annual event is devoted to various aspects of security, privacy, applied cryptography, and cryptographic engineering. This is indeed a very challenging field, requiring the expertise from diverse domains, ranging from mathematics to solid-state circuit design.

This year we received 57 submissions from 17 different countries, out of which 17 papers were accepted for presentation at the conference after an extensive review process. The submissions were evaluated based on their significance, novelty, technical quality, and relevance to the SPACE conference. The submissions were reviewed in a "double-blind" mode by at least three members of the Program Committee. The Program Committee was aided by 28 sub-reviewers. The Program Committee meetings were held electronically, with intensive discussions over a period of almost two weeks.

The program also included 9 invited talks and tutorials on several aspects of applied cryptology, delivered by world-renowned researchers: Jacob Appelbaum (Eindhoven University of Technology/The Tor Project), Daniel Bernstein (Eindhoven University of Technology/University of Illinois at Chicago), Claude Carlet (University of Paris 8), Trent Jaeger (The Pennsylvania State University) Rafael Boix Carpi & Vishwas Raj Jain (Riscure BV), Tanja Lange (Eindhoven University of Technology), Sri Parameswaran (University of New South Wales), Sandeep Shukla (Indian Institute of Technology Kanpur), Graham Steel (Inria), and Petr Švenda (Masaryk University), We sincerely thank the invited speakers for accepting our invitations in spite of their busy schedules.

Over the last five years, the SPACE conference has grown considerably, especially with respect to its appeal to the international applied security research community. SPACE 2015 was built upon the strong foundation laid down by dedicated academicians and industry professionals. In particular, we would like to thank the Program Chairs of the previous editions: Debdeep Mukhopadhyay, Benedikt Gierlichs, Sylvain Guilley, Andrey Bodganov, Somitra Sanadhya, Michael Tunstall, Marc Joye, Patrick Schaumont, and Vashek Matyas. Because of their efforts, SPACE is already in the "must submit" list of many leading researchers of applied security around the world. It still has a long way to go, but it is moving in the right direction.

Like its previous editions, SPACE 2015 was organized in co-operation with the International Association for Cryptologic Research (IACR). We are thankful to the Malaviya National Institute of Technology (MNIT) for being the gracious hosts of SPACE 2015. The conference was sponsored by the Defence Research and Development Organisation (DRDO), under the auspices of the Ministry of Defence (Govt. of India). The other sponsors are ISEA and MNIT. We would like to thank them for their generous financial support, which has helped us to avoid steep hikes in the registration fees in comparison with previous editions, thus ensuring wider participation, particularly from the student community of India.

There is a long list of volunteers who invested their time and energy to put together the conference, and who deserve accolades for their efforts. We are grateful to all the members of the Program Committee and the sub-reviewers for all their hard work in the evaluation of the submitted papers. Our heartiest thanks to Cool Press Ltd., owners of the EasyChair conference management system, for allowing us to use it for SPACE 2015. EasyChair was largely instrumental in the timely and smooth operation needed for managing such an international event. We also sincerely thank our publisher Springer for agreeing to continue to publish the SPACE proceedings as a volume in the Lecture Notes in Computer Science (LNCS) series. We are further very grateful to all the members of the Local Organizing Committee for their assistance in ensuring the smooth organization of the conference, especially M.S. Gaur, M.C. Govil, R.B. Battula, V. Laxmi, M. Tripathi, L. Bhargava, E.S. Pilli, and S. Vipparthi from MNIT Jaipur. Special thanks to our General Chairs, Adrian Perrig and Debdeep Mukhopadhyay, for their constant support and encouragement. We would also like to thank Vashek Matyas for managing the tutorials and the pre-conference workshop. We would like to thank Swarup Bhunia and R.B. Battula for taking on the extremely important role of Publicity Chairs. No words can express our sincere gratitude to Debdeep Mukhopadhyay for being constantly involved in SPACE since its very inception, and being the person most responsible for SPACE reaching its current status. We thank Durga Prasad for his commendable job in maintaining the website for SPACE 2015, and timely updates.

Last, but certainly not least, our sincere thanks go to all the authors who submitted papers to SPACE 2015, and to all the attendees. The conference is made possible by you, and it is dedicated to you. We sincerely hope you find the program stimulating and inspiring.

October 2015   Rajat Subhra Chakraborty
                                                        Peter Schwabe
                                                         Jon Solworth

Message from the General Chairs

We are pleased to extend a warm welcome to all participants of the Fifth International Conference on Security, Privacy, and Applied Cryptographic Engineering 2015 (SPACE 2015). Over the years, SPACE has progressed to become a major international forum for researchers to present and discuss ideas on challenging problems in the ever expanding field of security and applied cryptography. SPACE 2015 was held at Malaviya National Institute of Technology (MNIT), Jaipur, Rajasthan, India, during October 3–7, 2015, in cooperation with the International Association for Cryptologic Research (IACR). The proceedings was published by Springer as an LNCS volume.

The importance of SPACE, as a platform for the development and discussions on "engineering the system right" by researchers working in the areas of security, privacy, and applied cryptography, needs to be seen in the light of the revelations of Edward Snowden. These revelations demonstrate the ease with which current deployed security in today's connected world can be subverted. Society's trust in the increasing use of information systems in critical applications has been severely eroded. This is a challenge that needs to be addressed by the research community, to ensure that the necessary assurance about the adequacy of security technologies can be provided.

With emerging technologies and increasing complexity of hardware and software systems, security is not confined to a single layer but needs to be addressed across layers: hardware, microarchitecture, operating system, compiler, middleware, and application software. We are happy to report that over the years there has been a steady increase in the diversity of topics of the submissions to SPACE.

The Program Chairs, Rajat Subhra Chakraborty, Peter Schwabe, and Jon Solworth, deserve a special mention for their efforts in selecting an outstanding Program Committee and conducting a rigorous review process. Our sincere thanks go to the Program Committee members and sub-reviewers for their time and efforts in reviewing the submissions and selecting high-quality papers. The main technical program is accompanied by several tutorials, invited talks, and a two-day workshop. We are extremely grateful to DRDO, MNIT, ISEA, and all the other sponsors for their generous financial support. The conference would not have been possible without their support it. Last but not least, our special thanks to the Local Organizing Committee at MNIT, especially Prof. Manoj Gaur, for ensuring the smooth operation of the conference.

We hope you benefit from excellent technical and social interactions during the conference. Thank you for your participation, and we wish you an enjoyable and productive time at the conference.

October 2015

Adrian Perrig
Debdeep Mukhopadhyay

SPACE 2015

Fifth International Conference on
Security, Privacy, and Applied Cryptography Engineering
Malaviya National Institute of Technology (MNIT), Jaipur, India.
October 3–7, 2015.

In cooperation with the *International Association for Cryptologic Research*

General Co-chairs

Adrian Perrig   ETH Zurich, Switzerland
Debdeep Mukhopadhyay   IIT Kharagpur, India

Program Co-chairs

Rajat Subhra Chakraborty   IIT Kharagpur, India
Peter Schwabe   Radboud University, The Netherlands
Jon Solworth   University of Illinois at Chicago, USA

Organizing Co-chairs

Manoj Singh Gaur   MNIT Jaipur, India
Mahesh Chandra Govil   MNIT Jaipur, India

Tutorial Chair

Vashek Matyas   Masaryk University, Czech Republic

Publicity Co-chairs

Swarup Bhunia   Case Western Reserve University, USA
Ramesh Babu Battula   MNIT Jaipur, India

Finance Co-chairs

Veezhinathan Kamakoti   IIT Madras, India
Vijay Laxmi   MNIT Jaipur, India
Meenakshi Tripathi   MNIT Jaipur, India
Lava Bhargava   MNIT Jaipur, India

Program Committee

Ehab Al-Shaer	UNC Charlotte, USA
Lejla Batina	Radboud University, The Netherlands
Ramesh Babu Battula	MNIT Jaipur, India
Rajat Subhra Chakraborty	IIT Kharagpur, India
Jean-Luc Danger	Télécom ParisTech, France
Christian Doerr	TU Delft, The Netherlands
Praveen Gauravaram	Queensland University of Technology, Australia
Sylvain Guilley	Télécom ParisTech, France
Michael Hutter	Cryptography Research, USA
Vashek Matyas	Masaryk University, Czech Republic
Debdeep Mukhopadhyay	IIT Kharagpur, India
Michael Naehrig	Microsoft Research, USA
Ruchira Naskar	IIT Kharagpur, India
Antonio de La Piedra	Radboud University, The Netherlands
W. Michael Petullo	United States Military Academy, USA
Phuong Ha Nguyen	IIT Kharagpur, India
Emmanuel S. Pilli	MNIT Jaipur, India
Atul Prakash	University of Michigan, USA
Bimal Roy	ISI Kolkata, India
Somitra Sanadhya	IIT Delhi, India
Ravi Sandhu	University of Texas at San Antonio, USA
Palash Sarkar	ISI Kolkata, India
Peter Schwabe	Radboud University, The Netherlands
Prasad Sistla	University of Illinois at Chicago, USA
Jon Solworth	University of Illinois at Chicago, USA
Mostafa Taha	Assiut University, Egypt
A. Selcuk Uluagac	Florida International University, USA
Samuel M. Weber	Carnegie Mellon University, USA

External Reviewers

Mostafa Said Sayed Abd-Elrehim
Mahmoud Abd-Hafeez
Sk Subidh Ali
Hoda Alkhzaimi
Debapriya Basu Roy
Shivam Bhasin
Rishiraj Bhattacharyya
Melissa Chase
Craig Costello
Poulami Das
Benjamin Dowling

Thomas Eisenbarth
Nitesh Emmadi
Sen Gupta
Marc Juarez
Souvik Kolay
Qinyi Li
Patrick Longa
Wouter Lueks
Ahmed Medhat
Zakaria Najm
Mridul Nandi
Harika Narumanchi

Louiza Papachristodoulou
Kostas Papagiannopoulos
Goutam Paul
Sushmita Ruj
Sami Saab
Santanu Sarkar
Laurent Sauvage
Habeeb Syed
Michael Tunstall
Praveen Vadnala

Abstracts of Invited Talks

Boring Crypto

Daniel J. Bernstein

Department of Computer Science
University of Illinois at Chicago,
Chicago, IL 60607–7045, USA
djb@cr.yp.to

Abstract. Crypto is a thriving research area, full of excitement, which is exactly what the cryptographic user doesn't want.

Introduction to Security Analysis of Crypto APIs

Graham Steel

Cryptosense
19 Boulevard Poissonire
75002 Paris, France
graham.steel@cryptosense.com

Abstract. Using cryptographic APIs in a secure way has become a core competence in software development thanks to the more and more widespread use of crypto. In this tutorial we will give a short introduction to the security analysis of a crypto API. In particular, we will look at logical and cryptanalytic attacks on the most widely used API for key management in cryptographic hardware, PKCS#11. The tutorial will include implementing attacks on a software simulator of a Hardware Security Module (HSM). Some basic knowledge of C will be required.

The Tor Network: Free Software for a Free Society

Jacob Appelbaum

Department of Mathematics and Computer Science
Technische Universiteit Eindhoven
P.O. Box 513, 5600 MB Eindhoven, The Netherlands
jacob@appelbaum.net

Abstract. A detailed introduction to the Tor network, the software and open research questions for the world's largest anonymity network.

Post-Quantum Cryptography

Tanja Lange

Department of Mathematics and Computer Science
Technische Universiteit Eindhoven
P.O. Box 513, 5600 MB Eindhoven, The Netherlands
tanja@hyperelliptic.org

Abstract. Quantum computers will change the security of currently used cryptographic systems – the security level of most symmetric systems will drop to about half while the effects on RSA and ECC will be much more significant: the best quantum attacks run in polynomial time. This talk will highlight categories of other public-key systems that are significantly less affected by quantum computers and thus form the core or post-quantum cryptography.

Inferring Programmer Expectations to Protect Program Execution

Trent Jaeger

Department of Computer Science and Engineering
The Pennsylvania State University
344 IST Building
University Park, PA 16802, USA
tjaeger@cse.psu.edu

Abstract. Inferring Programmer Expectations to Prevent Confused Deputy Attacks Efficiently: Privileged programs are often vulnerable to confused deputy attacks, which enable an adversary to trick such programs into misusing their privileges. For example, a web server may be able to read the password file, so it must be careful not to be tricked into serving the password file to web clients. However, programmers have often failed to avoid creating confused deputy vulnerabilities, which account for 10-15% of vulnerabilities reported each year. Operating systems designers have proposed various mechanisms to prevent adversaries from exploiting these vulnerabilities, but these defenses either fail to account for programmer intent, require extensive program modifications, perform poorly, or incur false positives. We identify a fundamental reason that confused deputy vulnerabilities exist – a mismatch between programmer expectations and the actual deployment in which the program runs. In this talk, I will discuss a new approach that consists of two main tasks. First, we develop methods to build knowledge of the programmer expectations of security from the program. Second, we develop an enforcement mechanism that uses such knowledge to block confused deputy attacks efficiently. We evaluated our approach on several widely-used programs on Linux and found that programmers have many implicit expectations. Using programmer expectations, we found mismatches with deployments that led us to discover two previously-unknown vulnerabilities and a default misconfiguration in the Apache webserver. Our enforcement mechanism, called a Process Firewall, enforces programmer expectations for less than 5% overhead, thus blocking many confused deputy vulnerabilities efficiently and in a principled manner.

Side Channel Attacks: Types, Methods and Countermeasures

Sri Parameswaran

School of Computer Science and Engineering
University of New South Wales
Sydney NSW 2052, Australia
sridevan@cse.unsw.edu.au

Abstract. Deep devastation is felt when privacy is breached, personal information is lost, or property is stolen. Now imagine when all of this happens at once, and the victim is unaware of its occurrence until much later. This is the reality, as increasing amount of electronic devices are used as keys, wallets and files. Security attacks targeting embedded systems illegally gain access to information or destroy information. Advanced Encryption Standard (AES) is used to protect many of these embedded systems. While mathematically shown to be quite secure, it is now well known that AES circuits and software implementations are vulnerable to side channel attacks. Side-channel attacks are performed by observing properties of the system (such as power consumption, electromagnetic emission, etc.) while the system performs cryptographic operations. In this talk, differing power based attacks are described, and various countermeasures are explained.

Contents

Efficient Protocol for Authenticated Email Search

Sanjit Chatterjee, Sayantan Mukherjee, and Govind Patidar

Department of Computer Science and Automation,
Indian Institute of Science, Bangalore, India
{sanjit,sayantan.mukherjee,govind.patidar}@csa.iisc.ernet.in

Abstract. Executing authenticated computation on outsourced data is currently an area of major interest in cryptology. Large databases are being outsourced to untrusted servers without appreciable verification mechanisms. As adversarial server could produce erroneous output, clients should not trust the server's response blindly. Primitive set operations like union, set difference, intersection etc. can be invoked on outsourced data in different concrete settings and should be verifiable by the client. One such interesting adaptation is to authenticate email search result where the untrusted mail server has to provide a proof along with the search result. Recently Ohrimenko et al. proposed a scheme for authenticating email search. We suggest significant improvements over their proposal in terms of client computation and communication resources by properly recasting it in two-party settings. In contrast to Ohrimenko et al. we are able to make the number of bilinear pairing evaluation, the costliest operation in verification procedure, independent of the result set cardinality for union operation. We also provide an analytical comparison of our scheme with their proposal which is further corroborated through experiments.

Keywords: Authenticated email search, outsourced verifiable computation, bilinear accumulator, pairing-based cryptography.

1 Introduction

With the advent of internet, the amount of data available to an individual has gone up tremendously and is getting larger everyday. The idea of *cloud computing* allows us to keep the data in a third party server and access it as and when required. If the owner asks for certain function of data, the cloud server is expected to return the result correctly. To ensure correctness of the performed operation, the server needs to send cryptographic proof of correctness of the result as well. The proof must be efficiently verifiable by the client without performing the requested operation locally.

In a concrete setting like email, service providers (e.g. gmail, hotmail etc) provide huge amount of space to store the emails received by a client. Currently, clients trust the email server unconditionally not to modify or delete any mail or create new mails. For a search query on the email database (e.g. finding mails

© Springer International Publishing Switzerland 2015
R.S. Chakraborty et al. (Eds.): SPACE 2015, LNCS 9354, pp. 1–20, 2015.
DOI: 10.1007/978-3-319-24126-5_1

received on a specific date and/or from a specific person etc), the client also trusts the server blindly to return the correct result. Traditional authentication mechanisms (e.g. MAC or signature schemes) allow us to compute authenticated information of the *whole* dataset. Naturally they cannot be used to a scenario where an untrusted server computes *function* of the dataset and provide authenticated information about the result. Papamanthou et al. [1] presented the problem as a conjunction query of two *search parameters* i.e. keyword and time interval. In [2] a solution was proposed to verify mails that were received during a specific time interval and contains specific set of keywords. The solution is based on the idea of set operation verification technique proposed in [1]. The server has to return the result along with a cryptographic proof of the result which ensures *completeness* (all relevant mails are returned) and *soundness* (only relevant mails are returned).

Related Works. Some of the previous works on verifiable computation were done in [1–3]. In [1] the first public verification of set operations in a three-party settings with optimal efficiency was proposed. They posed a concrete problem [1, Section 11] to verify result of email search based on time interval and keyword (to search mails that were received during a specific time interval and contain specific set of keywords). Ohrimenko et al. [2] proposed a solution using the framework provided in [1]. The problem was instantiated in [2] using Merkle Hash Tree [4], Inverted Index List and Time Interval Tree. Informally speaking, they created an inverted index list for the keywords and the mails containing them and the time interval tree to efficiently find the mails received in different time intervals and a Merkle hash tree of the *dataset*. The client keeps some secret information to itself and makes search query to the server. Computation of the result is done using the inverted index list and the time interval tree. Along with the result, appropriate accumulation values [5], Merkle proof [4] of those accumulation values and witness [1] of correctness of the result are sent as proof. In [3] a verifiable computation mechanism for set operation was constructed which is more powerful than the basic framework [1] in terms of functionality as different composite queries were allowed. These extra functionalities [3] however incur extra cost in terms of computation and communication. Therefore we concentrate on [1] as the base framework that satisfies our requirement with better efficiency.

Our Contribution. We solely concentrate on the problem of email searching in this paper. The functionalities required from the email searching mechanism are discussed in Section 2.3. For this specific problem, we use [1] as the base of our improvement. Our primary observation is that in case of email searching, there are only two entities involved – Server[1] and Client. The key point to note is that client is not only the owner of the emails but also the verifier of the search results. Being the owner of the data client can use its own secret information to verify the result of the query efficiently. Thus allowing the client to have a small secret information leads to significant efficiency improvement as

---

[1] See Section 2.3 for the exact trust assumption of email server.

we can reduce number of bilinear pairing evaluations in intersection verification. In case of union operation we make a distinction between time interval-based union and keyword-based union where the former is essentially union verification for disjoint sets. Separate union verification for disjoint sets (i.e. time interval-based union) and general sets (i.e. keyword-based union) results in efficiency improvement for both. In general, it is reasonable to assume that the *cardinality of result set* ($|R| : R = \cup_i\{$mails containing keyword $k_i\}$) is greater than the *cardinality of query* (ℓ : query $= \{k_1, k_2, \ldots, k_\ell\}$ where k_i is a keyword). The union verification mechanism we propose achieves complexity with respect to *cardinality of query* which is a significant improvement over complexity with respect to *cardinality of result set* [2]. We improve upon the existing technique of email searching [2] based on these observations which is verified analytically as well through experiments.

Organization of the Paper. The rest of the paper is organized as follows. Section 2 deals with basic data structures, cryptographic primitives and a brief overview of the system. Next we present our proposal to efficiently verify basic operations like intersection, union and present a new scheme to verify email search query in Section 3. In Section 4, efficiency of our proposed framework, in terms of theoretical as well as practical, is briefly described. Section 5 concludes the paper with some possible future directions.

2 Preliminaries

This section describes basic cryptographic primitives and data structures that are used in our construction. Also, it provides a brief overview of the system.

2.1 Cryptographic Primitives and Complexity Assumptions

Let $\mathbb{G}$ and $\mathbb{G}_T$ be cyclic multiplicative groups of large prime order p and g be an arbitrary generator of group $\mathbb{G}$.

Bilinear Pairings. $e : \mathbb{G} \times \mathbb{G} \to \mathbb{G}_T$ is a cryptographic bilinear pairing [6] with the following properties:

1. Bilinearity: $e(X^a, Y^b) = e(X, Y)^{ab}$ where $a, b \in \mathbb{Z}_p$ and $X, Y \in \mathbb{G}$.
2. Non degeneracy: $e(g, g) \neq 1$.
3. Computability: The function e is efficiently computable.

Remark: The scheme in this work, similar to its precursors [1, 2], is described in symmetric pairing setting. Our primary motivation is a proof of concept instantiation of authentication mechanism for email search. For real world applications, the protocols should be recast in the most efficient Type-3 asymmetric pairing setting [7, 8].

Polynomial Interpolation with Fast Fourier Transform (FFT). Let $\prod_{i=1}^{n}(s + x_i) = \sum_{i=0}^{n} a_i s^i$ be a degree-n polynomial. The function interpolatePolyFFT computes the coefficients a_i for $0 \leq i \leq n$ with $O(n \log n)$ complexity given x_i ($1 \leq i \leq n$) [9]. If group elements $g, g^s, g^{s^2}, \ldots, g^{s^n}$ are given, any polynomial of degree upto n in exponent of g can be computed, given $(x_1, x_2, \ldots, x_n)$ without knowing the value of s.

Bilinear Accumulation Value. In [5], *accumulation value* of a set was computed based on bilinear pairing. The bilinear accumulator is a collision resistant accumulator [5] with efficient update operation. For a set $X = \{x_1, x_2, \ldots, x_\ell\}$, secret key s and arbitrary group generator g, the accumulation value ($Acc(X)$) is computed as $g^{\Pi_{x \in X}(s+x)}$. For a list (L) of sets, accumulation ($acc[i]$) and *digest* of ith element is $Acc(L[i])$ and $Acc(L[i])^{(s+i)}$ respectively.

Merkle Hash Tree. The Merkle Hash Tree [10] is a binary tree where each leaf node is hash of data value and each non-leaf node is hash of concatenation of its children's hash values. The hash function that computes hash of each node is collision resistant which results in unforgeability of *Merkle Hash value* (the hash value of the root of the tree). For a Merkle hash tree having root u_0, the *Merkle proof* of leaf u_ℓ is the cover [11] of u_ℓ. computeMerkleProof computes the Merkle proof as the ordered set (sibling(u_ℓ), sibling($u_{\ell-1}$), ..., sibling(u_1)) for the path ($u_0, u_1, \ldots, u_{\ell-1}, u_\ell$). Given a Merkle proof for u_ℓ, verifyProof ensures any malicious activity on the dataset can be identified efficiently.

Interval Tree. Interval Tree [12], as the name suggests, is an ordered tree with reference to different intervals. Given any event, it efficiently answers all the intervals when the event happened. It is implemented as a height balanced binary tree.

Bilinear q-Strong Diffie-Hellman Assumption. Given a bilinear pairing instance $(\mathbb{G}, \mathbb{G}_T, p, e, g)$ and the group elements $g, g^s, g^{s^2}, \ldots, g^{s^q} \in \mathbb{G}$ for $s \in_R \mathbb{Z}_p^*$, where $q = \text{poly}(\kappa)$, there is no polynomial time adversary that can output $(a, e(g, g)^{1/(s+a)})$ for some $a \in \mathbb{Z}_p$ except with negligible probability $\text{neg}(\kappa)$, for some security parameter κ. In other words, q-BSDH problem is intractable.

q-Strong Diffie-Hellman Assumption. For group $\mathbb{G}$, given $g, g^s, g^{s^2}, \ldots, g^{s^q}$ for $s \in_R \mathbb{Z}_p^*$, no polynomial time adversary can compute $(a, g^{1/(s+a)})$ efficiently. For a bilinear q-Strong Diffie-Hellman group $\mathbb{G}$, q-strong Diffie-Hellman (q-SDH) problem is intractable.

2.2   Authenticated Data Structure

In [1] the notion of authenticated data structure $auth(\mathcal{D})$ was defined to be the authenticated information of plaintext data structure ($\mathcal{D}$) that is efficiently searchable. An authenticated data structure supports queries and updates efficiently and provides efficient cryptographic mechanism to verify the results. We instantiate $\mathcal{D}$ using inverted index data structures indexed by keywords and time interval and $auth(\mathcal{D})$ using Merkle Hash Tree [10]. Informally speaking, the authenticated data structure we consider is a collection of five polynomial-time algorithms - genkey (generates secret (sk) and public key (pk)), setup (generates $auth(\mathcal{D})$ from $\mathcal{D}$ and Merkle hash value (r) of $\mathcal{D}$), update (performs insertion or deletion of data and correspondingly updates the authenticated data structures), query (performs search based on the query (q) and computes the proof ($\Pi(q)$) of the result ($\alpha(q)$)) and verify (verifies the result ($\alpha(q)$) using the proof ($\Pi(q)$)).

Correctness and Security Definitions. We follow the correctness and security definitions of an authenticated data structure from [1, Definition (2),(3)]. The correctness of the authenticated data structure ensures that $\mathsf{verify}(q, \Pi(q), \alpha(q), r, pk)$ accepts except with negligible probability when $\alpha(q)$ is correct result of q. The security of the authenticated data structure ensures $\mathsf{verify}(q, \Pi(q), \alpha(q), r, pk)$ accepts with negligible probability when $\alpha(q)$ is not a correct result of q.

2.3 System Overview

This section describes the system model and the protocol to be followed to compute set operations.

2.3.1 System Model

The system model we consider is same as [2] with two entities involved.

Client. The *client* processes keywords present in each mail and the time when it was received and constructs inverted index data structure (S). It constructs a Merkle hash tree where digest of each element of S is assigned a different leaf. The client keeps the secret key (s) and Merkle Hash value (r) to itself and sends the authentication information to the server.

Server. The *server* keeps the files (i.e. emails) and reconstructs all the data structures (the inverted index list of keywords, the interval tree [12] of time intervals and the Merkle hash tree). For a valid query asked by the client, the server computes the result using the inverted index data structures. Then it computes the cryptographic proof of the result based on the accumulation values and the Merkle hash tree.

In any email-based communication mechanism, the clients are the end users who send and receive emails. Each client needs to have a mail account in the mail server where all the mails received by that client will be stored and can be accessed only by itself when required. Our protocol deals with storing of emails in the server as well as getting back correct result computed by the server for a valid query. The server is trusted to deliver the emails correctly to the client when it is received for the first time. Once received, the client needs to keep track of the email so that if it is deleted or modified or not included in a search query result in spite of satisfying the query, the client can correctly identify the wrongdoing of the server. In general, one can consider a two-party scenario where client stores data on a cloud server and later executes queries on that data.

Here the client searches are based on predefined keywords and time intervals. On a valid query, the server answers with the mails that satisfy the query and corresponding accumulation values, Merkle proof and witnesses. The client verifies the accumulation values using received Merkle proof. The verification mechanism usually computes large number of bilinear pairings which in terms of complexity overshadows all other group operations performed – exponentiation, multiplication etc.

The search query can be abstracted as set operations naturally. For example, the query to find mails that contain keywords 'urgent' and 'cryptography' and was received in February, 2015 is expressed as $S[\text{'urgent'}] \cap S[\text{'cryptography'}] \cap \uplus_{t_i}(S[t_i])$ where t_i is i^{th} day of February, 2015. The client should verify witness for set union, intersection and composite operation.

2.3.2 Basic Operations
The basic set operations, the system described in Section 2.3.1 should support, are set union and set intersection verification.

Set Union. Set union verification was described in [1]. The proof of set union contains different witnesses along with the accumulation value and Merkle proof. The *membership witness* ensures that every element of resultant union is contained in some set for which client requested the union. The *subset witness* ensures that all the sets client requested union for, are subsets of the resultant union.

Set Intersection. The proof of set intersection contains different witnesses along with the accumulation value and Merkle proof. The *subset witness* [1] ensures that the result is a subset of all the sets for which the client requested intersection. The *complete witness* [1] ensures that there is no other element that is present in all the sets but not included in the intersection result. We use verification technique as mentioned in [1] after suitably modifying it for two-party settings.

2.3.3 Email Search
Verification of email search result is conceived by the basic set operations – set union verification and set intersection verification. On a query 'to find the mails that contain all the keywords $\{k_1, \ldots, k_\ell\}$', the server computes the result by computing *intersection* of the sets $S[k_1], \ldots, S[k_\ell]$. Along with the result, it also sends back corresponding accumulation value, Merkle proof, subset and complete witness. On a query 'to find the mails that were received in the time interval $[t_{begin}, t_{end})$', the server computes *union* of each of the $S[t_i]$-s where $t_{begin} \leq t_i < t_{end}$ and each t_i is distinct time interval. Along with the result, it also sends back corresponding accumulation value, Merkle proof, membership and subset witness. In reality, both the queries are often combined where the search is performed based on both the keywords and the time period. In [2] a solution was proposed based on a heuristic. They suggested to compute $I_k = \{$mails that contain all the keywords $\{k_1, \ldots, k_\ell\}\}$ and use it iteratively ($I_k \cap S[t_i]$ for all $t_{begin} \leq t_i < t_{end}$) to compute the result. The result is sent to the client along with the proofs and witnesses [2, Algorithm 4]. We propose algorithms to achieve better complexity in terms of bilinear pairing evaluation performed by the client while verifying the search result.

3   Proposed Protocol

In this section, we describe our proposal which improves upon the protocol proposed in [2].

Broadly, the client creates inverted index list (*IL*) indexed by unique keywords and interval tree (*IT*) indexed by distinct time intervals where $IL[k] = \{$mail-ids that contain keyword $k\}$ and $IT[t] = \{$mail-ids received in time interval $t\}$. Then it creates the *dataset* (*S*) (i.e. plaintext searchable data structure ($\mathcal{D}$)) by *merging* both *IL* and *IT*. The client then chooses secret key (s) uniformly at random from $\mathbb{Z}_p^*$ and computes the Merkle hash value (r) where *digest* ($D[i]$) of each entry of the dataset ($S[i]$) is assigned to a different (i^{th}) leaf. To preserve the integrity of an email, the client sets hash digest of the mail content as mail-id which also allows the client to uniquely identify the mail. The client sends the data structures S and D to the server and keeps only the secret key (s) and Merkle hash value (r) to itself. The server reconstructs the data structures using the information sent by the client and performs different operations as discussed in the following sections.

3.1   Setup

Similar to the setup function in [2], the client chooses an arbitrary generator $g \in \mathbb{G}$ and the secret key $s \in_R \mathbb{Z}_p^*$ using genkey function. It computes the accumulation values $Acc(S[i])$ for each $1 \leq i \leq |S|$ and computes Merkle hash value r using $D[i]$ (i.e. digest of each $S[i]$). It computes list $G = [g, g^s, g^{s^2}, \ldots, g^{s^q}]$ where $q = poly(\kappa)$ for security parameter κ. The client sends emails, S, $acc[i] = Acc(S[i])$ for each $1 \leq i \leq |S|$ and G to the server and keeps s and r to itself. Upon receiving the mails and the data structures, the server reconstructs Merkle hash tree M from $acc[i] = Acc(S[i])$ for each $1 \leq i \leq N$ and inverted index list (*IL*) and interval tree (*IT*) from S.

3.2   Update

We use the update function described in [2]. Addition or deletion of a mail is done based on the keywords present in it and the time interval it was received. Data structures IL and IT allow efficient updation of the dataset.

3.3   Intersection

The client asks the server for the mails that contain all the queried keywords ($V = \{k_1, \ldots, k_\ell\}$). The server computes the result $I = \cap_{v \in V} S[v]$ using inverted index list and computes the proof.

The server uses [2, Algorithm 2] to compute the set intersection and the accompanying proof. The proof contains *accsI* and *Mproof* which are accumulation value $acc[v]$ and Merkle proof of v respectively, $\forall v \in V$. It also contains the subset witness (*subs*) that ensures for all $v \in V$, $S[v] \subseteq I$ [1, Equation (6)]. The complete witness (*cmplt*) is also sent to prove that $\cap_{v \in V}(S[v] \setminus I) = \phi$ [1, Equation (7)].

We however, modify Algorithm 3 of [2] to improve efficiency of client verification in terms of number of bilinear pairing evaluation. We improve the verification of subsetwitness based on the observation that in two-party model the client knows the secret key s. In Algorithm 1, the client using verifyProof, verifies each of *accsI* by computing digest of each $v \in V$ and using the *Mproof* computes the root of the Merkle hash tree to compare with r. It uses *cmplt* and *subs* to ensure that mail-ids that were present in all of $S[v], v \in V$, are returned as I. Here Expo computes group element exponentiation in $\mathbb{G}$.

Algorithm 1. Verification of Set Intersection run by Client

Input: r, I, *accsI*, *Mproof*, *subs* and *cmplt*
Output: Accept/Reject
1: **for** $i \in \{0, 1, \ldots, |V| - 1\}$ **do**
2:     **if** verifyProof(r, *accsI*[i], *Mproof*[i]) rejects **then**
3:         **return** reject
4:     **end if**
5: **end for**
6: *len* = length(I)
7: *EvalPoly* = $(I[0] + s)(I[1] + s) \ldots (I[len-1] + s)$
8: **for** $i \in \{0, 1, \ldots, |V| - 1\}$ **do**
9:     *lefts* = Expo(*subs*[i], *EvalPoly*)
10:     *rights* = *accsI*[i]
11:     **if** *lefts* $\neq$ *rights* **then**
12:         **return** Reject and Abort
13:     **end if**
14: **end for**
15: *leftc* = 1
16: **for** $i \in \{0, 1, \ldots, |V| - 1\}$ **do**
17:     *leftc* $\times$ = e(*subs*[i], *cmplt*[i])
18: **end for**
19: *rightc* = $e(g, g)$
20: **if** *leftc* $\neq$ *rightc* **then**
21:     **return** Reject and Abort
22: **end if**
23: **return** Accept

Improvement. Being in a two-party settings, the client can evaluate the polynomial *EvalPoly* which allows the client to exponentiate *subs*[i] to *EvalPoly* for each $i \in [1, len]$. This results in significant reduction (see Section 4.1) of bilinear pairing evaluation as compared to [2, Algorithm 3].

Correctness. The correctness of Algorithm 1 follows from the correctness of verifyProof and witness verification.

For each $v \in V$, *accsI*[v] was returned which was used to compute digest of $S[v]$. If any of the digests was erroneous, the computed Merkle hash tree root r' will not be same as r except with negligible probability, due to collision resistant nature of Merkle hash tree. The correctness of subset and complete witness verification of Algorithm 1, as done in steps 7-14 and steps 15-22 respectively, follows from definitions [1, Section 3.1] of both the witnesses.

Security. Informally speaking, the scheme is secure if no polynomial time adversary can produce incorrect result and corresponding proof that will be verified correctly by the client except with negligible probability. Security is based on q-SDH and q-BSDH assumption as described below.

Claim 1. Under the assumption of q-SDH, given a set X and its accumulation value $Acc(X)$ no polynomial time adversary can find another set $Y \neq X$ but $Acc(Y) = Acc(X)$.

Proof. Let an adversary $\mathcal{A}$ exists that can generate $Y \neq X$ but $Acc(X) = Acc(Y)$ given a set X. We can construct a solver $\mathcal{B}$ of q-SDH problem.

Given a q-SDH problem instance $[g, g^s, g^{s^2}, \ldots, g^{s^q}]$ where $q = \mathsf{poly}(\kappa)$, $\mathcal{B}$ sends the set X and $[g, g^s, g^{s^2}, \ldots, g^{s^q}]$ to $\mathcal{A}$. $\mathcal{A}$ replies back with $Y \neq X$ such that $Acc(X) = Acc(Y)$.

As $X \neq Y$, without loss of generality $\exists\, y' \in Y$ st $y' \notin X$. Then the polynomial $(y' + s) \nmid \Pi_{x \in X}(x + s)$. By division theorem, $\Pi_{x \in X}(x + s) = q(s)(y' + s) + \lambda$ where λ is a constant. Since $Acc(X) = Acc(Y)$, $g^{\Pi_{x \in X}(x+s)} = g^{\Pi_{y \in Y}(y+s)}$ which implies $g^{q(s)(y'+s)+\lambda} = g^{\Pi_{y \in Y}(y+s)}$. Therefore $\mathcal{B}$ can compute $g^{\frac{1}{y'+s}} = g^{(\Pi_{y \neq y'}(y+s)-q(s))/\lambda}$.

$\mathcal{B}$ returns $(y', g^{\frac{1}{y'+s}})$ as the solution of the q-SDH instance. Due to hardness of q-SDH problem, such an efficient adversary $\mathcal{A}$ cannot exist except with negligible probability.

This ensures no efficient adversary can produce an incorrect result and corresponding incorrect subset witness and make the verification (steps 7-14) accept except with negligible probability.

We use [1, Lemma 6] to prove security of *complete witness* verification under q-BSDH assumption. For the sake of completeness we reproduce the proof here.

Claim 2. Under the assumption of q-BSDH, no polynomial time adversary can make complete witness verification accept wrong witness.

Proof. Let there be an adversary that generates an incomplete witness $CW[i](= g^{q_i(s)})$ corresponding to a subset witness $SW[i](= g^{P_i(s)})$ where each of $P_i(s)$ has a common factor $(w + s)$.

Then to make the client accept the verification of complete witness, $\Sigma_i q_i(s)P_i(s)$ needs to be equal to 1. As $P_i(s)$ shares a common factor $(w + s)$, there exists some polynomial $A(s)$ such that $(w + s)A(s) = 1$. Then $e(g, g)^{\frac{1}{w+s}} = e(g, g)^{A(s)}$ can be computed. It contradicts with hardness of q-BSDH problem.

3.4 Union

The client asks the server for the mails that contain any of the queried keywords $(V = \{k_1, \ldots, k_\ell\})$ or were received in any of the queried time intervals $(V = \{t_1, \ldots, t_\ell\})$. The server computes the result $U = \cup_{v \in V} S[v]$ using inverted index data structures and computes *accsU* and *Mproof* which are accumulation value $acc[v]$ and Merkle proof of v for all $v \in V$.

In case of a disjoint union query (e.g. union query on time intervals), the server sends the result (U), *accsU* and *Mproof* as described in Algorithm 2. In case of general union query (e.g. keyword-based union query), we design the server to compute the union as an iterative procedure and send back list of accumulation values of different sets as described in Algorithm 4. This kind of classification, leads to improvement in efficiency of both the cases (see Section 4.1).

3.4.1   Disjoint Union

In case of disjoint union query (e.g. time interval-based union query), the server computes the union (U) with corresponding proof in Algorithm 2 and sends them to the client.

Algorithm 2. Computation of Set Union run by Server

Input: V: $\{v : \cup_v S[v]$ is to be computed$\}$
Output: U: $S[v]$ for all $v \in V$
Output: *accsU*: $acc[v]$ for all $v \in V$
Output: *Mproof*: Merkle proof of $acc[v]$ for all $v \in V$

1: $j = 0$
2: **for** $v \in V$ **do**
3:     $U[j] = S[v]$
4:     $accsU[j] = acc[v]$
5:     $Mproof[j + +] = \mathsf{computeMerkleProof}(M, v)$
6: **end for**

The union result is sent as a list. The client verifies the accumulation values using Merkle proof, verifies $U[j]$ using the corresponding accumulation value and constructs the union result iteratively in Algorithm 3.

Algorithm 3. Verification of Set Union run by Client

Input: U, *accsU*, *Mproof* as output by Algorithm 2
Output: Computed Union

1: $j = 0$
2: **for** $v \in V$ **do**
3:     **if** $\mathsf{verifyProof}(r, accsU[v], Mproof[v])$ rejects **then**
4:         **return** Reject and Abort
5:     **end if**
6:     $acc = g^{\Pi_{x \in U[j]}(s+x)}$
7:     **if** $acc == accsU[v]$ **then**
8:         $R = R \uplus U[j]$
9:     **else**
10:         **return** Reject and Abort
11:     **end if**
12:     $j + +$
13: **end for**
14: **return** R

Correctness. The correctness of Algorithm 3 follows from collision resistance of Merkle hash tree and the resultant union is computed correctly in step 8 by the client as the sets concerned are disjoint in nature.

Security. The security of Algorithm 3 follows from Claim 1 as it ensures that no two different sets can have same accumulation value except with negligible probability.

3.4.2 General Union

In case of general union query (i.e. keyword-based union query), the server computes the union and sends it back along with the accumulation values of $S[v]$-s, Merkle proof and accumulation values ($accsA[v]$, $accsB[v]$, $accsC[v]$) as described in step 9 of Algorithm 4. In each step of iteration (v), the server computes sets as given in Table 1.

Table 1. verification list

$A[v] = PreU \setminus S[v]$ where $PreU = CurU[v-1]$ is the union computed in last iteration.
$B[v] = PreU \cap S[v]$
$R[v] = S[v] \setminus PreU$
$CurU[v] = CurU[v-1] \uplus R[v]$ where $CurU[v]$ is the union computed in current iteration.

Computation of general union and corresponding proof is described in Algorithm 4.

Algorithm 4. Computation of Set Union run by Server

Input: V: $\{v : \cup_v S[v]$ is to be computed$\}$
Output: R: $\{R[v]\}$ for all $v \in V$
Output: $accsR$: $Acc(S[v])$ for all $v \in V$
Output: $Mproof$: Merkle proof of $acc[v]$ for all $v \in V$
Output: $accsA$, $accsB$, $accsC$: $Acc(A[v])$, $Acc(B[v])$ and $Acc(CurU[v])$ for all $v \in V$
  1: $PreU = CurU[0] = \phi$
  2: **for** $v \in V$ **do**
  3:     $accsR[j] = Acc(S[v])$
  4:     $Mproof[j + +] = \mathsf{computeMerkleProof}(M, v)$
  5:     $R[v] = S[v] \setminus PreU$
  6:     $A[v] = PreU \setminus S[v]$
  7:     $B[v] = PreU \cap S[v]$
  8:     $CurU[v] = CurU[v - 1] \uplus R[v]$
  9:     compute $accsA[v]$, $accsB[v]$, $accsC[v]$ by computing the exponentiation of the polynomial representation of $A[v]$, $B[v]$ and $CurU[v]$ respectively.
 10:     $PreU = CurU[v]$
 11: **end for**

The verification technique we present here verifies union in three-party settings. The client needs to verify that for each iteration, all the conditions mentioned in Table 1 hold. The verification takes output of Algorithm 4 as input.

Algorithm 5. Verification of Set Union run by Client in three-party settings

Input: R, accsR, Mproof, accsA, accsB, accsC as output by Algorithm 4
Output: Computed Union

```
1: Res = φ
2: for i ∈ {0, 1, ..., |V| − 1} do
3:     accR = g^{Π_{x∈R[i]}(s+x)}.
4:     if verifyProof(r, accsR[i], Mproof[i]) rejects then
5:         return Reject and Abort
6:     end if
7:     if e(accsC[i − 1], accR) ≠ e(accsC[i], g) then
8:         return Reject and Abort
9:     end if
10:     if e(accsB[i], accR) ≠ e(accsR[i], g) then
11:         return Reject and Abort
12:     end if
13:     if e(accsR[i], accsA[i]) ≠ e(accsC[i], g) then
14:         return Reject and Abort
15:     end if
16:     Res = Res ⊎ R[i]
17: end for
18: return Res
```

Correctness. In verification, client needs to check:

$$e(accsC[i-1], \Pi_{x\in R[i]}(s+x)) \stackrel{?}{=} e(accsC[i], g) \tag{1}$$

$$e(accsB[i], \Pi_{x\in R[i]}(s+x))) \stackrel{?}{=} e(accsR[i], g) \tag{2}$$

$$e(accsR[i], accsA[i]) \stackrel{?}{=} e(accsC[i], g) \tag{3}$$

Equation (1) ensures that in each iteration, updation of elements ($PreU$, $R[i] \subseteq CurU$) in the union result, is performed correctly. Equation (2) ensures the membership condition ($B[i] \subseteq S[i]$) of union verification. Equation (3) ensures the subset condition ($S[i] \subseteq CurU$) of union verification. In every iteration, union result is updated correctly because of these conditions.

Even though, Algorithm 5 is devised in three-party settings, it can be recasted into two-party settings naturally. We can significantly reduce (see Table 3) the number of bilinear pairing evaluation based on the same observation (availability of secret key to the client) as suggested in the case of intersection verification (Section 3.3). To ensure correctness, the client needs to verify Expo($accsC[i-1]$, $accR$) = $accsC[i]$, Expo($accsB[i]$, $accR$) = $accsR[i]$ and $e(accsR[i], accsA[i])$ = $e(accsC[i], g)$, where $accR = \Pi_{x\in R[i]}(s+x)$.

Security. Claim 1 ensures that the server cannot send wrong $R[v]$ for all $v \in V$ except with negligible probability. Equations (1), (2) and (3) along with [1, Lemma 1] ensure that any wrong accumulation value present in either of $accsA[i]$ and $accsB[i]$ will not pass the verification except with negligible probability.

3.5 Composite Query

In case of composite query, as instantiated in [2], for any given $\{K, t_{begin}, t_{end}\}$, the server will compute $I_k = \cap_{k \in K} S[k]$ which will be used to compute $R[j] = I_k \cap S[t]$, where $tnum = |\{t \in [t_{begin}, t_{end})\}|$ and t is a time interval in between t_{begin} and t_{end} and $j \in \{1, \ldots, tnum\}$. The server sends I_k along with its proof, $R[j]\ \forall j$ and their proofs to the client. The client will verify I_k and all $R[j]$-s to compute $\cup_j R[j]$ to get back the result of the query.

In our protocol, the server computes $I_k = \cap_{k \in K} S[k]$, $T = \cup_{t \in [t_{begin}, t_{end})} S[t]$ and $R = I_k \cap T$. The server sends back I_k along with its proof, $Acc(T)$, proof of T, R and proof of R. The client will verify I_k and R. The client union verification operation needs to verify $Acc(T)$ without getting T form the server. To verify $Acc(T)$, we use *subset condition* [1, Equation (6)] in the following way and call it *superset condition*:

Let $T = S_1 \uplus S_2 \uplus \cdots \uplus S_\ell = \{y_1, y_2, \ldots, y_z\}$. The *superset condition* is to check $S_i \subseteq T,\ \forall i \in [1, \ell]$. The *completeness condition* is to ensure $\cap_{i \in [1, \ell]} (T \setminus S_i) = \phi$.

Algorithm 6. Email Search and Proof Computation by Server

Input: $K(= \{k_1, \ldots, k_r\}), t_{begin}, t_{end}$
Output: $I_k, accsI_k, MproofI_k, subsI_k, cmpltI_k$
Output: $accT, accsT, MproofT, supsT, cmpltT$
Output: $R, subsR, cmpltR$

1: $I_k = \cap_{i \in \{1, \ldots, r\}} S[k_i]$
2: $j = 0$
3: **for** $v \in V$ **do**
4:     $accsI_k[j] = Acc(S[v])$
5:     $MproofI_k[j + +] = \mathsf{computeMerkleProof}(M, v)$
6: **end for**
7: $j = 0$
8: **for** $v \in V$ **do**
9:     $subset = S[v] \setminus I$
10:     $scoeff[j] = \mathsf{interpolatePolyFFT}(subset)$
11:     $subsI_k[j] = 1$
12:     **for** $i \in \{0, \ldots, |V| - 1\}$ **do**
13:         $subsI_k[j] \times = \mathsf{Expo}(G[i], scoeff[j][i])$
14:     **end for**
15:     $j + +$
16: **end for**
17: $ccoeff = \mathsf{extendedEuclidean}(scoeff)$
18: **for** $j \in \{0, \ldots, |V| - 1\}$ **do**
19:     **for** $i \in \mathsf{length}(ccoeff[j])$ **do**
20:         $cmpltI_k[j] \times = \mathsf{Expo}(G[i], ccoeff[j][i])$
21:     **end for**
22: **end for**
23: $T = \cup_{t \in [t_{begin}, t_{end})} S[t]$
24: $j = 0$
25: **for** $t \in [t_{begin}, t_{end})$ **do**
26:     $accsT[j] = Acc(S[t])$

27:      $MproofT[j++] = \text{computeMerkleProof}(M, t)$
28: **end for**
29: $accT = Acc(T)$
30: $j = 0$
31: **for** $v \in V$ **do**
32:      $supset = T \setminus S[v]$
33:      $scoeff[j] = \text{interpolatePolyFFT}(supset)$
34:      $supsT[j] = 1$
35:      **for** $i \in \{0, \ldots, |V| - 1\}$ **do**
36:          $supsT[j] \times = \text{Expo}(G[i], scoeff[j][i])$
37:      **end for**
38:      $j++$
39: **end for**
40: $ccoeff = \text{extendedEuclidean}(scoeff)$
41: **for** $j \in \{0, \ldots, |V| - 1\}$ **do**
42:      **for** $i \in \text{length}(ccoeff[j])$ **do**
43:          $cmpltT[j] \times = \text{Expo}(G[i], ccoeff[j][i])$
44:      **end for**
45: **end for**
46: $R = I_k \cap T$
47: $Res = [I_k, T]$
48: **for** $j \in \{0, 1\}$ **do**
49:      $subset = Res[j] \setminus R$
50:      $subcoeff[j] = \text{interpolatePolyFFT}(subset)$
51:      $subsR[j] = 1$
52:      **for** $i \in \{0, 1\}$ **do**
53:          $subsR[j] \times = \text{Expo}(G[i], subcoeff[j][i])$
54:      **end for**
55:      $j++$
56: **end for**
57: $compcoeff = \text{extendedEuclidean}(subcoeff)$
58: **for** $j \in \{0, \ldots, |V| - 1\}$ **do**
59:      **for** $i \in \text{length}(ccoeff[j])$ **do**
60:          $cmpltR[j] \times = \text{Expo}(G[i], compcoeff[j][i])$
61:      **end for**
62: **end for**

The server returns $I_k = \cap_{k \in K} S[k]$, $accT = Acc(T)$ where $T = \cup_{t \in [t_{begin}, t_{end})} S[t]$ and $R = I_k \cap T$ and corresponding proofs. The verification is done by the client by verifying I_k and R using Algorithm 1. As the client does not have T (the server sent $Acc(T)$), we propose Algorithm 7 to verify $accT$ using the proof ($MproofT$, $supsT$, $cmpltT$).

Algorithm 7. Verification of time-interval-based union by Client

---

Input: r, $accT$, $accsT$, $MproofT$, $supsT$, $cmpltT$
Output: Accept/Reject
 1: **for** $i \in \{0, 1, \ldots, |V| - 1\}$ **do**
 2:      **if** verifyProof(r, $accsT[i]$, $MproofT[i]$) rejects **then**

```
 3:            return Reject and Abort
 4:        end if
 5: end for
 6: for i ∈ {0, 1, . . . , |V| − 1} do
 7:       lefts = e(sups[i], accsT[i])
 8:       rights = e(accT, g)
 9:       if lefts ≠ rights then
10:            return Reject and Abort
11:       end if
12: end for
13: leftc = 1
14: for i ∈ {0, 1, . . . , |V| − 1} do
15:       leftc × = e(sups[i], cmplt[i])
16: end for
17: rightc = e(g, g)
18: if leftc ≠ rightc then
19:       return Reject and Abort
20: end if
21: return Accept
```

Correctness. To verify I_k and R, the client uses Algorithm 1 which is correct as demonstrated in Section 3.3. The client uses Algorithm 7 to verify $T = \cup_{t \in [t_{begin}, t_{end})} S[t]$ although T is not provided. Given correct $sups[i]$ and $accsT[i]$ which correspond to partition of T (i.e. $T = sups[i] \uplus accsT[i]$), the verification satisfies. Correct $sups[i]$ and $cmplt[i]$ for all $1 \le i \le tnum$ ensures verification acceptance as each of the $S[t]$ are disjoint, sets corresponding to $sups[i], \forall i$ are also disjoint. The complete witness $cmplt$ verifies the disjointness.

Security. The verification of composite query response utilizes Algorithm 1 to verify I_k and R that was proven secure in Section 3.3. Therefore the security of verification by the client for such a combined query ($\{K, t_{begin}, t_{end}\}$) solely depends on the security of Algorithm 7.

Claim 3. Server has to send correct $accT$ to make the client accept the verification.

Proof. Let us assume the server can send an incorrect *accumulation value* ($accT'$) to make the client accept the verification. This can happen in two exhaustive way.

$\mathcal{E}1$: The server sends $accT'$ where $\exists z \in T$ but $z \notin T'$.

The verification of superset witness is done in lines [6-12] of Algorithm 7. In Algorithm 7, *lefts* depends on $accsT[i]$ which is verified by verifyProof using *MproofT*.

The server has to send such $sups[i]$ that when evaluating bilinear pairing will cancel the $(z + s)$ present in the exponent of $accsT[i]$ for some i (as $e(sups[i], accsT[i]) = e(accT', g)$) and there is no exponent $(z + s)$ in $accT'$).

Therefore the server has to compute $g^{r_i/(z+s)}$ and use it as $sups[i]$. By q-SDH assumption, computing such exponentiation of g is not possible except with negligible probability.

$\mathcal{E}2$: The server sends $accT'$ where $\exists w \in T'$ but $w \notin T$.

As $w \notin T$, none of the $accsT[i]$ will have $(w + s)$ in its exponent and $accT'$ has $(w + s)$ in its exponent. To make the client verify superset witness in steps 6-12 of Algorithm 7, all the $sups[i]$ must have a $(w + s)$ in the exponent. Therefore each of the corresponding polynomial $(P_i(s))$ of $sups[i]$ will have a zero at $(-w)$ where $1 \leq i \leq tnum$, $tnum = |\{t : t \in [t_{begin}, t_{end})\}|$. The GCD of the polynomials $(P_i(s))$ will be $m(w+s)$ where m is some polynomial.

To accept complete witness verification in steps 13-20 of Algorithm 7, the client needs $q_i(s)$, $1 \leq i \leq tnum$ st $\Sigma_i q_i(s)P_i(s) = 1$. As all the $P_i(s)$ share a common factor $(w + s)$, there exists some polynomial $A(s)$ such that $(w + s)A(s) = 1$. Then $e(g, g)^{\frac{1}{w+s}} = e(g, g)^{A(s)}$ can be computed. It contradicts with hardness of q-BSDH problem.

Union bound ensures that $\Pr[\mathcal{E}1 \cup \mathcal{E}2]$ is negligible.

4   Comparison

In this section we provide comparison between [2] and our protocol. We first provide an analytical comparison between both the protocols followed by experimental data supporting it.

4.1   Analytical Comparison

As discussed in Section 2.3.1, two parties are involved in the email search mechanism. The client has access to *secret key* (s) that can be used during verification of different queries. Number of bilinear pairing evaluation in case of intersection operation verification reduces to half (Algorithm 1). But it increases number of group exponentiation by *cardinality of the query* $(|V|)$.

Let's assume $m = $ *cardinality of the query* and $n = $ *cardinality of result set*. In general, for union, $m << n$. In Table 2 we show an asymptotic comparison of the scheme described in [1] and our scheme in case of disjoint union for two parties. In Table 3, however, we present an asymptotic comparison of scheme described in [1] and our scheme in case of general union.

4.1.1   Composite Query Verification Comparison

Here we present a comparative analysis between email search verification of [2] and our proposal. On query 'to find the mails that contain all the keywords $\{k : k \in K\}$ and were received in the time interval $[t_{begin}, t_{end}]$', let us define $knum := |\{k : k \in K\}|$ and $tnum := |\{t : t \in [t_{begin}, t_{end})\}|$.

Table 2. Comparison of number of operations required by the client for disjoint union

	[1]	Improved
Multiplication	$n - 1$	$n - m$
Exponentiation	n	m
Bilinear Pairing	$m + 1$	0
Communication cost	n	$m \log m$

Table 3. Comparison of number of operations required by the client for general union

	[1]	three party union	two party union
Multiplication	$n \log n$	$n \log n$	$n - m$
Exponentiation	$2n$	n	m
Bilinear Pairing	$2m + 2n$	$5m$	$2m$
Communication cost	n	$m \log m$	$m \log m$

Analysis of [2, Algorithm 4]. As described in [2, Algorithm 4], the server computes $I_k = \cap_{k \in K} S[k]$ and $R[j] = I_k \cap S[t]$ where t is a time interval between t_{begin} and t_{end} and sends all such $R[j]$ along with their proofs. $e(g, g)$ needed for every complete witness verification is precomputed.

To verify I_k, the client will need $2 * knum$ bilinear pairing evaluation for subset witness verification ($I_k \subseteq S[k_i], \forall k_i \in K$), $knum$ bilinear pairing computation for complete witness verification ($\cap_{k_i \in K}(S[k_i] \setminus I_k) = \phi$).

To verify $R[j]$, the client will need 4 bilinear pairings for subset witness verification (($(R[j] \subseteq I_k) \cap (R[j] \subseteq S[t])$)) and 2 bilinear pairing evaluation for complete witness verification (($(T_k \setminus R[j]) \cap (S[t] \setminus R[j]) = \phi$)). The client needs to verify every $R[j], 1 \leq j \leq tnum$ to compute their union to get back the result. Total number of bilinear pairings required to verify $R = [R[1], R[2], \dots, R[tnum]]$ is $(4 + 2) * tnum = 6 * tnum$.

Total number of bilinear pairing evaluation required is $(3 * knum + 6 * tnum)$ to verify email search query in [2].

Analysis of Verification of Composite Query (Section 3.5). Again $e(g, g)$ needed for every complete witness verification is precomputed.

To verify I_k, the client will need $knum$ group exponentiations in $\mathbb{G}$ for subset witness verification ($I_k \subseteq S[k_i], \forall k_i \in K$), $knum$ many bilinear pairing computation for complete witness verification ($\cap_{k_i \in K}(S[k_i] \setminus I_k) = \phi$) [1].

To verify T, the client will need $2 * tnum$ bilinear pairing evaluation for superset witness verification ($S[t] \subseteq T, \forall t \in [t_{begin}, t_{end})$) and $tnum$ bilinear pairing evaluation for complete witness verification ($\cap_{t \in [t_{begin}, t_{end})}(T \setminus S[t])$) [1].

To verify R, the client will need 4 bilinear pairings for subset witness verification ($R \subseteq I_k$ and $R \subseteq T$) and 2 bilinear pairing for complete witness verification (($(I_k \setminus R) \cap (T \setminus R) = \phi$) [1].

Total number of group exponentiations needed $= knum$.

Total number of bilinear pairings needed $= knum + 2*tnum + tnum + 4 + 2 = 6 + knum + 3*tnum$.

Thus our method roughly reduces number of pairing computation by a factor of $2*knum + 3*tnum$.

4.2 Experimental Results

Here we provide the experimental comparison of proposed verification protocols and [2]. The whole experiment is performed on 8-core Intel i7 3.4 GHz with 8GB RAM running 64-bit Ubuntu 12.04 and the algorithms were implemented using python. We used the pairing-based cryptographic library Charm-Crypto [13] available for python to implement the schemes. We use a symmetric curve with a 1024-bit base field ($\mathbb{F}_p$ for prime p of 1024 bit) for the bilinear groups. We have conducted the experiments on the Enron Email Dataset [14] (accessed Dec, 2014). For the experimental purpose we chose 200 random keywords from the corpus as done in [2]. We kept the interval fixed at 1 day only. The mail-id is SHA-2 hash digest of the content of the mail as mentioned in Section 3.

Table 4 shows the comparison between computation time required by the client in both the frameworks to verify email search based on intersection.

Table 4. Comparison of Intersection verification of [2] and our protocol

Cardinality of Query	Cardinality of Result	[2] (sec)	Our Protocol (sec)	Improvement Factor (X)
3	11	00.370204	00.199130	1.9
7	33	00.397503	00.227689	1.8
5	100	00.721012	00.418794	1.7
4	167	01.495034	01.392456	1.1
2	265	05.378835	04.268893	1.3

In Table 5, we compare computation time required by client in both the frameworks for verifying email search based on union of keywords.

Table 5. Comparison of Disjoint Union verification of [2] and our protocol

Cardinality of Query	Cardinality of Result	[2] (hr)	Our Protocol (hr)	Improvement Factor (X)
5	25	00:01:20.673509	00:00:00.113024	713
8	84	00:04:25.799064	00:00:00.115579	2300
10	225	00:32:20.001179	00:00:00.298521	6500
21	553	03:15:40.311964	00:00:00.446493	26300
32	1055	11:57:10.013695	00:00:01.403798	30650

Table 6 reflects comparison of computation time required by client in both the frameworks for verifying email search based on union of time intervals.

Table 6. Comparison of General Union verification of [2] and our protocol

Cardinality of Query	Cardinality of Result	[2] (hr)	Our Protocol (hr)	Improvement Factor (X)
8	174	00:22:11.700000	00:00:02.336589	570
9	238	00:40:40.063144	00:00:01.580584	1540
11	302	00:59:29.774574	00:00:01.512477	2360
14	458	02:25:33.486672	00:00:03.433091	2540
18	974	11:02:04.942754	00:02:28.052102	270

Note that amount of improvement is much higher in case of union verification query as it was mentioned in Section 4.1.

In Table 7, the comparison between verification time required by the client for email searching operation on queries that deal with both keywords and time intervals at the same time is shown.

Table 7. Comparison of Composite Query verification of [2] and our protocol

Cardinality of Query (keywords, time-intervals)	Cardinality of Result	[2] (sec)	Our Protocol (sec)	Improvement Factor (X)
(3, 17)	0	03.858381	02.454596	1.6
(4, 16)	4	03.168813	01.628256	2.0
(5, 12)	6	03.158784	01.661622	1.9
(3, 12)	8	04.744553	01.669637	2.8
(2, 20)	27	07.475947	04.155327	1.8

While our protocols always perform better than [2], the improvements are most pronounced for union operations as the number of pairing evaluation depends on *cardinality of query* rather than *cardinality of result* [2]. In case of intersection and composite query, even though the exact number of pairing evaluation is reduced, it still depends on *cardinality of result*. As mentioned in Section 3.5 and Section 4.1, there is a trade off between decrease in number of bilinear pairing and increase in number of group exponentiation which results in non-linearity in the efficiency improvement in our protocols for intersection and composite query verification.

5   Conclusion

In this paper we revisit the email search verification mechanism of [2] and propose an improved protocol. Along the way we improve efficiency of basic set union in three-party setting [1]. The proof computation by the server, although polynomial in the cardinality of a set, still takes significant time as shown in our experiments. It would be interesting to improve upon the practical computation time by the server, thereby improving the efficiency of the overall protocol.

References

1. Papamanthou, C., Tamassia, R., Triandopoulos, N.: Optimal verification of operations on dynamic sets. In: Rogaway, P. (ed.) CRYPTO 2011. LNCS, vol. 6841, pp. 91–110. Springer, Heidelberg (2011)
2. Ohrimenko, O., Reynolds, H., Tamassia, R.: Authenticating email search results. In: Jøsang, A., Samarati, P., Petrocchi, M. (eds.) STM 2012. LNCS, vol. 7783, pp. 225–240. Springer, Heidelberg (2013)
3. Canetti, R., Paneth, O., Papadopoulos, D., Triandopoulos, N.: Verifiable set operations over outsourced databases. In: Krawczyk, H. (ed.) PKC 2014. LNCS, vol. 8383, pp. 113–130. Springer, Heidelberg (2014)
4. Papamanthou, C., Tamassia, R., Triandopoulos, N.: Authenticated hash tables. In: Proceedings of the 15th ACM Conference on Computer and Communications Security, CCS 2008, pp. 437–448. ACM, New York (2008)
5. Nguyen, L.: Accumulators from bilinear pairings and applications. In: Menezes, A. (ed.) CT-RSA 2005. LNCS, vol. 3376, pp. 275–292. Springer, Heidelberg (2005)
6. Joux, A.: A one round protocol for tripartite Diffie–Hellman. In: Bosma, W. (ed.) ANTS 2000. LNCS, vol. 1838, pp. 385–393. Springer, Heidelberg (2000)
7. Chatterjee, S., Menezes, A.: On cryptographic protocols employing asymmetric pairings the role of revisited. Discrete Applied Mathematics 159(13), 1311–1322 (2011)
8. Galbraith, S.D., Paterson, K.G., Smart, N.P.: Pairings for cryptographers. Discrete Applied Mathematics 156(16), 3113–3121 (2008)
9. Preparata, F.P., Sarwate, D.V.: Computational complexity of fourier transforms over finite fields 31, 740–751 (1977)
10. Merkle, R.C.: A certified digital signature. In: Brassard, G. (ed.) CRYPTO 1989. LNCS, vol. 435, pp. 218–238. Springer, Heidelberg (1990)
11. Naor, D., Naor, M., Lotspiech, J.: Revocation and tracing schemes for stateless receivers. In: Kilian, J. (ed.) CRYPTO 2001. LNCS, vol. 2139, pp. 41–62. Springer, Heidelberg (2001)
12. Preparata, F.P., Shamos, M.I.: Computational Geometry: An Introduction. Springer-Verlag New York, Inc., New York (1985)
13. Akinyele, J., Garman, C., Miers, I., Pagano, M., Rushanan, M., Green, M., Rubin, A.: Charm: A framework for rapidly prototyping cryptosystems. Journal of Cryptographic Engineering 3(2), 111–128 (2013)
14. Klimt, B., Yang, Y.: The enron corpus: A new dataset for email classification research. In: Boulicaut, J.-F., Esposito, F., Giannotti, F., Pedreschi, D. (eds.) ECML 2004. LNCS (LNAI), vol. 3201, pp. 217–226. Springer, Heidelberg (2004)

Analyzing Traffic Features of Common Standalone DoS Attack Tools

Vit Bukac and Vashek Matyas

Centre for Research on Cryptography and Security
Faculty of Informatics
Masaryk University
Brno, Czech Republic
bukac@mail.muni.cz, matyas@fi.muni.cz

Abstract. Research on denial of service (DoS) attack detection is complicated due to scarcity of reliable, widely available and representative contemporary input data. Efficiency of newly proposed DoS detection methods is continually verified with obsolete attack samples and tools. To address this issue, we provide a comparative analysis of traffic features of DoS attacks that were generated by state-of-the-art standalone DoS attack tools. We provide a classification of different attack traffic features, including utilized evasion techniques and encountered anomalies. We also propose a new research direction for the detection of DoS attacks at the source end, based on repeated attack patterns recognition.

Keywords: denial of service tools, input features, traffic characteristics.

1 Introduction

Even though denial of service (DoS) attacks are steadily gaining on popularity among both cyber criminals and security researchers, there are only few studies collecting *thorough and truly representative characteristics* of DoS attack traffic. We observe a serious discrepancy between tools that are used by attack perpetrators and the tools that are used for testing DoS detection and mitigation solutions proposed by academia. The list of tools and techniques actively used in real environment contains advanced tools such as LOIC, HOIC or Slowloris.

Understanding how attacks evolve is a necessary step towards the design of appropriate DoS attack detection and mitigation systems. Conversely, academic concepts are notoriously evaluated with obsolete and in practice already forgotten tools, most notably TFN, TFN2k, Shaft, Trinoo, Knight, mstream and Stacheldraht that all date back to year 2000. We still encounter numerous research works that present these tools as representatives of modern DoS attacks, even in respectable periodics (e.g., [2,7,26]). These tools no longer reflect contemporary real DoS attacks. DoS attacks went through an incredible development not only in terms of overall performance, but also in terms of attack properties. A brand new class of slow application DoS attacks has emerged and gained on popularity.

© Springer International Publishing Switzerland 2015
R.S. Chakraborty et al. (Eds.): SPACE 2015, LNCS 9354, pp. 21–40, 2015.
DOI: 10.1007/978-3-319-24126-5_2

Simultaneously, contemporary labeled DoS attack datasets are sparse. Both DARPA and KDD99 datasets are still being used, despite being 15 years old and not representing current state in networks. For example, DoS category in KDD99 contains back, land, neptune, pod, smurf and teardrop attacks, none of which are seen in the wild any more. Other available datasets are produced by projects such as CAIDA, MAWI or ONTIC. However, these datasets either do not provide attack labeling or suffer from little DoS attack variability.

Our research focused on state-of-the art DoS tools, their DoS traffic properties, employed evasion techniques and further tools characteristics. Network traffic profiles of standalone DoS tools will help design detection methods that are based on valid assumptions. Also, by creating a database of attack tools, it will be possible to estimate what classes of DoS attacks can be detected by each proposed method.

Our traffic traces contain only attack traffic. Each trace file is labeled with the name of DoS tool that was used to generate the traffic, attack type and any attack configuration options. Therefore, our traces are suitable for evaluation of DoS detection and mitigation systems through attractive *overlay methodology*. Overlay methodology combines the separate attack traffic traces with the background traces from an arbitrary environment. This widespread methodology allows to recognize the ground truth and precisely determine the false positives rate and false negative rate of the evaluated detection system [5].

Our analysis will assist best to researchers focusing on *source-end DoS detection* solutions, such as D-WARD [17]. Mirkovic et al. argue that detecting DoS attacks directly at the source computers or first-mile routers brings benefits such as congestion avoidance, small collateral damage, easy traceback and the possibility to use sophisticated detection strategies due to more available resources [16]. Source-end solutions also bring significant advantages when applied in cloud environments, software-defined networking or untrustworthy networks. We believe the importance of source-end detection is proven by the development direction of host-based antimalware products. Security companies are gradually introducing more and more network analysis modules to their products, including DDoS detection modules, such as in the Symantec Endpoint Protection. Capability to detect outbound DoS attacks coupled with originator system process identification is a viable behavioral malware detection

This paper is supported by more technical details available in our technical report [8]. Our dataset of all PCAP traces and used DoS tools is freely available at [1]. Our paper presents the following contributions:

1. This is the first comparative study aimed exclusively at traffic properties of DoS attack tools. We overview existing state-of-the-art standalone DoS attack tools, their attack traffic properties and used evasion techniques. We provide conclusive evidence that no two DoS tools (of those we examined) generate DoS attack traffic with the same properties.
2. Identification of network traffic features that are suitable for the source-end DoS attack detection. We evaluated the importance of selected features for various classes of DoS attacks. We reject traffic randomization as an universal

answer to the DoS detection evasion. We propose a new area for detection of DoS attacks based on recognition of unique repeating patterns.
3. Support for the use of these traffic traces for evaluation of DoS intrusion detection systems in academic research thorough overlay methodology.

The remainder of this paper is organized as follows. Section 2 reviews relevant work in the traffic analysis of DoS tools. Section 3 describes our experiment and the selection of tools for analysis. Section 4 supplies our raw observations of the selected DoS traffic properties. Section 5 summarizes our results and highlights the impact of our analysis on DoS attacks detection. Section 6 concludes the paper.

2   Related Work

Exploration of detailed properties of DoS attacks in the wild received limited to none interest from academia. This may be because of an assumption that DoS attacks cannot notably alter their properties, otherwise they would have to sacrifice performance or increase visibility. On the other hand, some of the most prominent state-of-the-art DoS tools are occasionally examined by freelance security specialists or companies dealing with DDoS protection solutions. Such analyses are often thorough and descriptive, but lack a mutual comparison and frequently skip deriving general concepts.

The tools listed in this paper are extensively and routinely used by hacktivists to manifest their political opinions and by technically unsavvy users to harass other users. Bartolacci et al. describe the practice of "kicking", when online gamers use simple DoS tools to degrade their oponent's network connection or even force them out of the game [6].

Onut and Ghorbani argue there is a general lack of research on input features [19]. They investigated the effectiveness ranking of 673 network features for the detection of network attacks. Their evaluation concludes that for the detection of DoS attacks the best features are related to ICMP protocol. For TCP-based attacks, they emphasize the importance of SYN packet statistics and flow statistics. Another DARPA dataset traffic features analyzing paper was presented by Kabiri and Zargar [15]. They note the SYN flag presence, classification fields and protocol fields as most influential. Slightly enhanced DARPA 2000 dataset was analyzed by Zi et al. [27]. Their list of top 5 preferable features (in decreasing order) is TCP SYN occurrence, destination port entropy, entropy of source port, UDP protocol occurrence and packet volume. Unfortunately, the results based on DARPA and KDD datasets has been repeatedly criticized for not being a good representative sample of actual traffic in a network (e.g., [13,21]).

Thing et al. [23] performed a detailed source code analysis of selected then popular bots for distributed DoS (DDoS) attacks, namely Agobot, SDBot, RBot and Sybot. Authors emphasize the importance of randomization in creating a packet, which is a view we share. Given the source code availability, this analysis is very descriptive with a deep understanding of inner works of each tool, but the analysis does not provide a high-level overview of the traffic in real environments, study is not comparative and the scope is limited.

Traffic features that are significant for old TFN2k DoS tool traffic are examined by Dimitris et al. [11]. They put emphasis on the presence of SYN and URG flags, while simultaneously noticing that TTL and Window sizes provide almost no information. Conversely, our results indicate that the URG flag is not used by contemporary DoS tools anymore, probably because of its relative rarity, which would make the attack traffic easily identifiable [8].

Another study aimed at properties of DDoS bots has been performed by Edwards and Nazario [12]. The study focuses on families of DDoS botnet malware controlled predominantly from the Chinese IP space. An exhaustive summary of bot communication protocols is provided. Attacks supported by each bot are listed along with a high-level attack type taxonomy. However, from the perspective of attack traffic characteristics, only few unique properties of chosen bots are discussed and description of the traffic is overly general, without sufficient details to be used as an input in design of DDoS detection systems.

Slow DoS attacks form a class of stealthy attacks where attack hosts aim to allocate all available resources of the server for themselves, effectively denying the service for other hosts. Slow attacks require small bandwidth, are very stealthy and consist of fully established TCP connections. Cambiaso et al. classify slow attacks into four groups: pending requests DoS, long responses DoS, multi-layer DoS and mixed attacks [9]. Several representatives of slow DoS attacks have been discovered already, most notable being Slowloris [14] and Slow HTTP POST [10].

Basic properties of DDoS traffic are frequently listed with DDoS botnet analyses, such as the analysis of Dirt Jumper botnet [3] or Miner botnet [20]. Due to their primary focus on botnet properties, these studies only rarely provide sufficient technical details about the generated DDoS traffic. Although an overall description helps to understand the basic idea of an attack, missing technical details make it impossible to use this data as an input source for creation of new DDoS detection methods. Simultaneously, any estimate of effectiveness of existing DDoS detection methods against these attacks is difficult and unreliable.

3   Experiment

3.1   DoS Tools Selection

The full list of analyzed tools, versions, respective sources, supported attack types and tool identifiers used in later text is provided in Table 1. We are convinced that this list accurately represents the types of standalone DoS tools that can be currently encountered during real attacks.

Firstly, we selected a subset of existing standalone DoS tools based on their popularity and capabilities of attacking generic web servers. Arbor Networks Worldwide Infrastructure survey of 2014 notes that 78% of respondents have been targeted with various types of the HTTP GET flood, 55% with the HTTP POST flood, 43% with Slowloris attack, 38% with the LOIC DoS tool or its variants, 27% with the Apache Killer tool, 23% with the HOIC DoS tool or its

Table 1. Selected tools and supported attacks.

Name Version	Source	Tool ID	Attacks
Anonymous DoSer 2.0	OpUSA, OpMyanmar	AD	HTTP
AnonymousDOS	Representative	ADR	HTTP
BanglaDOS	Representative	BAD	HTTP
ByteDOS 3.2	OpIsrael, OpUSA	BD	SYN, ICMP
DoS 5.5	Representative	DS	TCP
FireFlood 1.2	OpMyanmar	FF	HTTP
Goodbye 3.0	OpUSA, ArborNetworks	GB3	HTTP
Goodbye 5.2	OpUSA, ArborNetworks	GB5	HTTP
HOIC 2.1.003	OpUSA, OpMyanmar	HO	HTTP
HULK 1.0	OpUSA, InfoSec	HU	HTTP
HTTP DoS Tool 3.6	Representative	HDT	slow headers, slow POST
HTTPFlooder	OpUSA	HF	HTTP
Janidos -Weak ed.-	ArborNetworks	JA	HTTP
JavaLOIC 0.0.3.7	OpUSA, OpMyanmar	JL	TCP, UDP, HTTP
LOIC 1.0.4.0	OpUSA, OpMyanmar	LO1	TCP, UDP, HTTP
LOIC 1.0.7.42	OpUSA, OpMyanmar	LO2	TCP, UDP, HTTP
LOIC 1.1.1.25	OpUSA, OpMyanmar	LO3	TCP, UDP, HTTP
LOIC 1.1.2.0b	OpUSA, OpMyanmar	LO4	TCP, UDP, HTTP, Re-Coil, slowLOIC
Longcat 2.3	Hacker forums	LC	TCP, UDP, HTTP
SimpleDoSTool	Representative	SD	TCP
Slowloris 0.7	OpIsrael, OpUSA	SL	HTTP
Syn Flood DOS	OpUSA	SF	SYN
TORSHAMMER 1.0b	OpIsrael, InfoSec	TH	HTTP
UnknownDoser 1.1.0.2	Hacker forums	UD	HTTP
XOIC 1.3	InfoSec	XO	TCP, UDP, ICMP

variants and 19% with the SIP Call-control flood. Among trailing attack types and tools are SlowPost, THC, nkiller, Hulk, RUDY and Recoil [4]. Secondly, we focused on tools that were used or allegedly used during publicized DDoS campaigns (OpUSA, OpIsrael, OpMyanmar). Thirdly, respected security companies often publish lists of DoS tools that are either popular or present a new step in development of DoS tools such as a by Curt Wilson of Arbor Networks [25].

We excluded any tools that are exclusive for a specific target application (e.g., Apache Killer) and tools that do not directly communicate with the target (e.g., DNS amplification attack tools). Lastly, we included several tools that are a popular choice on hacker forums (e.g., GoodBye, Janidos) or are created as open source in public software repositories (e.g., HTTP DoS Tool) or that take an extraordinary approach in causing a DoS effect (e.g., AnonymousDoS). Tools were selected in order to represent a full spectrum of existing types of TCP and HTTP DoS attacks.

Standalone tools are common inspirations for botnets. Even though most botnets rely on common volume-based attacks, such as generic HTTP GET flood,

HTTP POST attack or TCP SYN attack, succesful new attacks are occasionally incorporated as well. For example, since the first release of the Slowloris HTTP client in June 2009, the Slowloris attack code has been included in advanced DDoS bots such as Mariposa, Skunkx or SpyEye. Similarly, a slow POST attack known from the Torshammer tool has been added to the Solar botnet and the R-U-D-Y attack to the Cyclone botnet. Although we usually observe a delay between the creation of a new proof-of-concept tool and full weaponization, support for new attacks is indeed added to botnets. Also, while standalone DoS tools are mostly free and public, bot binaries may be cracked and therefore unreliable, may be missing crucial components or may not be available at all. Obtaining reasonable botnet DoS traffic samples under pre-defined conditions and with non-interfering background traffic might be extremely difficult. Therefore, we believe this paper will also be beneficial for research on contemporary botnet capabilities.

3.2   Environment

The virtual environment was used in order to minimize the influence of real intermediate network on measurements. Also, virtual machine snapshots allow returning to a conjoint initial stable state. Therefore, any measurements on a restored snapshot are not affected by artifacts from previous measurements (e.g., keep-alive packets sent by either side). Our virtual environment was built on a single physical server with Core i7 CPU and 16 GB RAM.

We created a simple point-to-point virtual network between two virtual machines. The attacker VM had the Windows 7 operating system and the victim was the IIS 7.0 webserver on the Windows Server 2008 R2. Firewalls on both machines were configured to allow all incoming traffic from the shared network. Default settings for other subnets were kept. Except for DoS attack tools and the operating system itself, no other legitimate network traffic was knowingly produced. Tools were executed through the Administrator account with UAC enabled.

Our analysis was performed in a controlled virtual environment with no background traffic. Background traffic was omitted in order to gain as clear view of ideal attack conditions as possible. Applying legitimate background traffic would invalidate our results for scenarios with background traffic differing from the one we generated. Also, from the perspective of source end DoS attack detection, the impact of background traffic is diminishing. A reasonable assumption is that the source host is sending the attack traffic towards only one victim. Therefore, any source end DoS detection system can be considering traffic of each source IP and destination IP pair separately.

Background traffic can only alter time distribution of traffic (sections 4.1, 4.2 and 4.3) and only for highly susceptible, usually low-volume, tools. Internal properties of flows (e.g., HTTP request URI, flow packet count) cannot be altered by background traffic at all (sections 4.4, 4.5 and 4.6). Given the placement of source end detectors directly on sending hosts or on first-mile routers, the complexity of intermediate networks or the number of attacking hosts is similarly irrelevant.

We used the CNN.com webpage from 11/19/2012 19:39 UTC, renamed to index.htm, as a testing target page. A popular existing webpage was selected in order to mimic real conditions under which DoS tools are launched. Saved webpage has 109 files and the total size is 3.3 MB including images.

3.3   Measurement

We review DoS attack tools from the viewpoint of source-end detection. While DoS mitigation systems are usually deployed on the victim side, the source-end side is more sound for the purpose of understanding the attack. Focusing on the source end enables deep and very precise understanding of inner works of tested tools without disturbances caused by an intermediate network.

Each tool has been tested with various configurations. The first configuration of each tool has been set with default tool settings if such exist. Configurations were chosen in order to test primarily settings that can alter the form of produced network traffic. We did not distinguish between successful and unsuccessful attacks. 60 and 300 second traffic samples were obtained for every tool configuration. The 300 second limit was chosen in order to track at least several iterations of even the most stealthy slow attacks. Oppositely, most DoS tools demonstrated their full traffic properties within first 15 seconds. Due to difficulties with packet recording at high packet transmission speeds, the measurement was focused on tool capabilities and traffic features, not performance comparison. Even though attack volume/performance is one of the cornerstones of victim end DDoS defense, its use in source end detection is problematic, mostly due to limited client bandwidth that is commonly saturated with legitimate network traffic.

DoS tools ran from a common initial state. Both outgoing and incoming network traffic was recorded with the dumpcap tool from the Wireshark suite directly at the attacker VM. We then performed our analyses offline on the collected PCAP files. Analyses consisted of two parts. First, the traffic was divided to 1-second intervals. Network features statistics (e.g., byterate, packetrate, TCP flag ratios) were then computed for each interval. Second, the PCAP file was processed packet by packet, network flows were reconstructed and flow statistics were computed (e.g., simultaneous flow count, packets per flow). We define flow as 5-tuple: source IP address, destination IP address, source TCP/UDP port, destination TCP/UDP port, protocol.

Graphs on the following pages represent values of respective metrics each second of the first minute of the attack. Tables contain tool IDs of tools representing each category. When an ID is found in multiple categories, the actual behavior is dependent on chosen tool settings. Identifiers GB and LO represent all versions of the respective tool.

4   DoS Traffic Properties

4.1   Traffic Burst Behavior

Traditionally, DoS attacks were believed to produce an excessively high volume of attack traffic in order to overwhelm the target. However, even though the peak volumes of observed DoS attacks are steadily increasing, the ratio of low-rate attacks is increasing as well [4].

Division of tools into classes by the packet rate shows that we can encounter both volume-rich tools and tools that produce hardly any traffic. Byte rate and packet rate values are especially interesting for tools that do not enable the attack intensity to be specified. For the vast majority of configurations the changes of byte rate value in time correspond to the changes of packet rate value. Note that the tool IDs are provided in Table 1 above.

In our set, a clear majority of tools employs an immediate full attack strength approach. Exceptions are LO and JL that may have an initiation period up to 10 seconds long (Fig. 4). We consider this revelation important, because it is a strong indicator that detection methods based on change detection can be widely adopted in real environments. Packet rates of many DoS tools in our set exhibit a burst behavior. We divide observed burst types into four types. Attribution of tools to each burstiness type is provided in Table 2.

Full burstiness: The attack traffic is delivered only in bursts. Minimal or no traffic is exchanged between bursts (Fig. 3). Full burstiness is also very popular with slow attacks, often probably due to guidance by an internal clock.

Regular peaks: Produced network traffic is very stable except for regular repeating anomalies (Fig. 1).

One-time extreme: At one point of the tool run, often at the beginning of the attack, the traffic characteristics are significantly different from the rest (Fig. 2).

None: The tool does not produce traffic that has observable bursts in packet rate.

Although according to our knowledge the burst behavior has not yet been used in the source end DoS attack detection, it could become a valid alternative to existing detection methods. A new method could be based on the detection of a burst behavior, recognition of repeated occurrences of bursts and on similarity comparisons of these bursts.

Table 2. Traffic burstiness.

Full burstiness	HDT, HU, LO4, SL, SF
Regular peaks	BD, HO, LO, LC, UD
One-time extreme	AD, BAD, DS, GB, HDT, TH
None	ADR, FF, HF, JA, JL, LO, LC, SD, UD, XO

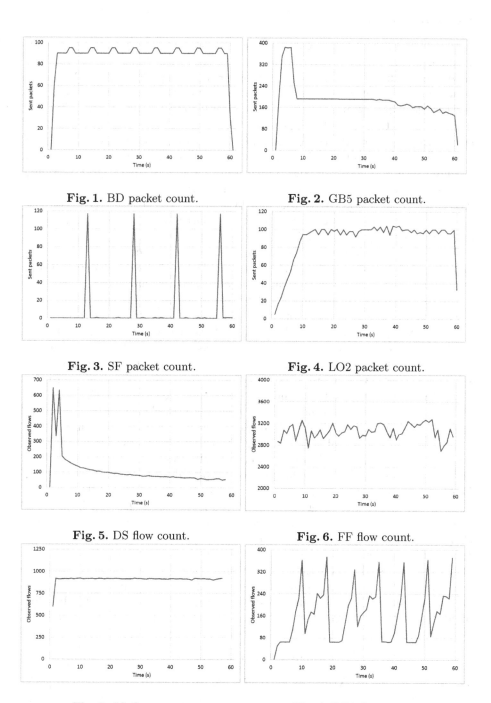

Fig. 1. BD packet count.

Fig. 2. GB5 packet count.

Fig. 3. SF packet count.

Fig. 4. LO2 packet count.

Fig. 5. DS flow count.

Fig. 6. FF flow count.

Fig. 7. JA flow count.

Fig. 8. LO2 flow count.

4.2 Flow Count

Attacker establishing many connections towards a victim is one of the most common assumptions about DoS attacks. Reasoning behind this assumption states that multiple connections imply higher (attack) performance. Also, some attacks are based on the number of connections or on the rate of their generation and therefore high number of flows is a desirable property. JL, SD and XO can generate more than 1000 flows per second without IP spoofing on a standard laptop. Depending on the configuration and the performance of the source host, several more tools can be used to reach such limit (e.g., HU, FF), especially when executed several times in parallel. Oppositely, without regards to tool versions, following tools can be configured to launch an attack with 100 or less flows: AD, BAD, HDT, LO (TCP, Recoil, SlowLOIC), LC (HTTP), SL, TH. Low flow counts make these tools stealthy for source-end intrusion detection systems that are based on flow count analysis.

Another important aspect of DoS traffic is the change in the number of flows in time. We classify configurations by the number of flows that were observed during initial 60 seconds of the attack. Four flow count patterns have been recognized. Attribution of tools to each flow count type is provided in Table 3.

Stability: Most tools exhibit only minor changes while the long term trend remains steady, e.g., FF or JA. While minor fluctuations can be expected (Fig. 6), the flow rate is extremely stable for most tools in an ideal closed environment (Fig. 7). This fact is emphasized in case of tools that require the operator to specify the flow rate prior to attack, be it directly as request per second ratio (e.g., BAD) or inderectly by the number of attack threads (e.g., LC, LO).

Pulsing: Intentionally pulsing attack is generally viewed as an attempt to stay undetected while maintaining a reasonable per host attack strength. Our analysis shows that pulsing can also be an integral part of the attack. Representatives are LO, which achieves pulsing by batch flow closures (Fig. 8) or HDT, which alternates between calm no-traffic periods and periods of batch packet sendings.

Decreasing count: Several tools such as DS (Fig. 5), GB and HDT tend to decrease the number of observable flows, even if the victim has not been made unavailable. The reason may be a poor design of the tool or inherent attack characteristics, especially in the case of slow attacks.

Increasing count: Although an attacker is expected to attempt using all available resources as soon as possible to overwhelm the victim, increasing strength could be used to circumvent reputation-based and some anomaly-based intrusion detection systems. A subtle attack start phase could lead to the attack being undetected for a prolonged time. Naturally, subtle attacks are not tempting for

Table 3. Flow count change.

Stability	AD, ADR, BAD, BD, FF, HF, HO, HDT, JA, JL, LC, LO, SD, XO
Pulsing	HDT, HU, JL, LO, SF, SL, UD
Decreasing count	DS, GB, HDT

hacktivists, who want the publicity of the attack. None of the tools in our set has shown an increasing strength trend, except for a short initialization period at the beginning of the attack.

4.3 Flow Parallelity

Results of flow parallelity measurements support our observations from the flow count measurement. The level of flow parallelity generally decreases with the decreasing flow count. Our observations show that a true parallelity is not common. Many tools actually produce flows in succession or in small batches of simultaneous flows. The outer effect of massive flow parallelity is caused by the length of the flow sampling interval. With a decreasing interval, thresholds for DoS detection via simultaneous flows count should be lowered in order to maintain detection accuracy, as the count of seemingly simultaneous flows will decrease. In contrast, the count of truly simultaneous flows would remain constant. Attribution of tools to each flow parallelity type is provided in Table 4.

All simultaneous: Flows that are initiated in a short succession and are never closed under normal circumstances. Attacker keeps these flows open for the duration of the attack and sends attack packets over them. Attacks with spoofed source IP address has been inserted into this group (e.g., SF).

Mostly simultaneous: Flows are closed after a prolonged time, usually by the victim after the connection timeout runs out. Many flows are open at the same time. Flow duration usually exceeds 60 seconds.

Long-term consecutive, many simultaneous: Generation and existence of flows themselves is one of the means of attack. Flows are generated rapidly, often by several process threads simulaneously. Flow duration varies with the performance of the attack tool, usually between several hundred milliseconds and several seconds.

Mostly consecutive: Flows are established and closed in succession, eventually only a few flows overlaps. Attacks aim to overwhelm the victim with flow generation rate. Flows have a very short duration.

Table 4. Flow parallelity.

All simultaneous	AD, BAD, LC, SF, SL
Mostly simultaneous	DS, GB, HDT, HU, LO4, TH, UD
Long-term consecutive	LO
Mostly consecutive	ADR, BD, FF, HF, HO, JA, JL, UD, XO

4.4 HTTP Requests Per Flow

Number of outgoing HTTP requests per flow for a single destination IP address can also be considered a decent detection metric. Normal non-DoS traffic consists both of TCP flows with only one HTTP request and of TCP flows that carry multiple HTTP requests along with respective responses. Therefore on average, the number of HTTP requests exchanged over destination port 80 is higher than the number of TCP flows with this destination port. This important characteristic is only rarely emulated by DoS tools. Volume-based HTTP attack tools produce many HTTP requests and their distribution between flows is often very straightforward, as can be seen in Table 5.

One per flow: Each established TCP flow is closed after at most one HTTP request is sent from the attacker to the victim. The ratio between the number of HTTP requests and the number of TCP flows carrying HTTP protocol messages converges to 1 (Fig. 9). Special case are slow attacks based on slow sending of HTTP header. Although these attacks take a long time, each flow contains only one HTTP request message that is slowly constructed.

Multiple per flow: Established TCP flows can carry one or more separate HTTP requests and respective responses. Of the tested tools, none has exhibited such behavior with chosen configurations.

Infinite per flow: TCP flows carrying attack HTTP requests are never closed under normal circumstances and the request sending has not been observed to be stopping during our analysis. The ratio between the number of HTTP requests and the number of TCP flows carrying HTTP protocol messages during each interval is much higher than 1. The ratio usually copies the packet rate curve (Fig. 10).

Table 5. HTTP requests per flow.

One per flow	ADR, FF, GB, HDT, HF, HO, HU, JA, JL, LO, SL, TH, UD
Infinite per flow	AD, BAD, LC

4.5   HTTP Request URIs

We are convinced that the HTTP uniform resource identifier (URI) monitoring can be used as one of the most important metrics to verify the presence of an outgoing DoS attack in a given traffic sample. Observing repeated similar URIs either within one HTTP flow or within multiple flows with very similar characteristics is a strong indication of internal relationship and possible evidence of an outgoing DoS attack. Even though simply storing of all observed URIs is inefficient, performance problems can be solved, for example, with counting Bloom filters. Our analysis shows that from the perspective of source end DoS detection, most DoS tools target only a very limited number of URIs. Observing such HTTP requests exceeding predefined threshold is a sufficient signal of an outgoing DoS attack in progress.

There are four basic techniques how DoS tools may process URIs. Attribution of tools to each of these techniques is provided in Table 6.

URI string set: The tool targets not just one URI on a selected victim server, but a predefined set of URIs. Using a set may slightly downgrade the attack efficiency, as not only the most resource demanding page is chosen to be the target, but also several others. If only one URI is accessed by the tool, the count

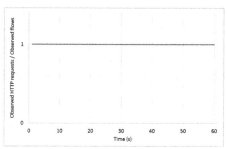

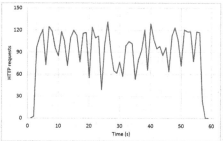

Fig. 9. FF HTTP requests per flow.   **Fig. 10.** LC HTTP requests per flow.

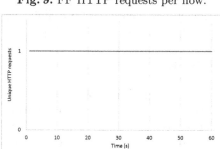

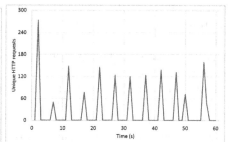

Fig. 11. JA unique HTTP request count.   **Fig. 12.** HU unique HTTP request count.

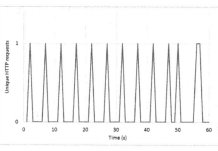

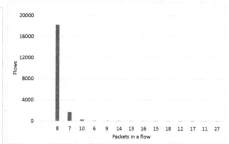

Fig. 13. HU requests without parameters.   **Fig. 14.** JL flow packet count distribution.

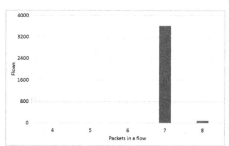

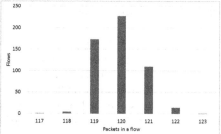

Fig. 15. UD flow packet count distribution.   **Fig. 16.** HO flow packet count distribution.

of unique HTTP requests in time is equal to 1 (Fig. 11). It is also not uncommon for tools to not allow the change of the target URI at all (i.e., a basic value such as index.htm is employed).

Page crawling: The tool starts with an initial URI and gets more URIs by parsing the links in the HTTP response. None of the tools in our analysis employed the page crawling.

Parameter change: The base domain and file path remain constant, but full URI is made unique by adding unique parameter values. Unique parameter values render webpage caching servers between the attacker and the victim useless, therefore make the attack mitigation more difficult. Figures 12 and 13 show the difference between capturing full URIs and without parameters.

Random URI: URI may be fully randomly generated. That presents a challenge for attack detection and mitigation, but attack effectiveness is severely degraded. A huge majority of responses is Error 400, therefore the web server does not saturate its outgoing bandwidth and also do not devote so much computational power to retrieve the response.

It should be noted that URI frequency monitoring is unreliable metric when the webpage in question is limited to only a few pages. Therefore a combination with other metrics, such as suspicious User-Agent string monitoring, is necessary.

Oppositely, an overly large number of hard-coded URIs negatively impacts the attack power. Although accessing a large number or URIs makes intermediate caching less effective, the attacker also partially sacrifices his attack potential. Different URI requests require different volume of resources to process. With the suggested approach not only resource-demanding requests (e.g., DB searches, form submits), but also generic requests are sent towards the victim, lowering the attack effectiveness.

Table 6. HTTP request URIs.

URI string set	ADR, FF, GB, HDT, HF, HO, JA, JL, LO, LC, SL, TH, UD
Parameter change	AD, BAD, HU
Random URI	JL, UD

4.6   Flow Packet Count

Packet count is one of the most important properties of every flow. We believe that it can be used to detect spoofed attacks, some classes of non-spoofed DoS attacks and, most importantly, it can serve as an indicator of similarity between seemingly unrelated flows. TCP attack tools produce traffic where all closed flows have exactly the same packet count (disregarding possible TCP retransmissions). We believe that when applied to high flow (count) tools (e.g., SD, XO, JL), this metric can be both very precise and computationally efficient. Configurable precision can be devised from how many flow counts must be correctly predicted in order to consider those flows being part of a DoS attack.

The purpose of normal traffic is to transmit data between communication participants. In terms of TCP, three packets are required to establish the connection and one or more packets to terminate the connection. Of those, two or more packets must be sent by connection initiator. Therefore, any closed connection with only two or less packets sent by the flow initiator could have not transmitted any data. Oppositely, TCP-based attacks usually transfer few packets per flow, aiming to exploit TCP rather than transmit data.

As is shown in Table 7, majority of tools can produce homogenous traffic from the point of flow packet count. For example, HTTP POST flooding attack by UD generates flows with vast majority having 7 packets after closure (Fig. 15). Oppositely, HO is one of the tools whose traffic does not provide any recognizable flow packet count (Fig. 16). Excluded were tools whose connections were never closed during the first minute of the attack (AD, BAD, HF).

Table 7. Flow packet count distribution.

All flows the same packet count	ADR, BD, DS, FF, GB, HDT, JA, JL, LC, LO1, SD, SF, SL, UD, XO
Minimal differences	LO, SD, UD
Significant differences	HDT, HO, HU, JL, LO, SD, TH, UD

5   Discussion

Most standalone DoS tools are single-purpose programs that are capable of only one type of attack. Moreover, even tools that support multiple attack types can rarely launch several attacks simultaneously. Majority of tools does not require root privileges and therefore can be executed on computers at work, school or internet cafe. Basic operations with DoS tools do not require advanced knowledge about the victim or the type of attack. Most tools allow for targeting only one victim at a time. This is an important observation for source-end detection, because statistics of multiple flows aimed at a single target can be included in detection.

5.1   Traffic Features and Aggregation

Network traffic generated by tools in our set presents a variety of DoS attacks. Even though it was possible to classify attacks by the basic concept, every attack was unique in some regard.

Although almost every traffic feature that we measured yielded some results, none proved to be sufficient on its own for the detection of DoS attacks in the source-end network. Every feature can detect only a subset of existing DoS attacks. Standalone features suffer from false positives, but more importantly, have an inherent limit of false negatives rate. Different classes of DoS attacks have different properties and none of the traffic features could be applied to all. Employing just one input feature for DoS detection results in an inability to detect many classes of attacks. Still prevalent assumptions about DoS traffic regarding traffic volume, flow composition or protocol compliance are obsolete and cannot be applied to DoS attacks in general, rather only to small DoS attack subclasses.

Therefore we believe that an aggregation of multiple features is necessary to be used for a general detection. We support the approach taken, for example, by [18,22] that collect multiple feature values and subsequently compute their aggregate importance.

Serious consideration must be given not only to the computational efficiency of the detection, but also to an efficient collection of input values. Features included in the NetFlow standard are therefore preferred. However, as our results show, this limited set of flow-based statistics and network layer features may not be sufficient for the reliable confirmation of some classes of DoS attacks (e.g., slow attacks cannot be detected with volume-based detection metrics). In order to balance the complexity of collection and processing of some features and potentially huge amounts of packets/flows for analysis, sampling and filtering of suspicious flows may be employed prior to the analysis. We believe that the analysis process separated into several stages as proposed, for example, by Wang et al. [24] is promising.

Traditional metrics such as a high bitrate and a high packetrate are by themselves not reliable options for the source-end detection. By definition, slow attacks are hardly detectable via metrics focused on high volumes. Also, many tools enable to specify the attack performance so it is possible to find a configuration which cannot be detected through volume-based metrics.

5.2   Repeating Patterns

Most important observation of this work is that standalone DoS attack tool *traffic comprises of repeating operations*. Every attack has a basic construction unit that is iterated in time, creating a series of similar operations. Although some characteristics of operations may change with each iteration, most defining properties are constant. Construction units may have a form of flows with distinct characteristics in case of TCP-based attacks or HTTP requests and according responses in case of HTTP-based attacks.

Noise traffic can be filtered out once DoS operations are identified. Subsequently, traffic can be analyzed on high scale. Patterns such as packet rate burst behavior, flow count in time or flow paralellity are recognizable. Existing DoS detection methods can be applied to the filtered traffic with increased accuracy.

Recognition of repeating patterns opens a new area of detecting outgoing DoS attacks at the source end. This novel approach presents challenges how to identify construction units in a traffic that contains both benign traffic and malicious traffic, how to determine which unit properties are constant and how to apply chosen pattern matching in time efficiently. Benefits are: high precision growing with each next correctly identified operation and possibility to detect yet unknown attacks. Since repeating patterns have been identified across all

classes of attacks, it can become a basis of a very broad detection method. For illustration, we provide example scenarios of this new approach to DoS detection.
Example 1 – BD. The traffic comprises of separate attack flows. Each flow is to be considered an operation. Each flow has the same packet count, packet size distribution and is carrying TCP segments. Each flow has the same TCP flag composition. The flow is always established via a correct TCP 3-way handshake (3WH) and terminated by the attacker with the TCP FIN segment, which is followed by the TCP RST segment from the victim. TCP segments don't carry any payload. All of the TCP header option fields of packets in one flow have the same values as the equivalent packets in other flows. All flows have a very short duration, 99% of them take between 0.1 and 0.12 seconds. None of the packets has the time to live (TTL) value altered or is using a spoofed IP address.
Example 2 – AD. The attacker opens a fixed number of simultaneous flows towards the victim. Repeated HTTP requests are sent over each flow. Each HTTP request is an operation. All packets with HTTP requests have the same length, TTL field value and packets are not fragmented. Header of every HTTP request contains the same fields with the same values. The referer field is always missing. The full URI comprises of a basic path and parameters. The path is similar across all flows. The parameter is numeric and is gradually rising, while the second parameter is a static string.

5.3   Evasion Techniques

Most standalone DoS tools do not support any type of detection evasion techniques. Even if supported, they are not enabled by default. Most frequent are various kinds of traffic properties randomization. Randomization is usually configurable only for the packet fields chosen by a tool creator. Therefore, the effect of randomization can frequently be negated if multiple input features/header fields are analyzed in conjunction.

A similar technique can be observed at URI randomization. Adding random parameters such as timestamps in Unix format (e.g., AD, BAD), random parameter values (e.g., LO) or even random parameters (e.g., HU) can be used both to evade simple DoS detection systems and to circumvent content caching between the attacker and the victim.

Randomization is a powerful weapon for attacker, but it is not almighty. Excessive or impromper randomization can be detrimental for the attacker by making his traffic more visible. For example, as noted above, attack tools commonly randomize User-Agent string of HTTP request header [8]. While this is reasonable for victim end detection systems, because User-Agent string cannot be used to classify attack traffic, it significantly raises suspicion of source end detection systems. Even more importantly, many attack traffic features cannot be randomized without severe degradation of attack performance (e.g., flow packet count for TCP SYN attack).

Employing evasion techniques for the network or transport ISO/OSI layer was rare. SF was the only tool in our set that employed IP spoofing. We assume that

IP spoofing is not popular with these tools, because it enforces the use of only the most primitive attacks, such as SYN flood.

5.4 Future Work

We perceive this work is a necessary prerequisite to our follow-up research on DDoS attack detection. Creation of this work was compelled by the lack of up-to-date traffic samples and sparse reliable information on traffic properties of contemporary DoS attacks. We are convinced that the persistent trend when DDoS detection methods are evaluated against well-understood, but ruefully outdated attack descriptions/attack tools, is inherently flawed. Even though the exact properties of each attack that we analyzed, varied, we have discovered a set patterns recurring among DoS tools from different creators. We believe these patterns will prevail for a longer time than simple attack signatures.

The key revelation is the presence of repeating operations in all analyzed DoS attack traffic. Therefore, we propose a new research area for the detection of DoS attacks at the source end that is based on repeated attack pattern recognition. We discuss overall DoS tool properties and employed detection evasion techniques. Since attack features are not mutually comparable due to inherent detection efficiency limitations, it is crucial that researchers include their DoS attack traffic assumptions and any possible evasion techniques in every research output/publication that is dealing with DoS attack detection.

Further research will be required to analyze why these patterns are prevalent. Possibly, this is because of focus of tools' creators on victim end defense. Even though thorough per-packet randomization is possible, it results in an increased load of the source host, brings implementation issues and most notably, it decreases an overall performance of the tool. We frequently encountered per-flow randomization or even randomization taking place only once when the tool was run. From the victim end perspective, this level of traffic randomization is usually sufficient, due to distributed nature of attacks. However, this behavior can be exploited by source end DDoS detection solutions, because it increases attack visibility near the source host.

The impact of randomization on detection metrics depending on the placement of detection sensors is another interesting area of further research.

Volumetric DoS attack traffic consists of repeated operations with minimal differences. We intend to explore the possibility of creating a grammar that would allow us to describe the attack traffic from the source host perspective in an easily understandable, yet precise notion. The grammar will give researchers a good understanding of what operations are common and how the attack traffic changes between different versions of one tool.

6   Conclusions

This paper encourages and supports the evaluation of new source end DDoS detection systems against contemporary DoS attacks. We have analyzed state-of-the-art standalone DoS tools that have been observed in real DoS attacks.

We provided detailed properties of attack traffic and emphasized notable traffic anomalies from the perspective of source end DoS detection. Attack traffic is classified by each input feature and overall characteristics of each class are listed. Attack traffic traces are suitable for evaluation of DoS detection and mitigation systems through overlay methodology. More details about our experiments can be found in our technical report [8]. The traces are available for download at [1].

References

1. DDoS-Vault project (2015). https://github.com/crocs-muni/ddos-vault/wiki
2. Alomari, E., Manickam, S., Gupta, B.B., Karuppayah, S., Alfaris, R.: Botnet-based Distributed Denial of Service (DDoS) Attacks on Web Servers: Classification and Art. International Journal of Computer Applications 49(7), 24–32 (2012)
3. Andrade, M., Vlajic, N.: Dirt Jumper: A New and Fast Evolving Botnet-for-DDoS. International Journal of Intelligent Computing Research 3(3), December 2012
4. Arbor Networks. Worldwide Infrastructure Security Report, vol. IX (2014)
5. Aviv, A.J., Haeberlen, A.: Challenges in experimenting with botnet detection systems. In: 4th USENIX Workshop on Cyber Security Experimentation and Test (CSET 2011) (2011)
6. Bartolacci, M.R., LeBlanc, L.J., Podhradsky, A.: Personal Denial Of Service (PDOS) Attacks: A Discussion and Exploration of a New Category of Cyber Crime. Journal of Digital Forensics, Security and Law 9(1), 19–36 (2014)
7. Bhuyan, M.H., Kashyap, H.J., Bhattacharyya, D.K., Kalita, J.K.: Detecting Distributed Denial of Service Attacks: Methods, Tools and Future Directions. The Computer Journal 57(4) (2013)
8. Bukac, V.: Traffic characteristics of common DoS tools. Masaryk University, Technical report FIMU-RS-2014-02, April 2014
9. Cambiaso, E., Papaleo, G., Aiello, M.: Taxonomy of slow DoS attacks to web applications. In: Thampi, S.M., Zomaya, A.Y., Strufe, T., Alcaraz Calero, J.M., Thomas, T. (eds.) SNDS 2012. CCIS, vol. 335, pp. 195–204. Springer, Heidelberg (2012)
10. Wong Onn Chee and Tom Brennan. H.....t.....t....p....p....o....s....t. In: OWASP AppSec DC 2010. The OWASP Foundation (2010)
11. Dimitris, G., Ioannis, T., Evangelos, D.: Feature selection for robust detection of distributed denial-of-service attacks using genetic algorithms. In: Vouros, G.A., Panayiotopoulos, T. (eds.) SETN 2004. LNCS (LNAI), vol. 3025, pp. 276–281. Springer, Heidelberg (2004)
12. Edwards, J., Nazario, J.: A survey of contemporary Chinese DDoS malware. In: Proceedings of the 21st Virus Bulletin International Conference (2011)
13. Engen, V., Vincent, J., Phalp, K.: Exploring Discrepancies in Findings Obtained with the KDD Cup 1999 Data Set. Intelligent Data Analysis 15(2), 251–276 (2011)
14. Hansen, R.: Slowloris HTTP DoS (2009). ha.ckers.org/slowloris/ (October 22, 2014)
15. Kabiri, P., Zargar, G.R.: Category-based selection of effective parameters for intrusion detection. International Journal of Computer Science and Network Security (IJCSNS) 9(9), 181–188 (2009)
16. Mirkovic, J., Prier, G., Reiher, P.: Source-end DDoS defense. In: Second IEEE International Symposium on Network Computing and Applications, NCA 2003, pp. 171–178 (2003)

17. Mirkovic, J., Reiher, P.: D-WARD: A Source-End Defense against Flooding Denial-of-Service Attacks. IEEE Transactions on Dependable and Secure Computing 2(3), March 2005
18. Öke, G., Loukas, G.: A Denial of Service Detector based on Maximum Likelihood Detection and the Random Neural Network. The Computer Journal 50(6), September 2007
19. Onut, I.-V., Ghorbani, A.A.: Features vs. attacks: A comprehensive feature selection model for network based intrusion detection systems. In: Garay, J.A., Lenstra, A.K., Mambo, M., Peralta, R. (eds.) ISC 2007. LNCS, vol. 4779, pp. 19–36. Springer, Heidelberg (2007)
20. Plohmann, D., Gerhards-Padilla, E.: Case study of the miner botnet. In: 4th International Conference on Cyber Conflict (CYCON). IEEE (2012)
21. Shiravi, A., Shiravi, H., Tavallaee, M., Ghorbani, A.A.: Toward developing a systematic approach to generate benchmark datasets for intrusion detection. Computers & Security 31(3) (2012)
22. Siaterlis, C., Maglaris, V.: Detecting incoming and outgoing DDoS attacks at the edge using a single set of network characteristics. In: 10th IEEE Symposium on Computers and Communications (ISCC 2005) (2005)
23. Thing, V.L., Sloman, M., Dulay, N.: A Survey of bots used for distributed denial of service attacks. In: Venter, H., Eloff, M., Labuschagne, L., Eloff, J. (eds.) New Approaches for Security, Privacy and Trust in Complex Environments. IFIP, vol. 232, pp. 229–240. Springer, Heidelberg (2007)
24. Wang, F., Wang, H., Wang, X., Su, J.: A new multistage approach to detect subtle DDoS attacks. Mathematical and Computer Modelling 55(1–2), 198–213 (2012)
25. Wilson, C.: Attack of the Shuriken: Many Hands, Many Weapons, Webpage (2012). http://asert.arbornetworks.com/ddos-tools/ (May 29, 2015)
26. Yu, J., Kang, H., Park, D.H., Bang, H.-C., Kang, D.W.: An in-depth analysis on traffic flooding attacks detection and system using data mining techniques. Journal of Systems Architecture 59(10), 1005–1012 (2013)
27. Zi, L., Yearwood, J., Wu, X.-W.: Adaptive clustering with feature ranking for DDoS attacks detection. In: 4th International Conference on Network and System Security (NSS), pp. 281–286, September 2010

Design of Cyber Security for Critical Infrastructures: A Case for a Schizoid Design Approach

Avik Dayal[1], Yi Deng[1], and Sandeep K. Shukla[2]

[1] FERMAT Lab, Virginia Tech, Blacksburg, VA 24061, USA
{ad6db,yideng56}@vt.edu
[2] Computer Science and Engineering Department,
Indian Institute of Technology Kanpur,
Kanpur, UP 208016, India
sandeeps@cse.iitk.ac.in

Abstract. In this invited talk, we argue that designing cyber security of critical infrastructure requires a spilt-personality approach to design as opposed to design for correctness or for performance. Designing a functionally correct system, or a performance constrained system is fundamentally different in the sense that such design requires us to build models and to systematically refine models towards implementation such that correctness is preserved between refinements, and performance optimizations are introduced during refinements. Designing systems with cyber-security properties requires us to not only build models from theoretical principles, but also require modeling possible behaviors of an adversary. Modeling adversarial behavior is akin to test-driven model refinement, and hence not so different from certain approaches used when our goal is functionally correct design. However, for cyber-physical systems, we often need to detect an ongoing cyber attack since safe guards for cyber security often depend on assumptions which can be invalidated (e.g., insider attacks may invalidate perimeter security assumptions). Detecting ongoing attacks requires detecting behavioral anomalies in the physical system under cyber control – thus requiring us to build models from data. Machine learning approaches could be used to build such models. This we view as a schizoid approach – since the designer has to not only model the system from physical principles, he/she also has to build nominal behavioral models from data. While arguing this point of view, we introduce a virtual SCADA (supervisory control and data acquisition) laboratory we have built to help design cyber security of critical systems. The majority of this talk focuses on describing this software based virtual laboratory called VSCADA. Most of this research is published in [8,11] and summarized here for the sake of exposition to the present audience.

1 Introduction

In the absence of cyber threats, designing functionally correct, and performance constrained cyber-physical systems usually follow model based engineering (MDE)

© Springer International Publishing Switzerland 2015
R.S. Chakraborty et al. (Eds.): SPACE 2015, LNCS 9354, pp. 41–54, 2015.
DOI: 10.1007/978-3-319-24126-5_3

approaches. In MDE approaches, the first step of the design process normally would be the construction of a physics based mathematical model of the physical system, and a control theoretic model of the control system. These are then put together in a formal or semi-formal framework (e.g., MATLAB/ Simulink, LabView, Ptolemy Models). Starting from such an abstract model, designers refine it down to an implementation model in several refinement steps. The refinements may be done manually or in a formal transformation framework. The implementation model is then validated for functional correctness, performance, real-time requirements etc. Functional Safety, robustness to input assumptions, reliability under fault assumptions, and resilience to unknown adversities are considered as good design goals. This worked well when the cyber-physical systems were placed in an air-gapped environment with strong physical security, and in the hands of trusted engineers.

With the increasing networked distributed control of large and geographically distributed critical infrastructures such as smart grid, smart transportation systems, air traffic control system etc., the world of critical infrastructure has changed drastically. The business network of a utility are often connected to the critical control network – a phenomenon known as IP-convergence. This has ushered an unprecedented exposure to network borne cyber-attacks. Further, insider attacks have been on the rise world wide. Therefore, design goals must include cyber-security and cyber defense as first class design objectives. In this talk, we argue that in order to do so, designers' approach must assume a dual personality. While designing for robustness, reliability, functional safety – a model driven engineering approach would work – whereas for designing for cyber-security and defense, the designer has to step into the shoes of a malicious attacker. This duality is not necessarily distinct because certain correct-by-construction design approaches – for example, test-driven development approach requires designers to think of an environment model which tries to bring the system under development to errorenous states. The main duality we speak of comes from physical principle driven model development vs. data-driven model development.

Examples of first kind of duality could be that one has to consider the various observation or sampling points of the system (e.g. sensors to read or sample the physical environment), and think how an attacker might compromise the unobservability of those points without authentication. Designer also has to worry about how much knowledge of the system dynamics or the control mechanism of the system might be actually reconstructed by the attacker by observing a few compromised sensors or actuators. Moreover, one has to consider the actuation points of the system, and ponder how many actuation points the attacker has to take over in order to disrupt the dynamics of the system enough to create considerable damage. One has to envision how to obfuscate the dynamics of the system even when certain sensing or actuation points are compromised.

The second type of duality that we emphasize here arises from that fact that a large percentage of attacks recently were induced by inside attackers. Perimeter defense to protect the sensors/actuators/network alone cannot defend the system from insider attacks. In such cases, the question that one is confronted with is whether there is enough indication of an ongoing attack in the dynamics of the physical system itself.

This approach to viewing the system from an adversarial position requires one to topple the design paradigm over its head, and we will need to build models from data, and not just generate data from models. The designer has to observe a system in action even through partial observations, and construct a model close enough to the real system model and then use the partial access to create damages to the because the approximate model allows her to do so. Almost like a schizophrenic duality, the engineer also has to wear the designers hat, and consider a game in which the observations are obfuscated enough to render it impossible for an attacker to build any useful model to induce clever attacks. The designer has to worry if she can construct from unobfuscated observations a dynamics quickly enough so that the difference between the expected dynamics and the real dynamics can trigger alarms to alert the system administrators. In this talk, while discussing this view of system design, we will also talk about VSCADA – a virtual distributed SCADA lab we created for modeling SCADA systems for critical infrastructures, and how to use such a virtual lab completely implemented in simulation – to achieve the cyber security and cyber defense objectives of critical infrastructures – through attack injections, attack detection, and experiments on new defense mechanisms.

In the rest of this paper, we do not discuss this dual-personality issue further – instead provide an exposition of an experimental virtual lab we constructed which we envisaged as a tool in the hands of designers of SCADA systems which are integral parts of critical infrastructures such as power grid, water/suage system, transportation systems etc. Since the designers of such SCADA systems has to consider cyber attacks while designing such systems, a modeling and experimentation framework might be useful. A number of national laboratories in the United States, and few academic institutes have built physical SCADA labs, where real equipments are networked, and a small scale physical system is controlled and monitored through the real SCADA which can then be used for experimenting with cyber security. However, building such a lab is capital intensive, and often not possible. Therefore, our goal is to provide an alternative solution which can be used at least for certain cyber security experiments, evaluating cyber-security solutions, and educating students, and engineers about the dual track approach to designing cyber secure critical systems. In this laboratory, the physical system is simulated with a domain specific simulator – for example, for a power grid, PSLF or any such simulator can be used as a back-end surrogate for a real physical power grid. The data collection, measurements, and control are then designed through a SCADA front-end. Various security measures can be then emulated in software, and in software simulation of the network using a network simulator. The approach of data-driven modeling of nominal behavior of the physical system is done by collecting data from the back-end simulator when no cyber attack is simulated, a nomimal behavioral model is built with machine learning techniques, and classification of behaviors to differentiate between a cyber-attack induced behavior vs. a nominal stochastic variation in behavioris learnt, and then used on-line to check for various cyber-attack scenarios. In what follows in the rest of the paper is a brief description of the architecture, and use cases for this virtual SCADA Lab.

1.1 Goals of Designing a Virtual SCADA Lab

Supervisory control and data acquisition (SCADA) systems are systems designed to provide real time data on production operations, implement efficient control paradigms, and reduce control costs of operation. Although these systems were originally built to be in isolation, with the use of advanced computing and communications technologies, more and more SCADA systems are connected to proprietary/commercial networks. This allows more information to be shared across platforms. To assess the efficiency, security, or resilience of the deployed systems, system engineers need to have a test bed to verify the correctness of their SCADA configurations. Such a test bed should be scalable, flexible, supporting many SCADA communication protocols, and support multiple scenarios [1].

Though SCADA is built on a myriad of communication protocols, all we attempt to classify the different methods of attacking and disrupting these protocols into attacks that target availability, integrity, and confidentiality. In general, SCADA systems have communication protocols at all layers of the OSI reference model: the Physical layer, MAC layer, Network and Transport Layers, and the Application layer [1]. Though attacks on other layers can be implemented in our SCADA system, we consider denial-of-service (DoS) attacks that occurs at the Network and Transport Layers. For the purposes of our test bed we consider scenarios that compromise three security objectives and experimentation on our test bed. In considering the cyber-security of SCADA networks, we classify malicious attacks into three types:

•Attacks targeting availability, also called DoS attacks that aim to delay or block SCADA communications.

•Attacks targeting integrity that aim to modify or disrupt the data exchange in the SCADA system

•Attacks targeting confidentiality, such as Man-in-the-Middle attacks that intend to acquire unauthorized information from the SCADA network.

2 Virtual SCADA Testbed Design Methodology

The distributed virtual SCADA test bed is built on several design main objectives that differentiate with other SCADA test bed. The primary advantages that this test bed offers are Reconfigurability, Virtualization, Standardization, and Scalability (RVSS):

• Reconfigurability the configurations of virtual remote devices, instruments, network simulators and network topologies are adjustable

• Virtualization all hardware devices and their behaviors are modeled and represented in software so that the users can easily extend the scale of the system.

• Standardization most commonly used communication protocols such as OPC, Modbus, etc. are capable of being implemented and integrated into this platform.

• Scalability heterogeneous systems, large-scale systems are modeled accurately and support multiple users simultaneously.

2.1 Distributed VSCADA Testbed System Architecture Design

In our framework, the scalable unified back-end infrastructure manipulates the generation of measurement data, and the application specific front-end infrastructure implements data visualization and SCADA control features. The back-end development usually has the application-specific simulation framework; whether it is a real-time simulator or non-real time simulator. A light-weight virtual machine (LVM) simulates the operating system of each sensor. The field database holds the generated information from the simulation engine, and a script takes changes in the simulation process depending on the messages sent from the front-end. First the back-end architecture is described, followed by the front-end. The entire architecture infrastructure is illustrated in Fig. 1. The network is also simulated through communications simulators, which can be connected to security analysis tools. These network analysis tools simulate ways possible attackers can gain information and compromise the SCADA system.

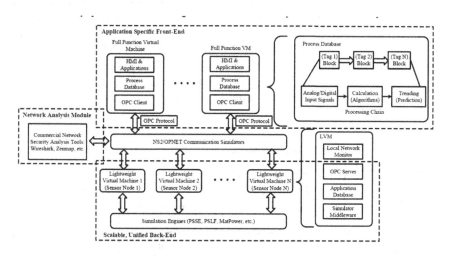

Fig. 1. Block diagram of the proposed Distributed Virtual SCADA

To handle the multiple Human Machine Interfaces (HMIs) that may run multiple simulations simultaneously, we use discrete event driven simulation to handle the system state. Discrete event driven simulation is when discrete events cause changes to the system. Usually, these events are anything relevant to a SCADA system and are unevenly distributed in time. A few examples include a load change in a power system or energy production in a nuclear control center.

Since there are variables constantly changing the simulation, we use an event scheduler in Python to the different instances of the simulation that is running. A simulation engine continuously creates scenarios dependent on changes to the HMI.

2.2   VSCADA Backend Architecture Design

Before the simulation starts, we initialize the system state and create a list of events. At the start of the simulation, an event scheduler records the current system time and event list. The events are stored with timestamps in the order of arrival. These events are sent over the communication network to the front-end after the start of the simulation. The scheduler replaces existing events with new events corresponding to the old event when the new simulation is started. After replacing the events, the scheduler updates the system time. The communication network then sends the information to the front-end, or HMI.

The figure below shows the backend infrastructure which consists of the network simulator, the sensor nodes, and the application simulators. Each sensor node is simulated in a lightweight virtual machine, which contains a local network monitor to interact with the network simulator, an OPC server, application database, and local network monitor. Each node gets sensor data from a database macro that controls the simulation engine.

In this SCADA system, OPC works as a communication protocol that works with the HMI and back-end simulator. If a change to the HMI, such as a load change, is made, the interactive agent picks up that new information and runs a new simulation. Both the variable change and the results of the new simulation are sent using the OPC protocol implemented by PyOPC. During the PyOPC processing, the system will first configure the initial states, and then design the system topology and system parameters, and finish the simulation control.

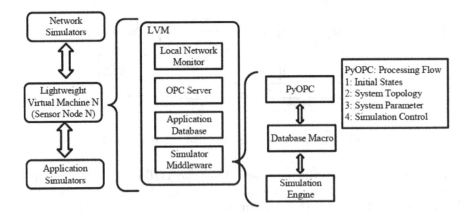

Fig. 2. Block diagram of back-end infrastructure and implementation of LVM with data flow of simulator middleware using PyOPC

NS2 is used to simulate the communication network. The interactive agent controls the simulation engines. The simulation engine runs a new simulation for a period of time and saves the new sensor values to a database. A script writes this time stamped values to tags that are read by PyOPC. Tags are blocks of information that are used by the HMI to allocate data. Each tag is capable of receiving information over some protocol and do some calculation and prediction.

Since in between simulations, there is the possibility of a loss of synchronization, an algorithm is used to update the simulation. This algorithm is shown in Fig. 3. The algorithm creates new simulations in an interrupt driven process, as shown below. After the simulation has started, a scheduling agent checks for changes in the HMI. The scheduling agent will continue to send out information until changes from the HMI are detected. The changes from the HMI correspond to new simulation parameters and creates a new set of simulation data. The scheduling agent then changes the pointer from the current time to the starting point of the new simulation.

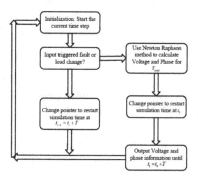

Fig. 3. An algorithm for synchronization between the simulation process and the interrupted new inputs

2.3 VSCADA Frontend Architecture Design

The SCADA HMI interacts with the communication network infrastructure by sending synchronized certain packets of data representing events in the system. Tags are used as inputs to the system, such as a load change or a fault. These tags are stored inside of a process database, which updates the HMI. Changes to the HMI are send to the scheduler and logged. Synchronization error is avoided with the use of an optimized global scheduler. Each tag is represented either as an analog or digital input and communicates over the network simulator. Each tag gets its data from the OPC Client software. The OPC client is part of the front-end design. The time for polling is predetermined by the HMI. Each tag connected to the OPC client corresponds to an identical tag on the OPC Server in the back-end infrastructure. The network delay in the HMI is simulated through different network simulators, discussed in the next section.

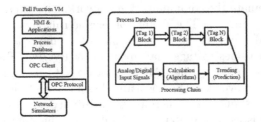

Fig. 4. Block diagram of front-end infrastructure and data flow of process database

2.4 Network Simulation/Emulation Architecture Design

When the simulation engine sends out values to the HMI, it is important to be capable of modeling the time delay in the cyber physical system. This could potentially be exploited in a cyber-attack. For this reason, we use a network simulator to model the delay paths that are involved in a large power system. This is especially prevalent for large scale distributed grids, which have large distances between nodes, corresponding to significant time delays between measurements. Thus, for each container, we have to add a delay in the in the network simulator that corresponds to the geographical distance from the HMI. Another important part of the network simulation is accurately representing the protocols used in the network. Since a vast majority of the protocols are implemented using a TCP/IP suite, we use that in this case, especially when implementing the OPC protocol over TCP/IP. We also emulate the different tools that are available to the potential hacker. With this reconfigurable lab, any potential user could gain or restrict access to certain parts of the network, which could test what damage an attacker could do with different knowledge about the network. It is important to consider scenarios where the attacker has detailed knowledge about the structure of the network, to account for sabotage. In this situation, we use Wireshark as a tool to observe and record information on the network.

3   VSCADA Implementation

The Virtual SCADA software test bed was divided into five parts: 1) the HMI; 2) the communications protocol, and the communications network 3) the SCADA master server, which will be represented using a local process database; 4) the sensors operating system, which are simulated in a lightweight Linux Container, and 5) the sensor values which are created in a simulation software. The platform consisted of computers running 64-bit version of Windows 7. However, the virtual machines and containers that that hosted the HMI and the sensor operating system, respectively, ran Linux. In the platform, we had one computer that served as the HMI, and another that served as the backend simulator. In simulating cyber-attacks, a third computer was used as an attacker to the network.

3.1   Human Machine Interface (HMI)

We use iFix as the software package to simulate the HMI. iFix is developed by General Electric and includes a SCADA engine, with an open architecture [9]. Since iFix is widely used by power utilities, it gives an advantage over other software packages. iFix gives the flexibility of communicating with multiple hardware components from a single server. It also provides VBA scripting and a scalable networking model. OPC is used as the communication protocol, though this can easily be modified to MODBUS or any other protocol. iFix receives simulation results from an OPC server running on a central server, and then display sensor values on the iFix GUI.

3.2   SCADA Master Control Server

We use the relational database that comes with the iFIX software that dictates that information be sent in the form of tags. Each tag corresponds to an aspect of the SCADA system, such as the voltage or phase of a bus. Over 400 tags can be stored in a database at once. As shown in Fig. 1, tags can also run some basic prediction algorithms.

Each tag corresponds to a particular item in the HMI. Tags can be triggered by alarms that inform the user if an item is out of a specified range. We also use tags to communicate between HMI and the server running the simulation. For example, the 39 bus example stores faults values in tags that alert the server about tripped fault lines. A tripped line creates a new simulation, Tags are given read/write capability and can be specified as either analog or digital values.

On the backend, an OPC server stores information from the tags. Tags in the OPC server each map to a tag on the client side. Though iFix has its own client software, a separate OPC server had to be used. For the 39-bus case, we used PyOPC as the server for the platform. PyOPC gives the ability to communicate with other applications through Python Scripting. This gives an added advantage of maintaining the same scripting language in the power system simulator as well as the communication standard.

3.3   Communication Protocol

For this application, we used PyOPC as the server for the platform. Using PyOPC, tags would be created that would correspond to aspects of the SCADA system. Data is stored in a database and sent over OPC to the HMI. PyOPC uses a platform-independent standard, OPC UA (Unified Architecture), which communicates by sending messages over local networks or internet. Any web standard supported by the OPC UA server can be used for communication between an OPC server and client [10].

3.4   Linux Containers/NS2 Interface

In order to properly simulate the operating system of each RTU, we run several Linux containers that each run a lightweight Linux operating system. Each operating system runs a PyOPC server that obtains information from the software simulator running on the main server. This PyOPC server then sends the particular sensor value information over the NS2 network simulator that connects the sensor data to the front-end and mimics the network protocol that is being used in the cyber-physical system.

NS2 is a communications network simulator that evaluates a network protocols performance. NS2 can be used as a discrete event simulator. It has a library of network models which covers all protocol layers except the physical layer in the network reference model. Most of NS2 is written in C++.

3.5   Software Simulators

To interact with the HMI, information is written into an Excel database with a Python script. The script is constantly updating the simulations from the simulation engine to a local database. If any input tags are updated the python script runs a new simulation and update its local database with a set of values corresponding to the changed power system. This script can be used across multiple platforms.

We use several different software suites to simulate the power flow and dynamics simulation. To simulate the power systems, we use Power System Simulator for Engineering (PSS/E) software for power system dynamic simulation. PSS/E is a power system software package designed by Siemens, which provides both steady state and dynamic power system simulations. PSS/E is written in Java and also gives a GUI to use for power system simulation, though this is not used. In addition there is a library of electromechanical dynamic models and can simulate a system with up to 60000 buses. Since Python can be used with PSS/E we use it for the 39-bus simulation and for the cascading failure example.

4   Cyber Security Case Study

We now present a scenario on our platform where we gain network access to the SCADA server through which we would be able to learn information about the structure of the system, and use that information to carry out an attack that could cripple the cyber-physical infrastructure. We assume that our network attack could obtain detailed system knowledge about the cyber-physical system. This system knowledge could be used to launch a data injection attack that leads to a cascading failure.

In creating these attacks, we simulate network vulnerabilities as well as system vulnerabilities. For each of these scenarios we assume that the attacker has disruption resources that enable it to make changes to the system, a prior system knowledge about critical buses required for stability, and disclosure resources that allow the attacker to observe the system for long periods of time. Since we control the simulation, we simulate attacks that require detailed knowledge of the cyber-physical system.

4.1 Network Security Scenario

When considering cyber security attacks, we assume the attacker has some knowledge of the network topology. Since our system uses the OPC protocol over the TCP/IP protocol suite, we assume that the attacker has some access to the network that is used to communicate with the devices.

We make a number of assumptions about the network in order for our attacker to be able to gain access to sensor information. The attacker would require nodes around the SCADA server to be vulnerable and time on the order of days to be able to both survey the network and capture the state information necessary for a data injection attack. Since the attacker has been observing the system, they are also to estimate the sequence numbers on the TCP/IP packets to account for the delay between observing the system and sending the false information. Such a powerful attacker is probably an insider. Since our attacker has a priori system knowledge, we assume they are targeting particular sensors that are critical to the system stability. To characterize the network, a large number of open source tools can be used to survey the network and find the range of IP addresses near the target server. In this case, we use a software tool Zenmap to use the TCP/IP protocol suite to isolate the IP address of the target server. This step would ordinarily require time and knowledge of the network in question to isolate the IP address of the OPC server. In our example, we find that the OPC server is located at 38.68.240.171. Since the OPC protocol was designed to operate using Microsofts DCOM standard, we use port 135 to initiate all connections across the network. Once gaining access to the network, we use Wireshark to make observations on the network and gather state information for a data injection attack. Wireshark is a network packet analyzer that can capture and display network packets in detail. Since it is cross-platform compatible, we are capable of using it to observe the network across all operating systems in our network. Wireshark also allows the ability to filter data and IP addresses, so a potential attacker could collect data and analyze data at certain points of time. This allows the attacker to record the system at different points in time that can be used in a replay attack or for information in a bad data injection attack.

We can relay the information gathered from the device to the actual OPC server by simultaneously running OPC client software. Doing this, we can create a model of the dynamic communication and control process in the SCADA network and create an attacker simulation of how the Power System works. Since we also have the actual values of the entire simulation, we can compare how similar an attacker model is to the actual power system. This entire process is illustrated in the Fig. 5.

4.2 Data Injection Attack Implementation

We now describe a data injection attack that could be launched on our system with knowledge obtained from observing critical sensor values. We assume the attacker has a priori knowledge of the structure of the power system, which means that they would know the critical nodes that would cause a cascading

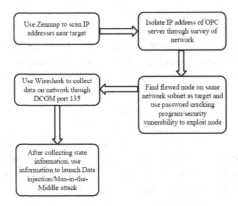

Fig. 5. Process of gaining access to network for attack

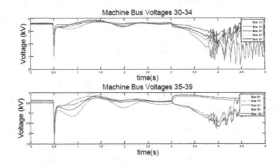

Fig. 6. Process of gaining access to network for attack

failure. An attacker injects false data that causes a wrong state estimation of the variables of the power system, which in turn causes cascading failures [13]. We use this network attack to create a cascading failure on our power system. On our VSCADA system, we use a compromised node on the same network to send faulty sensor data to the HMI. The simulation is run under steady state operating conditions. At 1 second in the simulation, we manipulate bus values to create a three-phase fault between buses 16 and 17. After 100 ms relays act and trip the line to clear the fault. This causes the system to become congested and few of the lines to overload. After three seconds, thermal limit relays act and trip the line between buses 15 and 16. This causes the generators to go out of synch with the power system completely failing. We demonstrate the results of this simulated attack in Fig. 6. VSCADA is also capable of simulating other attacks to SCADA systems. With access to the network we can launch denial-of-service and man-in-the-middle attacks with varying levels of security. We can also test the security firmware on the sensors, which can demonstrate how feasible it is to compromise different sensors. Different security protocols are also easily emulated and tested in this framework.

5 Conclusion

Our view regarding the design of cyber secure critical infrastructure is discussed in this talk in terms of a dual-personality design approach – which we see as a schizoid approach due to the split between traditional model driven engineering of such systems, vs. data-driven modeling based approach to security. In order to facilitate such a design, we are building a virtual laboratory, which we describe in the paper. We present a virtual test bed that integrates several SCADA applications into a single framework. We describe the framework and how it emulates the communication network that is used in the SCADA system. We also discuss a possible cyber security attack simulation usecases in this framework. This by no means is a complete solution, but captures our current thinking with regard to the science of design of secure critical infrastructures.

Acknowledgments. Authors would like to thank the organizers of the SPACE 2015 Conference for inviting us to deliver this invited talk.

References

1. Krutz, R.L.: Securing SCADA Systems. Wiley Publishing, Inc. (2005)
2. Craig Jr., P.A., Mortensen, J., Dagle, J.E.: Metrics for the National SCADA Test Bed Program, Report, Pacific Northwest National Laboratory, October 2008
3. Reaves, B., Morris, T.: An open virtual test bed for industrial control system security research. International Journal of Information Security 11(4), 215–229 (2012)
4. Davis, C.M., Tate, J.E., Okhravi, H., Grier, C., Overbye, T.J., Nicol, D.: SCADA cyber security test bed development. In: 38th North American Power Symposium, NAPS 2006, pp. 483–488, Septembe 17–19, 2006. doi:10.1109/NAPS.2006.359615
5. Bergman, D.C., Jin, D., Nicol, D.M., Yardley, T.: The virtual power system test bed and inter-test bed integration. In: Proceedings of the 2nd conference on Cyber security experimentation and test (CSET 2009), p. 5. USENIX Association, Berkeley (2009)
6. Giani, A., Karsai, G., Roosta, T., Shah, A., Sinopoli, B., Wiley, J.: A test bed for secure and robust SCADA systems. In: 14th IEEE Real-time and Embedded Technology and Applications Symposium (RTAS 2008) WIP session (2008)
7. Hong, J., Wu, S.-S., Stefanov, A., Fshosha, A., Liu, C.-C., Gladyshev, P., Govindarasu, M.: An intrusion and defense test bed in a cyber-power system environment. In: 2011 IEEE Power and Energy Society General Meeting, pp. 1–5, July 24–29, 2011
8. Dayal, A., Deng, Y., Tbaileh, A., Shukla, S.: VSCADA: A reconfigurable virtual SCADA testbed for simulating power utility control center operations. In: 2015 IEEE To Appear Power and Energy Society General Meeting, July 26–30, 2015
9. GE Intelligent Platforms, Proficy HMI/SCADA - iFIX, datasheet, GFA-562D, August 2012
10. Lian, F.-L., Moyne, J.R., Tilbury, D.M.: Performance evaluation of control networks: Ethernet, ControlNet, and DeviceNet. IEEE Control Systems 21(1), 66–83 (2001)

54   A. Dayal, Y. Deng, and S.K. Shukla

11. Deng, Y., Lin, H., Shukla, S., Thorp, J., Mili, L.: Co-simulating power systems and communication network for accurate modeling and simulation of PMU based wide area measurement systems using a global event scheduling technique. In: 2013 Workshop on Modeling and Simulation of Cyber-Physical Energy Systems (MSCPES), pp. 1–6, May 20–20, 2013
12. Siemens, Dynamic Simulation, White Paper, 02/2
13. Liu, Y., Reiter, M.K., Ning, P.: False data injection attacks against state estimation in electric power grids. In: Proc. 16th ACM Conf. Comput. Commun. Security, Chicago, IL, USA, p. 21, November 2009

Designing for Attack Surfaces: Keep Your Friends Close, but Your Enemies Closer

Trent Jaeger[1], Xinyang Ge[1], Divya Muthukumaran[2], Sandra Rueda[3],
Joshua Schiffman[4], and Hayawardh Vijayakumar[5]

[1] The Pennsylvania State University, University Park, PA, USA
[2] Imperial College, London, UK
[3] Universidad de Los Andes, Bogota, Colombia
[4] Hewlett-Packard Labs, Bristol, UK
[5] Samsung Research America, Mountain View, CA, USA

Abstract. It is no surprise to say that attackers have the upper hand on security practitioners today when it comes to host security. There are several causes for this problem ranging from unsafe programming languages to the complexity of modern systems at large, but fundamentally, all of the parties involved in constructing and deploying systems lack a methodology for reasoning about the security impact of their design decisions. Previous position papers have focused on identifying particular parties as being "enemies" of security (e.g., users and application developers), and proposed removing their ability to make security-relevant decisions. In this position paper, we take this approach a step further by "keeping the enemies closer," whereby the security ramifications of design and deployment decisions of all parties must be evaluated to determine if they violate security requirements or are inconsistent with other party's assumptions. We propose a methodology whereby application developers, OS distributors, and system administrators propose, evaluate, repair, and test their artifacts to provide a defensible *attack surface*, the set of entry points available to an attacker. We propose the use of a *hierarchical state machine* (HSM) model as a foundation for automatically evaluating attack surfaces for programs, OS access control policies, and network policies. We examine how the methodology tasks can be expressed as problems in the HSM model for each artifact, motivating the possibility of a comprehensive, coherent, and mostly-automated methodology for deploying systems to manage accessibility to attackers.

1 Introduction

It is no surprise to say that attackers have the upper hand on security practitioners today when it comes to host security. For the most part, security practitioners have little insight into where the next exploitable vulnerability will be found, so there seems to be little that they can do to detect and remove vulnerabilities before attackers. For example, a significant effort has been put into reengineering of network-facing servers (e.g., OpenSSH [45] and Postfix mail server [65]), but while these improvements have prevented a variety of new exploits against those daemons, there are so many programs that have access to network data that security practitioners are overwhelmed. On the

R.S. Chakraborty et al. (Eds.): SPACE 2015, LNCS 9354, pp. 55–74, 2015.
DOI: 10.1007/978-3-319-24126-5_4

positive side, many of these programs are run in unprivileged processes, so their compromise does not directly impact the system integrity. However, the negative side is that we (the security community) are even less effective at preventing local exploits than remote exploits.

Finding the root causes of such problems has been difficult. It appears that each party in the construction and deployment of a system is at fault for multiple poor decisions. Application developers clearly are not developing secure code. They still fail to prevent the same types of basic vulnerabilities (e.g., buffer overflows) that we have recognized for years. Further, when given type-safe languages with well-defined formal semantics, developers choose C and various scripting languages, which have all proven very difficult to use securely. OS distributors package the applications together into distributions, but historically, they abdicate responsibility for securing deployment of their distributions to application developers (it's the programs that have the bugs) or the system administrators (they cannot configure systems properly). Despite the introduction of comprehensive mandatory access control (MAC) systems [43, 63] in some distributions, we are still suffering from a variety of local exploits[1]. Finally, the system administrators are left to try to deploy a secure system from insecure parts. It is an impossible task of immense complexity. Currently, in order to deploy a system securely, a system administrator must understand the manner in which attackers can access their systems via the network (which they do pretty well), how the access control policy manages attackers' access to process (such policies are complex), and how programs handle untrusted input data (there are too many interfaces).

A variety of valuable security mechanisms have been developed, but these have not resulted in shifting the balance from the attackers to the defenders. For example, we have known about buffer overflows for many years, so a variety of mechanisms ranging from buffer overflow prevention [14, 44] to protecting the programs execution integrity [1, 10] to controlling the operating sequences that may be invoked [17, 29]. The expense of many of these services has prevented or delayed their adoption, so others have focused on bug detection and prevention (e.g., [5, 40, 46, 68]). Researchers have also developed models that enable reasoning about the integrity of systems [7, 12]. However, the assumptions underlying these models have been in conflict with the practice of deploying systems, and the security community has made little or no headway in changing such practice. Researchers again have developed other models that approximate classical integrity for conventional systems [28, 53, 57], but these require more effort that has not been forthcoming. Finally, system administrators are left to contemplate all the options and trade-offs without any coherent approach to reason about such options. Their task is far too complex.

Returning to the question of who is at fault, it appears that everyone is at one level or another, so the question is how to proceed forward. A number of approaches have been proposed to remove security decision-making from various parties. We agree that the user cannot be trusted to make anything but win-win security decisions [60], but what should be done about the application developers, OS distributors, and system adminis-

---

[1] Part of the problem is that to reduce the complexity of use, these systems are used incompletely, only to protect system services against network attackers, as proposed by other incomplete methods [36, 41].

trators? All need to make decisions that may impact security, but as with users, they also should only decide among win-win choices with respect to security. Wurster and van Oorschot argue this point for application developers [67], but we argue that this applies to all parties. The challenge is how to apply this approach to all parties. Solworth argues that this will require a fundamental change in systems and programming practice [56], and while we agree that some changes should be encouraged wholeheartedly, we argue that the revolutionary change must be accompanied by a tool-driven methodology that enforces any new requirements comprehensively and usably for each party. Building on the prior analogies, we refer to this approach as "keeping your friends close, but your enemies closer."[2] The idea is that the application developers, OS distributors, and system administrators must work by a methodology that supports decision-making among secure choices rather than giving insecure choices.

In this paper, we propose a methodology for constructing and deploying systems based on the concept of a *hierarchical state machine* [2] (HSM), a model used previously in software model checking. We find that application developers, OS distributors, and system administrators each make decisions that impact security and that these decisions build on one another, requiring a representation that enables checking of conflicts between different party's decisions. The HSM model represents a hierarchy of components (originally, code modules) and their interactions (calls and returns, and resultant data flows), but we find that this approach can be generalized to represent not only program modules, but the data flows that result from the combination of programs into an OS distribution with its access control policy and the data flows that result from the combination of OS distributions into systems of OS distribution instances (which we will call *hosts*, regardless of whether they run on physical or virtual machines) with its network policy (and optionally, virtual machine monitor policy). With the system's data flows expressed in an HSM, the question then is whether we can automate key decisions that these parties make. Our methodology identifies the types of decisions that must be made by each party, which turn out to be the same decisions on different artifacts, and we examine the possibility of automating or at least providing significant automated support for these decisions. While it is early, we are optimistic that such a view of system-wide management of data flow has potential as a new paradigm for achieving secure construction and deployment in practice.

The remainder of the paper is as follows. In Section 2, we examine problems with the current approach to configuring systems and discuss some trends that motivate our proposed approach. In Section 3, we define the concept of attack surfaces, which serves as the basis for decision-making for each party. In Section 4, we outline the proposed approach, showing that application developers, OS distributors, and system administrators need to make decisions that are test against security requirements and be able to build on each others' work effectively. In Section 5, we define our approach, based on the hierarchical state machine model [2] and examine the problems that need to be solved at each methodology task in detail to identify the opportunities and challenges in providing automated support for such tasks.

---

[2] There seems to be a lot of confusion about the origin of this quote, ranging from Sun-Tzu (Art of War), Machiavelli, and Petrarch, but we were not able to find a definitive source that predates its use in the movie, "The Godfather, Part II."

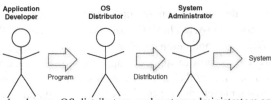

Fig. 1. Application developers, OS distributors, and system administrators are the main parties in constructing software components. The process of constructing a computing system involves the composition of programs into OS distributions and then into systems.

2 Background

In this section, we review how systems are currently configured, the recent trends that may change this situation (hopefully for the better).

2.1 System Configuration

Figure 1 shows the process of configuring a system in terms of the major parties. There would be no system to configure without programs, and application developers provide programs. A *program* consists of one or more executables and scripts, optional program-specific libraries, and deployment-independent data. Operating system (OS) distributors configure one or more programs for their system, including the definition of program packages for installation (including configurations) and security policies. Here, we focus mainly on the access control policy covering the program. System administrators compose systems from one or more OS distributions at a time. These distributions may run on one physical platform or more, thanks to ubiquitous virtualization. System administrators configure network policies to determine how the systems interact, may apply system hardening [6] to improve the security of the system beyond that of the OS distributor, and may change the configurations and access control policies over programs. Users are not shown in Figure 1, as, like many others, we assume that users do not make security-critical decisions [60].

Application developers have a tremendous challenge in building programs that protect themselves from attackers. Nearly any interesting program consists of multiple components, written in multiple languages, by many application developers. Also, software engineering practice has made design approaches that reuse components successful, but many bugs result from incorrect reuse of components. Further, the trade-offs that application developers make often involve compromises of security (e.g., features vs. security) that result in further vulnerabilities. The current state of application developer practice with respect to security is so dismal that Wurster and van Oorschot propose to take security-relevant programming decisions away from application developers through enforcement of best practices [67].

Operating system distributors have an even more difficult challenge in configuring their OS distributions in a manner that ensures security. Historically, the task of OS distributors is to provide an ecosystem for deploying applications easily, flexibly, and with good performance characteristics. While operating systems fundamentally provide protection mechanisms (e.g., address spaces and access control mechanisms), the aim was mainly to keep one program's failure from affecting another program's execution. As a result, security decisions were largely left in the hands of application developers in conventional systems. This approach is inherently incapable of enforcing security [31]. Some operating systems over the years deploy mandatory access control (MAC) for controlling, even malicious, programs, but mandatory access control systems that aim to enforce strong integrity guarantees [4, 12, 23, 30, 53] have not seen broad use, and the application of MAC enforcement to conventional systems [41, 43] has been hampered by complexity and enforcement of informal goals, such as least privilege [51]. Solworth argues for improved testing effectiveness and reduced complexity in operating systems [56], which we agree are insufficient in current MAC systems.

System administrators are left with the task of configuring the deployment of these OS distributions consisting of many such programs. System administration may consist of many tasks. First, system administrators specify the network policy, which determines how the deployed systems communicate among one another and the Internet at large. Second, they may determine the programs that are run on each system. Third, they may configure various system services based on the site's security requirements. Finally, system administrators are often responsible for the access control policies on their systems. Given that they have many physical machines to manage and they must respond to the non-deterministic behavior of their user community (and, of course, attackers), the security community's assumption that they can perform all of these tasks effectively on such complex systems is misplaced.

Thus, we find that none of these parties is capable of performing the tasks necessary to configure secure systems. Application developers do not ensure that their programs can defend themselves from attackers. OS distributors piece these programs together into systems without understanding the limitations that are built into programs nor configuring systems in a way that ensures any meaningful security property. Finally, system administrators are left with the responsibility to make all of this work. The semantic gap between the fine-grained security decisions in programs and those at the system-level make it impractical for even the best system administrators to configure a secure system unless they terminate all connections to attackers.

2.2   Trends in System Configuration

Despite our current situation, there are some trends that indicate that the kind of revolutionary change needed to develop systems that protect their integrity may be possible.

System Administrators Can Manage Firewalls. First, we start with a low-hanging fruit. It appears that network firewalls are an effective approach for protecting systems from attackers. We surmise that firewalls are effective for two reasons: (1) they actually are capable of reducing the accessibility of systems to attackers and (2) system administrators can define firewall policies with little knowledge about program or OS behavior. First, a firewall defines the first line of defense to a system, so its effectiveness is largely independent of how the system is configured behind the firewall. Thus, a firewall rule that denies an attacker access to a particular host prevents the host from being directly accessible to an attacker, regardless of how poorly the OS or programs are built Second, system administrators only need to understand the binding between ports and programs to configure a firewall. This information is standardized, so it is well-known. The result is that system administrators can do an effective job of defining firewall rules, even though these rulebases can get complex [66].

OS Distributors Define MAC Policies. MAC policy design unfortunately interacts more subtly with the system's programs, but recent trends in MAC policy configuration involve OS distributors learning more about their programs. MAC policies for SELinux are defined by a small group of experts in SELinux who define policies per program, implying that they study the permissions necessary for the program to run securely. This marks a major shift from OSes supporting arbitrary programs and their security requirements to OS distributors planning for the programs that their OS will run (for the security-relevant ones, anyway). A problem is that the permissions necessary for the program to run are easier to determine than the permissions necessary to protect the security of the system. Also, an artifact of the complexity of MAC policies is that users of such systems are no longer capable of modifying the OS distributors' policies. This may be a blessing in disguise, as this removes the responsibility of MAC policy specification from system administrators and places more demands on the OS distributors to assess programs. We have not yet seen the benefit from the former, as MAC policies for conventional systems are not designed to meet a security goal (e.g., Biba integrity [7], Clark-Wilson integrity [12], or even any practical approximation [28, 53, 57]) and OS distributors still lack the tools necessary to understand how a program's implementation may impact the security of the system at large.

Application Developers Can Follow Directions. A variety of software engineering methodologies have been developed, but it was not until recently that security improvement became a focus. Meta-compilation [68], ITS4 [61], and Prefast [34] were developed to find program bugs, including security bugs. However, such tools are unsound (i.e., do not find all bugs). More powerful approaches were developed to prove the correctness of complex software [47], such as drivers, although such techniques do not scale to large software components. We believe that programmers could be induced to follow a testing approach that scaled to the size of systems effectively. Many companies implement structured test procedures before releasing code, but that has not had a tangible effect on overall system security. Studies have shown that "test-driven development" [39] does have a significant impact on defect reduction, but our concern is that we are not doing the right testing in programs nor are we testing the composition of programs and OS distributions into systems.

Emerging Systems Architectures Might Enable Better Scalability in Administration. Say what one will about whether to trust your security-critical data to cloud systems [48], but the cloud architecture offers an opportunity to improve the scalability of system administrator decision-making. This occurs in two ways: (1) the cloud base platforms are defined by the cloud vendor, enabling a single configuration to apply to many systems, and (2) cloud vendors often provide a list of preconfigured OS distributions for their clients, aiming to encourage the use of known systems. In the first case, we envision that a single group of developers and administrators could define and manage the most secure system we can configure. Further, as this group could include the skills of application developers, OS distributors, and system administrators, they could cover the entire scope of security decisions. At present, however, few if any concrete security guarantees are offered by cloud vendors[3]. Second, by standardizing the OS distributions used, there is the potential that their configurations could be carefully designed to improve security. This will depend greatly on how well the OS distributors understand their programs' security defenses (or lack thereof).

Our claim is that the lack of a comprehensive methodology for designing and deploying systems that meet concrete security requirements prevents us from getting the upper-hand on attackers. As a result, everyone is the enemy of security. We have been looking for short-cuts, hoping that by incremental changes, we may be able to luck-out into the deployment of well-defended systems. However, the reality is otherwise. We need an approach based on concrete security goals. To date only information flow security models offer a precise and comprehensive understanding of possible attacks, as all the paths that attackers can use to access processes are identified by information flows. We need application developers to build their programs in such a way that they can understand the threats to their programs and evaluate the effectiveness of their defenses to such threats. We need OS distributors to be able to reason about program security in the context of their access control policy to determine if the threats they face are adequately addressed. Finally, we need a methodology where system administrators can make the decisions that they understand and leverage the improved efforts of the OS distributors and application developers effectively.

3   Attack Surfaces

We propose that the basis for security decisions should be the system's attack surface. An *attack surface* is defined as the entry points that are accessible to an attacker [20]. An attack surface was originally defined in the context of a program, but we use it in the context of programs, OS distributions, and systems, such that every design and deployment decision must account for the resulting attack surface and whether that attack surface can be adequately defended.

The key challenge regarding attack surfaces is to identify all the attack surfaces that may be used in a deployment. Consider the Apache web server program. The httpd-2.2.14 distribution including the Apache core and all the modules contains 2451 unique library calls. In theory, any of these library calls may cause an Apache process to input data from a system object (e.g., a network connect, an IPC, a file, etc.) accessible to an attacker. However, we may not want just any interface to be used to read data that may be modified by an attacker. Instead, the Apache team may consider only the interfaces that are known to be accessible to attackers, Apache's attack surface. A problem is that the Apache team's view of an attack surface may not correspond to the actual attack surfaces created when it is deployed.

Probably, the Apache team will consider the network interfaces among its attack surface, but an Apache process may also retrieve untrusted inputs from files, IPCs, etc.

---

[3] As a contrast, concrete claims regarding physical security, such as armed guards for the data center, are made [3].

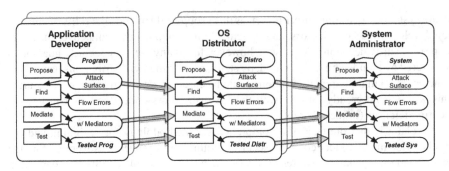

Fig. 2. The proposed approach for testing the composition of programs and OS distributions into systems.

For example, users may be able to provide content, including scripts, that Apache uses. In another case, when Apache forks a child process it creates a pipe to receive input from that child, but that child may be used to execute untrusted content, so such pipes may be the source of untrusted input. A recent vulnerability was found for this interface.

Previous work in identifying attack surfaces has focused on one component at a time, either on a program or an OS access control policy, but neither alone is sufficient to reason about attack surfaces accurately. First, researchers examined programs to identify possible attack surface interfaces and evaluate their significance [32]. In general, any program interface may define a location through which an attack may originate, so this work focused on identifying interfaces to valuable resources for attackers, hypothesizing that these would require the most attention for defense.

Second, others have used the system's access control policy to identify the programs that may have attack surfaces [11]. In this case, Linux systems with SELinux [43] and AppArmor [41] access control policies were compared based on the number of programs that were accessible to a network attacker and also had direct access to modify the Linux kernel (e.g., install a rootkit). What we want to know is whether attack surfaces created by the deployment conflict in some way with the expected attack surfaces of the program. For example, the OpenSSH daemon was carefully reengineered (privilege-separated) to limit the interfaces through which it receives untrusted input [45]. Nonetheless, a recent vulnerability was found caused by the incorrect parsing of users' authorized keys files. By looking at attack surfaces in the context of their deployment, we could locate this interface as a potential risk, rather than waiting for the attacker to identify it for us [62]. We also believe that examining OS distributions to identify attack surfaces in the context of their deployment, relative to network policies, is necessary to ensure that all decisions are acceptable for security.

4   Proposed Approach

What we want is to be able to test: (1) whether the attack surface expected for each component is consistent with its deployment and (2) that each component only permits authorized operations for its deployment. First, suppose that application developers constructed their program assuming that a program interface was adequately defended, but a vulnerability is found. In that case, OS distributors better design access control policies that prevent attackers from accessing that program interface. Second, the OS distributor must verify that the program when limited to this restricted attack surface only authorizes operations approved by the OS distributor.

The current approach to testing and the use of results of prior testing is inadequate to build secure systems. We surmise that program vulnerabilities are caused because: (1) the product was tested under an attack surface that differs (if any was identified) from the attack surface when deployed; (2) the product was not tested thoroughly enough to protect itself from threats at the "tested" interfaces; and/or (3) the OS distributors and system administrators do not know the extent of such testing, so their suggested deployment is a blind risk. A similar relationship between OS distributors and system administrators holds for determining whether an entire OS distribution will be deployed securely. Unfortunately, the testing of access control policies is even more ad hoc than for programs, as conventional systems that use MAC enforcement typically aim for least privilege [51], but that requirement cannot be precisely specified and tested. As a result, we are not surprised that the security community is in a reactive, rather than proactive mode of operation. The question is whether we can develop a methodology for *comprehensive testing of programs and distributions based on explicit assumptions that can be validated by parties that use these components.* We examine the roles that application developers, OS distributors, and system administrators would play (enabled by automated tools) to enable such a methodology.

Figure 2 shows the high-level view of the proposed approach. For each component, we see a sequence of steps consisting of: (1) (propose) propose the component's attack surface; (2) (find) identifying data (information) flows where an attacker affects the component's integrity, identifying a *flow error*; (3) (mediate) asserting *mediators* that comprehensively resolve all flow errors in the component; and (4) (test) testing the efficacy of the mediators to thwart all instances of the possible attacks from those flows. The aim is that each party inputs their component to this methodology and the methodology generates a security-tested version of that component. Any other party that uses a security-tested version obtains the proposed attack surface used in testing (from step 1), a summary of the information flows enabled by the component (from step 3), and the testing methodology used in determining the summary (from step 4). Thus, parties can test the use of others' components in their systems to obtain a comprehensive evaluation of security.

What we find intriguing is that the sequence of steps for each component is the same in this methodology, regardless of whether the component is a program, OS distribution, or system consisting of many OS distribution instances (hosts).

Application developers need to test their programs against the threats of attackers. First, they propose an attack surface for their program, which defines their assumption of the threats that are possible. An attack surface identifies low-integrity sources to the program. Second, application developers need to find what problems exist in their programs. In this case, a problem is where data from an attacker source may be used to modify data that is used for a high-integrity sink. That is, there is a data flow from the attacker to high-integrity program data. Third, the application developers must assert *mediation statements* to control such data flows. The problem is to determine what mediation statements to place at what locations in the code to address the illegal flow. The placement problem is non-trivial, as the application developer must make sure that all illegal flows are covered, this is difficult to ensure manually. Determining what mediation is necessary to prevent attacks is also difficult because such mediation is program-specific, in general. Fourth, we need to test that these mediations are adequate for the program. In general, testing is language and program-specific, but there is a rich literature in both testing methods and techniques for various problems, including security [5,27,34,54,68,70]. We envision that our methodology will leverage such methods and techniques, making them available to application developers. Eclipse [16] is a good foundation for integrating such testing for programmers.

We find that OS distributors have to perform similar tasks as those of application developers, but they construct a different artifact (an OS distribution) and they build this from others' components[4] (multiple programs). As mentioned in Section 2.2, a key trend is that OS distributors will have some prior knowledge about the programs (security-relevant ones) that run on their systems, so they will configure MAC policies for the programs running on their systems. For each program, the OS distributor first proposes an attack surface for their distribution. This typically consists of identifying the networked programs on their system, but some systems enable inter-VM communication via hypervisor operations, resulting in more operations to consider. Second, the OS distributor needs to compute the programs that may be accessible to attackers, particularly how attackers may impact how the valuable system data may be accessed. In this case, an information flow analysis is proposed to find how network processes create information flows in the distribution (e.g., computed from SELinux policies [19,22,52,59]). Rather than just using the access policy though, we envision that the information flows enabled by programs (from their data flows computed above) should be used to compute more accurate flows – not all program data flows, however, but a summary that expresses the information flows generated. Third, the OS distributor must identify where to resolve such information flow errors. In Biba integrity [7], such flows may be mediated by guards, but in conventional systems, the programs are expected to mediate their low-integrity inputs. In this case, the OS distributor needs information to make decisions about how to choose among such options based on what component attack surfaces they will accept. Fourth, the OS distributor must test the effectiveness of the selected mediation. Where such mediation depends on a program, we should leverage prior program testing in this evaluation.

Finally, the system administrators must configure systems consisting of one or more OS distributions into a coherently-defended whole. As described previously, system administrators' main focus is network policy (e.g., firewall). The question is how can configuration of a network policy build effectively on the work of the application developers and OS distributors. First, system administrators define the actual attack surface of the system from the network policy. However, they may not have as clear an understanding of what is valuable in the distributions that they use. Currently, OS deployments mix data (which belongs to the system administrator's organization) with

---

[4] Of course, application developers may have to compose programs from others' programs, so in those cases, they may have to adopt some aspects of the OS distributors' tasks described here.

code (which belongs to the OS distributor), so making this separation explicit and enabling each of the OS distributor and system administrator to define valuable data would make the security problem clearer. Second, while system administrators do not need to make any assumptions about what the attack surface might be, they must determine how the network policy enables attacks across hosts. A summary of the information flows generated by OS distributions, including their programs, should be constructed from which system-level information flows can be computed to identify information flow errors. Third, system administrators may need to assert network mediation, such as the placement of firewall rules to control information flow among individual distribution instances. At present, this seems like something that system administrators can do relatively well, but we may find that more accurate configuration of programs and systems may expose limitations in manual network configuration. Fourth, the system administrators must test the resultant configuration. A key ingredient in such testing is that it builds on the previous testing of OS distributors and application developers, but also informs system administrators of discrepancies between assumptions in attack surfaces that underlie any error.

5 Deploying the Approach

In this section, we propose that the *hierarchical state machine* (HSM) model [2] can serve as the formal foundation for our approach. First, we show that data flow in programs, distributions consisting of multiple programs, and systems consisting of multiple distributions can be expressed using an HSM. As a result, we can annotate an HSM representation with assumptions about attack surfaces, basically untrusted inputs to the representation. We then discuss the problem of inferring and resolving flow errors using data flow analyses of an HSM instance, based on the approach of the previous section.

5.1 Hierarchical State Machine Model

First, we define the hierarchical state machine (HSM) model [2].

Definition 1 *A hierarchical state machine K is a tuple $(K_1, ...K_n)$ of modules, where each module K_i has the following components:*

- *A finite set V_i of vertices, and a finite set B_i of boxes.*
- *Subsets I_i and O_i of V_i, respectively consisting of the entry vertices and exit vertices.*
- *An indexing function $Y_i : B_i \rightarrow \{i + 1, ..., n\}$ that maps each box of the i-th module to an index greater than i. That is, if $Y_i(b) = j$ for box b of module K_i, then b can be viewed as a reference to the definition of module K_j.*
- *If b is a box of the module K_i with $j = Y_i(b)$, then pairs of the form (b, u) with $u \in I_j$ are the calls of K_i and pairs of the form (b, v) with $v \in O_j$ are the returns of K_j.*
- *An edge relation E_i consisting of pairs (u, v), where the source u is either a vertex or a return of K_i and v is either a vertex or a call of K_i.*

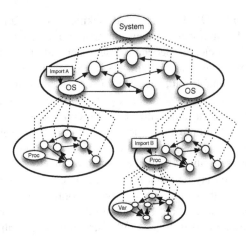

Fig. 3. A system of hosts (OS) and programs (proc) create an encapsulated, hierarchical system of information flows.

An HSM model represents an hierarchical structure of *modules* connected by interfaces, called *boxes*. Modules may have an arbitrary internal structure of connections, so they are represented by a graph. The HSM model is a well-known formalism in the model checking community, and we leverage it because it gives us a well-understood formalism on which to base our analysis.

We find that the HSM model maps directly to that of a system of hierarchically-arranged components, as ours is. We describe the intuition here, shown in Figure 3. What is important about the structure of such systems is that they are encapsulated, hierarchical systems. A system is *encapsulated* in that all interaction between components must be mediated by their reference validation mechanisms. Program information flows can only be propagated to other programs through operating system mechanisms. The hosts (i.e., instances of distributions) can only communicate via the network or virtual machine mechanisms (if on a VM system). These systems are also *hierarchical* in that the authority to make security decisions is monotonically-reduced from the root to the leaves. For example, processes cannot make a security decision unless their operating system authorizes them to make that decision.

Converting a program, distribution, or system to an HSM representation involves identifying each component that enforces its own information flow security policy, computing the authorized information flows of that component, and connecting the information flows between parent and child components. Figure 3 shows the resultant representation for a system. At the leaves are the programs that enforce information flow security. These programs include all the programs that have any attack surface. These programs must, at a minimum, ensure that low integrity data that they receive is sanitized effectively, although mandatory access control within programs is also practical now [38, 58]. Next, each OS distribution enforces its own access control policy, so if such a policy represents an enforcement of information flow security then it can be converted to an HSM module. Such policies must be mandatory access control policies that can be converted to an information flow representation, such as information

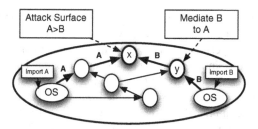

Fig. 4. A simple information flow graph where valuable data of integrity level A and attack data of integrity level B are imported. Vertex x has an attack surface caused by the graph's flows that is mediated at vertex y.

flow policies [7, 18], type enforcement policies [43, 63], approximations of information flow enforcement [28, 53, 57], or sandbox policies that confine enough processes to constrain information flow [41]. Dynamic information flow enforcement, such as the Decentralized Information Flow Control model [25, 69], may be converted to an HSM model, although program discretion about the creation of new attack surfaces must be modeled. Finally, virtual machine monitor and/or network policies control information flow among individual hosts in a system. Figure 3 shows just one level of hosts, where system policy controls information flow among hosts, using firewalls or VMM policies. For example, firewalls state communication paths between hosts, and VMM policies state which virtual resources may be shared by hosts running in VMs [13, 26, 50].

The most difficult task is to connect the information flows between parent and child modules. In constructing an HSM instance from a set of policies, we need to know how components at a parent layer (e.g., system) are connected to components at a child layer (e.g., hosts) and construct boxes to represent such connections (see Definition 1). This is fairly well-defined between the system and hosts by firewall and VMM policies. For example, firewalls state which ports can receive a packet, but many ports have well-known associations with processes. Nonetheless, such information may be ambiguous, so the use of labeled networking policies [21,35,42] is recommended, as these explicitly state the security labels of the processes that are authorized to use network connections. For VMMs, often any root process is typically authorized to make hypervisor calls, so these processes must be connected to the inter-VM flows authorized by a VMM policy. Fortunately, the only normal inter-VM interaction is between guest VMs and a single privileged VM, although this makes the privileged VM more complex. Finally, for programs, any program interface is authorized to access any resource that its process is authorized for (based on the process's security label). This presents a problem in that any interface may be part of that program's attack surface, although this is typically not expected to be the case. The HSM model makes this relationship explicit, and our approach aims to tease out the actual program attack surfaces.

5.2 Proposing Attack Surfaces

Assuming an attack surface for a program, distribution, or system involves identifying where an attacker may access that component. While the notion of "assuming" an attack surface is inherently incomplete and subject to change, it is important to state the assumptions under which one makes security decisions for a component. Others can then use a component under those assumptions or cause the assumptions to be re-evaluated. Neither task is performed in any principled manner currently.

An attack surface has a similar meaning for each component, but a different physical manifestation. All attack surfaces refer to the sources of untrusted data to the component. In the Common Criteria, these are called *imports*[5]. For a program, its attack surface consists of program interfaces (code instructions) that import data that may be modified by an attacker. For a host, its attack surface consists of a set of processes that have access to attacker data (e.g., data imported via devices, such as the network or disk, or program data downloaded with the distribution). For a system, its attack surface consists of the untrusted hosts and external components accessible to the system (e.g., via the network). Finally, we note that components also have valuable data, so imports must also identify key valuables (otherwise the attacker has nothing to attack). Elliciting imports with minimal manual effort is the goal, and we are exploring the development of a knowledge base to infer a conservative set of imports and their relative integrity relationships automatically [62].

The simple view of an attack surface in an HSM instance is shown in Figure 4. This figure shows that all these surfaces are represented by a set of imports to the graph, which represent set of entry vertices from boxes of its potential parent components. Imports are explicitly added to the HSM model to show where attacker data (level B) and valuable data (level A) originates.

5.3 Finding Flow Errors

Once we know we know where attacker data and valuable data are imported into the component, we need to identify flow errors, cases where an attacker can impact the component in unauthorized ways. While the security community has significant experience in inferring information flows and detecting information errors in programs and systems, we find that inferring information flow errors from OS attack surfaces may require different methods than for programs.

An information flow error occurs where a component tries to access unauthorized (i.e., lower integrity) data. For programs, information flows are inferred based on Denning's lattice model [15]. In this model, a component may either be bound to a security class (e.g., integrity level) statically or dynamically. If a component is bound to a security class statically and an access it performs violates the authorized flows in the lattice, then that access is a information flow error. If the component is dynamically bound to a security class, then the security class of the accessed data is combined with the current security class (e.g., using a least upper bound for the lattice) to assign a new security class to the component, if necessary. An error may then occur when the dynamically bound component is used by a component with a statically bound security class. This method of inference has been applied to identify information flow errors for both secrecy and integrity in programs [37].

For OS information flow policies, the bindings are typically all static (Biba and Clark-Wilson integrity [7,12]) or all dynamic (LOMAC [7,18]), although the IX system

---

[5] Exports are also a concern for secrecy.

allows dynamic binding with limits [33]. Thus, typical OS integrity policies bind or set bounds on each process or object *a priori*, or the entire OS is dynamically bound with no constraints. In conventional systems, integrity levels are not bound to each process or objects, so it is necessary to determine what each is supposed to be. However, manually binding each process or object to an integrity level is impractical, so the nature approach would be to bind some statically (e.g., attackers, which are low, and trusted components, which are high), and dynamically bind the rest using Denning's inference approach. Then, information flow errors can be found.

However, we find that this inference approach does not work well for non-information flow, OS policies, such as Type Enforcement [8]. If we bind processes that access the network to low integrity and the kernel to high integrity, we find that almost all the dynamically bound processes will be inferred to be low. This may be an accurate representation of modern, conventional operating systems, but we want to identify problems and fix them coherently. As an alternative, we propose an inference model where each process's integrity is determined by the transitive closure of the integrity levels that reach it [49]. This approach reflects a process's desire to remain high integrity, unless explicitly downgraded, but still shows that all processes are insecure (i.e., receive data of multiple integrity levels), unless mediation is performed somewhere. Using this inference approach, flow errors correspond to processes or objects (labels in a MAC policy) in the OS access control policy that receive multiple integrity levels of data.

Figure 4 shows how the HSM model is used to compute information flow errors. A layer-specific method is used to propagate imported integrity levels through the system. In practice, the application developer will focus only on their programs and the flow errors identified at that level, using Denning's inference. A number of programming languages have tools that provide such inference, including Java [38], OCaml [55], and C [6]. OS distribution and system layer analysis is either performed based on an information flow policy or based on the transitive closure approach above for a non-information flow policy. In Figure 4, transitive closure propagation shows that A and B both reach vertex X.

5.4 Mediating Flow Errors

Once flow errors are found, then the respective parties need to resolve such errors. The first decision is which party is assigned to fix the problem. For example, if the problem is a mismatch between the deployment attack surface and that which was assumed by the child component, then the question is whether to fix the policy or the attack surface. We assume that this decision has been made. Traditionally, resolution is a manual process, but the aim is to leverage the HSM model to automate some steps of the resolution process.

We have developed a method that generates placements for resolving data flow errors based on graph cuts [24]. In this method, the program is converted into an information flow graph, as above, and all paths from a source to a program location where a flow error occurs must be cut by a mediation statement (e.g., sanitizer or runtime check) that

---

[6] Since C is not type-safe, such inference only applies if the application developer is not adversarial.

resolves that error. This method is general for information flow graphs, so we propose to apply it to information flow graphs at different layers in the HSM model like the OS distribution layer. Figure 4 shows how a flow of level B is cut at vertex y removing all attack surfaces (not just the one shown at vertex X). However, for the approach to be practical, we must be able to construct complete cut problems. For this, we need to know the mediation statements, their possible locations, and costs (we can then use a min-cut algorithm). We also need to account for functionality, as we cannot simply cut access control policy flows, as they may be necessary for the system to work.

An advantage of reasoning about security in terms of information flows is that this reduces the number of options for resolving a flow error. We can either change a vertex or change the flows into or out of a vertex. Changes to vertex include removing it (e.g., removing a program from a distribution) or changing the information flows within the vertex (e.g., changing attack surface of the program). Changes to an edge include adding a sanitizer on an edge (e.g., *guard* process) or changing the integrity level of the imports (e.g., use more reliable inputs). We note that removing an edge alone is problematic in that this is likely to remove a necessary function for that vertex.

The problem of automating resolution is complex due to conflicting constraints. A system may both *require* particular information flows to occur for the system to function and *restrict* certain information flows from occurring. Finding solutions to constraint systems with positive and negative constraints, in our setting, will result in a PSPACE-hard branching-time model checking problem [2]. As a result, even with a small number of resolution options, if there are a large number of possible locations, then automating resolution will be computationally complex. Powerful solvers (e.g., SAT solvers) are now available that can search large solution spaces efficiently.

If the solution is to add a sanitizer or runtime check at a particular location, then the question is what this code should do. Historically, sanitization has been error-prone, so identifying locations is not sufficient to ensure error resolution. Further, researchers have found that simply placing one sanitizer may not be sufficient as different uses may require different sanitizations [5]. Thus, the purpose of the resolution must be clear enough to assess whether other mediation may also be required to satisfy security constraints. For example, if a sanitizer is for a web server to handle untrusted data, then that mediation may still permit data that is unsafe for the database (e.g., for SQL injections). Subsequent resolutions must be found for these "secondary" imports resulting from partial sanitization. Finally, while sanitization is inherently program-specific, a number of sanitizing functions have been identified over based on the type of error, programming language, etc. Tools based on this methodology should provide access to known sanitization functions to reduce the effort of the parties.

5.5   Testing the Resulting System

Finally, once the actor has decided on a resolution to any flow errors, it is necessary to test such resolutions, particularly for sanitization. Sanitization aims to allow a transformed version of an information flow that meets some requirements. Such requirements must be made explicit and test thoroughly. Fortunately, a variety of methods for testing sanitization procedures have been proposed, although most are language and bug-specific [5,64]. We envision that such procedures would be provided to application developers and sanitizer developers for systems, and that a required degree of testing would be enforced.

Testing of sanitizers involves conservative static analysis to ensure no false negatives (errors relative to requirements) and a supplementary runtime analysis to validate the existence of real errors [5]. Such testing is limited by the problem of identifying the sources of untrusted data, but the HSM model makes the sources of untrusted data explicit. Also, test cases need to be generated for the runtime validation. Fuzz testing tools generate inputs to programs to find vulnerabilities. One tool, EXE, automatically generates inputs that will crash a program [9]. It tracks possible values that variables can have symbolically. When an `assert` statement is reached, EXE checks if there is an input that causes the statement to become false.

6 Conclusions

Developing a software engineering methodology for security would be a significant undertaking. In addition to providing mechanisms to convert the relevant program, distribution, and system information into a canonical format (an HSM instance), algorithms must be developed to solve the problems highlighted above, and a user interface must be designed to convey this information clearly. Finally, testing tools must be integrated with the methodology to enable comprehensive testing for all the target languages and bugs.

Waiting for a "big bang" of all the technology above before we have a useful system pretty much guarantees that it will never happen, so the question is how should we proceed to provide a useful, but perhaps incomplete, functionality that leads to a desired goal. We envision that such tools must be integrated into a common, open software engineering ecosystem, such as Eclipse. We imagine that any initial methodology would enable testing of one component and the testing of its deployment, such as building a program and testing its deployment in an OS distribution. Finally, the security community will have to consider how to pull together the myriad of prior research into a coherent approach, whether for the proposed approach or another. The security community has undertaken similar challenges for defining assurance criteria, and this will be a similarly large undertaking.

References

1. Abadi, M., Budiu, M., Erlingsson, U., Ligatti, J.: Control-flow integrity. In: Proceedings of CCS 2005. ACM (2005)
2. Alur, R., Yannakakis, M.: Model checking of hierarchical state machines. ACM Trans. Program. Lang. Syst. 23(3) (2001)
3. Amazon. Amazon Web Services Security Center, http://aws.amazon.com
4. Ames, J., Gasser, S.R.M., Schell, R.R.: Security kernel design and implementation: An introduction. Computer 16(7), 14–22 (1983)
5. Balzarotti, D., et al.: Saner: Composing static and dynamic analysis to validate sanitization in web applications. In: Proceedings of the IEEE Symposium on Security and Privacy (2008)
6. The Bastille hardening program: Increased security for your OS, http://bastille-linux.sourceforge.net

7. Biba, K.J.: Integrity Considerations for Secure Computer Systems. Technical Report MTR-3153, MITRE (April 1977)
8. Boebert, W.E., Kain, R.Y.: A Practical Alternative to Hierarchical Integrity Policies. In: Proceedings of the 8th NCSC (1985)
9. Cadar, C., Ganesh, V., Pawlowski, P.M., Dill, D.L., Engler, D.R.: Exe: Automatically generating inputs of death. ACM Trans. Inf. Syst. Secur. 12(2) (2008)
10. Castro, M., Costa, M., Harris, T.: Securing software by enforcing data-flow integrity. In: Proceedings of OSDI 2006. USENIX Association (2006)
11. Chen, H., Li, N., Mao, Z.: Analyzing and Comparing the Protection Quality of Security Enhanced Operating Systems. In: Proceedings of NDSS 2009 (2009)
12. Clark, D.D., Wilson, D.: A Comparison of Military and Commercial Security Policies. In: 1987 IEEE Symposium on Security and Privacy (May 1987)
13. Coker, G.: Xen Security Modules (XSM). http://www.xen.org/files/xensummit_4/xsm-summit-041707_Coker.pdf
14. Cowan, C., et al.: Stackguard: Automatic adaptive detection and prevention of buffer-overflow attacks. In: Proceedings of the 7th USENIX Security Symp. (1998)
15. Denning, D.: A Lattice Model of Secure Information Flow. Communications of the ACM 19(5) (1976)
16. Eclipse. http://www.eclipse.org
17. Feng, H., et al.: Formalizing sensitivity in static analysis for intrusion detection. In: Proceeding of the 2004 IEEE Symposium on Security and Privacy (2004)
18. Fraser, T.: LOMAC: MAC you can live with. In: Proceedings of the FREENIX Track: USENIX Annual Technical Conference (June 2001)
19. Guttman, J.D., Herzog, A.L., Ramsdell, J.D., Skorupka, C.W.: Verifying Information Flow Goals in Security-Enhanced Linux. Journal of Computer Security 13(1) (2005)
20. Howard, M., Pincus, J., Wing, J.M.: Measuring Relative Attack Surfaces. In: Proceedings of Workshop on Advanced Developments in Software and Systems Security (2003)
21. Jaeger, T., Butler, K., King, D.H., Hallyn, S., Latten, J., Zhang, X.: Leveraging IPsec for Mandatory Access Control Across Systems. In: Proceedings of SecureComm 2006 (August 2006)
22. Jaeger, T., Sailer, R., Zhang, X.: Analyzing integrity protection in the SELinux example policy. In: Proceedings of the 12th USENIX Security Symp. (August 2003)
23. Karger, P., Zurko, M., Bonin, D., Mason, A., Kahn, C.: A retrospective on the VAX VMM security kernel. IEEE Trans. Softw. Eng. 17(11) (1991)
24. King, D., et al.: Automating security mediation placement. In: Proceedings of ESOP 2010, pp. 327–344 (2010)
25. Krohn, M.N., et al.: Information flow control for standard OS abstractions. In: Proceedings of the 21st ACM SOSP (October 2007)
26. KVM: Kernel based virtual machine. http://www.linux-kvm.org
27. Larochelle, D., Evans, D.: Statically detecting likely buffer overflow vulnerabilities. In: Proceedings of the 10th USENIX Security Symposium (2001)
28. Li, N., Mao, Z., Chen, H.: Usable Mandatory Integrity Protection For Operating Systems. In: Proceedings of the 2007 IEEE Symposium on Security and Privacy (May 2007)
29. Linn, C.M., Rajagopalan, M., Baker, S., Collberg, C., Debray, S.K., Hartman, J.H.: Protecting against unexpected system calls. In: Proceedings of the 14th Conference on USENIX Security Symposium (2005)
30. Lipner, S.B.: Non-discretionery controls for commercial applications. In: Proceedings of IEEE Symposium on Security and Privacy (1982)
31. Loscocco, P., et al.: The Inevitability of Failure: The Flawed Assumptions of Security Modern Computing Environments. In: Proceedings of the 21st National Information Systems Security Conference (1998)

32. Manadhata, P., Tan, K., Maxion, R., Wing, J.M.: An Approach to Measuring A System's Attack Surface. Technical Report CMU-CS-07-146, School of Computer Science, Carnegie Mellon University (2007)
33. McIlroy, D., Reeds, J.: Multilevel windows on a single-level terminal. In: Proceedings of the (First) USENIX Security Workshop (August 1988)
34. Microsoft. Prefast for drivers. http://www.microsoft.com/whdc/devtools/tools/prefast.mspx
35. Morris, J.: New secmark-based network controls for selinux. http://james-morris.livejournal.com/11010.html
36. MSDN. Mandatory Integrity Control (Windows). http://msdn.microsoft.com/en-us/library/bb648648%28VS.85%29.aspx
37. Myers, A.C., Liskov, B.: A decentralized model for information flow control. ACM Operating Systems Review 31(5) (October 1997)
38. Myers, A.C., Zheng, L., Zdancewic, S., Chong, S., Nystrom, N.: Jif: Java information flow (July 2001-2003). http://www.cs.cornell.edu/jif
39. Nagappan, N., Maximilien, E.M., Bhat, T., Williams, L.: Realizing quality improvement through test driven development: results and experiences of four industrial teams. Empirical Softw. Engg. 13(3), 289–302 (2008)
40. Newsome, J., Song, D.X.: Dynamic taint analysis for automatic detection, analysis, and signaturegeneration of exploits on commodity software. In: Proceedings of NDSS 2005 (2005)
41. Novell. AppArmor Linux Application Security. http://www.novell.com/linux/security/apparmor/
42. NetLabel - Explicit labeled networking for Linux. http://www.nsa.gov/selinux
43. Security-Enhanced Linux. http://www.nsa.gov/selinux
44. PaX homepage. http://pax.grsecurity.net
45. Provos, N., Friedl, M., Honeyman, P.: Preventing privilege escalation. In: Proceedings of the 12th USENIX Security Symp. USENIX Association (2003)
46. Qin, F., et al.: Lift: A low-overhead practical information flow tracking system for detecting security attacks. In: Proceedings of MICRO (2006)
47. Research, M.: SLAM - Microsoft Research
48. Ristenpart, T., et al.: Hey, you, get off of my cloud: exploring information leakage in third-party compute clouds. In: Proceedings of the 16th ACM CCS (2009)
49. Rueda, S., Vijayakumar, H., Jaeger, T.: Analysis of virtual machine system policies. In: Proceedings of SACMAT 2009 (2009)
50. Sailer, R., et al.: Building a MAC-Based Security Architecture for the Xen Open-Source Hypervisor. In: Proceedings of ACSAC 2005 (2005)
51. Saltzer, J.H., Schroeder, M.D.: The protection of information in computer systems. Proceedings of the IEEE 63(9) (September 1975)
52. Sarna-Starosta, B., Stoller, S.D.: Policy analysis for security-enhanced linux. In: Proceedings of the 2004 WITS (April 2004)
53. Shankar, U., Jaeger, T., Sailer, R.: Toward Automated Information-Flow Integrity Verification for Security-Critical Applications. In: Proceedings of the 2006 NDSS (February 2006)
54. Shankar, U., Talwar, K., Foster, J.S., Wagner, D.: Detecting format string vulnerabilities with type qualifiers. In: Proceedings of the 10th USENIX Security Symp. (2001)
55. Simonet, V.: The Flow Caml System: Documentation and User's Manual. Technical Report 0282, Institut National de Recherche en Informatique et en Automatique (INRIA), ©INRIA (July 2003)
56. Solworth, J.: Robustly secure computer systems: A new security paradigm of system discontinuity. In: Proceedings of NSPW 2007 (2007)
57. Sun, W., et al.: Practical proactive integrity preservation: A basis for malware defense. In: Proceedings of the 2008 IEEE Symposium on Security and Privacy (2008)

58. Tresys. Selinux userspace. `http://userspace.selinuxproject.org/trac/`
59. Tresys. SETools - Policy Analysis Tools for SELinux.
    `http://oss.tresys.com/projects/setools`
60. Vidyaraman, S., Chandrasekaran, M., Upadhyaya, S.: The user is the enemy. In: Proceedings of NSPW 2007 (2007)
61. Viega, J., Bloch, J.T., Kohno, T., McGraw, G.: Token-based scanning of source code for security problems. ACM Trans. Inf. Syst. Secur. 5(3), 238–261 (2002)
62. Vijayakumar, H., et al.: Integrity walls: Finding attack surfaces from mandatory access control policies. Technical Report Technical Report NAS-TR-0124-2010, Network and Security Research Center (February 2010)
63. Walker, K.M., et al.: Confining root programs with domain and type enforcement (DTE). In: Proceedings of the 6th USENIX Security Symp. (1996)
64. Wassermann, G., Su, Z.: Sound and precise analysis of web applications for injection vulnerabilities. SIGPLAN Not. 42(6), 32–41 (2007)
65. Venema, W.: Postfix Architecture Overview.
    `http://www.postfix.org/overview.html`
66. Wool, A.: A quantitative study of firewall configuration errors. IEEE Computer 37(6), 62–67 (2004)
67. Wurster, G., van Oorschot, P.C.: The developer is the enemy. In: Proceedings of NSPW 2008 (2008)
68. Yang, J., Sar, C., Twohey, P., Cadar, C., Engler, D.: Automatically generating malicious disks using symbolic execution. In: Proceedings of the 2006 IEEE Symposium on Security and Privacy (2006)
69. Zeldovich, N., Boyd-Wickizer, S., Kohler, E., Mazières, D.: Making information flow explicit in HiStar. In: Proceedings of the 7th OSDI (2006)
70. Zhang, X., Edwards, A., Jaeger, T.: Using CQUAL for static analysis of authorization hook placement. In: Proceedings of the 11th USENIX Security Symp. (2002)

Improving Application Security through TLS-Library Redesign*

Leo St. Amour[1] and W. Michael Petullo[2]

[1] Northeastern University
Boston, Massachusetts 02115, USA
[2] United States Military Academy
West Point, New York 10996, USA

Abstract. Research has revealed a number of pitfalls inherent in contemporary TLS libraries. Common mistakes when programming using their APIs include insufficient certificate verification and the use of weak cipher suites. These programmer errors leave applications susceptible to man-in-the-middle attacks. Furthermore, current TLS libraries encourage system designs which leave the confidentiality of secret authentication and session keys vulnerable to application flaws. This paper introduces libtlssep (pronounced lib·tē·el·sep), a new, open-source TLS library which provides a simpler API and improved security architecture. Applications that use libtlssep spawn a separate process whose role is to provide one or more TLS-protected communication channels; this child process assures proper certificate verification and isolates authentication and session keys in its separate memory space. We present a security, programmability, and performance analysis of libtlssep.

1 Introduction

Programs increasingly use Transport Layer Security (TLS) to protect communications. While TLS has long protected commerce and banking transactions, the protocol now routinely protects less sensitive services such as search and video streaming due to privacy concerns [23]. Researchers have even begun to investigate the notion of ubiquitous encryption [9, 14, 26]. TLS uses authentication and encryption to protect the confidentiality and integrity of communication channels, and its authentication makes use of asymmetric-key cryptography.

TLS provides server authentication through the use of X.509 identity certificates. In the most common model, some trusted Certificate Authority (CA) signs each identity certificate, ostensibly binding the public key present in the certificate to a hostname. Systems often rely on password-based client authentication which takes place after a TLS session initializes. However, TLS also supports client-side X.509-based authentication.

Yet attackers occasionally violate the confidentiality and integrity of communication channels despite the use of TLS. Studies by Vratonjic et al. [32],

---

* The rights of this work are transferred to the extent transferable according to title 17 U.S.C. 105.

© Springer International Publishing Switzerland 2015
R.S. Chakraborty et al. (Eds.): SPACE 2015, LNCS 9354, pp. 75–94, 2015.
DOI: 10.1007/978-3-319-24126-5_5

Georgiev et al. [15], and Fahl et al. [12] found that programmers consistently misuse TLS libraries in their applications. Such errors include:

(1) missing name verification,[1]
(2) trust of self-signed certificates,
(3) improper error handling,
(4) poor cipher-suite choices, and
(5) missing certificate revocation checks.

These vulnerabilities seem to arise from the Application Programming Interfaces (APIs) exported by contemporary TLS libraries. It seems that existing APIs leave too many responsibilities to the application programmer; the deceptive complexity of these steps overwhelm even those application programmers who do remember to attempt their implementation (over and over again, as they write each application). For example, Marlinspike showed how the different string encodings in X.509 and C give rise to a subtle attack on name verification [22].

Architectural choices also threaten TLS. In many cases, compromised control flow or ill information flow within an application can result in the compromise of a private cryptographic key. This is because many applications keep TLS processing and general logic in the same address space. While Heartbleed [24] attacked OpenSSL itself to compromise cryptographic keys, there are likely many more vulnerabilities present in application logic than there are present in the code included from TLS libraries. This is especially dangerous because systems often share TLS keys across several applications. For example, we counted 26 subject-alternative names plus a number of wildcards within the certificate which authenticates `bing.com` at the time of writing.

In this paper, we introduce `libtlssep` (pronounced lib·tē·el·sep), a TLS library that both simplifies the TLS API and utilizes privilege separation to increase communication security. By using `libtlssep`, an application forks a child process which is responsible for the application's TLS operations. Keeping private keys isolated in the child's separate memory space makes it more difficult for an application bug to result in a compromised key. We have released a research prototype of `libtlssep` under an open-source license, and we have made this prototype and its documentation available at `http://www.flyn.org/projects/libtlssep`.

In the following sections, we describe related work; summarize our threat model; present the design of `libtlssep`; and present security, programmability, and performance results.

2   Related Work

Our survey of related work focuses on (1) pitfalls resulting from the APIs provided by existing TLS libraries, (2) efforts to improve TLS APIs, (3) existing uses of privilege separation and similar architectures, and (4) systems which

---

[1] In this paper, we refer to verifying a *name* by which we mean verifying either a certificate's subject-common name or its subject-alternative name. Such names generally represent either a host or a user.

provide stronger or more universal cryptographic-key isolation than `libtlssep`, albeit not without tradeoffs.

2.1   API Pitfalls

Many researchers have studied the efficacy of TLS in practice [32, 15, 12]. From their work, we better understand a number of pitfalls which arise when using contemporary TLS libraries. Fahl et al. also provide evidence that the Internet is ripe with poor advice which results in programmers wrongly employing TLS libraries [13, §4.1]. We summarized the pitfalls of contemporary APIs in §1, and here we further describe this previous work.

A connection procedure which returns a TLS connection handle without first verifying the certificates involved seems to encourage omitting name verification, yet many contemporary APIs follow this pattern. Figure 1 shows in pseudo-code an example of an OpenSSL-based client. Note that a programmer could mistakenly begin calling `SSL_write` and `SSL_read` without first calling and checking the result of `SSL_get_verify_result` and `verify_name`. OpenSSL also provides a callback-type verification mechanism, but this similarly requires explicit use.

Marlinspike provided one example of why the design of X.509 makes implementing even `verify_name` difficult. Should any CA issue a certificate which contains an embedded NULL byte—such as `www.victim.com\0.attacker.com`—then it is possible that `attacker.com` could fraudulently assume the identity of `victim.com`. All that is necessary is for an application programmer to forget that NULL bytes are valid within X.509 strings but terminate C strings, such as by naïvely writing the application to use `strcmp` to compare the two as C strings. Fixed applications each duplicate strange but necessary checks such as the one found in `wget` [30]:

```
if (strlen (common_name) != (size_t) ASN1_STRING_length (sdata)) {
    /* Fail. */
}
```

Figure 2 shows in pseudo-code an example of an OpenSSL-based server. The program assumes that the client authenticates using a certificate. This requires more work from the application programmer: he would have to modify the client's logic to supply client-side certificates.

Researchers have found deployed applications which verify certificates yet trust self-signed certificates. Trusting self-signed certificates is rarely desirable except during the implementation and testing phases of development. In any case, these mistakes seem to arise from either ignorance of the dangers involved or programmers forgetting to deactivate the trust of self-signed certificates in their programs before deploying them. It is common in TLS libraries to rely on control-flow statements written by the application programmer to determine whether to honor self-signed certificates.

Additional dangers arise when the CA model itself breaks down; Durumeric et al. performed an extensive study of CA use in practice [11]. Research shows evidence that it is unreasonable for all Internet users to trust the same set of CAs [31, 21]. As CAs operate in the context of many juristictions and loyalties,

```
1   sock = create_socket(host) // Create BSD socket.
2   method = TLSv1_2_client_method()
3   ctx = SSL_CTX_new(method)
4   SSL_CTX_set_default_verify_paths(ctx)
5   ssl = SSL_new(ctx)
6   SSL_set_fd(ssl, sock)
7   SSL_connect(ssl)
8   cert = SSL_get_peer_certificate(ssl)
9   // Programmer must explicitly check certificate:
10  if cert != NULL
11    && X509_V_OK == SSL_get_verify_result(ssl)
12    && verify_name(cert, host) { // Cert. name == host?
13      SSL_write(ssl,request,len)
14      SSL_read(ssl, response, len)
15      handle(response)
16  }
17  SSL_shutdown(ssl)
18  SSL_free(ssl)
19  close(sock)
```

Fig. 1. Pseudocode to create a TLS connection using OpenSSL. Omits error handling, except for errors related to verification. The user-defined procedures are create_socket, verify_name, and handle. Beurdouche et al. provide a series of similar examples [7, Listing 1–3].

an individual is likely not well served by trusting all of them. Furthermore, CAs themselves have been the target of successful attacks [19]. Alternative models include PGP's web-of-trust model [34], DANE [18, 2], and certificate pinning, which closely resembles the model found in SSH [33]. Yet inspecting Figure 1 shows that programs which directly use OpenSSL each bear the responsibility of implementing verification logic from within their source code. This makes adopting emerging trust models across all applications cumbersome.

A certificate signatory ought to revoke certificates which are compromised or otherwise invalid, and part of the verification process should involve checking the revocation status of a certificate. However, existing TLS APIs permit the omission of these checks, and research has found such misuse in production applications [12, 15].

2.2   Improved APIs and Static Analysis

LibreSSL [4] aims to fix implementation errors in OpenSSL, and it also provides libtls. Libtls exports a simplified API; for example, it takes the approach of including certificate verification in the semantics of its tls_connect procedure, although a programmer can disable this name verification using a procedure named tls_config_insecure_noverifyname. Another library, s2n [29], has similar goals.[2]

Fahl et al. modified the Android software stack to employ a certificate-verification service which separately exists from each individual application [13,

---

[2] Amazon announced the s2n project during the final revisions of this paper.

```
1   sock = accept_connection() // Accept connection.
2   method = TLSv1_2_server_method()
3   ctx = SSL_CTX_new(method)
4   SSL_CTX_set_verify(ctx, SSL_VERIFY_PEER |
        SSL_VERIFY_FAIL_IF_NO_PEER_CERT, ignore);
5   SSL_CTX_use_certificate_file(ctx, cert, SSL_FILETYPE_PEM)
6   SSL_CTX_use_PrivateKey_file(ctx, key, SSL_FILETYPE_PEM)
7   SSL_CTX_check_private_key(ctx)
8   SSL_CTX_set_default_verify_paths(ctx)
9   ssl = SSL_new(ctx)
10  SSL_set_fd(ssl, sock)
11  SSL_accept(ssl)
12  cert = SSL_get_peer_certificate(ssl)
13  // Programmer must explicitly check certificate:
14  if cert != NULL
15   && X509_V_OK == SSL_get_verify_result(ssl)
16   && verify_user(cert) { // Cert. name permitted user?
17     SSL_read(ssl, request, len)
18     response = handle(request)
19     SSL_write(ssl,response,len)
20  }
21  SSL_shutdown(ssl)
22  SSL_free(ssl)
23  close(sock)
```

Fig. 2. Pseudocode to accept a TLS connection using OpenSSL. Omits error handling, except for errors related to verification. The user-defined procedures are accept_connection, verify_user, and handle.

§5.2]. Moving verification to a system-wide service reduces the possibility of a programmer accidentally circumventing verification, and it also simplifies the selection and configuration of verification techniques such as certificate pinning. Programmers can also—without modifying the program—configure the verification service to enable a per-application development mode which trusts self-signed certificates. This architecture also centralizes the management of certificate warnings.

CERTSHIM uses the LD_PRELOAD facility present in many Operating Systems (OSs) to assure certificate verification by replacing key TLS library procedures at runtime [3]. For example, CERTSHIM replaces OpenSSL's SSL_connnect with a version which adds certificate verification to its semantics. Applications do not require modifications to take advantage of CERTSHIM. CERTSHIM supports a number of verification techniques, and it makes use of a single configuration point which exists separately from each application's configuration.

The NaCl library provides two common cryptographic operations: public-key authenticated encryption and signatures [6]. NaCl pursues very-high performance, side-channel-free cryptography, and the library provides a vastly simpler API than contemporary cryptographic libraries. NaCl in its present form serves to replace the cryptographic-primitive procedures in TLS libraries, but it does not yet itself implement a protected network protocol. Work to build more-robust and higher-performance protocols around NaCl includes CurveCP [5] and MinimaLT [27], but these bear the cost of incompatibility with TLS.

Efforts such as the Fedora System-Wide Crypto Policy [1] seek to centralize the configuration of all cryptographic protections. This could simplify some portions of TLS configuration, although it will help less with verification because of the amount of application-specific verification code. The main beneficiary of this work will be cipher-suite selection.

SSLINT uses static analysis to determine if existing programs properly use TLS-library APIs [17]. This appears complimentary to `libtlssep`, as it can help convince programmers to fix API misuse, possibly opting to migrate to a library with an improved API. The researchers behind SSLINT discovered 27 previously-unknown vulnerabilities in deployed programs.

2.3   Privilege Separation

Researchers have produced a number of models which increase security by using separate processes to isolate components; these designs are often described as providing *privilege separation*. The OpenSSH dæmon's privileged component can access the host's private key, open pseudo-terminals, and service change-of-identity requests [28]. Unprivileged components within OpenSSH then make indirect use of these capabilities through carefully-defined interfaces, for example by receiving pseudo-terminal file descriptors via file-descriptor passing. OpenBSD provides a framework called `imsg` [25] which aims to ease the explicit programming of communication between privileged-separated components.

The Plan 9 operating system provides a process called `factotum` which negotiates service authentication on behalf of applications [10]. `Factotum` isolates authentication keys as well as the code required for performing authentication in a separate memory space. Concentrating security code within a single program increases the programmer's ability to verify that the code is correctly written, facilitates executing the code with the least privilege required, and makes it easier to update security software. Most importantly, a logical flaw in a complicated program cannot directly lead to the compromise of an authentication key because of privilege separation. Plan 9 does not subsume from applications the work of verifying certificates.

2.4   Specialized Cryptographic Key Isolation

Other systems provide stronger cryptographic key isolation, albeit with more intrusive requirements. One example, Mimosa [16], uses the properties of transactional memory to protect cryptographic keys from attacks originating both in user and kernel space. Yet Mimosa requires modifications to the OS kernel as well as hardware transactional memory.

Ethos is a novel OS kernel which provides digital-signature and encrypted-networking system calls [26]. This allows the kernel to universally isolate cryptographic keys from applications, and it also makes the kernel aware of the location in memory of all cryptographic keys. Ethos is clean-slate and thus requires applications to be rewritten for all of its unique interfaces, and this burden is greater than the smaller changes required by merely porting to a new TLS API (this is a tradeoff between expediency and Ethos' stronger security properties).

Plan 9 also provides special facilities for isolating authentication keys. The system will not swap `factotum` to disk and protects `factotum`'s entry in the `/proc` filesystem. Many versions of UNIX support an encrypted swap space for similar reasons.

3   Threat Model

Our threat model includes very powerful Man-in-the-Middle (MitM) attackers who can capture, modify, and deny the transmission of the messages communicated between two hosts. Specifically, our attacker can respond to the requests intended for another recipient, generate self-signed certificates, present legitimate certificates for the domains he controls, or capture legitimate certificates for the domains he does not control. Thus our goal is to use strong, *properly-applied* cryptography to provide confidentiality and integrity protections despite these attacks, namely to (1) blind the attacker to the messages we send and receive and (2) detect any attacker-manipulated traffic.

Our design removes a number of TLS misuses, and thus reduces the burden on programmers so that they can focus on the correctness of their program's core logic. It is not possible to protect against *all* programmer errors, yet we expect that the attacker will try to exploit these errors too. Such errors are orthogonal to the use of TLS, and thus they are outside of our threat model, except that we wish to avoid them compromising a cryptographic key.

We also ignore attacks on the host OS, OS access controls, the privileged account, a virtual machine monitor (if present), and hardware. We assume that the applications which make use of TLS do not do so with elevated privileges. Finally, while we are concerned about programmers selecting weak cipher suites, we ignore attacks on the TLS cryptographic protocol itself. Here there is some overlap [7], but in any case the techniques we used in `libtlssep` could likely aid in crafting libraries to support protected-networking protocols other than TLS.

4   Design of `libtlssep`

4.1   `Libtlssep` Architecture

We designed our architecture to employ the isolation facilities already present in mainstream OSs to engender more robust applications. The architecture of `libtlssep` follows from the suggestions of Provos et al. [28], as it aims to aid in crafting applications which make use of privilege separation. Like SSH, `libtlssep` uses file-descriptor passing to transmit capabilities (BSD-socket connections in the case of `libtlssep`) from one process to another.

As with Plan 9's `factotum`, `libtlssep` aims to apply SSH-style privilege separation to many applications in a convenient way. `Factotum` is more general but isolates only authentication secrets; `libtlssep` spans both authentication and encryption, isolates the session key negotiated between two parties, and provides a TLS-focused API.

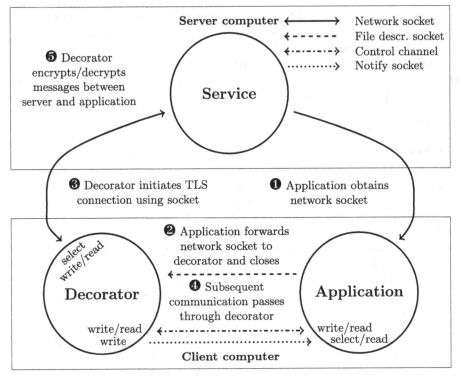

Fig. 3. Our Architecture

Libtlssep's use of a separate process also resembles Fahl's certificate-verification service, but the latter does not isolate session keys. Libtlssep targets C on POSIX instead of Java on Android, and while it leaves the particulars of error presentation to application programmers, an untrusted connection will result in an error code rather than proceeding.

The libtlssep architecture breaks applications into (at least) two processes: (1) a process containing authentication and encryption functionality, provided by libtlssep 's *network decorator*; and (2) a process containing program logic, provided by the application programmer. The decorator itself makes use of OpenSSL, but could be ported to any existing TLS implementation without requiring further application changes; nonetheless the decorator simplifies the use of the underlying implementation. Unlike with the direct use of OpenSSL, the decorator—like LibreSSL's libtls—assures the verification of certificates and hides a number of disparate OpenSSL procedure calls behind around a dozen libtlssep procedures. Figure 3 depicts libtlssep's architecture.

Libtlssep uses three channels to facilitate communication between an application and its decorator: (1) a UNIX-domain socket used by the application to pass file descriptors to its decorator, (2) a shared-memory- and event-file-descriptor-based control channel which allows the application to make Remote Procedure Calls (RPCs) to its decorator, and (3) a UNIX-domain notification socket which allows the application to poll for available data. The application provides yet another file descriptor—the network file descriptor—over which TLS messages flow between the decorator and remote service.

To use `libtlssep`, an application first initiates a connection with some service using the BSD-socket API. Next, the application calls the `tlssep_init` and `tlssep_connect` (or `tlssep_accept`) procedures. `Tlssep_init` executes the decorator process and initiates the control and file-decriptor-passing channels with it. `Tlssep_connect` passes the network socket and a notification socket to the decorator, and the decorator uses the network socket to initiate a TLS connection with the service. One decorator can support a number of `tlssep_connect` calls to different end points; thus two of the communication channels mentioned are per-run (i.e., the control and file-decriptor-passing channels) and two are per-TLS-connection (i.e., the network and notification sockets).

From this point on, the application communicates with the service through the decorator using `libtlssep`'s API: the application makes read and write RPCs across the control channel by calling `tlssep_read` and `tlssep_write` (possibly employing `select` on the notification socket), and the decorator wraps/unwraps the contents of these calls using TLS, passing/receiving them to/from the service.

4.2   Libtlssep **API and Configuration**

API: `Libtlssep` provides around a dozen procedures which we summarize here. Most of the procedures take a `tlssep_desc_t` argument which describes an established `libtlssep` connection. The fields within the `tlssep_desc_t` structure are meant to be opaque, with the exception of the notification file descriptor which bears the field name `notificationfd`.

```
tlssep_status_t tlssep_init (tlssep_context_t *context)
```

The `tlssep_init` procedure initializes a context structure, executes the decorator process, and establishes the control and file-descriptor-passing channels described in §4.1. Upon execution, the decorator reads its configuration and begins polling the control socket.

```
tlssep_status_t tlssep_connect (tlssep_context_t *context,
                                int file_descriptor,
                                const char *expected_name,
                                char *name,
                                tlssep_desc_t *desc)
```

The `tlssep_connect` procedure provides the decorator with a network file descriptor, expected name, and the per-TLS-connection notification socket described in §4.1. After providing this information to the decorator, `libtlssep` closes the application-side copy of the network file descriptor; thereafter the application can determine if network data is available for `tlssep_read` by polling the per-TLS-connection notification socket.

Given these parameters, the decorator initiates a TLS connection and adds the given network file descriptor to the set of file descriptors it polls. Finally, the decorator verifies the certificate received from the server against `expected_name`, aborting the process if the certificate does not satisfy the configured verification engine. Upon receiving notification of a successful connection, tlssep_connect initializes the connection descriptor named desc and copies the server's true name into the buffer pointed to by name.

```
tlssep_status_t tlssep_accept (tlssep_context_t *context,
                               int file_descriptor,
                               const char *expected_name,
                               char *name,
                               tlssep_desc_t *desc)
```

The tlssep_accept procedure serves the same purpose as tlssep_connect, except that it implements the server side.

```
tlssep_status_t tlssep_write (tlssep_desc_t *desc,
                              const void *buf,
                              int buf_size,
                              int *bytes_written)
```

The tlssep_write procedure provides the decorator with a number of bytes to write on the given TLS connection.

```
tlssep_status_t tlssep_read (tlssep_desc_t *desc,
                             void *buf,
                             int buf_size,
                             int *num_read)
```

The tlssep_read procedure requests from the decorator a number of bytes to be read from the given TLS connection.

```
tlssep_status_t tlssep_peek (tlssep_desc_t *desc,
                             void *buf,
                             int buf_size,
                             int *num_read)
```

The tlssep_peek procedure serves the same purpose as tlssep_read, except that the returned bytes will remain in the decorator's buffer and thus remain available for subsequent reads/peeks.

```
tlssep_status_t tlssep_poll (tlssep_desc_t *desc,
                             unsigned int timeout)
```

The tlssep_poll procedure polls the notification socket associated with the TLS connection, blocking until the decorator has data for the application. Alternatively, a programmer can directly use UNIX's select system call since the desc structure contains the notification socket file descriptor.

```
tlssep_status_t tlssep_setnonblock (tlssep_desc_t *desc)
```

The tlssep_setnonblock procedure sets the mode of the decorator's network file descriptor to non-blocking.

```
tlssep_status_t tlssep_close (tlssep_desc_t *desc)
```

The `tlssep_close` procedure instructs the decorator to close the given TLS connection and remove its file descriptor from the set of file descriptors it polls. The procedure also frees any state associated with the connection.

```
tlssep_status_t tlssep_terminate (tlssep_context_t *context)
```

The `tlssep_terminate` procedure instructs the decorator to exit.

```
char *tlssep_strerror (tlssep_status_t error)
```

The `tlssep_strerror` transforms a `tlssep_status_t` status code into a human-readable string.

```
1   sock = create_socket(hostname)
2   tlssep_init(ctx)
3   status = tlssep_connect(ctx, sock, hostname, NULL, desc)
4   if TLSSEP_STATUS_OK == status {
5       tlssep_write(desc, request, len)
6       tlssep_read(desc, response, len)
7       handle(response)
8       tlssep_close(desc)
9   }
10  tlssep_terminate(desc)
```

Fig. 4. Pseudocode to create a TLS connection using `libtlssep`. Omits error handling, other than to check that the server's certificate satisfies `tlssep_connect`. The user-defined procedures are `create_socket` and `handle`.

```
1   sock = accept_connection()
2   tlssep_init(ctx)
3   status = tlssep_accept(ctx, sock, NULL, user_name, desc)
4   if TLSSEP_STATUS_OK == status && user_auth(user_name) {
5       tlssep_read(desc, request, len)
6       response = handle(request)
7       tlssep_write(desc, response, len)
8       tlssep_close(desc)
9   }
10  tlssep_terminate(desc)
```

Fig. 5. Pseudocode to accept a TLS connection using `libtlssep`. Omits error handling, other than to check that the client is authorized to connect. The user-defined procedures are `accept_connection`, `user_auth`, and `handle`.

Figure 4 shows in pseudo-code an example of a `libtlssep`-based client, and Figure 5 shows a server. In a real application, the programmer would check the status code returned from each `libtlssep` call; here we show only those checks required to perform authentication. §5.1 will describe the security advantages of `libtlssep`'s API.

Configuration: CERTSHIM provided the inspiration for `libtlssep`'s configuration engine. Figure 6 lists a sample `libtlssep` configuration as is typically found at `/etc/tlssep-decorator-`*api-version*`.cfg`, where *api-version* represents the major and minor version numbers of `libtlssep`. Lines 1–3 specify the global configuration parameters, in this case the path to a certificate and private key as well as the default certificate-trust model.

The application-specific statement beginning on line 5 overrides the configuration when `tlssep-decorator` acts on behalf of `/usr/bin/my-prototype` so that the program chains two verification techniques: the traditional CA model and self-signed certificates, with the latter presumably supported for development purposes. Here the meaning of the **enough** parameter resembles CERTSHIM's **vote**: satisfying *one* of either CA or self-signed verification is sufficient for this application.

Had the administrator set **enough** to 2, the application would require that *both* verifications be successful; in the absence of an **enough** parameter, `tlssep-decorator` will enforce *all* of the specified verification techniques. An administrator could select other trust models here without making any changes to application source code.

```
1   certpath = "/etc/pki/tls/certs/cert.pem";
2   privkeypath = "/etc/pki/tls/certs/key.pem";
3   verification = ( "ca" );

5   programs = ({
6       path = "/usr/bin/my-prototype";
7       verification = ( "ca", "self-signed" );
8       enough = 1;
9   })
```

Fig. 6. Sample `libtlssep` configuration.

5   Security, Programmability, and Performance

5.1   Security Benefits of `libtlssep`'s API and Architecture

Table 1 summarizes the security advantages of `libtlssep` which we further describe here. Libtlssep contributes to application robustness for two reasons: (1) it has a simple API which we designed to provide clear failure semantics, and (2) it results in applications which make use of privilege separation to protect secret cryptographic keys.

Our design represents a tradeoff: for example, combining another TLS library with OpenBSD's `imsg` would provide more flexibility, but such a composition requires the programmer to design a privilege-separation architecture. With

Table 1. Comparison of OpenSSL and `libtlssep`.

	OpenSSL	`libtlssep`
Certificate verification	Left to application programmer; trust model (including trust of self-signed certificates) embedded in application logic	Follows from semantics of library; trust model selected by configuration
Name verification	Application programmer must check that the certificate's name matches the expected name	Follows from semantics of library
Error reporting	Inconsistent API [15, §4.1]	Consistent API
Key isolation	Key compromise follows from application compromise	Architecture isolates keys in separate memory space
Configuration	Each application has its own configuration mechanism	Single configuration point for all applications
OS access controls	OS has difficulty discerning between encrypted and cleartext connections	OS can restrict applications such that they can only perform network reads and writes through decorator
Cipher suite choices	Left to application programmer; includes `null` cipher	Library designers choose cipher suite

`libtlssep`, programmers benefit from the architecture we designed to protect cryptographic keys without needing to reason about privilege separation.

Libtlssep's API promotes better application security. Recall Figures 1, 2, 4, and 5 which show examples of using OpenSSL and `libtlssep`. Figure 1 shows that a client application programmer who makes direct use of OpenSSL must call a number of procedures to set up the TLS connection. Most significantly, explicit code is required to verify the peer certificate involved in the connection; this involves obtaining the peer certificate using `SSL_get_peer_certificate`, verifying it through a call to `SSL_get_verify_result`, and further checking the certificate's name by implementing and calling `verify_name`. We discussed in §2 Marlinspike's attack on subtle flaws in `verify_name`-like procedures, and contemporary TLS APIs cause such procedures to be repeated across many applications.

Figure 4 shows that `libtlssep` requires fewer procedure calls, and thus allows less ill composition. Here the programmer does not have to explicitly call a verification routine. Instead, verification follows from the semantics of `tlssep_connect` (or `tlssep_accept`), as with LibreSSL's `tls_connect`. Libtlssep does not return a valid TLS connection handle if verification fails.

By using libtlssep instead of directly using OpenSSL, an application remains simpler, because libtlssep absolves the application programmer of the responsibility of verification. Libtlssep also makes error handling more clear as its procedures report errors in a consistent manner, unlike many existing APIs [15, §4.1].

With libtlssep, all network messages subsequent to the initial connection establishment pass through the decorator. The decorator isolates both long-term authentication keys and session keys in its own address space. This reduces the likelihood that an application compromise will result in the compromise of a cryptographic secret. This design is intended to address issues which stem from a combination of (1) implementation flaws which allow for applications to be compromised and (2) design flaws which allow long-term keys to exist in an application's memory space. We do not claim to fix all attacks, but our implementation will help with those that exploit application code to retrieve long-term keys.

In other architectures, both verification code and configuration settings are duplicated throughout a number of applications. Bugs fixed in one application are left latent in others, and administrators must learn each application's TLS-configuration syntax. With libtlssep, the API and decorator consolidates verification code, ensures applications cannot ignore verification failures, and consolidates trust-model configuration. Programmers are accustomed to deploying different configuration files than those used while developing their software, so this will reduce the likelihood of deploying an application which trusts self-signed certificates. Furthermore, upgrading libtlssep and modifying the library's configuration file can add new certificate trust models without modifying applications. This can also centralize efforts to address emerging threats—such as with the triple-handshake attack [8]—which with other libraries require updates to each application.

Libtlssep's decorator will exist in a filesystem with its setuid bit set. This ensures that the decorator runs as a different user than the application. The decorator's user should have special read access to the appropriate cryptographic keys, but should not necessarily have full superuser privileges.

Libtlssep's architecture allows OSs to better constrain applications which make use of the library. For example, Security-Enhanced Linux (SELinux) or another fine-grained access-control system could forbid an application from reading or writing cleartext network connections, instead permitting only TLS-protected communication through the libtlssep decorator. This forces applications to communicate over the network only in an encrypted manner. Current architectures make it difficult to discern between encrypted and cleartext connections from within OS access controls. Existing techniques rely on weaker transport-layer-port filtering or attempts at runtime packet inspection.

Our design does not allow programmers to pick the cipher suites their applications use. This allows libtlssep to avoid cryptographic disasters such as weak ciphers, disabled cryptography, or ill-composed cryptographic primitives [6].

5.2 Programmability

To assess the programmability of libtlssep, we ported two common applications: the wget client [30] and the lighttpd [20] server.

Porting wget required the addition of 231 lines of code—31 of which were comments—and the removal of three lines (wget totals around 39,000 lines). A number of these additions involved properly implementing error handling and following good programming practices. We benefited from the fact that wget already supports multiple TLS backends, so our additions took the form of a libtlssep backend and modified only two source files. The libtlssep backend comprises of 159 lines of code while the OpenSSL backend consumes 590.

Porting lighttpd required the addition of 352 lines and the removal of 15 lines (lighttpd totals around 40,000 lines). Lighttpd was not written to support multiple TLS backends, which slightly added to the difficulty of our port. Here we ended up replacing OpenSSL procedure calls with libtlssep procedure calls in seven source files.

Modifying wget and lighttpd to use our library shows that existing applications—both client- and server-side—can easily gain the security benefits provided by libtlssep. In both cases, we completed the port without having previously studied the application's source code. The use of CERTSHIM with existing applications requires even less effort, but CERTSHIM does not provide the architectural security benefits of libtlssep. New applications will immediately benefit from choosing libtlssep's simpler API.

5.3 Performance

To evaluate libtlssep's performance, we measured latency and throughput while comparing libtlssep with pure OpenSSL. We made use of a computer with a 3.4-GHz four-core Intel Core i7-3770 processor and 32 GB of memory. We ran our tests by requesting data from a local HTTPS server using the loopback interface; thus our results amplify the performance differences between libtlssep and OpenSSL because they omit real network latency.

For testing purposes, we created four HTTPS clients: for each of OpenSSL and libtlssep, we implemented a latency- and throughput-testing client. Lighttpd 1.4.36 (compiled to use pure OpenSSL, not libtlssep) provided the HTTPS server for our test clients. Each benchmark uses the same cipher suite: ephemeral elliptic-curve Diffie-Hellman, RSA, 128-bit AES, and SHA-256. We also performed tests using wget and lighttpd, each compiled to use both pure OpenSSL and libtlssep.

Latency Performance: Each of our latency benchmarks repeats the process of initiating a TLS connection, reading one byte, and then closing the connection. We measured the time that it took each application to complete 10,000 iterations. Table 2a summarizes the results of this experiment. We present the results of 10 full runs, along with the mean and standard deviation. The OpenSSL implementation had an average runtime of 49.580 seconds with a standard deviation of 0.403. The libtlssep implementation had an average runtime of 50.894 seconds

Table 2. Latency and throughput measurements. Both client and server ran on the same machine and communicated using the loopback interface.

	Runtime (seconds)	
#	OpenSSL	libtlssep
1	49.341	50.903
2	49.474	51.178
3	49.112	50.783
4	49.358	50.945
5	49.457	50.604
6	50.563	51.212
7	49.818	50.594
8	49.764	51.075
9	49.563	51.028
10	49.353	50.616
μ	49.580	50.894
σ	0.403	0.235

(a) Runtime of 10,000 serial connections using OpenSSL and libtlssep.

	Runtime (seconds)					
	OpenSSL			libtlssep		
#	10^1 MB	10^2 MB	10^3 MB	10^1 MB	10^2 MB	10^3 MB
1	0.061	0.193	1.517	0.071	0.205	1.625
2	0.061	0.193	1.517	0.070	0.205	1.557
3	0.061	0.193	2.420	0.070	0.206	1.589
4	0.061	0.193	1.521	0.079	0.294	1.585
5	0.061	0.194	1.517	0.070	0.212	1.841
6	0.061	0.194	1.521	0.070	0.212	1.557
7	0.061	0.194	1.559	0.070	0.294	2.446
8	0.061	0.193	1.519	0.071	0.206	1.554
9	0.061	0.194	1.518	0.070	0.207	1.563
10	0.061	0.194	2.417	0.070	0.295	2.456
μ	0.061	0.194	1.703	0.071	0.234	1.777
σ	0.000	0.000	0.378	0.003	0.042	0.365

(b) Single download time of file sizes indicated using OpenSSL and libtlssep.

with a standard deviation of 0.235 seconds. On average, libtlssep initiates TLS connections at 97.4% the rate measured with pure OpenSSL.

Throughput Performance: Our throughput benchmarks read files of varying sizes over a TLS connection. Each creates a single connection, reads 1,024 MB at a time until the entire file is read, and then closes the connection. We measured the time that it took each application to download 10 MB, 100 MB, and 1,000 MB files.

Table 2b summarizes the results of this experiment. For the 1,000 MB file, the pure OpenSSL implementation took an average of 1.703 seconds with a standard deviation of 0.378, while the libtlssep implementation took an average of 1.777 seconds with a standard deviation of 0.365.

Based on these results, the throughput of libtlssep is 95.8% of that measured with pure OpenSSL. The slight difference is due to the added overhead of scheduling an additional process as well as the additional memcpys and RPC-related shared-memory communication involved. Libtlssep's throughput during our experiments exceeded 4,610 Mb/s.

We also performed benchmarks using both our libtlssep and the upstream-OpenSSL versions of lighttpd and wget. Here we used variations of the following command (note that the libtlssep version of wget presently ignores the --no-check-certificate option):

Table 3. Single download time of a 1,000 MB file using the OpenSSL and `libtlssep` versions of `wget` and `lighttpd`.

#	Runtime (seconds) OpenSSL server OpenSSL client	OpenSSL server libtlssep client	libtlssep server OpenSSL client	libtlssep server libtlssep client
1	1.601	2.643	2.066	2.722
2	1.597	2.565	2.055	2.704
3	1.599	2.566	2.247	2.732
4	1.598	2.559	2.040	2.645
5	1.598	2.584	2.056	2.865
6	1.600	2.590	2.052	2.581
7	1.597	2.565	2.103	2.643
8	1.596	2.563	2.051	2.977
9	1.608	2.564	2.054	2.736
10	1.829	2.619	2.059	2.855
μ	1.622	2.582	2.078	2.746
σ	0.073	0.028	0.062	0.120

Table 4. Total download time of three simultaneous transfers of a 1,000 MB file from OpenSSL/`libtlssep` `lighttpd` to OpenSSL `wget`s.

#	Runtime (seconds) OpenSSL server	libtlssep server
1	4.466	6.449
2	4.470	6.203
3	4.479	6.558
4	4.545	6.621
5	4.622	6.809
6	4.438	6.667
7	4.428	6.725
8	4.432	6.445
9	4.519	6.494
10	4.455	6.310
μ	4.485	6.528
σ	0.061	0.187

```
time wget --quiet --no-http-keep-alive --no-check-certificate \
    -O /dev/null https://127.0.0.1/1000M
```

We summarize our `lighttpd`-to-`wget` results in Tables 3 and 4. The former table contains measurements of a single 1,000 MB download, and the latter table contains measurements of three simultaneous 1,000 MB downloads. A single serial `libtlssep`-to-`libtlssep` download provides approximately 59% the throughput of its pure-OpenSSL counterpart when transfering over our computer's loopback interface. This rate would benefit from increasing the size of the buffers used within `lighttpd` and `wget` to reduce the number of RPCs `libtlssep` must invoke to transfer data (also recall that our previous experiments used `libtlssep` only on one side of the connection). Simultaneous transfers fare better; here `libtlssep` approaches within 68% of OpenSSL's throughput. This performance would also benefit from tuning the buffer sizes within `lighttpd` and `wget`.

6   Conclusion

`Libtlssep` provides application programmers with a simpler API and more secure design for adding TLS support to their applications. `Libtlssep` is less ambitious than other projects; it exists between contemporary TLS libraries and projects such as NaCL [6] and MinimaLT [27]. `Libtlssep` serves as an easy-to-integrate, near-term replacement for existing TLS libraries. Nonetheless, `libtlssep` provides better isolation of cryptographic secrets and reduces the number of pitfalls faced by network programmers.

Future work on `libtlssep` will include further performance optimizations, a review of the library's source code, and additional application ports. Previous performance improvements came from replacing our use of Open Network Computing (ONC) RPC with a custom RPC implementation, moving from a UNIX-socket-based to a shared-memory-based RPC channel, and reusing a single decorator process across multiple connections within an application. `Libtlssep`'s decorator would also benefit from an implementation in a strongly typed language such as Go. Once we are satisfied with our implementation and API we will announce a stable release; our research prototype is already available at `http://www.flyn.org/projects/libtlssep`.

Acknowledgments. We thank Suzanne Matthews, Kyle Moses, and Christa Chewar for their comments on our early work, our anonymous referees for comments on subsequent drafts, and the United States Military Academy for their support. We are also grateful to Colm MacCárthaigh who encouraged us to pursue using shared memory to improve the performance of `libtlssep`'s RPC channel.

References

[1] Fedora system-wide crypto policy. `http://fedoraproject.org/wiki/Changes/CryptoPolicy` (accessed Mach 22, 2014)

[2] Barnes, R.L.: DANE: Taking TLS authentication to the next level using DNSSEC. IETF Journal, October 2011. `http://www.internetsociety.org/articles/dane-taking-tls-authentication-next-level-using-dnssec` accessed June 22, 2015)

[3] Bates, A., Pletcher, J., Nichols, T., Hollembaek, B., Tian, D., Butler, K.R., Alkhelaifi, A.: Securing SSL certificate verification through dynamic linking. In: Proceedings of the 2014 ACM SIGSAC Conference on Computer and Communications Security, CCS 2014, pp. 394–405. ACM, New York (2014)

[4] Beck, B.: LibreSSL: The first 30 days and the future. In: presentation at the 11th BSDCan Conference, May 2014

[5] Bernstein, D.J.: CurveCP: Usable security for the Internet. CurveCP: Usable security for the Internet. http://curvecp.org (accessed July 9, 2015)

[6] Bernstein, D.J., Lange, T., Schwabe, P.: The security impact of a new cryptographic library. In: Hevia, A., Neven, G. (eds.) LatinCrypt 2012. LNCS, vol. 7533, pp. 159–176. Springer, Heidelberg (2012)

[7] Beurdouche, B., Bhargavan, K., Delignat-Lavaud, A., Fournet, C., Kohlweiss, M., Pironti, A., Strub, P.Y., Zinzindohoue, J.K.: A messy state of the union: Taming the composite state machines of TLS. In: Proc. IEEE Symp. Security and Privacy. IEEE Computer Society Press, Washington, DC, May 2015

[8] Bhargavan, K., Lavaud, A., Fournet, C., Pironti, A., Strub, P.: Triple handshakes and cookie cutters: Breaking and fixing authentication over TLS. In: Proc. IEEE Symp. Security and Privacy, pp. 98–113. IEEE Computer Society Press, Washington, DC, May 2014

[9] Bittau, A., Hamburg, M., Handley, M., Mazières, D., Boneh, D.: The case for ubiquitous transport-level encryption. In: Proceedings of the 19th USENIX Security Symposium. USENIX Association, Berkeley, August 2010

[10] Cox, R., Grosse, E., Pike, R., Presotto, D., Quinlan, S.: Security in Plan 9. In: Proc. of the USENIX Security Symposium, pp. 3–16. USENIX Association, Berkeley (2002)

[11] Durumeric, Z., Kasten, J., Bailey, M., Halderman, J.A.: Analysis of the HTTPS certificate ecosystem. In: Proceedings of the 2013 Conference on Internet Measurement, IMC 2013, pp. 291–304. ACM, New York (2013)

[12] Fahl, S., Harbach, M., Muders, T., Smith, M., Baumgärtner, L., Freisleben, B.: Why eve and mallory love android: an analysis of android SSL (in)security. In: Proceedings of the 2012 ACM Conference on Computer and Communications Security, pp. 50–61. ACM, New York (2012)

[13] Fahl, S., Harbach, M., Perl, H., Koetter, M., Smith, M.: Rethinking SSL development in an appified world. In: Proceedings of the 2013 ACM SIGSAC Conference on Computer and Communications Security, CCS 2013, pp. 49–60. ACM, New York (2013)

[14] Electronic Frontier Foundation: HTTPS everywhere. https://www.eff.org/https-everywhere (accessed August 26, 2013)

[15] Georgiev, M., Iyengar, S., Jana, S., Anubhai, R., Boneh, D., Shmatikov, V.: The most dangerous code in the world: validating SSL certificates in non-browser software. In: Proceedings of the 2012 ACM Conference on Computer and Communications Security, CCS 2012, pp. 38–49. ACM, New York (2012)

[16] Guan, L., Lin, J., Luo, B., Jing, J., Wang, J.: Protecting private keys against memory disclosure attacks using hardware transactional memory. In: Proc. IEEE Symp. Security and Privacy. IEEE Computer Society Press, Washington, DC, May 2015

[17] He, B., Rastogi, V., Cao, Y., Chen, Y., Venkatakrishnan, V., Yang, R., Zhang, Z.: Vetting SSL usage in applications with SSLINT. In: Proc. IEEE Symp. Security and Privacy. IEEE Computer Society Press, Washington, DC, May 2015

[18] Hoffman, P., Schlyter, J.: RFC 6698: The DNS-based Authentication of Named Entities (DANE) Transport Layer Security (TLS) protocol: TLSA, August 2012. http://www.ietf.org/rfc/rfc6698.txt (accessed June 22, 2015), status: PROPOSED STANDARD

[19] IOerror: DigiNotar damage disclosure. The Tor Blog, September 2011. https://blog.torproject.org/blog/diginotar-damage-disclosure (accessed May 20, 2015)

[20] Kneschke, J., et al.: lighttpd. http://www.lighttpd.net/ (accessed Jun 22, 2015)

[21] Leavitt, N.: Internet security under attack: The undermining of digital certificates. Computer 44(12), 17–20 (2011)

[22] Marlinspike, M.: Null-prefix attacks against SSL/TLS certificates. Presentation at Black Hat USA, July 2009. http://www.blackhat.com/presentations/bh-usa-09/MARLINSPIKE/BHUSA09-Marlinspike-DefeatSSL-PAPER1.pdf accessed June 22, 2015)

[23] Naylor, D., Finamore, A., Leontiadis, I., Grunenberger, Y., Mellia, M., Munafò, M., Papagiannaki, K., Steenkiste, P.: The cost of the 'S' in HTTPS. In: Proceedings of the 10th ACM International on Conference on Emerging Networking Experiments and Technologies, CoNEXT 2014, pp. 133–140. ACM, New York (2014)

[24] NIST National Vulnerability Database: CVE-2014-0160, Decembe 2013. http://web.nvd.nist.gov/view/vuln/detail?vulnId=CVE-2014-0160 (accessed April 15, 2014)

[25] OpenBSD manual pages: imsg_init(3). http://www.openbsd.org/cgi-bin/man.cgi/OpenBSD-current/man3/imsg_init.3 (accessed July 8, 2015)

[26] Petullo, W.M., Solworth, J.A.: Simple-to-use, secure-by-design networking in Ethos. In: Proceedings of the Sixth European Workshop on System Security, EUROSEC 2013. ACM, New York, April 2013

[27] Petullo, W.M., Zhang, X., Solworth, J.A., Bernstein, D.J., Lange, T.: MinimaLT: Minimal-latency networking through better security. In: Proceedings of the 2013 ACM SIGSAC Conference on Computer and Communications Security, CCS 2013. ACM, New York, Novembe 2013

[28] Provos, N., Friedl, M., Honeyman, P.: Preventing privilege escalation. In: Proc. of the USENIX Security Symposium, pp. 231–242. USENIX Association, Berkeley, August 2003

[29] Schmidt, S.: Introducing s2n, a new open source TLS implementation. Amazon Web Services Security Blog, June 2015. https://blogs.aws.amazon.com/security/post/TxCKZM94ST1S6Y/Introducing-s2n-a-New-Open-Source-TLS-Implementation (accessed July 1, 2015)

[30] Scrivano, G., et al.: wget. http://www.gnu.org/software/wget/ (accessed June 22, 2015)

[31] Soghoian, C., Stamm, S.: Certified lies: Detecting and defeating government interception attacks against SSL (Short paper). In: Danezis, G. (ed.) FC 2011. LNCS, vol. 7035, pp. 250–259. Springer, Heidelberg (2012)

[32] Vratonjic, N., Freudiger, J., Bindschaedler, V., Hubaux, J.P.: The inconvenient truth about web certificates. In: Proceedings of the 10th Workshop on the Economics of Information Security (June 2011)

[33] Ylonen, T.: SSH—secure login connections over the Internet. In: Proc. of the USENIX Security Symposium, pp. 37–42. USENIX Association, San Jose (1996)

[34] Zimmermann, P.R.: The Official PGP Users Guide. MIT Press, Boston (1995)

How Not to Combine RC4 States

Subhadeep Banik[1] and Sonu Jha[2]

[1] DTU Compute, Technical University of Denmark, Lyngby 2800, Denmark
subb@dtu.dk
[2] National Informatics Center, Sector V, Salt Lake, Kolkata 91, India
jhasonu1987@yahoo.com

Abstract. Over the past few years, an attractive design paradigm has emerged, that aims to produce new stream cipher designs, by combining one or more independently produced RC4 states. The ciphers so produced turn out to be faster than RC4 on any software platform, mainly because the average number of internal operations used in the cipher per byte of keystream produced is usually lesser than RC4. One of the main efforts of the designers is to ensure that the existing weaknesses of RC4 are not carried over to the new ciphers so designed. In this work we will look at two such ciphers RC4B (proposed by Zhang et. al.) and Quad-RC4/m-RC4 (proposed by Maitra et. al.). We will propose distinguishing attacks against all these ciphers, and look at certain design flaws that made these ciphers vulnerable.

Keywords: RC4, RC4B, Quad-RC4, m-RC4, Distinguishing Attacks, Stream Cipher.

1 Introduction

From over the past two decades, RC4 has been one of the most extensively used stream ciphers in many popular protocols like WEP, TLS, TCP etc. The reason behind the popularity of this byte oriented stream cipher was the simplicity of its design. Using a very few number of operations, RC4 is able to provide fast enough encryption in software. It is not very surprising that such an elegant cipher wrapped in just 4 lines of code was going to gain the attention of the researchers from all over the world. As a result, several attempts have been made to cryptanalyze this stream cipher (see [7, 8]). Apart from the analysis point of view, there has also been several proposals of new RC4-like stream ciphers by introducing some number of modifications on the original RC4 design paradigm. The major motivations behind these new proposals were to protect the cipher against some well known cryptanalytic results shown on the RC4 stream cipher keeping also in mind that the average number of operational steps taken by those new introduced designs in order to encrypt the data is not much more than the number of steps taken by RC4 itself. For example, the RC4+ stream cipher [6] proposed by Maitra et. al. introduced a modified version of RC4 with a complex 3-phase key schedule and a more complex output function in order to protect the new design against the above mentioned well known attacks with

© Springer International Publishing Switzerland 2015
R.S. Chakraborty et al. (Eds.): SPACE 2015, LNCS 9354, pp. 95–112, 2015.
DOI: 10.1007/978-3-319-24126-5_6

the speed being marginally slower in software compared to RC4. Similarly there were interesting stream cipher proposals (such as VMPC [16], GGHN [3] etc.) with the introduction of various modifications to achieve faster encryption in software and to protect the design of the cipher against the potential vulnerabilities reported in literature. Nevertheless, some distinguishing attacks on all of the above mentioned ciphers have already been reported [2, 9, 15].

An interesting advancement proposed by some researchers towards the modifications in the RC4 design has been to increase the number of RC4 states, i.e., to increase the number of permutations in order to make the output generation dependent on more random variables which minimizes the correlation between the bytes produced. This approach has the added advantage that the number of steps performed per keystream byte produced may be made smaller than RC4 itself. This makes the ciphers designed under this paradigm faster than RC4 in software. Ciphers like RC4A [12], RC4B [4], Quad-RC4 [11] etc. have been introduced to fulfill such needs. In this paper we will concentrate on the analysis of two stream ciphers namely RC4B and Quad-RC4. The RC4B stream cipher is similar to RC4's exchange shuffle model i.e. RC4A. It also uses two different arrays of permutations. The Key-Scheduling Algorithm (KSA) of RC4B is same as that of RC4A. The Pseudo-Random Keystream Generation Algorithm (PRGA) of RC4B differs slightly from that of RC4A. In order to prevent the strong distinguisher biases [4, 14], the authors of RC4B choose to mix the two array's states. A detailed description of the RC4B stream cipher will be given in Section 2.

Quad-RC4 was first presented at a session in Indocrypt 2012 [5]. Its design focuses on building a 32-bit RC4 for a 32-word machine, however the basic 8-bit RC4 is used as a building block at every round of keystream generation. The KSA of Quad-RC4 is similar to the 3-layer KSA+ of RC4+. Since Quad-RC4 uses four different 8-bit identity permutations, the authors run the KSA+ routine on four identity permutations independently to generate four scrambled permutations over $\mathbb{Z}_{256}$. In the PRGA, the four scrambled pseudo random permutations are merged into a single array of size 256 where each element is a 32 bit number. The output byte is then produced following a certain number of operations. See Section 3 for a detailed description of the Quad-RC4 stream cipher. A description of the m-RC4 stream cipher will also be given in section 3.3 in which the authors propose a model of combining m number of different 8-bit pseudo random permutations.

1.1   Contribution and Organization of the Paper

In this paper, we analyze the security of RC4B and Quad-RC4 stream ciphers by mounting distinguishing attacks on them. The RC4B stream cipher uses two independent RC4 states in its encryption scheme. In Section 2, we will show that the probability that the first two output bytes produced by RC4B are both 0 is approximately $\frac{2}{N^2}$ ($N = 256$) which is twice the expected probability in the ideal case. In Section 3, we will show that any r-th 4-byte output word Z_r (for $r \geq 1$) produced by the Quad-RC4 stream cipher is biased and the probability that it is equal to 0 is around $\frac{3}{N^2}$. Since in the ideal case, this probability should have been $\frac{1}{N^4}$, this represents a huge bias in the distribution. The authors of Quad-RC4 also proposed a scheme of combining m number of independent RC4 states (m-RC4) which would produce output bytes of size m bytes. We will also analyze the m-RC4 stream cipher by mounting distinguishing attacks and show that this design is still vulnerable for any m. In fact we will show that for the case of m being even (Section 3.4), the r-th output word Z_r produced by the stream cipher is biased towards 0. Furthermore in Section 3.5, we will show for the case of any m in general ($m > 2$), the probability of the first two output bytes Z_1 and Z_2 being equal is also biased. Lastly, in Section 3.6, we will discuss some flaws in the design of these stream ciphers which made them vulnerable to distinguishing attacks. We tabulate some experimental results in Section 4. We will conclude the paper in Section 5.

2 Description and Analysis of the RC4B Stream Cipher

In this section we give a detailed description of RC4B stream cipher. In addition we also analyze the stream cipher by mounting distinguishing attack on its first two output bytes Z_1 and Z_2.

2.1 Description of RC4B

The RC4B stream cipher is similar to the RC4A [12], and uses two RC4 states namely S_1 and S_2. RC4B uses the same Key Scheduling Algorithm (KSA) as RC4 and RC4A. The KSA routine is used to construct two permutations S_1 and S_2 using two keys K_1 and K_2 respectively (K_2 is usually derived as some pseudorandom function of K_1). The PRGA of RC4B is different from RC4A. Unlike RC4A, RC4B mixes the two arrays of the state. The arrays in RC4A evolve independent of the other, i.e. the *index pointers* used to update the array S_1 are generated by S_1 itself, and similarly the *index pointers* used to update S_2 are generated by S_2. This makes the cipher design vulnerable to distinguishing attacks. Therefore in RC4B this trend is reversed, the elements to be swapped in a particular array is determined by the other array. Algorithm 1 describes the PRGA of RC4B.

The key scheduling algorithm or KSA takes an array S to derive a permutation of $\{0, 1, 2, \ldots, N-1\}$ using a variable size key K. The byte-length of the Secret Key K is denoted by l. Please note that all the addition operations are done in the integer ring $\mathbb{Z}_{256}$. Three byte indices i, j_1 and j_2 are used. After performing the KSA on S_1 and S_2, the PRGA begins which produces two pseudo-random bytes Z_1 and Z_2 using the two permutations derived from KSA. The authors claim that RC4B generates keystreams faster than RC4 itself, since the number of operations performed per byte of keystream produced is lesser than that of RC4. The state space of RC4B is $N! \cdot N! \cdot N^3$ which is approximately 2^{2388} since $N = 256$. Hence it is hard to perform state recovery attack on RC4B.

Input: Pseudorandom Permutations S_1, S_2
Output: Keystream bytes Z_1, Z_2

$i \leftarrow 0$, $j_1 \leftarrow 0$, $j_2 \leftarrow 0$;
while Keystream is required **do**
$\quad$ $i \leftarrow i + 1$;
$\quad$ $j_1 \leftarrow j_1 + S_2[i]$;
$\quad$ Swap($S_1[i], S_1[j_1]$);
$\quad$ $Z_1 = S_2[S_1[i] + S_1[j_1]]$;
$\quad$ $j_2 \leftarrow j_2 + S_1[i]$;
$\quad$ Swap($S_2[i], S_2[j_2]$);
$\quad$ $Z_2 = S_1[S_2[i] + S_2[j_2]]$;
end

Algorithm 1. PRGA

2.2 Analysis of RC4B

In this Subsection, we analyze the RC4B stream cipher. We refer to the PRGA Algorithm 1 of RC4B. Let the initial states of RC4B PRGA be denoted by S_1 and S_2.

Lemma 1. *Let S_1 and S_2 be random permutations on $\{0, 1, 2, \ldots, 255\}$. If $S_1[1]$ $= 0$, $S_2[1] = X$, $S_1[X] = Y$ and $S_2[Y] = 0$, (where $X \neq 1$, $Y \neq 0$ are any two byte values) then the first two output bytes Z_1 and Z_2 are always 0.*

Proof. According to the PRGA algorithm described in Algorithm 1, initially $i = j_1 = j_2 = 0$. In the next step, the index i is incremented as $i = i + 1$. The secret index j_1 is incremented as

$$j_1 = j_1 + S_2[i] = 0 + S_2[1] = X. \tag{1}$$

After following the swap operation, $S_1[1] = Y$ and $S_1[X] = 0$. In the next step, the first output byte Z_1 is produced as

$$Z_1 = S_2[(S_1[1] + S_1[X])] = S_2[Y + 0] = 0. \tag{2}$$

The second secret index j_2 is incremented as

$$j_2 = j_2 + S_1[i] = 0 + S_1[1] = Y. \tag{3}$$

After following the next swap operation, $S_2[1] = 0$ and $S_2[Y] = X$. Thereafter, the next output byte Z_2 is given as

$$Z_2 = S_1[(S_2[1] + S_2[Y])] = S_1[X + 0] = 0. \tag{4}$$

Hence the first 2 output bytes Z_1 and Z_2 are always 0.

$\square$

Theorem 1. *Let S_1 and S_2 be random permutations on $\{0, 1, 2, \ldots, 255\}$. The probability that $Z_1 = Z_2 = 0$ is given by the equation $\Pr[Z_1 = Z_2 = 0] = \frac{2}{N^2} - \frac{1}{N^4}$ where $N = 256$.*

Proof. Let E denote the event "$S_1[1] = 0$, $S_2[1] = X$, $S_1[X] = Y$ and $S_2[Y] = 0$". Then we have,

$$\Pr[\mathsf{E}] = \frac{1}{(N-1)} \cdot \frac{1}{(N-1)} \approx \frac{1}{N^2}.$$

From Lemma 1, we know $\Pr[Z_1 = Z_2 = 0 | \mathsf{E}] = 1$. By standard randomness assumptions and by performing extensive computer experiments using up to 2^{25} keys, we have verified $\Pr[Z_1 = Z_2 = 0 | \mathsf{E}^c] = \frac{1}{N^2}$ (E^c denotes the complement of the Event E). Hence the final probability is given as

$$\begin{aligned}
\Pr[Z_1 = Z_2 = 0] &= \Pr[Z_1 = Z_2 = 0 | \mathsf{E}] \cdot \Pr[\mathsf{E}] + \\
&\quad \Pr[Z_1 = Z_2 = 0 | \mathsf{E}^c] \cdot \Pr[\mathsf{E}^c] \\
&= 1 \cdot \frac{1}{N^2} + \frac{1}{N^2} \cdot (1 - \frac{1}{N^2}) \\
&= \frac{2}{N^2} - \frac{1}{N^4}.
\end{aligned}$$

(5)

$\square$

For an ideal cipher, the probability $\Pr[Z_1 = Z_2 = 0]$ should be only $\frac{1}{N^2}$, so we can see that in RC4B, this probability is twice that of an ideal cipher. We now state the following theorem from [7], which outlines the number of output samples required to distinguish two distributions X and Y.

Theorem 2. *(Mantin-Shamir [7]) Let X, Y be distributions, and suppose that the event e happens in X with probability p and in Y with probability $p(1 + q)$. Then for small p and q, $O\left(\frac{1}{pq^2}\right)$ samples suffice to distinguish X from Y with a constant probability of success.*

Distinguishing RC4B from Random Sources. Let X be the probability distribution of Z_1, Z_2 in an ideal random stream, and let Y be the probability distribution of Z_1, Z_2 in streams produced by RC4B for randomly chosen keys. Let the event e denote $Z_1 = Z_2 = 0$, which occurs with probability of $\frac{1}{N^2}$ in X and $\frac{2}{N^2} - \frac{1}{N^4} \approx \frac{2}{N^2}$ in Y. By using the Theorem 2 with $p = \frac{1}{N^2}$ and $q = 1$, we can conclude that we need about $\frac{1}{pq^2} = N^2 = 2^{16}$ output samples to reliably distinguish the two distributions.

3   Description and Analysis of Quad-RC4 and m-RC4 Stream Ciphers

In this section we describe Quad-RC4 and m-RC4 stream ciphers. We also demonstrate distinguishing attacks on Quad-RC4 and m-RC4 by proving biases in their output bytes.

3.1   Description of Quad-RC4

The rationale behind the design of Quad-RC4 was the optimal utilization of the resources on the modern processors which are mostly 32 bits. The authors take a single l-byte key ($16 \leq l \leq 30$) which is used to drive 4 different key scheduling in parallel to obtain 4 different permutations over $\mathbb{Z}_{256}$. Two byte indices i and j are used where j is kept secret. The authors of Quad-RC4 argue that their scheme is more secure than the basic RC4 encryption scheme. The key scheduling for Quad-RC4 is same as the KSA+ of the stream cipher RC4+ [6]. The KSA+ consists of 3 layers: the basic scrambling of the first layer of KSA+ is similar to the RC4 KSA. Algorithms 2 and 3 describes the other two layers namely IV Scrambling and Zig-Zag Scrambling of the KSA+ respectively. All the addition operations are performed in $\mathbb{Z}_{256}$ and $\oplus$ denotes the bitwise XOR. The array V used in the Algorithm 2 is of length $N = 256$ and is defined as

$$V[i] = \begin{cases} IV[\frac{N}{2} - 1 - i] & \text{if } \frac{N}{2} - l \leq i \leq \frac{N}{2} - 1 \\ IV[i - \frac{N}{2}] & \text{if } \frac{N}{2} \leq i \leq \frac{N}{2} + l - 1 \\ 0 & \text{otherwise} \end{cases}$$

Input: S, K, V
Output: Scrambled S

---

for $i = N/2 - 1$ to 0 **do**
　$j = (j + S[i]) \oplus (K[i] + V[i]);$
　Swap($S[i]$,$S[j]$);
end

for $i = N/2 to N - 1$ **do**
　$j = (j + S[i]) \oplus (K[i] + V[i]);$
　Swap($S[i]$,$S[j]$);
end

Algorithm 2. Mix-IV

Input: S, K
Output: Scrambled S

---

for $y = 0$ to $N - 1$ **do**
　if $y \equiv 0 \mod 2$ **then**
　　$i = \frac{y}{2};$
　end
　else
　　$y = N - \frac{y+1}{2};$
　end
　$j = (j + S[i] + K[i]);$
　Swap($S[i]$,$S[j]$);
end

Algorithm 3. Zig-Zag

Let S_1, S_2, S_3 and S_4 denote the 4 pseudo random permutations over $\mathbb{Z}_{256}$ produced after running the key scheduling algorithm. They are merged into a single array S of size 256, where the i-th entry of S is an 32-bit number formed by concatenating the 4 bytes $S_1[i], \ldots, S_4[i]$. Algorithm 4 describes the PRGA of Quad-RC4. Please note that $\ll$ and $\gg$ denotes left and right bitwise shifts respectively. The | and & signs represent bitwise OR and AND whereas $\oplus$ represents the bitwise XOR.

Input: 4 pseudo random permutations over $\mathbb{Z}_{256}$
Output: 32-bit output words

$i = j = 0$;
for $i = 0$ to 255 **do**
| $S[i] = (S_1[i] \ll 24)|(S_2[i] \ll 16)|(S_3[i] \ll 8)|S_4[i]$;
end
while Keystream is required **do**
| $i = (i + 1) \mod 256$;
| $j = (j + S_4[i]) \mod 256$;
| Swap($S[i]$, $S[j]$);
| $t = (S[i] + S[j]) \mod 2^{32}$;
| $t_1 = t\&\text{0xFF}$;
| $t_2 = (t \gg 8)\&\text{0xFF}$;
| $t_3 = (t \gg 16)\&\text{0xFF}$;
| $t_4 = (t \gg 24)\&\text{0xFF}$;
| Output $Z = S[t_1] \oplus S[t_2] \oplus S[t_3] \oplus S[t_4]$;
| $\{a, b\}$ =Next pair of permutations in turn;
| Swap($S_a[i],S_a[t_a]$);
| Swap($S_b[i],S_b[t_b]$);
end

Algorithm 4. Quad-RC4 PRGA Routine

The authors introduce some additional swaps to break the symmetry in the swaps of the individual permutations. Two permutations S_a and S_b are selected at every round. Thereafter the i-th and the t_a-th bytes of S_a and the i-th and the t_b-th bytes of S_b are swapped. Note that t_a and t_b are the a-th and the b-th bytes of $t = t_1\|\ldots\|t_4$. Note that 2 permutations out of 4 can be selected in 6 ways.

3.2   Analysis of Quad-RC4

In this subsection we present the analysis of the Quad-RC4 stream cipher by demonstrating a distinguishing attack. We refer to the PRGA of Quad-RC4 presented in Algorithm 4.

Some Notations: Let the initial states of four 8-bit RC4 state permutations be represented as S_1, S_2, S_3 and S_4. Let S denote the 256-element array whose i-th entry is formed by concatenating the i-th bits of these four RC4 states. Let $t_1, \ldots, t_4$ denotes variables of size 1 byte each and $t = t_1\|\ldots\|t_4$ be a 32-bit variable. Before proceeding, let us define the event E_τ described as follows.

The Event: *Consider the four elements t_1, t_2, t_3, t_4. Partition these elements into 2 groups G_1, G_2 (there are $\frac{\binom{4}{2}}{2} = 3$ ways to do so). The event E_τ will be said to have occurred if one of the two conditions are satisfied:*

1. All the t_i's are equal i.e. $t_1 = t_2 = t_3 = t_4$.
2. All the t_i's are not equal but the two elements in G_1 are equal and the two elements in G_2 are also equal.

Lemma 2. *If the event E_τ described above occurs, the 4-byte output word Z_r in any PRGA round r is always equal to* 0.

Proof. In any PRGA round r of Quad-RC4, the variable t is assigned a value as follows

$$t = (S[i] + S[j]) \mod 2^{32}$$

In the subsequent operations, $t_1, \ldots, t_4$ are assigned the values

$$t_1 = t \& \texttt{0xFF}, \quad t_2 = (t \gg 8) \& \texttt{0xFF}, \quad t_3 = (t \gg 16) \& \texttt{0xFF}, \quad t_4 = (t \gg 24) \& \texttt{0xFF}.$$

Now the event E_τ can occur in 2 ways:

1. If $t_1 = t_2 = t_3 = t_4 = a$ (say). In that case $Z_1 = S[a] \oplus S[a] \oplus S[a] \oplus S[a] = 0$.
2. If two elements of G_1 are equal and the two elements of G_2 are also equal. Without loss of generality assume that G_1 consists of t_1, t_2 and G_2 of t_3, t_4 and $t_1 = t_2 = a$ and $t_3 = t_4 = b$. In this case

$$Z_r = S[a] \oplus S[a] \oplus S[b] \oplus S[b] = 0 \oplus 0 = 0$$

So it is evident that the value of Z_r is always going to be 0 under the occurrence of E_τ. $\qquad\square$

In general, the number of ways one can divide 4 things in 2 groups where each group has 2 things is $\frac{\binom{4}{2}}{2}$. For each such group, say (t_1, t_2) and (t_3, t_4) as shown earlier, let's have $t_1 = t_2 = a$ and $t_3 = t_4 = b$. Here a can take N values and b can take $N - 1$ values ($N = 256$) giving $N \cdot (N - 1) \cdot \frac{\binom{4}{2}}{2} = 3N^2 - 3N$ total ways the elements can be partitioned. Also $t_1 = t_2 = t_3 = t_4$ can occur in exactly N ways, and so the event E_τ can occur in total $3N^2 - 3N + N = 3N^2 - 2N$ ways. The probability that E_τ occurs if we choose the indices t_1, t_2, t_3, t_4 randomly is therefore given as $\Pr[E_\tau] = \frac{3N^2 - 2N}{N^4}$.

Theorem 3. *The probability that the 4-byte output word Z_r, produced by Quad-RC4 in any PRGA round r, is equal to 0 is given by the equation* $\Pr[Z_r = 0] \approx \frac{3}{N^2}$.

Proof. We have established that $\Pr[E_\tau] = \frac{3N^2 - 2N}{N^4}$. Since Z_r is always 0 under the event E_τ, therefore we have $\Pr[Z_r = 0 | E_\tau] = 1$. By the results of the extensive computer experiments performed using 2^{30} keys, we have verified that $\Pr[Z_r = 0 | E_\tau^c] = \frac{1}{N^4}$. Therefore the final probability can be given as

$$\begin{aligned}
\Pr[Z_r = 0] &= \Pr[Z_r = 0 | E_\tau] \cdot \Pr[E_\tau] + \Pr[Z_r = 0 | E_\tau^c] \cdot \Pr[E_\tau^c] \\
&= 1 \cdot \frac{3N^2 - 2N}{N^4} + \frac{1}{N^4} \cdot (1 - \frac{3N^2 - 2N}{N^4}) \\
&= \frac{3N^2 - 2N + 1}{N^4} \approx \frac{3}{N^2}.
\end{aligned}$$

$$(6)$$

$\qquad\square$

Thus we see a huge bias present in the output words produced Quad-RC4. In an ideal cipher, the probability of Z_r being equal to 0 was required to be $\frac{1}{N^4}$. Thus in Quad-RC4, the value of $\Pr[Z_r = 0]$ is $3N^2 \approx 2^{17.5}$ times that of an ideal cipher. It is clear that the design paradigm of the stream cipher is vulnerable. This has long term implications in the broadcast scenario, in which a single plaintext is encrypted by several randomly generated secret keys, and broadcast over a network. The attacker can perform a ciphertext only plaintext recovery attack if Quad-RC4 is used for encryption. For example if an attacker can collect around 2^{20} broadcast ciphertexts, then following our analysis we can say that any r-th 4-byte word of the plaintext would have been encrypted with around $\frac{3 \cdot 2^{20}}{N^2} \approx 48$ zeroes. Thus the attacker can do a simple statistical test: the most frequent r-th ciphertext word is also likely to be the r-th plaintext word. Since the attack works for any r, it makes the entire plaintext easily recoverable. In the upcoming subsection we will generalize our results for m-RC4 and present our analysis for odd and even m.

3.3 Description of m-RC4

The m-RC4 stream cipher is similar to the Quad-RC4 stream cipher explained in the previous section with the difference being the number of different 8-bit RC4 states to be combined here is m and the output bytes produced through a suitable function h which takes the quantities $S[t]$, $S[i]$, $S[j]$ and $S[t_p]$ where $p = 1, \ldots, m$. However the authors argue that if h simply returns the bitwise XOR

Input: m pseudo random permutations over $\mathbb{Z}_{256}$
Output: $8m$-bit output words

$i = j = 0$;
for $i = 0$ to 255 **do**
  | $S[i] = (S_1[i] \ll 8(m-1)) | \ldots | (S_{m-1}[i] \ll 8) | S_m[i]$;
end
while Keystream is required **do**
  | $i = (i + 1) \mod 256$;
  | $j = (j + S_m[i]) \mod 256$;
  | $t = (S[i] + S[j]) \mod 2^{8m}$;
  | $t_1 = t \& \texttt{0xFF}; t_2 = (t \gg 8) \& \texttt{0xFF}; \ldots t_m = (t \gg 8(m-1)) \& \texttt{0xFF}$;
  | Swap($S[i]$, $S[j]$);
  | Output $Z = h(S[t], S[i], S[j], S[t_1], S[t_2], \ldots, S[t_m])$;
  | $\{a, b\}$ =Next pair of permutations in turn;
  | Swap($S_a[i], S_a[t_a]$);
  | Swap($S_b[i], S_b[t_b]$);
end

Algorithm 5. m-RC4 PRGA Routine

of its quantities, then the keystreams produce is not perfectly random. Thus the design of h with good randomness properties is left by the authors as an open problem. The PRGA of m-RC4 takes m different pseudo random permutations over $\mathbb{Z}_{256}$ produced by applying m number of key scheduling namely KSA+. Let $S_1, \ldots, S_m$ be the pseudo random permutations produced. They are merged into a single array S of size 256, where the i-th entry of S is an $8m$-bit number formed by concatenating the m many bytes $S_1[i], \ldots, S_m[i]$. Algorithm 5 describes the PRGA of the m-RC4 stream cipher.

3.4   Analysis for Even m

In this subsection we present an analysis for even m. The analysis is similar to that for Quad-RC4. Before presenting the analysis, we will go through some general notations which will be used by us during the proofs.

Some Notations and Assumptions: Let the initial states of m 8-bit RC4 state permutations be represented as $S_1, S_2, S_3, \ldots, S_m$. Let S denote the 256-element array whose i-th entry is formed by concatenating the i-th bits of these m RC4 states. Let $t_1, \ldots, t_m$ denotes variables of size 1 byte each and $t = t_m \| \ldots \| t_1$ be an $8m$-bit variable. Since the design of an output function (namely h in Algorithm 5) with good randomness properties is left by the authors as an open problem, in our analysis we will assume that as in Quad-RC4, the function simply returns the bitwise XOR of $S[t_1], S[t_2], \ldots, S[t_m]$.

The Event: *We will start with the definition of the event E_τ for m-RC4, along similar lines as in Quad-RC4. Consider the m elements $t_1, t_2, \ldots, t_m$. Partition these elements into k groups $G_1, G_2, \ldots, G_k$ ($1 \le k \le \frac{m}{2}$), such that the cardinality of each group G_i is even. The event E_τ will be said to have occurred if the following occurs:*

1. *The elements in each of the $G_i's$ are equal.*

Note that when $k = 1$, it denotes the degenerate case when all the $t_i's$ are equal. So this definition is consistent with the definition of E_τ given for Quad-RC4.

So, there are exactly $f(\frac{m}{2})$ ways in which the groups G_i can be formed, where f denotes the well-known partition function (i.e. the number of ways of writing an integer as sum of positive integers) [1]. For example, when $m = 6$, the number of partitions are $f(3) = 3$, i.e., 6, $4 + 2$ and $2 + 2 + 2$. In the first case we have $t_1 = t_2 = \ldots = t_6$ and it can happen in N ways where $N = 256$. In the second case, we need to divide the 6 elements into 2 groups of 4 and 2. Without loss of generality let us have $t_1 = t_2 = t_3 = t_4 = a$ and $t_5 = t_6 = b$. The number of ways we can divide 6 elements in groups of 4 and 2 is $\binom{6}{2} = 15$ and the number of ways we can select a, b is $N \cdot (N - 1)$. So the total number of ways is $15 \cdot N \cdot (N - 1)$. Lastly we have 2 elements in each of the 3 groups and the number of ways it can happen is given as $\frac{\binom{6}{2} \cdot \binom{4}{2}}{3!} = 15$ and the number of ways the elements of each group can be selected is $N \cdot (N-1) \cdot (N-2)$ and so the total number of combinations is $15 \cdot N \cdot (N-1) \cdot (N-2)$. Therefore the total number of ways for all the partitions can be given as $15 \cdot N \cdot (N-1) \cdot (N-2) + 15 \cdot N \cdot (N-1) + N$, and so the for $m = 6$, we have

$$\Pr[E_\tau] = \frac{15 \cdot N \cdot (N-1) \cdot (N-2) + 15 \cdot N \cdot (N-1) + N}{N^6}$$

Similarly, when $m = 8$, the number of partitions are $f(4) = 5$ which are 8, $6+2$, $4+2+2$, $4+4$ and $2+2+2+2$. For an arbitrary even value of $m = 2p$, it is difficult to analytically determine the value of $\Pr[E_\tau]$. However, we can find a lower bound for this probability. In the case of $m = 2p$, we know that total partition is denoted by $f(p)$. However, the dominant partition, that is the one that will contribute the maximum number of combinations will be

$$\underbrace{2 + 2 + \ldots + 2}_{p \text{ times}}.$$

We call this event as E_m which denotes the situation when $t_1, \ldots, t_m$ are divided into p groups having 2 elements each and elements of any given group are equal to each other. The number of ways of dividing $m = 2p$ items in p groups of 2 each is

$$\frac{\binom{2p}{2} \cdot \binom{2p-2}{2} \cdot \ldots \cdot \binom{2}{2}}{p!} = \frac{2p!}{p!2^p} = \prod_{i=1}^{p}(2i-1) = B_m \text{ (say)}. \tag{7}$$

B_m is therefore the product of the first $\frac{m}{2} = p$ odd integers. So the number of ways in which the event E_m can occur is given by

$$B_m \cdot N \cdot (N-1) \cdot (N-2) \ldots (N-p+1) \approx B_m \cdot N^p. \tag{8}$$

Therefore we have

$$\Pr[E_\tau] \approx \Pr[E_m] = \frac{B_m \cdot N^p}{N^m} = \frac{B_m}{N^p}$$

Lemma 3. *If the event E_τ described above occurs, the any m-byte output word Z_r, produced in PRGA round r, is always equal to 0.*

Proof. The proof is similar to Lemma 2, and follows from the definition of E_τ. If E_τ occurs then the t_i's are divided into k groups each having an even number of elements which are equal. In that case the output byte Z_r is given as

$$Z_r = (S[a_1] \oplus \cdots S[a_1]) \oplus (S[a_2] \oplus \cdots S[a_2]) \oplus \cdots \oplus (S[a_k] \oplus \cdots S[a_k]) = 0. \tag{9}$$

$\square$

Theorem 4. *The probability that $Z_r = 0$ in m-RC4, is given by the equation $\Pr[Z_r = 0] = \frac{B_m}{N^p}$ where $\frac{m}{2} = p$.*

Proof. We know that $\Pr[E_\tau] = \frac{B_m}{N^p}$. Since Z_r is always 0 under the event E_τ, therefore we have $\Pr[Z_r = 0 | E_m] = 1$. By the results of the extensive computer experiments performed using 2^{30} keys, we have verified $\Pr[Z_r = 0 | E_m^c] = \frac{1}{N^m}$. Therefore the final probability can be given as

$$
\begin{aligned}
\Pr[Z_r = 0] &= \Pr[Z_r = 0 | E_m] \cdot \Pr[E_m] + \Pr[Z_r = 0 | E_m^c] \cdot \Pr[E_m^c] \\
&= 1 \cdot \frac{B_m}{N^p} + \frac{1}{N^m} \cdot (1 - \frac{B_m}{N^p}) \\
&= \frac{B_m}{N^p}.
\end{aligned}
$$

(10)

Note that in an ideal cipher the probability $\Pr[Z_r = 0]$ was required to be $\frac{1}{N^m} = \frac{1}{N^{2p}}$. So in m-RC4 this probability is $B_m \cdot N^p$ times that of an ideal cipher. For example in 10-RC4, this figure is $945 \cdot 2^{40} \approx 2^{50}$. So as m increases the design becomes increasingly weaker. $\square$

3.5   Analysis for General m

Previously we demonstrated our analysis for m-RC4 in case when m was an even number. In this subsection we will present our analysis in case when m is any integer greater than equal to 4. We will show that the probability of the first and the second output bytes being equal is biased.

Some Other Notations: We we will denote the m 8-bit RC4 state permutations at the beginning of PRGA round r as $S_1^r, S_2^r, S_3^r, \ldots, S_m^r$. Similarly S^r denotes the the state of 256-element array S (whose i-th entry is formed by concatenating the i-th bits of these m RC4 states) at the beginning of round r. Similarly $t_1^r, \ldots, t_m^r$ and t^r denote the values of the variables $t_1, \ldots, t_m$ and t respectively in round r.

Lemma 4. *If $S_m^1[1] = 2$ and $S_m^1[2] = N - 1$, then*

  a) *The value of the of the variables t^1 and t^2 are both equal,*
  b) *The values of t_1^1 and t_1^2 are both equal to 1.*

Proof. We refer to the PRGA (5) of m-RC4. The index pointers i and j are incremented as $i = 0 + 1 = 1$ and $j = 0 + S_m^1[1] = 2$. Let us denote $S^1[1] = x$ and $S^1[2] = y$ (where x, y are distinct m-byte integers). The variable t^1 is updated in the next step as follows

$$
t^1 = S^1[1] + S^1[2] \bmod 2^{8m} = x + y \bmod 2^{8m}
$$

We also have

$$t_1^1 = t^1 \ \& \ \texttt{0xFF} = (S^1[1] + S^1[2]) \ \& \ \texttt{0xFF}$$
$$= (S^1[1] \ \& \ \texttt{0xFF}) + (S^1[2] \ \& \ \texttt{0xFF}) \ \text{mod} \ 256$$
$$= S_m^1[1] + S_m^1[2] \ \text{mod} \ 256 = 1.$$

In the next operation, $S^1[1]$ and $S^1[2]$ are swapped. After the swap we have $S^2[1] = y$ and $S^2[2] = x$. Then in the next round, the index pointers i and j are incremented as $i = 1+1 = 2$ and $j = 2 + S_m^2[1] = 2 + S_m^1[1] = 2 + N - 1 \ \text{mod} \ 256 = 1$. The above follows, because as per the specifications of m-RC4, the array S_m is not shuffled in the first round, and so $S_m^1 = S_m^2$. The variable t^2 is updated in the next step as:

$$t^2 = S^2[2] + S^2[1] \ \text{mod} \ 2^{8m} = x + y \ \text{mod} \ 2^{8m} = t^1.$$

Again we have,
$$t_1^2 = t^2 \ \& \ \texttt{0xFF} = t^1 \ \& \ \texttt{0xFF} = t_1^1 = 1. \tag{11}$$

□

Since it was established in Lemma 4, that $t^1 = t^2$, we automatically have $t_1^1 = t_1^2$, $t_2^1 = t_2^2, \ldots, t_m^1 = t_m^2$. Furthermore it has already been shown that $t_1^1 = t_1^2 = 1$. For convenience let us denote $t_k^1 = t_k^2 = b_k$ for all $2 \le k \le m$. Hence we can write

$$Z_1 = S^1[1] \oplus S^1[b_2] \oplus S^1[b_3] \oplus \cdots \oplus S^1[b_m]$$

$$Z_2 = S^2[1] \oplus S^2[b_2] \oplus S^2[b_3] \oplus \cdots \oplus S^2[b_m]$$

From the proof of Lemma 4, it is also clear that the array S^1 and S^2 differ in only two locations which are 1 and 2. We have $S^1[1] = S^2[2] = x$ and $S^1[2] = S^2[1] = y$. For all other k not equal to 1 or 2 we have $S^1[k] = S^2[k]$. So consider the following non-intersecting cases:

Case 1. If the number of $1's$ among $b_2, b_3, \ldots, b_m$, is odd and the number of $2's$ among $b_2, b_3, \ldots, b_m$ is even. In this case

$$Z_1 = \underbrace{\bigoplus S^1[1]}_{even} \oplus \underbrace{\bigoplus S^1[2]}_{even} \oplus \underbrace{\bigoplus_{b_k \ne 1,2} S^1[b_k]}_{} = \underbrace{\bigoplus_{b_k \ne 1,2} S^1[b_k]}_{}$$

$$Z_2 = \underbrace{\bigoplus S^2[1]}_{even} \oplus \underbrace{\bigoplus S^2[2]}_{even} \oplus \underbrace{\bigoplus_{b_k \ne 1,2} S^2[b_k]}_{} = \underbrace{\bigoplus_{b_k \ne 1,2} S^2[b_k]}_{}$$

where $\bigoplus_{even} u$ denotes the bitwise XOR of u even number of times which is obviously 0. Since $S^1[b_k] = S^2[b_k]$ if b_k is different from 1 or 2 we have $Z_1 = Z_2$.

Case 2. If the number of $1's$ among $b_2, b_3, \ldots, b_m$, is even and the number of $2's$ among $b_2, b_3, \ldots, b_m$ is odd. Let the number of $1's$ be c and the number of $2's$ be d, where c is even and d is odd. Without loss of generality, let $c + 1 \geq d$. In this case

$$Z_1 = \bigoplus_d \left(S^1[1] \oplus S^1[2] \right) \oplus \bigoplus_{c+1-d} S^1[1] \oplus \bigoplus_{b_k \neq 1,2} S^1[b_k]$$

$$= (x \oplus y) \oplus \bigoplus_{b_k \neq 1,2} S^1[b_k]$$

$$Z_2 = \bigoplus_d \left(S^2[1] \oplus S^2[2] \right) \oplus \bigoplus_{c+1-d} S^2[1] \oplus \bigoplus_{b_k \neq 1,2} S^2[b_k]$$

$$= (x \oplus y) \oplus \bigoplus_{b_k \neq 1,2} S^2[b_k]$$

Here $\bigoplus_n u$ denotes the bitwise XOR of u, a total of n times which is 0 if n is even and u if n is odd. Since d is odd and $c + 1 - d$ is even, the above result follows. Again since $S^1[b_k] = S^2[b_k]$ if b_k is different from 1 or 2 we have $Z_1 = Z_2$.

Lemma 5. *The event E_μ will said to have occurred if both the events occur simultaneously.*

a) $S_m^1[1] = 2$ *and* $S_m^1[2] = N - 1$,
b) *Either* **Case 1** *or* **Case 2**, *described above holds true.*

The probability that $\Pr[E_\mu] \approx \frac{2(m-1)}{N^3}$.

Proof. First of all, from all the previous discussion we have established that $\Pr[Z_1 = Z_2 | E_\mu] = 1$. Turning our attention to **Case 1/Case 2**, we can make the following observation:

- Both **Case 1** and **Case 2**, involve fixing an odd number of values among $b_2, b_3, \ldots, b_m$ to either 1 or 2.

Starting with **Case 1**, if the number of fixed values is 1, this implies only one of the $b_k's$ equal 1. Hence, the number of combinations is $C_1 = \binom{m-1}{1} \cdot (N - 2)^{m-2}$. The above holds since, the index to be set to 1 can be chosen in $\binom{m-1}{1}$ ways and the remaining $m - 2$ indices can be set to any value other than 1 or 2. Similarly, if the number of fixed values is 3, this implies either three $1's$ or one 1 and two $2's$. The total number of combinations is therefore

$$C_3 = \binom{m-1}{3} \cdot (N - 2)^{m-4} + \binom{m-1}{3} \cdot \frac{3!}{2!} \cdot (N - 2)^{m-4}$$

It is clear that if m is much smaller that N then, C_1 is much larger than C_3. Similarly, C_3 would be much larger than C_5, i.e. the number of combinations when 5 indices are fixed, and so on. Hence C_1 contributes the maximum number of combinations to **Case 1** and we have $C_1 \approx (C_1 + C_3 + C_5 + \cdots)$. So we have

$$\Pr[\textbf{Case 1}] \approx \frac{C_1}{N^{m-1}} = \frac{\binom{m-1}{1} \cdot (N-2)^{m-2}}{N^{m-1}} \approx \frac{m-1}{N}$$

Analogously, similar arguments can be made about **Case 2**, and since these cases are non-intersecting we have

$$\Pr[\textbf{Case 1} \vee \textbf{Case 2}] \approx \frac{2(m-1)}{N}.$$

And so that the events $S_m^1[1] = 2$ and $S_m^1[2] = N-1$ and **Case 1** $\vee$ **Case 2** are independently distributed, we have

$$\Pr[E_\mu] = \Pr[(S_m^1[1] = 2) \wedge (S_m^1[2] = N-1) \wedge (\textbf{Case 1} \vee \textbf{Case 2})]$$
$$= \frac{1}{N} \cdot \frac{1}{N-1} \cdot \frac{2(m-1)}{N} \approx \frac{2(m-1)}{N^3}.$$

$\square$

Theorem 5. *The probability that $Z_1 = Z_2$ in m-RC4 (for $m > 2$), is given by the equation* $\Pr[Z_1 = Z_2] = \frac{2(m-1)}{N^3}$.

Proof. We have already established that $\Pr[Z_1 = Z_2|E_\mu] = 1$. By the results of the extensive computer experiments performed using 2^{30} keys, we have verified $\Pr[Z_1 = Z_2|E_\mu^c] = \frac{1}{N^m}$. Therefore the final probability can be given as

$$\Pr[Z_1 = Z_2] = \Pr[Z_1 = Z_2|E_\mu] \cdot \Pr[E_\mu] + \Pr[Z_1 = Z_2|E_\mu^c] \cdot \Pr[E_\mu^c]$$
$$= 1 \cdot \frac{2(m-1)}{N^3} + \frac{1}{N^m} \cdot \left(1 - \frac{2(m-1)}{N^3}\right)$$
$$\approx \frac{2(m-1)}{N^3}.$$

(12)

In an ideal cipher $\Pr[Z_1 = Z_2]$ was required to be $\frac{1}{N^m}$. So, in m-RC4 this probability is $2(m-1) \cdot N^{m-3}$ times that of an ideal cipher. For example in 3-RC4 this figure is 4, for 7-RC4 this figure is $12 \cdot 2^{32} \approx 2^{36}$. This underscores the point that the design is vulnerable for any m.

$\square$

3.6 The Flaws in the Design

In this subsection we will discuss the flaws in the design of Quad-RC4/m-RC4 which results in highly biased output bytes.

Simple XOR operation in Output Function. The output function based on simple bitwise XOR of $S[t_1], S[t_2], \ldots, S[t_m]$ when m is even is clearly not a good idea. From our analysis presented in the Section 3.4 for even m, one can clearly understand that the reason for the high bias in Z_r is the simplicity of the output function is a simple XOR. The output function also contributes to bias in $Z_1 = Z_2$ for any general value of m. Thus the output function needs to be changed to some operation which would involve modular addition, rotation and XOR (ARX functions). This may result in some degradation of performance in software with respect to speed, but this is one correction that the design must make to be secure.

The "not so random" S. Referring to the PRGA of m-RC4 given in Algorithm 5, it is clear that the main array S used in the algorithm is only updated by swaps. In original RC4, swap update works because RC4 state is a permutation on $\mathbb{Z}_{256}$. Each swap makes the original RC4 state a new permutation on $\mathbb{Z}_{256}$, and therefore the total entropy in the state is $\log_2 256! \approx 1684$ bits. However, the array S used in m-RC4 is not a permutation on $\mathbb{Z}_{2^{8m}}$. Once the cipher array enters the PRGA phase, the array S is updated by only swap operations, this means that during the entire PRGA phase S contains the same elements. So for a fixed Key/IV, thee entropy of the state space comes only from the permutation of the 256 elements of S, which is again 1684 bits. Once m-RC4 states are used, thee designers would have wanted the entropy of the State Space to be as close to $1684m$ bits as possible. However due to the simplistic state update function which consists of only swaps, the entropy never increases. This implies that the for the design to be secure, a more complicated state update was necessary.

The effect on t. This effect of the reduced state entropy is directly felt on the $8m$-bit variable t. The designers had probably intended t to be a pseudorandom index with entropy close to $8m$ bits. However t is calculated as $S[i] + S[j] \mod 2^{8m}$. Because of the simplistic nature of the state-update, the array S, contains the same N elements during the entire evolution of the PRGA. As a result $S[i], S[j]$ can take at most N values each, and hence t can take at most N^2 values. Due to this the entropy of t is only $\log_2 N^2 = 16$ bits for any value of m. Thus the probability that the values of t in two successive PRGA rounds are equal is only about $\frac{1}{N^2}$, and it can be seen that this directly contributes to the bias in the distribution of $Z_1 = Z_2$, as described in Section 3.5. This further emphasizes the point that in a design like Quad-RC4/m-RC4, which combines several RC4 states by simple concatenation, the state update can *not* be a simple swap operation. A more complicated update using modular addition/XOR is necessary. This would again involve decrease of software speed, but this is again a necessary correction that the design must make to be secure.

4   Experimental Results

We will now tabulate some experimental results to validate our theoretical findings. The results can be found in Table 1. All the experiments were performed

Table 1. Experimental Results

#	Cipher	Event	Theoretical Value	Experimental Result	N
1	RC4B	$\Pr[Z_1 = Z_2 = 0]$	$2/N^2$	$1.99/N^2$	256
2	Quad-RC4	$\Pr[Z_1 = 0]$	$3/N^2$	$2.94/N^2$	256
	6-RC4		$15/N^3$	$15.53/N^3$	64
3	Quad-RC4	$\Pr[Z_1 = Z_2]$	$6/N^3$	$6.13/N^3$	128
	5-RC4		$8/N^3$	$7.84/N^3$	128

with 2^{30} randomly chosen Keys, and in certain cases we have reported the probability values for reduced variants of the actual cipher i.e. for $N = 64, 128$ in place of 256. This was done only because the computational resources required to perform the experiments on the full ciphers were unavailable. As can be seen in Table 1 the experimental results are in accordance with our theoretical findings.

5 Conclusion

In this paper we discuss the stream ciphers which are designed by combining one or more independently produced RC4 states. We study three such stream ciphers namely RC4B, Quad-RC4 and m-RC4 (where m can be odd or even), and demonstrate distinguishing attacks on them by showing biases in the output bytes produced by each of these stream ciphers. In addition we also discuss the scenarios which leads to such vulnerabilities present in the output bytes of these stream ciphers. Combining multiple stream cipher states to produce new stream ciphers which perform better than the original stream cipher seems to be an attractive research discipline as evidenced by numerous papers in this area [4, 10, 11]. As far as combining RC4 states are concerned, much can be achieved if the problem is addressed judiciously. This does seem to be an area worth looking into.

References

1. Partition (Number Theory),
   http://en.wikipedia.org/wiki/Partition_%28number_theory%29
2. Banik, S., Sarkar, S., Kacker, R.: Security analysis of the RC4+ stream cipher. In: Paul, G., Vaudenay, S. (eds.) INDOCRYPT 2013. LNCS, vol. 8250, pp. 297–307. Springer, Heidelberg (2013)
3. Gong, G., Gupta, K.C., Hell, M., Nawaz, Y.: Towards a general RC4-like keystream generator. In: Feng, D., Lin, D., Yung, M. (eds.) CISC 2005. LNCS, vol. 3822, pp. 162–174. Springer, Heidelberg (2005)
4. Lv, J., Zhang, B., Lin, D.: Distinguishing Attacks on RC4 and A New Improvement of the Cipher. Cryptology ePrint Archive: Report 2013/176
5. Maitra, S.: Four Lines of Design to Forty Papers of Analysis: The RC4 Stream Cipher, http://www.isical.ac.in/~indocrypt/indo12.pdf

6. Maitra, S., Paul, G.: Analysis of RC4 and proposal of additional layers for better security margin. In: Chowdhury, D.R., Rijmen, V., Das, A. (eds.) INDOCRYPT 2008. LNCS, vol. 5365, pp. 27–39. Springer, Heidelberg (2008)

7. Mantin, I., Shamir, A.: A practical attack on broadcast RC4. In: Matsui, M. (ed.) FSE 2001. LNCS, vol. 2355, pp. 152–164. Springer, Heidelberg (2002)

8. Maximov, A., Khovratovich, D.: New state recovery attack on RC4. In: Wagner, D. (ed.) CRYPTO 2008. LNCS, vol. 5157, pp. 297–316. Springer, Heidelberg (2008)

9. Maximov, A.: Two linear distinguishing attacks on VMPC and RC4A and weakness of RC4 family of stream ciphers. In: Gilbert, H., Handschuh, H. (eds.) FSE 2005. LNCS, vol. 3557, pp. 342–358. Springer, Heidelberg (2005)

10. Paul, G., Chattopadhyay, A.: Designing stream ciphers with scalable data-widths: a case study with HC-128. J. Cryptographic Engineering 4(2), 135–143 (2014)

11. Paul, G., Maitra, S., Chattopadhyay, A.: Quad-RC4: Merging Four RC4 States towards a 32-bit Stream Cipher. IACR Cryptology eprint Archive 2013: 572 (2013)

12. Paul, S., Preneel, B.: A new weakness in the RC4 keystream generator and an approach to improve the security of the cipher. In: Roy, B., Meier, W. (eds.) FSE 2004. LNCS, vol. 3017, pp. 245–259. Springer, Heidelberg (2004)

13. Paul, S., Preneel, B.: On the (In)security of stream ciphers based on arrays and modular addition. In: Lai, X., Chen, K. (eds.) ASIACRYPT 2006. LNCS, vol. 4284, pp. 69–83. Springer, Heidelberg (2006)

14. Sarkar, S.: Further non-randomness in RC4, RC4A and VMPC. Cryptography and Communications 7(3), 317–330 (2015)

15. Tsunoo, Y., Saito, T., Kubo, H., Shigeri, M., Suzaki, T., Kawabata, T.: The Most Efficient Distinguishing Attack on VMPC and RC4A. In: SKEW 2005 (2005), http://www.ecrypt.eu.org/stream/papers.html

16. Zoltak, B.: VMPC one-way function and stream cipher. In: Roy, B., Meier, W. (eds.) FSE 2004. LNCS, vol. 3017, pp. 210–225. Springer, Heidelberg (2004)

Preimage Analysis of the Maelstrom-0 Hash Function

Riham AlTawy and Amr M. Youssef

Concordia Institute for Information Systems Engineering,
Concordia University, Montréal, Québec, Canada

Abstract. Maelstrom-0 is the second member of a family of AES-based hash functions whose designs are pioneered by Paulo Baretto and Vincent Rijmen. According to its designers, the function is designed to be an evolutionary lightweight alternative to the ISO standard Whirlpool. In this paper, we study the preimage resistance of the Maelstrom-0 hash function using its proposed 3CM chaining construction. More precisely, we apply a meet-in-the-middle preimage attack on the compression function and combine it with a guess and determine approach which allows us to obtain a 6-round pseudo preimage for a given compression function output with time complexity of 2^{496} and memory complexity of 2^{112}. Then, we propose a four stage attack in which we adopt another meet-in-the-middle attack and a 2-block multicollision approach to defeat the two additional checksum chains and turn the pseudo preimage attack on the compression function into a preimage attack on the hash function. Using our approach, preimages of the 6-round reduced Maelstrom-0 hash function are generated with time complexity of 2^{505} and memory complexity of 2^{112}.

Keywords: Cryptanalysis, Hash functions, Meet in the middle, Preimage attack, Maelstrom-0, 3CM.

1 Introduction

The attacks of Wang *et al.* [27, 28] which broke a large cluster of widely used hash functions have proven to be most effective against Add-Rotate-Xor (ARX) based hash functions. The success of such attacks on ARX constructions is attributed to the possibility of finding differential trails that propagate for a significant number of rounds with acceptable probabilities. Moreover, considerable improvement in the attack complexity can be achieved using message modification techniques [28] which take advantage of the independence of consecutive message words which may span over a relatively large number of rounds. On the other hand, the Advanced Encryption Standard (AES) wide trail strategy [7] continues to show solid resistance to standard differential attacks. This fact has made AES-based hash functions a favorable direction when considering new designs. Indeed, at the same time when most of the standardized ARX-based hash functions were failing to resist the techniques introduced by Wang *et al.*, the already existing

© Springer International Publishing Switzerland 2015
R.S. Chakraborty et al. (Eds.): SPACE 2015, LNCS 9354, pp. 113–126, 2015.
DOI: 10.1007/978-3-319-24126-5_7

ISO standard Whirlpool [23] was not affected by these attacks. This conceptual shift in hash function designs was clearly evident among the SHA-3 competition proposals [22] (e.g., the SHA-3 finalists Grøstl [12] and JH [29], and LANE [16]). Additionally, Whirlwind [6] and Streebog [20], the new Russian hash standard which is officially known as GOST R 34.11-2012, are also among the recently proposed AES-based hash functions.

Maelstrom-0 is an AES-based hash function that adopts a modified chaining scheme called 3CM [8]. The function is proposed by Filho, Barreto, and Rijmen as an evolutionary lighter alternative to its predecessor Whirlpool. Maelstrom-0 is considered the second member of a family of hash functions which is preceded by Whirlpool and followed by Whirlwind. The design of Maelstrom-0 is heavily inspired by Whirlpool but adopts a simpler key schedule and takes into account the recent development in hash function cryptanalysis. Particularly, the designers consider those attacks where the cryptanalytic techniques which are applicable on the compression function can be easily mapped to the hash function due to the simplicity of the Merkle-Damgård construction used by Whirlpool. In addition to adopting a simpler key schedule which makes Maelstrom-0 more robust and significantly faster than Whirlpool, the designers employ the Davis-Mayer compression mode which is the only mode among the twelve secure constructions that naturally allows the compression function to accept a message block size different from the chaining value size, thus allowing faster hashing rate [8]. Also, all the remaining eleven constructions XOR the message and the chaining value block, thus forcing either truncation or padding to cope with the different sizes, and it is unclear to what extent truncation or padding might adversely affect the security analysis.

The most important feature in the design of Maelstrom-0 is the proposal of a new chaining construction called 3CM which is based on the 3C/3C+ family [13]. This construction computes two checksums from the generated intermediate chaining values, concatenates them, and as a finalization step processes the result as a message block in the last compression function call. This finalization step aims to thwart some generic attacks on the MD construction used in Whirlpool such as long second preimage and herding attacks, and also inhibits length extension attacks. According to the designers of Maelstrom-0, the proposed finalization step mitigates the applicability of extending attacks on the compression function to the hash function. Unfortunately, this is not the case in our attack where we employ a 4-stage approach that uses a modified technique which defeats the 3CM chaining construction [9–11] and combines it with another meet-in-the-middle (MitM) attack to extend a pseudo preimage attack on the compression function to a preimage attack on the hash function.

Literature related to the cryptanalysis of Maelstrom-0 include the analysis of the collision resistance of its compression function by Kölbl and Mendel [18] where the weak properties of the key schedule were used to produce semi free-start collision for the 6 and 7 round reduced compression function and semi free-start near collision for the 8 and 10-rounds compression function. Finally, Mendel *et al.* used the rebound attack to show how employing a message block whose size is double that of the chaining state is used to present a free start collisison on the 8.5 reduced round compression function [21].

In this work, we investigate the security of Maelstrom-0 and its compression function, assessing their resistance to the MitM preimage attacks. Employing the partial matching and initial structure concepts [24], we present a pseudo preimage attack on the 6-round reduced compression function. In the presented attack, we employ a guess and determine approach [26] to guess parts of the state. This approach helps in maintaining partial state knowledge for an extra round when all state knowledge is lost due to the wide trail effect. The proposed 6-round execution separation maximizes the overall probability of the attack by balancing the chosen number of starting values and the guess size. Finally, we propose a four stage approach which combines a 2-block multicollision attack [9, 10] with a second MitM attack to bypass the effect of the 3CM checksum used in the finalization step. Our approach is successfully used to generate preimages of the 6-round reduced Maelstrom-0 hash function using the presented pseudo preimage attack on the last compression function. Up to our knowledge, our analysis is the first to consider the hash function and not only the compression function of Maelstrom-0.

The rest of the paper is organized as follows. In the next section, a brief overview of the related work regarding MitM preimage attacks and the used approaches is provided. The description of the Maelstrom-0 hash function along with the notation used throughout the paper are given in Section 3. Afterwards, in Sections 4, we provide detailed description of the pseudo preimage attack on the compression function. In Section 5, we show how preimages of the hash function are generated using our four stage approach and the attack presented in Section 4. Finally, the paper is concluded in Section 6.

2 Related Work

A pseudo preimage attack on a given a compression function CF that processes a chaining value h and a message block m is defined as follows: Given x, one must find h and m such that $CF(h, m) = x$. The ability to generate a pseudo preimage for the compression function has always been regarded as a certificational weakness as its local effect on the overall hash function is not important . However, as we are going to show in Section 5, when a pseudo preimage attack on the compression function is combined with other attacks, it can be used to build a preimage for the whole hash function.

The MitM preimage attack was first proposed by Aoki and Sasaki [5]. The main concept of the proposed MitM attacks is to separate the attacked rounds at a starting point into two independent executions that proceed in opposite directions (forward and backward chunks). The two executions must remain independent until the point where matching takes place. To maintain the independence constraint, each execution must depend on a different set of inputs, e.g., if only the forward chunk is influenced by a change in a given input, then this input is known as a forward neutral input. Consequently, all of its possible values can be used to produce different outputs of the forward execution at the matching point. Accordingly, all neutral inputs for each execution direction attribute to the number of independent starting values for each execution. Hence, the output of the forward and the backward executions can be independently calculated and stored at the matching point. Similar to all MitM attacks, the matching point is where the outputs of the two separated chunks meet to find a solution, from both the forward and backward directions, that satisfies both executions. While for block ciphers, having a matching point is achieved by employing both the encryption and decryption oracles, for hash function, this is accomplished by adopting the cut and splice technique [5] which utilizes the employed mode of operation. In other words, given the compression function output, this technique chains the input and output states through the feedforward as we can consider the first and last states as consecutive rounds. Subsequently, the overall attacked rounds behave in a cyclic manner and one can find a common matching point between the forward and backward executions and consequently can also select any starting point.

Ever since their inception, significant improvements on MitM preimage attacks have been proposed. Such improvements include the initial structure approach [24, 25] which allows the starting point to span over few successive transformations where bytes in the states are allowed to belong to both the forward and backward chunks. Additionally, the partial matching technique [5] enables only parts of the state to be matched at the matching point which extends the matching point further by not restricting full state knowledge at the matching point. Once a partial match is found, the starting values of both executions are selected and used to evaluate the remaining undetermined parts of the state at the matching point to check for a full state match. Figure 1 illustrates the MitM preimage attack approaches for a compression function operating in the Davis-Mayer mode. The red and blue arrows denote the forward and backward executions on the message state, respectively. S_0 is the first state initialized by h and S_i is the last attacked state.

The MitM preimage attack was applied on MD4 [5, 14], MD5 [5], HAS-160 [15], and all functions of the SHA family [3, 4, 14]. The attack exploits the weak key schedules of ARX-based functions where some of the expanded message blocks are used independently in each round. Thus, one can determine which message blocks affect each execution for the MitM attack. Afterwards, the MitM

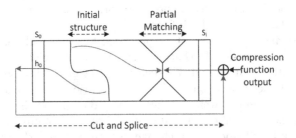

Fig. 1. MitM preimage attack techniques used on a Davis-Mayer compression function.

preimage attack was adapted on the AES block cipher in hashing modes [24]. The attack was then applied to Whirlpool and a 5-round pseudo preimage attack on the compression function was used for a second preimage attack on the whole hash function in the same work. In the sequel, Wu *et al.* [30] improved the time complexity of the 5-round attack on the Whirlpool compression function. Moreover, they applied the MitM pseudo preimage attack on Grøstl and adapted the attack to produce pseudo preimages of the reduced hash function. Afterwards, a pseudo preimage attack on the 6-round Whirlpool compression function and a memoryless preimage attack on the reduced hash function were proposed in [26]. Finally, AlTawy and Youssef employed MitM pseudo preimages of the compression function of Streebog to generate preimages of the reduced hash function [1], the complexity of their attack was later improved in [19]. They also presented a second preimage analysis of Whirlwind [2].

3 Specifications of Maelstrom-0

Maelstrom-0 is an AES-based iterative hash function designed by Filho, Barreto and Rijmen [8]. Its compression function processes 1024-bit message blocks and a 512-bit chaining value. As depicted in Figure 2, the message M is padded by 1 followed by zeros to make the length of the last block 768. Then the remaining 265 bits are used for the binary representation of the message length $|M|$. Hence the padded message has the form $M = m_1||m_2||\cdots||m_k$, where the last 256-bits of m_k denote $|M|$. The compression function is iterated in the 3CM chaining mode which is based on 3C/3C+ family [13]. Given that h_i denotes the internal state value after processing the message block m_i, i.e., $h_i = f(m_i, h_{i-1})$ with $h_0 = IV$, this chaining mode generalizes the Merkle-Damgård construction by maintaining three chains h_i, s_i, t_i instead of only h_i. The extra two chains are transformed into an additional message block $m_{k+1} = s_k||t_k$. The second chain s_i is a simple XOR accumulation of all intermediate compression function outputs, recursively defined as $s_0 = 0$, $s_i = h_i \oplus s_{i-1}$. The third chain is recursively defined as $t_0 = IV$, $t_i = h_i \oplus \zeta(t_{i-1})$ where an LFSR is employed by ζ to update t_{i-1} by left shifting it by one byte followed by a one byte XOR. More precisely, we compute the hash value h_i in the following way:

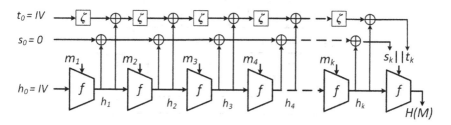

Fig. 2. The Maelstrom-0 hash function.

$$h_0 = IV,$$
$$h_i = f(h_{i-1}, m_i), \text{ for } i = 1, 2, ..., k,$$
$$H(M) = f(h_k, s_k \| t_k).$$

The compression function, f, employs a block cipher, E and uses the Davis-Mayer mode of operation. The internal cipher is based on the one used in Whirlpool where it only differs in the key schedule. The round function which operates on 8×8 byte state is initially loaded with the input chaining value. As depicted in Figure 3, the state is updated through 10 rounds and one key addition at the beginning. One round of the state update function consists of the application of the following four transformations:

- The nonlinear layer γ: A transformation that consists of parallel application of a nonlinear Sbox on each byte using an 8-bit Sbox. The used Sbox is the same as the one used in Whirlpool.
- The cyclical permutation π: This layer cyclically shifts each column of its argument independently, so that column j is shifted downwards by j positions, $j = 0, 1, \cdots, 7$.
- The linear diffusion layer θ: A MixRow operation where each row is multiplied by an 8×8 MDS matrix over F_{2^8}. The values of the matrix are chosen such that the branch number of MixRow is 9. Therefore the total number of active bytes at both the input and output is at least 9.
- The key addition σ: A linear transformation where the state is XORed with a round key state.

The key schedule takes as input the 1024-bit message block and generates the 512-bit round keys, $K_0, K_1, \cdots, K_{10}$. Since the key scheduling process is not relevant to our attack, we do not give a detailed description of the round key generation function. For more details on the specification of Maelstrom-0, the reader is referred to [8].

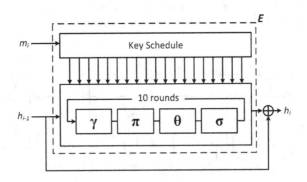

Fig. 3. The Maelstrom-0 compression function.

Notation: Let X be (8×8) byte state denoting the internal state of the function. The following notation is used in our attacks:

- X_i: The message state at the beginning of round i.
- X_i^U: The message state after the U transformation at round i, where $U \in \{\gamma, \pi, \theta, \sigma\}$.
- $X_i[r, c]$: A byte at row r and column c of state X_i.
- $X_i[\text{row } r]$: Eight bytes located at row r of state X_i.
- $X_i[\text{col } c]$: Eight bytes located at column c of state X_i.

4 Pseudo Preimage Attack on the 6-Round Reduced Compression Function

In our analysis of the compression function, we are forced to adopt a pseudo preimage attack because the compression function operates in Davis-Mayer mode. Consequently, using the cut and splice technique causes updates in the first state which is initialized by the chaining value. In our attack, we start by dividing the two execution chunks around the initial structure. More precisely, we separate the six attacked rounds into a 3-round forward chunk and a 2-round backward chunk around the starting round represented by the initial structure. The proposed chunk separation is shown in Figure 4. The number of the forward and backward starting values in the initial structure amounts for the complexity of the attack. Accordingly, one must try to balance the number starting values for each chunk and the number of known bytes at the matching point at the end of each chunk. The total number of starting values in both directions should produce candidate pairs at the matching point to satisfy the matching probability.

To better explain the idea, we start by demonstrating how the initial structure is constructed. The main objective of the MitM attack separation is to maximize the number of known bytes at the start of each execution chunk. This can be achieved by selecting several bytes as neutral so that the number of corresponding output bytes of the θ and θ^{-1} transformations at the start of both chunks that are constant or relatively constant is maximized. A relatively constant byte is a byte whose value depends on the value of the neutral bytes in one execution direction but remains constant from the opposite execution perspective. As depicted in Figure 5, we want to have six constants in the lowermost row in state a, then we need to evaluate the possible values of the corresponding red row in state b such that the values of the selected six constants in state a hold. The values of the lowermost red row in state b are the possible forward starting values. For the lowermost row in state b, we randomly choose the six constant bytes in $a[\text{row } 7]$ and then evaluate the values of red bytes in $b[\text{row } 7]$ so that after applying θ^{-1} on $b[\text{row } 7]$, the chosen values of the six constants hold. Since we require six constant bytes in the lowermost row in state a, we need to maintain six variable bytes in $b[\text{row } 7]$ in order to solve a system of six equations when the other two bytes are fixed. Accordingly, for the last row in state b, we can randomly choose any two red bytes and compute the remaining six so that the

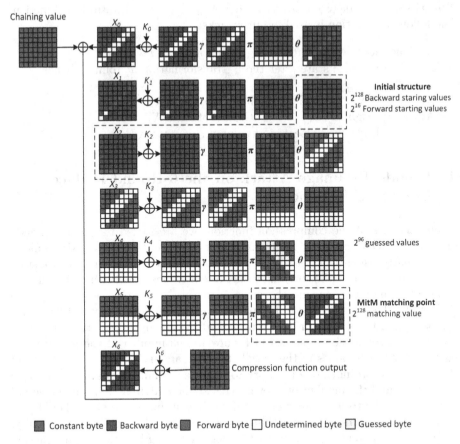

Fig. 4. Chunk separation for a 6-round MitM pseudo preimage attack the compression function.

output of θ^{-1} maintains the previously chosen six constant bytes at state a. To this end, the number of forward starting values is 2^{16}. Similarly, we choose 40 constant bytes in state d and for each row in state c we randomly choose two blue bytes and compute the other five such that after the θ transformation we get the predetermined five constants at each row in d. However, the value of the five shaded red bytes in each row of state d depends also on the one red byte in the rows of state c. We call these bytes relative constants because their final values cannot be determined until the forward execution starts and these values are different for each forward execution iteration. Specifically, their final values are the predetermined constants acting as offsets which are XORed with the corresponding red bytes multiplied by the MDS matrix coefficients. In the sequel, we have two free bytes for each row in c which means 2^{128} backward starting values.

Following Figure 4, due to the wide trail strategy where one unknown byte results in a full unknown state after two rounds, we lose all state knowledge after

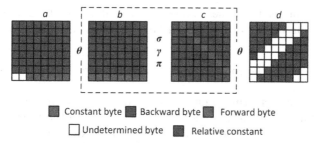

Constant byte ■ Backward byte ■ Forward byte
□ Undetermined byte ■ Relative constant

Fig. 5. Initial structure used in the attack on the 6-round compression function.

applying θ on X_4^π. To maintain partial state knowledge in the forward direction and reach the matching point at X_5^π, we adopt a guess and determine approach [26], by which, we can probabilistically guess the undetermined bytes in some rows of the state at round 4 before the linear transformation. Thus, we maintain knowledge of some state rows after the linear transformation θ which are used for matching. One have to carefully choose the number of guessed bytes and both starting values in the initial structure to result in an acceptable number of correctly guessed matching pairs. Accordingly, we guess the twelve unknown yellow bytes in state X_4^π. As a result, we can reach state X_5^π with four determined bytes in each row where matching takes place.

As depicted in Figure 4, the forward chunk begins at X_2^θ and ends at X_5^π which is the input state to the matching point. The backward chunk starts at X_1^π and ends after the feedforward at X_5^θ which is the output state of the matching point. The red bytes denote the bytes which are affected by the forward execution only and thus can be independently calculated without the knowledge of the blue bytes. White words in the forward chunk are the ones whose values depend on the blue bytes of the backward chunk. Accordingly, their values are undetermined. Same rationale applies to the blue bytes of backward execution. Grey bytes are constants which can be either the compression function output or the chosen constants in the initial structure.

At the matching point, we partially match the available row bytes from the forward execution at X_5^π with the corresponding row bytes from the backward execution at X_5^θ through the linear θ transformation. In each row, we have four and six bytes from the forward and backward executions, respectively. Since the linear mapping is performed on bytes, we compose four byte linear equations in two unknown bytes. Then we evaluate the values of the two unknown bytes from two out of the four equations and substitute their values in the remaining two equations. With probability 2^{-16} the two remaining byte equations are satisfied. Hence, the matching probability for one state row is 2^{-16}. Thus, the partial matching probability for the whole state is $2^{8 \times -16 = -128}$.

For our attack, the chosen number for the forward and backward starting values, and the guessed values are 2^{16}, 2^{128}, and 2^{96}, respectively. Setting these parameters fixes the number of matching values to 2^{128}. The chosen parameters maximize the attack probability as we aim to increase the number of starting forward values and keep the number of backward and matching values as close as possible and larger than the number of guessed values. In what follows, we give a description of the attack procedure and complexity based on the above chosen parameters:

1. Randomly choose the constants in X_1^π and X_2^θ and the input message block value.
2. For each forward starting value fw_i and guessed value g_i in the 2^{16} forward starting values and the 2^{96} guessed values, compute the forward matching value fm_i at X_5^π and store (fw_i, g_i, fm_i) in a lookup table T.
3. For each backward starting value bw_j in the 2^{128} backward starting values, we compute the backward matching value bm_j at X_5^θ and check if there exists an $fm_i = bm_j$ in T. If found, then a partial match exists and the full match should be checked. If a full match exists, then we output the chaining value h_{i-1} and the message m_i, else go to step 1.

The complexity of the attack is evaluated as follows: after step 2, we have $2^{16+96} = 2^{112}$ forward matching values which need 2^{112} memory for the look up table. At the end of step 3, we have 2^{128} backward matching values. Accordingly, we get $2^{112+128} = 2^{240}$ partial matching candidate pairs. Since the probability of a partial match is 2^{-128} and the probability of a correct guess is 2^{-96}, we expect $2^{240-128-96} = 2^{16}$ correctly guessed partially matching pairs. To check for a full match, we want the partially matching starting values to result in the correct values for the 48 unknown bytes in both X_5^π and X_5^θ that make the blue and red words hold. The probability that the latter condition is satisfied is $2^{48 \times -8} = 2^{-384}$. Consequently, the expected number of fully matching pairs is 2^{-368} and hence we need to repeat the attack 2^{368} times to get a full match. The time complexity for one repetition is 2^{112} for the forward computation, 2^{128} for the backward computation, and 2^{16} to check that partially matching pairs fully match. The overall time complexity of the attack is $2^{368}(2^{112} + 2^{128} + 2^{16}) \approx 2^{496}$ and the memory complexity is 2^{112}.

5   Preimage of the Maelstrom-0 Hash Function

In this section, we propose a 4-stage approach by which we utilize the previously presented pseudo preimage attack on the Maelstrom compression function to produce a preimage for the whole hash function. The designers of Maelstrom-0 proposed the 3CM chaining scheme that computes two additional checksum chains specifically to inhibit the ability of extending attacks on the compression function to the hash function. The two additional checksums are computed from a combination of the XOR of the intermediate chaining values, then the two results are concatenated and processed as the input message block of the last compression function call in the hash function. At first instance, this construction seems to limit the scope of our attack to the compression function. Nevertheless, employing the 4-stage approach, a preimage of the hash function can be found when we consider a large set of messages that produce different combinations of intermediate chaining values and thus different checksums and combine it with

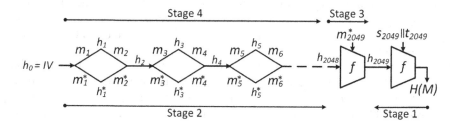

Fig. 6. A 4-stage preimage attack on the Maelstrom-0 hash function.

a set of pseudo preimage attacks on the last compression function call. Hence, another MitM attack can be performed on both sets to find a message that correspond to the retrieved checksums. As depicted in Figure 6, the attack is divided into four stages:

1. Given the hash function output $H(M)$, we produce 2^p pseudo preimages for the last compression function call. The output of this step is 2^p pairs of the last chaining value and the two checksums $(h_{2049}, s_{2049}, t_{2049})$. We store these results in a table T.

2. In this stage, we construct a set of 2^{1024} of 2-block messages such that all of them collide at h_{2048}. This structure is called a 2-block multicollision of length 1024 [10, 17]. More precisely, an n-block multicollisison of length t is a set of 2^t messages where each message consists of exactly $n \times t$ blocks and every consecutive n application of the compression function results in the same chaining value. Consequently, we have 2^t different possibilities for the intermediate chaining values and all the 2^t n-block messages lead to the same $h_{n \times t}$ value. Constructing a 2^t n-block mulitcollision using exhaustive collision search requires a time complexity of $t(2(n-1)+2^{b/2})$, where b is the chaining state size, and a memory complexity of $t(2 \cdot n)$ message to store t two messages of n-block each. In our case, we build 2^{1024} 2-block multicollision where each 2-block collision gives us two choices for the checksum of two consecutive chaining values. In other words, in the first 2-block collision, we either choose (h_1, h_2) or (h_1^*, h_2) and thus two choices for the checksum chains. To this end, we have 2^{1024} different 2-block massages stored in $1024 \cdot 2 \cdot 2 = 2^{12}$ memory and hence 2^{1024} candidate chaining checksums.

3. At this stage, we try to connect the resulting chaining value, h_{2048}, from stage 2 to one of 2^p chaining values, h_{2049}, stored in T which was created in stage 1, using the freedom of choosing m_{2049}. Specifically, we randomly choose 512 bit of m_{2049}^*, then properly pad it and append the message length, and using h_{2048} generated by the multicollison, we compute h_{2049}^* and check if it exists in T. As T contains 2^p entries, it is expected to find a match after 2^{512-p} evaluations of the following compression function call:

$$h_{2049}^* = f(h_{2048}, m_{2049}^*).$$

Once a matching h_{2049}^* value is found in T, the corresponding checksums s_{2049}^*, t_{2049}^* are retrieved. Hence the desired checksums at the output of the multicollision, s_{2048} and t_{2048} are equal to $s_{2049}^* \oplus h_{2049}^*$ and $\zeta^{-1}(t_{2049}^* \oplus h_{2049}^*)$, respectively.

4. At the last stage of the attack, we try to find a message M out of the 2^{1024} 2-block messages generated in stage 2 that results in checksums equal to the ones retrieved in stage 3. For this, we form a system of 1024 equations in 1024 unknowns to select one combination from the 2^{1024} different combinations of possible chaining checksums which make the retrieved two checksums hold. Note that, the algorithm proposed in [9] which employs 2^{512} 2-block multicollision and treats the two checksums independently by solving two independent systems of 512 equations cannot work on 3CM, as the two checksums are dependent on each other. This algorithm only works on the 3C chaining construction [10, 11] because it utilizes only one checksum. Accordingly, in our solution, we adopt 1024 2-block messages to find a common solution for the two checksums simultaneously, hence, having the required freedom to satisfy two bit constraints for each bit position in the two checksums. The time complexity of this stage is about $1024^3 = 2^{30}$.

The time complexity of the attack is evaluated as follows: we need $2^p \times$ (complexity of pseudo preimage attack) in stage 1, $1024 \times 2^{256} + 2048 \approx 2^{266}$ to build the 2-block multicollision at stage 2, 2^{512-p} evaluations of one compression function call at stage 3, and finally 2^{30} for stage 4. The memory complexity for the four stages is as follows: 2^p 3-states to store the pseudo preimages in stage 1 and 2^{112} for the pseudo preimage attack, and 2^{12} for the multicollision in stage 2. Since the time complexity is highly influenced by p, so we have chosen $p = 8$ to maximize the attack probability. Accordingly, preimages for the 6-round Maelstrom-0 hash function can be produced with a time complexity of $2^{8+496} + 2^{266} + 2^{512-8} + 2^{30} \approx 2^{505}$. The memory complexity of attack is dominated by the memory requirements of the pseudo preimage attack on the compression function which is given by 2^{112}.

6   Conclusion

In this paper, we have investigated Maelstrom-0 and its compression function with respect to MitM preimage attacks. We have shown that with a carefully balanced chunk separation and the use of a guess and determine approach, pseudo preimages for the 6-round reduced compression function are generated with time complexity of 2^{496} and memory complexity of 2^{112}. Moreover, we have analyzed the employed 3CM chaining scheme which is designed specifically to inhibit the ability of extending attacks on the compression function to the hash function, and proposed a 4-stage approach to bypass its effect and turn the pseudo preimage attack on the compression function to a preimage attack on the hash function. Accordingly, 6-round hash function preimages are generated with time complexity of 2^{505} and a memory complexity of 2^{112}. It should be noted that, if one considers removing the linear transformation from the last round similar to AES, the attack could be extended to cover seven rounds.

Acknowledgment. The authors would like to thank the anonymous reviewers for their valuable comments and suggestions that helped improve the quality of the paper. This work is supported by the Natural Sciences and Engineering Research Council of Canada (NSERC).

References

1. AlTawy, R., Youssef, A.M.: Preimage attacks on reduced-round stribog. In: Pointcheval, D., Vergnaud, D. (eds.) AFRICACRYPT. LNCS, vol. 8469, pp. 109–125. Springer, Heidelberg (2014)
2. AlTawy, R., Youssef, A.M.: Second preimage analysis of whirlwind. In: Lin, D., Yung, M., Zhou, J. (eds.) Inscrypt 2014. LNCS, vol. 8957, pp. 311–328. Springer, Heidelberg (2015)
3. Aoki, K., Guo, J., Matusiewicz, K., Sasaki, Y., Wang, L.: Preimages for step-reduced SHA-2. In: Matsui, M. (ed.) ASIACRYPT 2009. LNCS, vol. 5912, pp. 578–597. Springer, Heidelberg (2009)
4. Aoki, K., Sasaki, Y.: Meet-in-the-middle preimage attacks against reduced SHA-0 and SHA-1. In: Halevi, S. (ed.) CRYPTO 2009. LNCS, vol. 5677, pp. 70–89. Springer, Heidelberg (2009)
5. Aoki, K., Sasaki, Y.: Preimage attacks on one-block MD4, 63-step MD5 and more. In: Avanzi, R.M., Keliher, L., Sica, F. (eds.) SAC 2008. LNCS, vol. 5381, pp. 103–119. Springer, Heidelberg (2009)
6. Barreto, P., Nikov, V., Nikova, S., Rijmen, V., Tischhauser, E.: Whirlwind: a new cryptographic hash function. Designs, Codes and Cryptography 56(2-3), 141–162 (2010)
7. Daemen, J., Rijmen, V.: The Design of Rijndael: AES- The Advanced Encryption Standard. Springer (2002)
8. Filho, D., Barreto, P., Rijmen, V.: The Maelstrom-0 hash function. In: VI Brazilian Symposium on Information and Computer Systems Security (2006)
9. Gauravaram, P., Kelsey, J.: Cryptanalysis of a class of cryptographic hash functions. Cryptology ePrint Archive, Report 2007/277 (2007), http://eprint.iacr.org/
10. Gauravaram, P., Kelsey, J.: Linear-XOR and additive checksums dont protect Damgård-Merkle hashes from generic attacks. In: Malkin, T. (ed.) CT-RSA 2008. LNCS, vol. 4964, pp. 36–51. Springer, Heidelberg (2008)
11. Gauravaram, P., Kelsey, J., Knudsen, L.R., Thomsen, S.: On hash functions using checksums. International Journal of Information Security 9(2), 137–151 (2010)
12. Gauravaram, P., Knudsen, L.R., Matusiewicz, K., Mendel, F., Rechberger, C., Schläffer, M., Thomsen, S.S.: Grøstl – a SHA-3 candidate. NIST submission (2008)
13. Gauravaram, P., Millan, W.L., Dawson, E., Viswanathan, K.: Constructing secure hash functions by enhancing Merkle-Damgård construction. In: Batten, L.M., Safavi-Naini, R. (eds.) ACISP 2006. LNCS, vol. 4058, pp. 407–420. Springer, Heidelberg (2006)
14. Guo, J., Ling, S., Rechberger, C., Wang, H.: Advanced meet-in-the-middle preimage attacks: First results on full Tiger, and improved results on MD4 and SHA-2. In: Abe, M. (ed.) ASIACRYPT 2010. LNCS, vol. 6477, pp. 56–75. Springer, Heidelberg (2010)
15. Hong, D., Koo, B., Sasaki, Y.: Improved preimage attack for 68-step HAS-160. In: Lee, D., Hong, S. (eds.) ICISC 2009. LNCS, vol. 5984, pp. 332–348. Springer, Heidelberg (2010)

16. Indesteege, S.: The Lane hash function. Submission to NIST (2008), http://www.cosic.esat.kuleuven.be/publications/article-1181.pdf
17. Joux, A.: Multicollisions in iterated hash functions. Application to cascaded constructions. In: Franklin, M. (ed.) CRYPTO 2004. LNCS, vol. 3152, pp. 306–316. Springer, Heidelberg (2004)
18. Kölbl, S., Mendel, F.: Practical attacks on the Maelstrom-0 compression function. In: Lopez, J., Tsudik, G. (eds.) ACNS 2011. LNCS, vol. 6715, pp. 449–461. Springer, Heidelberg (2011)
19. Ma, B., Li, B., Hao, R., Li, X.: Improved cryptanalysis on reduced-round GOST and Whirlpool hash function. In: Boureanu, I., Owesarski, P., Vaudenay, S. (eds.) ACNS 2014. LNCS, vol. 8479, pp. 289–307. Springer, Heidelberg (2014)
20. Matyukhin, D., Rudskoy, V., Shishkin, V.: A perspective hashing algorithm. In: RusCrypto (2010) (in Russian)
21. Mendel, F., Rechberger, C., Schläffer, M., Thomsen, S.S.: The rebound attack: Cryptanalysis of reduced Whirlpool and Grøstl. In: Dunkelman, O. (ed.) FSE 2009. LNCS, vol. 5665, pp. 260–276. Springer, Heidelberg (2009)
22. NIST: Announcing request for candidate algorithm nominations for a new cryptographic hash algorithm (SHA-3) family. In: Federal Register, vol. 72(212), November 2007, http://csrc.nist.gov/groups/ST/hash/documents/FR_Notice_Nov07.pdf
23. Rijmen, V., Barreto, P.S.L.M.: The Whirlpool hashing function. NISSIE submission (2000)
24. Sasaki, Y.: Meet-in-the-middle preimage attacks on AES hashing modes and an application to Whirlpool. In: Joux, A. (ed.) FSE 2011. LNCS, vol. 6733, pp. 378–396. Springer, Heidelberg (2011)
25. Sasaki, Y., Aoki, K.: Finding preimages in full MD5 faster than exhaustive search. In: Joux, A. (ed.) EUROCRYPT 2009. LNCS, vol. 5479, pp. 134–152. Springer, Heidelberg (2009)
26. Sasaki, Y., Wang, L., Wu, S., Wu, W.: Investigating fundamental security requirements on Whirlpool: Improved preimage and collision attacks. In: Wang, X., Sako, K. (eds.) ASIACRYPT 2012. LNCS, vol. 7658, pp. 562–579. Springer, Heidelberg (2012)
27. Wang, X., Yin, Y.L., Yu, H.: Finding collisions in the full SHA-1. In: Shoup, V. (ed.) CRYPTO 2005. LNCS, vol. 3621, pp. 17–36. Springer, Heidelberg (2005)
28. Wang, X., Yu, H.: How to break MD5 and other hash functions. In: Cramer, R. (ed.) EUROCRYPT 2005. LNCS, vol. 3494, pp. 19–35. Springer, Heidelberg (2005)
29. Wu, H.: The hash function JH (2011), http://www3.ntu.edu.sg/home/wuhj/research/jh/jh-round3.pdf
30. Wu, S., Feng, D., Wu, W., Guo, J., Dong, L., Zou, J.: (Pseudo) preimage attack on round-reduced Grøstl hash function and others. In: Canteaut, A. (ed.) FSE 2012. LNCS, vol. 7549, pp. 127–145. Springer, Heidelberg (2012)

Meet-in-the-Middle Attacks
on Round-Reduced Khudra

Mohamed Tolba, Ahmed Abdelkhalek, and Amr M. Youssef

Concordia Institute for Information Systems Engineering,
Concordia University, Montréal, Quebéc, Canada

Abstract. Khudra is a hardware-oriented lightweight block cipher that is designed to run efficiently on Field Programmable Gate Arrays. It employs an 18-rounds Generalized type-2 Feistel Structure with a 64-bit block length and an 80-bit key. In this paper, we present Meet-in-the-Middle (MitM) attacks on 13 and 14 round-reduced Khudra. These attacks are based on finding a distinguisher that is evaluated offline independently of the key. Then in an online phase, some rounds are appended before and after the distinguisher and the correct key candidates for these rounds are checked whether they verify the distinguisher property or not. Using this technique, we find two 6-round distinguishers and use them to attack 13 and 14 rounds of Khudra with time complexity of $2^{66.11}$ and $2^{66.19}$, respectively. Both attacks require the same data and memory complexities of 2^{51} chosen plaintexts and $2^{64.8}$ 64-bit blocks, respectively.

Keywords: Cryptanalysis, Meet-in-the-middle attacks, Generalized type-2 Feistel Structure.

1 Introduction

Recently, the design and cryptanalysis of lightweight block ciphers have received a lot of attention due to the demand for cryptographic protection in the increasingly used resource constrained devices such as RFIDs and wireless sensor networks. Designing an efficient hardware-oriented lightweight block cipher is a challenging task. Therefore, novel design criteria were proposed such as the use of a simple round function along with a simple key schedule. Examples of lightweight block ciphers that use these new techniques are HIGHT [16], PRESENT [3], KATAN/KTANTAN [5], KLEIN [12], Zorro [11], TWINE [19], and Khudra [17]. With such simple design, lightweight block ciphers should be deeply scrutinized in order to guarantee their security.

Unlike Application-Specific Integrated Circuits (ASICs), low cost Field Programmable Gate Arrays (FPGAs) are reconfigured and upgraded easily and therefore are now used extensively in numerous network applications. Consequently, lightweight block ciphers have to be designed with the goal of being integrated with FPGA applications in order to guarantee their security. Khudra is a new lightweight block cipher that was proposed by Kolay and Mukhopadhyay at SPACE 2014 [17] in order to address the issue of efficient lightweight block

© Springer International Publishing Switzerland 2015
R.S. Chakraborty et al. (Eds.): SPACE 2015, LNCS 9354, pp. 127–138, 2015.
DOI: 10.1007/978-3-319-24126-5_8

ciphers that operate on FPGAs. To have an efficient lightweight block cipher for deployment on FPGAs, a new design criterion, namely, recursive structure was proposed. Khudra has a 64-bit block length and employs an 80-bit key. Its structure inherits the Generalized type-2 Feistel Structure (GFS) that was proposed by Hoang and Rogaway [15]. In particular, it uses 4 branches each of 16-bit length.

In 1977, Diffie and Hellman proposed the MitM attack to be used in the cryptanalysis of Data Encryption Standard (DES) [9]. The MitM attack is one of the major attacks on block ciphers as it requires low data complexity. Its time complexity is, however, very close to that of an optimized exhaustive key search. Hence, enhancing its time complexity and increasing the number of attacked rounds have always been hot topics in cryptanalysis. For example, Bogdanov and Rechberger proposed the 3-Subset MitM attack and applied it to the full KTANTAN cipher [4]. Zhu and Guang presented multidimensional MitM against KATAN32/48/64 [20]. Demirci and Selçuk attacked 8 rounds of both AES-192 and AES-256 using MitM techniques [6]. The main drawback of their attack is the high memory requirement. To tackle the high memory requirement issue, Dunkelman, Keller and Shamir put forward a couple of new ideas. Particularly, they presented the concepts of differential enumeration and multisets [10] that have drastically decreased the high memory requirement of the attack of Demirci and Selçuk. Later on, Derbez *et al.* enhanced the attack and decreased the memory requirement even further which made it possible on AES-128 [7]. The MitM techniques, which were developed to attack AES and Substitution Permutation Network (SPN) based block ciphers such as Hierocrypt-3 [1] and mCrypton [14], were also proven to be equally powerful on Feistel constructions, as exemplified by the generic work done by Guo *et al.* [13] and Lin *et al.* [18]. Finally, at FSE 2015, two MitM attacks based on the Demirci and Selçuk approach were presented on the SPN structure PRINCE [8] and the Feistel construction TWINE [2].

In this paper, we present MitM attacks on 13 and 14 rounds of Khudra. In the attack on 13 rounds, we first construct a 6-round distinguisher, append three rounds at the top and four rounds at the bottom. To attack 14 rounds, the same distinguisher would require the whole key to be guessed, therefore we construct a different 6-round distinguisher, and append three rounds at the top and five rounds at the bottom. The time complexities of these attacks are $2^{66.11}$ to attack 13 rounds and $2^{66.19}$ to attack 14 rounds, respectively. Both attacks require the same data and memory complexities of 2^{51} chosen plaintext and $2^{64.8}$ 64-bit blocks. To the best of our knowledge, these are the best attacks on Khudra so far.

The rest of the paper is organized as follows. In section 2, we provide a brief description of Khudra and the notations used throughout the paper. Our attacks are presented in section 3 and the paper is concluded in section 4.

2   Specifications of Khudra

Khudra is an iterated lightweight block cipher that operates on 64-bit blocks using an 80-bit key and employs a Generalized Feistel Structure (GFS). It has four branches of 16-bit each, i.e., the state is divided into four words and each word is 16-bit long. The cipher iterates over 18 rounds where in every round, an unkeyed 16×16-bit F-function is applied on two words. This unkeyed F-function, designed to be efficient when deploying Khudra on FPGAs, uses a 6-round GFS as depicted in the right side of Figure 1. Each round of these 6-round GFS has two 4×4-bit SBoxes identical to the SBox used in PRESENT [3]. After applying the F-functions of round i, two 16-bit round keys RK_{2i} and RK_{2i+1} are xored to the state along with the other two words to generate the two new words of round $i + 1$ for $i = 0, 1, \cdots, 17$. Additionally, two pre-whitening keys WK_0 and WK_1 are xored with the plaintext before the first round and two other post-whitening keys WK_2 and WK_3 are xored with the internal state after the last round and before generating the ciphertext.

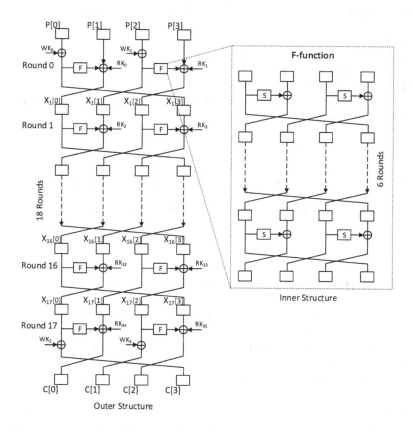

Fig. 1. Structure of Khudra

The key schedule of Khudra takes an 80-bit master key K and splits it into five keys k_i of 16-bit each where $K = k_0||k_1||k_2||k_3||k_4$. Then, it generates 16-bit 36 round keys $RK_i, 0 \leqslant i < 36$, two per round, and four 16-bit whitening keys $WK_i, 0 \leqslant i < 4$, as shown in Algorithm 1.

Data: Key Scheduling$(k_0, k_1, k_2, k_3, k_4)$
Result: $WK_i, 0 \leqslant i < 4$ and $RK_i, 0 \leqslant i < 36$
$WK_0 \leftarrow k_0, WK_1 \leftarrow k_1, WK_2 \leftarrow k_3, WK_3 \leftarrow k_4$;
for $i \leftarrow 0$ *to* 35 **do**
$\quad RC_i \leftarrow 0||i_{(6)}||00||i_{(6)}||0$;
$\quad RK_i \leftarrow k_{i \bmod 5} \oplus RC_i$;
end

Algorithm 1. The Key Schedule employed in Khudra [17]

2.1 Notations

The following notations will be used throughout the rest of the paper:

- K: The master key.
- k_i: The ith 16-bit of K, where $0 \leq i < 5$.
- RK_i: The 16-bit key used in round $\lfloor i/2 \rfloor$.
- WK_i: The 16-bit whitening key, where $0 \leq i < 4$.
- X_i: The 64-bit input to round i, where $0 \leq i \leq 18$, X_0 is the plaintext P and X_{18} is the ciphertext C.
- $X_i[l]$: The lth 16-bit word of X_i, where $0 \leq l < 4$.
- $\Delta X_i, \Delta X_i[l]$: The difference at state X_i and word $X_i[l]$, respectively.
- X_i^j: The jth state of the 64-bit input to round i.
- $X_i^j[l]$: The lth 16-bit word of the jth state of the 64-bit input to round i.

We measure the memory complexity of our attacks in number of 64-bit Khudra blocks and the time complexity in terms of the equivalent number of round-reduced Khudra encryptions.

3   MitM Attacks on Round-Reduced Khudra

In our MitM attacks, Khudra is split into three sub-ciphers such that $E_K(P) = E_{K_2} \circ E_{dis} \circ E_{K_1}(P)$, where E_{dis} is the middle part which exhibits a distinguishing property. In the offline phase, that particular property is evaluated independently of the keys used in the middle rounds. Then in the online phase, correct K_1 and K_2 key candidates are checked whether they verify this distinguishing property or not.

The b-δ-set concept [13], as captured by Definition 1, is used to build our distinguisher. Using a b-δ-set enables us to reduce the memory and data complexities of our distinguisher.

Definition 1. *(b-δ-set, [13]). A b-δ-set is a set of 2^b state values that are all different in b state bits (the active bits) and are all equal in the remaining state bits (the inactive bits).*

In the following subsections, we demonstrate our attacks on 13 and 14 rounds of Khudra in details.

3.1 A MitM Attack on 13-Round Khudra

A *b-δ-set* is employed in our MitM attack where we set $b = 3$, i.e., 3 active bits. b is chosen in order to reduce the memory and data requirements of the attack without increasing its time complexity. In our 13-round attack, the active word is $P[1]$, i.e., the second word. The 3 active bits can take any position in this 16-bit word. Such 3-δ-set enables us to build a 6-round distinguisher, as depicted in Figure 2, by the following proposition:

Proposition 1. *Consider the encryption of 3-δ-set $\{P^0, P^1, ..., P^7\}$ through six rounds of Khudra. The ordered sequence $[X_6^0[3] \oplus X_6^1[3], X_6^0[3] \oplus X_6^2[3], ..., X_6^0[3] \oplus X_6^7[3]]$ is fully determined by the following 4 16-bit parameters, $X_1^0[0]$, $X_2^0[0]$, $X_3^0[0]$ and $X_4^0[0]$.*

The above proposition means that we have $2^{4 \times 16} = 2^{64}$ ordered sequences out of the $2^{(2^3-1) \times 16} = 2^{112}$ theoretically possible ones.

Proof. The knowledge of the 3-δ-set $= \{P^0, P^1, \cdots, P^7\}$ allows us to determine $[P^0 \oplus P^1, P^0 \oplus P^2, \cdots, P^0 \oplus P^7]$. In what follows we show how the knowledge of the 4 16-bit parameters mentioned in proposition 1 is enough to compute the ordered sequence of the differences at $X_6[3]$. As there is no F-function involved in the first round, the difference $\Delta P[1]$ is propagated through the first round as is. The knowledge of $X_1^0[0]$ enables us to bypass the F-function of the second round to compute $\Delta X_2[0]$. Then, the knowledge of $X_2^0[0]$ enables us to bypass the F-function of the third round to compute $\Delta X_3[0]$ and the previous steps are repeated until we compute $\Delta X_6[3]$. It is to be noted that after the third (resp. fourth) round, $X_3[3]$ (resp. $X_4[3]$) should have non-zero difference because $X_2[0]$ (resp. $X_3[0]$) has non-zero difference. However, these differences are omitted from Figure 2 since they do not impact the ordered sequence at $X_6[3]$.

The previous proposition is utilized to attack 13-round Khudra by appending 3 rounds on top of it and 4 rounds below it, as illustrated in Figure 3. The attack has two phases and proceeds as follows:

Offline Phase. Build the distinguisher property by determining all the 2^{64} ordered sequences as illustrated in Proposition 1 and save them in a hash table H.

Online Phase. As illustrated in Figure 3, the online phase advances as follows:

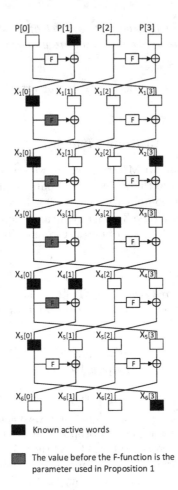

Fig. 2. 6-Round distinguisher to attack 13-round Khudra

1. A plaintext P^0 is chosen to act as a reference to all the differences in the 3-δ-set.
2. The 3-δ-set P^0, P^1, $\cdots$, P^7 is determined by guessing the state variables $X_1^0[3]$, $X_1^0[1]$, $X_1^0[0]$, $X_2^0[2]$ to decrypt the 3-δ-set differences $[X_3^0[1] \oplus X_3^1[1]$, $X_3^0[1] \oplus X_3^2[1], \cdots, X_3^0[1] \oplus X_3^7[1]]$.
3. The corresponding ciphertexts C^0, C^1, $\cdots$, C^7 are requested.
4. The differences in $[X_9^0[3] \oplus X_9^1[3], X_9^0[3] \oplus X_9^2[3], \cdots, X_9^0[3] \oplus X_9^7[3]]$ are determined by guessing the state variables $X_9^0[2]$, $X_{10}^0[0]$, $X_{11}^0[0]$, $X_{11}^0[2]$, $X_{12}^0[0]$, $X_{12}^0[2]$ that are required to decrypt the ciphertext differences $[C^0 \oplus C^1, C^0 \oplus C^2, \cdots, C^0 \oplus C^7]$.
5. The guessed state variables are filtered by checking if the computed ordered sequence exists in H or not.

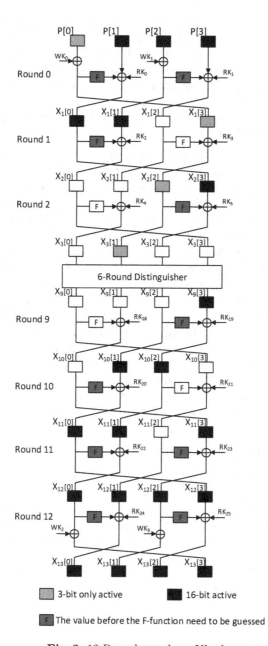

Fig. 3. 13-Round attack on Khudra

Steps 2 and 4 require the guessing of 10 words and the attack time complexity would then exceed the exhaustive key search. Therefore, we investigate the key schedule aiming to find relations between the round keys and thus reduce the number of guessed words. Indeed, we find that by guessing k_0, k_1, k_3, and with the knowledge of P^0, we can compute $X_1^0[3]$, $X_1^0[1]$, $X_1^0[0]$, $X_2^0[2]$ and by guessing k_0, k_3, k_4, and with the knowledge of C^0, C^1, $\cdots$, C^7 and $[C^0 \oplus C^1, C^0 \oplus C^2, \cdots, C^0 \oplus C^7]$, we can compute $X_9^0[2]$, $X_{10}^0[0]$, $X_{11}^0[0]$, $X_{11}^0[2]$, $X_{12}^0[0]$, $X_{12}^0[2]$. Therefore, instead of guessing 10 words, only 4 key words k_0, k_1, k_3, k_4 are to be guessed. The probability of a wrong key resulting in an ordered sequence in H is $2^{64-(7\times16)} = 2^{-48}$. As we have 2^{64} key guesses, we expect that only $2^{64-48} = 2^{16}$ keys will remain. Hence, we guess k_2 to fully recover the master key and test it using two plaintext/ciphertext pairs.

Attack Complexity. The memory complexity of the attack is determined by the memory required to store the hash table H in the offline phase. This table has 2^{64} entries where each entry contains seven 16-bit words, i.e., 112 bits. Therefore, the memory complexity is given by $2^{64} \times 112/64 = 2^{64.8}$ 64-bit blocks. The data complexity is determined from step 2. As shown in Figure 3, after the decryption of step 2, three words are fully active, i.e., they assume all the 2^{16} possible values while the fourth word has only three active bits, i.e., assumes 2^3 possible values only in correspondence to the 3-δ-set. Therefore, the data complexity of the attack is upper bounded by 2^{51} chosen plaintext. The time complexity of the offline phase is determined by the time required to build the hash table H and is estimated to be $2^{64} \times 8 \times 4/(2 \times 13) = 2^{64.3}$. The complexity of the online phase includes the time required to filter the key space and is estimated to be $2^{64} \times 8 \times (4+6)/(2 \times 13) = 2^{65.62}$. It also includes the time to exhaustively search through the remaining key candidates along with the guess of k_2 using two plaintext/ciphertext pairs and is estimated to be $2 \times 2^{(64-48)} \times 2^{16} = 2^{33}$. Therefore, the overall time complexity of the attack is estimated to be $2^{64.3} + 2^{65.62} + 2^{33} \approx 2^{66.11}$ 13-round Khudra encryptions.

3.2   A MitM Attack on 14-Round Khudra

Reusing the same distinguisher to extend our attack by one round requires guessing the 5 words of the key. Therefore, we construct another distinguisher, depicted in Figure 4, to attack 14-round reduced Khudra without the post-whitening keys. The active word in this new distinguisher is $P[3]$. It is built according to proposition 2 below and, as in the previous attack, b is set to 3.

Proposition 2. *Consider the encryption of 3-δ-set $\{P^0, P^1, \cdots, P^7\}$ through six rounds of Khudra. The ordered sequence $[X_6^0[1] \oplus X_6^1[1], X_6^0[1] \oplus X_6^2[1], \cdots, X_6^0[1] \oplus X_6^7[1]]$ is fully determined by the following 4 16-bit parameters $X_1^0[2]$, $X_2^0[2]$, $X_3^0[2]$ and $X_4^0[2]$.*

By appending three rounds on top of this new distinguisher and five rounds beneath it, we are able to attack 14-round Khudra. The attack proceeds as the previous one, as illustrated in Figure 5, with the exception that the active word is $X_3[3]$ rather than $X_3[1]$ in the 13-round attack and the ordered sequence is calculated at $X_9[1]$ instead of $X_9[3]$. Guessing k_0, k_1, k_2 with the knowledge of

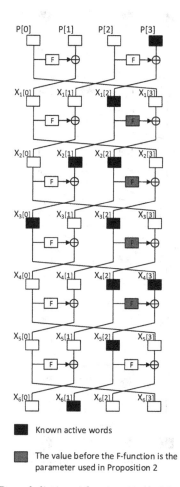

Fig. 4. 6-Round distinguisher to attack 14-round Khudra

P^0 enables us to compute the state variables needed to determine the 3-δ-set. In order to determine the ordered sequence, we need to guess k_0, k_1, k_2, k_4. Therefore, guessing the four key words, k_0, k_1, k_2, k_4 allows us to mount an attack on 14-round Khudra.

Attack Complexity. The memory and data complexities of this attack are similar to the previous one, i.e., $2^{64.8}$ 64-bit blocks and 2^{51} chosen plaintext, respectively. The time complexity is $2^{64} \times 8 \times 4/(2 \times 14) + 2^{64} \times 8 \times (4+8)/(2 \times 14) + 2 \times 2^{(64-48)} \times 2^{16} = 2^{64.19} + 2^{65.78} + 2^{33} \approx 2^{66.19}$ 14-round Khudra encryptions.

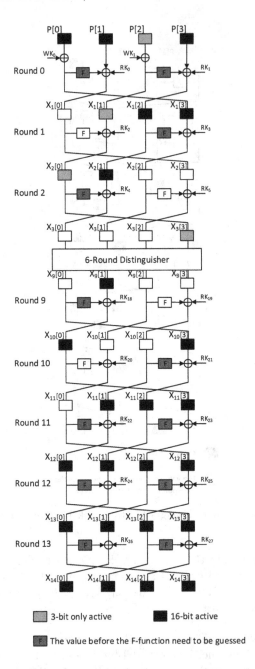

■ 3-bit only active   ■ 16-bit active

■ The value before the F-function need to be guessed

Fig. 5. 14-Round attack on Khudra

4   Conclusion and Discussion

We presented MitM attacks on Khudra. The time complexities of the attacks are given by $2^{66.11}$ and $2^{66.19}$ for the 13-round and 14-round reduced cipher, respectively. Both attacks have the same data and memory complexities of 2^{51} chosen plaintext and $2^{64.8}$ 64-bit blocks, respectively. To the best of our knowledge, these are the best known attacks on Khudra.

Finally, we briefly discuss why we did not use the notion of differential enumeration. In the attack of Dunkelman et al. [10], the differential enumeration technique helps reduce the number of parameters by using the differential property of the SBox over one round. In Feistel constructions, the differential property of the SBox can be utilized over at least two rounds and can be extended further depending on the specific structure of the scheme. However, in the case of Khudra, differential enumeration does not help reduce the number of parameters because propagating the difference backward requires a set of parameters that is different than the set of parameters needed to compute the ordered sequence. In other words, using the differential enumeration technique reduces the number of parameters by using the differential property of the SBox but at the same time, incurs additional parameters to be guessed in order to propagate the difference backward. Since Khudra has an 80-bit key, the number of parameters is limited to 4 16-bit parameters. Using the differential enumeration technique, the best 6-round distinguisher that we are able to construct requires 6 parameters which renders the attack worse than exhaustive key search.

References

1. Abdelkhalek, A., Altawy, R., Tolba, M., Youssef, A.M.: Meet-in-the-middle attacks on reduced-round hierocrypt-3. In: LatinCrypt. LNCS. Springer (2015, to appear)
2. Biryukov, A., Derbez, P., Perrin, L.P.: Differential analysis and meet-in-the-middle attack against round-reduced TWINE. In: Leander, G. (ed.) FSE 2015. LNCS, vol. 9054, pp. 3–27. Springer, Heidelberg (2015)
3. Bogdanov, A.A., Knudsen, L.R., Leander, G., Paar, C., Poschmann, A., Robshaw, M., Seurin, Y., Vikkelsoe, C.: PRESENT: An ultra-lightweight block cipher. In: Paillier, P., Verbauwhede, I. (eds.) CHES 2007. LNCS, vol. 4727, pp. 450–466. Springer, Heidelberg (2007)
4. Bogdanov, A., Rechberger, C.: A 3-subset meet-in-the-middle attack: Cryptanalysis of the lightweight block cipher KTANTAN. In: Biryukov, A., Gong, G., Stinson, D.R. (eds.) SAC 2010. LNCS, vol. 6544, pp. 229–240. Springer, Heidelberg (2011)
5. De Cannière, C., Dunkelman, O., Knežević, M.: KATAN and KTANTAN - A family of small and efficient hardware-oriented block ciphers. In: Clavier, C., Gaj, K. (eds.) CHES 2009. LNCS, vol. 5747, pp. 272–288. Springer, Heidelberg (2009)
6. Demirci, H., Selçuk, A.A.: A meet-in-the-middle attack on 8-round AES. In: Nyberg, K. (ed.) FSE 2008. LNCS, vol. 5086, pp. 116–126. Springer, Heidelberg (2008)
7. Derbez, P., Fouque, P.-A., Jean, J.: Improved key recovery attacks on reduced-round AES in the single-key setting. In: Johansson, T., Nguyen, P.Q. (eds.) EUROCRYPT 2013. LNCS, vol. 7881, pp. 371–387. Springer, Heidelberg (2013)

8. Derbez, P., Perrin, L.: Meet-in-the-middle attacks and structural analysis of round-reduced PRINCE. In: Leander, G. (ed.) FSE 2015. LNCS, vol. 9054, pp. 190–216. Springer, Heidelberg (2015)

9. Diffie, W., Hellman, M.E.: Special feature exhaustive cryptanalysis of the NBS data encryption standard. Computer 10(6), 74–84 (1977)

10. Dunkelman, O., Keller, N., Shamir, A.: Improved single-key attacks on 8-round AES-192 and AES-256. In: Abe, M. (ed.) ASIACRYPT 2010. LNCS, vol. 6477, pp. 158–176. Springer, Heidelberg (2010)

11. Gérard, B., Grosso, V., Naya-Plasencia, M., Standaert, F.-X.: Block ciphers that are easier to mask: How far can we go? In: Bertoni, G., Coron, J.-S. (eds.) CHES 2013. LNCS, vol. 8086, pp. 383–399. Springer, Heidelberg (2013)

12. Gong, Z., Nikova, S., Law, Y.W.: KLEIN: A new family of lightweight block ciphers. In: Juels, A., Paar, C. (eds.) RFIDSec 2011. LNCS, vol. 7055, pp. 1–18. Springer, Heidelberg (2012)

13. Guo, J., Jean, J., Nikolić, I., Sasaki, Y.: Meet-in-the-middle attacks on generic Feistel constructions. In: Sarkar, P., Iwata, T. (eds.) ASIACRYPT 2014. LNCS, vol. 8873, pp. 458–477. Springer, Heidelberg (2014)

14. Hao, Y., Bai, D., Li, L.: A meet-in-the-middle attack on round-reduced mCrypton using the differential enumeration technique. In: Au, M.H., Carminati, B., Kuo, C.-C.J. (eds.) NSS 2014. LNCS, vol. 8792, pp. 166–183. Springer, Heidelberg (2014)

15. Hoang, V.T., Rogaway, P.: On generalized feistel networks. In: Rabin, T. (ed.) CRYPTO 2010. LNCS, vol. 6223, pp. 613–630. Springer, Heidelberg (2010)

16. Hong, D., et al.: HIGHT: A new block cipher suitable for low-resource device. In: Goubin, L., Matsui, M. (eds.) CHES 2006. LNCS, vol. 4249, pp. 46–59. Springer, Heidelberg (2006)

17. Kolay, S., Mukhopadhyay, D.: Khudra: A new lightweight block cipher for FPGAs. In: Chakraborty, R.S., Matyas, V., Schaumont, P. (eds.) SPACE 2014. LNCS, vol. 8804, pp. 126–145. Springer, Heidelberg (2014)

18. Lin, L., Wu, W.: Improved Meet-in-the-Middle Distinguisher on Feistel Schemes. IACR Cryptology ePrint Archive, 2015/051 (2015). https://eprint.iacr.org/2015/051.pdf

19. Suzaki, T., Minematsu, K., Morioka, S., Kobayashi, E.: TWINE: A lightweight block cipher for multiple platforms. In: Knudsen, L.R., Wu, H. (eds.) SAC 2012. LNCS, vol. 7707, pp. 339–354. Springer, Heidelberg (2013)

20. Zhu, B., Gong, G.: Multidimensional meet-in-the-middle attack and its applications to KATAN32/48/64. IACR Cryptology ePrint Archive, 2011/619 (2011). https://eprint.iacr.org/2011/619.pdf

Improved Key Recovery Attack on Round-reduced Hierocrypt-L1 in the Single-Key Setting

Ahmed Abdelkhalek, Mohamed Tolba, and Amr M. Youssef

Concordia Institute for Information Systems Engineering,
Concordia University, Montréal, Quebéc, Canada

Abstract. Hierocrypt-L1 is a 64-bit block cipher with a 128-bit key. It was selected among the Japanese e-Government 2003 recommended ciphers list and has been reselected in the 2013 candidate recommended ciphers list. In this work, we cryptanalyze Hierocrypt-L1 in the single-key setting. In particular, we construct a 5 S-box layers distinguisher that we utilize to launch a meet-in-the-middle attack on 8 S-box layers round-reduced Hierocrypt-L1 using the differential enumeration technique. Our attack allows us to recover the master key with data complexity of 2^{49} chosen plaintexts, time complexity of $2^{114.8}$ 8-Sbox layers Hierocrypt-L1 encryptions and memory complexity of 2^{106} 64-bit blocks. Up to the authors' knowledge, this is the first cryptanalysis result that reaches 8 S-box layers of Hierocrypt-L1 in the single-key setting.

Keywords: Cryptanalysis, Hierocrypt-L1, Meet-in-the-Middle attack, Differential Enumeration.

1 Introduction

Hierocrypt-L1 (HC-L1) [24,10,29], designed by Toshiba Corporation in 2000, is a 64-bit block cipher with a 128-bit key. The cipher employs a nested Substitution Permutation Network (SPN) structure [24], where each S-box in a higher SPN level encompasses the lower-level SPN structure. HC-L1 was submitted to the New European Schemes for Signatures, Integrity, and Encryption (NESSIE) project [23]. In 2003, HC-L1 was selected as one of the Japanese e-Government recommended ciphers [9], and its security was reaffirmed by CRYPTREC in 2013 where it was included in the candidate recommended ciphers list [8].

The best known attack on HC-L1 in the single-key setting is the square attack on 7 S-box layers which was proposed by the designers [19] and independently by Barreto *et al.* [5]. Later, Cheon *et al.* proposed a 4 S-box layers impossible differential [29] and utilized it to attack HC-L1 reduced to 6 S-box layers. In the related-key setting, Taga *et al.* utilized a differential characteristic in the key scheduling of HC-L1 to attack 8 S-box layers [28].

The meet-in-the-middle (MitM) attack, first proposed by Diffie and Hellman in 1977, is considered as one of the major attacks on cryptographic primitives.

© Springer International Publishing Switzerland 2015
R.S. Chakraborty et al. (Eds.): SPACE 2015, LNCS 9354, pp. 139–150, 2015.
DOI: 10.1007/978-3-319-24126-5_9

Following its introduction, a number of variants has been developed to study the security of many block ciphers such as DES [15], XTEA, [27], KTANTAN [7], LBlock [2], and Twine [6]. MitM attacks were also employed in the cryptanalysis of a number of hash functions [17,26,3] and public key cryptosystems [18].

A new line of research was opened when Demirci and Selçuk presented the first MitM attack on AES at FSE 2008 [12]. They presented small data complexity attacks on 8-round AES-256 and 7-round AES-192 using time/memory trade-off. The major downside of their attack is the high memory required to store a precomputation table. The issue of the high memory requirement remained severe untill Dunkelman, Keller, and Shamir [14] introduced the notions of multisets and differential enumeration that have reduced the memory requirement drastically but with higher data complexity. Furthermore, Derbez, Fouque and Jean revised Dunkleman et al.'s attack, by borrowing ideas from the rebound attack [22], rendering the attack feasible on AES-128 [13]. Then, Li, Jia and Wang [20] presented attacks on 9-round AES-192 and 8-round PRINCE using a key-dependent sieving. MitM attacks were also applied on other block ciphers such as Hierocrypt-3 [1] and mCrypton [16].

In this work, we first construct a 5 S-box layers truncated differential characteristic for HC-L1. Then, we utilize this characteristic as a distinguisher to launch a MitM attack based on the differential enumeration technique against HC-L1 reduced to 8 S-box layers. Unlike the majority of existing MitM attack results, the matching step in our attack is performed around the linear transformation. Particularly, in the offline phase, we compute two specific bytes of the input of the linear transformation and store their xor in a precomputation table. Then, in the online phase, we compute two particular bytes of the output of that linear transformation, compute their xor which is equivalent to the xor of the two input bytes, and look for a match in the precomputation table. If no match is found, the key is discarded. Our attack recovers the master key with data complexity of 2^{49} chosen plaintexts, time complexity of $2^{114.8}$ 8-Sbox layers HC-L1 encryptions and memory complexity of 2^{106} 64-bit blocks.

The rest of the paper is organized as follows. Section 2 provides a description of HC-L1 and the notations adopted in the paper. Section 3 describes our 5 S-box layers distinguisher and how it is used to launch our MitM attack to recover the master key. Then, our conclusion is provided in Section 4.

2 Specification of Hierocrypt-L1

HC-L1 is an iterated block cipher with 64-bit blocks and 128-bit key. It adopts a nested SPN construction which embeds a lower level SPN structure within a higher SPN one. It has 6 rounds where the last round is slightly different than the others. As shown in Figure 1, the higher SPN level of HC-L1 consists of the following three operations:

- AK: Mixes 64-bit layer key with the 64-bit internal state.
- XS: Two 32×32-bit keyed substitution boxes that are applied simultaneously to the internal state.

- MS: A diffusion layer consisting of a byte-wise linear transform defined by the matrix

$$MDS_H = \begin{pmatrix} 1 & 0 & 1 & 0 & 1 & 1 & 1 & 0 \\ 1 & 1 & 0 & 1 & 1 & 1 & 1 & 1 \\ 1 & 1 & 1 & 0 & 0 & 1 & 1 & 1 \\ 0 & 1 & 0 & 1 & 1 & 1 & 0 & 1 \\ 1 & 1 & 0 & 1 & 0 & 1 & 0 & 1 \\ 1 & 1 & 1 & 0 & 1 & 0 & 1 & 0 \\ 1 & 1 & 1 & 1 & 1 & 1 & 0 & 1 \\ 1 & 0 & 1 & 0 & 1 & 0 & 1 & 1 \end{pmatrix}.$$

The lower SPN level, i.e., the two 32×32-bit XS-boxes, as shown in Figure 1, comprises of:

- SB: A nonlinear byte bijective mapping layer which applies the same 8×8-bit S-box 8 times in parallel.
- MC: A diffusion layer consisting of a byte-wise linear transform defined by a 4×4 matrix called mds_l which is a Maximum Distance Separable (MDS) matrix [21,25].
- AK: The 64-bit layer key is divided into halves and each half is mixed with the 32-bit internal state of one XS box.
- SB: Another nonlinear byte bijective mapping layer which applies the same 8×8-bit S-box 8 times in parallel.

Each round of HC-L1 includes two S-box layers. The last round of HC-L1 is an output transformation where the MS linear transformation is substituted by an xor layer with a layer key. The full encryption function of HC-L1 where the ciphertext C is computed from the plaintext P is given by:

$$C = AK[K_1^{(7)}] \circ ((SB \circ AK[K_2^{(6)}] \circ MC \circ SB) \circ AK[K_1^{(6)}])$$
$$\circ \cdots \circ (MS \circ (SB \circ AK[K_2^{(1)}] \circ MC \circ SB) \circ AK[K_1^{(1)}])(P)$$

To facilitate the understanding of our attacks, we represent the internal state of HC-L1 as a 4×2 matrix, as depicted in Figure 2, where each 8-bit word in the ith row and the jth column of this matrix represent a state byte. Consequently, MC, similar to the MixColumns operation in AES, operates column-wise and MS affects the entire matrix. Moreover, we exploit the fact that both the linear transformations (MC, MS), and the key addition AK are linear and swap their order. In such case, the input data is first xored with an equivalent layer key, denoted by EK_i, and then the linear transformation is applied. The equivalent layer key at any given S-box layer i is evaluated by $EK_i = MC^{-1}(K_i)$ when i is odd and $EK_i = MS^{-1}(K_i)$ when i is even. In addition, we use the following property of the S-box:

Proposition 1 (Differential Property of S). *Given Δ_i and Δ_o two non-zero differences in $\mathbb{F}_{256}$, the equation: $S(x) + S(x + \Delta_i) = \Delta_o$ has one solution on average. This property also applies to S^{-1}.*

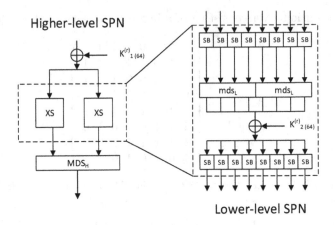

Fig. 1. One round of Hierocrypt-L1

Key Schedule. The input to the key schedule is the 128-bit master key and the output is 13 64-bit layer keys (1 key per S-box layer in addition to the final key). The master key initializes the first key state denoted by $V_{1(32)}^{(-1)} \| V_{2(32)}^{(-1)} \| V_{3(32)}^{(-1)} \| V_{4(32)}^{(-1)}$ which then undergoes 8 rounds relying on a Feistel construction and linear transformations to generate the layer keys where the first round is a bit special as it omits a linear function and does not produce any layer keys. Then, depending on the employed function, the other rounds form two groups, which we mark as 'type A' and 'type B'. The two 32-bit key state words $V_{3(32)}$ and $V_{4(32)}$ are updated linearly in each round, while the other two 32-bit key state words $V_{1(32)}$ and $V_{2(32)}$ are updated using a Feistel construction with additional input from $V_{3(32)}$ and $V_{4(32)}$. Specifically, as shown in Figure 3, one round of 'type A' of the key schedule can be described by:

$$(V_{3(32)}^{(r)}, V_{4(32)}^{(r)}) \leftarrow L(V_{3(32)}^{(r-1)}, V_{4(32)}^{(r-1)});$$
$$V_{1(32)}^{(r)} \leftarrow V_{2(32)}^{(r-1)};$$
$$V_{2(32)}^{(r)} \leftarrow V_{1(32)}^{(r-1)}; \oplus F_\sigma(V_{2(32)}^{(r-1)} \oplus V_{3(32)}^{(r)}), \quad r = 0, 1, \cdots, 7$$

where L is a linear function and the function F_σ is a level of S-boxes succeeded by another linear transformation. Then, the 64-bit layer keys $K_{1(64)}^{(r)}$ $(k_{1(32)}^{(r)} \| k_{2(32)}^{(r)})$ and $K_{2(64)}^{(r)}$ $(k_{3(32)}^{(r)} \| k_{4(32)}^{(r)})$ are generated in every round of 'type A' as follows:

$$k_{1(32)}^{(r)} \leftarrow V_{1(32)}^{(r-1)} \oplus F_\sigma(V_{2(32)}^{(r-1)} \oplus V_{3(32)}^{(r)});$$
$$k_{2(32)}^{(r)} \leftarrow V_{3(32)}^{(r)} \oplus F_\sigma(V_{2(32)}^{(r-1)} \oplus V_{3(32)}^{(r)});$$
$$k_{3(32)}^{(r)} \leftarrow V_{4(32)}^{(r)} \oplus F_\sigma(V_{2(32)}^{(r-1)} \oplus V_{3(32)}^{(r)});$$
$$k_{4(32)}^{(r)} \leftarrow V_{4(32)}^{(r)} \oplus V_{2(32)}^{(r-1)}, \quad\quad\quad\quad r = 0, 1, \cdots, 7$$

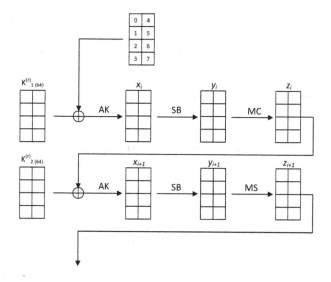

Fig. 2. Alternative representation of one round of Hierocrypt-L1

The round function of 'type B' is almost equivalent to the inversion of the 'type A' round function but the linear function that operates on $V_{3(32)}$ and $V_{4(32)}$ is different. It is to be noted that in our attacks, we number the layer keys sequentially from K_1 up to K_{13} where $K_i = K_{1(64)}^{\lceil i/2 \rceil}$ when i is odd and $K_i = K_{2(64)}^{\lceil i/2 \rceil}$ when i is even.

For further details regarding the S-box, the linear transformations or the key schedule, the reader is referred to [29].

The following notations are used throughout the paper:

- x_i: The internal state at the input of layer i
- y_i: The internal state after the SB of layer i.

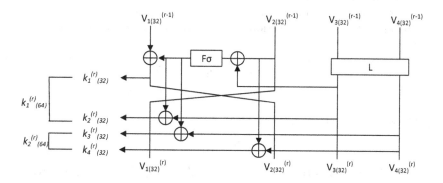

Fig. 3. 1 Round of Hierocrypt-L1 key schedule

- z_i: The internal state after the MC (resp. MS) of layer i when i is odd (resp. even).
- z_i': The internal state after the AK of layer i with an equivalent key EK_i.
- $x_i[j]$: The jth byte of the state x_i, where $j = 0, 1, \cdots, 7$, and the bytes are indexed as described in Figure 2.
- $x_i[j \cdots k]$: The bytes between the jth position and k^{th} position of the state x_i.
- $\Delta x_i, \Delta x_i[j]$: The difference at state x_i and byte $x_i[j]$, respectively.
- $X_{(n)}$: An n-bit word X. Such notation is specifically used in describing the key schedule.

The memory and time complexities of our attack are measured as 64-bit HC-L1 blocks and round-reduced HC-L1 encryptions, respectively.

3   A Differential Enumeration MitM Attack on HC-L1

Generally, in a MitM attack, a round reduced block cipher E_K is split into 3 successive parts, such that $E_K = E_{K_2}^2 \circ E_m \circ E_{K_1}^1$, where E_m exhibits a distinguishing property. The exploited property is used to identify the correct key by checking whether each guess of subkey (K_1, K_2) yields the property or not. In our attacks, we use a truncated differential characteristic as the distinguishing property, such that its input is a δ-set [11] captured by Definition 1. While in most of the published MitM attacks the matching is performed around a specific byte or word, adopting such approach on HC-L1 requires a time complexity that exceeds that of the exhaustive search. Therefore, as explained in details below, we opt for matching on a single equation that relates two input bytes of the linear transformation MS with two bytes at its output.

Definition 1 (δ-set of HC-L1). *Let a δ-set be a set of 256 HC-L1 states that are all different in one state byte (the active byte) and all equal in the other state bytes (the inactive bytes).*

In our MitM attack, we use the 5 S-box layers distinguisher embedded in the truncated differential characteristic, illustrated in Figure 4. It starts at x_2 and ends at the input of the linear transformation MS of layer 6, i.e., z_6'. We exploit the simplicity of the MS operation by observing the below equations of two of its output bytes:

$$z_i[0] = y_i[0] \oplus y_i[2] \oplus y_i[4] \oplus y_i[5] \oplus y_i[6] \tag{1}$$

$$z_i[7] = y_i[0] \oplus y_i[2] \oplus y_i[4] \oplus y_i[6] \oplus y_i[7] \tag{2}$$

Therefore, from (1) and (2), we have

$$z_i[0] \oplus z_i[7] = y_i[5] \oplus y_i[7] \tag{3}$$

Consequently, it follows that $x_7[0] \oplus x_7[7] = z_6'[5] \oplus z_6'[7]$ (see Figure 4) which is the single equation upon which the matching is performed as will be explained in the attack procedure. Proposition 2, below, is the core of our attack.

Proposition 2. *If a message m belongs to a pair of states conforming to the truncated differential characteristic of Figure 4, then the ordered sequence of differences $\Delta z_6'[5] \oplus \Delta z_6'[7]$ obtained from the δ-set constructed from m in $x_2[3]$ is fully determined by the following 14 bytes: $x_2[3], \Delta x_2[3], x_3[1,3,4,6], y_5[4\cdots7], \Delta y_6[5], \Delta y_6[7], y_6[5]$ and $y_6[7]$.*

Proof. The proof is based on rebound-like arguments adopted from the cryptanalysis of hash functions [22] and used in [13]. Assuming that (m, m') is a pair that follows the truncated differential characteristic in Figure 4. In the sequel, we manifest that knowing these specific 14 bytes is sufficient to compute the ordered sequence of differences $\Delta z_6'[5] \oplus \Delta z_6'[7]$. To conform to the differential characteristic in Figure 4, the 14 bytes $x_2[3], \Delta x_2[3], x_3[1,3,4,6], y_5[4\cdots7], \Delta y_6[5], \Delta y_6[7], y_6[5]$ and $y_6[7]$ can take as many as $2^{8\times13} = 2^{104}$ possible values only. This is because $\Delta y_6[5]$ must equal $\Delta y_6[7]$ in order to result in a difference in just $x_7[0,7]$. Then for each of these 2^{104} values, we can determine all the differences shown in Figure 4.

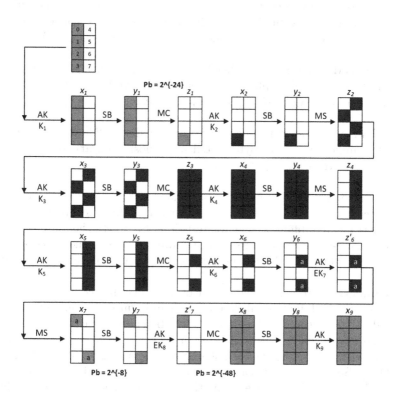

Fig. 4. The differential characteristic used in the MitM attack on HC-L1 using differential enumeration. Offline bytes are colored in black while online bytes are colored in gray.

- The value $x_2[3]$ with the difference $\Delta x_2[3]$ enable us to bypass the S-box of layer 2 and then propagate the difference linearly through MS to compute $\Delta x_3[1, 3, 4, 6]$.
- By knowing $x_3[1, 3, 4, 6]$, we can bypass the S-box of layer 3 to reach y_3, then linearly through MC to compute $\Delta x_4[0 \cdots 7]$.
- Similarly in the other direction, the differences $\Delta y_6[5]$ and $\Delta y_6[7]$ with the values $y_6[5]$ and $y_6[7]$ enable us to bypass the S-box of layer 6 and compute the difference $\Delta z_5[5, 7]$, then linearly through MC^{-1} we compute $\Delta y_5[4 \cdots 7]$.
- By knowing $y_5[4 \cdots 7]$, we bypass the S-box of layer 5 to compute $\Delta z_4[4 \cdots 7]$ and then linearly through MS^{-1} we can compute $\Delta y_4[0 \cdots 7]$.
- Now, we have the differences $\Delta x_4[0 \cdots 7]$ and $\Delta y_4[0 \cdots 7]$. Hence, by the differential property of the HC-L1 S-box (Proposition 1), there is, on average, one solution for each of the 8 bytes of x_4.

To build the ordered sequence for each of the 2^{104} possible values of the 14 bytes from proposition 1, we consider all the $2^8 - 1$ possible values for the difference $\Delta x_2[3]$ and propagate them until z_6' with the help of the internal state solutions we have. This creates an ordered sequence of $2^8 - 1$ differences in $\Delta z_6'[5, 7]$.

Attack Procedure. Similar to other MitM attacks, our attack has 2 phases; an offline phase and an online phase that result in recovering the 64-bit last layer key K_9, 2 bytes of $EK_8 = MC^{-1}(K_8)$ and 4 bytes of K_1.

Offline Phase. In the offline phase, we compute all the 2^{104} values of $\Delta z_6'[5] \oplus \Delta z_6'[7]$ determined by the 14 bytes listed in proposition 1 and store them in a precomputation table T.

Online Phase. The online phase can be divided into two stages; data collection and key recovery. The data collection stage aims at finding pairs of messages that follow the truncated differential characteristic in Figure 4. Then, for each of the found pairs, a δ-set is created, its corresponding ordered sequence is computed and tested for a match in T to identify the correct key in the key recovery stage.

Data Collection. To generate one pair of messages that conforms to the 8 S-box layers truncated differential characteristic in Figure 4, the encryption oracle is queried with structures of chosen plaintexts. In a given structure, bytes $[0 \cdots 3]$ take all the 2^{32} possible values while the other 4 bytes are fixed to some, possibly different, constants and hence, each structure generates $2^{32} \times (2^{32} - 1)/2 \approx 2^{63}$ pairs. Our 8 S-box layers truncated differential characteristic has a probability of $2^{-3 \times 3 \times 8 - 1 \times 8} = 2^{-80}$ because of the three $4 \to 1$ transitions over MC in addition to the probability that $\Delta x_7[0]$ equals $\Delta x_7[7]$, marked as a in Figure 4. Consequently, in order to find one pair that follows our chosen 2^{-80} probability truncated differential characteristic, 2^{80} pairs are needed which is equivalent to 2^{80-63}, i.e., 2^{17} structures of 2^{32} messages, each. Briefly, $2^{17+32} = 2^{49}$ messages are sent to the encryption oracle to generate the required 2^{80} pairs. It is to be noted that the distinguisher was chosen to start at $x_2[3]$ because this specific byte results into just 4 differences, i.e., $z_2[1, 3, 4, 6]$ after the application of the MS transformation (cf. 4th column of MDS_H).

Key Recovery. The key bytes: $K_9[0 \cdots 7]$, $EK_8[0, 7]$ and $K_1[0 \cdots 3]$ can take $2^{(2+1+1) \times 8} = 2^{32}$ possible values for each of the 2^{80} pairs. This is justified as follows:

- The difference $\Delta y_7[0, 7]$ is guessed and propagated linearly through MC to compute $\Delta x_8[0 \cdots 7]$.
- The difference $\Delta y_8[0 \cdots 7]$ is equal to the difference $\Delta x_9[0 \cdots 7]$ which, in turn, is the difference in the ciphertext pair.
- As we have the difference $\Delta x_8[0 \cdots 7]$ and $\Delta y_8[0 \cdots 7]$, the differential property of the S-box is used to deduce a solution for each byte of x_8 and y_8 which yields 2^{16} key candidates for the whole K_9 by simply xoring y_8 with the ciphertext.
- Then, $x_8[0 \cdots 7]$ is propagated linearly through MC^{-1} to deduce $z'_7[0 \cdots 7]$.
- Afterwards, the difference $\Delta y_6[5, 7]$ which, as explained before, assumes 2^8 values only is guessed and propagated through MS to get the difference $\Delta x_7[0, 7]$.
- As we have $\Delta x_7[0, 7]$ and $\Delta y_7[0, 7]$ were already guessed in the first step above, the differential property of the S-box is used to deduce a solution for $y_7[0, 7]$ which with $z'_7[0 \cdots 7]$, computed above, enables us to deduce 2^8 candidates for $EK_8[0, 7]$.
- Next, the difference $\Delta x_2[3]$ is guessed and propagated linearly through MC^{-1} to compute $\Delta y_1[0 \cdots 3]$.
- The difference $\Delta x_1[0 \cdots 3]$ is actually the difference in the plaintext pair. Therefore, knowing the differences $\Delta x_1[0 \cdots 3]$ and $\Delta y_1[0 \cdots 3]$ enables us to deduce 2^8 candidates for $K_1[0 \cdots 3]$ using the differential property of the S-box.

All in all, guessing 4 bytes helps deduce 14 key bytes. In other words, these 14 key bytes have just 2^{32} possible values for each of the 2^{80} pairs. Then, in order to recover the key, we enumerate each of the 2^{80} candidate pairs we obtained in the data collection stage and deduce the corresponding 2^{32} possible key suggestions. Next, we build the plaintext δ-set and compute its corresponding ordered sequence of $\Delta x_7[0] \oplus \Delta x_7[7]$ and look for a match in T and if no match is found, this key suggestion is discarded.

A valid ordered sequence can be generated by a wrong key with a negligible probability, $2^{80+32+104-255 \times 8} = 2^{-1824}$, which can be relaxed. Therefore, we use the partial sequence matching idea proposed in [4]. Instead of matching $2^8 - 1$ bytes ordered sequence, we match b bytes such that $b < 2^8$ and the probability of error, chosen to be 2^{-32}, is still small enough to be able to identity the right key. In that case, the number of required bytes b is calculated by $2^{-32} = 2^{80+32+104-8b}$ which yields $b = 31$. Therefore, it is enough to match 31 bytes of the ordered sequence to identify the right key with a negligible error probability of 2^{-32}.

So far, we have recovered 14 key bytes; the 8-byte K_9, 2 bytes of EK_8 and 4 bytes of K_1. To recover the master key, 6 bytes of EK_8 are guessed to get 2^{48} suggestions for K_8, which, using the key schedule notations, means that there are 2^{48} candidates for the keys $k_{3(32)}^{(4)}, k_{4(32)}^{(4)}$. Along with K_9 or rather $k_{1(32)}^{(5)}$ and $k_{2(32)}^{(5)}$, these keys are computed as follows:

$$k_{3(32)}^{(4)} = V_{4(32)}^{(4)} \oplus F_\sigma(V_{2(32)}^{(3)} \oplus V_{3(32)}^{(4)}) \tag{4}$$

$$k_{4(32)}^{(4)} = V_{4(32)}^{(4)} \oplus V_{2(32)}^{(3)} \tag{5}$$

$$k_{1(32)}^{(5)} = V_{1(32)}^{(4)} \oplus F_\sigma(V_{2(32)}^{(4)} \oplus V_{3(32)}^{(5)}) \tag{6}$$

$$k_{2(32)}^{(5)} = V_{3(32)}^{(5)} \oplus F_\sigma(V_{2(32)}^{(4)} \oplus V_{3(32)}^{(5)}) \tag{7}$$

Then, the 32-bit $V_{2(32)}^{(3)}$ is guessed and $V_{4(32)}^{(4)}$ is computed from equation (5) and, in turn, $V_{3(32)}^{(4)}$ is deduced from equation (4). According to the key schedule, the knowledge of $V_{3(32)}^{(4)}$ and $V_{4(32)}^{(4)}$ results in knowing $V_{3(32)}^{(5)}$ and $V_{4(32)}^{(5)}$. Next, since $V_{1(32)}^{(4)} = V_{2(32)}^{(3)}$, $V_{2(32)}^{(4)}$ is computed from equation (6) and then equation (7) is used as a 2^{-32} filter to get one solution for $V_{2(32)}^{(3)}, V_{1(32)}^{(4)}, V_{2(32)}^{(4)}, V_{3(32)}^{(4)}$, $V_{4(32)}^{(4)}, V_{3(32)}^{(5)}$ and $V_{4(32)}^{(5)}$. As we recover one full intermediate state of the key schedule and its round is bijective, we can recover the master key and get 2^{48} candidates for the master key corresponding to the 2^{48} K_8 suggestions. The correct master key is found by exhaustively searching through these 2^{48} candidates using 2 plaintext/ciphertext pairs with no significant impact on the attack overall time complexity.

Attack Complexity. The size of the precomputation table T created in the offline phase determines the memory requirement of the attack. T contains 2^{104} ordered sequences, each of $8 \times 31 = 248$ bits by using the partial sequence matching technique. Therefore, the memory complexity of the attack is $2^{104} \times 248/64 \approx 2^{106}$ 64-bit blocks. The data collection stage of the online phase sets the data complexity of the attack to 2^{49} chosen plaintexts. The offline phase time complexity to build T is attributed to executing 2^{104} partial encryptions on 32 messages, which is equivalent to $2^{104+5} \times 11/(8 \times 8) = 2^{106.46}$ encryptions. The online phase time complexity to recover 14 key bytes is determined by the time needed to partially decrypt the 2^5 values in a δ-set with all the 2^{32} key suggestions for all the 2^{80} generated pairs which is equivalent to $2^{80+32+5} \times (4 + 10)/(8 \times 8) = 2^{114.8}$. Finding the correct master key among the 2^{48} candidates using 2 plaintext/ciphertext pairs requires $2 \times 2^{48} = 2^{49}$ encryptions. Therefore, the time complexity of the attack is equivalent to $2^{114.8} + 2^{106.46} + 2^{49} \approx 2^{114.8}$.

4   Conclusion

In this paper, we have analyzed one of the Japanese e-Government 2013 candidate recommended block ciphers; Hierocrypt-L1 using the meet-in-the-middle (MitM) attack in the single-key setting. Our attack employs the differential enumeration technique and is launched against 8 S-box layers using a 5 S-box layers distinguisher. The attack recovers the master key with data complexity of 2^{49} chosen plaintexts, time complexity of $2^{114.8}$ 8 S-box layers Hierocrypt-L1 encryptions and memory complexity of 2^{106} 64-bit blocks. To the best of our knowledge, this is the first attack on Hierocrypt-L1 in the single-key setting that reaches 8 S-box layers.

References

1. Abdelkhalek, A., AlTawy, R., Tolba, M., Youssef, A.M.: Meet-in-the-Middle Attacks on Reduced-Round Hierocrypt-3. In: Lauter, K., Rodríguez-Henríquez, F. (eds.) LatinCrypt 2015. LNCS, vol. 9230, pp. 187–203. Springer, Heidelberg (2015)
2. AlTawy, R., Youssef, A.M.: Differential Sieving for 2-step matching meet-in-the-middle attack with application to LBlock. In: Eisenbarth, T., Öztürk, E. (eds.) LightSec 2014. LNCS, vol. 8898, pp. 126–139. Springer, Heidelberg (2015)
3. AlTawy, R., Youssef, A.M.: Preimage Attacks on Reduced-Round Stribog. In: Pointcheval, D., Vergnaud, D. (eds.) AFRICACRYPT. LNCS, vol. 8469, pp. 109–125. Springer, Heidelberg (2014)
4. AlTawy, R., Youssef, A.M.: Meet in the Middle Attacks on Reduced Round Kuznyechik. Cryptology ePrint Archive, Report 2015/096 (2015), http://eprint.iacr.org/
5. Barreto, P.L.M., Rijmen, V., Jr. Nakahara, J., Bart, P., Joos, V., Kim, H.Y.: Improved Square Attacks against Reduced-Round Hierocrypt. In: Matsui, M. (ed.) FSE 2001. LNCS, vol. 2355, pp. 165–173. Springer, Heidelberg (2002)
6. Biryukov, A., Derbez, P., Perrin, L.P.: Differential Analysis and Meet-in-the-Middle Attack against Round-Reduced TWINE. Fast Software Encryption (2015) (to appear)
7. Bogdanov, A., Rechberger, C.: A 3-Subset Meet-in-the-Middle Attack: Cryptanalysis of the Lightweight Block Cipher KTANTAN. In: Biryukov, A., Gong, G., Stinson, D.R. (eds.) SAC 2010. LNCS, vol. 6544, pp. 229–240. Springer, Heidelberg (2011)
8. CRYPTEC. e-Government Candidate Recommended Ciphers List (2013). http://www.cryptrec.go.jp/english/method.html.
9. CRYPTEC. e-Government Recommended Ciphers List (2003). http://www.cryptrec.go.jp/english/images/cryptrec_01en.pdf
10. CRYPTEC. Specification on a Block Cipher: Hierocrypt-L1. http://www.cryptrec.go.jp/cryptrec_03_spec_cypherlist_files/PDF/04_02espec.pdf
11. Daemen, J., Knudsen, L.R., Rijmen, V.: The block cipher SQUARE. In: Biham, E. (ed.) FSE 1997. LNCS, vol. 1267, pp. 149–165. Springer, Heidelberg (1997)
12. Demirci, H., Selçuk, A.A.: A meet-in-the-middle attack on 8-round AES. In: Nyberg, K. (ed.) FSE 2008. LNCS, vol. 5086, pp. 116–126. Springer, Heidelberg (2008)

13. Derbez, P., Fouque, P.-A.: Improved Key Recovery Attacks on Reduced-Round AES in the Single-Key Setting. In: Johansson, T., Nguyen, P. (eds.) Advances in Cryptology EUROCRYPT 2013. LNCS, vol. 7881, pp. 371–387. Springer, Heidelberg (2013)
14. Dunkelman, O., Keller, N., Shamir, A.: Improved Single-Key Attacks on 8-Round AES-192 and AES-256. In: Abe, M. (ed.) ASIACRYPT 2010. LNCS, vol. 6477, pp. 158–176. Springer, Heidelberg (2010)
15. Dunkelman, O., Sekar, G., Preneel, B.: Improved meet-in-the-middle attacks on reduced-round DES. In: Srinathan, K., Rangan, C.P., Yung, M. (eds.) INDOCRYPT 2007. LNCS, vol. 4859, pp. 86–100. Springer, Heidelberg (2007)
16. Hao, Y., Bai, D., Li, L.: A Meet-in-the-Middle Attack on Round-Reduced mCrypton Using the Differential Enumeration Technique. In: Au, M.H., Carminati, B., Kuo, C.-C.J. (eds.) NSS 2014. LNCS, vol. 8792, pp. 166–183. Springer, Heidelberg (2014)
17. Hong, D., Koo, B., Sasaki, Y.: Improved Preimage Attack for 68-Step HAS-160. In: Lee, D., Hong, S. (eds.) Information, Security and Cryptology ICISC 2009. LNCS, vol. 5984, pp. 332–348. Springer, Heidelberg (2010)
18. Howgrave-Graham, N.: A Hybrid Lattice-Reduction and Meet-in-the-Middle Attack Against NTRU. In: Menezes, A. (ed.) CRYPTO 2007. LNCS, vol. 4622, pp. 150–169. Springer, Heidelberg (2007)
19. Ohkuma, K., Sano, F., Muratani, H., Motoyama, M., Kawamura, S.: On security of block ciphers Hierocrypt-3 and Hierocrypt-L1. In: The 2001 Symposium on Cryptography and Information Security (SCIS 2001), 11A-4 (January 2001)
20. Li, L., Jia, K., Wang, X.: Improved Meet-in-the-Middle Attacks on AES-192 and PRINCE. Cryptology ePrint Archive, Report 2013/573 (2013). http://eprint.iacr.org/
21. MacWilliams, F.J., Sloane, N.J.A.: The theory of error correcting codes, vol. 16. Elsevier (1977)
22. Mendel, F., Rechberger, C.: The Rebound Attack: Cryptanalysis of Reduced Whirlpool and Grøstl. In: Dunkelman, O. (ed.) Fast Software Encryption. LNCS, vol. 5665, pp. 260–276. Springer, Heidelberg (2009)
23. New European Schemes for Signatures, Integrity, and Encryption. https://www.cosic.esat.kuleuven.be/nessie.
24. Ohkuma, K., Muratani, H., Sano, F., Kawamura, S.: The Block Cipher Hierocrypt. In: Stinson, D.R., Tavares, S. (eds.) SAC 2000. LNCS, vol. 2012, pp. 72–88. Springer, Heidelberg (2001)
25. Rijmen, V.: Cryptanalysis and design of iterated block ciphers. PhD thesis, Doctoral Dissertation, October 1997, KU Leuven (1997)
26. Sasaki, Y., Wang, L., Wu, S., Wu, W.: Investigating fundamental security requirements on whirlpool: Improved preimage and collision attacks. In: Wang, X., Sako, K. (eds.) ASIACRYPT 2012. LNCS, vol. 7658, pp. 562–579. Springer, Heidelberg (2012)
27. Sekar, G., Mouha, N., Velichkov, V., Preneel, B.: Meet-in-the-Middle Attacks on Reduced-Round XTEA. In: Kiayias, A. (ed.) Topics in Cryptology CT-RSA 2011. LNCS, vol. 6558, pp. 250–267. Springer, Heidelberg (2011)
28. Taga, B., Moriai, S., Aoki, K.: Differential and Impossible Differential Related-Key Attacks on Hierocrypt-L1. In: Susilo, W., Mu, Y. (eds.) ACISP 2014. LNCS, vol. 8544, pp. 17–33. Springer, Heidelberg (2014)
29. Toshiba Corporation. Block Cipher Family Hierocrypt. http://www.toshiba.co.jp/rdc/security/hierocrypt/index.htm

S-boxes, Boolean Functions and Codes for the Resistance of Block Ciphers to Cryptographic Attacks, with or without Side Channels

Claude Carlet

LAGA, Universities of Paris 8 and Paris 13; CNRS, UMR 7539;
Department of Mathematics,University of Paris 8, 2 rue de la liberté,
93526 Saint-Denis cedex 02, France
claude.carlet@univ-paris8.fr

Abstract. The choice of functions $S : \mathbb{F}_2^n \mapsto \mathbb{F}_2^m$ to be used as substitution boxes (S-boxes), fastly implementable and contributing to resisting attacks is a crucial question for the design of block ciphers. We summary the state of the art in this domain, considering also the case $m < n$ which has been less studied. We also recall the method for protecting block ciphers against side channel attacks (SCA) by masking, and how the S-boxes can be processed in order to ensure this protection. We state a related open problem, also interesting for its own sake. We eventually see how Boolean functions, vectorial functions and error correcting codes can be used in different ways for reducing the cost of masking while keeping the same resistance to some SCA and also for allowing resisting fault injection attacks (FIA).

1 Introduction

If a block cipher has linear (or affine) relationship between its input (the plaintext) and its output (the cipher text), algorithms from linear algebra are able to recover the unknown key bits in polynomial time. Substitution boxes (S-boxes) are often included in the design of block ciphers to provide nonlinear relationship between the input bits and the output bits, ensuring what Shannon called confusion [69]. These S-boxes are functions from $\mathbb{F}_2^n$ to $\mathbb{F}_2^m$ (called (n, m)-functions). They were used in the DES [59], and are used in most modern block ciphers such as AES [36], Serpent [4], PRESENT [10], CLEFIA [70], CAMELLIA [3], MISTY [57], KASUMI [41], CAST [1], KN [61]. S-boxes in block ciphers with the Substitution-Permutation-Network (SPN) structure must be bijective (with $n = m$, then). Those used in the Feistel structure can be defined with $m < n$ or even $m > n$ but are better balanced (an (n, m)-function F is *balanced* if it takes every value of $\mathbb{F}_2^m$ the same number 2^{n-m} of times, which needs $m \leqslant n$), since a cipher with unbalanced S-boxes needs heavier diffusion layers, see [63].

Even when the relationship between the input bits and the output bits is nonlinear, the block cipher may be weak against more sophisticated attacks: the differential and linear attacks [8,56], other versions of these attacks such as truncated differential cryptanalysis, impossible differential cryptanalysis, boomerang

© Springer International Publishing Switzerland 2015
R.S. Chakraborty et al. (Eds.): SPACE 2015, LNCS 9354, pp. 151–171, 2015.
DOI: 10.1007/978-3-319-24126-5_10

attack, multidimensional linear attacks (see [48]), and the higher order differential attack [47]. Nyberg has introduced in [60] criteria to measure the resistance of block ciphers against such attacks: the S-boxes must have high nonlinearity and low differential uniformity to resist linear and differential attacks, respectively, provided that other components of the block cipher contribute to a good diffusion. The S-boxes in these block ciphers would also better have an algebraic degree larger than 2 (and even than 3, since cryptographers like to have a security margin) to avoid the higher order differential attack, within a trade-off between robustness and efficiency. Summarizing, the design criteria for S-boxes in block ciphers are:

1. bijectivity when used in SPN, and if possible balancedness when used in Feistel ciphers,
2. high nonlinearity (for the resistance to linear attacks),
3. low differential uniformity (for the resistance to differential attacks),
4. not too low algebraic degree (for the resistance to higher order differential attacks).

Satisfying the criteria 1-4 above is not sufficient for an S-box. It needs also to be fastly computable, since it is not always possible to use a look-up-table for implementing it; this depends on the device.

The set of (n, m)-functions is denoted by $\mathcal{B}_{n,m}$. Such function F being given, the Boolean functions $f_1, \ldots, f_m$ defined by $F(x) = (f_1(x), \ldots, f_m(x))$ at every $x \in \mathbb{F}_2^n$ are called the *coordinate functions* of F. When the numbers m and n are not specified, (n, m)-functions are called *multi-output Boolean functions*, *vectorial Boolean functions* or *S-boxes*. There exist several possible representations of (n, m)-functions [19] allowing to represent them with uniqueness:

- a multivariate representation called the *algebraic normal form* (ANF):

$$F(x) = \sum_{I \subseteq \{1, 2, \ldots, n\}} a_I \left(\prod_{i \in I} x_i \right) \quad \text{where} \quad a_I \in \mathbb{F}_2^m,$$

  (this sum being calculated in $\mathbb{F}_2^m$, in characteristic 2)
- a univariate representation: $\mathbb{F}_2^n$ being endowed with the structure of the finite field $\mathbb{F}_{2^n}$, (n, m)-functions where m divides n are viewed as mapping elements of the finite field $\mathbb{F}_{2^n}$ to itself and are represented in the form $F(x) = \sum_{i=0}^{2^n-1} a_i x^i$, $a_i \in \mathbb{F}_{2^n}$. The coefficients can be obtained by applying Lagrange's interpolation. When m does not divide n, the m-bit outputs of F can be embedded into $\mathbb{F}_2^{m'}$ where $m' \geqslant m$ divides n, by padding. This ensures that any function $h \in \mathcal{B}_{n,m}$ can be evaluated as a polynomial over $\mathbb{F}_{2^n}$. If padding has been used, then it can be removed after the polynomial evaluation by mapping the output from $\mathbb{F}_{2^n}$ to $\mathbb{F}_2^n$.
- Representations hybrid between these two ones; for instance, when n is even, an $(n, n/2)$-function can be viewed as a bivariate polynomial over $\mathbb{F}_{2^{n/2}}$, and for every n, an $(n, n-1)$-function can be viewed as mapping elements of $\mathbb{F}_{2^{n-1}} \times \mathbb{F}_2$ to $\mathbb{F}_{2^{n-1}}$.

In multivariate representation, the *algebraic degree* $d°(F) = \max\{|I|; a_I \neq 0\}$ (the global degree of the ANF) equals the maximum algebraic degree of the coordinate Boolean functions, and also equals the maximum algebraic degree of their linear combinations with non-all zero coefficients, called the *component functions* of F. A function is called *affine* (respectively *quadratic, cubic*) if it has an algebraic degree equal to 1 (respectively 2, 3). In univariate representation, it can be shown, see e.g. [19], that the algebraic degree equals the maximum Hamming weight $HW(i)$ of those (binary expansions of) exponents with nonzero coefficients a_i. The algebraic degree must then not be confused with the classical notion of polynomial degree which is the integer value $\max_{a_i \neq 0}(i)$. The algebraic degree plays an important role in counter-measures to side channel attacks, as well as the notion of higher-order derivative (see Section 3). For any positive integer t and any t-tuple $(a_1, a_2, \ldots, a_t) \in (\mathbb{F}_2^n)^t$, the (n, m)-function $D_{a_1, a_2, \ldots, a_t} F$ which maps any $x \in \mathbb{F}_{2^n}$ to $\sum_{I \subseteq [\![1, t]\!]} F\left(x + \sum_{i \in I} a_i\right)$ is called the tth-*order derivative* of F with respect to $(a_1, a_2, \ldots, a_t)$. Any t^{th}-order derivative of a function of algebraic degree s has an algebraic degree bounded above by $s - t$. We denote by $\varphi_F^{(t)}$ the function:

$$\varphi_F^{(t)} : (a_1, a_2, \ldots, a_t) \mapsto D_{a_1, a_2, \ldots, a_t} F(0) \, . \tag{1}$$

If F has algebraic degree s, then $\varphi_F^{(t)}$ is s-linear symmetric and equals zero for any family of a_i linearly dependent over $\mathbb{F}_2$. Conversely, if $\varphi_F^{(s)}$ is s-linear, then the algebraic degree of F is at most s.

The *Hamming distance* between two (n, m)-functions F and G is the size of the set $\{x \in \mathbb{F}_2^n | F(x) \neq G(x)\}$. The *nonlinearity*, which is the parameter quantifying the resistance of the S-box to the linear attack, equals the minimum Hamming distance between the component functions of the S-box and all affine functions. The larger the nonlinearity, the better the resistance to this attack.

The *differential uniformity*, which is the parameter quantifying the resistance of the S-box to the differential attack, equals the maximum number of solutions $x \in \mathbb{F}_2^n$ of the equations $F(x + a) + F(x) = b$ where $a \in \mathbb{F}_2^n$, $a \neq 0$, and $b \in \mathbb{F}_2^m$. This number is even since if x is a solution then $x + a$ is also a solution. We denote it by δ_F. Given an integer δ, the function is called *differentially δ-uniform* if $\delta_F \leqslant \delta$. The smaller the differential uniformity, the better the resistance to differential attacks. Nyberg [60] observed that $\delta_F \geqslant 2^{n-m}$ if $n > m$ and $\delta_F \geqslant 2$ if $n \geqslant m$. Moreover, she proved that $\delta_F = 2^{n-m}$ (that is, all first-order derivatives $D_a F(x) = F(x) + F(x + a)$, $a \in \mathbb{F}_2^{n*}$, that we shall simply call *derivatives*, are balanced) if and only if F has the optimal nonlinearity $2^{n-1} - 2^{n/2-1}$. In this case, F is called *bent* or *perfect nonlinear* (PN). Bent (n, m)-functions exist if and only if n is even and $m \leqslant \frac{n}{2}$ [60].

The (n, n)-functions which contribute to optimal resistance to differential attacks, that is, differentially 2-uniform functions, are called *almost perfect nonlinear* (APN). All their derivatives $D_a F$, $a \in \mathbb{F}_2^{n*}$, are 2-to-1 (every element of $\mathbb{F}_2^n$ has 0 or 2 pre-images by $D_a F$).

The implementation of cryptographic algorithms in devices like smart cards, FPGA or ASIC leaks information on the secret data, leading to very powerful side channel attacks (SCA) if countermeasures are not included. The most commonly used counter-measure is *masking*. Counter-measures are costly in terms of running time and of memory when they need to resist higher order SCA.

In this paper, we first recall in Section 2 what are the known S-boxes achieving high nonlinearity and low differential uniformity. We then recall in Section 3 the principle of side channel attacks and of the counter-measure of masking. We describe the known methods for evaluating and masking S-boxes. Eventually in Section 4, we recall methods using vectorial or Boolean functions and codes for making the masking less costly, while keeping the same resistance to the most efficient side channel attacks.

2   Known S-boxes with Good Properties

Several infinite classes of APN functions are known. All are defined over the finite field $\mathbb{F}_{2^n}$ rather than the vector space $\mathbb{F}_2^n$; this allows using multiplication to define the functions. Table 1 lists all the known classes of non-quadratic APN (n,n)-functions, up to composing by linear automorphisms of $\mathbb{F}_2^n$ (such as field automorphisms $x \mapsto x^{2^i}$ of $\mathbb{F}_{2^n}$), to adding an affine function, and to replacing permutations by their compositional inverses. These APN functions are power functions (and are then bijective if and only if n is odd, as proved by Dobbertin), that is, have the form $F(x) = x^d$ for some powers d, and are then more easily implementable than general functions (it is difficult to say if their particular structure is an advantage for the designer only, since it could be an advantage for the attacker if a possibility is found of exploiting the structure). There are other known infinite classes of APN functions, e.g. *Gold* functions x^{2^i+1}, $\gcd(i,n) = 1$ [43], but they are quadratic.

Table 1. Table of known non-quadratic classes of APN (n,n)-functions

Name	$F(x)$	Conditions	References
Kasami	$x^{2^{2i}-2^i+1}$	$\gcd(i,n) = 1$	[46]
Welch	x^{2^t+3}	$n = 2t+1$	[37]
Niho (even)	$x^{2^t+2^{\frac{t}{2}}-1}$	$n = 2t+1$, t even	[38]
Niho (odd)	$x^{2^t+2^{\frac{3t+1}{2}}-1}$	$n = 2t+1$, t odd	[38]
Inverse	$x^{2^{2t}-1}$	$n = 2t+1$	[60,6]
Dobbertin	$x^{2^{4t}+2^{3t}+2^{2t}+2^t-1}$	$n = 5t$	[39]

There has been considerable efforts in order to classify APN (n,n)-functions and this could be done for $n = 4,5$. Bijectivity (which is required for SPN) is easily achieved for n odd, because of Dobbertin's result recalled above. Bijective

APN $(7,7)$- and $(9,9)$-functions are used for the design of the two S-boxes of the MISTY block cipher [57] and its variant KASUMI [41] (which have a Feistel structure). But (see below) n even is in general preferred. Only one APN bijective (n,n)-function in even dimension was found, for $n = 6$, but it has a complex representation [15], and 8 variables would be preferred. The question of finding an APN bijective (n,n)-function for even $n > 6$ is still open.

The best situation for the implementation in finite fields being when n equals a power of 2 (this allows decomposing the computation of multiplication in subfields whose order level can be chosen according to the device to which the implementation is devoted), many designers have preferred using permutations (over $\mathbb{F}_{2^4}$ or $\mathbb{F}_{2^8}$) which are not APN but are differentially 4-uniform. The known families of differentially 4-uniform bijective (n,n)-functions are presented in Table 2. Other classes of differentially 4-uniform (n,n)-functions exist, mostly obtained by modifying power (n,n)-functions.

Table 2. Table of known differentially 4-uniform bijective (n,n)-functions

$F(x)$	Conditions	Ref
x^{2^i+1}	$n = 2k$, k is odd, $\gcd(i,n) = 2$	[43]
$x^{2^{2i}-2^i+1}$	$n = 2k$, k is odd, $\gcd(i,n) = 2$	[46]
$x^{2^{2t}-2}$	$n = 2t$	[60]
$x^{2^{2t}+2^t+1}$	$n = 4t$, t is odd	[11]
$\begin{cases} X + (X+\alpha+1)^{-1} + (X+\alpha+1)^{-2} \\ X \in \mathbb{F}_{2^n+1}, Tr_1^{n+1}(X) = 0 \end{cases}$	n is odd, $Tr_1^{n+1}(\alpha) = 1$	[20]
$\alpha x^{2^s+1} + \alpha^{2^m} x^{2^{-m}+2^{m+s}}$	$n = 3m$, $m/2$ is odd, $\gcd(s,n) = 2$, $3\mid(m+s)$, α primitive element of $\mathbb{F}_{2^n}$	[12]
$x^{-1} + Tr_1^n\left(x + (x^{-1}+1)^{-1}\right)$	$n = 2t$	[73]
$x^{-1} + Tr_1^n\left(x^{-3(2^k+1)} + (x^{-1}+1)^{3(2^k+1)}\right)$	$n = 2t$, $2 \leqslant k \leqslant t-1$	[73]
$\sum_{k=0}^{2^n-3} x^k$	$n = 2t$, t is odd	[76]
$x^{-1} + t(x^{2^s} + x)^{2^{sn}-1}$	s is even, $t \in \mathbb{F}_{2^s}^*$, or s, n are odd, $t \in \mathbb{F}_{2^s}^*$	[77]
$x^{2^k+1} + t(x^{2^s} + x)^{2^{sn}-1}$	n, s are odd, $t \in \mathbb{F}_{2^s}^*$, $\gcd(k,sn) = 1$	[75]

The *Walsh transform* of an (n,m)-function F maps any ordered pair $(u,v) \in \mathbb{F}_2^n \times \mathbb{F}_2^m$ to the sum (calculated in $\mathbb{Z}$): $\sum_{x \in \mathbb{F}_2^n}(-1)^{v \cdot F(x)+u \cdot x}$, where the same symbol "$\cdot$" is used to denote inner products in $\mathbb{F}_2^n$ and $\mathbb{F}_2^m$. Note that the function $v \cdot F$ is a component function of F when $v \neq 0$. The *Walsh spectrum* of F is the multi-set of all the values of the Walsh transform of F, for $u \in \mathbb{F}_2^n, v \in \mathbb{F}_2^{m*}$ (where $\mathbb{F}_2^{m*} = \mathbb{F}_2^m \setminus \{0\}$). We call *extended Walsh spectrum* of F the multi-set of their absolute values.

The nonlinearity $nl(F)$ satisfies:

$$nl(F) = 2^{n-1} - \frac{1}{2} \max_{v \in \mathbb{F}_2^{m*}; \ u \in \mathbb{F}_2^n} \left| \sum_{x \in \mathbb{F}_2^n} (-1)^{v \cdot F(x) + u \cdot x} \right|.$$

The two main known upper bounds on the nonlinearity are:
- the *covering radius bound*:

$$nl(F) \leqslant 2^{n-1} - 2^{n/2-1}$$

which is tight for n even and $m \leqslant n/2$, as recalled above (achieved with equality by bent functions);
- the *Sidelnikov-Chabaud-Vaudenay bound*, valid only for $m \geqslant n - 1$:

$$nl(F) \leqslant 2^{n-1} - \frac{1}{2} \sqrt{3 \times 2^n - 2 - 2 \frac{(2^n - 1)(2^{n-1} - 1)}{2^m - 1}}$$

which is identical to the covering radius bound when $m = n - 1$ and is strictly better when $m \geqslant n$. It is tight only for $m = n$ (in which case it states that $nl(F) \leqslant 2^{n-1} - 2^{\frac{n-1}{2}}$), with n odd (the functions achieving it with equality are called *almost bent* AB).

According to Chabaud-Vaudenay's proof of the Sidelnikov-Chabaud-Vaudenay bound, any AB function is APN.

The nonlinearity and the δ-uniformity are invariant under affine, extended affine and CCZ equivalences (in increasing order of generality). Two functions are called *affine equivalent* if one is equal to the other, composed on the left and on the right by affine permutations. They are called *extended affine equivalent* (EA-equivalent) if one is affine equivalent to the other, added with an affine function. They are called *CCZ-equivalent* if their graphs $\{(x, y) \in \mathbb{F}_2^n \times \mathbb{F}_2^n \mid y = F(x)\}$ and $\{(x, y) \in \mathbb{F}_2^n \times \mathbb{F}_2^n \mid y = G(x)\}$ are affine equivalent, that is, if there exists an affine automorphism $L = (L_1, L_2)$ of $\mathbb{F}_2^n \times \mathbb{F}_2^n$ such that $y = F(x) \Leftrightarrow L_2(x, y) = G(L_1(x, y))$.

2.1   The Case $m < n$

Little theoretical work has been done on (n, m)-functions when m does not equal n, even though these functions can play a role in Feistel ciphers, and actually play a role in several block ciphers; for instance, the S-boxes of the DES [59], found by computer investigations, are $(6, 4)$-functions; their differential uniformities have all the same value 16.

A way of designing differentially 2^{n-m+1}-uniform (n, m)-functions is to take them of the form $L \circ F$ where F is an APN (n, n)-function and L is an affine surjective (n, m)-function. Such functions have optimal differential uniformity for $m = n - 1, n \geqslant 3$ (recall that when n is odd and when $m > n/2$, no differentially 2^{n-m}-uniform (n, m)-function exists, that is, no bent or PN function exists).

Other types of differentially 4-uniform $(n, n-1)$-functions exist. It is observed in [21] that taking two APN $(n - 1, n - 1)$-functions F and G, the function

$(x, x_n) \in \mathbb{F}_{2^{n-1}} \times \mathbb{F}_2 \mapsto x_n F(x) + (1 + x_n) G(x)$ is differentially 4-uniform if and only if, for every $a \in \mathbb{F}_{2^{n-1}}$, the function $F(x) + G(x + a)$ is at most 2-to-1 (i.e. each value in the image set has at most two pre-images) or equivalently $F(x + a) + G(x)$ is at most 2-to-1.

In [21] is deduced the following construction: let i be a positive integer coprime with $n - 1$. The function $(x, x_n) \mapsto x^{2^i + 1} + x_n x$ is differentially 4-uniform. This function has also good nonlinearity, but it is not balanced and has also the drawback of being quadratic.

A construction in [2], based on the same structure, allows obtaining non-quadratic balanced highly nonlinear differentially 4-uniform $(n, n-1)$-functions, whatever is the parity of n: for every $n > 3$, the function $(x, x_n) \mapsto (1 + x_n) x^{2^n - 2} + x_n \alpha x^{2^n - 2}$, where $x, \alpha \in \mathbb{F}_{2^{n-1}}, \alpha \notin \mathbb{F}_2, x_n \in \mathbb{F}_2$, is differentially 4-uniform if and only if $tr_{n-1}(\alpha) = tr_{n-1}\left(\frac{1}{\alpha}\right) = 1$. This same paper gives constructions of similar differentially 8-uniform $(n, n-2)$-functions.

For $m \leqslant n - 2$, the existence of δ_F-uniform functions with $2^{n-m} < \delta_F < 2^{n-m+1}$ for n even and $m > n/2$ or for n odd is an open question. In particular, it is an open problem to determine whether differentially 6-uniform $(n, n-2)$-functions exist for $n > 4$.

3   Protection of S-boxes against Side Channel Attacks

The implementation of cryptographic algorithms over devices like smart cards, FPGA, ASIC, leaks information on the secret data, leading to *side channel attacks* (SCA). These attacks exploit the running-time, the power consumption or the electromagnetic radiations of a cryptographic computation and apply statistical methods to determine the most probable values of well-chosen bits of the data processed by the algorithm. The model of attacker for these attacks is the so-called *grey-box model*, where a *leakage* coming from inside the algorithm can be measured. This leakage can be for instance a noisy version of the Hamming weight of some *sensitive variable* depending on a few bits of the secret key. SCA are often more efficient than cryptanalyses mounted in the so-called *black-box model* where no leakage occurs, in particular in the case of iterative ciphers like block ciphers since it is possible to attack the first round, when the diffusion is not yet optimal. In particular, *continuous side-channel attacks*, in which the adversary gets information at each invocation of the cryptosystem, are especially threatening. They allow recovering the key from few plaintext-ciphertext pairs in a few seconds if no counter-measure is included in the algorithm and/or the device.

Many implementations of block ciphers have been practically broken by continuous side-channel analysis — see for instance [49,13,58,53] — and securing them has been a longstanding issue for the embedded systems industry.

3.1   Masking

The most commonly used counter-measure to SCA is a secret-sharing method called *masking*. It is efficient for implementations both in smart cards (which are software implementations including a part of hardware) and in hardware (FPGA, ASIC) [9,68]. This approach consists in splitting each sensitive variable Z of the implementation (*i.e.* each variable depending on the secret key, or better for the attacker, on a small part of it, and of data known by the attacker, such as the plaintext) into $d + 1$ shares $M_0, \ldots, M_d$, where d is called the *masking order*, such that Z can be recovered from these shares but no information can be recovered from less than $d + 1$ shares. In other words, the sensitive variable Z is a deterministic function of all the M_i, but is independent of $(M_i)_{i \in I}$ if $|I| \leqslant d$. The simplest way of achieving this is to draw $M_1, \ldots, M_d$ at random (they are then called *masks*) and to take M_0 such that $M_0 + \cdots + M_d$ equals the sensitive variable, where $+$ is a relevant group operation (in practice, the bitwise XOR). It has been shown that the complexity of mounting a successful side-channel attack against a masked implementation increases exponentially with the masking order [31]. The design of efficient *masking schemes at higher order d*, aims at specifying how to update the sharing of the internal state throughout the processing while ensuring that (1) the final sharing corresponds to the expected ciphertext, and (2) the dth-order security property is satisfied, in the sense of the *probing security* model introduced in [45], which states that every tuple of d or less intermediate variables is independent of the secret parameter of the algorithm. When satisfied, it guarantees that no attack of order lower than or equal to d is possible. A weaker notion of order of security exists, called *HO-CPA resistance*, where HO-CPA stands for the higher-order correlation power analysis by Waddle and Wagner [74], which is the most efficient known univariate attack (univariate meaning that a single instantaneous leakage is exploited), when the Gaussian noise is high and the model of leakage is known, see [16]. The dth-order correlation power analysis consists in testing if a given power $d > 0$ of the leakage $\mathscr{L}$ statistically depends on the plaintext; the attacker has a model of $\mathscr{L}$, for instance the Hamming weight of a sensitive variable added with a white Gaussian noise, and checks for the feasibility of a dth-order attack by studying the variation of the function of x equal to the mean of $\mathscr{L}^d$ when the plaintext is fixed to x, and by selecting the smallest d such that such variation happens.

Most block ciphers apply several times a same transformation, called *round*, composed of a key addition, one or several linear transformation(s) and one or several non-linear transformation(s) called S-box(es). Key addition and linear transformations are easily handled as linearity enables to process each share independently. The main difficulty in designing masking schemes for block ciphers hence lies in masking the S-box(es). The scheme must take at input a $(d+1)^{\text{th}}$-order sharing of the input(s) and return a $(d+1)^{\text{th}}$-order sharing of the output, while ensuring that any d-tuple of intermediate results during the processing is independent of the unshared input, or at least (in the weaker version of security) does not allow a dth-order attack of practicable complexity.

3.2   Masking Schemes

There currently exist four masking schemes which have not been broken, due to Genelle, Prouff and Quisquater [42] (mixing additive and multiplicative sharings), to Prouff and Roche [64] (using multi-party computation), to Coron [33] (extending the *table re-computation technique* introduced in the original paper by Kocher *et al.* [49]) and to Carlet, Goubin, Prouff, Quisquater and Rivain [26].

The first method, dedicated to the AES S-box, seems difficult to generalize efficiently to S-boxes not affinely equivalent to power functions. The second one is much less efficient than the other schemes (but, contrary to them, remains secure even in presence of hardware perturbations called glitches [52]). The third one has a RAM memory consumption which can quickly exceed the memory capacity of the hosted device (*e.g.* a smart card). The only method which is in the same time practical and general is then the fourth one. It generalizes the method from [66], which was dedicated to power functions, and was adapting the techniques proposed in [45] for Boolean circuits by Ishai, Sahai and Wagner (ISW). It decomposes the S-box into a sequence as short as possible of field multiplications and $\mathbb{F}_2$-linear operations, and then secures these operations independently. The complexity of the masking scheme for an $\mathbb{F}_2$-linear operation (satisfying $f(x+y) = f(x) + f(y)$ for any pair (x, y), e.g. a squaring) is $O(d)$. The complexity for a non-$\mathbb{F}_2$-linear multiplication is $O(d^2)$, and the constant terms in these complexities are greater for the multiplication than for the $\mathbb{F}_2$-linear operations.

Processing a Multiplication: Time/memory trade-offs exist in the literature for implementing multiplications: for hardware implementations and large dimensions n, the Omura-Massey method [62], the Sunar-Koc method [72] and the Karatsuba algorithm [40]; for software implementations in small dimensions (*e.g.* $n \leqslant 10$), the *log-alog* method, which assumes that the functions $log : x \in \mathbb{F}_{2^n} \mapsto i = \log_\alpha(x)$ and $alog : i \mapsto x = \alpha^i$ have been tabulated in ROM and processes $alog[(log[a] + log[b]) \bmod 2^n - 1]$; and the *Tower Fields* approach, which works recursively as long as n is even, $n = 2m$, and represents $\mathbb{F}_{2^n}$ has the degree-2 extension $\mathbb{F}_{2^m}[X]/(p''(X))$, where $p''(X) = X^2 + X + \beta$ is irreducible over $\mathbb{F}_{2^m}$.

Masking a Multiplication: the inputs a and b being additively shared into $(a_0, a_1, \cdots, a_d)$ and $(b_0, b_1, \cdots, b_d)$ respectively, the scheme from [45,66] involves $2d(d + 1)$ additions and $(d + 1)^2$ multiplications in $\mathbb{F}_{2^n}$.

Algorithm 1: Higher-Order Masking Scheme for the Multiplication (Additive Sharing)

Input : $(d + 1)^{\text{th}}$-order sharings $(a_0, a_1, \cdots, a_d)$ and $(b_0, b_1, \cdots, b_d)$ of a and b in $\mathbb{F}_{2^n}$
Output: a $(d + 1)^{\text{th}}$-order sharing $(c_0, c_1, \cdots, c_d)$ of $c = a \times b$

1   Randomly generate $d(d + 1)/2$ elements $r_{ij} \in \mathbb{F}_{2^n}$; $0 \leqslant i < j \leqslant d$
2   **for** $i = 0$ **to** d **do**
3   **for** $j = i + 1$ **to** d **do**
4       $r_{j,i} \leftarrow (r_{i,j} + a_i \times b_j) + a_j \times b_i$

5   **for** $i = 0$ **to** d **do**
6     $c_i \leftarrow a_i \times b_i$
7   **for** $j = 0$ **to** d, $j \neq i$ **do**
8       $c_i \leftarrow c_i + r_{i,j}$

9   **return** $(c_0, c_1, \ldots, c_d)$

An alternative to Algorithm 1 exists, proposed by Ben-Or *et al.* in [5], and based on Shamir's polynomial sharing [68]. It has higher complexity but stays secure even in the presence of glitches. More generaly, as observed by Massey [55], given any linear $[\ell + 1, k]$-code C (where $\ell + 1$ is the code length and k its dimension) whose dual $C^\perp$ has minimum distance $d^\perp \geqslant 2$, one can define a linear ℓ-sharing of any $a \in \mathbb{F}_{2^n}$ from a systematic generator matrix $G = [I_{\ell+1} \mid M]$ and a $(\ell - 1)$-tuple of random values $(r_0, r_1, \cdots, r_{\ell-1})$ by $(a, a_0, a_1, \cdots, a_{\ell-1}) = (a, r_0, \cdots, r_{\ell-1}) \times G$. This sharing [32] defeats any side channel attack of order lower than or equal to $d^\perp - 2$.

Processing an S-box: For reducing the cost of the sharing counter-measure, we need, when choosing the S-boxes, to minimize, in their processing, the number of field multiplications which are non-linear. The *masking complexity* of an S-box corresponds to the minimal number of non-linear multiplications needed to evaluate it. Following a brute force approach using that the complexity is the same for all powers in the same cyclotomic class, [26] exhibited the masking complexity for all monomials in $\mathbb{F}_{2^n}$ with $n \leqslant 8$ and addressed the masking complexity of polynomials by two methods:

- The *cyclotomic method* which consists in writing $P(x) = u_0 + \sum_{i=1}^{q} L_i(x^{\alpha_i}) + u_{2^n-1} x^{2^n-1}$ where $(L_i)_{i \leqslant q}$ is a family of linearized polynomials. The masking complexity of $\sum_{i=1}^{q} L_i(x^{\alpha_i})$ equals the number of non-linear multiplications required to evaluate all the monomials x^{α_i} and is then bounded above by the number of cyclotomic classes in $\mathbb{F}_{2^n}$ minus 2. Coron, Roy and Vivek have deduced in [35] that for every n, there exists a polynomial $P(x) \in \mathbb{F}_{2^n}[x]$ with masking complexity at least $\sqrt{\frac{2^n}{n}} - 2$.
- *Knuth-Eve's method* which consists in applying recursively the decomposition $P(x) = P_1(x^2) + P_2(x^2)x$, where $P_1(x)$ and $P_2(x)$ have degrees at most $2^{n-1} - 1$. Eventually, the masking complexity of $P(x)$ is bounded above by
$$\begin{cases} \frac{3}{2} 2^{n/2} - 2 & \text{if } n \text{ is even} \\ 2^{(n+1)/2} - 2 & \text{if } n \text{ is odd} \end{cases}$$
More recently, methods were found which improved upon these two ones:

- *Roy-Vivek's method* [67] consists in recursively decomposing $P(x)$ as follows: $P(x) = (x^{kt} + C_0(x)) \times Q_0(x) + x^{k(t-1)} + S_0(x)$, where, assuming that $P(x)$ has degree $k(2t - 1)$, $S_0(x)$ and $Q_0(x)$ have degree at most $kt - 1$.
- *Coron-Roy-Vivek's (CRV) method* proposed in [35] is an extension of [67] building a union $\mathcal{C}$ of cyclotomic classes of 2 in $\mathbb{Z}/(2^n - 1)\mathbb{Z}$ such that all the powers of the monomials in $P(x)$ are in $\mathcal{C} + \mathcal{C}$, and, denoting by $\mathcal{P}$ the subspace of $\mathbb{F}_{2^n}[x]$ spanned by all the monomials whose exponents belong to $\mathcal{C}$, fixing a set of r polynomials $P_1(x), ..., P_r(x)$ in $\mathcal{P}$ and searching $r + 1$ polynomials $P_{r+1}(x), ..., P_{2r+1}(x)$ in $\mathcal{P}$ such that:

$$P(x) = \sum_{i=1}^{r} P_i(x) \times P_{r+i}(x) + P_{2r+1}(x) . \tag{2}$$

This can be done by solving the linear system of 2^n equations over $\mathbb{F}_{2^n}$ implied by the evaluation of Equation (2) at every $x \in \mathbb{F}_{2^n}$. The size ℓ of $\mathcal{C}$ is taken such that the number of equations is smaller than or equal to the number of unknowns: $2^n \leqslant \ell \times (r+1)$. The complexity of this heuristic but efficient method in terms of the number of non-linear multiplications is $O(\sqrt{2^n/n})$, which is asymptotically better than the complexity $O(\sqrt{2^n})$ of Knuth-Eve's method. A comparison with $\sqrt{\frac{2^n}{n}} - 2$ shows that Coron-Roy-Vivek's method is asymptotically optimal. The method is applied for the first DES S-box and leads to an evaluation with only 4 non-linear multiplications. The method is also applied to the S-boxes of CLEFIA and PRESENT, leading to a complexity of 10 and 2 respectively (which improves all previous methods).

- *Carlet-Prouff-Rivain-Roche's method* proposed in [30] consists in a first step: decompose the S-box by means of functions of low algebraic degree s, and a second step: evaluate these low degree functions. The first step starts by deriving a family of generators G_i as follows: $\begin{cases} G_1(x) = F_1(x) \\ G_i(x) = F_i(G_{i-1}(x)) \end{cases}$ where the F_i are random polynomials of algebraic degree s. Then it randomly generates t polynomials Q_i of the form $\sum_{j=1}^r L_j \circ G_j$, where the L_j are linearized polynomials. Eventually, it searches for t polynomials P_i of algebraic degree s and for $r+1$ linearized polynomials L_i such that the polynomial univariate representation of the S-box equals:

$$P(x) = \sum_{i=1}^t P_i(Q_i(x)) + \sum_{i=1}^r L_i(G_i(x)) + L_0(x) \ . \tag{3}$$

This involves $r+t$ evaluations of polynomials of algebraic degrees at most s (the F_i and the P_i), plus some linear operations. As in the CRV method, the search of polynomials P_i and L_i satisfying (3) for given polynomials G_i and Q_i amounts to solve a system of linear equations over $\mathbb{F}_{2^n}$: $A \cdot b = c$. The target vector c has 2^n coordinates which are the values taken by $P(x)$ for all x over $\mathbb{F}_{2^n}$. The coordinates of the vector b are the variables of the system that represent the solutions for the coefficients of the polynomials P_i and L_i.

Masking an S-box: In the frameworks of the cyclotomic method, Knuth-Eve's method, Roy-Vivek's method and Coron-Roy-Vivek's (CRV) method, the masking strategy is clear:

- each affine function is masked by applying it to each share (and, in the case the number of shares is even, adding the constant equal to the value of the function at 0),
- each nonlinear multiplication is masked by Algorithm 1.

We need now to describe how the masking is performed in Carlet-Prouff-Rivain-Roche's method, on a function F of algebraic degree at most s. The definition of $\varphi_F^{(s)}$:

$$\varphi_F^{(s)}(a_1, a_2, \ldots, a_s) = \sum_{I \subseteq [\![1,s]\!]} F\left(\sum_{i \in I} a_i\right)$$

allows deducing (see the full version of [30]) that for every $d \geqslant s$:

$$F\left(\sum_{i=1}^{d} a_i\right) = \sum_{1 \leqslant i_1 < \cdots < i_s \leqslant d} \varphi_F^{(s)}(a_{i_1}, \ldots, a_{i_s}) + \sum_{j=0}^{s-1} \eta_{d,s}(j) \sum_{\substack{I \subseteq [\![1,d]\!] \\ |I|=j}} F\left(\sum_{i \in I} a_i\right) ,$$

where $\eta_{d,s}(j) = \binom{d-j-1}{s-j-1} \bmod 2$ for every $j \leqslant s - 1$, and this gives then:

$$F\left(\sum_{i=1}^{d} a_i\right) = \sum_{j=0}^{s} \mu_{d,s}(j) \sum_{\substack{I \subseteq [\![1,d]\!] \\ |I|=j}} F\left(\sum_{i \in I} a_i\right) ,$$

where $\mu_{d,s}(j) = \binom{d-j-1}{s-j} \bmod 2$ for every $j \leqslant s$.

Hence, for any $d \geqslant s$, the evaluation of a function $F \in \mathcal{B}_{n,m}$ of algebraic degree s on the sum of d shares can be expressed as several evaluations of F on sums of at most s shares. Afterwards, a secure scheme of sharing compression combines the obtained shares of all the $F(\sum_{i \in I} a_i)$, with $I \subseteq [\![1, d]\!]$ such that $|I| \leqslant s$ and $\mu_{d,s}(|I|) = 1$, into a d-sharing of $F(a)$, see [30]. It is shown in this same paper that whenever $d \equiv s \bmod 2^\ell$ with $\ell = \lfloor \log_2 s \rfloor + 1$ (which is a weak assumption for low algebraic degrees) the whole masking represents the following operation count (where "#add" and "#rand" respectively denote the number of additions and the number of sampled random values in the sharing compression).

#SecureEval	#add	#rand
$\binom{d}{s}$	$\left(s\binom{d}{s} - d\right)(d+1)$	$\frac{1}{2}\left(s\binom{d}{s} - d\right)(d-1)$

where SecureEval is a primitive that performs a secure evaluation of F on a j-sharing input for any $j \leqslant s$.

Moreover, in the particular case of a quadratic function, it is possible to use an improved sharing compression inspired from ISW, which gives the following complexity:

# add	# eval$_F$	# mult	# rand
$\frac{9}{2}d(d-1)+1$	$d(2d-1)$	-	$d(d-1)$

3.3   An Open Problem with Multiple Facets

Both CRV and Carlet-Prouff-Rivain-Roche's methods are heuristic. Proving that these two methods actually work with high probability under some assumptions is open. In general, the problem of decomposing a function by means either of low algebraic degree functions or of functions with prescribed exponents is interesting to study, not only in the framework of masking but also for its own sake.

Let us consider for instance the problem of characterizing those families of polynomials $(Q_1, \ldots, Q_t)$ (which can be taken of algebraic degrees at most s or not) such that any polynomial $P(x) = \sum_{j=0}^{2^n-1} a_j x^j \in \mathbb{F}_{2^n}[x]$ can be decomposed in the form

$$P(x) = \sum_{i=1}^{t} P_i(Q_i(x)) = \sum_{i=1}^{t} \sum_{\substack{j \in \mathbb{Z}/(2^n-1)\mathbb{Z} \\ HW(j) \leqslant s}} p_{i,j} [Q_i(x)]^j , \qquad (4)$$

where each $P_i(x) = \sum_{\substack{j \in \mathbb{Z}/(2^n-1)\mathbb{Z} \\ HW(j) \leqslant s}} p_{i,j} x^j$ has algebraic degree at most s. This problem seems difficult. We make a few elementary observations.

Finding the $P_i(x)$, given the $Q_i(x)$, amounts to find the $t \times \sum_{j=0}^{s} \binom{n}{j}$ coefficients $p_{i,j}$ as the solutions of a linear system of 2^n equations and $t \times \sum_{j=0}^{s} \binom{n}{j}$ unknowns. Such a system admits a solution for every choice of $P(x)$ if and only if its rank is 2^n, which implies the following inequality as a first necessary condition: $t \times \sum_{j=0}^{s} \binom{n}{j} \geqslant 2^n$. Note that if (4) has a solution for every (n,n)-function then it has one for every Boolean function and conversely (this is easily checked by decomposing over an $\mathbb{F}_2$-basis).

If the mapping $Q : x \in \mathbb{F}_{2^n} \mapsto (Q_1(x), \ldots, Q_t(x)) \in \mathbb{F}_{2^n}^t$ is non-injective, then for every $x \neq x'$ such that $(Q_1(x), \ldots, Q_t(x)) = (Q_1(x'), \ldots, Q_t(x'))$, the two equations (4) corresponding to x and x' are identical and the system of equations (4) has rank strictly less than 2^n. Hence a second necessary condition is that Q be injective. We shall assume this condition satisfied in the sequel.

A third necessary condition, which is clearly a necessary and sufficient condition, expresses that no non-zero $\mathbb{F}_{2^n}$-linear combination of the equations (4) completely vanishes: for every non-zero function $\varphi : \mathbb{F}_{2^n} \mapsto \mathbb{F}_{2^n}$, there exists $i \in \{1, \ldots, t\}$ and $j \in \mathbb{Z}/(2^n-1)\mathbb{Z}$ such that:

$$HW(j) \leqslant s \text{ and } \sum_{x \in \mathbb{F}_{2^n}} \varphi(x)[Q_i(x)]^j \neq 0.$$

Note that, if each Q_i is bijective, then $\sum_{x \in \mathbb{F}_{2^n}} \varphi(x)[Q_i(x)]^j = \sum_{x \in \mathbb{F}_{2^n}} \varphi \circ Q_i^{-1}(x)x^j$, and the condition is equivalent to: for every non-zero function φ, there exists i such that $\varphi \circ Q_i^{-1}$ has algebraic degree at least $n - s$. Equivalently, denoting $\phi(x) = (Q_1^{-1}(x), \ldots, Q_t^{-1}(x))$ and $\underline{\varphi}(y_1, \ldots, y_t) = (\varphi(y_1), \ldots, \varphi(y_t))$, the function $\underline{\varphi} \circ \phi : \mathbb{F}_{2^n} \mapsto \mathbb{F}_{2^n}^t$ has algebraic degree at least $n-s$. Let us take an example: we view ϕ as valued in $\mathbb{F}_{2^{nt}}$ and, given $a \in \mathbb{F}_{2^{nt}} \setminus \mathbb{F}_{2^n}$, we define $\phi(x) = (ax+1)^{2^{nt}-2} = \left((ax+1)^{2^{nt-1}-1}\right)^2 = \left(\sum_{k=0}^{2^{nt-1}-1}(ax)^k\right)^2$; $x \in \mathbb{F}_{2^n}$. Then we have $x^{2^n} = x$ and $\phi(x)$ equals then $1 + \left(\sum_{k=1}^{2^n-1}\left(\sum_{l=0}^{\left\lfloor \frac{2^{nt-1}-k-1}{2^n-1}\right\rfloor} a^{(2^n-1)l}\right)(ax)^k\right)^2 = 1 + \left(\sum_{k=1}^{2^n-1} \frac{1+a^{(2^n-1)\left(\left\lfloor \frac{2^{nt-1}-k-1}{2^n-1}\right\rfloor+1\right)}}{1+a^{2^n-1}}(ax)^k\right)^2$. The problem would be to deter-

mine if, for every n and $s < n$, there exists t such that, for some basis $(u_1, \ldots, u_t)$ of $\mathbb{F}_{2^{nt}}$ over $\mathbb{F}_{2^n}$, all functions $tr_n^{nt}(u_i \phi(x))$, where tr_n^{nt} is the trace function from $\mathbb{F}_{2^{nt}}$ to $\mathbb{F}_{2^n}$, are bijective and for every $\varphi \neq 0$, the function $\varphi \circ \phi$ has algebraic degree at least $n - s$. We could then take $Q_i^{-1}(x) = tr_n^{nt}(u_i \phi(x))$.

Coming back to the general case and taking for φ a Boolean function over $\mathbb{F}_{2^n}$, we have the necessary condition:

$$\forall f : \mathbb{F}_{2^n} \mapsto \mathbb{F}_2, f \neq 0, \exists i \in \{1, \ldots, t\}, \exists j \in \mathbb{Z}/(2^n - 1)\mathbb{Z};$$

$$HW(j) \leqslant s \text{ and } \sum_{x \in \mathbb{F}_{2^n}; f(x)=1} [Q_i(x)]^j \neq 0.$$

In other words, if S is the support of f, denoting by $Q_i[S]$ the set of those elements in $Q_i(S) = \{Q_i(x), x \in S\}$ which are matched an odd number of times, for every non-empty subset S of $\mathbb{F}_{2^n}$, there exists i such that the indicator of $Q_i[S]$ has algebraic degree at least $n - s$. In particular (still assuming that $\mathcal{Q} = (Q_1, \ldots, Q_t)$ is injective):

for every S of size 2^{s+1}, there exists i such that $Q_i[S]$ is not empty nor

the indicator of an affine subspace of $\mathbb{F}_{2^n}$ of dimension $s + 1$.   (5)

Note that, given any function $Q : \mathbb{F}_{2^n} \mapsto \mathbb{F}_{2^n}$, if there exists j such that $HW(j) \leqslant s$ and $\sum_{x \in \mathbb{F}_{2^n}} [Q(x)]^j \neq 0$, then $[Q(x)]^j$ has algebraic degree n and Q has algebraic degree at least $\frac{n}{s}$. Hence, a necessary condition is that for every non-zero Boolean function f over $\mathbb{F}_{2^n}$, there exists i such that the function fQ_i has algebraic degree at least $\frac{n}{s}$ (for $f = 1$, this implies that at least one function Q_i has algebraic degree at least $\frac{n}{s}$). We are led to study those functions $\mathcal{Q} : \mathbb{F}_2^n \mapsto \mathbb{F}_2^m$ such that, for every non-zero n-variable Boolean function f, the function $f\mathcal{Q}$ has algebraic degree at least $\frac{n}{s}$.

4   Boolean Functions, Vectorial Boolean Functions and Error Correcting Codes for Improving Counter-Measures to SCA

Counter-measures to SCA are costly in terms of running time (more in software applications), of implementation area (in hardware applications) and program executable file size (in software), all the more if they need to resist higher order side channel attacks. A new role is played in cryptography by Boolean functions, vectorial functions and error correcting codes for reducing this cost.

4.1   Correlation Immune Boolean Functions, Vectorial Functions with Correlation Immune Graphs, Complementary Information Set Codes

Correlation immune functions are those Boolean functions f whose Walsh transform $W_f(a) = \sum_{x \in \mathbb{F}_2^n} (-1)^{f(x)+a \cdot x}$ vanishes for every vector a of Hamming weight between 1 and some integer called the correlation immunity order. They allow the pseudo-random generators using them as combiners in stream ciphers to resist Siegenthaler's correlation attack [71]. They allow reducing, at least in two possible ways, the overhead of masking while keeping the same resistance to d^{th}-order HO-CPA (see Subsection 3.1), when the leakage is simply (a noisy version of) a linear combination over the reals of the bits of the sensitive variable:

- *leakage squeezing*, introduced in [50] and further studied in [51], allows achieving with one single mask the same protection as with d ones in the framework of HO-CPA resistance. It uses a bijective vectorial function F; the mask M is not processed as is in the device, but in the form of $F(M)$. The condition for achieving resistance to d^{th}-order SCA is that the graph indicator of F, that is, the $2n$-variable Boolean function whose support equals the graph $\{(x, y) \in \mathbb{F}_2^n \times \mathbb{F}_2^n; \ y = F(x)\}$ of F, is d^{th}-order correlation immune. Such graph is a *complementary information set* code (CIS code for short): it admits (at least) two information sets which are complement of each other. The condition that the indicator of this CIS code is d^{th}-order correlation immune is equivalent to saying that the dual distance of this code is at least $d + 1$. CIS codes have been studied in [25]. Leakage squeezing has been later generalized in [23] to several masks and the corresponding higher-order CIS codes have been studied in [24].

- an alternative way of resisting higher order SCA with one single mask consists in avoiding processing the mask at all: for every sensitive variable Z which is the input to some box S in the block cipher, Z is replaced by $Z + M$ where M is drawn at random, and $Z + M$ is the input to a "masked" box S_M whose output is a masked value of $S(Z)$. This method, called *Rotating S-box Masking* (RSM), obliges, for each box S in the cipher, to implement a look-up table for each masked box S_M, which is costly for nonlinear boxes. To reduce the cost, M is drawn at random in a subset of binary vectors of the same length as Z. The condition for achieving resistance to d^{th}-order SCA is that the indicator of this set is a dth-order correlation immune function. The size of the overhead due to the masked look-up tables is proportional to the Hamming weight of this d^{th}-order correlation immune function and we wish then to choose this function with lowest possible weight.

In both cases, we need correlation-immune functions of low weights (or equivalently, orthogonal arrays of small sizes, see [17]), and additionally, in the second case, with a support equal to the graph of a permutation. Most of the numerous studies made until now on correlation immune functions dealt with balanced correlation immune functions (called resilient functions). The known constructions of resilient functions do not work for constructing low weight correlation immune functions; see more in [7,27].

4.2   Linear Complementary Dual Codes

Implementations of cryptographic algorithms are not only prone to SCA, but also to fault injection attacks (FIA). Non-invasive FIA perturb internal data (for example with electromagnetic impulses), without damaging the system and can, thanks to this perturbation, extract sensitive data, without leaving evidence that they have been perpetrated.

Few generic protections, demonstrably provable against both threats of SCA and FIA, have been proposed. A recently proposed one uses Linear Complementary Dual (LCD) codes [29]. Let C and D be two supplementary vector subspaces of $\mathbb{F}_2^n$, where n is larger than the length of the sensitive data. The strategy of this protection is to take the mask in D and the sensitive data in C (whose dimension is then supposed to equal the number of bits to be protected against SCA). The data processed by the algorithm is the sum of the sensitive data and the mask. Considering generator matrices G and G' of C and D respectively, every vector $z \in \mathbb{F}_2^n$ can be written in a unique way as $z = xG + yG'$, $x \in \mathbb{F}_2^k, y \in \mathbb{F}_2^{n-k}$, where k is the dimension of C. If C and D are furthermore orthogonal with respect to the usual inner product, i.e., if $D = C^\perp$, that is, if the *hull* $C \cap C^\perp$ equals $\{0\}$, then C is said complementary dual (see [54]). G' is then a parity-check matrix of C, that is, $GG'^\mathsf{T} = 0$, where G'^T is the transposed matrix; we denote then G' by H. As shown by Massey [54], the three following properties are equivalent:

1. C is LCD,
2. the matrix HH^T is invertible,
3. the matrix GG^T is invertible.

and x and y can be recovered from z by the formulae: $x = zG^\mathsf{T}(GG^\mathsf{T})^{-1}, y = zH^\mathsf{T}(HH^\mathsf{T})^{-1}$.

The masked word z conceals the information x at first degree if for all leakage function $\mathscr{L} : \mathbb{F}_2^n \to \mathbb{R}$ of unitary numerical degree [18], all the averages of $\mathscr{L}(z)$ over the masks $y \in D$ for a given x are equal irrespective of x. This means that for all $x \in \mathbb{F}_2^k$, the sums $\sum_{y \in \mathbb{F}^{n-k}} \mathscr{L}(xG + yH)$ are the same, i.e., equal $\sum_{y \in \mathbb{F}^{n-k}} \mathscr{L}(yH)$. More generally, a masking countermeasure is of *degree at least* d if for all $x \in \mathbb{F}_2^k$, the sums $\sum_{y \in \mathbb{F}^{n-k}} \mathscr{L}(xG + yH)$ equal $\sum_{y \in \mathbb{F}^{n-k}} \mathscr{L}(yH)$ for all $\mathscr{L}$ of numerical degrees at most d. The greater the degree of the countermeasure, the harder to pass a successful SCA. Actually, it is known from [14] that the countermeasure is $(d - 1)^{\text{th}}$degree secure if D has dual distance d, i.e., if C has minimum distance d. This result has been independently validated in [44] for $d \in \{1, 2\}$.

Let us now consider a fault injection attack (FIA). The state z is modified into $z + \varepsilon$. By supplementarity of C and D, there exists a unique ordered pair $(e, f) \in \mathbb{F}_2^k \times \mathbb{F}_2^{n-k}$ such that $\varepsilon = eG + fH$. Checking whether or not the mask has been altered, i.e., $zH^\mathsf{T}(HH^\mathsf{T})^{-1} = y$, is a harmless detection strategy since y does not contain information. An undetected fault happens if and only if $f = 0$, i.e., $\varepsilon \in C$. Harmful faults only happen if $\varepsilon \in C \backslash \{0\}$. In particular, the Hamming weight of ε must be greater or equal to the minimum distance d of code C for the fault not to be detected. Hence having C of greatest possible minimum distance simultaneously improves the resistance against SCA and FIA.

Side-channel analysis starts to be difficult even at low degrees (e.g., $d = 2, 3, 4$). The same applies to FIA: if all faults on $d = 1, 2, 3, 4$ bits are detected, then the success of FIA is compromised. The counter-measure also allows protection against *hardware trojan horses* (HTHs), which are gates added by an adversary (e.g., a silicon foundry) into the design at fabrication time, allowing to deliver a malicious payload when some activation condition on the value of some bits of the circuit is satisfied [22]. In a circuit protected by an LCD code C of minimum distance d, the HTH must connect to at least d bits. Consequently, the HTH must modify at least d bits to bypass an integrity check. The minimum distance d of LCD codes must be then set has high as possible.

The problem is thus the following: for a given dimension k (architecture parameter) and minimum distance d (security parameter), find a LCD code of length n as small as possible (and therefore, of *rate* k/n as large as possible). It has been studied in [29].

References

1. Adams, C.M.: Constructing symmetric ciphers using the CAST design procedure. Designs, Codes, and Cryptography (12), 283–316 (1997)
2. Al Salami, Y.: Constructions with High Algebraic Degree of Differentially 4-uniform (n, n − 1)-Functions and Differentially 8-uniform (n, n − 2)-Functions. Preprint (2015)
3. Aoki, K., Ichikawa, T., Kanda, M., Matsui, M., Moriai, S., Nakajima, J., Tokita, T.: Camellia: A 128-Bit Block Cipher Suitable for Multiple Platforms - Design and Analysis. In: Stinson, D.R., Tavares, S. (eds.) SAC 2000. LNCS, vol. 2012, pp. 39–56. Springer, Heidelberg (2001)
4. Anderson, R., Biham, E., Knudsen, L.: Serpent: A proposal for the advanced encryption standard (1998).
   http://www.cl.cam.ac.uk/ftp/users/rja14/serpent.pdf
5. Ben-Or, M., Goldwasser, S., Wigderson, A.: Completeness theorems for non-cryptographic fault-tolerant distributed computation. In: STOC 1988: Proceedings of the Twentieth Annual ACM Symposium on Theory of Computing, pp. 1–10. ACM, New York (1988)
6. Beth, T., Ding, C.: On almost perfect nonlinear permutations. In: Helleseth, T. (ed.) EUROCRYPT 1993. LNCS, vol. 765, pp. 65–76. Springer, Heidelberg (1994)
7. Bhasin, S., Carlet, C., Guilley, S.: Theory of masking with codewords in hardware: low weight d-th order correlation-immune functions. IACR ePrint Archive 2013/303
8. Biham, E., Shamir, A.: Differential cryptanalysis of DES-like cryptosystems. Journal of Cryptology 4(1), 3–72 (1991)
9. Blakley, G.: Safeguarding cryptographic keys. In: National Comp. Conf., vol. 48, pp. 313–317. AFIPS Press, New York (1979)
10. Bogdanov, A., Knudsen, L.R., Leander, G., Paar, C., Poschmann, A., Robshaw, M.J.B., Seurin, Y., Vikkelsoe, C.: PRESENT: An Ultra-Lightweight Block Cipher. In: Paillier, P., Verbauwhede, I. (eds.) CHES 2007. LNCS, vol. 4727, pp. 450–466. Springer, Heidelberg (2007)
11. Bracken, C., Leander, G.: A highly nonlinear differentially 4 uniform power mapping that permutes fields of even degree. Finite Fields and their Applications 16(4), 231–242 (2010)
12. Bracken, C., Tan, C.H., Tan, Y.: Binomial differentially 4-uniform permutations with high nonlinearity. Finite Fields Applications 18, 537–546 (2012)
13. Brier, E., Clavier, C., Olivier, F.: Correlation Power Analysis with a Leakage Model. In: Joye, M., Quisquater, J.-J. (eds.) CHES 2004. LNCS, vol. 3156, pp. 16–29. Springer, Heidelberg (2004)
14. Bringer, J., Carlet, C., Chabanne, H., Guilley, S., Maghrebi, H.: Orthogonal Direct Sum Masking - A Smartcard Friendly Computation Paradigm in a Code, with Builtin Protection against Side-Channel and Fault Attacks. In: Naccache, D., Sauveron, D. (eds.) WISTP 2014. LNCS, vol. 8501, pp. 40–56. Springer, Heidelberg (2014)

15. Browning, K., Dillon, J.F., McQuistan, M.T., Wolfe, A.J.: An APN permutation in dimension six. Contemporary Mathematics 58, 33–42 (2010)
16. Bruneau, N., Guilley, S., Heuser, A., Rioul, O.: Masks Will Fall Off. In: Sarkar, P., Iwata, T. (eds.) ASIACRYPT 2014, Part II. LNCS, vol. 8874, pp. 344–365. Springer, Heidelberg (2014)
17. Camion, P., Carlet, C., Charpin, P., Sendrier, N.: On correlation-immune functions. In: Feigenbaum, J. (ed.) CRYPTO 1991. LNCS, vol. 576, pp. 86–100. Springer, Heidelberg (1992)
18. Carlet, C.: The monography "Boolean Models and Methods in Mathematics, Computer Science, and Engineering". In: Crama, Y., Hammer, P.L. (eds.) Boolean Functions for Cryptography and Error Correcting Codes, pp. 257–397. Cambridge University Press (2010), Preliminary version available at http://www.math.univ-paris13.fr/$\sim$carlet/pubs.html
19. Carlet, C.: The monography Boolean Models and Methods in Mathematics, Computer Science, and Engineering. In: Crama, Y., Hammer, P.L. (eds.) Vectorial boolean functions for cryptography, pp. 398–469. Cambridge University Press (2010), Preliminary version available at
http://www.math.univ-paris13.fr/~carlet/pubs.html
20. Carlet, C.: On Known and New Differentially Uniform Functions. In: Proceedings of Information Security and Privacy - 16th Australasian Conference (ACISP) 2011, Melbourne, pp. 1–15 (2011)
21. Carlet, C., Al Salami, Y.: A New Construction of Differentially 4-uniform (n,n − 1)-Functions. To appear in Advances in Mathematics of Communications (2015)
22. Carlet, C., Daif, A., Danger, J.-L., Guilley, S., Najm, Z., Thuy Ngo, X., Porteboeuf, T., Tavernier, C.: Optimized Linear Complementary Codes Implementation for Hardware Trojan Prevention. In: Proceedings of ECCTD (2015, to appear)
23. Carlet, C., Danger, J.-L., Guilley, S., Maghrebi, H.: Leakage Squeezing of Order Two. In: Galbraith, S., Nandi, M. (eds.) INDOCRYPT 2012. LNCS, vol. 7668, pp. 120–139. Springer, Heidelberg (2012)
24. Carlet, C., Freibert, F., Guilley, S., Kiermaier, M., Kim, J.-L., Solé, P.: Higher-order CIS codes. IEEE Transactions on Information Theory 60(9), 5283–5295 (2014)
25. Carlet, C., Gaborit, P., Kim, J.-L., Solé, P.: A new class of codes for Boolean masking of cryptographic computations. IEEE Transactions on Information Theory 58(9), 6000–6011 (2012)
26. Carlet, C., Goubin, L., Prouff, E., Quisquater, M., Rivain, M.: Higher-order masking schemes for S-boxes. In: Canteaut, A. (ed.) FSE 2012. LNCS, vol. 7549, pp. 366–384. Springer, Heidelberg (2012)
27. Carlet, C., Guilley, S.: Correlation-immune Boolean functions for easing countermeasures to side channel attacks. In: Proceedings of the Workshop "Emerging Applications of Finite Fields" Part of the Semester Program on Applications of Algebra and Number Theory, Linz, December 9-13. Algebraic Curves and Finite Fields, Radon Series on Computational and Applied Mathematics, pp. 41–70. Published by de Gruyter (2014)
28. Carlet, C., Guilley, S.: Side-channel indistinguishability. In: Proceedings of HASP 2013, 2nd International Workshop on Hardware and Architectural Support for Security and Privacy, Tel Aviv, Israel, pp. 9:1–9:8. ACM, New York (2013)
29. Carlet, C., Guilley, S.: Complementary Dual Codes for Counter-Measures to Side-Channel Attacks. In: 4th International Castle Meeting, Palmela Castle, Portugal, September 15-18. CIM Series in Mathematical Sciences, vol. 3 (2014) (Submitted to the post-proceedings to appear in AMC)

30. Carlet, C., Prouff, E., Rivain, M., Roche, T.: Algebraic Decomposition for Probing Security. In: Gennaro, R., Robshaw, M. (eds.) Proceedings of CRYPTO 2015. LNCS, vol. 9215, pp. 742–763. Springer, Heidelberg (2015)

31. Chari, S., Jutla, C., Rao, J., Rohatgi, P.: Towards Sound Approaches to Counteract Power-Analysis Attacks. In: Wiener, M. (ed.) CRYPTO 1999. LNCS, vol. 1666, pp. 398–412. Springer, Heidelberg (1999)

32. Chen, H., Cramer, R., Goldwasser, S., de Haan, R., Vaikuntanathan, V.: Secure computation from random error correcting codes. In: Naor, M. (ed.) EUROCRYPT 2007. LNCS, vol. 4515, pp. 291–310. Springer, Heidelberg (2007)

33. Coron, J.-S.: Higher order masking of look-up tables. In: Nguyen, P.Q., Oswald, E. (eds.) EUROCRYPT 2014. LNCS, vol. 8441, pp. 441–458. Springer, Heidelberg (2014)

34. Coron, J.-S., Giraud, C., Prouff, E., Renner, S., Rivain, M., Vadnala, P.K.: Conversion of security proofs from one leakage model to another: A new issue. In: Schindler, W., Huss, S.A. (eds.) COSADE 2012. LNCS, vol. 7275, pp. 69–81. Springer, Heidelberg (2012)

35. Coron, J.-S., Roy, A., Vivek, S.: Fast Evaluation of Polynomials over Finite Fields and Application to Side-channel Countermeasures. In: Batina, L., Robshaw, M. (eds.) CHES 2014. LNCS, vol. 8731, pp. 170–187. Springer, Heidelberg (2014); J. Cryptographic Engineering 5(2), 73–83 (2015)

36. Daemen, J., Rijmen, V.: The design of Rijndael: AES: The advanced encryption standard. Springer (2002)

37. Dobbertin, H.: Almost perfect nonlinear power functions over $GF(2^n)$: the Welch case. IEEE Transactions on Information Theory 45, 1271–1275 (1999)

38. Dobbertin, H.: Almost perfect nonlinear power functions over $GF(2^n)$: the Niho case. Information and Computation 151, 57–72 (1999)

39. Dobbertin, H.: Almost perfect nonlinear power functions on $GF(2^n)$: a new case for n divisible by 5. In: Proceedings of Finite Fields and Applications Fq5, Augsburg, Germany, pp. pp. 113–121. Springer (2000)

40. Karatsuba, A., Ofman, Y.: Multiplication of many-digital numbers by automatic computers. Proceedings of the USSR Academy of Sciences 145, 293–294 (1962); Translation in the academic journal Physics-Doklady, 7, pp. 595–596 (1963)

41. European Telecommunications Standards Institute. Technical Specification 135 202 V9.0.0: Universal mobile telecommunications system (UMTS); LTE; specification of the 3GPP confidentiality and integrity algorithms; Document 2: KASUMI specification (3GPP TS 35.202 V9.0.0 Release 9)

42. Genelle, L., Prouff, E., Quisquater, M.: Thwarting higher-order side channel analysis with additive and multiplicative maskings. In: Preneel, B., Takagi, T. (eds.) CHES 2011. LNCS, vol. 6917, pp. 240–255. Springer, Heidelberg (2011)

43. Gold, R.: Maximal recursive sequences with 3-valued recursive cross-correlation functions. IEEE Transactions on Information Theory 14, 154–156 (1968)

44. Grosso, V., Standaert, F.-X., Prouff, E.: Low Entropy Masking Schemes, Revisited. In: Francillon, A., Rohatgi, P. (eds.) CARDIS 2013. LNCS, vol. 8419, pp. 33–43. Springer, Heidelberg (2014)

45. Ishai, Y., Sahai, A., Wagner, D.: Private Circuits: Securing Hardware against Probing Attacks. In: Boneh, D. (ed.) CRYPTO 2003. LNCS, vol. 2729, pp. 463–481. Springer, Heidelberg (2003)

46. Kasami, T.: The weight enumerators for several classes of subcodes of the second order binary Reed-Muller codes. Information and Control 18, 369–394 (1971)

47. Knudsen, L.R.: Truncated and higher order differentials. In: Preneel, B. (ed.) FSE 1994. LNCS, vol. 1008, pp. 196–211. Springer, Heidelberg (1995)

170   C. Carlet

48. Knudsen, L.R., Robshaw, M.: The block cipher companion. Springer (2011)
49. Kocher, P., Jaffe, J., Jun, B.: Differential Power Analysis. In: Wiener, M. (ed.) CRYPTO 1999. LNCS, vol. 1666, pp. 388–397. Springer, Heidelberg (1999)
50. Maghrebi, M., Guilley, S., Danger, J.-L.: Leakage Squeezing Countermeasure Against High-Order Attacks. In: Ardagna, C.A., Zhou, J. (eds.) WISTP 2011. LNCS, vol. 6633, pp. 208–223. Springer, Heidelberg (2011)
51. Maghrebi, H., Carlet, C., Guilley, S., Danger, J.-L.: Optimal first-order masking with linear and non-linear bijections. In: Mitrokotsa, A., Vaudenay, S. (eds.) AFRICACRYPT 2012. LNCS, vol. 7374, pp. 360–377. Springer, Heidelberg (2012)
52. Mangard, S., Popp, T., Gammel, B.M.: Side-Channel Leakage of Masked CMOS Gates. In: Menezes, A. (ed.) CT-RSA 2005. LNCS, vol. 3376, pp. 351–365. Springer, Heidelberg (2005)
53. Mangard, S., Pramstaller, N., Oswald, E.: Successfully Attacking Masked AES Hardware Implementations. In: Rao, J.R., Sunar, B. (eds.) CHES 2005. LNCS, vol. 3659, pp. 157–171. Springer, Heidelberg (2005)
54. Massey, J.L.: Linear codes with complementary duals. Discrete Mathematics 106-107, 337–342 (1992)
55. Massey, J.L.: Minimal Codewords and Secret Sharings. In: Sixth Joint Sweedish-Russian Workshop on Information Theory, pp. 246–249 (1993)
56. Matsui, M.: Linear cryptanalysis method for DES cipher. In: Helleseth, T. (ed.) EUROCRYPT 1993. LNCS, vol. 765, pp. 386–397. Springer, Heidelberg (1994)
57. Matsui, M.: Block encryption algorithm MISTY. In: Biham, E. (ed.) FSE 1997. LNCS, vol. 1267, pp. 54–68. Springer, Heidelberg (1997)
58. Messerges, T.: Using Second-order Power Analysis to Attack DPA Resistant software. In: Paar, C., Koç, Ç.K. (eds.) CHES 2000. LNCS, vol. 1965, pp. 238–251. Springer, Heidelberg (2000)
59. National Institute of Standards and Technology. Data encryption standard (AES). Federal Information Processing Standards Publication 49-3. United States National Institute of Standards and Technology (NIST). Reaffirmed on October 25, 1999
60. Nyberg, K.: Perfect nonlinear S-boxes. In: Davies, D.W. (ed.) EUROCRYPT 1991. LNCS, vol. 547, pp. 378–386. Springer, Heidelberg (1991)
61. Nyberg, K., Knudsen, L.R.: Provable security against a differential attack. Journal of Cryptology 8(1), 27–37 (1995)
62. Omura, J., Massey, J.L.: Computational method and apparatus for finite field arithmetic. Technical report, Omnet Associates, Patent Number 4,587,627 (May 1986)
63. Piret, G., Roche, T., Carlet, C.: PICARO - A block cipher allowing efficient higher-order side-channel resistance. In: Bao, F., Samarati, P., Zhou, J. (eds.) ACNS 2012. LNCS, vol. 7341, pp. 311–328. Springer, Heidelberg (2012)
64. Prouff, E., Roche, T.: Higher-order glitches free implementation of the aes using secure multi-party computation protocols. In: Preneel, B., Takagi, T. (eds.) CHES 2011. LNCS, vol. 6917, pp. 63–78. Springer, Heidelberg (2011)
65. Prouff, E., Rivain, M., Bevan, R.: Statistical Analysis of Second Order Differential Power Analysis. IEEE Trans. Computers 58(6), 799–811 (2009)
66. Rivain, M., Prouff, E.: Provably secure higher-order masking of aes. In: Mangard, S., Standaert, F.-X. (eds.) CHES 2010. LNCS, vol. 6225, pp. 413–427. Springer, Heidelberg (2010)
67. Roy, A., Vivek, S.: Analysis and improvement of the generic higher-order masking scheme of fse 2012. In: Bertoni, G., Coron, J.-S. (eds.) CHES 2013. LNCS, vol. 8086, pp. 417–434. Springer, Heidelberg (2013)

68. Shamir, A.: How to Share a Secret. Commun. ACM 22(11), 612–613 (1979)
69. Shannon, C.E.: Communication theory of secrecy systems. Bell System Technical Journal 28, 656–715 (1949)
70. Shirai, T., Shibutani, K., Akishita, T., Moriai, S., Iwata, T.: The 128-Bit Block-cipher CLEFIA. In: Biryukov, A. (ed.) FSE 2007. LNCS, vol. 4593, pp. 181–195. Springer, Heidelberg (2007)
71. Siegenthaler, T.: Decrypting a Class of Stream Ciphers Using Ciphertext Only. IEEE Transactions on Computer C-34(1), 81–85 (1985)
72. Sunar, B., Koç, Ç.K.: An efficient optimal normal basis type ii multiplier. IEEE Trans. Computers 50(1), 83–87 (2001)
73. Tan, Y., Qu, L., Tan, C., Li, C.: New families of differentially 4-uniform permutations over $\mathbb{F}_{2^{2k}}$. In: Helleseth, T., Jedwab, J. (eds.) SETA 2012. LNCS, vol. 7280, pp. 25–39. Springer, Heidelberg (2012)
74. Waddle, J., Wagner, D.: Towards Efficient Second-Order Power Analysis. In: Joye, M., Quisquater, J.-J. (eds.) CHES 2004. LNCS, vol. 3156, pp. 1–15. Springer, Heidelberg (2004)
75. Xu, G., Cao, X., Xu, S.: Constructing new differentially 4-uniform permutations and APN functions over finite fields. To appear in Cryptography and Communications - Discrete Structures, Boolean Functions and Sequences (2015)
76. Yu, Y., Wang, M., Li, Y.: Constructing low differential uniformity functions from known ones. Chinese Journal of Electronics 22(3), 495–499 (2013)
77. Zha, Z., Hu, L., Sun, S.: Constructing new differentially 4-uniform permutations from the Inverse function. Finite Fields Applications 25, 64–78 (2014)

Simulations of Optical Emissions for Attacking AES and Masked AES

Guido M. Bertoni, Lorenzo Grassi, and Filippo Melzani

STMicroelectronics Agrate Brianza (MB), Italy
{guido.bertoni,filippo.melzani}@st.com, lorenzo.grassi3@hotmail.com

Abstract. In this paper we present a novel attack based on photonic emission analysis targeting software implementations of AES. We focus on the particular case in which the attacker can collect the photonic emission of a limited number of sense amplifiers (e.g. only one) of the SRAM storing the S-Box. The attack consists in doing hypothesis on the secret key based on the knowledge of the partial output of the SubBytes operation. We also consider the possibility to attack a masked implementation of AES using the photonic emission analysis. In the case of masking, the attacker needs 2 leakages of the same encryption to overcome the randomization of the masks. For our analysis, we assume the same physical setup described in other previous works. Reported results are based on simulations with some hypothesis on the probability of photonic emission of a single transistor.

Keywords: Photonic side channel, Side channel analysis, Light emission, AES, Boolean Masking, Chosen plaintext attack, Full key recovery.

1 Introduction

Some physical parameters, such as power consumption, electromagnetic radiations, or execution time, depend on processed data and on the performed operations. In the context of cryptographic devices, these data-dependent quantities are called *side-channel leakages*. If the attacker is able to detect vulnerable leakage points and to measure side-channel emanations, she can exploit this dependence to extract information about the secret key. *Side Channel Attacks* (SCA) are the cryptanalytic techniques that consist of analyzing the physical leakage (i.e. measurements of such parameters) produced during the execution of a cryptographic algorithm embedded on a physical device. Example of SCA are Differential/Correlation power analysis (see [5]) and Electro-magnetic analysis.

Protection against these attacks has become a very important and challenging task. In the context of symmetric cryptographic algorithms, the most well-established countermeasure to thwart attacks based on power consumption is masking. The core idea is to mix the sensitive variables with some random values (called *masks*) in order to render every intermediate variable of the computation statistically independent of any sensitive variable. In this way, the measurements of the side-channel leakages are unpredictable to the attacker due to the presence of the masks.

© Springer International Publishing Switzerland 2015
R.S. Chakraborty et al. (Eds.): SPACE 2015, LNCS 9354, pp. 172–189, 2015.
DOI: 10.1007/978-3-319-24126-5_11

Another possible leakage that can be used to set up a side channel attack is the optical emission. The light emission phenomenon has been mainly studied for failure analysis during the last 25 years and many techniques have been developed to extract and process the light emitted by the electronic components in order to localize different kinds of defects. One of the first uses of photonic emissions in CMOS in a security application was presented in [3], where the authors demonstrate the possibility to set up an attack based on light emitted by the sense amplifiers in order to recover the secret key stored in the microcontroller RAM. In particular, the authors utilize Picosecond Imaging Circuit Analysis (PICA), i.e. one kind of the detector technologies in use today, to spatially recover information about exclusive or operations ($\oplus$) related to the initial AddRoundKey operation of AES. A similar attack has been presented in [9]. In both these works, the authors suppose that an attacker has complete information about the photonic emission, that is she is able to observe the photonic emission of all the sense amplifiers during the reading or/and the writing operations of the SRAM.

Starting from these works, we consider the particular case in which the attacker has only partial information on the photonic emission. The possibility to recover the secret key using only the emissions of a single transistor was already suggested in [6], in [7] and in [2]. In the former paper, the authors perform a Simple Photonic Emission Analysis (SPEA) of a proof-of-concept AES implementation, and they have been able to recover the full AES secret key by monitoring accesses to the S-Box, directly exploiting the side channel leakage of a single transistor of the row inverter. In the second paper (and similarly in the third one), the authors present a Differential Photonic Emission Analysis (DPEA), that is a differential side channel analysis technique applied to the photonic emission measurement of a limited number of sense amplifiers. In particular, they analyze the emission traces of data-dependent regions of the datapath to recover a single bit of the S-Box output and, subsequently, they apply a Difference of Means to recover the full AES secret key. In these previous works, the authors suppose that the S-Box is stored into the SRAM.

In our work, we set up a simple photonic emission attack in the case in which the attacker can observe the photonic emission of a limited number (e.g. only one) of sense amplifiers, that is the photonic emission corresponding to the output of the SubBytes operation. In particular, we focus on the case in which each row of the SRAM stores only one byte (i.e. it is composed of 8 memory cells), which is the same model studied in [3] and [9]. Moreover, in order to minimize the number of plaintexts (and of the tests) that the attacker needs to discover the secret key, we set up a chosen plaintext attack. Finally we consider the possibility to use our Photonic Emission Analysis to attack a software AES implementation protected against first order SCA, even in the previous case of limited knowledge about the photonic emission of the attacker. For our analysis, we have assumed the physical setup described in [6], [7] and [9], and we have focused on the results of these works in order to show our improvements and our new results, which are obtained using a theoretical approach.

The paper is organized as follow. In Sections 2 and 3 we present additional background information on the underlying physics of the photonic emissions in CMOS, the optical emission during the read operation of a SRAM, the AES and the Masked AES algorithm. In section 4 we detail our proposed attack against software implementations of AES-128 in the case of partial information about the photonic emissions, and we set up a chosen plaintext attack. Next, in Section 5 we consider photonic emission analysis on AES with masks as power analysis countermeasure. We conclude in Section 6.

2 Background on Photonic Emission

Currently, most digital circuits are based on CMOS (i.e. Complementary-MOS) technology. CMOS circuits use a combination of complementary and symmetrical pairs of p-type and n-type MOSFETs transistors to implement logic gates and other digital circuits. We restrict photonic emission to CMOS case only.

2.1 Photonic Emissions in CMOS

One of the particularities of CMOS transistors is that photons are emitted during their commutation. Indeed, when a current flows between the source and the drain, the electrons gain energy and accelerate due to the electrical field. At the drain edge of the channel where the field is most intense, this energy is released in radiative transitions, generating photons. The optical emission from a n-channel transistor takes place when the output goes from high to low state, and from a p-channel when it goes from low to high, that is when the transistor opens. This hot-carrier luminescence is dominant in n-type transistors due to the higher mobility of electrons as compared to holes (the photonic emission in a p-type transistor is usually too low to be acquired). Consequently, this phenomenon produces an asymmetric light emission profile that can be used to extract relevant information from the circuit (for more details, see [10] and [12]).

To observe the light emitted, the chip needs to be opened from its backside. The silicon substrate is then mechanically thinned down and polished, in order to decrease the absorption rate of the silicon substrate. The photons emission can be collected by a specific device equipped with a high sensitivity photon sensor mounted on the optical axis of a conventional microscope (see [14] and [13]).

The number of photons emitted by MOS transistors depends on many complex physical aspects, the most important of which are the number of electrons flowing through the MOSFET channel, the probability of each electron to emit a photon and the physical size of the MOSFET. Approximately, the number of emitted photons for each switching transition varies from 10^{-2} to 10^{-4}, but in general only about 5% of the emitted photons reach the detector. Moreover, when they come to the sensor itself, photons are only registered with a certain probability called quantum efficiency (for more details, see [11] and [9]).

Consequently, in contrast to power consumption and electromagnetic field emissions, not every switching of a transistor results in emission of photons.

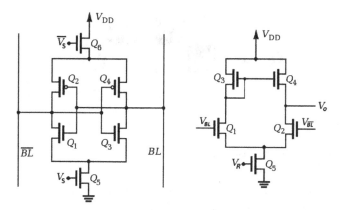

Fig. 1. (a) A sense amplifier with positive feedback - (b) A differential MOS amplifier with a current-mirror load

Thus, the absolute number of detectable photons must be integrated over multiple tests.

2.2 Photons Emission by the SRAM during the Reading Operation

Static random-access memory (SRAM) is a type of semiconductor memory that uses bistable latching circuitry to store each bit. The major part of a memory chip consists of cells in which bits are stored (one bit for each memory cell), and are typically organized in a matrix.

Each cell in the array is connected to one of the 2^M row lines, known as word lines, and to one of the 2^N column lines, known as bit lines. A particular cell is selected for reading or writing by activating its word line, via the row-address decoder, and its bit line, via the column-address decoder. The content of the selected cell is detected by the *sense amplifier*, which provides a full-swing version of it to the data-output terminal of the chip.

During the reading and the writing operations, few photons are emitted both by the memory cell and by the sense amplifier. For both cases, the photonic emission is different (in term of location) if the read bit is a 0-logic or a 1-logic. Thus, knowing the photonic emission during the reading or/and the writing operations, it is possible to discover which bit has been read or/and written. Since a sense amplifier is in general bigger than a memory cell and since the intensity of current flowing through a sense amplifier is greater than that passing through a memory cell, the number of photons that are emitted by a sense amplifier is greater than those emitted by a memory cell.

Sense amplifiers are essential to the proper operations of SRAMs and a variety of sense-amplifier designs are in use. The two most common models of sense amplifier (shown in Fig. 1) are:

Fig. 2. (a) Schematically representation of a *Sense Amplifier with Positive Feedback* - (b) Photons emission when a 0-logic is read - (c) Photons emission when a 1-logic is read

- Sense Amplifier with Positive Feedback;
- Differential MOS Amplifier with a Current-Mirror Load.

In the following, we study the photonic emission of these two models of sense amplifier during the reading operation. Observe that optical emission analysis allows direct observation of the data processed inside semiconductor chips (e.g. data stored in SRAM can be extracted). For more details about the SRAM and the Sense Amplifiers, see [8] (chapter 15).

Sense Amplifier with Positive Feedback. The sense amplifier with positive feedback is a latch formed by cross-coupling two CMOS inverters. Referring to Fig. 2, one inverter is implemented by transistors Q_1 and Q_2, and the other by transistors Q_3 and Q_4. In particular, transistors Q_1 and Q_3 are n-MOS type, while transistors Q_2 and Q_4 are p-MOS type. During the read operation, it can be proven that if the stored bit is a 0-logic, then photons are emitted by transistors Q_2 and Q_3, while they are emitted by transistors Q_1 and Q_4 if the stored bit is a 1-logic (remember that photons are emitted only by MOS in which current flows). Thus, there is a difference in term of location of the photonic emission, but the total number of emitted photons doesn't change.

An example of a real photonic emission described previously can be found in [6], Fig. 3. In this image, you can observe the optical emission of the SRAM cells during the reading operation (remember that the design of a sense amplifier with positive feedback is very similar to that of a memory cell, and that the photonic emission of a memory cell is analogous to that of this kind of sense amplifier in the case of a reading operation). In particular, in this image it is very simple to note the difference (in term of location) of the photonic emission between the case in which the read bit is a 0-logic and the case in which it is a 1-logic.

Numerical Model. We want to build a simplified and approximated model that describes the photonic emission of a sense amplifier with positive feedback. Let p the following probability:

$$p = Prob(\text{at least one photon is emitted by the transistor during the} \tag{1}$$
reading operation of a bit and it is detected by the collector).

Since the number of photons emitted by a p-MOS transistor is negligible compared to the number of photons emitted by a n-MOS transistor, p is well approximated by the probability that at least one photon is emitted by the n-MOS

Fig. 3. (a) Schematically representation of a *Differential MOS Amplifier with a Current-Mirror Load* - (b) Photons emission when a 0-logic is read - (c) Photons emission when a 1-logic is read

transistor during the reading operation of a bit and that it is detected by the collector. Let us suppose to read the same bit N times and to integrate the photonic emission over the multiple tests, then:

$$Prob(\text{at least one photon is emitted and detected by the collector in } N \text{ reads}) = 1 - (1 - p)^N. \tag{2}$$

Let P_{min} the minimum *chosen* probability that at least one photon is emitted and detected by the collector in N reads. To collect at least one emitted photon in N tests with probability P_{min}, N has to satisfy the following condition:

$$N \geq \frac{\log(1 - P_{min})}{\log(1 - p)}. \tag{3}$$

Differential MOS Amplifier with a Current-Mirror Load. The differential MOS amplifier with a current-mirror load is composed of two identical n-MOS transistors Q_1 and Q_2, as illustrated schematically in Fig. 3. During the reading operation, it can be proven that photons are (mainly) emitted only by the transistor Q_1 if the stored bit is a 1-logic, and that no photons are emitted if the read bit is a 0-logic. Thus, the number of emitted photons depends on which bit has been read.

An example of a real photonic emission described previously can be found in [9], Fig. 7 and 8. In these images, it is very simple to note that there is an optical emission only when the read bit is a 1-logic.

Finally, observe that the photonic emission of a differential MOS amplifier with a current-mirror load can be described by the previous numerical model. Indeed, for a chosen probability P_{min}, let us suppose as before to read the same bit N times (where N is defined in (3)), and to integrate the photonic emission over the multiple tests. Then, the read bit is a 1-logic if at least one photon is emitted in N reads, otherwise it is a 0-logic with probability P_{min}.

3   Background on AES

The Advanced Encryption Standard (AES) is a secret key encryption algorithm based on the Rijndael cipher [1]. AES can process data blocks of 128 bits, using cipher keys with lengths of 128, 192 and 256 bits, and operates on a 4×4 matrix of bytes, named the state. The algorithm is specified as a number of identical rounds (except for the last one) that transform the input plaintext into the ciphertext. AES consists of 10, 12 and 14 rounds for 128-, 192- and 256-bit keys, respectively.

Since our attack exploits the leakage obtained during the beginning of the first round of AES, we present only the two beginning operations that are executed until then, namely *AddRoundKey* and *SubBytes*. In the AddRoundKey step, each byte of the plaintext is combined with the corresponding byte of the secret key, using the exclusive or operation ($\oplus$). In the SubBytes step, each byte of the state is replaced with another according to a fixed 8-bit lookup table, denoted S-Box. The used S-Box is constructed by combining the multiplicative inverse function over $GF(2^8)$ (known to have good non-linearity properties) with an invertible affine transformation. This operation provides the non-linearity in the algorithm.

3.1 The Masked AES Algorithm

The core idea of masking is to conceal all intermediate values with some random values called *masks*, in order to make the leakage measurements unpredictable. For every execution of the algorithm, new masks are generated. Hence, the attacker does not know the masks. The masks are added at the (very) beginning of the algorithm to the plaintext. During the execution of the algorithm, one needs to take care that every intermediate value stays masked. Obviously, a correct masking scheme doesn't have to modify the ciphering.

For our work we decided to focus on the first order masking AES proposed by *C. Herbst et al.* in [4]. We only present the masking scheme of AddRoundKey and SubBytes operations of the beginning of the first round of AES.

In this scheme, we use two (byte) masks, M and M', as the input and the output masks for the masked SubBytes operation. At the start of each AES encryption, we pre-compute a masked SubBytes table S-Box$'$ such that $\forall x \in GF(2^8)$

$$\text{S-Box}'(x \oplus M) = \text{S-Box}(x) \oplus M'. \tag{4}$$

At the beginning of the first round, the plaintext byte p is masked with M (i.e. $p_M = p \oplus M$), and then the AddRoundKey operation is performed on p_M. Then, the SubBytes operation with the table S-Box$'$ is performed and this changes the mask to M' (indeed: S-Box$'(p_M \oplus k) = $ S-Box$(p \oplus k) \oplus M'$).

4 Photonic Side Channel Attacks on AES

The typical strategy of side channel attacks is to reveal each byte of the key separately. Thus, for the following we work on a fixed but arbitrary single byte of the key, of the plaintext and of the intermediate state.

If an attacker is able to know the photons emission of all the sense amplifiers of the SRAM, she can use this knowledge to find the key in a very simple way. In particular, she can discover the secret key using the photons that are emitted by the sense amplifiers during the reading of the secret key from the SRAM, for instance when needed for the AddRoundKey operation (see [3] and [9] for a detailed exposition).

Let us suppose now that an attacker is only able to collect the photons that are emitted by a limited number of sense amplifiers. In this case, if the attacker can know at least 6 bits for each byte of the secret key (that is 96 bits of the complete key) using for example the previous method, then she can simply discover the remaining 32 bits (and so the complete secret key) using a brute force attack. Otherwise, in general the attacker is not able to discover the complete secret key using only the knowledge of the photons that are emitted by less than 6 sense amplifiers during its reading.

To discover the secret key in this case we concentrate on the output of the SubBytes operation, and in particular on the photons that are emitted by (some) sense amplifiers during the reading of the output of the SubBytes operation. Indeed, note that the knowledge of one bit of the output of the S-Box allows the attacker to do some hypothesis on the input of the S-Box (and so on the byte of the secret key), because each bit of the output of the S-Box depends on all the bits of its input.

We emphasize that the possibility to recover a single bit of the S-Box output by analyzing emission traces of data-dependent regions of the datapath has been proven in [7]. More generally, the possibility to recover a bit by analyzing the photonic emission and using the techniques described in subsection 2.2 has already been proven in practice in [6] and [9].

4.1 Monitoring the SRAM

We consider the case in which the S-Box is contained within the SRAM, which led us to consider possible side channels that exist within this memory. As in [6], our attack needs an initial spatial analysis to allow for at least a basic understanding of the chip's functionality and the organization of the SRAM to identify the S-Box within memory. We refer to [6] for a detailed explanation of the initial spatial analysis of the SRAM.

We start showing our attack in the simple case in which each row of the SRAM is composed by 8 memory cells, i.e. each row of the SRAM stores one byte (observe that this is the same model studied in [3] and [9]). Then we will generalize the models considered for the attack.

In the simple model, we suppose that there is an area of the SRAM where each row stores one byte of the S-Box and where all the r-th bits of each byte of the S-Box are on the r-th bit line. That is, during the read operation, the r-th bit of the output of the SubBytes operation is read and amplified by the r-th sense amplifier. Moreover, we suppose that the attacker can observe only the sense amplifier of the single (fixed) column r of the SRAM, i.e. she is only able to collect the photons that are emitted by the r-th sense amplifier. Thus, using this photonic emission, the attacker is able to discover the r-th bit of the output of the SubBytes operation. In the next subsection, we describe how she can use this knowledge to do hypothesis on the secret key.

4.2   Key Recovery in the Simple Model

Let us suppose that an attacker discovers that the r-th bit of the output of the S-Box for an input message m is b. Using this information she can eliminate all the candidates $k \in GF(2^8)$ of the secret key byte such that

$$\text{S-Box}(m \oplus k)_r \neq b, \tag{5}$$

where $\text{S-Box}(x)_r$ denotes the r-th bit of the output of S-Box(x).

The idea is to repeat this simple operation with different plaintexts m until the attacker recovers the byte k of the secret key.

Let m_1 the first plaintext used by the attacker, and let b_1 the r-th bit of the output of the SubBytes operation of the exclusive or of m_1 and of the secret key byte. We define K_1 as the set of all possible candidates of the secret key byte after the first step:

$$K_1 = \{k \in GF(2^8) \mid \text{S-Box}(m_1 \oplus k)_r = b_1\}, \tag{6}$$

It is simple to verify that $|K_1| = \frac{1}{2}|GF(2^8)| = 128$ for each choice of m_1 (remember that the S-Box is a bijective function), where $|K|$ denotes the cardinality of the set K.

If the attacker iterates this procedure using different plaintexts, she can discover the secret key. Indeed, let us suppose to be at the $(h-1)$-th step (where $h \geq 2$) and let K_{h-1} the set of all the possible candidates of the key byte at this step (where $|K_{h-1}| > 1$). As previously, using the h-th plaintext byte m_h (where $m_h \neq m_1, ..., m_{h-1}$), she can eliminate other candidates of the key byte. Thus, starting from K_{h-1}, let K_h defined as:

$$K_h = \{k \in K_{h-1} \mid \text{S-Box}(m_h \oplus k)_r = b_h\}, \tag{7}$$

where b_h is defined as before. Observe that $|K_h| \leq |K_{h-1}|$. If $|K_h| = 1$, then the attacker has found the secret key byte, otherwise she has to repeat this procedure for a new plaintext byte m_{h+1}.

The attacker surely discovers the byte of the secret key using a finite number of different plaintext bytes. Indeed, we have verified by computer simulations that for each $k_1, k_2 \in GF(2^8)$ such that $k_1 \neq k_2$ and for each $r \in \{1, ..., 8\}$, there exists at least one $m \in GF(2^8)$ such that

$$\text{S-Box}(k_1 \oplus m)_r \neq \text{S-Box}(k_2 \oplus m)_r.$$

This implies that for each sequence $m_1, m_2, ..., m_{256}$, there exists an integer h such that $2 \leq h \leq 256$ and $|K_h| = 1$.

The number of plaintexts that an attacker needs to discover the byte of the secret key is not fixed if the plaintexts are chosen in a random way. In particular, using computer simulations, we found that if she chooses the plaintexts in a random way, then:

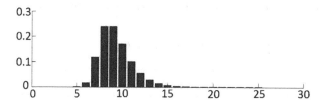

Fig. 4. The histogram shows (on the vertical axis) the probability that an attacker needs a certain number of plaintexts (on the horizontal axis) to recover the byte of the secret key. The histogram was obtained with 250 000 simulations.

- the average number of plaintexts she needs to recover the secret key is about 9.3;
- in the best case, she needs only 5 (different) plaintexts to recover the secret key;
- in the worst case, she needs up to 146 (different) plaintexts to recover the secret key.

The probability that an attacker needs a certain number of plaintexts to recover the byte of the secret key is showed in the histogram in Fig. 4.

To explain the fact that the number of plaintexts is not constant if they are chosen in a random way, consider the following example. Let the secret key byte $k = 0x65$, the first plaintext byte $m_1 = 0x27$ and $r = 6$. The number of key candidates after the first step is 128. Let m_2 the second plaintext byte. Then, the number of possible keys after the second step depends on the choice of m_2:

- if $m_2 = 0x2B$, the number of key candidates after the second step is 72;
- if $m_2 = 0x10$, the number of key candidates after the second step is 64;
- if $m_2 = 0xC5$, the number of key candidates after the second step is 60.

This situation also occurs in the next steps and this is the reason why the number of plaintexts that the attacker needs is not constant.

4.3   Chosen Plaintext Attack in the Simple Model

If the attacker has the possibility to do a chosen plaintext attack, she can choose the plaintexts $m_1, m_2, \ldots$ in order to minimize the number of plaintexts that she needs to recover the byte of the secret key. In the following, we show a way to choose the plaintexts such that the attacker needs only 8 different plaintexts to recover the secret key. Moreover, the following algorithm (to choose the plaintexts) can be easily generalized to more generic models.

The first plaintext byte m_1 can be chosen in a random way, because, as we have seen, any choice of m_1 halves the number of the candidates of the secret key.

The h-th plaintext byte m_h ($h \in \{2, ..., 8\}$) has to satisfy the following condition[1]:

$$|\{k \in K_{h-1} \,|\, \text{S-Box}(m_h \oplus k)_r = 0\}| = \\ = |\{k \in K_{h-1} \,|\, \text{S-Box}(m_h \oplus k)_r = 1\}|. \tag{8}$$

Observe that this condition implies that $m_h \neq m_1, ..., m_{h-1}$. If m_h satisfies the condition (8) and if K_h is defined as in (7), it is simple to verify that

$$|K_h| = \frac{1}{2}|K_{h-1}| = \frac{1}{2^h}|GF(2^8)| = \frac{256}{2^h}.$$

Thus $|K_8| = 1$, that is K_8 contains only the secret key.

If there is no m_h that satisfies (8), the idea is to choose m_h that minimizes the following quantity:

$$abs(|\{k \in K_{h-1} \,|\, \text{S-Box}(m_h \oplus k)_r = 0\}| - \\ |\{k \in K_{h-1} \,|\, \text{S-Box}(m_h \oplus k)_r = 1\}|). \tag{9}$$

In this case, the number of plaintexts that the attacker needs to find the byte of the secret key can be greater than 8, but using this method she can still minimize the number of plaintexts.

Why does m_h have to satisfy the condition (8)? We define:

$$A = \{k \in K_{h-1} \,|\, \text{S-Box}(m_h \oplus \tilde{k})_r = 0\},$$

$$B = \{k \in K_{h-1} \,|\, \text{S-Box}(m_h \oplus \tilde{k})_r = 1\},$$

where $\tilde{k}$ is the secret key. Observe that $|A| + |B| = |K_{h-1}|$. It is simple to prove that if $|A| > \frac{1}{2}|K_{h-1}|$ (or $|A| < \frac{1}{2}|K_{h-1}|$), the number of the key candidates after the h-th step is greater than $\frac{1}{2}|K_{h-1}|$ with probability 0.5 (or it is less than $\frac{1}{2}|K_{h-1}|$ with probability 0.5, respectively). Instead if $|A| = |B| = \frac{1}{2}|K_{h-1}|$, then the number of the key candidates after the h-th step is equal to $\frac{1}{2}|K_{h-1}|$ with probability 1.

We repeated the previous computer simulations using the method described above. In all these tests the attacker always needs 8 plaintexts to find the secret key. From computer simulations, we can say that:

- the random choice is better in 13.3% of cases;
- the two methods are equivalent in 24.0% of cases;
- the above method is better in 60.7% of cases.

It is simple to note that the plaintext bytes $m_1, ..., m_8$ can be precomputed for each possible output bit sequence $b_1, ..., b_8$.

---

[1] The condition (8) is equivalent to the following condition:

$$\sum_{k \in K_{h-1}} \text{S-Box}(m_h \oplus k)_r = \frac{|K_{h-1}|}{2}.$$

Another Way to Choose the Second Plaintext m_2. Given K_1 and m_1, an equivalent condition that the second plaintext m_2 has to satisfy is:

$$|\{k \in K_1 \mid k \oplus m_1 \oplus m_2 \in K_1\}| =$$
$$= |\{k \in K_1 \mid k \oplus m_1 \oplus m_2 \notin K_1\}|. \tag{10}$$

It is very important to observe that this condition works only for the choice of the second plaintext m_2. Additionally one can observe that the condition (10) is independent from the S-Box functionality.

To prove this condition, we introduce two sets A and B:

$$A = \{k \in GF(2^8) \mid \text{S-Box}(m_1 \oplus k)_r = j\}$$

$$B = \{k \in GF(2^8) \mid \text{S-Box}(m_2 \oplus k)_r = l\},$$

where $j, l \in \{0, 1\}$. Using:

- $|A \cap B| + |A \cap B^C| = |A|$,
- if $j = l$, then

$$|A \cap B| = |\{k \in A \mid k \oplus m_1 \oplus m_2 \in A\}|$$
$$|A \cap B^C| = |\{k \in A \mid k \oplus m_1 \oplus m_2 \notin A\}|,$$

- if $j \neq l$, then

$$|A \cap B^C| = |\{k \in A \mid k \oplus m_1 \oplus m_2 \in A\}|$$
$$|A \cap B| = |\{k \in A \mid k \oplus m_1 \oplus m_2 \notin A\}|,$$

it is simple to prove the condition (10).

4.4   Key Recovery in the Generic Model

The method described in the previous subsections can be extended to more generic models. In particular, if the attacker can observe S ($1 \leq S \leq 8$) sense amplifiers, our method changes very little (only in the definition of (7)) and the number of plaintexts/tests that the attacker needs to recover the secret key decreases.

More interesting is the case in which the number of sense amplifiers is greater than 8 (that is they are 2^N with $N > 3$). In this case, the idea is to repeat our attack in the same way. Anyway, it works efficiently only when the attacker can observe at least one of every 8 sense amplifiers. We plan to further investigate more specifically the attack for this case in a forthcoming work.

In both the previous cases, it is easy to generalize and to adapt the chosen plaintext attack described in the previous subsection to these generic models.

Finally, if the attacker can observe both the photonic emission of the row decoder and of the sense amplifiers, she can combine our attack with the one described in [6].

5   Photonic Side Channel Attacks on Masked AES

As we said before, the common approach to secure implementations of symmetric cryptographic algorithms against power analysis attacks is randomize the key-dependent data by the addition of one or several random *masks*. Our goal is to understand if AES with power analysis countermeasure can be considered secure against photonic side channel attacks. In particular, for our work we consider the efficient first order masking AES proposed in [4] and explained in subsection 3.1.

As previously, we focus on the case in which each row of the SRAM stores one byte (that is each row is composed of 8 memory cells) and we suppose that the masks are stored into the SRAM. However, the following analysis holds for more generic models.

5.1   Key Recovery

Let us suppose for the moment that an attacker can observe all the sense amplifiers of the SRAM, which means that she is able to collect the photons that are emitted by all the sense amplifiers. In this case, the masking scheme for the AES is completely useless against photonic emission analysis. Indeed, as in the case of unmasked AES, the attacker can discover the secret key using the photons that are emitted by the sense amplifiers during the reading of the key from the SRAM (required for the AddRoundKey operation). Since the read secret key is always the same, she can repeat this operation as many time as she wants, in order to integrate the photonic emission over multiple tests (remember that the number of detectable photons is so low that it needs to be averaged over multiple tests). Using this procedure, she can obtain the secret key in the same way as the unmasked AES.

Consider now the case in which an attacker can observe only a limited number (e.g. one) of sense amplifiers of the SRAM, that is she is only able to know the photons emission of a limited number (e.g. one) of sense amplifiers. As previously, a possible way to discover all bits of each byte of the secret key is to attack the output of the SubBytes operation. However, using this method there is an important difference between the masked and the unmasked case that must be taken into account. In the case of unmasked AES, an attacker can repeat the encryption as many time as she wants, and she can integrate the photonic emissions over multiple tests in order to recover the read bit. Instead, in the case of masked AES, the attacker can not do this, because the intermediate values (and so the photonic emissions) are different for every encryption due to the presence of the masks. Thus, if an attacker is not able to understand if the read bit is 0- or 1-logic with only one photonic emission, she can not attack masked AES using the output of the SubBytes operation in this particular case. For the following, we assume that it is sufficient one photonic emission to understand if the read bit is 0- or 1-logic. Observe that this assumption is (at the moment) unrealistic (for example it means that there is no noise), but it is the best situation for the attacker.

With this assumption, the attacker must use two leakages to attack the masked AES, due to the presence of the masks. It is very important to note that these two leakages must be of the same encryption, that is the masks of the two leakages have to be the same. There are several possibilities about the leakages that can be used to implement the attack. We consider the two following cases:

- two different bytes of the masked message (with the same masks);
- one byte of the masked message and of the associated mask.

Another interesting possibility is to attack the key schedule to recover the secret key (remember that each round key depends on the initial secret key): we plan to further investigate this possibility in a forthcoming work.

5.2 Two Different Bytes of the Masked Message (with the Same Masks)

Let us suppose that an attacker knows the r-th bit of the i-th and of the j-th byte of the output of the masked SubBytes operation $(i \neq j)$. We denote respectively by b_i and b_j these two bits, and by m_i and m_j the i-th and the j-th byte of the plaintext. As before, the idea is to use this information to eliminate some key candidates. The procedure is very similar to that explained in section 4, but in this case we attack two different bytes of the secret key simultaneously.

Let K_1 the set of all the possible candidates of the i-th and of the j-th byte of the secret key after the first step[2]:

$$K_1 = \{(k_i, k_j) \in GF(2^8) \times GF(2^8) \mid \text{S-Box}(m_i \oplus k_i)_r \\ \oplus \text{S-Box}(m_j \oplus k_j)_r = b_i \oplus b_j\}. \tag{11}$$

Observe that for each $x, y \in GF(2^8)$:

$$\text{S-Box}'(x)_r \oplus \text{S-Box}'(y)_r = \text{S-Box}(x)_r \oplus \text{S-Box}(y)_r.$$

Using different couples of plaintext bytes m_i and m_j, the attacker can eliminate other candidates of the key repeating the above procedure, until she finds the secret key. We define K_h as the set of all possible candidates of the key after the h-th step:

$$K_h = \{(k_i, k_j) \in K_{h-1} \mid \text{S-Box}(m_i \oplus k_i)_r \oplus \text{S-Box}(m_j \oplus k_j)_r = b_i \oplus b_j\}. \tag{12}$$

Also in this case, if the attacker chooses the plaintext in a random way, the number of plaintexts that she needs to discover the secret key is not constant. At the h-th step, if she has the possibility to do a chosen plaintext attack, the chosen plaintext bytes m_i and m_j have to satisfy the following condition:

$$|\{(k_i, k_j) \in K_{h-1} \mid \text{S-Box}(m_i \oplus k_i)_r \oplus \text{S-Box}(m_j \oplus k_j)_r = 0\}| = \\ = |\{(k_i, k_j) \in K_{h-1} \mid \text{S-Box}(m_i \oplus k_i)_r \oplus \text{S-Box}(m_j \oplus k_j)_r = 1\}|,$$

---

[2] In this subsection, we omit the index (h) of the step on m and on b for an easier reading.

in order to minimize the number of plaintexts that the attacker needs to recover the bytes of the secret key. It is simple to prove that if m_i and m_j satisfy the previous condition, then $|K_h| = \frac{1}{2}|K_{h-1}|$.

5.3   One Byte of the Masked Message and of the Associated Mask

Let us suppose that an attacker knows the r-th bit of the output of the masked SubBytes operation for a plaintext byte m (denoted b) and the r-th bit of the masked M' (denoted $M'^{(r)}$). Also in this case, she can use these information to eliminate some candidates of the key and to discover the byte of the secret key. In this particular case, the attack is completely equivalent to that described in section 4. For this reason, we refer to that section for a complete explanation of the attack, and we limit ourselves to re-define the set K_h used in (7) and in (8).

We define K_1 as the set of all the possible candidates of the secret key byte after the first step:

$$K_1 = \{k \in GF(2^8) \mid \text{S-Box}(m_1 \oplus k)_r = b_1 \oplus M_1'^{(r)}\}, \tag{13}$$

and, in the same way, let K_h the set of all the possible candidates of the secret key byte after the h-th step:

$$K_h = \{k \in K_{h-1} \mid \text{S-Box}(m_h \oplus k)_r = b_h \oplus M_h'^{(r)}\}, \tag{14}$$

where, as before, $m_h \neq m_1, ..., m_{h-1}$. Remember that:
S-Box$'(x)_r = $ S-Box$(x)_r \oplus M'^{(r)}$ for each $x \in GF(2^8)$.

If the attacker has the possibility to do a chosen plaintext attack, she can choose the plaintexts using the algorithm (8) described in subsection 4.3, in order to minimize the number of plaintexts/tests.

Observe that, during the encryption, the mask M' could be read several times depending on how masked AES is implemented. For example, during the pre-computation of the masked S-Box$'$, the mask can be read 256 times, i.e. one for each input/output of the S-Box, or it can be read only 1 time and then stored in a working register. If the mask M' is read more times, then the attacker may have more opportunities to have two photons emissions (one for the mask and one for the plaintext) in the same encryption.

5.4   Numerical Model and Comparison

We want to compare the number of acquisitions required by an attacker in order to discover one or more bits of the output of the SubBytes operation, both in the unmasked and in the masked AES case. In this second case, we consider only the case in which the attacker uses the two leakages of one byte of the masked message and of the associated mask M': remember that the two leakages have to be of the same encryption (i.e. the masks of the two leakages must be the same). Moreover, in both cases we suppose that the knowledge of at least 1 emitted photon is sufficient for the attacker to discover which bit has been read.

Table 1. The following table gives an estimate of the number of tests that the attacker needs to do in order to discover the key for different values of p, P_{min} and R. Remember that these numbers are obtained with simple and approximated models.

p	P_{min}	(unmasked) AES	Masked AES & $R = 256$	Masked AES & $R = 1$
10^{-4}	95 %	29 960	1 170 210	299 573 230
10^{-4}	99.99 %	92 100	3 597 785	921 034 050
10^{-5}	95 %	299 575	117 020 795	29 957 322 740
10^{-5}	99.99 %	921 050	359 778 930	92 103 403 750

In the unmasked AES case, the required number of tests for each plaintext is given by the equation (3). In a similar way, it can be proven that the required number of encryptions/tests for each plaintext in the masked AES case is given by

$$N \geq \frac{\log(1 - P_{min})}{\log(1 - R \cdot p^2)}, \tag{15}$$

where p is defined in (1), P_{min} is the chosen probability that at least one photon is emitted and detected by the collector in N encryptions, and R is the number of times that the mask M' is read during the encryption process. Observe that the probability that there is at least one photonic emission in R reads of the same bit of the mask M' is given by $1 - (1 - p)^R$, but since $0 < p \ll 1$, then $1 - (1 - p)^R \simeq 1 - (1 - R \cdot p) = R \cdot p$. The quantity p^2 in (15) depends on the fact that the attacker needs at least two photonic emissions (respectively, at least one for the bit $M'^{(r)}$ of the mask and at least one for the bit S-Box$'(p_M \oplus k)_r$) for the same encryption.

Table 1 gives an estimation of the minimum number of tests that an attacker needs to do in order to discover the secret key for some different values of p, P_{min} and R. We emphasize that these numbers are obtained with simple and approximated models, and they are useful only in order to do a simple comparison between the unmasked and masked case.

The relationship between the number of tests in the masked and in the unmasked AES case is given by:

$$\frac{N_{\text{masked AES}}}{N_{\text{(unmasked) AES}}} = \frac{\log(1 - p)}{\log(1 - R \cdot p^2)} \simeq \frac{1}{R \cdot p} > 1. \tag{16}$$

If $(R \cdot p)^{-1} \gg 1$, then the number of tests in the masked case is much bigger than in the unmasked case. In this case, the time that the attacker needs to collect the two leakages in the same encryption can be so long that the attack can become unworkable.

6   Conclusion

In this work we have presented a novel attack based on photonic emission analysis against software implementations of AES-128. We have mainly analyzed the case

188 G.M. Bertoni, L. Grassi, and F. Melzani

in which the attacker can collect the photonic emission of a limited number (e.g. only one) of sense amplifiers and in which each row of the SRAM stores only one byte. Based on the state of the art and on the capability of the real equipment, the analysis of a single spot is shown to be a realistic scenario. The presented attack can easily be adopted to AES-192 and AES-256.

Attacking masked AES is another novel result reported in this paper. In this case the attacker needs 2 leakages of the same encryption to overcome the randomization of the masks. Moreover, the number of acquisitions needed by the attacker increases by a factor proportional to p^{-1} with respect to the unmasked AES case, where p is the probability that at least one photon is emitted by the transistor and detected by the collector during the read operation. Since p is practically very low and since it is not possible to integrate the photonic emission over multiple tests, a simple photonic emission analysis seems to be not practical to attack masked AES.

Acknowledgement. The work has been supported in part by the Austrian Science Fund (project P26494-N15).

References

1. Daemen, J., Rijmen, V.: The design of Rijndael: AES - the Advanced Encryption Standard. Springer Verlag (2002)
2. Di-Battista, J., Courrege, J.C., Rouzeyre, B., Torres, L., Perdu, P.: When Failure Analysis Meets Side-Channel Attacks. In: Mangard, S., Standaert, F.-X. (eds.) CHES 2010. LNCS, vol. 6225, pp. 188–202. Springer, Heidelberg (2010)
3. Ferrigno, J., Hlaváč, M.: When AES blinks: introducing optical side channel. Information Security, IET 2(3), 94–98 (2008)
4. Herbst, C., Oswald, E., Mangard, S.: An AES Smart Card Implementation Resistant to Power Analysis Attacks. In: Zhou, J., Yung, M., Bao, F. (eds.) ACNS 2006. LNCS, vol. 3989, pp. 239–252. Springer, Heidelberg (2006)
5. Kocher, P.C., Jaffe, J., Jun, B., Rohatgi, P.: Introduction to differential power analysis. Journal of Cryptographic Engineering 1(1), 5–27 (2011)
6. Schlösser, A., Nedospasov, D., Krämer, J., Orlic, S., Seifert, J.-P.: Simple Photonic Emission Analysis of AES. In: Prouff, E., Schaumont, P. (eds.) CHES 2012. LNCS, vol. 7428, pp. 41–57. Springer, Heidelberg (2012)
7. Schlösser, A., Nedospasov, D., Krämer, J., Orlic, S., Seifert, J.-P.: Differential Photonic Emission Analysis. In: Prouff, E. (ed.) COSADE 2013. LNCS, vol. 7864, pp. 1–16. Springer, Heidelberg (2013)
8. Sedra, A.S., Smith, K.C.: Microelectronic Circuits, vol. 6. Oxford University Press (2009)
9. Skorobogatov, S.P.: Using Optical Emission Analysis for Estimating Contribution to Power Analysis. In: 6th Workshop on Fault Diagnosis and Tolerance in Cryptography (FDTC), pp. 111–119. IEEE Computer Society (2009)
10. Stellari, F., Zappa, F., Cova, S., Vendrame, L.: Tools for non-invasive optical characterization of CMOS circuits. In: Electron Devices Meeting, IEDM 1999. Technical Digest. International, pp. 487–490 (December 1999)

11. Stellari, F., Zappa, F., Ghioni, M., Cova, S.: Non-Invasive Optical Characterisation Technique for Fast Switching CMOS Circuits. In: Proceeding of the 29th European Solid-State Device Research Conference, vol. 1, pp. 172–175 (September 1999)
12. Tosi, A., Stellari, F., Zappa, F., Cova, S.: Hot-carrier luminescence: comparison of different CMOS technologies. In: 33rd Conference on European Solid-State Device Research, ESSDERC 2003, pp. 351–354 (September 2003)
13. Tsang, J., Fischetti, M.: Why hot carrier emission based timing probes will work for 50 nm, 1V CMOS technologies. Microelectronics Reliability 41(9-10), 1465–1470 (2001)
14. Villa, S., Lacaita, A.L., Pacelli, A.: Photon emission from hot electrons in silicon. Phys. Rev. B 52, 10 993–10 999 (1995)

Fault Tolerant Infective Countermeasure for AES

Sikhar Patranabis, Abhishek Chakraborty, and Debdeep Mukhopadhyay

Department of Computer Science and Engg., IIT Kharagpur, India
{sikhar.patranabis,abhishek.chakraborty,debdeep}@cse.iitkgp.ernet.in

Abstract. Infective countermeasures have been a promising class of fault attack countermeasures. However, they have been subjected to several attacks owing to lack of formal proofs of security and improper implementations. In this paper, we first provide a formal information theoretic proof of security for one of the most recently proposed state of the art infective countermeasures against DFA, under the assumption that the adversary does not change the flow sequence or skip any instruction. Subsequently, we identify weaknesses in the infection mechanism of the countermeasure that could be exploited by attacks which change the flow sequence. Furthermore, we propose an augmented infective countermeasure scheme obtained by introducing suitable randomizations that reduce the success probabilities of such attacks. All the claims have been validated by supporting simulations and real life experiments on a SASEBO-W platform. We also compare the fault tolerance provided by our proposed countermeasure scheme against that provided by the existing scheme.

Keywords: Infective Countermeasure, AES, Randomization, Instruction Skip, Fault Attack, Fault Tolerant.

1 Introduction

With fault attacks now being an established threat to the security of cryptosystems, sound countermeasures are needed to protect them. Recent research has demonstrated two major flavors of countermeasures - detection based and infection based. Detection based countermeasures such as time and hardware redundancy [1, 2] are vulnerable against attacks to the comparison step itself and also against attacks using biased fault models [3]. Infective countermeasures, on the other hand, avoid the use of comparison by diffusing the effect of the fault to render the ciphertext unexploitable. However, deterministic diffusion based infective countermeasures are vulnerable to attacks as demonstrated by Lomné et.al [4]. A random variation of the infective countermeasure was proposed by Gierlichs et.al [5]. However, the infection method employed by this countermeasure has a number of shortcomings, as demonstrated by Battistello and Giraud [6], and in greater detail by Tupsamudre et.al [7]. Tupsamudre et.al have also proposed an improved infective countermeasure that avoids all the pitfalls of [5]

© Springer International Publishing Switzerland 2015
R.S. Chakraborty et al. (Eds.): SPACE 2015, LNCS 9354, pp. 190–209, 2015.
DOI: 10.1007/978-3-319-24126-5_12

and thwarts DFA. However, no formal proof of security has been provided for the proposed scheme. Moreover, fault attacks that allow an adversary to change the flow sequence of an algorithm by methods such as instruction skips have also not been considered.

Recent research on microcontrollers and embedded processors has revealed that fault models in which an adversary can skip one or more instructions is practically observable on various architectures [8, 9] using different fault injection techniques [10–12]. Hence, such a fault model is a realistic threat to embedded applications. We demonstrate in this paper that the instruction skip fault model weakens the infective countermeasure scheme proposed in [7] and allows easy key recovery. Thus, it is important to make infective countermeasure tolerant against attacks that change the flow sequence of the algorithm. This paper proposes an augmented infective countermeasure scheme with suitable randomizations that reduce the probability of occurrence such faults considerably.

Contributions: In this paper, we first present a formal information theoretic proof of security for the infective countermeasure scheme proposed by Tupsamudre *et. al* [7] against single and multiple fault injection models, under the assumption that an adversary cannot change the flow sequence or skip instructions. We then investigate in detail the threats posed to this countermeasure by the instruction skip fault model and formally analyze the information leakage as a result of the attack. We also examine in detail the drawbacks of the original scheme that makes it vulnerable to instruction skips, and then propose an augmented countermeasure scheme by incorporating necessary randomizations in the existing algorithm to reduce the probability of such attacks. All the claims have been validated by supporting simulations and real-life experiments on a SASEBO-W platform that compare the existing and augmented versions of the infective countermeasures both in terms of performance and security.

2   Preliminaries: The Infective Countermeasure

In this section, we briefly introduce the infective countermeasure scheme proposed by Tupsamudre *et. al* [7]. Table 1 summarizes the notations used in the rest of this paper. For the description of the countermeasure scheme, we use the same notations used in the original paper. Algorithm 1 depicts the infective countermeasure proposed in [7] for AES-128. In the event of a fault in any of the computation rounds (redundant or cipher), the algorithm detects the difference in values of R_0 and R_1 during the execution of the cipher round. The value of R_0 is then set to R_2 as described in step 11 of the algorithm. If, on the other hand, the adversary attacks the dummy round, $(R_2 \oplus \beta)$ evaluates to 1 and R_0 is once again set to R_2. In the event of undisturbed execution, the algorithm outputs the correct ciphertext. In the following section, we formally examine the security of the countermeasure scheme against single and multiple fault injections under the assumption that adversary cannot alter the flow of execution of the algorithm.

Table 1. Notations

$RoundFunction$	The round function of AES128 block cipher which operates on a 16 byte state matrix and 16 byte round key
S	The SubByte operation in the $RoundFunction$
SR	The ShiftRow operation in the $RoundFunction$
MC	The MixColumn operation in the $RoundFunction$
n	The total number of computation rounds (n = 11 for AES128)
t	The total number of rounds for the infective algorithm
I^i	The 16 byte input to the ith round of AES128, where $i \in \{0, \ldots, 10\}$
K	The 16 byte secret key used in AES128
k^j	The 16 byte matrix that represents $(j-1)^{th}$ round key, $j \in \{1, \ldots, 11\}$, derived from the main secret key K
β	The 16 byte secret input to the dummy round
k^0	The 16 byte secret key used in the computation of dummy round
$rstr$	A 't' bit random binary string, consisting of $(2n)$ 1's corresponding to AES rounds and $(t-2n)$ 0's corresponding to dummy rounds
$BLFN$	A Boolean function that maps a 128 bit value to a 1 bit value (0 input is mapped to 0; all other inputs are mapped to 1)
γ	A one bit comparison variable to detect fault injection in AES round
δ	A one bit comparison variable to identify a fault injection in dummy round
$\cdot$	A multiplication operation
$\wedge$	A bitwise logical AND operation
$\vee$	A bitwise logical OR operation
$\neg$	A bitwise logical NOT operation
$\oplus$	A bitwise logical XOR operation
X	A discrete random variable
x_i	A specific value that X may take
$Pr(X = x)$ or $Pr(x)$	The probability that a random variable X takes a value x
hline $Pr(x|y)$	The conditional probability that $X = x$ given $Y = y$
$H(X)$	The entropy of random variable X
$H(X|Y)$	The conditional entropy of X given Y
$I(X|Y)$	The mutual information of random variables X and Y
K	The secret key used by AES
Δ	The differential of the fault-free and faulty ciphertexts
N	The total number of possible values for K and Δ
$\{k_1, k_2, \cdots, k_N\}$	The sample space from which K takes its values
$\{\Delta_1, \Delta_2, \cdots, \Delta_N\}$	Sample space from which Δ can take its value

3   Information Theoretic Evaluation of the Infective Countermeasure

In Differential Fault Analysis (DFA), the adversary uses a fault model of her choice and obtains both fault-free and faulty ciphertexts. The basic assumption underlying the DFA principle is that the differential of the correct and faulty ciphertext leaks some information about the secret key used in the algorithm. The adversary then infers the key by analyzing the fault propagation under the assumption of a fault model. However, if the differential provides no additional information about the key, then obtaining the faulty ciphertext does not give the adversary any advantage at all. Thus, the capability of a countermeasure

Algorithm 1. Infective Countermeasure [7]

Inputs : P, k^j for $j \in \{1, \ldots, n\}$, (β, k^0), $(n = 11)$ for AES128
Output : $C = BlockCipher(P, K)$

1. State $R_0 \leftarrow P$, Redundant state $R_1 \leftarrow P$, Dummy state $R_2 \leftarrow \beta$
2. $i \leftarrow 1$, $q \leftarrow 1$
3. $rstr \leftarrow \{0, 1\}^t$ // $\#1(rstr) = 2n$, $\#0(rstr) = t - 2n$
4. while $q \leq t$ do
5. $\lambda \leftarrow rstr[q]$ // $\lambda = 0$ implies a dummy round
6. $\kappa \leftarrow (i \wedge \lambda) \oplus 2(\neg \lambda)$
7. $\zeta \leftarrow \lambda \cdot \lceil i/2 \rceil$ // ζ is actual round counter, 0 for dummy
8. $R_\kappa \leftarrow RoundFunction(R_\kappa, k^\zeta)$
9. $\gamma \leftarrow \lambda(\neg(i \wedge 1)) \cdot BLFN(R_0 \oplus R_1)$ // check if i is even
10. $\delta \leftarrow (\neg \lambda) \cdot BLFN(R_2 \oplus \beta)$
11. $R_0 \leftarrow (\neg(\gamma \vee \delta) \cdot R_0) \oplus ((\gamma \vee \delta) \cdot R_2)$
12. $i \leftarrow i + \lambda$
13. $q \leftarrow q + 1$
14. end
15. return(R_0)

---

scheme to thwart DFA, can be evaluated by formally quantifying the **mutual information** between the output differential and the key. The lesser the mutual information, the stronger is the countermeasure scheme.

In this section, we first describe in greater detail the aforementioned information theoretic security evaluation methodology for countermeasures. We then evaluate the information leakage from infective countermeasure depicted in Algorithm 1 using this framework under single and multiple fault injection models. Table 1 summarizes some of the notations used in this section.

3.1 The Evaluation Methodology

Definition 1. *In information theory, the **mutual information** of two discrete random variables X and Y is defined as:*

$$I(X; Y) = H(X) - H(X|Y) \tag{1}$$

where $H(X)$ denotes the entropy of the random variable X and $H(X|Y)$ denotes the conditional entropy of X given Y.

Again, entropy and conditional entropy are represented using the following formulations:

$$H(X) = \sum_{i=1}^{N} Pr(x_i) \log(Pr(x_i)) \tag{2}$$

$$H(X \mid Y) = \sum_{i=1}^{N} \sum_{j=1}^{N} Pr(y_j) Pr(x_i \mid y_j) \log(Pr(x_i \mid y_j)) \tag{3}$$

Using this information theoretic measure, we can compute how much information a differential fault attack technique leaks about the key, for a given fault model. Let Δ is the fault observed at the output of a block cipher and K is the key used in the encryption. Then $I(K; \Delta)$ provides the mutual information between Δ and K. Using formulations 1, 2 and 3, we have :

$$I(K;\Delta) = \sum_{i=1}^{N}\sum_{j=1}^{N} Pr(\Delta_j)Pr(k_i \mid \Delta_j)\log Pr(k_i \mid \Delta_j) - \sum_{i=1}^{N} Pr(k_i)\log Pr(k_i) \qquad (4)$$

where Δ and K can take values from the sets $\{\Delta_1, \Delta_2, \cdots, \Delta_N\}$ and $\{k_1, k_2, \cdots, k_N\}$ respectively. Further, using Bayes' Theorem, we have $Pr(k_i \mid \Delta_j) = \frac{Pr(\Delta_j|k_i)Pr(k_i)}{Pr(\Delta_j)}$. Thus, using the information theoretic measure, one can evaluate the security of a countermeasure scheme against DFA. We next perform this analysis for the infective countermeasure in the forthcoming discussion.

3.2   Evaluating the Security of the Infective Countermeasure against DFA

Assumptions about the Fault Model: In the information theoretic evaluation of the security of the infective countermeasure, we make the following assumptions about the fault model:

1. The flow sequence of the algorithm, that is, the order in which the redundant, cipher and dummy computations are executed for various rounds is determined solely by the sequence of bits in $rstr$ and does not change during the course of execution of the algorithm via instruction skip or any other methodology.
2. The number of rounds of execution of the algorithm is not in any way affected, that is, we have exactly 11 pairs of redundant and cipher computations, with the redundant computation always preceding the cipher computation.
3. The values of internal variables and registers other than the state registers R_0, R_1 and R_2 are not updated except as required by the algorithm.

We now use the mutual information formalism to evaluate the security of the infective countermeasure proposed by Tupsamudre *et.al.* Before delving into a rigorous analysis, we make an important observation about the algorithm.

Observation 1. *In the event of a fault injection in a single round of the algorithm, the entire cipher state is affected and is in fact replaced by a random matrix β which is entirely independent of the key K.*

A single fault injection could occur in either a redundant computation round, or a cipher computation round, or a dummy round. The correctness of observation 1 can be easily verified by considering each scenario individually.

1. **Redundant round affected:** In this case, R_1 stores the faulty output after the redundant round computation. When the computation of the corresponding cipher round takes place, R_0 stores a value different from the current content of R_1. Hence $R_0 \oplus R1$ evaluates to a non-zero value in step 9 of the algorithm. Hence γ is 1 and R_0 is replaced by β.

2. **Cipher round affected:** In this case, R_0 stores the faulty output after the original round computation, while R_1 stores the correct output. Hence $R_0 \oplus R1$ evaluates to 1 in step 9 of the algorithm. Hence γ is 1 and R_0 is replaced by β.

3. **Dummy round affected:** In this case, R_2 stores the faulty output after the original round computation, which is different from β. Hence $R_2 \oplus \beta$ evaluates to 1 in step 9 of the algorithm. Hence δ is 1 and R_0 is once again replaced by β.

3.3 Security against Single Fault Injections

Since the outcome of fault injection in any of the rounds is thus essentially the same, we present a common analysis for all three scenarios. *Assuming that the adversary cannot affect the number of rounds of computation*, a single fault injection must be detected and the infection will occur. Consequently, the output differential is of the form $\Delta = C \oplus \hat{\beta}$, for fault injection into either the redundant, cipher or dummy rounds, C being the fault free ciphertext output and $\hat{\beta}$ being a random 128 bit matrix. Since $\hat{\beta}$ and K are independent random variables, we have:

$$Pr(\hat{\beta} = \hat{\beta}_k \mid K = k_i) = Pr(\hat{\beta} = \hat{\beta}_k) \tag{5}$$

Consequently , the conditional probability $Pr(\Delta_j \mid k_i)$ takes the form :

$$\begin{aligned} Pr(\Delta_j \mid k_i) &= Pr(\hat{\beta} = \Delta_j \oplus C \mid k_i) \\ &= Pr(\hat{\beta} = \Delta_j \oplus C) \\ &= Pr(\Delta_j) \end{aligned} \tag{6}$$

Thus Bayes' theorem and 6 together establish the conditional independence of K and Δ as:

$$Pr(k_i \mid \Delta_j) = Pr(k_i) \tag{7}$$

Substituting $Pr(k_i)$ in equation 4 yields the following.

$$\begin{aligned} I(K; \Delta) &= \sum_{i=1}^{N} \sum_{j=1}^{N} Pr(\Delta_j) Pr(k_i \mid \Delta_j) \log Pr(k_i \mid \Delta_j) - \sum_{i=1}^{N} Pr(k_i) \log Pr(k_i) \\ &= \sum_{i=1}^{N} \sum_{j=1}^{N} Pr(\Delta_j) Pr(k_i) \log Pr(k_i) - \sum_{i=1}^{N} Pr(k_i) \log Pr(k_i) \\ &= \sum_{i=1}^{N} Pr(k_i) \log Pr(k_i) - \sum_{i=1}^{N} Pr(k_i) \log Pr(k_i) \\ &= 0 \end{aligned} \tag{8}$$

3.4   Security against Multiple Fault Injection

Let e' be the event that the adversary beats the countermeasure by success-fully injecting identical faults in a redundant-cipher round pair. Then, by a similar analysis, the information leakage is found to be $Pr(e')(\log N - \log M + \log Pr(e')) + (1 - Pr(e')) \log (1 - Pr(e'))$, where M is the number of output differentials possible due to fault injection for any given key k_i and $M < N$. The leakage is thus low if $Pr(e')$ is low. Figure 1 summarizes the double fault injection attack probability on rounds p and q of the algorithm. An important assumption for the analysis presented in this section was that *the adversary cannot in any way disturb the order in which the rounds are executed.* If the adversary chooses to mount an attack that, instead of affecting the cipher state, *disturbs the round counter and prevents the infection from affecting the cipher state,* she could gain access to intermediate cipher state values and exploit it to decipher the key in a much simpler fashion. In the next section, we show that the instruction skip fault model indeed allows such an attack that exploits the vulnerability of the round counter.

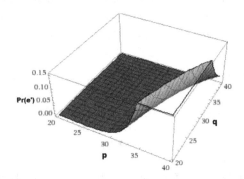

Fig. 1. Variation of $Pr(e')$ with target rounds p and q

4   Instruction Skip Threats to the Infective Countermeasure

We now look in detail at the threat posed to Algorithm 1 by the instruction skip fault model. We begin by looking at possible threats to the infective countermeasure other than traditional DFA attacks, on of which is the instruction skip attack. We next introduce in brief the instruction skip fault model, followed by a description of how the instruction skip fault model could be used by the adversary to disturb the number of executed rounds in Algorithm 1. Finally we focus on the loopholes in the algorithm that allow the adversary to mount such an attack.

4.1 Possible Attacks on the Infective Countermeasure: Affecting Flow Sequence

The formal proof of security of the infective countermeasure 1, presented in section 3, makes some assumptions about the fault model of the adversary. One of these is that the number of rounds and the order of their execution are not affected by the adversary. However, in a practical implementation of the infective countermeasure, the adversary could attack the round counter itself to try and upset the normal execution of the algorithm. As demonstrated in [13, 14], round reduction and fault round modification allow the adversary to obtain the key with a relatively small number of computations. Thus, although Algorithm 1 thwarts traditional DFA, it could be vulnerable to this flavor of attacks where the adversary could play around with the number of effectively executed rounds.

One of the major drawbacks of the infective countermeasure depicted in Algorithm 1 is that there is no validation check for the round counters q and i. If the value of either of these counters is affected by the adversary, the algorithm would not be able to detect the fault, which in turn would affect the order of round execution. There are many ways in which the adversary could inject such a fault. One approach is to affect the state of either the counter variables q and i, or other variables affecting them, such as λ. The stuck-at fault model makes such attacks practically feasible. Alternatively, the adversary could choose to simply skip the round counter updation step(s), that is, steps 12 and/or 13 of Algorithm 1. Such attacks come under the purview of the *instruction skip fault model*. In the forthcoming discussion, we look in greater detail at the threat posed by the instruction skip fault model, the corresponding information leakage as well the loopholes in the infective countermeasure scheme that make such an attack possible.

4.2 The Instruction Skip Fault Model

The instruction skip fault model is a subset of the more general instruction replacement fault model, in which the adversary is able to replace one instruction by another. Previous research has shown that it is possible to perform instruction replacement on embedded processors by a variety of fault injection means [10, 15]. However, precise control over instruction replacement demands very accurate fault injection means and is not of much practical significance. However, a specific category of instruction replacement is the instruction skip fault model, in which the adversary replaces an instruction by another one that does not affect any useful register [16] and has the same effect as a NOP. Instruction skips have been achieved by a number of fault injection schemes on a variety of architectures - via clock glitches [8, 10] and electromagnetic glitches [11] on 8-bit AVR microcontroller, via voltage glitches on a 32-bit ARM9 processor [9] and via laser shots on a 32-bit ARM Cortex-M3 processor [12]. Hence, instruction skips are considered as a practically achievable fault model and have been used for cryptanalysis in recent research [17, 18]. We now look into how the adversary may use the instruction skip fault model to attack Algorithm 1.

4.3   Instruction Skip Attack on the Infective Countermeasure

The attack presented here exploits the fact that a redundant round computation in Algorithm 1 does not involve any infection to the state of the cipher R_0. The adversary targets skipping instruction 12 of Algorithm 1 after the execution of the last redundant round. As a result of this attack, the final cipher round is replaced by another redundant computation round. Since a redundant round does not involve any infection and does not affect the output register R_0, the algorithm simply returns the output of the penultimate cipher round, that is the output of round 9. The adversary can then exploit this faulty ciphertext to recover the key by making hypotheses over each key byte.

Description of the Attack Strategy: We now describe the proposed instruction skip attack strategy on Algorithm 1 in greater detail. The adversary skips instruction 12 of the algorithm in the last (or the nth) redundant round (which is the penultimate computation round). As a result i is not incremented while q is incremented as usual in the next step. Since the affected round is the last redundant round, it is followed by dummy rounds and a single cipher round. We claim and establish in the forthcoming discussions that in any of these rounds, the state register R_0 is not infected despite the presence of the fault. Note that after the instruction skip attack has been mounted in the redundant round, R_0 holds the correct output of the 9th round while R_1 holds the correct output of the 10th round.

- For a dummy round ($\lambda = rstr[q] = 0$), we have $\gamma = 0$ as $\lambda = 0$, and $\delta = 0$ as no fault has been injected in the dummy round and $R_2 = \beta$. So R_0 is not infected and still contains the output of the 9th round.
- For the cipher round ($\lambda = rstr[q] = 1$), we have $\gamma = 0$ because the oddity of i did not change in the preceding redundant computation due to the instruction skip. Additionally, $\delta = 0$ as before. Thus, the algorithm mistakes the cipher computation for a redundant computation and R_0 still holds the correct output of the 9th round.

Since the algorithm definitely terminates due to normal increment of the round counter q, the adversary obtains the output of the 9th round. A trivial DFA now leaks the last round key. Since the key scheduling algorithm of AES is reversible, the adversary can now obtain the master key from the last round key so obtained.

4.4   The Information Leakage : A Formal Quantification

We now evaluate the security of the infective countermeasure in the light of the instruction skip attack event e. We denote by $\bar{e}$ the event that the adversary fails to perform the instruction skip attack and the state of the cipher is randomized due to the infection which breaks any correlation that the output differential Δ has with the key K. Given that e occurs, for a particular key k_i, there is a unique output differential Δ_i. Thus we have the conditional probability distribution of occurrence of a random output differential Δ_j given key k_i as $Pr(\Delta_j \mid k_i, \bar{e}) = \frac{1}{N}$ (since the infection breaks all correlation with the key) and

$$Pr(\Delta_j \mid k_i, e) = \begin{cases} 1, & \text{if } j = i \\ 0, & \text{otherwise} \end{cases}$$

The modified conditional fault probability distribution expression takes the form

$$Pr(\Delta_j \mid k_i) = Pr(\Delta_j \mid k_i, e)Pr(e) + Pr(\Delta_j \mid k_i, \bar{e})Pr(\bar{e})$$

$$= \begin{cases} Pr(e) + \frac{1}{N}(1 - Pr(e)), & \text{if } j = i \\ \frac{1}{N}(1 - Pr(e)), & \text{otherwise} \end{cases} \tag{9}$$

The marginal probability distributions are again unaltered and are given by $Pr(\Delta_j) = Pr(k_i) = \frac{1}{N}$. From Bayes' Theorem, we obtain $Pr(k_i \mid \Delta_j) = Pr(\Delta_j \mid k_i)Pr(k_i)/Pr(\Delta_j) = Pr(\Delta_j \mid k_i)$. Finally using the mutual information formalism, we have the following expression for the mutual information $I(K; \Delta)$.

$$I(K; \Delta) = \sum_{i=1}^{N} \sum_{j=1}^{N} Pr(\Delta_j)Pr(k_i \mid \Delta_j) \log Pr(k_i \mid \Delta_j) - \sum_{i=1}^{N} Pr(k_i) \log Pr(k_i)$$

$$= \sum_{i=1}^{N} \sum_{\substack{j=1 \\ j \neq i}}^{N-1} (1 - Pr(e))/N^2 \log \frac{(1 - Pr(e))}{N}$$

$$\tag{10}$$

$$+ \sum_{i=1}^{N} ((1 - Pr(e))/N^2 \log \frac{(1 - Pr(e))}{N} + Pr(e)/N(\log Pr(e))) + \sum_{i=1}^{N} 1/N \log \frac{1}{N}$$

$$= (1 - Pr(e))(\log (1 - Pr(e)) - \log N) + Pr(e) \log Pr(e) + \log N$$

$$= Pr(e)(\log N + \log Pr(e)) + (1 - Pr(e))(\log (1 - Pr(e)))$$

Once again, it can be easily verified that when $Pr(e) = 0$ the mutual information $I(K; \Delta) = 0$, while for any non-zero value of $Pr(e)$ the value of $I(K; \Delta) > 0$. In particular, for $Pr(e) = 1$, that is, for a sure attack, $I(K; \Delta) = N$ and the entire key is leaked. Thus we have formally established that a successful instruction skip attack leaks information about the key to the adversary. The amount of information leakage depends on the value of $Pr(e)$ as is evident from Equation 10.

The Attack Probability $Pr(e)$: We now analyze the probability that the adversary successfully performs the aforementioned attack on the infective countermeasure. Let e be the event that the adversary performs a successful instruction skip in the nth redundant round by attacking the qth loop of Algorithm 1. *Note that the attack is only deemed to be successful if instruction 12 of Algorithm 1 is skipped. Any other instruction skip causes an infection and the adversary gains no information about the key.* Also, if the nth redundant round coincides with the qth iteration of the algorithm, then the bit string $rstr$ has - $(2n - 2)$ positions set to 1 among the first $q - 1$ positions, has the qth bit set and exactly 1 more bit set among the remaining $t - q$ bits. The probability of this is given by $\binom{q-1}{2n-2}\binom{t-q}{1}/\binom{t}{2n}$. Since there are a total of 9 steps in one iteraton of which only one is to be skipped, assuming single instruction skip, $Pr(e) = \frac{1}{9} \times \binom{q-1}{2n-2}\binom{t-q}{1}/\binom{t}{2n}$ Moreover, $Pr(e)$ could be further augmented to $Pr(e,r)$ by repeating the fault injection experiment independently r times, such that $Pr(e,r) = 1 - (1 - Pr(e))^r$. Note that $Pr(e,r)$ is essentially the probability of obtaining at least one useful faulty ciphertext in r fault injections. It is also interesting to note that for this attack, as the number of dummy rounds increases $Pr(e)$ decreases.

4.5   The Loopholes in the Infective Countermeasure : A Closer Look

There are two major loopholes in the countermeasure that allow the adversary to mount the aforementioned attack :

Table 2. Computation of Algorithm 1

Step	Redundant Round	Cipher Round	Dummy Round
5.	$\lambda = 1$, i is odd	$\lambda = 1$, i is even	$\lambda = 0$
6.	$\kappa \leftarrow 1$	$\kappa \leftarrow 0$	$\kappa \leftarrow 2$
7.	$\zeta \leftarrow \lceil i/2 \rceil$	$\zeta \leftarrow \lceil i/2 \rceil$	$\zeta \leftarrow 0$
8.	$R_1 \leftarrow RoundFunction(R_1, k^\zeta)$	$R_0 \leftarrow RoundFunction(R_0, k^\zeta)$	$R_2 \leftarrow RoundFunction(R_2, k^0)$
9.	$\gamma \leftarrow 0$	$\gamma \leftarrow BLFN(R_0 \oplus R_1)$	$\gamma \leftarrow 0$
10.	$\delta \leftarrow 0$	$\delta \leftarrow 0$	$\delta \leftarrow BLFN(R_2 \oplus \beta)$
11.	$R_0 \leftarrow R_0$	$R_0 \leftarrow (\neg(\gamma) \cdot R_0) \oplus ((\gamma) \cdot R_2)$	$R_0 \leftarrow (\neg(\delta) \cdot R_0) \oplus ((\delta) \cdot R_2)$
12.	$i \leftarrow i + 1$	$i \leftarrow i + 1$	$i \leftarrow i + 0$
13.	$q \leftarrow q + 1$	$q \leftarrow q + 1$	$q \leftarrow q + 1$

1. An inherent drawback of the infective countermeasure is the inability to immediately detect a fault injection in the redundant round. The algorithm must wait until the corresponding cipher round in order to detect the presence of the fault. On the other hand, a fault injection in a cipher round or a dummy round is detected immediately. After a faulty redundant round, R_0 still contains the output of the previous round and is not infected. The phenomenon is made clear in the highlighted row of Table 2 that captures the execution flow of the algorithm in the redundant, cipher and dummy rounds respectively.

2. The execution of the redundant round is merely decided by the fact that the variable i is odd and $\lambda = 1$. There is no way to verify if the redundant round being executed is indeed a valid one. This makes the round counter vulnerable to attacks by a malicious agent who can manipulate the value of the internal variables, as done in the aforementioned attack via an instruction skip, and trick the algorithm into believing that the round to be executed is a redundant one. This allows the adversary to skip the final cipher round, and thus avoid fault detection and infection altogether.

An interesting observation about Algorithm 1 is that the order of the redundant and cipher rounds is fixed. For a given round, the redundant computation always precedes the cipher computation. This is because both the redundant and the cipher rounds are denoted by a set bit in the bit vector $rstr$ and are distinguished by the oddity of i. The randomness is thus limited to the occurrence of the dummy rounds in between, represented by the 0's in $rstr$. Thus the adversary is guaranteed to obtain the output of the penultimate round if she can skip the last cipher round and replace it by a redundant round. If, on the other hand, the relative ordering of the redundant and cipher computations corresponding to a single round could also be randomized and the output masked, then the adversary would have to perform additional instruction skips to get the unmasked output of the penultimate round. In the following section, we present a modified version of Algorithm 1 that achieves this randomization.

5   A Modified Infective Countermeasure

In this section we present a modified infective countermeasure algorithm. The idea is to reduce the probability of the instruction skip attack by making it more uncertain as to whether the fault is introduced in the redundant or cipher round of computation. Unlike in the original scheme where the redundant round always precedes the corresponding cipher round, in the modified version, the order of the redundant and cipher rounds is scrambled and is encoded by an additional bit string $cstr$ of length $2n$. Each 1 bit in $cstr$ corresponds to a redundant round and each 0 bit corresponds to a cipher round. Since cipher and redundant pair of computations are still necessary for each round, $cstr$ is a sequence of $(1,0)$ and $(0,1)$ pairs. The $cstr$ vector may be populated by randomly filling out the odd positions with 0 or 1 and then setting each even position to the negation of its preceding odd position. Additionally, in the modified algorithm, both R_0 and R_1 are masked at the end of each odd computation round and unmasked at the beginning of the corresponding even computation round. The mask m is a 128 bit vector and is generated randomly at the beginning of each odd computation round. Algorithm 2 details the steps of the modified countermeasure,

---

Algorithm 2. Modified Infective Countermeasure

Inputs : P, k^j for $j \in \{1, \ldots, n\}$, (β, k^0), $(n = 11)$ for AES128
Output : $C = \text{BlockCipher}(P, K)$

1. State $R_0 \leftarrow P$, Redundant state $R_1 \leftarrow P$, Dummy state $R_2 \leftarrow \beta$
2. $i \leftarrow 1, q \leftarrow 1$
3. $rstr \leftarrow \{0,1\}^t$ // $\#1(rstr) = 2n, \#0(rstr) = t - 2n$
4. $cstr \leftarrow \{0,1\}^{2n}$ // $\#1(cstr) = n, \#0(cstr) = n$
5. while $q \leq t$ do
6. $\lambda \leftarrow rstr[q]$ // $\lambda = 0$ implies a dummy round while $\lambda = 1$ implies a computation round
7. $\kappa \leftarrow (\lambda \cdot cstr[i]) \oplus 2(\neg\lambda)$ // $\kappa = 0$ or 1 depending on $cstr[i]$
8. $\zeta \leftarrow \lambda \cdot \lceil i/2 \rceil$ // ζ is actual round counter, 0 for dummy
9. $m \leftarrow (\neg(\lambda) \cdot m) \oplus (\lambda \cdot (((\neg(i \wedge 1)) \cdot m) \oplus ((i \wedge 1).RAND())))$ // new m if λ is 1 and i is odd
10. $R_\kappa \leftarrow RoundFunction(R_\kappa \oplus (\neg(i \wedge 1) \cdot m), k^\zeta)$ // unmask R_κ if i is even
11. $\gamma \leftarrow \lambda(\neg(i \wedge 1)) \cdot BLFN(R_0 \oplus R_1 \oplus (\neg(i \wedge 1) \cdot m))$ // unmask $R_{\hat{\kappa}}$ if i is even
12. $\delta \leftarrow (\neg\lambda) \cdot BLFN(R_2 \oplus \beta)$
13. $R_0 \leftarrow (\neg(\gamma \vee \delta) \cdot (R_0 \oplus ((i \wedge 1) \cdot m))) \oplus ((\gamma \vee \delta) \cdot R_2)$ // mask R_0 if i is odd
14. $R_1 \leftarrow (\neg(\lambda) \cdot R_1) \oplus (\lambda \cdot (R_1 \oplus ((i \wedge 1) \cdot m)))$ // mask R_1 if i is odd and λ is 1
15. $i \leftarrow i + \lambda$
16. $q \leftarrow q + 1$
17. end
18. return(R_0)

---

while Table 3 summarizes the functioning of Algorithm 2. The major differences between Algorithms 1 and 2 are summarized below:

1. In Algorithm 1 no infection occurs during the redundant round since the redundant round always occurs prior to the cipher round. On the other hand, in Algorithm 2, the infection occurs (upon fault detection) in the round that occurs later, which may be either cipher or redundant, depending on the content of $cstr$. This makes the treatment of the redundant and cipher rounds more symmetric.
2. In Algorithm 2 both R_0 and R_1 are masked in the end of an odd round and unmasked in the beginning of the corresponding even round computations. This ensures that neither R_0 nor R_1 exposes the output of the previous round after the end of an odd computation round.
3. In Algorithm 1 between each pair of redundant and cipher computations, R_0 retains the unmasked output of the previous round, which could be exploited by an adversary. On the other hand, in Algorithm 2, R_0 holds the masked output of a previous round only if the bit pair in $cstr$ corresponding to the current round is $(1,0)$, the probability of which is $\frac{1}{2}$.

Table 3. Computation of Algorithm 2

Step	Computation Round 1	Computation Round 2	Dummy Round
6.	$\lambda = 1$, i is odd	$\lambda = 1$, i is even	$\lambda = 0$
7.	$\kappa \leftarrow 1$	$\kappa \leftarrow 0$	$\kappa \leftarrow 2$
8.	$\zeta \leftarrow \lceil i/2 \rceil$	$\zeta \leftarrow \lceil i/2 \rceil$	$\zeta \leftarrow 0$
9.	$m \leftarrow RAND()$	$m \leftarrow m$	$m \leftarrow m$
10.	$R_{cstr[i]} \leftarrow RoundFunction(R_{cstr[i]}, k^{\zeta})$	$R_{cstr[i]} \leftarrow RoundFunction((R_{cstr[i]} \oplus m), k^{\zeta})$	$R_2 \leftarrow RoundFunction(R_2, k^0)$
11.	$\gamma \leftarrow 0$	$\gamma \leftarrow BLFN(R_0 \oplus R_1 \oplus m)$	$\gamma \leftarrow 0$
12.	$\delta \leftarrow 0$	$\delta \leftarrow 0$	$\delta \leftarrow BLFN(R_2 \oplus \beta)$
13.	$R_0 \leftarrow R_0 \oplus m$	$R_0 \leftarrow (\neg(\gamma) \cdot R_0) \oplus ((\gamma) \cdot R_2)$	$R_0 \leftarrow (\neg(\delta) \cdot R_0) \oplus ((\delta) \cdot R_2)$
14	$R_1 \leftarrow R_1 \oplus m$	$R_1 \leftarrow R_1$	$R_1 \leftarrow R_1$
15.	$i \leftarrow i + 1$	$i \leftarrow i + 1$	$i \leftarrow i + 0$
16.	$q \leftarrow q + 1$	$q \leftarrow q + 1$	$q \leftarrow q + 1$

Note: The formal proof of security presented for Algorithm 1 in Section 3 also holds good for Algorithm 2 under the same assumptions that the attacker cannot alter the flow sequence or skip instructions. A security analysis for the bit string $cstr$ is presented in Appendix A. We now analyze the impact of the instruction skip fault model on Algorithm 2 as well as corresponding attack probabilities.

5.1   Instruction Skip Attack on the Modified Algorithm

We now analyze in greater detail the probability that the adversary can still mount the same instruction skip attack on Algorithm 2 and obtain the output of the penultimate round. Note that the adversary would have to skip step 15 of Algorithm 2, which corresponds to the increment of the variable i. Since the order of redundant and cipher rounds is now random, we simply assume that the adversary skips step 15 in the penultimate computation round, which could be either a redundant or cipher round. It is to be noted that irrespective of whether a cipher or redundant round is targeted by the adversary, the value of i corresponding to this round is odd(as it is the penultimate round). So at the beginning of this round, a new random value of mask m is generated, and both R_0 and R_1 are thus masked at the end of this round. Thus, we have the following scenarios:

Scenario 1: The Penultimate Computation Is Redundant Computation
If the instruction is skipped during the redundant computation, then the the last cipher round is replaced by a redundant round. Thus, in this scenario, the adversary gets a ciphertext which is the output of the penultimate encryption round XOR-ed with two distinct random values of m generated in the two consecutive redundant rounds. Thus, the obtained ciphertext gives the adversary no extra information about the key.

Scenario 2: The Penultimate Computation Is Cipher Computation
Conversely, if the instruction is skipped during the cipher computation, then the last redundant round is replaced by a cipher round. Thus, the obtained ciphertext is the output of an extra encryption round, but again XOR-ed with two distinct random values of m generated during the two consecutive cipher rounds. Hence, even in this scenario, the ciphertext so obtained gives the adversary no information about the key.

Note that the masking step is important; otherwise in either scenario, the attacker would get the key easily, either from the output of the penultimate cipher round or the output of the additional cipher round. In the presence of the masking step, the only way for the adversary to get the output of the penultimate or the extra round is to also skip the masking step (step 13) in the second redundant/cipher round. Note that Algorithm 2 has 11 instructions in each iteration, out of which exactly one instruction is to be skipped in either round. Thus, if the instruction skip attacks are now made in rounds q and q', the new probability of a successful attack $Pr(\hat{e})$ becomes $\frac{1}{11^2} \times \frac{\binom{q-1}{2n-2}\binom{t-q}{1}}{\binom{t}{2n}} \times \frac{\binom{q'-1}{2n-1}}{\binom{t}{2n}}$ which is less than the original attack probability. Moreover, even if the attacker skips the desired instructions, the output so obtained is either the output of the penultimate round or the output of the additional round with probability $\frac{1}{2}$. This increases the computational complexity of the attack. Figure 2 presents a theoretical comparison of the variation of the two attack probabilities $Pr(e)$ (on the original infective scheme) and $Pr(e')$ (on our proposed infective scheme) with the target rounds q and q'. The comparison assumes a specific instance of both schemes with 30 dummy rounds, that is, $t = 52$ and $n = 11$. The analysis clearly reveals that the range of values of $Pr(\hat{e})$ is much lesser compared to $Pr(e)$ for similar attack scenarios. Finally, as the attack probability on the proposed countermeasure is lower than on the original scheme, the attack on the proposed countermeasure should intuitively lead to a lesser information leakage. This is indeed the case as is proved formally in the following discussion.

A Formal Analysis of the Leakage from the Modified Countermeasure.
We now formally analyze the information leakage due to instruction skip at-

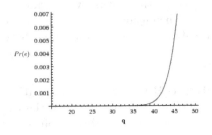

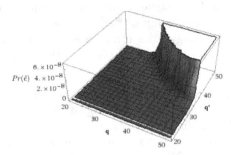

(a) Attack Probability on Original Cou termeasure

(b) Attack Probability on Modified Countermeasure

Fig. 2. Instruction Skip Attack Probabilities on the Original and Modified Countermeasure Schemes

tacks on the augmented infective countermeasure scheme. In the presence of the masking step, the only way for the adversary to get the output of the penultimate or the extra round is to also skip the masking step in the second redundant/cipher round We consider the following mutually exclusive and exhaustive events:

- Event $\hat{e}_1$: The adversary skips neither the increment step in the penultimate computation round nor the masking step in the final computation round of Algorithm 2. Thus in this scenario, the output is either the correct ciphertext or an infected value that has no correlation with the key.
- Event $\hat{e}_2$: The adversary skips only the increment step in the penultimate computation round but not the masking step in the final computation round of Algorithm 2. In this scenario, the adversary will obtain the output of the 9th or 11th cipher round; however the output so obtained will be masked with a random value that has no correlation with the key.
- Event $\hat{e}$: As mentioned already in the preceding discussion, The adversary skips both the increment step in the penultimate computation round as well as the masking step in the final computation round of Algorithm 2. In this scenario, the adversary will obtain the unmasked output of the 9th or 11th cipher round which can then be used to obtain the key, as discussed in Section 5.1.

Quite evidently $\hat{e}_1 \cup \hat{e}_2 = \bar{\hat{e}}$. Given that $\hat{e}_1$ occurs, the output differential Δ has no correlation with the key K because of the infection. Similarly, given that $\hat{e}_2$ occurs, the output differential Δ again has no correlation with the key K due to the presence of the masking.

The scenario is different for the event $\hat{e}$. Here for each given key, there are exactly two output differentials possible, one for the 9th round output and the other for the 11th round output. Since the output differential depends on the $(2n-1)^{th}$ bit value of the bit string *cstr*, each of these occur with probability

$1/2$. We denote this set of possible output differentials corresponding to the key k_i as Δ^i, where $\mid Delta^i \mid = 2$.

The modified conditional fault probability distribution expression takes the form

$$Pr(\Delta_j \mid k_i) = Pr(\Delta_j \mid k_i, \hat{e})Pr(\hat{e}) + Pr(\Delta_j \mid k_i, \bar{\hat{e}})Pr(\bar{\hat{e}})$$

$$= \begin{cases} \frac{1}{2}Pr(\hat{e}) + \frac{1}{N}(1 - Pr(\hat{e})), & \text{if } \Delta_j \in \Delta^i \\ \frac{1}{N}(1 - Pr(\hat{e})), & \text{otherwise} \end{cases} \quad (11)$$

The marginal probability distributions are again unaltered and are given by $Pr(\Delta_j) = Pr(k_i) = \frac{1}{N}$. From Bayes' Theorem, $Pr(k_i \mid \Delta_j) = Pr(\Delta_j \mid k_i)Pr(k_i)/Pr(\Delta_j) = Pr(\Delta_j \mid k_i)$. Finally using the mutual information formalism, we have Equation 12 for the mutual information $I(K; \Delta)$. Once again, it can be easily verified that when $Pr(\hat{e}) = 0$ the mutual information $I(K; \Delta) = 0$, while for any non-zero value of $Pr(\hat{e})$ the value of $I(K; \Delta) > 0$. Note that the factor of 2 in $N/2$ comes due to the randomization provided by the bit sting cstr. This implies even if $Pr(\hat{e}) = 1$ the information leakage is only $N/2$ bits of the key and not all N bits. This emphasizes the advantage of randomizing the order of cipher and redundant rounds using the bit string cstr.

$$I(K; \Delta) = \sum_{i=1}^{N}\sum_{j=1}^{N} Pr(\Delta_j)Pr(k_i \mid \Delta_j) \log Pr(k_i \mid \Delta_j) - \sum_{i=1}^{N} Pr(k_i) \log Pr(k_i)$$

$$= \sum_{i=1}^{N} \sum_{\substack{j=1 \\ \Delta_j \notin \Delta^i}}^{N-2} (1 - Pr(\hat{e}))/N^2 \log \frac{(1 - Pr(\hat{e}))}{N}$$

$$+ \sum_{i=1}^{N} \sum_{\substack{j=1 \\ \Delta_j \in \Delta^i}}^{2} ((1 - Pr(\hat{e}))/N^2 \log \frac{(1 - Pr(\hat{e}))}{N} + Pr(\hat{e})/2N(\log \frac{Pr(\hat{e})}{2})) \quad (12)$$

$$+ \sum_{i=1}^{N} 1/N \log \frac{1}{N}$$

$$\approx (1 - Pr(\hat{e}))(\log(1 - Pr(\hat{e})) - \log N) + Pr(\hat{e})(\log Pr(\hat{e}) - 1) + \log N$$
$$= Pr(\hat{e})(\log(N/2) + \log Pr(\hat{e})) + (1 - Pr(\hat{e})) \log(1 - Pr(\hat{e}))$$

6   Simulation and Experimental Results

In this section, we present results of performed instruction skip attacks mounted on the three different versions of the infective countermeasures for AES128 - Algorithm 1 and Algorithm 2. The results involve both simulation studies as well as real-life experimental results using a Xilinx MicroBlaze soft-core processor in Spartan 6 FPGA of SASEBO-W board.

6.1   Simulation Results

The simulation experiments involved inflicting random instruction skips on 10^5 runs of C implementations of each countermeasure scheme for a given number of

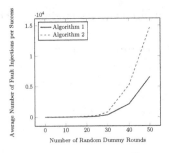

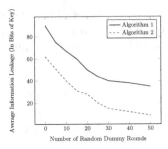

(a) Attack Efficiency vs Dummy Rounds

(b) Information Leakage vs Dummy Rounds

Fig. 3. Simulation results

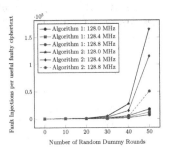

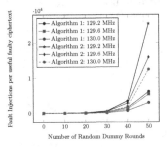

(a) Results at Lower Frequencies

(b) Results at Higher Frequencies

Fig. 4. Experimental Results

dummy rounds. The 128 bit plaintext and the 128 bit key were both randomly chosen, but the same input-key pair was used across all countermeasure schemes for normalization of results. Figures 1a and 1b summarize the results thus obtained. We note that for the same number of dummy rounds, the number of fault injections required by Algorithm 2 is approximately double the number of fault injections required for Algorithm 1, while the information leakage is about $30-40\%$ less for Algorithm 2. This is in accordance with the fact that the probability of a successful fault injection in Algorithm 2 is less than the corresponding probability for Algorithm 1 for a given number of dummy rounds.

6.2 Experimental Results

The experimental set up consisted of an FPGA (Spartan-6 XC6SLX150) on a SASEBO-W platform, Xilinx SDK and an external arbitrary function generator (Tektronix AFG3252). The FPGA had a DUT (Device Under Test) block, which consisted of an infective countermeasure implementation for AES128 on a Xilinx MicroBlaze softcore processor. Instruction skip faults were injected in the DUT using clock glitches. The external clock signal clk_{ext} was supplied from the function generator. The high frequency clock signal clk_{fast} was then derived from the clk_{ext} signal via a Xilinx Digital Clock Manager (DCM) module and supplied to the DUT. We inflicted instruction skip attacks on each of the three infective countermeasure implementations by causing critical path violations using clk_{fast}. We compared the number of fault injections required per useful faulty ciphertext for each of the countermeasure schemes at six different clk_{fast} frequencies and for the number of the dummy rounds set at 0, 10, 20, 30, 40 and 50 respectively. We performed the fault injection trials in a range of clk_{fast} frequencies such that the faulty ciphertexts thus obtained were *useful* ones. Figures 2a and 2b summarize the experimental results. It is observed that the number of fault injections per useful ciphertext increases with an increase in the number of dummy rounds for each version of infective countermeasures. Also, the number of fault injections per useful ciphertext decreases with an increase in clock frequency due to increased fault occurrences.

7   Conclusions

The paper shows that a recently proposed infective countermeasure is formally secure against DFA under the assumption that an attacker cannot subvert the control flow or skip instructions. The paper identifies that such threats against the countermeasure exist because the scheme has a fixed ordering of the redundant and cipher rounds, leading to the fact that a fault in the redundant round is detected in the subsequent cipher round. This leads to the exposure of the previous round output which can lead to trivial attacks. Furthermore, the validity of a redundant round is not checked in the proposal. The paper then proposes a countermeasure scheme against instruction skip attacks. In order to reduce the attacker's success probability, the paper proposes suitable randomizations in the ordering of the redundant and cipher rounds, along with masking the previous round outputs. Detailed simulations and real life experiments have been performed on a MicroBlaze implementation of the countermeasure schemes on a SASEBO-W board, injected with faults via clock glitches. The experiments have demonstrated that the overall resistance to fault attacks is higher for the proposed version of the infective countermeasure scheme as compared to the already existing scheme.

References

1. Malkin, T., Standaert, F.-X., Yung, M.: A comparative cost/security analysis of fault attack countermeasures. In: Breveglieri, L., Koren, I., Naccache, D., Seifert, J.-P. (eds.) FDTC 2006. LNCS, vol. 4236, pp. 159–172. Springer, Heidelberg (2006)
2. Maistri, P., Leveugle, R.: Double-data-rate computation as a countermeasure against fault analysis. IEEE Transactions on Computers 57(11), 1528–1539 (2008)
3. Patranabis, S., Chakraborty, A., Nguyen, P.H., Mukhopadhyay, D.: A Biased Fault Attack on the Time Redundancy Countermeasure for AES. In: Mangard, S., Poschmann, A.Y. (eds.) COSADE 2015. LNCS, vol. 9064, pp. 189–203. Springer, Heidelberg (2015)

4. Lomné, V., Roche, T., Thillard, A.: On the Need of Randomness in Fault Attack Countermeasures - Application to AES. In: Bertoni, G., Gierlichs, B. (eds.) Fault Diagnosis and Tolerance in Cryptography – FDTC 2012, pp. 85–94. IEEE Computer Society (2012)

5. Gierlichs, B., Schmidt, J.-M., Tunstall, M.: Infective Computation and Dummy Rounds: Fault Protection for Block Ciphers without Check-before-Output. In: Hevia, A., Neven, G. (eds.) LatinCrypt 2012. LNCS, vol. 7533, pp. 305–321. Springer, Heidelberg (2012)

6. Battistello, A., Giraud, C.: Fault Analysis of Infective AES Computations. In: Fischer, W., Schmidt, J.-M. (eds.) Fault Diagnosis and Tolerance in Cryptography – FDTC 2013, pp. 101–107. IEEE Computer Society Press (2013)

7. Tupsamudre, H., Bisht, S., Mukhopadhyay, D.: Destroying fault invariant with randomization. In: Batina, L., Robshaw, M. (eds.) CHES 2014. LNCS, vol. 8731, pp. 93–111. Springer, Heidelberg (2014)

8. Schmidt, J., Herbst, C.: A practical fault attack on square and multiply. In: 5th Workshop on Fault Diagnosis and Tolerance in Cryptography, FDTC 2008, pp. 53–58. IEEE (2008)

9. Barenghi, A., Bertoni, G.M., Breveglieri, L., Pelosi, G.: A fault induction technique based on voltage underfeeding with application to attacks against aes and rsa. Journal of Systems and Software 86(7), 1864–1878 (2013)

10. Balasch, J., Gierlichs, B., Verbauwhede, I.: An in-depth and black-box characterization of the effects of clock glitches on 8-bit mcus. In: 2011 Workshop on Fault Diagnosis and Tolerance in Cryptography (FDTC), pp. 105–114. IEEE (2011)

11. Dehbaoui, A., Dutertre, J.-M., Robisson, B., Tria, A.: Electromagnetic transient faults injection on a hardware and a software implementations of aes. In: 2012 Workshop on Fault Diagnosis and Tolerance in Cryptography (FDTC), pp. 7–15. IEEE (2012)

12. Trichina, E., Korkikyan, R.: Multi fault laser attacks on protected crt-rsa. In: 2010 Workshop on Fault Diagnosis and Tolerance in Cryptography (FDTC), pp. 75–86. IEEE (2010)

13. Choukri, H., Tunstall, M.: Round reduction using faults. FDTC 5, 13–24 (2005)

14. Dutertre, J.-M., Mirbaha, A.-P., Naccache, D., Ribotta, A.-L., Tria, A., Vaschalde, T.: Fault round modification analysis of the advanced encryption standard. In: 2012 IEEE International Symposium on Hardware-Oriented Security and Trust (HOST), pp. 140–145. IEEE (2012)

15. Moro, N., Dehbaoui, A., Heydemann, K., Robisson, B., Encrenaz, E.: Electromagnetic fault injection: towards a fault model on a 32-bit microcontroller. In: 2013 Workshop on Fault Diagnosis and Tolerance in Cryptography (FDTC), pp. 77–88. IEEE (2013)

16. Heydemann, K., Moro, N., Encrenaz, E., Robisson, B.: Formal verification of a software countermeasure against instruction skip attacks. In: PROOFS 2013 (2013)

17. Schmidt, J., Medwed, M.: A fault attack on ecdsa. In: 2009 Workshop on Fault Diagnosis and Tolerance in Cryptography (FDTC), pp. 93–99. IEEE (2009)

18. Barenghi, A., Breveglieri, L., Koren, I., Naccache, D.: Fault injection attacks on cryptographic devices: Theory, practice, and countermeasures. Proceedings of the IEEE 100(11), 3056–3076 (2012)

A   Security of the Bit String *cstr* in the Modified Countermeasure

Algorithm 2 uses an additional bit string *cstr* to randomize the order of redundant and cipher computations. Hence it is important to examine the security of *cstr* as well. Note that *cstr* is a sequence of 01 and 10 pairs, because the countermeasure must duplicate the computation of each round for fault detection. It is only the order of the redundant and cipher computations for each round that is scrambled using *cstr*. An adversary might therefore try to upset the order of round execution by performing bit flips or stuck-at fault attacks on *cstr*.

- **Bit-Flips:** *A single bit flip in cstr would result in either two consecutive redundant rounds or two consecutive cipher rounds.* In either scenario, the same register would be updated twice in both rounds - R_1 for redundant or R_0 for cipher round respectively. The algorithm will automatically detect the fault in the second computation, as one of R_0 or R_1 will contain the output of the current round while the other still contains the output of the previous round. Thus as long as the variable i is incremented appropriately after each round computation, the algorithm is fault-tolerant to single bit upsets on *cstr*. However, the adversary could reverse the order of the redundant and original computations corresponding to a round r by flipping both the $(2r-1)^{th}$ and $(2r)^{th}$ bits. In such a scenario, the algorithm cannot detect that the order of the redundant and cipher computations has been reversed. However, in that case, the adversary must make sure that both the bits of *cstr* that are flipped correspond to computations for the same round, which demands slightly greater precision than a naive two bit flip attack. For the naive attack, the probability of appropriate bit flips is $(n-1)/\binom{n}{2}$, which is much smaller than the single bit flip probability. It is important to note that the adversary cannot skip any round by only attacking the bit string *cstr* because it only decides the order of the redundant and cipher computation. Moreover, since the adversary has no idea about the content of *cstr*, the probability that the rth bit pair is 01 or 10 is still $1/2$ and gives the adversary no extra advantage towards other fault attacks such as instruction skips.
- **Stuck-at Faults:** A possible stuck at fault on the bit string *cstr* would be to set the last bit pair to 01 or 10 thus fixing the relative order of the last redundant-cipher round pair. Any other instance of stuck-at fault attack including single bit stuck-at faults would be easily discoverable and would either result in infection or normal operation (depending on if the fault has flipped the bit value). Fixing the relative order of the final pair of computation rounds reduces the uncertainty but as in Algorithm 1 the adversary would still have to perform a successful instruction skip to take advantage of this reduction. Due to the presence of the masking the probability of the instruction skip attack on the modified countermeasure would be less as compared to the original countermeasure. Moreover, achieving a stuck-at-zero fault on one of the bits and a stuck-at-one fault on the other requires high precision and the attack probability is as low as $\frac{1}{n^2}$.

Modified Transparency Order Property: Solution or Just Another Attempt

Stjepan Picek[1,2], Bodhisatwa Mazumdar[3],
Debdeep Mukhopadhyay[4], and Lejla Batina[2,5]

[1] Faculty of Electrical Engineering and Computing, University of Zagreb, Croatia
[2] ICIS - Digital Security Group, Radboud University Nijmegen, The Netherlands
[3] New York University Abu Dhabi, Abu Dhabi
[4] Department of Computer Science and Engineering,
IIT Kharagpur, Kharagpur, India
[5] ESAT/COSIC, KU Leuven, Belgium

Abstract. S-boxes are usual targets of side-channel attacks and it is an
open problem to develop design techniques for S-boxes with improved
DPA resistance. One result along that line is the transparency order, a
property that attempts to characterize the resilience of S-boxes against
DPA attacks. Recently, it was shown there exist flaws with the original
definition of transparency, which resulted in the new definition - modified
transparency order. This paper develops techniques for constructions using the modified transparency as a guiding metric. For the 4×4 size,
we significantly improve modified transparency order while remaining in
the optimal classes. Experimental results are provided assuming a noisy
HW leakage model to show the proposed S-boxes are more resistant than
the original one of the PRESENT algorithm. We conclude with reports
on 4×4 and 8×8 S-boxes where the results indicate that the modified
transparency order could be a more useful metric than the transparency
order. However, both measures are far from definitive solution on how
to improve the DPA resistance.

Keywords: S-box, Modified transparency order, DPA-resilience,
Lightweight cryptography.

1 Introduction

When discussing the security of modern block ciphers, it is often natural to
discuss it through the prism of resilience against certain cryptographic attacks.
Alongside differential [1] and linear [2] cryptanalysis, it is expected today that the
algorithm possesses resistance also against side-channel attacks [3]. In order to
defend against the first two types of cryptanalysis, Substitution Boxes (S-boxes)
play a significant role. In fact, in many block ciphers, S-box is the only nonlinear
part and therefore fundamental for the security of a whole cipher [4]. Somewhat
surprising, in recent years researchers found that S-boxes have inherent resistance
against side-channel analysis (SCA) (some more and some less). Naturally, there

© Springer International Publishing Switzerland 2015
R.S. Chakraborty et al. (Eds.): SPACE 2015, LNCS 9354, pp. 210–227, 2015.
DOI: 10.1007/978-3-319-24126-5_13

exist numerous countermeasures such as various hiding and masking schemes that improve the algorithm resiliency to SCA [5].

First property that connected S-boxes and their resistance against side-channel attacks was SNR (DPA) [6]. Next, Prouff introduced transparency order [7], a property that characterizes the resistance of S-boxes to the SCA or more precisely to differential power analysis (DPA) [8]. Later, Fei introduced confusion coefficient where it is possible to separate the target device, the number of traces and the algorithm under the examination [9–12]. Up to now, transparency order received the most interest so we can speak about a whole line of research about the transparency order property as it is detailed below in Section 1.1.

Recently, Chakraborty et al. showed that the original transparency order definition is flawed and they proposed amendments to it that resulted in the modified transparency order property. However, until now, there has been no practical examination of this new property.

In accordance with that, in this paper we concentrate on generating S-boxes that have good values of modified transparency order property. By good values, we mean such values that are better than those found in currently used S-boxes. When generating S-boxes we concentrate on the two most widely used S-box sizes; more precisely, 4×4 and 8×8. The first one is used in lightweight cryptographic algorithms like PRESENT [13] or PRINCE [14] while the second one is used in what is probably the most well-known cryptographic algorithm in the world - AES [15]. In doing so, we experiment with three different approaches when generating S-boxes: random search, heuristics and affine transformation.

After presenting the newly generated S-boxes for both sizes, we also give SCA experiments, but only for 4×4 size. This is due to the two reasons: the first one is that our new S-box has all the same properties as the S-boxes currently used except it is superior in modified transparency order property. The second reason is that our S-box is possible to implement only as a lookup table which does not represent a difficulty for that size. When considering 8×8 size, both of those arguments do not hold.

1.1   Related Work

Leander and Poschmann classify all optimal 4×4 S-boxes [4]. Some examples of algorithms using optimal S-boxes are PRESENT [13], PRINCE [14] and Noekeon [16].

Regarding modified transparency order property, except for the paper that presented the property [17], there are currently no other works. However, when discussing the original transparency order property there are many (sometimes contradicting) results. After Prouff in 2005 defined transparency order [7], for a couple of years this property did not attract a lot of attention. However, from 2012 there have been several works exploring that property. Mazumdar et al. construct rotation symmetric S-boxes with high nonlinearity and DPA resistance [18]. The same authors use constrained random search to find S-boxes with low transparency order and high nonlinearity [19]. Picek et al. use heuristics to evolve S-boxes that have improved values of transparency order property for 8×8 size [20] and 4×4 size [21]. The same authors investigate one more measure, namely, confusion coefficient that characterizes the resilience of S-boxes against DPA attacks [22]. Evci and Kavut show the minimal affine transformation needed to change transparency order property [23]. Nguyen et al. investigate the influence of transparency order property on Serpent-type S-boxes [24].

1.2 Our Contributions

There are two main contributions in this paper. Our first contribution is that, to our best knowledge, we are the first to generate S-boxes with improved values of modified transparency order property. In order to do that we use two techniques; heuristics and affine transformation. For the 4×4 size, we find the best possible value of modified transparency order as well as lower and upper bounds for all 16 optimal classes. The second contribution is extensive DPA analysis of several newly generated S-boxes as well as their comparison with the PRESENT S-box.

The remainder of this paper is organized as follows: Section 2 gives basic information about cryptographic properties of S-boxes. In Section 3, we present S-boxes that have improved values of modified transparency order. Furthermore, we give a comparison between several methods capable of generating S-boxes. Side-channel analysis of a number of S-boxes with improved modified transparency order values as well as PRESENT S-box is presented in Section 4. Finally, in Section 5, we conclude the paper.

2   Preliminaries

Here, we present basic notions about cryptographic properties of S-boxes that are of direct interest in this research.

2.1 Optimal S-boxes

First, it would be beneficial to offer an answer which S-boxes are actually suitable in practice. When considering 4×4 S-boxes, there exist in total 16! bijective S-boxes which is approximately 2^{44} options to search from. Leander and Poschmann define optimal S-boxes as those that are bijective, have linearity equal to 8 and δ-uniformity equal to 4. Since the linearity that equals 8 is the same as nonlinearity of 4, we continue using the nonlinearity property instead of the linearity. By using some shortcuts they found that all optimal S-boxes belong to 16 classes, i.e. all optimal S-boxes are affine equivalent to one of those 16 classes [4].

Therefore, for the 4×4 S-box size, we concentrate only on optimal S-boxes as those of practical interest. Indeed, as far as the authors know, all ciphers that use 4×4 S-boxes actually use optimal S-boxes [13, 14, 16, 25].

For the 8×8 size, there exists no such classification, but in general it is believed that nonlinearity of 112 is the maximum possible and therefore the best S-boxes should reach that nonlinearity [26]. There are other conditions except the nonlinearity property, but highly nonlinear S-boxes usually also have other classical properties with good values [26, 27]. In accordance to that, for the 8×8 size, we restrict our attention to the same properties as for the 4×4 size.

2.2 Cryptographic Properties of S-boxes

Here, we discuss the properties that are used to define optimal S-boxes: bijectivity, nonlinearity and δ-uniformity [4]. Besides those properties, we also formally introduce two properties that constitute the core of this research: transparency order and modified transparency order.

The addition modulo 2 is denoted as " $\oplus$ ". The inner product of vectors $\bar{a}$ and $\bar{b}$ is denoted as $\bar{a} \cdot \bar{b}$ and equals $\bar{a} \cdot \bar{b} = \oplus_{i=1}^{n} a_i b_i$.

Function F, called S-box or vectorial Boolean function, of size (n, m) is defined as any mapping F from $\mathbb{F}_2^n$ to $\mathbb{F}_2^m$ [7].

The Hamming weight HW of a vector $\bar{a}$, where $\bar{a} \in \mathbb{F}_2^n$, is the number of non-zero positions in the vector.

An (n, m)-function is called balanced if it takes every value of $\mathbb{F}_2^m$ the same number 2^{n-m} of times [26]. Balanced (n, n)-functions are permutations on $\mathbb{F}_2^n$.

Nonlinearity NL_F of an (n, m)-function F equals the minimum nonlinearity of all non-zero linear combinations $\bar{b} \cdot F$ of its coordinate functions f_i, where $\bar{b} \neq 0$ [28]:

$$NL_F = 2^{n-1} - \frac{1}{2} max_{\substack{\bar{a} \in \mathbb{F}_2^n \\ \bar{v} \in \mathbb{F}_2^{m*}}} |W_F(\bar{a}, \bar{v})|. \tag{1}$$

Here, $W_F(\bar{a}, \bar{v})$ represents the Walsh-Hadamard transform of F [7]:

$$W_F(\bar{a}, \bar{v}) = \sum_{\bar{x} \in \mathbb{F}_2^n} (-1)^{\bar{v} \cdot F(\bar{x}) \oplus \bar{a} \cdot \bar{x}}. \tag{2}$$

Differential delta uniformity δ represents the largest value in the difference distribution table without counting the value 2^n in the first row and first column position [1, 26, 29].

Prouff introduced transparency order property of S-boxes which can be defined for a (n, m)-function as follows [7]:

$$T_F = max_{\bar{\beta} \in \mathbb{F}_2^m} (|m - 2HW(\bar{\beta})| - \frac{1}{2^{2n} - 2^n}$$
$$\sum_{\bar{a} \in \mathbb{F}_2^{n*}} | \sum_{\substack{\bar{v} \in \mathbb{F}_2^m \\ HW(\bar{v}) = 1}} (-1)^{\bar{v} \cdot \bar{\beta}} W_{D_a F}(\bar{0}, \bar{v})|). \tag{3}$$

Here, $W_{D_a F}$ represents Walsh-Hadamard transform of the derivative of F with respect to a vector $a \in \mathbb{F}_2^n$. For further information about the transparency order property, we refer readers to [7, 28].

Recently, researchers presented modified transparency order property in order to deal with some errors in the original definition [17]. This new, modified transparency order property equals:

$$MT_F = max_{\bar{\beta} \in \mathbb{F}_2^m}(m - \frac{1}{2^{2n} - 2^n} \sum_{\bar{a} \in \mathbb{F}_2^{n*}}$$

$$\sum_{j=1}^{m} |A_{F_j}(a) + \sum_{i=1, i \neq j}^{m} (-1)^{\beta_i \oplus \beta_j} C_{F_i, F_j}(a)|), \qquad (4)$$

where $A_{F_j}(a)$ represents the autocorrelation function of F and $C_{F_i, F_j}(a)$ represents the crosscorrelation function. The crosscorrelation $C_{F_i, F_j}(a)$ between functions F_i and F_j equals:

$$C_{F_i, F_j}(a) = \sum_{x \in \{0,1\}^n} (-1)^{F_i(x) \oplus F_j(x \oplus a)}. \qquad (5)$$

We do not give an exhaustive explanation behind the modified transparency order, but rather we enumerate main problems with the original definition of transparency order which are corrected in the new, modified measure. In [19], it was shown that the autocorrelation spectra properties of the coordinate functions have a bearance on the resistivity of the S-box towards power analysis attacks. Further, the crosscorrelation term in the modified transparency order show that the coordinate functions when selected in a pairwise fashion, also affect the resistance to the power based side-channel attacks. Therefore, along with the differential uniformity [30], several cryptographic properties of an S-box such as the autocorrelation spectra and the crosscorrelation spectra properties also determine the side-channel resistivity of an S-box.

In the transparency order property, there is a maximization over all values of β which is shown to be redundant. Next, the crosscorrelation terms between coordinate functions is assumed to be 0 in the original definition which is not the case in general. Finally, when considering lower bound in the original transparency order, it is calculated for bent functions, but the property itself is defined only for balanced functions [17]. In the original definition of the transparency order, the coordinate functions of an S-box are assumed to be balanced, which though correct for popular S-boxes in block ciphers, is not correct on the entire space of S-box functions. This makes the definition of original transparency order incorrect for S-boxes with unbalanced coordinate functions like bent functions. For instance, it was shown in Chakraborty et al. that for an S-box with pairwise complement coordinate functions which are bent, DPA is not possible [17]. But from the definition, transparency order is maximum for such S-boxes, which indicates high vulnerability towards the DPA attacks. This contradiction renders the original definition of transparency order incorrect.

2.3   Affine Equivalence

For two (n, n)-functions S_1 and S_2 to be affine equivalent, the following equation needs to hold:

$$S_2(x) = B(S_1(A(x) \oplus a)) \oplus b, \qquad (6)$$

where A and B are invertible $n \times n$ matrices and a, b are constants in $\mathbb{F}_2^n$.

Picek et al. showed that affine transformation can be used to generate affine equivalent S-boxes that have different values of the transparency order and the confusion coefficient properties [21, 22].

3 Generating S-boxes

In this section, we use several techniques to generate S-boxes with improved modified transparency order. Furthermore, we conduct a comparison between those methods and give an analysis of the lower and upper bounds for the modified transparency order of 4×4 S-boxes.

3.1 Random Search

For random search, solutions are generated by creating uniformly at random a permutation list of values from 0 to 2^{n-1}. Distribution of the random S-boxes values is shown in Table 1 for the 4×4 size and Table 2 for 8×8 size.

Table 1. Distribution of random S-boxes property values, 4×4, 5 000 evaluations.

Property	Max	Min	Mean	Std. dev.
NL_F	4	0	2.1	0.69
δ-uniformity	16	4	6.7	1.37
MT_F	2.93	1.6	2.44	0.14

Table 2. Distribution of random S-boxes property values, 8×8, 1 000 evaluations.

Property	Max	Min	Mean	Std. dev.
NL_F	98	84	92.57	2.13
δ-uniformity	16	10	11.37	1.21
MT_F	6.9	6.83	6.86	0.01

3.2 Genetic Algorithm

In accordance with the related works, e.g. [21,31], we experiment with heuristics to evolve S-boxes that have good modified transparency order values. For the algorithm of the choice, we use genetic algorithm (GA) since it proved to be a good choice in related works. We emphasize that the genetic algorithm does not necessarily represent the best possible approach how to solve this problem, but rather an option one has at his disposal. For a detailed explanation about genetic algorithms, we refer interested readers to [32].

To represent the problem, we use a permutation representation where an S-box is represented with decimal values between 0 and $2^n - 1$, where each of those values is one entry for the S-box lookup table. For the permutation representation, a mutation operator is selected uniformly at random between insert and inversion mutation [32]. Recombination operator is selected uniformly at random between the partially mapped crossover (PMX) [33] and order crossover OX [34]. Both of those crossover operators are among the most common ones for the permutation encoding.

Fitness Functions. When investigating 4×4 size, fitness function combines all the properties that the optimal S-box must have plus the modified transparency order. The goal is to *maximize* the following function:

$$fitness = NL_F + (n - MT_F) + (2^n - \delta). \tag{7}$$

We subtract MT_F and δ-uniformity values from the maximum obtainable values since we represent the problem as a maximization problem and those properties need to be as small as possible.

For the 8×8 case, fitness function equals the sum of nonlinearity (N_F) and modified transparency order as follows:

$$fitness = NL_F + (n - MT_F). \tag{8}$$

For this size, we do not add δ-uniformity to the equation since all our experiments show that it does not help in converging to better solutions, but just makes the evolution process longer.

Common Parameters. Parameters for the GA are the following: the sizes of (n, n)-function are 4 and 8, number of independent runs for each evolutionary experiment is 50 and the population size is 50. Tournament size in steady-state tournament selection is equal to 3. Mutation probability is set to 0.3 per individual. This mutation rate is set on a basis of tuning phase where it showed good results. The evolution process lasts until there is 50 generations without improvement of the best solution. Common parameters are additionally given in Table 3.

3.3   Evolved S-boxes

For the 4×4 size, the best value of modified transparency order we found with the genetic algorithm is 1.9 for an optimal S-box. The transparency order and the modified transparency order values for our evolved S-box as well as for the PRESENT S-box and random S-box are presented in Table 4.

Next, in Table 5, we display a solution that have the best modified transparency order (1.9) property that we found with the genetic algorithm and that belongs to the one of the optimal classes.

As it can be seen, for the 4×4 size, it is possible to obtain S-box that has significantly lower value of modified transparency order while remaining in one

Table 3. Common parameters for GA.

Parameter	Parameter value
Tournament size k	3
Population size	50
Number of experiments	50
Mutation probability	0.3 per individual
Stopping criterion	50 generations without improvement

Table 4. Properties of evolved S-boxes, modified transparency order, 4×4.

S-box	MT_F	T_F
PRESENT	2.467	3.53
Random S-box	2.44	3.47
Evolved S-box	1.9	3.267

Table 5. S-box evolved with the genetic algorithm.

x	0	1	2	3	4	5	6	7	8	9	10	11	12	13	14	15
S(x)	2	0	C	6	A	E	F	7	3	1	8	4	9	D	B	5

of the optimal classes. Next, we display results for the 8×8 size in Table 6. As it can be seen, in this case properties like the nonlinearity, δ-uniformity, GAC (Δ_F and σ_F) [35] significantly deteriorate for the evolved S-boxes. In Figures 1 and 2, we display results for random, AES and evolved S-boxes for sizes 4×4 and 8×8, respectively.

3.4 Affine Transformations

It has been shown that the transparency order property is not affine invariant under certain affine transformations [21]. Therefore, we investigate whether the same applies when considering modified transparency order property. We apply four affine transformations as given in [21], where we see that the transformations 3 and 4 change the modified transparency order values (as is the case for the transparency order property [21]). Those affine transformations are based on Eq. (6).

By following the reasoning from [23], we observe that we can apply the same transformation as in that work in order to conduct an exhaustive search. That affine transformation has the following form:

$$S_2(x) = B(S_1(x)). \tag{9}$$

Note that the affine transformation in Eq. (9) is the special form of transformations 3 and 4 from [21] where constants c and d equal 0 and matrix B is the identity matrix.

Table 6. Properties of evolved S-boxes, modified transparency order, 8 × 8.

S-box	NL_F	MT_F	T_F	δ	Δ_F	σ_F
AES S-box	112	6.916	7.86	4	32	133120
Random S-box	92	6.869	9.173	12	96	272128
Evolved S-box 1	100	6.815	7.761	10	104	258304
Evolved S-box 2	98	6.67	7.7	14	96	272896

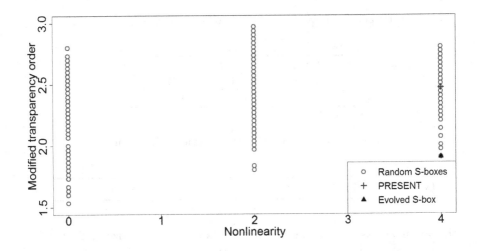

Fig. 1. Nonlinearity versus modified transparency order, 4 × 4.

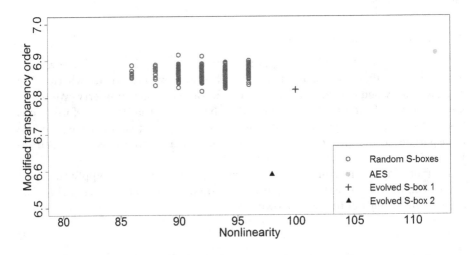

Fig. 2. Nonlinearity versus modified transparency order, 8 × 8.

Results of exhaustive search for all 16 optimal classes' lower and upper bounds are given in Table 7. Additionally, we offer results for class representatives where G_1 to G_{15} are the usual acronyms for the 16 optimal S-box classes.

Table 7. Modified transparency values, 4×4 size.

S-box	MT_F		
	Min	Max	Class representative
G_0	2.067	3	2.23
G_1	1.9	2.8	2.53
G_2	2.03	2.867	2.56
G_3	2.4	2.8	2.46
G_4	2.3	2.83	2.56
G_5	2.33	2.93	2.53
G_6	2.23	2.73	2.46
G_7	2.26	2.7	2.53
G_8	2.03	2.867	2.3
G_9	2.167	2.8	2.5
G_{10}	2.167	2.767	2.36
G_{11}	2.23	2.667	2.46
G_{12}	2.33	2.83	2.5
G_{13}	2.26	2.9	2.66
G_{14}	2.2	2.93	2.6
G_{15}	2.13	2.9	2.5

We see there is only one class that reaches the minimal value of 1.9 and there are 10 different maximal values over all classes. In Figure 3, we give a frequency distribution of all values under the affine transformation from Eq. (9) for the optimal class G_1.

Note that the best value from the exhaustive search is the same as from the genetic algorithm. This shows that such heuristics should present a viable choice when generating S-boxes of comparable sizes. For larger sizes we believe heuristics like genetic algorithms are not appropriate. This stems from two important facts. The first one is that the generated S-boxes have significantly worse values for properties like the nonlinearity and δ-uniformity. The second reason is that the equation for calculating the modified transparency order is much more complex and computationally demanding than in the case of e.g. original transparency order property. This results in relatively slow evaluation of the modified transparency order property, a fact not so important when it is necessary to

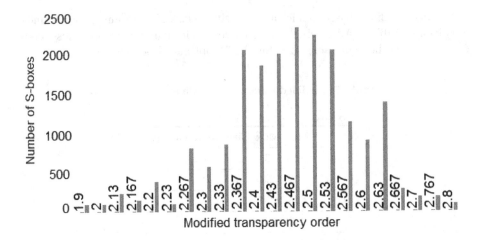

Fig. 3. Frequency distribution of MT_F values for the class G_1.

run the equation only a several times. However, for heuristics like genetic algorithm where the number of evaluations can be rather large, this means the whole process will be long.

When considering 8×8 size, it is not possible to conduct an exhaustive search since the search space is still to large. Therefore, we run experiment with the affine transformation as for the 4×4 size, but for 1 000 randomly generated B matrices. The best value we found equals 6.89 (while AES S-box has 6.916).

4   Success Rate Evaluation of DPA Attacks on the Synthesized S-boxes

In this section, we evaluate the generated 4×4 S-boxes when these S-boxes are subjected to key-recovery attacks like differential power analysis (DPA) in the form of statistical analysis of the physically observables like power traces to efficiently discriminate the secret key. In this set of experiments, we consider Pearson's coefficient as the statistical analysis parameter.

In this experiment, we consider the standalone module of an S-box to which the input is the XOR of the secret key and the input message. We employ the security metric called success rate to measure how easily the physical observable can be turned into a successful attack [36]. The efficiency of a side-channel attack to reach a certain success rate (e.g. 80%) is the minimum average number of queries such that the success rate of this attack attains the value (80%). Here, we measure this efficiency of the DPA attacks in terms of number of queries required to extract the secret key.

We inspect the Gaussian noise distribution $\mathbf{N}$ with zero mean and standard deviation σ added to the Hamming weight of the S-box output $S(x \oplus k)$ as the physically observable power trace. From the literature, this is the standard power model for hardware implementation and as for the software implementation, this power model in the microprocessor is applied on each instruction execution [3].

In order to evaluate the success rate, we observe the number of successful attempts to extract the secret key out of several random attempts to attack on an average. The success rate of the correlation analysis DPA attacks with noise with standard deviation values from 0.1 to 2.0 on the synthesized S-boxes is shown in Fig. 4. We also perform the same experiment on the PRESENT 4×4 S-box whose results are shown in Fig. 5. In comparison of success rate results in both the figures, we find that in the presence of noise with high standard deviation, the success rate of DPA attacks of the synthesized S-boxes is less than that of the PRESENT S-boxes.

From Table 8, for Gaussian noise with standard deviation as high as 2.0, the maximum success rate attained in our class of synthesized S-boxes is less than half of that of PRESENT S-box. In the case the standard deviation of the Gaussian noise is small, the number of queries required to attain a success rate of 80% in case of our synthesized S-boxes is lesser compared to the PRESENT S-box. Furthermore, in the same table we give data about the transparency order and confusion coefficient values for all S-boxes. We can observe that the properties are not in line, e.g. different properties point that different S-boxes have the best DPA resistance. Further, the success rate for small number of queries is very small in both PRESENT S-box as well as our class of synthesize S-boxes. Also, contrary to the fact that the success rate of correlation DPA should increase with increasing number of queries, the dip in success rates (especially for PRESENT S-box) is significant for some regions of increasing queries. Similar results were observed in existing literature for classification rates of S-boxes with increasing number of queries [37].

Table 8. Comparison of modified transparency order parameter with success rates of the DPA attacks

S-box	T_F	MT_F	Conf. coeff.	# queries to reach 100% success rate (SD=0.1)	Max success rate (SD=2.0)
PRESENT	3.533	2.467	1.709	8	65%
S-box 1	3.267	1.9	1.145	8	28%
S-box 2	3.4	2.167	1.615	10	32%
S-box 3	3.333	2.2	1.615	8	35%
S-box 4	3.4	2.233	1.145	7	34%
S-box 5	3.467	2.267	1.145	6	32%
S-box 6	3.467	2.3	0.956	11	34%

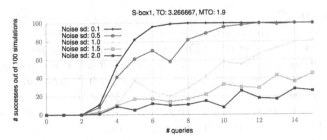

(a) Success rate plots for the correlation analysis DPA on simulated power traces of S-box 1.

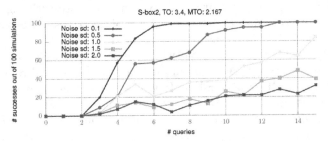

(b) Success rate plots for the correlation analysis DPA on simulated power traces of S-box 2.

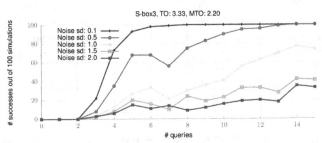

(c) Success rate plots for the correlation analysis DPA on simulated power traces of S-box 3.

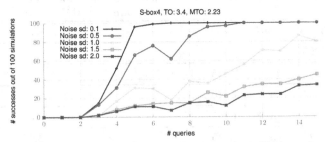

(d) Success rate plots for the correlation analysis DPA on simulated power traces of S-box 4.

Fig. 4. Success rate plots for the correlation analysis DPA on simulated power traces of the generated S-boxes.

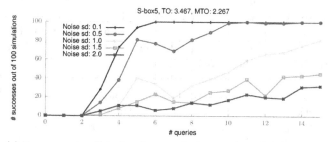

(e) Success rate plots for the correlation analysis DPA on simulated power traces of S-box 5.

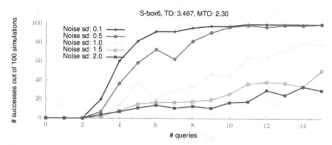

(f) Success rate plots for the correlation analysis DPA on simulated power traces of S-box 6.

Fig. 4. (Continued)

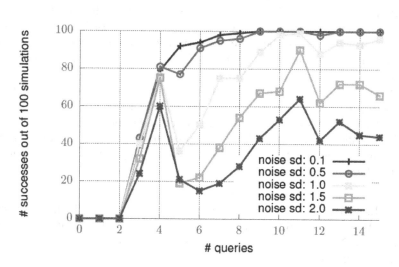

Fig. 5. Success rate plots for the correlation analysis DPA on simulated power traces of PRESENT S-box.

Although smaller modified transparency order should result in an S-box with better DPA resistivity, our experiments show that in the case of small differences in modified transparency, such behavior is hard to obtain. This behavior is similar to that what can be observed when examining original transparency order measure. However, there are at least two advantages of using the modified transparency order. The first one is the fact the researcher would use the correct formula (although, sometimes practical results do not show significant differences between properties). The second advantage is that the correlation between the modified transparency order values and max. success rates is more easily noticeable, although not linear. The answer whether the modified transparency order property is a sufficient countermeasure against DPA attacks highly depends on the level of noise in the settings. However, we believe it is not enough (similar to other DPA related S-box properties), but instead should be used in combination with some other countermeasures like masking.

5   Conclusion

In this work, we consider the influence of the modified transparency order property to the DPA resistance of S-boxes. We generate S-boxes that have improved values of the modified transparency order where for the 4×4 size, we remain in the optimal classes. When considering 8×8 size, the improvement in the modified transparency comes at the cost of the deterioration of other properties like the nonlinearity or δ-uniformity. Furthermore, we show the minimal necessary affine transformation needed to change the modified transparency order value. Based on that transformation, we show that the value obtained by our genetic algorithm is indeed the optimal one. In doing so, we also show that only one of 16 optimal classes for the 4×4 size can reach the best possible value for modified transparency. We use the same affine transformation to find the upper and lower bound for modified transparency order for all 16 optimal classes. Finally, we conduct practical SCA experiments with our new S-boxes as well as with the PRESENT S-box. From the results, we observe that the number of necessary traces for the successful attack is significantly lower for our S-boxes than for the PRESENT S-box in the presence of noise. Although our results indicate that the modified transparency order is more reliable measure than the original transparency order, we still do not deem it sufficiently strong to be considered without other countermeasures.

Acknowledgments. This work was supported in part by the Technology Foundation STW (project 12624 - SIDES), The Netherlands Organization for Scientific Research NWO (project ProFIL 628.001.007) and the ICT COST action IC1204 TRUDEVICE.

References

1. Biham, E., Shamir, A.: Differential Cryptanalysis of DES-like Cryptosystems. In: Menezes, A., Vanstone, S.A. (eds.) CRYPTO 1990. LNCS, vol. 537, pp. 2–21. Springer, Heidelberg (1991)
2. Matsui, M., Yamagishi, A.: A new method for known plaintext attack of FEAL cipher. In: Rueppel, R.A. (ed.) EUROCRYPT 1992. LNCS, vol. 658, pp. 81–91. Springer, Heidelberg (1993)
3. Mangard, S., Oswald, E., Popp, T.: Power Analysis Attacks: Revealing the Secrets of Smart Cards (Advances in Information Security). Springer-Verlag New York, Inc (2007)
4. Leander, G., Poschmann, A.: On the Classification of 4 Bit S-Boxes. In: Carlet, C., Sunar, B. (eds.) WAIFI 2007. LNCS, vol. 4547, pp. 159–176. Springer, Heidelberg (2007)
5. Mangard, S., Oswald, E., Popp, T.: Power Analysis Attacks: Revealing the Secrets of Smart Cards (Advances in Information Security). Springer-Verlag New York, Inc., Secaucus (2007)
6. Guilley, S., Pacalet, R.: Differential Power Analysis Model and Some Results. In: Proceedings of CARDIS, pp. 127–142. Kluwer Academic Publishers (2004)
7. Prouff, E.: DPA Attacks and S-Boxes. In: Gilbert, H., Handschuh, H. (eds.) FSE 2005. LNCS, vol. 3557, pp. 424–441. Springer, Heidelberg (2005)
8. Kocher, P., Jaffe, J., Jun, B.: Differential Power Analysis. In: Wiener, M. (ed.) CRYPTO 1999. LNCS, vol. 1666, pp. 388–397. Springer, Heidelberg (1999)
9. Fei, Y., Luo, Q., Ding, A.A.: A statistical model for dpa with novel algorithmic confusion analysis. In: Prouff, E., Schaumont, P. (eds.) CHES 2012. LNCS, vol. 7428, pp. 233–250. Springer, Heidelberg (2012)
10. Fei, Y., Ding, A.A., Lao, J., Zhang, L.: A statistics-based fundamental model for side-channel attack analysis. IACR Cryptology ePrint Archive 2014, 152 (2014)
11. Luo, Q., Fei, Y.: Algorithmic collision analysis for evaluating cryptographic systems and side-channel attacks. In: 2011 IEEE International Symposium on Hardware-Oriented Security and Trust (HOST), pp. 75–80 (2011)
12. Ding, A.A., Zhang, L., Fei, Y., Luo, P.: A statistical model for higher order dpa on masked devices. IACR Cryptology ePrint Archive 2014, 433 (2014)
13. Bogdanov, A., Knudsen, L.R., Leander, G., Paar, C., Poschmann, A., Robshaw, M.J., Seurin, Y., Vikkelsoe, C.: PRESENT: An Ultra-Lightweight Block Cipher. In: Paillier, P., Verbauwhede, I. (eds.) CHES 2007. LNCS, vol. 4727, pp. 450–466. Springer, Heidelberg (2007)
14. Borghoff, J., Canteaut, A., Gneysu, T., Kavun, E., Knezevic, M., Knudsen, L., Leander, G., Nikov, V., Paar, C., Rechberger, C., Rombouts, P., Thomsen, S., Yaln, T.: PRINCE: A Low-Latency Block Cipher for Pervasive Computing Applications. In: Wang, X., Sako, K. (eds.) ASIACRYPT 2012. LNCS, vol. 7658, pp. 208–225. Springer, Heidelberg (2012)
15. Daemen, J., Rijmen, V.: The Design of Rijndael. Springer-Verlag New York, Inc., Secaucus (2002)
16. Daemen, J., Peeters, M., Assche, G.V., Rijmen, V.: Nessie proposal: the block cipher Noekeon. Nessie submission (2000), http://gro.noekeon.org/
17. Chakraborty, K., Sarkar, S., Maitra, S., Mazumdar, B., Mukhopadhyay, D., Prouff, E.: Redefining the transparency order. In: Coding and Cryptography, International Workshop, WCC 2015, Paris, France, April 13-17 (2015)

18. Mazumdar, B., Mukhopadhyay, D., Sengupta, I.: Design and implementation of rotation symmetric S-boxes with high nonlinearity and high DPA resilience. In: 2013 IEEE International Symposium on Hardware-Oriented Security and Trust (HOST), pp. 87–92 (2013)
19. Mazumdar, B., Mukhopadhyay, D., Sengupta, I.: Constrained search for a class of good bijective s-boxes with improved DPA resistivity. IEEE Transactions on Information Forensics and Security 8(12), 2154–2163 (2013)
20. Picek, S., Ege, B., Batina, L., Jakobovic, D., Chmielewski, L., Golub, M.: On Using Genetic Algorithms for Intrinsic Side-channel Resistance: The Case of AES S-box. In: Proceedings of the First Workshop on Cryptography and Security in Computing Systems, CS2 2014, pp. 13–18. ACM, New York (2014)
21. Picek, S., Ege, B., Papagiannopoulos, K., Batina, L., Jakobovic, D.: Optimality and beyond: The case of 4x4 s-boxes. In: 2014 IEEE International Symposium on Hardware-Oriented Security and Trust, HOST 2014, Arlington, VA, USA, May 6-7, pp. 80–83 (2014)
22. Picek, S., Papagiannopoulos, K., Ege, B., Batina, L., Jakobovic, D.: Confused by Confusion: Systematic Evaluation of DPA Resistance of Various S-boxes. In: INDOCRYPT 2014. LNCS, vol. 8885, pp. 374–390. Springer, Heidelberg (2014)
23. Evci, M.A., Kavut, S.: DPA Resilience of Rotation-Symmetric S-boxes. In: Yoshida, M., Mouri, K. (eds.) IWSEC 2014. LNCS, vol. 8639, pp. 146–157. Springer, Heidelberg (2014)
24. Nguyen, C., Tran, L., Nguyen, K.: On the resistance of serpent-type 4 bit s-boxes against differential power attacks. In: 2014 IEEE Fifth International Conference on Communications and Electronics (ICCE), pp. 542–547 (July 2014)
25. Gong, Z., Nikova, S., Law, Y.: A new family of lightweight block ciphers. In: Juels, A., Paar, C. (eds.) RFIDSec 2011. LNCS, vol. 7055, pp. 1–18. Springer, Heidelberg (2012)
26. Crama, Y., Hammer, P.L.: Boolean Models and Methods in Mathematics, Computer Science, and Engineering, vol. 1. Cambridge University Press, New York (2010)
27. Braeken, A.: Cryptographic Properties of Boolean Functions and S-Boxes. PhD thesis, Katholieke Universiteit Leuven (2006)
28. Carlet, C.: On highly nonlinear S-boxes and their inability to thwart DPA attacks. In: Maitra, S., Veni Madhavan, C.E., Venkatesan, R. (eds.) INDOCRYPT 2005. LNCS, vol. 3797, pp. 49–62. Springer, Heidelberg (2005)
29. Nyberg, K.: Perfect Nonlinear S-Boxes. In: Davies, D.W. (ed.) EUROCRYPT 1991. LNCS, vol. 547, pp. 378–386. Springer, Heidelberg (1991)
30. Heuser, A., Rioul, O., Guilley, S.: A theoretical study of kolmogorov-smirnov distinguishers - side-channel analysis vs. differential cryptanalysis. In: Constructive Side-Channel Analysis and Secure Design - 5th International Workshop, COSADE 2014, Paris, France, April 13-15, pp. 9–28 (2014) (Revised Selected Papers)
31. Picek, S., Ege, B., Batina, L., Jakobovic, D., Chmielewski, L., Golub, M.: On Using Genetic Algorithms for Intrinsic Side-channel Resistance: The Case of AES S-box. In: Proceedings of the First Workshop on Cryptography and Security in Computing Systems, CS2 2014, pp. 13–18. ACM, New York (2014)
32. Eiben, A.E., Smith, J.E.: Introduction to Evolutionary Computing. Springer, Heidelberg (2003)
33. Goldberg, D.E., Lingle, R.: Alleles, loci, and the traveling salesman problem. In: Proc. of the International Conference on Genetic Algorithms and their Applications, Pittsburgh, PA, pp. 154–159 (1985)

34. Davis, L.: Applying adaptive algorithms to epistatic domains. In: Proceedings of the 9th International Joint Conference on Artificial Intelligence, IJCAI 1985, pp. 162–164. Morgan Kaufmann Publishers Inc., San Francisco (1985)
35. Zhang, X., Zheng, Y.: GAC-the criterion of global avalanche characteristics of cryptographic functions. Journal of Universal Computer Science 1(5), 316–333 (1995)
36. Standaert, F.X., Malkin, T.G., Yung, M.: A unified framework for the analysis of side-channel key recovery attacks. In: Joux, A. (ed.) EUROCRYPT 2009. LNCS, vol. 5479, pp. 443–461. Springer, Heidelberg (2009)
37. Kim, Y., Sugawara, T., Homma, N., Aoki, T., Satoh, A.: Biasing power traces to improve correlation in power analysis attacks. In: First International Workshop on Constructive Side-Channel Analysis and Secure Design COSADE 2010, pp. 77–80 (2010)

Investigating SRAM PUFs
in large CPUs and GPUs*

Pol Van Aubel[1], Daniel J. Bernstein[2,3], and Ruben Niederhagen[3]

[1] Radboud University
Digital Security Group
P.O. Box 9010, 6500 GL Nijmegen, The Netherlands
radboud@polvanaubel.com
[2] Department of Computer Science
University of Illinois at Chicago
Chicago, IL 60607–7045, USA
djb@cr.yp.to
[3] Department of Mathematics and Computer Science
Technische Universiteit Eindhoven
P.O. Box 513, 5600 MB Eindhoven, The Netherlands
ruben@polycephaly.org

Abstract. Physically unclonable functions (PUFs) provide data that can be used for cryptographic purposes: on the one hand randomness for the initialization of random-number generators; on the other hand individual fingerprints for unique identification of specific hardware components. However, today's off-the-shelf personal computers advertise randomness and individual fingerprints only in the form of additional or dedicated hardware.

This paper introduces a new set of tools to investigate whether intrinsic PUFs can be *found* in PC components that are not advertised as containing PUFs. In particular, this paper investigates AMD64 CPU registers as potential PUF sources in the operating-system kernel, the bootloader, and the system BIOS; investigates the CPU cache in the early boot stages; and investigates shared memory on Nvidia GPUs. This investigation found non-random non-fingerprinting behavior in several components but revealed usable PUFs in Nvidia GPUs.

Keywords: Physically unclonable functions, SRAM PUFs, randomness, hardware identification.

---

* This work was supported by the European Commission through the ICT program under contract INFSO-ICT-284833 (PUFFIN), by the Netherlands Organisation for Scientific Research (NWO) under grant 639.073.005, by the U.S. National Science Foundation under grant 1018836, and by the Dutch electricity transmission system operator TenneT TSO B.V. Permanent ID of this document: 2580a85505520618ade3cd462a3133702ae673f7. Date: 2015.07.09.

R.S. Chakraborty et al. (Eds.): SPACE 2015, LNCS 9354, pp. 228–247, 2015.
DOI: 10.1007/978-3-319-24126-5_14

1   Introduction

Commonly used consumer computing devices, such as desktop computers and laptop computers, need a multitude of cryptographic primitives, e.g., cryptographic operations with secret keys, keyed hash functions, secure randomness, and, in some cases, remote attestation and identification capabilities. In this paper we focus on two seemingly conflicting aspects: The generation of *random bit strings*, which requires indeterministic behavior, and the generation of *unique identifiers*, which requires deterministic behavior.

Randomness is required for several purposes in cryptography. For example, random bit sequences are used to generate secret encryption keys and nonces in cryptographic protocols in order to make them impossible for an attacker to guess. Many cryptographic primitives assume the presence of a secure random source; however, most processing chips are designed to be deterministic and sources of randomness are rare [12, 15].

Unique identifiers can be used to deterministically derive an identity-based cryptographic key. This key can be used for authentication and data protection. For example, it would be possible to use these keys as an anti-counterfeiting measure. Bloomberg Business reports in [13] that "an 'epidemic' of bogus chips, routers, and computers costs the electronics industry up to \$100 billion annually", and Business Wire reports in [1] that "as many as one in ten IT products sold may actually be counterfeit". Having the ability to identify a chip as legitimate by comparing some PUF to a database provided by the manufacturer may help reduce this problem. As another example, it is possible to use this key for hard disk encryption: The hard drive, i.e., the bootloader, operating system, and user data, are encrypted with this secret intrinsic key and can only be decrypted if the unique identifier is available. The identifier thus must be protected from unauthorized access.

Currently, these features are provided by accompanying the device with dedicated hardware: randomness is offered, e.g., by the RDRAND hardware random number generator; identification, e.g., by a Trusted Platform Module (TPM). However, these solutions can only be used if a dedicated TPM is available in the device or if the CPU supports the RDRAND instruction which only recently was introduced with Intel's Ivy Bridge CPUs. Furthermore, they do not help in cases where the cryptographic key should be bound to the identity of a specific chip itself.

However, for these cryptographic functionalities additional hardware is not necessarily required: randomness as well as identification can be derived from individual physical characteristics inherent to a silicon circuit by the use of physically unclonable functions (PUFs). PUFs can be derived from, e.g., ring oscillators [10], signal delay variations [14, 23], flip-flops [16], latches [22], and static random-access memory (SRAM) [11, 4]. While most of these require dedicated circuits, SRAM is already used for other purposes in many general-purpose, mass-market chips.

SRAM PUFs were initially identified in FPGAs. The PUF characteristics of SRAM are derived from the uninitialized state of SRAM immediately after power-up. When unpowered SRAM cells are powered up, they obtain a value of 0 with a certain probability P_0, or 1 with probability $P_1 = 1 - P_0$. The individual probabilities of each SRAM cell depend on minor manufacturing differences and are quite stable over time. Some of the cells have a probability close to 1 for either P_0 or P_1 and thus tend to give the same value at every power-up. Because of this stability, and because the pattern of this stability is different for every block of SRAM, they can be used for fingerprinting. Other cells have a probability close to 0.5 for both P_0 and P_1 and thus tend to give a different value at each power-up. Since their behavior is unstable, they are a good source for randomness.

Before the power-up state of SRAM can be used as PUF, an enrollment phase is required: the SRAM is powered up several times in order to measure which SRAM cells are suitable for randomness and which for fingerprinting. For the actual use of the SRAM PUF some postprocessing is performed, e.g., a feedback loop can be used in order to avoid bias in the generated random bit sequence and an error correction code in order to compensate for occasional bit errors in the fingerprint.

At TrustED 2013, researchers demonstrated in [24] that SRAM-based PUFs exist in various brands of popular microcontrollers, such as AVR and ARM, which are commonplace in mobile and embedded devices. More recently [20] used this to secure a mobile platform.

We want to investigate the possible presence of PUFs in commonly used desktop and laptop computers. For this purpose, the two most attractive targets are the Central Processing Unit (CPU) and the Graphics Processing Unit (GPU), since they are present in almost every desktop machine commonly in use, and they are the chips most directly accessible by the software running on the machine. Research into PUFs on GPUs was suggested independently by [7].

The most common CPU architecture today for large computing devices, such as laptop computers, desktop computers, and servers, is the AMD64 architecture. The AMD64 architecture, also known as x86-64 and x64, was introduced by AMD in 1999 as a backwards-compatible successor to the pervasive x86 architecture. SRAM is used in abundance in the caches and registers of AMD64 CPUs. Therefore, they may carry intrinsic PUFs. In [18] the authors propose an instruction-set extension to utilize this SRAM to build a secure trusted computing environment within the CPU. However, research on existing PUFs in AMD64 CPUs appears non-existent. The obvious question is whether such PUF capabilities are currently also exhibited by (i.e., available and accessible in) x86 and AMD64 CPUs. The documentation of these processors contains a number of statements which suggest that — even though such SRAM PUFs may exist — they are impossible to access from software running on those CPUs.

This paper introduces new tools to investigate whether it is indeed impossible to use registers and caches of AMD64 CPUs as PUFs. The result of our investigation is a negative one, in the sense that for the specific CPU we investigated fully (an AMD E350) we have to confirm that even at the earliest boot stages we cannot use registers or caches as PUFs.

However, the situation is vastly different for older-generation GPUs. Many desktop and laptop computers include hardware dedicated to processing computer graphics, the GPU. The chips on this hardware are tailored toward parallel computation for graphics processes (e.g., vectorized floating-point operations), rather than the general-purpose computation done in CPUs. Typically, GPUs have large amounts of SRAM. Contrary to the CPU, which provides security features such as memory protection and therefore has clear reasons to prevent direct access to the SRAM, GPUs often expose their SRAM directly to the programmer, and also do not have the same reasons to clear the SRAM after reset. GPU memory and registers leak sensitive data between processes, as observed in [21] and later in [8]; the absence of memory zeroing between processes, where sensitive data may be handled, suggests that zeroing to prevent reading *uninitialized* memory is also absent.

We therefore think that it will be easier to find and read uninitialized SRAM on GPUs than on CPUs. In this paper we explore the possibilities for this on the Nvidia GTX 295 and find that it is indeed possible to extract enough uninitialized SRAM to build PUFs. On the other hand, we did not find PUFs on a newer generation GPU.

To enable reproducibility of our results, and to allow other researchers to investigate other CPUs, we place all our modifications to the software described in this paper into the public domain. The source code and patches are available at https://www.polvanaubel.com/research/puf/x86-64/code/.

This paper is structured as follows: In the next section, we describe our experimental setup for the CPU, i.e., the AMD64 processor architecture and our test mainboard, the ASRock E350M1. In Section 3 we describe how we investigate if CPU registers can be accessed sufficiently early in the boot process in order to read their power-on state and use them as SRAM PUFs. In Section 4 we investigate the suitability of the CPU cache as SRAM PUF during BIOS execution when the processor is in the *cache-as-RAM* mode. In Section 5 we describe the experimental setup for the GPU, i.e., the Nvidia GTX 295 GPU architecture. Finally, in Section 6 we describe the experiments conducted on the GPU. Finally, in Section 7 we discuss our results.

2   Experimental Setup for the CPU

Our main experimental setup consisted of a single mainboard with an AMD64 CPU.

AMD64 Architecture. Computers based on the x86 and AMD64 architectures have a long history, tracing back to the IBM PC. The most common setup today, visualized in Figure 1, is based on a motherboard that has a socket for an AMD64 architecture CPU, a memory controller and slots for Random Access Memory, several communication buses such as PCI and PCI Express and associated slots for expansion cards, non-volatile memory for storing the system's boot firmware, and a "chipset" tying all these together. This chipset consists of a Northbridge, handling communication between the CPU and high-speed peripherals such as

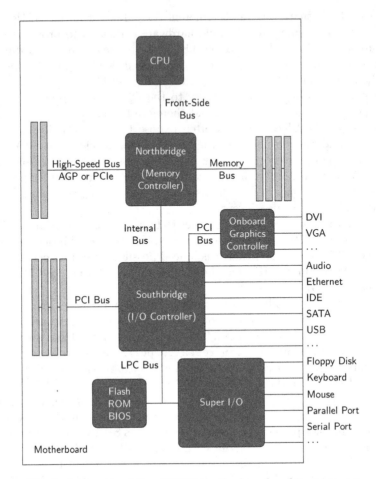

Fig. 1. Schematic of the AMD64 motherboard architecture.

graphics hardware and main memory, and the Southbridge, handling everything else, with the Northbridge as an intermediary to the CPU.

Finally, there is the Super I/O chip. This chip condenses many I/O features which were traditionally handled by different circuits into one chip. This is the reason that the current iteration of AMD64 motherboards still supports many features found on boards from 20 years ago, such as serial port I/O, floppy-disk drives, and parallel ports, next to relatively new features such as Serial ATA and PCI Express. However, some of these features might not be exposed to the user: The Super I/O chip that is used to drive these subsystems often supports the entire range of "old" functionalities, but only those which the motherboard manufacturer deems worthwhile to offer are actually exposed through sockets on the board. The serial port, for example, is still exposed as a header on most boards, or at least as a solder-on option. Since these are relatively simple I/O devices, they are often the first to be initialized after system startup and can be used for output of, e.g., system diagnostics during the early boot stage before the graphics hardware has been initialized.

In recent years, functions the Northbridge used to handle, such as memory control and graphics-hardware control, were integrated into the CPU. This was done to reduce overhead and speed limitations caused by having to go through an intermediary chip. Since this lifted most of the high-speed demands from the Northbridge, this development has caused manufacturers to integrate the few remaining functions of the Northbridge and the functions of the Southbridge into a single chip. The main principles of operation of the motherboard, however, remain the same.

Test Mainboard. Our main test board is the E350M1, manufactured by AS-Rock. On it runs an AMD E-350 APU (Accelerated Processing Unit, a package embedding a CPU and graphics controller) which was first manufactured in 2011, with an AMD A50M chipset. It has an exposed serial port header and a socketed 4 MiB Winbond 25Q32FVAIQ NVRAM chip for the UEFI or BIOS firmware. The board has on-board flash capabilities for this chip. The form factor is mini-ITX. The E-350 APU itself has two processor cores, with 32 KiB level-1 data cache, 32 KiB level-1 instruction cache, and 512 KiB of level-2 cache per core.

As explained later in Section 3.4, the main reasons for picking this mainboard are that it supports a fairly recent AMD CPU, has a socketed NVRAM chip, and is supported by the open-source BIOS implementation coreboot [26].

The integration of graphics hardware, combined with the small form factor, make this a board suited for general-purpose home computing and multimedia computers.

We acquired two sets of replacement NVRAM chips. The first set consisted of five MXIC MX25L3206EPI. These chips closely match the original chip's specifications, yet are from a different manufacturer. They failed to boot the board with anything other than the original UEFI firmware. The second set consisted of two Winbond 25Q64FVSIG chips. These chips are almost identical to the original, with only two major differences: they have twice the storage size (8 MiB), and a different form factor (SOIC8 instead of DIP8). Therefore, they required an adapter circuit to fit the form factor. However, these chips served the purpose of booting the board with modified firmware. The three different types of chips can be seen in Figure 2. For flashing these chips under Linux, we used the open-source software flashrom.

For mass storage (bootloader and operating system) we used a simple USB stick. For I/O we used a normal setup of keyboard, mouse and screen, but also attached a serial socket to the serial port header, and used a serial-to-USB adapter to get serial output from BIOS and bootloader. The test setup can be seen in Figure 3.

Finally, power was supplied by a normal ATX power supply, and we powered, unpowered and reset the board by shorting the corresponding pins with a metal tab. Measurements were taken by manually powercycling the board and reading the measurement output from screen (kernel) or serial output (BIOS and bootloader).

Fig. 2. Chips used on the E350M1 motherboard. Left: the original Winbond 25Q32FVAIQ. Center: The unsuitable replacement MX25L3206EPI. Right: The working replacement Winbond 25Q64FVSIG

Fig. 3. Photograph of the E350M1 motherboard.

3   CPU Registers

There are indications that both Intel and AMD use SRAM to build the register banks present in their CPUs [5], although this is not explicitly mentioned in the specification charts for their CPUs. The register banks contain, among others, general-purpose registers, MMX vector registers, and XMM vector registers. Of these, the general-purpose registers are likely to be heavily used from the moment of system start, since many of them are required to be used in basic instructions. The XMM registers, however, can only be accessed by the use of the Streaming SIMD Extensions (SSE) instruction set, which is unlikely to be used by the system startup code. They are therefore good candidates to check for PUF behavior.

However, the *AMD64 Architecture Programmer's Manual Volume 2: System Programming* [2] contains several statements which give reason to believe that it would be extremely hard, if not outright impossible, to get to the power-on state of the register banks. For instance, Table 14-1 of that document shows the initial processor state that follows RESET or INIT. The table lists a deterministic state for all the general-purpose registers, most of which get initialized to 0. The 64-bit media state (MMX registers) and the SSE state (XMM registers) are also initialized to 0 after RESET. After INIT, however, they are apparently not modified, but since it is not possible to initialize a processor without going through power-on RESET at the beginning, this does not help either. Volume 1 of the *Programmer's Manual* also states that, upon power-on, all YMM/XMM registers are cleared. This confirms the conclusions drawn from the table in Volume 2.

Experimental results show that the register banks are indeed not usable as PUFs on our testing machines. To explain this conclusion, we will describe the x86/AM64 boot process, and discuss how to dump the state of the XMM registers during different stages of the boot procedure.

3.1   Boot Process

The boot process for an AMD64-based machine consists of several steps. The Southbridge loads the initial firmware code (BIOS or UEFI), and the processor starts executing from the RESET vector (address 0xFFFFFFF0). This code performs CPU initialization and initialization of other mainboard components such as the Super-IO chip, responsible for input-output through devices such as the serial port, and the memory controller, responsible for driving and communicating with main memory. Next, it searches for all bootable devices and finally loads the bootloader from the desired location.

The bootloader allows the user to select between different operating systems, loads the desired operating-system kernel and any other required resources, and then hands over control to this kernel. From this moment on the operating system is in control.

One of the main differences between BIOS and UEFI boot options is that a BIOS system will, in order to start the bootloader, drop the CPU back into 16-bit real mode, whereas a UEFI system can directly load the bootloader in 32-bit protected or 64-bit long mode. We have looked at systems using the BIOS model, but our findings apply to the UEFI model as well since the UEFI model is not different from the BIOS model in how it initializes the CPU, Super-I/O, and memory controller. For the rest of this paper, when discussing bootloader and boot firmware, we assume the BIOS model.

This division of stages in the boot process is also reflected in the complexity of the software running in each stage. The BIOS is small, very specialized, and designed to work for specific hardware. The bootloader, in turn, is somewhat larger, somewhat more portable, but still has a very limited set of tasks. Finally, an operating-system kernel is often large and complex, and designed to deal with many different hardware configurations and many different use cases. If PUF behavior can easily be exposed at the operating system level, without edits to the underlying layers, this enables wide deployment with relatively little development. If, however, the BIOS needs to be edited, then deploying a system using these PUF results would require edits to each mainboard that the system will use. The tradeoff here is that a solution which does not require edits to the BIOS and bootloader would implicitly trust these components, whereas a solution where the BIOS needs to be edited would be able to work with a much smaller trusted base system.

Because of these considerations, we decided to explore all three options. In the following sections, we first look at the kernel level, before going to the bootloader, and finally to the BIOS.

3.2   Kernel

The operating-system kernel is started by a bootloader in our test setup. We can only be sure to read potentially uninitialized values from registers if we read the state of the registers as early as possible, before they are used either by the operating system or by user processes. Thus, the register state must be stored during the startup-process of the operating system. This requires us to modify the source code of the operating-system kernel. Therefore, the obvious choice is to use an open-source kernel. We decided to use Linux.

Our code that reads out and displays the contents of the XMM registers consists of two parts: a kernel patch that stores the content of the XMM registers right after those registers have been made available and a kernel module that gives access to the stored data after the boot process has been finished.

Kernel Patch. Before XMM registers can be accessed, the processor must be switched to the correct mode using the CR0 and CR4 control registers [2, Page 433]. This happens in fpu_init in file arch/x86/kernel/i387.c of the Linux kernel. Before this function is called, the kernel does not have access to the XMM registers. Thus, it is not possible that the XMM registers have been used before within the kernel and that potential PUF data in those registers has been overwritten by the kernel.

We are storing the data of all XMM registers into memory right after the control registers have been set, in order to ensure that our code is the first kernel code that accesses the registers. We use the instruction FXSAVE in order to save all the FPU and XMM registers to memory at once; the kernel patch adds only 5 lines of source code.

Kernel Module. Displaying or permanently storing data in the very early phase of the kernel boot process is tedious. Therefore, we simply store the data at boot time and make it available to user space applications once the boot process is finished via a kernel module. The kernel module provides entries (one for each CPU core) in the proc file system that can simply be read in order to obtain and display the XMM register data.

Results. We tested our code on two AMD64-based machines, first on a surplus office machine with an AMD Athlon 64 X2 3800. Later, we re-ran the tests on the dedicated test-board with an AMD E350 CPU described in Section 2. Both CPUs are dual-core CPUs. On both boards, all XMM registers on the second

CPU core contained all 0. The registers on the first CPU core contained some data, some of it stable over several reboots, some of it varying. However, some of the registers obviously contained ASCII code, e.g., the strings "GNU core", "GB.UTF-8", and ": <%s>". This indicates that the XMM registers have been used by the boatloader — if not directly in the source code then maybe by C standard-library calls like memcpy, memcmp, or string operations; disassembling the GRUB boatloader shows many occurrences of vector instructions on XMM registers.

Thus, at the time of kernel startup, the initial status of the registers has been modified and they cannot be used as PUF. Therefore, in the next step we investigated the status of the XMM registers before the kernel is started, i.e., in the early stages of the bootloader.

3.3   GRUB

The bootloader is a user-controlled piece of software, often installed into the boot sector of one of the hard disk drives. However, it runs still fairly early in the boot process. This combination of factors makes it a good candidate for attempting to find uninitialized SRAM in the XMM registers of a CPU.

GRUB Patch. GRUB (GRand Unified Bootloader) is a free open-source bootloader for AMD64 systems [9]. It is one of the most popular bootloaders used to boot Linux systems and fairly easy to modify. After GRUB starts, it switches the CPU back into 32-bit protected mode as soon as possible. Then it does some more machine initialization and checks, during which it initializes the terminal console, either over the VGA output or serial output. Next, it loads all the modules it requires, loads its configuration, and displays the boot menu for the user to select an operating system.

In the previous section, we mentioned that disassembly of GRUB shows many uses of the XMM registers. However, at the moment when GRUB starts, the CPU is still in 16-bit real mode. Therefore no XMM registers are available to be used. In order to be early enough to read uninitialized registers, we changed the GRUB source code so that immediately after machine and terminal initialization, we enable access to the XMM registers ourselves, then read the register contents of the XMM registers XMM0 to XMM7. Next, we write them to the terminal. First we allocate a block of memory with a size of 1024 bits (128 bits for each register) and fill it with a known pattern. Next, we enable SSE-instructions on the CPU in the first asm-block. Immediately after that we copy the contents of each register to the memory region allocated before, in the second asm-block. We do not use the FXSAVE instructions here, rather, we perform a single MOVUPD instruction for each register we want to store. Finally, we write the values from memory to the console. Disassembly of the resulting GRUB image shows that, indeed, our reading of the XMM registers is the first use of these registers within GRUB.

Results. Again, we tested our code on the surplus office machine described above and later also on the dedicated test mainboard. Unfortunately, on the first test-machine the contents of all registers except for XMM0 were 0. XMM0 was filled with a static value which turned out to be a fill-pattern used in the initialization code of main memory in AMD-supplied BIOS code. These values were stable over repeated tests. This indicates that at this point the registers have been zeroed and that at least register XMM0 has been used already by the BIOS. For the same reasons as before, this means that at this point the XMM registers cannot be used as PUF, neither for randomness nor for fingerprinting. Therefore, as the next step we turned to the BIOS in the attempt to read data usable as a PUF from the registers.

3.4   Coreboot

As stated before, the BIOS is the first code run by the CPU. It detects and initializes the hardware and firmware, puts the CPU in the correct mode, runs software that makes it possible to configure the BIOS itself, and loads and runs the bootloader. The BIOS is the earliest step in the boot process that can be controlled, unless one has access to the CPU microcode.

The BIOS is loaded from an NVRAM chip. Often, its machine code is readable by reading out the NVRAM chip or by dumping the contents of BIOS updates. However, it is not easy to edit the BIOS code without access to its source code, which most mainboard vendors do not provide. Luckily, it is not necessary to reverse-engineer the closed-source BIOS provided by the mainboard vendors; there is an alternative: coreboot, formerly linuxBIOS, is a free open-source machine-initialization system [26]. It is modularly built so that it can function as a BIOS, a UEFI system, or in several other possible configurations.

Mainboard Selection. Coreboot, despite its modularity, needs to be ported to every individual new mainboard for which support is desired. This is caused by subtle differences in hardware configuration, and is even required if a board uses chips which are all already supported by coreboot. Instead of porting coreboot to the AMD Athlon 64 X2 3800 mainboard mentioned before that we already had "in stock", we decided to acquire a board that coreboot had already been ported to by the community; our first requirement for the board was that it must support modern AMD64 CPUs.

Since the BIOS resides in an NVRAM chip on the mainboard, the only way to install a new BIOS is by flashing this chip. Most modern mainboards have this flash-capability built into the mainboard itself and software running in the operating system can flash the BIOS in order to enable user-friendly BIOS updates. However, should a modification to the BIOS source code render the system unbootable, this on-board capability will obviously not be available. Therefore an additional requirement was that the mainboard that we were going to use must have a socketed NVRAM chip rather than one soldered onto the board. This would allow us to boot the board with a "good" chip, then switching the chips and re-flashing the bad one.

Because of these requirements, our choice was the ASRock E350M1 mainboard described in Section 2.

Coreboot Patch. The coreboot boot process begins the same as described in Section 3.1: the Southbridge loads the coreboot image, then the CPU starts processing from the `RESET` vector. The first thing coreboot does is to put the CPU into 32-bit protected mode. It then does some additional CPU initialization, initializes the level-2 cache as RAM for stack-based computing, initializes the Super-IO chip for serial port output, and then starts outputting diagnostic and boot progress information over the serial port. It initializes the memory controller, and eventually it loads the payloads stored in NVRAM, which can vary: a VGA ROM to enable VGA output, a BIOS or UEFI implementation, an operating-system kernel directly, or several other possibilities.

As soon as the cache-as-RAM initialization is done, memory is available to store the values of the XMM registers. We changed coreboot similar to how we changed GRUB. First, we allocate a buffer of 1024 bits of memory and fill them with a known pattern. Then we copy the contents of the XMM registers to the buffer. At this point, there is no interface initialized to send data out of the CPU, except for a very rudimentary POST code interface which can send one byte at a time and requires a special PCI card to read it. This is inconvenient at best, so we allow coreboot to continue machine initialization until the serial port is enabled. Then, we write the values previously read from the registers out over the serial console.

Results. This time, all the registers contain 0 on our test machine. Manual analysis of a disassembly of the coreboot firmware image flashed to the device shows that `XMM0` and `XMM1` are at some earlier point used to temporarily store data, but `XMM2`–`XMM7` are not used before being copied by the modified code. This matches the documentation, and implies that there is no way to get access to uninitialized SRAM state by using XMM registers.

4   CPU Cache

The AMD64 architecture defines the possibility of several levels of cache, while leaving the exact implementation to manufacturers of actual CPUs. As mentioned before, caches are usually implemented as SRAM. Therefore, reading the bootup-state of cache could be another source of PUF behavior.

4.1   Cache Operation

During normal operation of an AMD64-based machine, main memory is available through a memory controller. The use of caches speeds up memory accesses by granting the CPU fast read and write access to recently touched data which would otherwise have to be fetched from main memory. On the AMD64 architecture, the data stored in caches is always the result of a read from main memory or a write to main memory; caches act as a fast temporary buffer. It is not possible for software to explicitly write to, or read from, cache. If software needs to use data from a certain address in main memory, the corresponding cache line is first loaded into cache, then accessed and potentially modified by the software, and eventually modifications may be written back to main memory. Thus, the cache contains a copy of the data that should be in main memory, but that might not be the exact same data as what *is* in main memory because the writeback has not happened yet. When exactly reads from and writes to main memory are performed, depends on the *memory type* assigned to the section of main memory being handled. For the purposes of this paper, we will only examine the memory type *writeback* [2, Page 173].

On multicore systems and cache-coherent multi-socket systems, another problem is that the data in cache itself might not be the most up-to-date copy of the data. Because of this, the cache controller must keep track of which data is stored in which location (a specific cache or in main memory) at what time. In order to keep track of this, the MOESI protocol is used that allows cache lines to be in one of five different states: *Modified*, *Owned*, *Exclusive*, *Shared*, and *Invalid* [2, Pages 169–176].

Many modern AMD64 CPUs support what is known as cache-as-RAM operation. This uses the level-2 cache in each CPU core to enable stack-based computing during the early boot process. At this point the memory controller has not yet been initialized, so main memory is unavailable [3, Pages 32–33]. In cache-as-RAM operation mode, the memory state *writeback* is assigned to all available memory addresses. After the CPU received a RESET signal, the entire cache is in the state *Invalid*. In writeback mode Invalid state, any memory read will trigger a "read miss", which would normally cause a read from memory into cache, and put the cache line in either *Shared* or *Exclusive* state. Any memory write will cause a "write miss", since the line needs to be modified and held as Modified in cache. Therefore, a write miss would normally cause a read from memory, modify the corresponding data, and put the cache line in *Modified* state [2, Pages 169–171]. However, the documentation does not state what happens when these misses are encountered during the early boot process when the memory controller is still disabled. It could be the case that any read from main memory will be handled within the CPU to return some static value, e.g., zero. It could also be the case that the cache is not actually modified on a read, in which case reading a block of memory might give us the power-on state of the SRAM cells in the cache.

4.2   Coreboot

The cache-as-RAM initialization code used by coreboot, written by AMD, contains instructions to explicitly zero out the cache area used as stack. Furthermore, a comment on lines 51–58 of src/cpu/x86/16bit/entry16.inc (one of the source files used to define the earliest stages of the coreboot boot process before the CPU is switched to 32-bit protected mode) implies that coreboot used to explicitly invalidate the cache at that point, but no longer does for performance reasons. This could imply that power-on values from the cache are indeed readable after cache-as-RAM initialization, if the instructions to explicitly zero the cache are removed.

Coreboot Patch. To test this, we replaced the instructions zeroing out the cache with instructions filling it with a known pattern. Then we allowed the boot process to continue until initialization of the serial console. As soon as the serial console was available, we output the entire contents of the memory region used as stack, and confirmed that the known pattern was there. This ensures that we were modifying the correct code, and that the values were not being changed between the initialization of the cache and the output. After this test, we simply removed the instructions writing the pattern entirely to get the power-on state of the SRAM. These patches to coreboot should be applied separately from the earlier, register-related patches.

Results. Unfortunately, as in the previous experiments, the output consisted mostly of zeroes, and the parts that were non-zero were clearly deterministic and at the top of the memory region. This part of the memory most likely is the region of the stack that already has been used by function calls before and during serial console initialization. Therefore, also cache-as-RAM does not provide access to SRAM in bootup state; the CPU transparently takes care of wiping the cache before the first read access.

5   GPU Experimental Setup

Our experimental setup for the GPUs consisted of several modern desktop machines, each running one or two GPU cards based on the Nvidia GTX 295. We used the CUDA SDK version 4.0.

Graphics Processing. Graphics cards used to provide only operations for graphics processing. However, in the past decade, a shift has taken place tailored to expose this power, providing a more general-purpose instruction set along with heavily vectorized, parallel computation. Because of this, non-graphical programs have started to utilize this power by offloading certain computations to the GPU that would previously have been done by the CPU.

Graphics programming is usually done using various high-level graphics APIs, such as OpenGL and DirectX. However, the more general-purpose use of their operations is done through other semi-portable high-level programming interfaces, such as CUDA [6] and OpenCL. The CPU, and therefore any normal user program, does not have direct access to the GPU's SRAM memory. Furthermore, the public documentation for the actual low-level instruction sets is not as extensive as for CPUs. For example, one of the ways Nvidia card programming is done is by writing programs in CUDA, which then compiles into still semi-portable, high-level, "assembly-language-like" PTX [19], still hiding most of the hardware details. The PTX is in turn compiled by the GPU card's driver to a binary "kernel" which is run on the card itself.

On the other hand, GPUs evolved as single-user devices, dedicated to processing (non-sensitive) graphics data, without many of the security features of CPUs. Considering those features, such as virtual memory, address space separation, and memory protection, it is unsurprising that the CPU indeed clears its

SRAM and makes it unavailable to any outside applications. Since GPUs do not have to take this into consideration, it is possible that there will be no logic to clear the SRAM or make it unavailable to outside applications. On top of that, in contrast with their instruction sets, GPU hardware tends to be documented as well as or better than CPUs. There also exists research into the non-documented aspects of the architecture, see e.g. [25].

Nvidia GTX 295 GPU Card. The Nvidia GTX 295 GPU card contains two graphics processing devices. Each of these devices has 896MiB of DDR3 RAM — "global memory" — and 30 multiprocessors (MPs). Each of the MPs, in turn, has 8 arithmetic logic units (ALUs), 16384 32-bit registers, and 16KiB SRAM — "shared memory". Nvidia GPUs can be programmed for general-purpose computing using the CUDA framework.

6 GPU Multiprocessor Shared Memory

Even though more SRAM is available in the registers, the shared memory SRAM is easier to access. The main cause of this is that CUDA and PTX make it easy to access the shared memory through a linear address space, but there is no real assembly language provided by NVIDIA that would allow to directly access registers.

Using Nvidia's CUDA language, we developed an SRAM readout tool. CUDA hides most of the hardware details, but it provides enough control to access specified locations in SRAM. The tool works by copying the shared memory SRAM to global memory DRAM, after which the code running on the host CPU reads this data. The actual size of the SRAM is 16384 bytes, but the first 24 bytes are reserved for kernel parameters (e.g., the thread id) and for the function parameters passed to the kernel. Thus, only the latter $16384 - 24$ bytes can be accessed from CUDA code. The resulting loop doing this is very simple:

```
#define MAX (16384 - 24)

__global__ void read(unsigned char *data)
{
    __shared__ unsigned char d[MAX];

    for (int i = 0; i < MAX; i++) {
        data[blockIdx.x * MAX + i] = d[i];
    }
}
```

Results. The power-on SRAM contents appear to contain large amounts of random data. Powering off and on again produces a similar, but not identical, SRAM state. Overwriting the SRAM state and resetting the GPU again produces a similar state, as if the SRAM state had never been overwritten. A different GTX 295 GPU has a different power-on SRAM state. These observations were consistent with what one would expect from uninitialized SRAM.

In the end, we were able to read out 490800 bytes out of the 491520 bytes of shared memory in each GPU. We repeated this experiment on 17 devices.

Figure 4 shows an example of a GPU SRAM PUF from device 0, MP 0 on the machine "antilles0". We took 17 measurements, each after a power-off reboot. The figure shows different colors for each bit of the first 64×64 bits of the SRAM; white pixels indicate that a bit was 1 on each power-up, black pixels indicate that the bit was 0; different shades of red indicate the ratio of 1 versus 0 on each power-on. Thus, the corresponding bits of black/white pixels can be used to identify the SRAM and thus the device, while the bits of the red pixels can be used to derive randomness from the device. The first accessible 64 bits are allways 0 and thus appear to be cleared on kernel launch when kernel parameters are copied to the SRAM.

Figure 5 shows the within-class Hamming distance from 18 different traces taken from each MP of device 0 on the machine "antilles2". Each measurent is compared to the "enrollment" measurement 0. The Hamming distance for each comparison is around 5% which indicates that the device can be identified with high accuracy. Figure 6 shows the between-class Hamming distance pairwise between all of our measurements. The Hamming distance varied between 40% and 60%, which again indicates that the difference between distinct devices is high and that each individual device can be recognized accurately. In particular, there is no general bias that maps certain bits of the SRAM to the same value for all devices. These measurements and analysis show no obstacle to building a usable PUF on top of these devices.

Fig. 4. antilles0, device 0, MP 0, 17 traces.

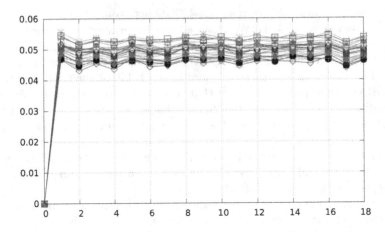

Fig. 5. Within-class Hamming distance for antilles2, device 0, MPs 0–29.

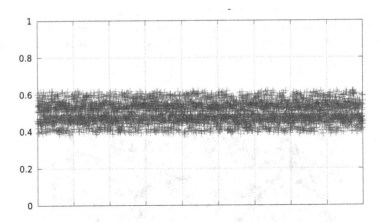

Fig. 6. Between-class Hamming distance for all devices.

7   Discussion

Although we did not find a way to access and read either CPU registers or CPU caches before they are initialized, technically it would be possible to use them as SRAM PUFs. Thus, CPU vendors could enable these hardware features for the use as PUFs probably with relatively small modifications to their chip designs.

As we explained, the situation seems to be different with at least older-generation GPUs, yielding a usable PUF on the Nvidia GTX 295.

However, these SRAM PUFs in both CPU and GPU, if available to be read by software either within the BIOS code or in the bootloader or operating system, would not be protected against an attacker with any kind of root access to the machine. In case the attacker is able to read the PUF, he would be able to reproduce the fingerprint and to impersonate the machine. In case the attacker is able to deploy malware in the early boot process, he would be able to manipulate the PUF state and thus he could influence, e.g., random number generation based on the PUF. Strong software security is thus a prerequisite for truly secure use of these PUFs.

Our explorations on the GPU encountered challenges when we upgraded to a different version of the Nvidia GPU drivers. These drivers appeared to clear large amounts of GPU SRAM, presumably in an effort to reduce the amount of undocumented behavior exposed to GPU applications. Explicit memory zeroing is among the recommended countermeasures against data leakage in [8]. Unfortunately, this also prevents using it as a PUF. Furthermore, when we ran the same tests on a newer generation Nvidia card, we were no longer able to retrieve the SRAM data. On ATI cards, we were never able to read uninitialized SRAM data. This suggests that here, vendors are actually trying to suppress this PUF-like behavior in their devices.

If CPU and GPU vendors decide to provide access to uninitialized SRAM state for use as PUFs, further protection of their data is required. However, data leakage should be prevented, as explained in [8], so maybe direct access is not the best solution. An instruction-set extension as proposed in [18], where the PUF data never leaves the CPU, could also be applied to GPUs and seems to be the best way to implement this.

We have shown that the embedded SRAM in AMD64 CPUs, at least for the model we tested, is indeed not usable as a PUF. For this, we have made modifications to several open-source software packages. We release these modifications into the public domain; they are available online. We have also shown that PUFs are present in the Nvidia GTX 295 graphics card, and conclude that they may be present in other graphics devices.

7.1 Future Work

We have noticed the following phenomenon on a Lenovo ThinkPad X1 Carbon laptop, 2014 edition, with an Intel Core i7-4600U CPU and a 2560×1440 screen; note that this CPU contains a capable GPU embedded inside the CPU. After the BIOS boot stage, approximately the lower third of the screen is temporarily filled with what appear to be randomly colored pixels. This indicates possible presence of a PUF inside the video buffer on the GPU. The obvious next step is to use high-resolution photographic equipment to check the Hamming distance between the colors after multiple power cycles.

246   P. Van Aubel, D.J. Bernstein, and R. Niederhagen

References

1. AGMA Urges Manufacturers to Take Steps to Protect Products from Counterfeiters, http://businesswire.com/news/home/20071003005260/en/AGMA-Urges-Manufacturers-Steps-Protect-Products (October 2007)
2. AMD64 Architecture Programmer's Manual Volume 2: System Programming. 3.23. AMD (May 2013)
3. BIOS and Kernel Developer's Guide (BKDG) for AMD Family 14h Models00h-0Fh Processors. 3.13. AMD (February 2012)
4. van den Berg, R., Škorić, B., van der Leest, V.: Bias-based modeling and entropy analysis of PUFs. In: Armknecht, F., Seifert, J.-P. (eds.) Proceedings of Trust-Worthy Embedded Devices — TrustED 2013, pp. 13–20. ACM (2013)
5. Bohr, M.: 22nm SRAM announcement, http://download.intel.com/pressroom/kits/events/idffall_2009/pdfs/IDF_MBohr_Briefing.pdf (September 2009)
6. CUDA C Programming Guide: Design Guide. 7.0. Nvidia (March 2015)
7. Chauvet, J.-M., Mahe, E.: Secrets from the GPU. ArXiv e-prints (2013), See also: [17]. arXiv:1305.3699
8. Di Pietro, R., Lombardi, F., Villani, A.: CUDA Leaks: Information Leakage in GPU Architectures. ArXiv e-prints (2013). arXiv:1305.7383
9. GNU GRUB, https://www.gnu.org/software/grub/
10. Gassend, B., Clarke, D., van Dijk, M., Devadas, S.: Silicon physical random functions. In: Atluri, V. (ed.) Proceedings of Computer and Communications Security — CCS 2002, pp. 148–160. ACM (2002)
11. Guajardo, J., Kumar, S.S., Schrijen, G.-J., Tuyls, P.: FPGA Intrinsic PUFs and Their Use for IP Protection. In: Paillier, P., Verbauwhede, I. (eds.) Workshop on Cryptographic Hardware and Embedded Systems — CHES 2007. LNCS, vol. 4727, pp. 63–80. Springer, Heidelberg (2007)
12. Heninger, N., Durumeric, Z., Wustrow, E., Alex Halderman, J.: Mining Your Ps and Qs: Detection of Widespread Weak Keys in Network Devices. In: Proceedings of the 21st USENIX Security Symposium, p. 35. USENIX Association (2012)
13. King, R.: Fighting a Flood of Counterfeit Tech Products, http://www.bloomberg.com/bw/stories/2010-03-01/fighting-a-flood-of-counterfeit-tech-productsbusinessweek-business-news-stock-market-and-financial-advice (March 2010)
14. Lee, J.W., Lim, D., Gassend, B., Edward Suh, G., van Dijk, M., Devadas, S.: A technique to build a secret key in integrated circuits for identification and authentication applications. In: Symposium on VLSI Circuits 2004, pp. 176–179. IEEE (2004)
15. Lenstra, A.K., Hughes, J.P., Augier, M., Bos, J.W., Kleinjung, T., Wachter, C.: Public Keys. In: Safavi-Naini, R., Canetti, R. (eds.) Advances in Cryptology — CRYPTO 2012. LNCS, vol. 7417, pp. 626–642. Springer, Heidelberg (2012)
16. Maes, R., Tuyls, P., Verbauwhede, I.: Intrinsic PUFs from Flip-flops on Reconfigurable Devices. In: Workshop on Information and System Security — WISSec 2008 (2008)
17. Mahé, E., Chauvet, J.-M.: Secrets from the GPU. Journal of Computer Virology and Hacking Techniques 10(3), 205–210 (2014)
18. Owusu, E., Guajardo, J., McCune, J., Newsome, J., Perrig, A., Vasudevan, A.: OASIS: On Achieving a Sanctuary for Integrity and Secrecy on Untrusted Platforms. In: Proceedings of Computer and Communications Security — CCS 2013, pp. 13–24. ACM (2013)

19. Parallel Thread Execution ISA: Application Guide. 4.2. Nvidia (March 2015)
20. Schaller, A., Arul, T., van der Leest, V., Katzenbeisser, S.: Lightweight Anti-counterfeiting Solution for Low-End Commodity Hardware Using Inherent PUFs. In: Holz, T., Ioannidis, S. (eds.) Trust and Trustworthy Computing — TRUST 2014. LNCS, vol. 8564, pp. 83–100. Springer, Heidelberg (2014)
21. Schwabe, P.: Graphics Processing Units. In: Markantonakis, K., Mayes, K. (eds.) Secure Smart Embedded Devices: Platforms and Applications, pp. 179–200. Springer (2014)
22. Su, Y., Holleman, J., Otis, B.P.: A Digital 1.6 pJ/bit Chip Identification Circuit Using Process Variations. Journal of Solid-State Circuits 43(1), 69–77 (2008)
23. Suzuki, D., Shimizu, K.: The Glitch PUF: A New Delay-PUF Architecture Exploiting Glitch Shapes. In: Mangard, S., Standaert, F.-X. (eds.) Workshop on Cryptographic Hardware and Embedded Systems — CHES 2010. LNCS, vol. 6225, pp. 366–382. Springer, Heidelberg (2010)
24. Van Herrewege, A., van der Leest, V., Schaller, A., Katzenbeisser, S., Verbauwhede, I.: Secure PRNG Seeding on Commercial Off-the-shelf Microcontrollers. In: Armknecht, F., Seifert, J.-P. (eds.) Proceedings of Trustworthy Embedded Devices — TrustED 2013, pp. 55–64. ACM (2013)
25. Wong, H., Papadopoulou, M.-M., Sadooghi-Alvandi, M., Moshovos, A.: Demystifying GPU microarchitecture through microbenchmarking. In: Performance Analysis of Systems Software (ISPASS), pp. 235–246. IEEE (2010)
26. coreboot, http://www.coreboot.org/

Reconfigurable LUT: A Double Edged Sword for Security-Critical Applications

Debapriya Basu Roy[1], Shivam Bhasin[3], Sylvain Guilley[2,4], Jean-Luc Danger[2,4], Debdeep Mukhopadhyay[1], Xuan Thuy Ngo[2], and Zakaria Najm[2]

[1] Secured Embedded Architecture Laboratory (SEAL)
Department of Computer Science and Engineering,
Indian Institute of Technology Kharagpur
{deb.basu.roy,debdeep}@cse.iitkgp.ernet.in
[2] Institut MINES-TELECOM, TELECOM ParisTech, CNRS LTCI (UMR 5141)
{sylvain.guilley,danger,znajm}@enst.fr,
xuan-thuy.ngo@telecom-paristech.fr
[3] Temasek Laboratories, NTU, Singapore
sbhasin@ntu.edu.sg
[4] Secure-IC S.A.S., 80 avenue des Buttes de Coësmes, 35 700 Rennes, France

Abstract. Modern FPGAs offer various new features for enhanced reconfigurability and better performance. One of such feature is a dynamically Reconfigurable LUT (RLUT) whose content can be updated internally, even during run-time. There are many scenarios like pattern matching where this feature has been shown to enhance the performance of the system. In this paper, we study RLUT in the context of secure applications. We describe the basic functionality of RLUT and discuss its potential applications for security. Next, we design several case-studies to exploit RLUT feature in security critical scenarios. The exploitation are studied from a perspective of a designer (e.g. designing countermeasures) as well as a hacker (inserting hardware Trojans).

Keywords: Reconfigurable LUT (RLUT), FPGA, CFGLUT5, Hardware Trojans, Side-Channel Countermeasures, Secret Ciphers.

1 Introduction

Field Programmable Gate Arrays (FPGAs) have had a significant impact on the semiconductor market in recent years. FPGAs came into the VLSI industry as successor of programmable read only memories (PROMs) and programmable logic devices (PLDs) and has been highly successful due to its reconfigurable nature. A standard FPGA can be defined as islands of configurable logic blocks (CLBs) in the sea of programmable interconnects. However, with time, FPGAs have become more sophisticated due to the addition of several on-chip features such as high-density block memories, DSP cores, PLLs, etc. These features coupled with their core advantage of reconfigurability and low-time to market have made FPGA an integral part of the semiconductor industry, as

© Springer International Publishing Switzerland 2015
R.S. Chakraborty et al. (Eds.): SPACE 2015, LNCS 9354, pp. 248–268, 2015.
DOI: 10.1007/978-3-319-24126-5_15

an attractive economic solution for low to medium scale markets like defense, space, automotive, medical, etc. The key parameters for FPGA manufacturers still remain area, performance and power. However, during these recent years, FPGA manufacturers have started considering security as the fourth parameter. Most recent FPGAs support bitstream protection by authentication and encryption schemes [1]. Other security features like tamper resistance, blocking bitstream read-back, temperature/voltage sensing, etc. are also available. FPGA has also been a popular design platform for implementations of cryptographic algorithms due to its reconfigurability and in house security. Apart from the built-in security features, designers can use FPGA primitives and constraints to implement their own designs in a secure manner. In [2], authors show several side-channel countermeasures which could be realized on FPGAs to protect one design. Another work [3] demonstrates the efficient use of block RAMs to implement complex countermeasures like masking and dual-rail logic. DSPs in FPGAs have also been widely used to design public-key cryptographic algorithms like ECC [4, 5] and other post-quantum algorithms [6]. Moreover, papers like [7] have used FPGA constraints like *KEEP, Lock_PINS* or language like *XDL* to design efficient physical countermeasures.

The basic building block of an FPGA is logic slices. Typically a logic slice contains look up tables (LUTs) and flip-flops. LUTs are used to implement combinational logics whereas flip-flops are used to design sequential architectures. Every LUT contains an *INIT* value which is basically the truth table of the combinational function implemented on that LUT. This *INIT* value is set during the programming of the FPGA through bitstream. Generally this *INIT* value is considered to be constant until the FPGA is reprogrammed again. However, in recent years, a new feature has been added to the FPGAs which allows the user to modify the *INIT* value of some special LUTs in the run time, without any FPGA programming. These special LUTs are known as reconfigurable LUTs or RLUTs as they can be reconfigured during the operation phase to change the input-output mapping of the LUT. To the best of our knowledge, RLUTs have found relevant use in pattern matching and filter applications [8]. Side channel protection methodology using RLUT is presented in [9] where the authors have combined different side channel protection strategies with RLUTs and have developed leakage resilient designs. However, in that work the authors have concentrated mainly on constructive use of RLUTs, not on destructive applications which is covered by our paper.

In this paper, we aim to study the impacts and ramifications of these RLUTs on cryptographic implementations. We have provided a detailed study of RLUTs and have deployed it in many security related applications. We propose several industry-relevant applications of RLUT both of constructive and destructive nature. For example, an RLUT can be easily (ab)used by an FPGA IP designer to insert a hardware Trojan. On the other hand, using RLUT, a designer can provide several enhanced features like programming secret data on client-side. The contribution of the paper can be listed as follows:

- This paper provides a detailed analysis of RLUTs and how it can be exploited to create extremely stealthy and serious hardware security threats like hardware Trojans (destructive applications).
- Moreover, we also propose design methodologies which uses RLUTs to redesign efficient and lightweight existing side channel countermeasures to mitigate power based side channel attacks (constructive applications)
- Thus, in this paper we show that how RLUTs provide a gateway of creating efficient designs for both adversary and normal users and act as double-edged swords for security applications. To the best of our knowledge, this is the first study which provides a detailed security analysis of RLUTs from both constructive and destructive points of view.

The rest of the paper is organized as follows: Sec. 2 describes the rationale of an RLUT and discusses its advantages and disadvantages. Thereafter several destructive and constructive applications of RLUT are demonstrated in Sec. 3 and Sec. 4 respectively. Finally conclusions are drawn in Sec. 5.

2   Rationale of the RLUT

RLUT is a feature which is essentially known to be found in *Xilinx* FPGAs. A *Xilinx* RLUT can be inferred into a design by using a primitive cell called *CFGLUT5* from its library. This primitive allows to implement a 5-input LUT with a single output whose configuration can be changed. *CFGLUT5* was first introduced in Virtex-5 and Spartan-6 families of *Xilinx* FPGAs. As we will show later in this section, the working principle of *CFGLUT* is similar to the shift register or the more popularly known *SRL* primitives. Moreover, some older families of Xilinx which do not support *CFGLUT5* as a primitive, can still implement RLUT using the *SRL16* primitive. In the following, for sake of demonstration, we stick to the *CFGLUT5* primitives. Nevertheless the results should directly apply to its alternatives as well.

As stated earlier, a RLUT can be implemented in Virtex-5 FPGAs using a *CFGLUT5* primitive. The basic block diagram of CFGLUT5 is shown in Fig. 1. It is a 5-input and a 1-output LUT. Alternatively, a CFGLUT5 can also be modeled as a 4-input and 2-output function. The main feature of CFGLUT5 is that it can be configured dynamically during the run-time. Every LUT is loaded with a $INIT$ value, which actually represents the truth table of the function implemented on that LUT. A CFGLUT5 allows the user to change the $INIT$ value at the run-time, thus giving the user power of dynamic reconfiguration internally. This reconfiguration is performed using the CD_I port. A 1-bit reconfiguration data input is shifted serially into $INIT$ in each clock cycle if the reconfiguration enable signal (CE) is set high. The previous value of $INIT$ is flushed out serially through the CD_O port, 1-bit per clock cycle. Several CFGLUT5 can be cascaded together using reconfiguration data cascaded output port (CD_O).

The reconfiguration property of CFGLUT5 is illustrated in Fig. 2 with the help of a small example. In this figure, we show how the value of $INIT$ gets modified:

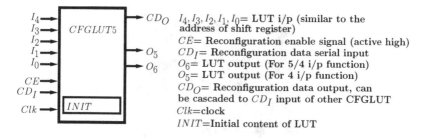

I_4, I_3, I_2, I_1, I_0= LUT i/p (similar to the address of shift register)
CE= Reconfiguration enable signal (active high)
CD_I= Reconfiguration data serial input
O_6= LUT output (For 5/4 i/p function)
O_5= LUT output (For 4 i/p function)
CD_O= Reconfiguration data output, can be cascaded to CD_I input of other CFGLUT
Clk=clock
$INIT$=Initial content of LUT

Fig. 1. Block diagram of CFGLUT5

- from value $O = (O_0, O_1, O_2, \ldots, O_{30}, O_{31})$,
- to a new value $N = (N_0, N_1, N_2, \ldots, N_{30}, N_{31})$.

This reconfiguration requires 32 clock cycles. As it is evident from the figure, reconfiguration steps are basic shift register operations. Hence if required, reconfiguration of LUT content can be executed by using shift register primitives ($SRL16E\_1$) in earlier device families. The CD_O pin can also be fed back to the CD_I pin of the same $CFGLUT5$. In this case, the original $INIT$ value can be restored after a maximum of 32 clock cycles without any overhead logic. We will exploit this property of RLUT later to design hardware Trojans.

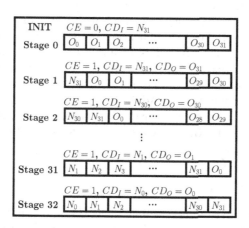

Fig. 2. $INIT$ value reconfiguration in CFGLUT5

There are two different kinds of slices in a Xilinx FPGA i.e., $SLICE\_M$ and $SLICE\_L$. Whereas a simple LUT can be synthesized in either of the slices, CFG-LUT5 can be implemented only in $SLICE\_M$. $SLICE\_M$ contains LUTs which can be configured as memory elements like shift register, distributed memory along with combinational logic function implementation. The LUTs of $SLICE\_L$

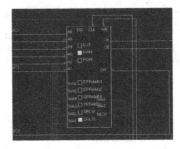

Fig. 3. CFGLUT5 mapped in LUT as SRL32 as shown from Xilinx FPGA Editor

can only implement combinational logic. CFGLUT5, when instantiated, is essentially mapped into a *SLICE_M*, configured as shift register (*SRL*32) as shown in Fig 3.

2.1   Comparison with Dynamic Configuration

Another alternative to reconfigure FPGA in run-time is to use partial or dynamic reconfiguration. This reconfiguration can also be exploited to implement secure architectures [10]. In partial reconfiguration, a portion of the implemented design is changed without disrupting operations of the other portion of the FPGA. This operation deploys an Internal Configuration Access Ports (ICAP) and the design needing reconfiguration must be mapped into a special *reconfigurable region* [11]. Reconfiguration latency is in order of milliseconds. Partial reconfiguration is helpful when significant modification of the design is required. However, for small modification, using RLUT is advantageous as it has very small latency (maximum 32 clock cycles) compared to partial reconfiguration. RLUT is configured internally and no external access to either JTAG or Ethernet ports are required for reconfiguring RLUTs. Additionally, traditional DPR (Dynamic Partial Reconfiguration) requires to convey an extra bit file which is not required in case of RLUT, making RLUT ideal for small reconfiguration of the design, in particular for Trojans.

2.2   RLUT and Security

Since we have described the functioning of RLUT in detail, we can clearly recognize some properties which could be helpful or critical for security. A typical problem of cryptographic implementations is its vulnerability to statistical attacks like Correlation Power Analysis (CPA) [12]. For instance, CPA tries to extract secret information from static cryptographic implementations by correlating side-channel leakages to estimated leakage models. A desirable feature to protect such implementations is reconfiguration of few internal features. A RLUT would be a great solution in this case as it has the power to provide reconfigurability at minimal overhead and with no external access. It is important to reconfigure internally to avoid the risk of any eavesdropping. On the other hand, RLUT can also be used as a security pitfall. For example, an efficient designer can simply replace a LUT with RLUT in a design keeping the same *INIT* value. Until reconfiguration, RLUT would compute normally. However upon reconfiguration, the RLUT can be turned into a potential Trojan. The routing of the design is actually static, only the functionality of the LUT is modified upon reconfiguration. In the following sections, we would show some relevant applications of constructive or deadly nature. Of course it is only a non-exhaustive list of RLUT applications into security.

3   Destructive Applications of RLUT

In earlier sections, we have presented the basic concepts of RLUTs with major emphasis on *CFGLUT5* of Xilinx FPGAs. Though *CFGLUT5* provides user unique opportunity of reconfiguring and modifying the design in run-time, it also gives an adversary an excellent option to design efficient and stealthy hardware Trojan. In this section, we focus on designing tiny but effective hardware Trojan exploiting reconfigurability of RLUTs.

A hardware Trojan is a malevolent modification of a design, intended for either disrupting the algorithm operation or leaking secret information from it. The design of hardware Trojan involves efficient design of Trojan circuitry (known as payload) and design of trigger circuitry to activate the Trojan operation. A stealthy hardware Trojan should have negligible overhead, ideally zero, compared to the original *golden* circuit. Moreover, probability of Trojan getting triggered during the functional testing should be very low, preventing accidental discovery of the Trojan. The threat of hardware Trojans is very realistic due to the fabless model followed by the modern semiconductor companies. In this model, the design is sent to remote fabrication laboratories for chip fabrication. It is very easy for an adversary to make some small modification in the design without violating the functionality of the design. The affected chip will give desired output in normal condition, but will leak sensitive information upon being triggered. More detailed analysis of hardware Trojans can be found in [13–15].

Researchers have shown that it is possible to design efficient hardware Trojans on FPGAs. In [16] the authors have designed a Trojan on a Basys FPGA board which get triggered depending upon the 'content and timing' of the signals. On the other hand, authors in [17] have designed a hardware Trojan which can be deployed on the FPGA via dynamic partial reconfiguration to induce faults in an AES circuitry for differential fault analysis.

In this section, we will focus on effective design of hardware Trojan payload using RLUT. But before going into the design methodologies of payload using RLUTs, we will first describe the other two important aspects of the proposed hardware Trojans: Adversary model and Trigger methodologies.

3.1   Adversary Model

It is a common trend in the semiconductor industry to acquire proven IPs to reduce time to market and stay competitive. We consider an adversary model where a user buys specific proven IPs from a third party IP vendor. By proven IPs, we mean IPs with well-established performance and area figures. Let us consider that the IP under consideration is a cryptographic algorithm and the target device is an FPGA. An untrusted vendor can easily insert a Trojan in the IP which can act as a backdoor to access sensitive information of other components of the user circuit. For instance, an IP vendor can provide a user with an obfuscated or even encrypted netlist (encrypted *EDIF* (Electronic Design Interchange Format)). Such techniques are popular and often used to protect the rights of the IP vendor. A Trojan in an IP is very serious for two major reasons. First, the Trojan will affect all the samples of the final product and secondly it is almost impossible to get a golden model. Moreover, research in Trojan detection under the given attack model is quite limited. The user does not have a golden circuit to compare, thus making hardware Trojan detection using side channel methodology highly unlikely. Additionally, this adversary model also makes the Trojan design challenging. Generally, before buying an IP, user will analyze IPs from different IP vendors for performance comparison. This competitive scenario does not leave a big margin (gate-count) for Trojans.

Using RLUT, we can design extremely lightweight hardware Trojan payload as we can reconfigure the same LUTs, used in the crypto-algorithm implementation, from correct value to malicious value. This reduces the overhead of the hardware Trojan and makes it less susceptible to detection techniques based on visual inspection [18]. We can also restore the original value of RLUT to remove any trace of Trojan, of course, at minor overheads. An IP designer can easily replace a normal LUT with RLUT. In this case, the designer has only one restriction of replacing a LUT implemented in *SLICE_M*. It is not difficult to find such a LUT in a medium to big-scale FPGA which is often the case with cryptographic modules. Moreover, if the designer chooses to insert the trojan at RTL level, the present restriction would not even apply. Additionally, if the access to the client bitstream is available, the adversary can reverse engineer the bitstream [19] and can replace a normal LUT with RLUT.

Instantiation of *CFGLUT5* does not report any special element in the design summary report, **but a LUT modeled as *SRL32*.** A shift register has many usages on the circuit. For example, a counter can be very efficiently designed on a shift register using one hot encoding. Moreover, lightweight ciphers employs extensive usage of shift registers for serialized architectures. Thus any suspicion of malicious activity will not arise in the user's mind by seeing the design report.

The only requirement is efficient triggering and a reconfiguration logic which will generate the malicious value upon receiving trigger signal. However, in this paper we will show that once triggered, **malicious value for the hardware Trojan can be generated without any overhead**, thus giving us extremely lightweight and stealthy design of hardware Trojans. The basic methodology is same for all the Trojans, which can be tabulated as follows:

- Choose a sensitive sub-module of the crypto-algorithm. For example, one can choose a 4×4 Sbox (can be implemented using 2 LUTs) as the sensitive sub module.

- Replace the LUTs of the chosen sub-module with *CFGLUT5s* without altering the functionality. A 4 × 4 Sbox can also be implemented using two *CFGLUT5*.
- Modify the *INIT* value upon trigger. As shown in Fig. 1, reconfiguration in *CFGLUT5* takes place upon receiving the *CE* signal. By connecting the trigger output to the *CE* port, an adversary can tweak the *INIT* value of *CFGLUT5* and can change it to a malicious value. For example, the 4 × 4 Sboxes, implemented using *CFGLUT5* can be modified in such a way that non-linear properties of the Sboxes get lost and the crypto-system becomes vulnerable to standard cryptanalysis. The malicious *INIT* value can be easily generated by some nominal extra logic. However, in the subsequent sections, we will show that it is possible to generate the malicious *INIT* value without any extra logic.
- Upon exploitation, restore original *INIT* value.

3.2 Trigger Design the Hardware Trojans

A trigger for a hardware Trojan is designed in a way that the Trojan gets activated in very rare cases. The trigger stimulus can be generated either through output of a sensor under physical stress or some well controlled internal logic. The complexity of trigger circuit also depends on the needed precision of the trigger in time and space. Several innovative and efficient methods were introduced as a part of Embedded Systems Challenge (2008) where participants were asked to insert Trojans on FPGA designs. For instance, one of the the proposition was *content & timing* trigger [16], which activates with a correct combination of input and time. Such triggers are considered practically impossible to simulate. Other triggers get activated at a specific input pattern. A more detailed analysis with example of different triggering methodologies and their pros and cons can be found in [20].

Moreover, modern devices are loaded with physical sensors to ensure correct operating conditions. It is not difficult to find voltage or temperature sensors in smart-cards or micro-controllers. Similarly, FPGA also come with monitors to protect the system for undesired environmental conditions, Virtex-5 FPGAs contain *system monitor*. Though system monitor is not a part of cipher, they are often included in the SoC for tamper/fault/ temperature variation detection. These sensors are programmed to raise an alarm in event of unexpected physical conditions like overheating, high/low voltage etc. Now an adversary can use this system monitor to design an efficient and stealthy hardware Trojan trigger methodology. The trick is to choose a trigger condition which is less than threshold value but much higher than nominal conditions. For instance, a chip with nominal temperature of $20°C - 30°C$ and safety threshold of $80°C$, can be triggered in a small window chosen from the range of $40°C - 79°C$. Similarly, user deployed sensors like the one proposed in [21] can also be used to trigger a Trojan. In our case study, we used the temperature sensor of Virtex-5 FPGAs *system monitor* to trigger the Trojan, more precisely on SASEBO-GII boards.

The heating required to trigger the Trojan can be done by a simple \$5 hair-dryer easily available in the market. The triggering mechanism is explained in Appendix A. In the following to not deviate from the topic, we focus mainly on the payload design of the Trojan using RLUT. We let the designer choose any of the published techniques (including one proposed in Appendix A) or innovate one. We precisely propose the design of the Trojan and the required triggering conditions.

3.3   Trojan Description

Before designing Trojan payload for a given hardware, we first demonstrate the potential of RLUT in inserting malicious activity. Let us consider a buffer which is a very basic gate. Buffers are often inserted in a circuit by CAD tools to achieve desired timing requirements. For FPGA designers, another equivalent of buffer is route-only LUT. These buffers can be inserted in any sensitive wires without raising an alarm. In fact, sometimes the buffers might already exist.

These buffers are implemented in a *LUT6* with `INIT=0xAAAAAAAAAAAAAAAA` and can be easily replaced by *CFGLUT5*. A simple Trojan would consist in changing the *INIT* value of CFGLUT5 to `0xAAAAAAAA` and feedback CD_O output to CD_I input (see Fig 1). The *CE* input is connected to the trigger of the Trojan. Now, when the Trojan is triggered once (one clock), *INIT* value changes to `0x55555555` which changes the functionality of the gate to **inverter**. Another trigger brings back the *INIT* value to `0xAAAAAAAA` i.e., a **buffer**. The operations are illustrated in Fig. 4, where red block shows Trojan inverter and black blocks show a normal buffer. Thus by precisely controlling the trigger, an adversary can interchange between a buffer and inverter. Such a Trojan can be used in many scenarios like injecting single bit faults for Differential Fault Attacks [22] or controlling data multiplexers or misreading status flags, etc.

In the above example, we see how a buffer can be converted to an inverter by reconfiguring the *CFGLUT5* upon receiving the trigger signal. One important observation is that we do need need any extra reconfiguration logic to modify the *INIT* value of the *CFGLUT5*. The modification of the *INIT* value is achieved by the connecting the reconfiguration input port CD_I to the reconfiguration data output port CD_O. In other words, we can define the malicious *INIT* value in following way

$$INIT_{malicious} = CS_i(INIT_{normal})$$

where CS_i denotes cyclic right shift by i bits. The approach of RLUT is harder to detect because the malicious payload does not exist in the design. It is configured when needed and immediately removed upon exploitation. In normal LUT, the malicious design is hardwired (requires extra logic) and risk detection, whereas RLUT modifies existing resources and enables us to design design hardware Trojans without any extra reconfiguration logic. We will use similar methodologies for all the proposed hardware Trojans in this paper.

Next, we target a basic *AES* IP as a Trojan target. The architecture of the AES design is shown in Fig. 5. The AES takes 128 bits of plaintext and key

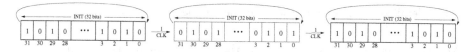

Fig. 4. Operations of CFGLUT5 to switch from a buffer to inverter and back

as input and produce 128 bit cipher-text in 11 clock cycles. The control unit of the AES encryption engine is governed by a 4 bit mod-12 counter and generates three different control signals which are as follows:

1. *load:* It is used to switch between plaintext and MixColumns output. During the start of the encryption, this signal is made high to load the plaintext in the AES encryption engine.
2. *S.R/M.C:* It is used to switch between the ShiftRows and MixColumns output in the last round of AES.
3. *done:* It is used to indicate the end of encryption.

These signals are set high for different values of the counter. In our Trojan design, we mainly target the control unit of the AES architecture to disrupt the flow of the encryption scheme so that we can retrieve the AES encryption key. For this, we have developed four different Trojans and have deployed them on the *AES* implementation. The objective of the developed Trojan is to retrieve the *AES* key with only one execution of hardware Trojan or single bad encryption. Indeed, it has been shown that only one faulty encryption, if it is accurate in time, suffices to extract a full 128-bit key [23]. Triggering conditions can be further relaxed if several bad encryptions are acceptable. Each Trojan has trigger with different pulse-width or number of clock cycles. For different payloads, the RLUT content varies, hence variation in the trigger.

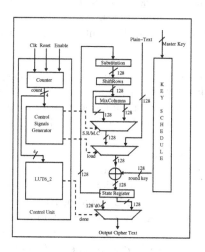

Fig. 5. AES architecture without Trojans

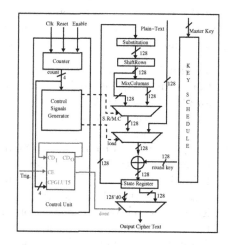

Fig. 6. AES architecture with Trojan 1

The detailed description of the developed Trojans are as follows:

Trojan 1. As we have stated earlier, the control unit of *AES* is based on a counter which also generates a *done* flag to indicate completion of the encryption cycle and is set to high only if counter value reaches 11. Signal *done* as shown in Fig. 5, is driven by a LUT6_2, which takes 4 bit counter value as input, and under normal operation it should contain *INIT* value 0x00000800 (it means only the 11th bit is set to one i.e. condition required for *done* signal). To insert a Trojan we replace this LUT with *CFGLUT5* with INIT=0x80000800. It must be noted that though the *INIT* value of LUT6_2 and *INIT* value of CFGLUT5 are not same, both will essentially produce the same output upon receiving the 4 bit counter value. This is because truth-table of a function of 4 variables consists of 16 bits only, hence any change in the upper 16 bits of the *INIT* value will not change the functionalities of the LUT.

The CD_O output is feedback into CD_I input as in the example above. A trigger of 2 clock cycles at the CE input activates the Trojan (INIT=0x00002002) and produces the round 0 output (at round 0, counter value is 1) as the ciphertext. The round 0 output is actually same as *plaintext XOR key* and by knowing the plaintext, one can easily extract the full key with one wrong encryption. Again, we can see that malicious value of the *INIT* is generated by cyclic shift of the original *INIT* value of the *CFGLUT5*, hence we do not need any extra logic to generate the new *INIT* value. After extracting the key, a trigger of 10 clock cycles will restore the normal operations of the AES (INIT=0x00800800). This *INIT* value need not to be the same value, with which we started the computation (INIT=0x80000800), as long as the LUT generates correct output. The transition of *INIT* to activate the Trojan and restore back is shown in Fig 7(a) and the modifications in the AES architecture is shown in Fig. 6.

In the above Trojan description, we need 2 clock cycles to modify the *CFG-LUT5* to malicious Trojan configuration and 10 clock cycles to restore it to the original correct value. So in total, we require 12 clock cycles.

Keeping this in mind, we have implemented three different versions of the same Trojan, depending on the precision of the trigger.

1. **Trojan 1a** needs a 1 cycle trigger synchronized with the start of the encryption. This trigger is used to enable a FSM which generates 12 clock cycles for CE of the $CFGLUT$, in order to activate the Trojan and restore it back after exploitation. Because of this, the overhead of the developed Trojan is **6 LUTs and 4 flip-flops**.
2. **Trojan 1b** is a **zero** overhead Trojan. It assumes an adversary to be slightly stronger than Trojan 1a who can generate a trigger signal active for precisely 12 cycles and synchronized with the start of encryption. This overhead is absent in Trojan 1b as the trigger itself act as the CE signal of RLUT.
3. **Trojan 1c** relaxes the restriction on the adversary seen at previous case. It assumes that there are some delays of $n \gg 10$ clock cycles between two consecutive encryption. The choice of $n \gg 10$ is due to the fact that we need 2 clock cycles to reconfigure the RLUT into malicious Trojan payload,

and 10 clock cycles to restore it back to good value. Hence the gap between two consecutive AES encryption should be greater than 10. The adversary provides a trigger of two clock cycles (not necessarily consecutive) before the start of current encryption. After the faulty encryption is complete, the adversary generates 10 trigger cycles (again not necessarily consecutive) to restore back the cipher operations. The overhead for this Trojan is 2 **LUTs**, due to routing of RLUT.

Trojan 2. This Trojan targets a different signal in the control unit of the *AES* design. As shown in Fig. 5, the design contains a multiplexer which switches between MixColumns output and input plaintext depending on the round/count value. The output of the multiplexer is produced at input of AddRoundKey operation. Under normal operation, multiplexer passes the input plaintext in round 0 (*load* signal of multiplexer is set to 1) and MixColumns output (ShiftRows output in the last round) in other rounds (*select* signal of multiplexer is set to 0). To design the Trojan, we have replaced the LUT6_2 (with INIT=0x00000002) which generates *load* signal of the multiplexer with *CFGLUT5*, containing INIT= 0x00400002. As we have observed for Trojan 1, the difference in the *INIT* value in LUT6_2 and *INIT* value of *CFGLUT5* will essentially produce the same output.

In this case also CD_O port of *CFGLUT5* is connected to CD_I port, enabling cyclic shift of the *INIT* value. Upon a trigger of 10 clock cycles, the *INIT* value gets modified to INIT=0x80000400 (it means load will set to one during the last round). This actually changes the multiplexer operation, modifying it to select the plaintext in the last round computation. From the resulting ciphertext of this faulted encryption, we can easily obtain the last round key, given the plaintext. Further a trigger of 2 clock cycles restores the normal operation (INIT=0x00001002) as shown in Fig 7(b). Again the value over bit position 12 is not a problem as the *select* signal is controlled by a mod-12 counter and the value is never reached. The counter value 0 indicates idle state, $1 - 10$ encryption and 11 indicates end of encryption. This Trojan also has a **zero** overhead as reconfiguration of the CFGLUT5 is obtained by cyclic right shifting of *INIT*.

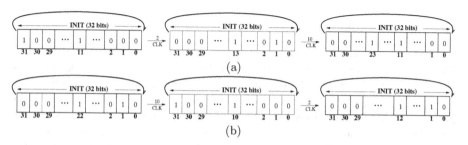

Fig. 7. Operations of CFGLUT5 to activate the Trojan and restore to normal operations for (a) Trojan 1; (b) Trojan 2. Bit positions not shown contain '0'

Table 1. Area overhead of the Trojans on Virtex-5 FPGA. Trigger is given in clock cycles and s subscript indicates trigger must be consecutive synchronized with the start of encryption.

Trojan	Trigger	LUT	Registers	Payload Overhead	Frequency (MHz)
AES (No Trojan)		1594	260	X	212.85
Trojan 1a	1_s	1600	264	6 LUTs & 4 flip-flops	212.85
Trojan 1b	12_s	1594	260	0	212.85
Trojan 1c	12	1596	260	2 LUTs	212.85
Trojan 2	12_s	1594	260	0	212.85

But the trigger signal need to be precise and should be available for consecutive 12 clock cycles. Hence, triggering cost is same as Trojan 1b.

Tab. 1 summarizes the nature, trigger condition and cost of the four Trojans.

The above described Trojans can also be designed using normal LUTs. The zero overhead Trojans described above can be designed using 2 LUT overhead (One LUT for Trojan operation and other for selecting between Trojan and normal operations). But such Trojan designs can be easy to detect as the Trojan operated LUT is always present on the design unlike CFGLUT5, where the Trojan operated LUT is created by run time reconfiguration.

In this section, we have presented different scenarios where CFGLUT5 can be employed as hardware Trojans and can leak secret information from crypto-IPs like AES. We specifically have targeted multiplexers and FSMs of the circuit. It is also possible to design sophisticated Trojans using CFGLUT5 where the developed Trojan will work in conjunction with side channel attacks or fault injections to increase the vulnerability of the underlying crypto-system.

4   Constructive Applications for RLUT

In the previous section, we discussed some application of RLUT for hardware Trojans into third party IPs. However, RLUT do have a brighter side to their portfolio. The easy and internal reconfigurability of RLUT can surely be well exploited by the designers to solve certain design issues. In the following, we detail two distinct cases with several applications, where RLUT can be put to good use.

4.1   Customizable Sboxes

A common requirement in several industrial application is dynamic or cutomizable substitution boxes (Sboxes) of a cipher. One such scenario which is often encountered by IP designers who design **secret ciphers** for industrial application. A majority of secret ciphers use a standard algorithm like AES with modified specification like custom Sboxes or linear operations. Sometimes the client is not comfortable to disclose these custom specifications to the IP designer. Common solutions either have a time-space overhead or resort to dynamic reconfiguration, to allow the client to program secret parameters at their facilities. A RLUT can come handy in this case.

There are several algorithms where the Sboxes can be secret. The former Soviet encryption algorithm GOST 28147-89 which was standardized by the Russian standardization agency in 1989 is a prominent example [24]. The A3/A8 GSM algorithm for European mobile telecommunications is another example. In the field of digital rights management, Cryptomeria cipher (C2) has a secret set of Sboxes which are generated and distributed to licencees only.

There are certain encryption schemes like DRECON [25], which offers DPA resistance by construction, exploiting tweakable ciphers. In this scheme, users exchange a set of tweak during the key exchange. The tweak is used to choose the set of Sboxes from a bigger pool of precomputed Sboxes. In the proposed implementation [25], the entire pool of Sboxes must be stored on-chip. Using RLUT, the Sboxes can be easily computed as a function of the tweak and stored on the fly. Similarly, a low-cost masking scheme RSM [3] can also benefit from RLUT to achieve desired rotation albeit at the cost of latency. Thus there exist several applications where customizable Sboxes are needed.

Architecture of Sbox Generator: As a proof of concept, we implement the Sbox generation scheme of [25]. The original implementation generates a pool of 32 4×4 Sboxes and stores it into BRAMs, while only 16 are used for a given encryption. It uses a set of Sboxes which are affine transformations of each other. For a given cryptographically strong Sbox $S(\cdot)$, one can generate 2^n strong Sboxes by following: $F_i(x) = \alpha S(x) \oplus i$ for all $i = 0, \cdots, 2^n - 1$, where α is an invertible matrix of dimension $n \times n$. α can also be considered a function of the tweak value t i.e. $\alpha = f(t)$. Since affine transformation does not change most of the cryptographic properties of Sboxes, all the generated Sboxes are of equal cryptographic strength [25].

The Sbox computation scheme of [25] can be very well implemented using RLUT as follows. The **main objective** of this Sbox generator is to compute a new affine Sbox from a given reference Sbox, and store it in the same location. The architecture is shown in Fig 8. As we have stated earlier, each $CFGLUT5$ can be modeled as 2 output 4 input function generator, we can implement a 4×4 Sbox using two $CFGLUT5$ as shown in Fig 8. We consider that the reference 4×4 Sbox is implemented using 2 $CFGLUT5$. We compute the new Sbox and program it in the same 2 $CFGLUT5$. The reconfiguration of the Sbox is carried through following steps:

1. Read the value of the Sbox for input 15.
2. Compute the new value (4-bits $\{3,2,1,0\}$) of the Sbox using affine transformer for the Sbox input 15.
3. Now $CFGLUT5$ is updated by the computed value, 2 bits for each $CFGLUT5$ ($\{3,2\},\{1,0\}$). However, only one bit can be shifted in $CFGLUT5$ in one clock cycle. Hence we shift in two bits, 1-bit in each CFGLUT5 ($\{0,2\}$) and store the other 2-bit ($\{1,3\}$) in two 16 bit registers.

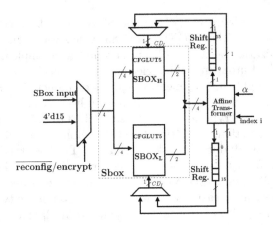

Fig. 8. Architecture of Sbox Computation using affine transformation and storing in RLUT

4. After the 2-bits ({0,2}) of new value of Sbox is shifted in to position 0 of each *CFGLUT5*, old value for the position 15 is flushed out. The old value at position 14 is moved up to position 15. Thus the address is hard-coded to 4'd15.
5. Repeat steps 1 − 4 until whole old Sbox is read out i.e. 16 clock cycles.
6. After 16 clock cycles, we start to shift in the data which we stored in the shift register bits ({1,3}) for 16 Sbox entries, which takes another 16 clock cycles. This completes Sbox reconfiguration.

The architecture requires **56 LUTs, 38 flip-flops with a maximum operating frequency of 271 MHz.** To reconfigure one Sbox, we need 32 clock cycles. Now depending on the application and desired security the sbox recomputation can be done after several encryption or every encryption or every round. It is a purely security-performance trade-off.

4.2 Sbox Scrambling for DPA Resistance

RLUT also have the potential to provide side-channel resistance. The reconfiguration provided by RLUT can be very well used to confuse the attackers. A beneficial target would be the much studied masking countermeasures [2] which suffer from high overhead due to the requirement of *regular mask refresh*. One of the masking countermeasures which was fine-tuned for FPGA implementation is Block Memory content Scrambling (BMS [2]). This scheme claims first-order security and, to our knowledge, no practical attack has been published against it. However, Sbox Scrambling using BRAM is inefficient on lightweight ciphers with 4x4 sboxes due to underutilization of resources. Hence we propose a novel architecture using RLUT to address this. Nevertheless, this mechanism can easily be translated to AES also.

The side channel countermeasure using RLUT, shown in [9] is different from the proposed design architecture. The design of [9] implements standard Boolean

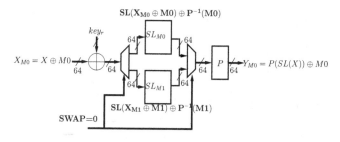

Fig. 9. Architecture of Modified PRESENT Round. SL_{M0} is the (precomputed) active SLayer while SL_{M1} is being computed as in Fig. 10.

masking scheme, where each round uses a different mask. Here, we propose a lightweight architecture of SBox scrambling scheme presented in [2]. These two countermeasures have similar objectives but quite different designs.

The BMS scheme works as follows: let $Y(X) = P(SL(X))$ be a round of block cipher, where X is the data, $P(\cdot)$ is the linear and $SL(\cdot)$ is the non-linear layer of the block cipher. For example in PRESENT cipher [26], the non-linear layer is composed of 16 4×4 Sboxes and the linear layer is bit-permutation. According to the BMS scheme, the masked round can be written as $Y_M(X) = P(SL_M(X_M))$, where X_M is masked data $X \oplus M$ and $SL_M(\cdot)$ is the Sbox layer of 16 scrambled Sbox. Now each Sbox $S_m(\cdot)$ in SL_M is scrambled with one nibble m of the 64-bit mask M. The scrambled Sbox $S_m(\cdot)$ can be simplified as $S_m(x_m)) = S(x_m \oplus m) \oplus P^{-1}(m)$, where x is one nibble of round input X. Next in a dual-port BRAM which is divided into an active and inactive segment, where the active segment contains $SL_{M0}(\cdot)$ i.e. Sbox scrambled with mask $M0$ is used for encryptions. Parallely, another Sbox layer $SL_{M1}(\cdot)$ scrambled with mask $M1$ is computed in an encryption-independent process and stored in the inactive segment. Every few encryption, the active and inactive contents are swapped and a new Sbox scrambled with a fresh mask is computed and stored in the current inactive segment. This functioning is illustrated in Fig. 9.

BMS is an efficient countermeasure and shown to have reasonable overhead of 44% for LUTs, 2× BRAMs and roughly 3× extra flip-flops in FPGA. Another advantage of BMS is that it is generic i.e., it can be applied to any cryptographic algorithm. BMS can be viewed as a *leakage resilient* implementation, where the cipher is not called enough with a fixed mask for an attack to succeed. The memory contexts are swapped again with a fresh mask. However, for certain algorithms BMS could become unattractive. For example in a lightweight algorithm like PRESENT, a 4×4 Sbox can be easily implemented in 4 LUTs. In newer FPGA families which support 2-output LUT, 2 LUTs are enough to implement a Sbox. Using a BRAM in such a scenario would lead to huge wastage of resources.

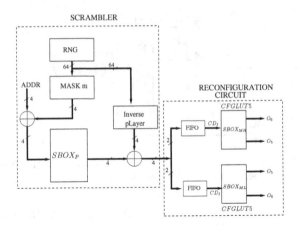

Fig. 10. Architecture of Sbox Scrambler

Table 2. Area and Performance Overhead of Scrambling Scheme on Virtex-5 FPGA

Architecture	LUTs	Flip-flops	Frequency (MHz)
Original	208	150	196
Scrambled	557	552	189
Overhead	2.67×	3.68×	1.03×

Sbox Scrambling Using RLUT: In the following, we use RLUT to implement BMS like countermeasure. Precisely we design a PRESENT cryptoprocessor protected with a BMS like scrambling scheme but using RLUTs to store scrambled Sboxes. The rest of the scheme is left same as [2]. The architecture of Sbox scrambler using RLUT is shown in Fig 10. $SBOX_P$ is the PRESENT Sbox. A mod16 counter generates the Sbox address $ADDR$ which is masked with Mask m of 4-bits. The output of Sbox is scrambled with the inverse permutation of the mask to scramble the Sbox value. Please note that the permutation must be applied on the whole 64-bits of the mask to get 4-bits of the scrambling constant for each Sbox. Each output of the scrambler is 4-bits. As stated before, each 4×4 Sbox can be implemented in 2 CFGLUT5 each producing 2-bits of the Sbox computation. Let us call the CFGLUT5 producing bits $0, 1$ as $SBOX_{ML}$ and bits $2, 3$ as $SBOX_{MH}$. The 4-bit output of the scrambler is split into two buses of 2-bits ($\{3,2\},\{1,0\}$). Bits $\{3,2\}$ and $\{1,0\}$ are then fed to the CD_I of $SBOX_{ML}$ and $SBOX_{MH}$ respectively, through a FIFO. The same scrambler is used to generate all the 16 Sboxes one after the other and program CFGLUT5. In total it requires 16×32 clock cycles to refresh all 16 inactive Sboxes. We implement two parallel layers of SBoxes. When the active layer is computing the cipher, the inactive one is being refreshed. Thus cipher operation is not stalled. 16×32 clocks (16 encryptions) are needed to refresh the inactive layer and this means that we can swap active and inactive SBoxes after every 16 encryptions. Swap means that active SBox become inactive and vice versa. The cipher design uses active SBox only. The area overhead comes from the scrambler circuit and multiplexers used to swap active/inactive Sboxes. We implemented a PRESENT crypto-processor and protected it with Sbox scrambling countermeasure. The area and performance figures of the original design and its protected version are summarized in Tab. 2. It should be noted that proposed design has more overhead compared to original BMS scheme in terms of LUT and flip-flops, but does not require any block RAMs which are essential part of original BMS scheme.

5 Conclusions

This paper addresses methods to exploit reconfigurable LUTs (RLUTs) in FPGAs for secure applications, with both views: destructive and constructive. First it has been shown that the RLUT can be used by an attacker to create Hardware Trojans. Indeed the payload of stealthy Trojans can be inserted easily in IP by untrusted vendors. The Trojans can be used to inject faults or modify the control signals in order to facilitate the key extraction. This is illustrated by a few examples of Trojans in AES. Second the protective property of RLUT has been illustrated by increasing the resiliency of the Sboxes of cryptographic algorithms. This is accomplished either by changing dynamically the Sboxes of customized algorithms or scrambling the Sboxes of standard algorithms. These type of design techniques are extremely useful for lightweight block ciphers with SBox of smaller dimension. Moreover, generating Sboxes in runtime is an attractive design choice for the designer employing ciphers with secret Sboxes.

To sum up, this paper clearly shows that RLUT is a double-edged sword for security applications on FPGAs. Due to the obvious positive application of RLUTs in security, one cannot simply restrict the use of RLUT in secure applications. This motivates further research in two principal directions. Firstly, there is need for Trojan detection techniques at IP level. This detection techniques should be capable of distinguishing a RLUT based optimizations from potential Trojans. Finally certain new countermeasures totally based on RLUTs can be studied.

Bibliography

1. Trimberger, S.M., Moore, J.J.: FPGA Security: Motivations, Features, and Applications. Proceedings of the IEEE 102(8), 1248–1265 (2014)
2. Güneysu, T., Moradi, A.: Generic side-channel countermeasures for reconfigurable devices. In: Preneel, B., Takagi, T. (eds.) CHES 2011. LNCS, vol. 6917, pp. 33–48. Springer, Heidelberg (2011)
3. Bhasin, S., He, W., Guilley, S., Danger, J.-L.: Exploiting FPGA block memories for protected cryptographic implementations. In: ReCoSoC, pp. 1–8. IEEE (2013)
4. Güneysu, T., Paar, C.: Ultra High Performance ECC over NIST Primes on Commercial FPGAs. In: Oswald, E., Rohatgi, P. (eds.) CHES 2008. LNCS, vol. 5154, pp. 62–78. Springer, Heidelberg (2008)
5. Roy, D.B., Mukhopadhyay, D., Izumi, M., Takahashi, J.: Tile before multiplication: An efficient strategy to optimize DSP multiplier for accelerating prime field ECC for NIST curves. In: The 51st Annual Design Automation Conference, DAC 2014, San Francisco, CA, USA, June 1-5, pp. 1–6. ACM (2014)

6. Güneysu, T.: Getting Post-Quantum Crypto Algorithms Ready for Deployment. https://www.cosic.esat.kuleuven.be/ecrypt/cryptofor2020/program.shtml
7. He, W., Otero, A., de la Torre, E., Riesgo, T.: Automatic generation of identical routing pairs for FPGA implemented DPL logic. In: ReConFig, pp. 1–6. IEEE (2012)
8. Kumm, M., Möller, K., Zipf, P.: Reconfigurable FIR filter using distributed arithmetic on FPGAs. In: 2013 IEEE International Symposium on Circuits and Systems (ISCAS 2013), Beijing, China, May 19-23, pp. 2058–2061. IEEE (2013)
9. Sasdrich, P., Moradi, A., Mischke, O., Güneysu, T.: Achieving Side-Channel Protection with Dynamic Logic Reconfiguration on Modern FPGAs. In: IEEE International Symposium on Hardware Oriented Security and Trust, HOST 2015, Washington, DC, USA, May 5-7, pp. 130–136 (2015)
10. Madlener, F., Sotttinger, M., Huss, S.A.: Novel hardening techniques against differential power analysis for multiplication in gf(2n). In: International Conference on Field-Programmable Technology, FPT 2009, pp. 328–334 (December 2009)
11. Xilinx. Xilinx Partial Reconfiguration User Guide (UG702), http://www.xilinx.com/support/documentation/sw_manuals/xilinx14_1/ug702.pdf
12. Brier, E., Clavier, C., Olivier, F.: Correlation Power Analysis with a Leakage Model. In: Joye, M., Quisquater, J.-J. (eds.) CHES 2004. LNCS, vol. 3156, pp. 16–29. Springer, Heidelberg (2004)
13. Ali, S., Chakraborty, R.S., Mukhopadhyay, D., Bhunia, S.: Multi-level attacks: An emerging security concern for cryptographic hardware. In: Design, Automation and Test in Europe, DATE 2011, Grenoble, France, March 14-18, pp. 1176–1179 (2011)
14. Chakraborty, R.S., Narasimhan, S., Bhunia, S.: Hardware Trojan: Threats and Emerging solutions. In: IEEE International High Level Design Validation and Test Workshop, HLDVT 2009, San Francisco, CA, USA, November 4-6, pp. 166–171 (2009)
15. Tehranipoor, M., Forte, D.: Tutorial T4: All You Need to Know about Hardware Trojans and Counterfeit ICs. In: 2014 27th International Conference on VLSI Design and 2014 13th International Conference on Embedded Systems, Mumbai, India, January 5-9, pp. 9–10 (2014)
16. Chen, Z., Guo, X., Nagesh, R., Reddy, A., Gora, M., Maiti, A.: Hardware trojan designs on basys fpga board
17. Johnson, A.P., Saha, S., Chakraborty, R.S., Mukhopadhyay, D., Gören, S.: Fault Attack on AES via Hardware Trojan Insertion by Dynamic Partial Reconfiguration of FPGA over Ethernet. In: Proceedings of the 9th Workshop on Embedded Systems Security, WESS 2014, pp. 1:1–1:8. ACM, New York (2014)
18. Bhasin, S., Danger, J.-L., Guilley, S., Ngo, X.T., Sauvage, L.: Hardware Trojan Horses in Cryptographic IP Cores. In: Fischer, W., Schmidt, J.-M. (eds.) FDTC, pp. 15–29. IEEE (2013)
19. Note, J.-B., Rannaud, É.: From the Bitstream to the Netlist. In: Proceedings of the 16th International ACM/SIGDA Symposium on Field Programmable Gate Arrays, FPGA 2008, pp. 264–264. ACM, New York (2008)
20. Benchmarks. https://www.trust-hub.org/resources/benchmarks (accessed: January 30, 2015)
21. Homma, N., Hayashi, Y.-i., Miura, N., Fujimoto, D., Tanaka, D., Nagata, M., Aoki, T.: EM Attack Is Non-invasive? - Design Methodology and Validity Verification of EM Attack Sensor. In: Batina, L., Robshaw, M. (eds.) CHES 2014. LNCS, vol. 8731, pp. 1–16. Springer, Heidelberg (2014)

22. Piret, G., Quisquater, J.-J.: A Differential Fault Attack Technique against SPN Structures, with Application to the AES and KHAZAD. In: Walter, C.D., Koç, Ç.K., Paar, C. (eds.) CHES 2003. LNCS, vol. 2779, pp. 77–88. Springer, Heidelberg (2003)
23. Ali, S., Mukhopadhyay, D., Tunstall, M.: Differential fault analysis of AES: towards reaching its limits. J. Cryptographic Engineering 3(2), 73–97 (2013)
24. Poschmann, A., Ling, S., Wang, H.: 256 Bit Standardized Crypto for 650 GE – GOST Revisited. In: Mangard, S., Standaert, F.-X. (eds.) CHES 2010. LNCS, vol. 6225, pp. 219–233. Springer, Heidelberg (2010)
25. Hajra, S., Rebeiro, C., Bhasin, S., Bajaj, G., Sharma, S., Guilley, S., Mukhopadhyay, D.: DRECON: DPA Resistant Encryption by Construction. In: Pointcheval, D., Vergnaud, D. (eds.) AFRICACRYPT. LNCS, vol. 8469, pp. 420–439. Springer, Heidelberg (2014)
26. Bogdanov, A.A., Knudsen, L.R., Leander, G., Paar, C., Poschmann, A., Robshaw, M., Seurin, Y., Vikkelsoe, C.: PRESENT: An Ultra-Lightweight Block Cipher. In: Paillier, P., Verbauwhede, I. (eds.) CHES 2007. LNCS, vol. 4727, pp. 450–466. Springer, Heidelberg (2007)
27. Xilinx. Virtex-5 fpga system monitor, http://www-inst.eecs.berkeley.edu/~cs150/fa13/resources/ug192.pdf

A   Trigger Generation for Hardware Trojans

For the hardware Trojan trigger signal, we exploit directly the temperature sensor measurement to generate the *trigger* signal. The device, used for this experiment, is Xilinx Virtex 5 FPGA mounted on SASEBO-GII boards. As described in the documentation [27], the temperature measurement is read directly on 10 bits signal output of system monitor. This output allows a value which varies from 0 to 1023. System monitor measurement allows to sense a temperature in range of $[-273°C, +230°C]$ hence the LSB of the 10 bits output is equal to $1/2°C$. At the normal operating temperature ($25°C$), system monitor output is around $605 = b'1001011101$. Thanks to this observation, we decided to use directly the 7th bit of system monitor output as hardware Trojan trigger signal. The hardware Trojan will be activated when 7th bit of monitor output is high, i.e., when the monitor output is superior to $640 = b'1010000000$. This value corresponds to $42°C$. Therefore the trigger signal will be active when FPGA temperature is higher than $42°C$. The trigger temperature can be easily changed according to the design under test. In our case study, a simple hair dryer of cost \$5 is enough to heat the FPGA and reach this temperature. We assume that a system monitor is already instantiated in the design, to monitor device working conditions and the alarm is raised at a temperature higher than $42°C$. In such a scenario, the hardware Trojan trigger part does not consume much extra logic and would result in a very low-cost hardware Trojan example.

Whenever we need to trigger the Trojan, we bring the heater circuit close to the FPGA. The FPGA heats up slowly to the temperature of $42°C$ and raises the output bit to '1'. At this point, we switch-off the heater. Now this output bit stays '1' till the FPGA cools down below $42°C$, therefore we cannot precisely control the duration of trigger in terms of cycle count. We further process this output bit of the system monitor to generate a precise duration trigger. This can be done with some extra logic. In other words, we need a small circuit which can generate a precise trigger signal when the output bit of system monitor goes to '1'. For the Trojans in Tab 1, we either need a trigger of 1 clock cycle or 12 clock cycles. Both these triggers can be generated by deploying one LUT and one flip-flop to process output bit of system monitor. Thus, we can generate a very small trigger circuit to trigger a zero-overhead hardware Trojan.

Architecture Considerations for Massively Parallel Hardware Security Platform
Building a Workhorse for Cryptography as a Service

Dan Cvrček[1] and Petr Švenda[2]

[1] Enigma Bridge, Cambridge, Great Britain
[2] Masaryk University, Faculty of Informatics, Czech Republic
dan@enigmabridge.com, svenda@fi.muni.cz

Abstract. Cryptography as a service (CaaS) provides means for executing sensitive cryptographic operations when the primary computing platform does not offer the required level of trust and security. Instead of executing operations like document signing directly by an application running in untrusted environment, the operation keys are only present in trusted environment used by CaaS. Once the operation keys are put in place, the applications use a CaaS interface to obtain results of sensitive operations - document signatures - executed by CaaS. A typical scenario is the use of virtual computing platform in the cloud. Use of CaaS reduces impact of the potential compromise of this virtual platform and simplifies subsequent recovery. The attacker will not learn the value of sensitive keys (e.g., signing keys) and is only able to use the keys for a limited time. The CaaS is enabling technology for a large number of use cases where security is important. The concept of scalable and universally available CaaS has also far-reaching usability, security, legal, and economics consequences of cloud use. In this position paper, we focus on requirements for building a CaaS platform – what are the options and challenges to build hardware and software components for CaaS suitable for usage scenarios with different load patterns and user requirements. We propose a suitable architecture for CaaS that can be shared by a large number of concurrent users, i.e., providing access to a large number of cryptographic keys. We also provide practical results from our prototype implementation[1].

1 Introduction

There is a strong demand for a secure cryptographic platform for the cloud and mobile computing to support a variety of sensitive applications. When used in large scale distributed environments, one of the options is to provide cryptographic operations as a service (CaaS) instead of implementing sensitive computations on end-user device. There are several advantages of this approach,

---

[1] Full details and paper's supplementary material can be found at
http://crcs.cz/papers/space2015.

© Springer International Publishing Switzerland 2015
R.S. Chakraborty et al. (Eds.): SPACE 2015, LNCS 9354, pp. 269–288, 2015.
DOI: 10.1007/978-3-319-24126-5_16

as recognized in [17], particularly, end-user device might be more vulnerable to compromise or lack of entropy source for key generation.

When CaaS is discussed in research literature, performance considerations are often omitted or neglected. One of such assumptions is that when a CaaS provider is fully trusted by users, it can have unlimited access to cryptographic keys. This assumption allows the provider easy scaling of computation power for cryptographic operations, as there are no security constraints. But the performance becomes quickly an issue when the CaaS provider is untrusted - it can execute cryptographic operations, but it cannot access keys directly and it becomes subject of constraints introduced by the API providing access to keys. Execution of sensitive operations is in this case provided by a specialized trusted hardware module (HSM) that ensures the cryptographic material cannot be accessed directly. Current HSMs provide reasonable computational performance for closed, centralized systems (high-end HSMs can perform up to 9,000 RSA 1024b signatures per second) under certain conditions. But implementing scalable CaaS supporting a range of operations and concurrent use of a large number of keys of CaaS users poses a number of challenges.

So far, high-performance cryptographic hardware platform, providing high level of shareability was not discussed in details in research literature. In this work, we summarize existing challenges and introduce open research questions for alternative architectures capable to host a large number of applications, cryptographic material and concurrent users. Our paper provides considerations and proposes a suitable architecture for CaaS supporting many users and many key scenarios, architecture based on secure processors with protected between processors. The experience obtained from building such a platform will also be discussed.

The paper is organized as follows: The next section provides a short introduction to cryptography as a service (CaaS) and defines main usage scenarios with related requirements on the high-performance cloud-based CaaS platform. Section 3 reviews different hardware options available and challenges present to provide high-performance trustworthy computation CaaS platform. The proposed architecture using high number of parallel secure processors connected with secure channels is described. Section 4 presents case-study of HMAC-based one-time password provided via proposed architecture together with practical results from prototype build. Possible future directions are summarized in Section 5 with conclusions given in Section 6.

2 Cryptography as a Service (CaaS)

Information systems face many security threats. Some of them are almost universal and all systems and business applications have to deal with them, some are specific. Every designer has to assess risks of their existing or new application and consider methods to mitigate those risks.

Running applications in the cloud introduces a number of universal threats that one does not have to think about while he/she runs their applications from own servers. All those new threats are related to the fact that the cloud introduces new entities into the system model of cloud applications - the cloud provider.

Threat modelling is is a subject on its own (refer to [6] for foundations of cloud security) but we need to introduce some initial assumptions that we use below for reasoning about security of CaaS and definitions of security levels. Our initial classification is based on system components.

The list of components is as follows:

Application – the software application providing beneficial functionality for Client.

Application Owner – an entity that develops the application itself and is responsible for its correct operation. In many cases the application owner will be the client of the application as well.

Client – user of the application; when client is different from application owner the client would expect the application to provide certain business functionality. Security aspects may be still an issue though as secure processing and storage of data is hard to verify through the business functionality provided by the application.

CaaS Provider – an entity that provides functionality of CaaS including support and management of CaaS, e.g., system updates. While CaaS provider would be typically independent of Cloud Provider but it may be Application Owner.

Cloud Provider – the entity that controls the physical platform on which the application runs. The platform has several layers of components with each layer potentially provided a different entity.

Internet – communication between entities of the system (e.g., via web services API).

2.1 Levels of Trust and Security

We are able to define the following levels of trust for CaaS – using a system architecture with components defined in the previous section. Let us first assume different levels of trust in CaaS.

- *Client Trust* – users may or may not trust CaaS provider directly. The trust, if it exists, may be complete or based on an assumption of split control between CaaS provider and Application Owner – an assumption that data of Client can only be compromised if both parties cooperate. Based on our empirical experience, CaaS should be trusted more than Application Owner as CaaS would provide security as its main business and as such have more expertise needed for implementing security measures correctly.
- *Application Owner Trust* – if Application Owner trusts CaaS, it can use its relationship with Clients to leverage own trust in CaaS for persuading Clients that the use of CaaS increases the security of their data.
- *Cloud Provider Trust* – from practical point of view it is irrelevant whether Cloud Provider trusts or distrusts CaaS. It has, however, means to disable access to CaaS from applications using its platform.

Use of CaaS can be either enforced by compliance requirements or by concerns of Clients. The former will require Application Owner Trust that may be based on external validations of CaaS. Such validations would have to be sufficient for compliance. Concerns of Clients may either prompt Application Owner to use CaaS or find a way to use CaaS on top of the application.

In terms of dataflows, Client may trust parts of dataflows involving its data:

- *Client* – computers and/or networks under the control of Client.
- *CaaS* – systems that implement cryptographic functions for an application must be trusted by Client and usually by Application Owner as well.
- *Application Owner* – trust in systems of Application Owner would be limited – either by Clients or even by Application Owner itself.
- *Internet* – it is generally untrusted; it is possible to relax requirements on data protection only if the data itself are not confidential or Client's security requirements allow for some security properties to be ignored.

The trust balance between Client systems and CaaS is important in terms of the CaaS setup for Application. In general, we can assume that CaaS will provide full life-cycle support for applications but Client may decide not to fully trust CaaS and keep some aspects of cryptography under its own control.

If Client trusts its computers and/or information systems, it can use it for enrolment or other bootstrapping operations that are otherwise manageable for it information systems. A generation of application keys may be one of such examples.

2.2   Usage Scenarios

The typical usage scenario influences significantly properties required for a CaaS platform as well as imposing restrictions and limitations of the hardware/software architecture behind the CaaS platform. We will discuss possible usage scenarios with respect to a number of parallel users and a number of distinct cryptographic keys used by every user. Note that other classifications are possible, e.g., w.r.t. the amount of transmitted data (short packets vs. long data streams), number of messages to finalize a single logical operation (e.g., decryption of single packet vs. multi-packet challenge-response protocol) or list of required cryptographic algorithms to name a few. We choose a number of users, and distinct keys because these factors are the most specific for situation where a CaaS platform is significantly shared between a number of different entities – a typical "cloud" scenario that already proved its viability for general purpose computing (but we will not limit our description only to such scenario).

Note that in the following classification, we will talk about a *service* rather than a CaaS platform, as some categories would not classify as CaaS as commonly defined, but make sense to list them because of distinct features and security/performance considerations introduced.

We also use count quantifiers 1, few (M) and many (N) to describe concept categories, e.g., *many users* or *a few keys per user* as different hardware devices used to facilitate service are capable to store and handle different numbers of cryptographic contexts of a particular type (e.g., AES or RSA). When more contexts than a device is able to hold internally are required, contexts must be offloaded from device when not used and load in again later, introducing potential delay and additional requirements like the need for out-of-device secure storage or key wrapping. A provider of a service can utilize more hardware devices to linearly increase the number of contexts that can be maintained at the same time. When we use *many* keyword, its strictly more than number of contexts that can be fit into available hardware device(s).

S1: One user, few keys (1:M) – no sharing of the target service, as only a single user with a single key (or very few keys) is using it. Because of exclusive use and a small number of keys, there is no need to switch cryptographic contexts (pre-scheduled keys, initialized cryptographic engines...) before serving a new request and the whole cryptographic context can reside directly inside a service computational device(s). There is little need for CaaS to provide scalability, while secure remote access, use in virtualized environments and suitable API (e.g., application oriented rather than low-level PKCS#11) requirements remain. Example: a payment card physically owned by the user with a payment authentication key or an HTTPS TLS accelerator with one private key.

S2: One user, many keys (1:N) - this use case does not require service sharing, but it does imply frequent changes of cryptographic contexts because of a high number of keys involved. If the number of used keys is significantly higher than the number of contexts that can fit into the underlying hardware, then cryptographic contexts may need to be changed even with every request. Context loading, cryptographic engine initialization and key scheduling may significantly contribute to the overall time required to complete a requested operation. Subsequent performance degradation with the factor of 2-5 is well known from benchmarks for encryption throughput measuring the effects of varying message length (bulk encryption vs. small messages). The performance degradation is even more severe in the case of secure switching of cryptographic contexts between the secure processor and untrusted memory. Use considerations of CaaS are similar to the 1:M scenario. However, as the higher number of keys amplifies generic key management issues, CaaS may offer better overall usability. Example: PIN verification procedure performed inside an HSM on behalf of card issuing bank.

S3: Few users, few keys (M:M) – limited sharing of the target service while every user uses only a few keys. This is the first use case where service's computational devices are shared by mutually distrusting users. An additional overhead is introduced due to a need to securely erase sensitive values before the context switch between users may occur. As only few keys exist in the system overall, there is no need to offload cryptographic contexts. Example: Amazon CloudHSM [4] where a small number of users (e.g., 16) is sharing same physical hardware device performing cryptographic operations.

S4: Few users, many keys (M:N) - an extension of *S3: Few users, few keys (M:M)* scenario with a need to perform cryptographic context offload due to a high number of used keys. As only a few users are present, secure offload can be done relatively quickly as wrapping and unwrapping engines on service devices can be left initialized and ready to process next request at all times.

S5: Many users, many keys (N:N) – CaaS service serves many users, each of them with few keys, resulting in many keys in total. High-level of sharing of hardware resources of service. Includes also scenarios where primary keys from many users are used to derive and use new (session) keys based on a user input. Example: TLS accelerator with different session keys established for every different user after an initial TLS handshake with the server's private key. Note that number of keys can be further amplified if TLS accelerator is shared as CaaS service between multiple web servers with different private keys. See Section 4 for details of another example providing HMAC-based one-time password verification.

2.3   Typical Operations Needed for CaaS

Although many different algorithms and protocols can be implemented and provided by CaaS, we can identify a short list of common generic operations:

1. **Generate/derive new key** – new key K (symmetric, asymmetric or other secret) is generated by CaaS service. The key then either never leaves the CaaS service (analogy with on-card non-exportable private key for digital signatures) or alternatively can be exported back to the Client (e.g., in encrypted blob).
2. **Import new key** – Client provides a key K to be imported and later used by CaaS. Transfer of a key K can be protected for confidentiality, integrity and freshness.
3. **Process input data** – Client provides input data M, processed inside a CaaS service by a key K and cryptographic algorithm F, where $C = F(M, K)$. Input data M and output data C (returned to a Client) may be protected for confidentiality, integrity and freshness.
4. **Obtain usage statistics** – how many times was a particular key K used? Requires authorization of process input data requests and protection of usage data.
5. **Remove key from service** – when Client doesn't need to use the key K any more, key is removed. Key removal might be on a Client request, automatic (time-limited exposure) or as a result of compliance requirements (e.g., reset the device at least once every 24 hours if it contains Client's keys)

2.4   Preferred Properties of Cloud-Based High-Performance CaaS

There is no single unified CaaS architecture which would ideally fit all scenarios described in Section 2.2. In this paper, we focus on scenario *S5: Many users, many keys* as we believe this scenario is difficult to support with current technology on a sufficient level of security. We believe that the most important principles for a secure and scalable CaaS platform are as follows:

P1: Untrusted CaaS provider for handling of cryptographic secrets – if the provider of CaaS doesn't need to be trusted to preserve secrecy of cryptographic material, the attack surface is significantly reduced (highlight for the Client). Provider itself will not be subject of internal and external attacks due to its low impact on CaaS security (highlight for provider). Some system designs require to trust only provider with physical access to CaaS as they mitigate threats of corrupted operator with only logical access [5]. If operator can't compromise security of CaaS and its cryptographic material, we can achieve higher level of overall security. Note that this principle is also beneficial for CaaS provider as it decrease its attractivity as a target for compromise.

P2: Easy to use API – because platform will be used as a service, a well-defined and simple interface is vital for fast adoption. Care should be taken to provide API not only easy to integrate, but also easy to use securely [8].

P3: Secure import of cryptographic material – secure way to import initial cryptographic material is required in majority of use case scenarios. Even when a key is generated directly inside the CaaS service as a result of Client request, additional shared keys are usually required to authenticate subsequent process input requests.

P4: Low latency of responses in the presence of many requests from many parallel user – as a platform will be significantly shared, low latency should not deteriorate even when many parallel requests are served. The tolerable latency range is specific to the particular usage scenario and in turn affects limits on the sharing of a given platform.

P5: High performance in the presence of frequent key change – significant level of sharing between many users, everyone with potentially distinct cryptographic keys introduces a high number of expected key scheduling before request can be processed. In an extreme (but not uncommon) scenario, every request may cause initialization and key scheduling of several cryptographic engines. Overall platform performance is expected to decrease with more users/requests scale reasonably.

P6: Authentication of input/output requests – once cryptographic material is (securely) imported into a CaaS platform, actual use of the imported key should be authorized by the Client and performed only on data provided by authorized Client. Verification of authorization itself should not significantly impact platform performance. Usually achieved by requests authorization by separate shared request authorization keys (commonly called "API keys"). An output data provided by service back to the Client should be authenticated as well to provide strong assurance that Client's original request was really processed by the imported key.

P7: Confidentiality of input and output data – if sensitive data are transmitted as part of request and corresponding response, confidentiality should be protected (again, "API keys" can be used).

P8: Easy recovery from client-side compromise – as Client can be compromised with the assumption that the key imported to CaaS was not, procedure to recover from a compromise should be easy to perform (e.g., fresh re-installation of client environment and transparent change of request authorization keys with perfect forward secrecy property). Eventually, frequent automatic recovery process can be executed as a preventive measure for undetected compromises.

P9: Robust audit trail of key usages – because CaaS is offered as a service, pay-per-use model may be utilized and Client should be provided with robust audit trail how often imported key was used. Another important reason for audit trails steams from potential compromise of client software together with authorization keys for requests. An attacker can then use an imported key without a user's consent. Once the compromise is detected, the user might be interested in realizing an exact extend of service usage during the compromise period.

P10: Limit on maximum key usages (before re-authorization) – once a key is imported and request authorization keys are compromised, an attacker can issue a large number of requests unless limited by another factor. To limit an extend of expected malicious usages of imported key, a Client can import key together with a number of "credits" limiting the maximum number of requests which can be served by service. Again, the provider of the service should not be able to manipulate with credits already used.

P11: Tolerance to occasional hardware/software failures – large level of sharing and high number of requests will inevitably result in occasional failures of the platform components, which should not impact other parallel users significantly. Natural requirement, but might be harder to achieve, if CaaS provider is not trusted and thus cannot inspect the full results of operation for errors itself. Also, move of Client request from failed to functioning device is more difficult if relevant contexts are cryptography bound to a single device.

3   Building Hardware for CaaS Back-End

In this section, we will discuss various options for building hardware platform which will satisfy principles described in Section 2.4. Different architectures are discussed both from performance and security perspective with the focus on *S5: Many users, many keys* scenario.

3.1   Designing CaaS

There are many ways how to build computational platform for CaaS. The following list shows some of the more obvious options:

1. *Use of general-purpose hardware*, e.g., high-performance multi-core server processor and implementation of the required cryptographic functionality in software. The advantage is fast development and deployment with existing

cryptographic libraries like OpenSSL [2] or cryptlib++ [1] and medium expected performance. The main disadvantage is need to trust CaaS provider as all cryptographic secrets and input/output data are easily accessible inside the CaaS implementation. Note that the level of trust to provider with logical-only access can be limited by a combination of virtualization and trusted computing [5]. In this particular case, a modified Xen hypervisor is used to make standard TPM available for secret-less virtual machine resulting in significant decrease in the size of trusted computational base (TCB).

2. *Use of generic programable hardware* (e.g., Field-programmable gate array (FPGA) or Graphics processing unit (GPU)) with cryptographic operations accelerated by programmable hardware with advantage of higher performance. The disadvantage is increased difficulty of implementation and deployment due to lower number of readily available cryptographic implementations. Note that GPU architectures like nVidia CUDA [3] provides top throughput only when the same program (including data-dependent branching) is executed over multiple input data blocks in parallel. As selected cryptographic operations are heavily data/key dependent (e.g., public-key algorithms based on modular multiplication like RSA) performance gain may be more difficult to achieve [11]. The need for trust to provider is still present although more advanced skills may be required to extract cryptographic secrets from less common architectures, possibly via side-channel attacks. Additionally, a more complex architecture makes more difficult evaluation of security assurances when a single device is shared by mutually distrusting Clients.

3. *Use of dedicated cryptographic circuits*, e.g., application-specific integrated circuit (ASIC) can provide very high performance implementation for selected cryptographic algorithms. The disadvantage is a significant increase in the cost of design and development if required circuits are not readily available. High-speed cryptographic circuits were proposed and sometimes built for brute-force cracking of algorithms with insufficient length of key of used password like Copacobana (based on FPGA) [12]. Note that brute-force cracking architectures are usually not designed to handle high input/output traffic. If cryptographic circuit is not additionally protected, trust to provider is still required.

4. *Use of secure processors*, e.g., cryptographic smart cards or hardware security modules (HSM) can significantly limit level of trust put on CaaS provider. HSMs are able to provide high performance for certain use-cases (see 2.2) while providing good security for cryptographic keys even for attackers with physical access to CaaS. Use from virtualized environments is also possible – Virtual HSM project [15] provides remote physical HSM via PKCS#11 API.

5. *Use of fully homomorphic encryption* (FHE) – all architectures mentioned so far except secure processors required trust to CaaS provider. Fully homomorphic encryption [10] provides a way to perform sensitive computations on untrusted platform – a feature well suited for CaaS as well as cloud-based computations in general. While performance of FHE schemes has been significantly improving in recent years [13], including highly optimized implementations for

FPGAs [7] , the overall performance is still several orders of magnitude slower when compared to unprotected implementations.

3.2 The Proposed Design

As discussed in previous section, dedicated high-performance hardware offers the best overall performance, but also comes with a high additional cost to verify required security properties in an auditable manner.

We instead propose to build CaaS from simple and small secure processing units that are easier to test for security assurances. A large number ($10^2 - 10^4$) of these secure processing units are connected in a massively parallel multi-processor device[2]. Every secure processor has limited persistent storage and may provide acceleration of some cryptographic operations. The design has to take care of all communication between secure processors if needed and to provide data confidentiality, integrity and freshness with the use of secure processors. Due to limited computational resources of secure processors, CaaS design will have to carefully separate untrusted storage for secure off-loading of sensitive dat from secure processors, provide untrusted connectivity of CaaS components, allocate of secure processors to tasks, and so on. Overall resiliency of CaaS can be high if failed or malfunctioning secure processing units are quickly and efficiently isolated.

In the rest of the section, we will describe how the proposed design can be implemented from a large number of modern cryptographic smart cards (secure processors) and how the principles laid out in Section 2.4 can be achieved with an example test application for computing OATH HOTP values [9] provided in Section 4.

The proposed architecture has the following key properties:

1. **High number of secure processors** – depending on the required performance, at least $10^2 - 10^4$ processors. Each processor is able to withstand focused physical and logical attacks as required by FIPS140-2 Level 3 or 4, CC EAL 4+, or similar. Attacker should not be able to learn any cryptographic secrets stored inside secure processors, read any sensitive input/output data even with direct physical access or modify applications running inside secure processors.
2. **Small trusted computing base** – every secure processor contains a small application capable of processing requests coming from Client using previously imported cryptographic secrets.
3. **Untrusted controller** – software responsible for efficient distribution of Client requests and storage of data offloaded from secure processors. The

---

[2] Note that analogy with the current multi-core graphic processing units (GPUs) ends with the high number of cores. Parallel cores of GPUs are not designed for use as secure processors (both for performance and cost reasons). GPU cores share both memory and program's instructions. Also, the GPU is not specifically built to accelerate cryptographic operations (although high-speed encryption, etc. is possible – especially when only single key and large data are processed).

controller is untrusted, i.e., it must not be able to access plain values of any cryptographic material or input/output data supplied by Client for processing. If the controller is compromised, no secrets are revealed.

4. **Secure channels between secure processors** – if sensitive data is to be transferred between secure processors, end-to-end secure channels have to be established and used. A secure channel should be as lightweight as possible, yet able to withstand common attacks on network layer, such as packet replay.

5. **High-speed I/O data interface** – large number of requests imply significant volumes of data traffic in the order of gigabits per second. Note that because of a high number of parallel processors, it would be natural to create logical or physical clusters of processors with dedicated I/O interface to keep traffic volume within current technology capabilities.

6. **Initialization phase** – before a CaaS device is ready for operational use, it has to be securely initialised. This includes bare hardware and other components' configuration, upload and installation of verified application packages, exchange of initial secrets needed for secure processors' communication, generation and certification of keys and public keys. Initialisation phase is the single most critical operation of any CaaS device and its correct and secure execution must be independently verifiable at any time afterwards.

7. **Operational phase** – after a trusted initialization, a CaaS device is switched into operational mode and starts serving Client requests. Only code inside secure processors has to be trusted for processing Client's cryptographic secrets and data, once in operation mode.

8. **Restricting use and audit trail** – trust is the single most important aspect of CaaS. While CaaS has to provide maximum security, it must also offer means to audit and verify its operation. One of the approaches is to use authorisation tokens that has to be regularly, or on demand, re-issued. Client cryptographic secrets are then imported together with authorisation tokens limited use of secrets. Issued tokens can be then matched against a trusted audit trail produced by secure cryptographic processors. This not only allows independent verification of CaaS operation but it also gives Clients an efficient way to disable or even remove their secrets from CaaS – simply by not refreshing authorisation tokens.

3.3   Why Smart Cards?

Cryptographic smart cards [16] were designed to withstand attacks in completely hostile environment under full control of attackers. Cryptographic smart cards have following significant advantages in comparison to common CPU: 1) Secure runtime environment (an attacker cannot directly inspect executed code or manipulated data values including cryptographic keys); 2) Dedicated cryptographic coprocessors to speedup operations (especially relevant for asymmetric cryptography); 3) Secure on-card TRNG generator (usable for on-card keys generation); 4) Secure on-card storage (but limited in size); 5) Reasonable price per unit (when bought in larger quantities).

But smart cards are generally perceived as being quite slow and usable only for a single holder (user), not as a potential component for high-performance computation. Although it might be true when one compares single card with a performance of desktop CPU, small size, low energy consumption, relatively low price and inherent advantage of secure contained environment make smart cards good candidate for powerful, yet secure computational device following principles defined in Section 2.4 – if a large number of cards can be utilized as array of secure processors.

In Table 1, raw performances of selected cryptographic algorithms are presented[3], showing that especially for RSA algorithm, smart cards have decent performance on its own. If an array of hundreds to thousands of smart cards can be run in parallel, high-performance composite device can be obtained.

Table 1. The raw performance of Cipher engine with AES-128 key in CBC encryption mode and RSA-1024/2048 in PKCS1 sign mode with SHA-1 hash function. The raw performance is performance achievable when only time spend inside cryptographic coprocessor itself is assumed – no transfer of input data to card, key scheduling, engine init and startup etc. For AES algorithm, raw performance was computed from the difference between an encryption time for 512 and 256 bytes. For RSA algorithm, sole time to execute single sign operation on-card was measured.

Card type	AES-128 CBC encrypt	RSA-1024 sign	RSA-2048 sign
NXP CJ2A081 (2014)	36.5kB/sec	10.5 signs/sec	2.3 signs/sec
NXP CJ3A080 v2.4.1 (2013)	17.6kB/sec	6.3 signs/sec	1.6 signs/sec
Gemalto GXP R4 72K (2008)	10.8kB/sec	2.5 signs/sec	0.6 signs/sec
NXP JCOP4.1 v2.2.1 72K (2008)	N/A	9.3 signs/sec	1.6 signs/sec

4   The Case Study: HMAC-Based One-Time Password

HMAC-based one-time password protocol (HOTP) [14] is widely used algorithm for generation of one-time passwords for an authentication. HOTP authentication code is based on a secret key shared between an authentication server and user and changing counter value incremented after every one-time password generation. HOTP is widely used, e.g., as a basic building block for Initiative For Open Authentication (OATH) [9]. We selected HOTP as example which involves not only single operation (e.g., RSA signature), but also maintenance of updated state (which must be offloaded outside physical card) and need for protected input and output from the Client (authentication server in this case) of a CaaS service.

---

[3] Note that provided comparison is meant only to demonstrate achievable level of performance and not as the exact comparison between various cards (there are differences between batches of cards). The more detailed comparison is provided in [18].

HOTP algorithm (RFC4226 [14]) is defined as sequence of four logical steps:

1. $HMAC(K, C) = SHA1(K \oplus 0x5c5c \ldots | SHA1(K \oplus 0x3636 \ldots | C))$, where K is a secret key shared between user and authentication server, C is counter incremented after every authentication attempt, HMAC is construction defined in RFC2104, and SHA1 is a cryptographic hash function.
2. $HOTP(K, C) = Truncate(HMAC(K, C)) \& 0x7FFFFFFF$, where *Truncate function* selects 4 bytes in a deterministic way from HMAC output.
3. $HOTP - Code = HOTP(K, C) \, mod \, 10^d$ where d is desired number of digits of resulting code (system parameter).
4. $HOTP - Code$ generated by user is compared with expected $HOTP - Code$ generated by the authentication server.

4.1   Why Would HOTP Will Benefit from CaaS?

Because both server and user need to store and use same secret key value K used during every authentication attempt, not only the user, but also server becomes a plausible attacker's target when the value of the secret key is of interest. When an authentication server is temporarily compromised, an attacker can learn the secret keys for all of its users – or at least for those authenticated during the compromise period. An attacker can then use obtained secret keys to impersonate legitimate users later. To mitigate this threat, authentication server can utilize CaaS for HOTP code verification instead of computing expected HOTP code on its own. When a user provides HOTP code, authentication server asks CaaS service to compute expected code and verify it against supplied user code. An authentication server is then just notified about the verification result and does not need to be able to compute expected HOTP code itself. Even when authentication server is temporarily compromised, an attacker will not learn used secret key(s) (although may issue requests to CaaS on behalf of compromised server).

To learn a secret key, an attacker needs to attack CaaS platform, which can utilize secure hardware (e.g., HSM) to protect manipulated secrets. Authentication server can also utilize secure hardware itself – but because of associated upfront costs and management issues, only some will do while others stay with computation of HOTP in software. Additionally, when the authentication server runs as a virtual image in a public cloud environment, options to connect own secure hardware into datacenter are limited or not available at all.

4.2   Moving HOTP into CaaS

Four main operations are required to facilitate HOTP as a CaaS:

1. **Import new server's context** – done once for every authentication server. Contains keys used to protect user states and authenticate requests from authentication server to CaaS.
2. **Generation of initial, wrapped user state** – done once for every user of a particular authentication server. Contains HOTP specific state for given user including key K and initial value of counter C.

3. **Verification of user-supplied HOTP code** – done for every user authentication request. Generates and compares expected and supplied HOTP code.

4. **Establishment and use of secure channels** – used to facilitate distribution of secrets and authorizations inside CaaS itself. Necessary to limit the overall number of HOTP verifications and provide cryptographic audit trail (principles P9 and P10).

4.3 HOTP Implementation

To measure a real cost of HOTP verification in secure hardware using proposed architecture, we implemented HOTP verification as CaaS service, including all required operations as a part of CryptoHive design described in Sections 3.2 and 4.6. Using our implementation, we measured detailed time required to perform single HOTP verification as well as performance of the whole CryptoHive prototype.

Note that we excluded overhead related to transmission of Client request to CaaS service and back as overhead values are highly dependent on platform settings (e.g., how many credits are uploaded at once before costly recharge credits operation is invoked or how often is signed audit trail for performed operations generated).

We also intentionally excluded operations performed by the authentication server (Client) as this presents no load CryptoHive. We also did not include operations related to managing user contexts in untrusted part of CryptoHive where generic computational resources can be made powerful enough to match required load.

The following data blobs are present and processed: *Initial import of authentication server* with imported communication keys (256 bytes in total), *Authentication server context* with imported keys (4x AES128b keys, unchanged during the request, stored on CaaS platform in rewrapped form after initial import, only some keys shared with the authentication server, 88 bytes in total), *user HOTP state* (updated with every request, stored but unreadable by the authentication server, 40 bytes in total), input/output data with *user HOTP code* or verification result respectively (new with every request, provided and readable by authentication server, 24 bytes in total).

Following cryptographic keys are used: 1) The communication keys for encryption $K_{commEnc}$ and integrity $K_{commMAC}$ used for authorization and protection of data exchanged between the authentication server and CaaS (generated and used by authentication server). 2) The keys for protection of user HOTP state $K_{stateEnc}$ and $K_{stateMAC}$ (generated by CryptoHive and not shared with authentication server). 3) The authentication key K_{auth} for given user (stored inside user HOTP state, generated by CryptoHive and not shared with authentication server). 4) The CaaS internal keys $K_{authServerCtxEnc}$ and $K_{authServerCtxMAC}$ for protection of offloaded authentication server contexts with $K_{commEnc}$, $K_{commMAC}$, $K_{stateEnc}$

and $K_{stateMAC}$) (generated by CryptoHive and not shared with authentication server) – note that these keys can be used to protect multiple authentication server contexts[4]. 5) RSA-2048b keypair K_{pubCG} and K_{privCG} for import of initial import of authentication server context (generated by CryptoHive with public key K_{pubCG} distributed to authentication server).

4.4   Performance Results – A Single Card

At first, we provide performance results for primitive operations used as building blocks to implement whole HOTP in CaaS, followed by the discussion about possible speedups.

Table 2 provides list of times required to finish HOTP operations[5]. HOTP verification operation is measured in two settings – in the first case (called *Clean call*) verification is performed with full initialization of all keys and cryptographic engines – corresponding to the situation when a given user was not authenticated recently and no pre-initialized engines can be used. In the second case (called *Repeat call*), card already have relevant keys initialized from the previous *Clean call* – corresponding to the situation when controller was able to keep secrets on card (e.g., due to low service load or dedicated card for target authentication server and user – kind of caching).

4.5   Improving Expected Performance

Based on the measured results we can identify the steps which consumes most of the time to process. At first, *Verify HOTP code* operation is the dominating operation as all others are executed only once for every authentication server (*Import authentication server context*) or limited number of times (*Generate HOTP state for a new user* once for every user). The *Verify HOTP code* operation can be further divided into a data transmission (about 18 %), setup and clear of cryptographic engines and key objects (about 54 %), encryption/decryption and MAC operation (about 20 %) and remaining functionality like HMAC, dynamic truncation or comparison of expected and supplied HOTP code (about 8 %).

The time required for data transmission can be significantly reduced by increase in communication speed between smart card and reader (default value negotiated is 38400bps, but some smart cards can support 307200bps or more if the capable reader or custom build reader can be used).

The largest fraction of a time on the card for HOTP verification is clearly consumed by the preparation of cryptographic engines and not by the cryptographic operation itself (confirmed also by the performance comparisons for a wider range of different smart cards [18]). The fixed time required to initialize

---

[4] Unwrap keys and engines can be preinitialized as are shared between multiple contexts. Additionally, limited number of unwrapped authentication server contexts can be also left on-card to decrease latency of subsequent requests.

[5] Detailed description of measurements with results for other variants can be found at http://crcs.cz/papers/space2015

Table 2. The performance of operations required to complete single HOTP code verification request performed by NXP CJ2A081 smart card. The measured time is an average taken from 100 independent measurements. Note that results on different cards may differ, see [18]. Prepare&use means: prepare key object(s), initialize cryptographic engine(s) with prepared key(s) and decrypt/encrypt and sign/verify data.

Operation	Length (bytes)	Clean call	Repeat call
Verify HOTP code	**I/O:157/66B**	**288ms**	**134ms**
1. Transfer authentication server context, input data and user state into card	5+88+40+24	34ms	34ms
2. Unwrap authentication server context – use: $K_{authServerCtxEnc}$ and $K_{authServerCtxMAC}$	88	14ms	14ms
3. Unwrap user state (HOTP counter, failed attempts, settings, HMAC key) – prepare&use: $K_{stateEnc}$ and $K_{stateMAC}$	40	65ms	11ms
4. Unwrap input data (HOTP code provided by user) – prepare&use: $K_{commEnc}$ and $K_{commMAC}$	24	63ms	10ms
5. Compute HMAC&truncation over current value of counter obtained from user state– prepare&use: K_{auth}	-	20ms	20ms
6. Compare expected and supplied HOTP code, update failed attempts count, update counter	-	4ms	4ms
7. Wrap output data with status of HOTP code verification (correct/incorrect) – prepare&use: $K_{commEnc}$ and $K_{commMAC}$	16	33ms	10ms
8. Wrap updated user state – prepare&use: $K_{stateEnc}$ and $K_{stateMAC}$	32	36ms	12ms
9. Transfer output data and user state outside card	40+24+2	19ms	19ms

Table 3. The performance of operations required to complete single import of authentication server context by NXP CJ2A081 smart card. Resulting rewrapped context is later used in other HOTP operations.

Operation	Length (bytes)	Time (ms)
Import authentication server context	**I/O:261/90B**	**534ms**
1. Transfer wrapped authentication server context into card	5+256	64ms
2. Unwrap initial authentication server context – use: K_{privCG}	256	430ms
3. Create internal authentication server context and generate keys $K_{stateEnc}$ and $K_{stateMAC}$	32+32	4ms
4. Wrap authentication server context by internal keys – use: $K_{authServerCtxEnc}$ and $K_{authServerCtxMAC}$	88	14ms
5. Transfer internal authentication server context outside card	88+2	22ms

and setup the engine is especially significant when relatively short data blocks are processed. The required time can be decreased, if initialized keys and engines already present on a card are used as demonstrated by *Repeat call* measurements in Table 2 – e.g., when multiple requests for the same cryptographic context are performed in close sequence (requires proper optimization of distribution of requests to same set of cards). Design and implementation should also use lowest possible (yet secure) number of keys for different operations.

Table 4. The performance of operations required to complete creation of context (HOTP state) for new user of given authentication server by NXP CJ2A081 smart card. Resulting user HOTP state is later used in *Verify HOTP code* operation.

Operation	Length (bytes)	Time (ms)
Generate HOTP state for a new user	**I/O:12/42B**	**70ms**
1. Transfer user state information into card	5+7	14ms
2. Prepare new HOTP state for user and generate new K_{auth} key	28	3ms
3. Wrap user HOTP state – prepare&use: $K_{stateEnc}$ and $K_{stateMAC}$	40	36ms
4. Transfer user HOTP state outside card	40+2	17ms

4.6   Performance Results – Network of Processors

So far, we focused on performance of one secure processor – smart card. Even single card can be suitable platform for smaller uses with ability to serve more then 300,000 authentications per day. Still, we need to increase transaction rate significantly to provide CaaS service shared between many users.

We built a prototype "CryptoHive" as described in Section 3.2 to show scalability of our approach. The enclosure is a standard 1U rack-mount with a standard Intel i5 processor, 4GB of RAM, 2x 120GB SSD disk, and 2x 1Gbps ethernet interface. The first version used a set of smart cards and smart-card readers connected to this untrusted controller via USB ports. Prototype characteristics:

- standard size of 1U server, Intel i5, 4GB RAM;
- 45x NXP CJ2A081 smart cards (JavaCard 2.2.2 platform);
- Omnikey 6121 USB SIM Reader as smart card readers;
- 8x active USB hub with 7 ports - connected in a two-level tree; and
- AES128/256 CBC, CBC-MAC/ RSA 2048 as main internal cryptographic algorithms.

We have encountered several difficulties with this architecture, namely:

- only 10 or 16 card readers are detected by default on OS Windows 7/8 and Linux (Ubuntu 15.04) respectively;
- parallel requests are inherently serialized by the communication stack (i.e., PC/SC interface);
- compatibility issues with some USB hubs and selected readers;
- relatively high failure rate of smart-card readers.

We have eventually overcome these difficulties and created a functional prototype suitable for long-term tests. The experience was used for design of an improved version. Smart cards are connected via internal Ethernet hub and a custom communication layer that allow to maximise performance of smart cards plugged in the "CryptoHive" and significantly improve reliability of the whole architecture.

Even with relatively small number (45) of smart cards, the only efficient implementation of the untrusted controller is a fully asynchronous version. It turned out that 30-40 smartcards were able to serve sufficient amount of requests to create significant synchronisation bottlenecks when the system with partially synchronous implementation was used.

Asynchronous controller was able to utilise secure cryptographic processors near to physical maximum – at about 98 % of the theoretical maximum. This in effect demonstrates almost linear scalability of the computational power of the "CryptoHive".

We have introduced an additional overhead to provide auditable audit trails and key use dependent on the presence of authorisation tokens but their impact on the system throughput is in the region of 1-2% with authorisations renewed on average every 30 seconds.

5   Future Directions

We believe that CaaS is only at its beginnings and there are a large number of research as well as engineering problems that need to be solved. Some particular issues we encountered while working on this problem include:

Efficient secure channel context management – the question is to find an efficient mechanism to protect and efficiently access cryptographic contexts with only a limited secure resources (computational power, memory space). Scaling of CaaS means that the number of contexts greatly exceeds the size of secure memory. This is closely related to efficient offload and restore of intermediate cryptographic context including fully scheduled keys and initialized engine. Such a feature is not currently supported by smart cards because in single holder scenario, keys are changed infrequently and will all fit into available on-card memory. Also, offloading intermediate state extends an attack surface to mount various side-channel or fault attacks. But benefits of such a would be high as preparation of cryptographic contexts accounts for more then half of total time of HOTP verification.

Highly accessible distributed shared state with updates – freshness of requests in highly distributed environment, where updates have to be instantly distributed to a large number of processing units. The classic option is either to limit modification of the state data only to single processor (which would decrease performance) or to combine partial state updates into a final state later. Delayed combination of state can be performed either in secure processors (increasing latency to serve request) or in untrusted controller (which requires suitable secure scheme).

Robust architecture tolerant to hardware/software failures – the architecture must be be fault tolerant and be able to recover automatically; if a particular secure computational resource fails permanently, the system has to adapt to that and continue safe and secure operation.

Encryption and authentication schemes – establishment of cryptographic contexts is an expensive operation and ability to merge multiple atomic cryptographic operations into single invocation of cryptographic engine provides immediate computational boost. For example, it is faster to encrypt and transmit 256B of data then encrypt and then MAC only 32B of data. If some precomputation of data otherwise done by service (e.g., keystream) can be done by Client and transmitted inside encrypted request to service, performance gain can be obtained.

6 Conclusions

As more and more services are being moved into cloud environment, user has less control over his/her sensitive data including cryptographic keys. Cryptography as a Service (CaaS) is an attempt to offer cryptographic functions in a similar manner as a generic computation is offered in cloud. There has been little systematic discussion yet about actual user needs in such a context as well as design of new architectures able to fulfil those needs.

We described several usage scenarios of CaaS and discussed its properties. We believe that scenario with many users and many cryptographic keys fits the best situation when secure hardware is shared among many users in the cloud computing. For such *many users, many keys* scenario, we defined set of principles which should be followed by platform offering CaaS functionality. Based on these principles, we discussed various available hardware architectures which can be used to provide computational resources for CaaS.

We propose scalable secure architecture for CaaS based on large numbers of secure processors, interconnected by secure channels to facilitate information exchange via untrusted surrounding environment and provide hierarchical control yet retains high performance. The proposed architecture was implemented as a prototype called "CryptoHive" using an array of cryptographic smart cards and evaluated on HMAC-based one-time password authentication (HOTP) protocol. We identified frequent switch of the cryptographic context switching (key scheduling, cryptographic engine initialization) as the major performance impactor in the HOTP as well as other usage scenarios. Based on the practical experience, a set of tips for improving performance are discussed together with possible future directions.

References

1. CryptLib++ project, http://www.cryptlib.com/ (July 12, 2015)
2. OpenSSL project, https://openssl.org (July 12, 2015)
3. NVIDIAs next generation CUDA compute architecture: Fermi. NVIDIA (2009)
4. Amazon AWS. CloudHSM, https://aws.amazon.com/cloudhsm/ (July 12, 2015)
5. Bleikertz, S., Bugiel, S., Ideler, H., Nürnberger, S., Sadeghi, A.-R.: Client-Controlled Cryptography-as-a-Service in the Cloud. In: Jacobson, M., Locasto, M., Mohassel, P., Safavi-Naini, R. (eds.) ACNS 2013. LNCS, vol. 7954, pp. 19–36. Springer, Heidelberg (2013)
6. Chow, R., Golle, P., Jakobsson, M., Shi, E., Staddon, J., Masuoka, R., Molina, J.: Controlling data in the Cloud: Outsourcing computation without outsourcing control. In: ACM Workshop on Cloud Computing Security (CCSW 2009), pp. 85–90. ACM (2009)

7. Doroz, Y., Ozturk, E., Sunar, B.: Accelerating fully homomorphic encryption in hardware. IEEE Transactions on Computers 64(6), 1509–1521 (2015)
8. Focardi, R., Luccio, F.L., Steel, G.: An introduction to security API analysis. In: Aldini, A., Gorrieri, R. (eds.) FOSAD 2011. LNCS, vol. 6858, pp. 35–65. Springer, Heidelberg (2011)
9. Initiative for open authentication (OATH), http://www.openauthentication.org/ (July 12, 2015)
10. Gentry, C.: Fully homomorphic encryption using ideal lattices. In: 41st ACM Symposium on Theory of Computing (STOC), pp. 169–178. ACM (2009)
11. Jang, K., Han, S., Han, S., Moon, S., Park, K.: SSLSshader: cheap SSL acceleration with commodity processors. In: 8th USENIX Conference on Networked Systems and Implementation, NSDI 2011. USENIX Association (2011)
12. Kumar, S., Paar, C., Pelzl, J., Pfeiffer, G., Schimmler, M.: Breaking ciphers with COPACOBANA –a cost-optimized parallel code breaker. In: Goubin, L., Matsui, M. (eds.) CHES 2006. LNCS, vol. 4249, pp. 101–118. Springer, Heidelberg (2006)
13. Lepoint, T., Naehrig, M.: A comparison of the homomorphic encryption schemes FV and YASHE. In: Pointcheval, D., Vergnaud, D. (eds.) AFRICACRYPT. LNCS, vol. 8469, pp. 318–335. Springer, Heidelberg (2014)
14. M'Raihi, D., Bellare, M., Hoornaert, F., Naccache, D., Ranen, O.: HOTP: An HMAC-based one-time password algorithm. In: RFC 4226. IETF (2005)
15. OpenVZ. VirtualHSM project, https://openvz.org/virtual_hsm (July 12, 2015)
16. Rankl, W., Effing, W.: Smart Card Handbook. Wiley (2004) ISBN 9780470856680
17. Robinson, P.: Cryptography as a service. In: RSAConference Europe 2013 (2013)
18. Švenda, P.: JCAlgTester project, http://www.fi.muni.cz/ xsvenda/jcsupport.html (July 12, 2015)

Efficient and Secure Elliptic Curve Cryptography for 8-bit AVR Microcontrollers

Erick Nascimento, Julio López, and Ricardo Dahab

Institute of Computing, University of Campinas, Campinas, Brazil
ra032483@students.ic.unicamp.br,
{jlopez,rdahab}@ic.unicamp.br

Abstract. The AVR family of 8-bit microcontrollers is widely used in several applications demanding secure communications and protection against physical attacks, such as side-channel analysis. In this context, processing, storage and energy demands of cryptographic software must be low, requirements which are met by ECC. At the 128-bit security level, two recently proposed curves are an attractive option for 8-bit microcontrollers: Curve25519 for Diffie-Hellman key exchange, and Ed25519 for signature. Simple power analysis is a significant threat to AVR applications, but efficient and side-channel tested implementations of SPA countermeasures for ECC protocols have not yet been dealt with in this platform, in the literature. This paper describes an efficient implementation of ECDH-Curve25519 and EdDSA-Ed25519-SHA512 for the ATmega328P platform. Our implementation provides protection against timing attacks, SPA and template SPA. The resistance against SPA is evaluated through the test vector leakage assessment (TVLA) methodology based on Welch's t-test, using the Chipwhisperer platform.

Keywords: Public-key cryptography, elliptic curves, ECDH, EdDSA, embedded system, AVR, side-channel attack, timing analysis, simple power analysis, SPA, template SPA, countermeasure.

1 Introduction

Elliptic Curve Cryptography (ECC) is a class of public-key cryptosystems proposed by Koblitz [32] and Miller [40], which provides significant efficiency advantages for microcontrollers, due to small key sizes which may improve speed, memory and power. For example, some industry standards require 2048-bit keys for RSA, whereas the equivalent security for ECC demands 224-bit keys. In fact, ECC-based protocols are used in many embedded applications, such as payment, pay-TV, wireless sensors, medical and identification systems.

Passive side-channel attacks (SCA) are a class of implementation attacks exploiting physical leakages of a device during the execution of a cryptographic operation, such as: timing [33], power consumption [34] and electromagnetic radiation [47,21]. They present a realistic threat to cryptographic applications, and have demonstrated to be very effective against smart cards without proper

© Springer International Publishing Switzerland 2015
R.S. Chakraborty et al. (Eds.): SPACE 2015, LNCS 9354, pp. 289–309, 2015.
DOI: 10.1007/978-3-319-24126-5_17

290 E. Nascimento, J. López, and R. Dahab

countermeasures [37]. Evaluation of SCA resistance is mandatory in some current and upcoming standards: Common Criteria [17], FIPS 140-3 [43] and others [31]. SCA attacks can be classified in two categories: *Simple Side-Channel Analysis* (SSCA) [33], in which measurements (traces) obtained for a single or few runs of a private key operation (e.g., signing or decryption) are acquired, and the differences in the measured physical quantity depending on the value of the secret key are analyzed; and *Differential Side-channel Analysis* (DSCA) [34], which is based on statistical analysis to retrieve information about the private key based on a large number of traces. SSCA is considered the main side-channel threat against implementations of public key cryptographic algorithms.

Current cryptographic standards require a work factor around 128 bits [2,11] [44,45]. Curve25519 [5] and Ed25519 [6] are two curves at the 128 bit security level that have achieved promising industry adoption. Curve25519 is a curve in the Montgomery model over the 255-bit prime field $\mathbb{F}_p$, for $p = 2^{255} - 19$, suitable for ECDH. Ed25519 is a curve in the twisted Edwards model also defined over $\mathbb{F}_p$, but designed for the EdDSA (Edwards DSA) signature scheme [6].

Related Work. The closest related works that can be directly compared to ours are the port of the NaCl library to AVR by Hutter and Schwabe [27], which includes constant time implementations of both EdDSA-Ed25519 (23 216 241 cycles for signing and 32 634 713 cycles for verification) and ECDH-Curve25519 (22 791 579 cycles for computing a shared secret key using Montgomery ladder) protocols, and the faster version [19] of ECDH-Curve25519 (13 900 397 cycles using Montgomery ladder). Other implementations of ECC for twisted Edwards or Montgomery curves for 8-bit AVRs in the literature cannot be directly compared to ours, because they target different curves. Chu et al [14] implemented ECC for twisted Edwards curves over 160 and 192 bits Optimal Prime Fields (OPFs), but do not implement any countermeasures against SCA. Liu et al [35] described an implementation of ECC for Montgomery curves over OPFs with field sizes ranging from 160 to 256 bits[1]. Liu et al [36] described constant time, variable and fixed-base scalar multiplications for twisted Edwards and Montgomery curves over OPFs, the latter uses a highly regular comb algorithm.

Our Contributions. We describe implementations of fixed and variable-base elliptic curve scalar multiplication algorithms for Ed25519, and of EdDSA-Ed25519-SHA512 signature generation and verification for AVR microcontrollers, which are efficient, timing analysis resistant through constant time implementation, and SPA-protected by the randomized coordinates countermeasure. Our EdDSA-Ed25519-SHA512 implementation improves the current state of the art [27] performance for signing in 17.2%, with 19 221 517 cycles (constant time, randomized coordinates, and with a lookup-protected precomputed table of 8 points), and for verification in 5.7%, with 30 776 942 cycles. We also test the SPA leakage of our constant time implementation of the Montgomery Ladder scalar multiplication algorithm for Curve25519 with the randomized coordinates countermeasure by

---

[1] They used a version of the binary Extended Euclidean Algorithm for field inversion which is not constant time, and no SPA-specific countermeasure was applied.

running CRI's test vector leakage assessment methodology (TVLA) [22,50]. To the best of our knowledge, this is the first work to provide a SPA leakage assessment of an implementation of ECC on AVR. Finally, we also show that addresses of loads from Flash memory leak through power, and that such leakage can be exploited by template SPA.

2 Side-Channel Analysis on the AVR

2.1 Timing Analysis

Timing attacks against implementations of cryptographic algorithms exploit the fact that the elapsed time typically varies and depends on the specific value of the input data being processed on the particular run, for fixed (e.g., key) or variable (e.g., plaintext or ciphertext) data. Vulnerability to timing analysis implies vulnerability to power analysis, as time differences can be visually detected in power traces. The following are recommendations to prevent timing analysis [7].

Avoiding Secret-Dependent Load Addresses. This is necessary when the architecture has a memory hierarchy. It is not the case of AVR architecture, which has just one memory level, the SRAM, and in which all accesses take the same time. Thus, we do not implement this recommendation.

Avoiding Secret-Dependent Branch Conditions. In other words, to avoid data flow from secret data to branch conditions. In the case of AVR, there is no branch prediction mechanism, so this problem could be solved by balancing the number of instructions executed in the two conditions of the branch, but it has to be done at the assembly level, is tedious and error prone. Instead, we solve it by using conditional move operations implemented with logical operations.

2.2 Simple Power Analysis

Generally speaking, power analysis exploits the fact that the instantaneous power consumption of a device depends on both the data processed and the operation performed [37,34]. Power analysis attacks are classified as SPA even if the attacker needs to obtain more than one trace to succeed, maybe from different input data values, provided statistical analysis of the traces are not required [37].

Power analysis countermeasures for both SPA and DPA are based on the reduction or elimination of the dependency between the power consumption of a cryptographic device and the intermediate values used by the algorithm, and are classified in two main groups: hiding and masking [37]. In this work we apply both kinds of countermeasures. Hiding is employed through highly regular[2] [30] scalar multiplication algorithms, which also do not assume that

---

[2] An algorithm is said to be highly regular when: (i) it always executes the same instructions, in the same order, for all possible input values; and (ii) there is no dummy instructions, i.e., all instructions are effective.

distinct operations have the same leakage characteristics[3]. Masking is applied by randomizing the point coordinate representation, to protect against SPA and template SPA [39].

3   Prime Field Arithmetic

Curve25519 and Ed25519. Curve25519 [5] is the Montgomery curve $E(\mathbb{F}_p)$: $y^2 = x^3 + 48662x^2 + x$ over the prime field $\mathbb{F}_p$, $p = 2^{255} - 19$. Ed25519 [6] is a twisted Edwards curve birationally equivalent to Curve25519, defined by $E'(\mathbb{F}_p) : -x^2 + y^2 = 1 - \frac{121665}{121666}x^2y^2$ over the same prime field $\mathbb{F}_p$.

Prime field $\mathbb{F}_{2^{255}-19}$. Following the representation proposed in [9], we also represent an element of $\mathbb{F}_p$ as an integer modulo $2^{256} - 38$ during field operations, as do previous implementations of Curve25519 and Ed25519 in AVR [27,19]. This redundant representation allows for a more efficient reduction than reducing directly modulo p. Only in the end of the scalar multiplication calculation, if the integer is not already in $\mathbb{F}_p$, we subtract p in constant time.

Field Multiplication and Squaring. Multi-precision multiplication (256-bit) is implemented as a 3-level subtractive Karatsuba [10,28]. This variant of Karatsuba avoids the carry bits when computing the middle partial product, but it requires the computation of two absolute differences of the low and high halves of the operands, $|A_L - A_H|$ and $|B_L - B_H|$, and one conditional negation of the product of these differences. The bottom 32-bit multiplier is fully unrolled. Field squaring is implemented as a 3-level subtractive Karatsuba, in which case there is no conditional negation of M. The 32-bit multiplier from the multiplication is reused here, through a function call, at the bottom level. Both operations are implemented in assembly, are branch-free and partially unrolled.

Multiplication by Constant 121666. This multiplication is required for the group arithmetic in Curve25519. Since the constant representation requires 3 bytes (1 ∥ DB ∥ 42), multiplying it by a single word takes only 2 multiplications and a few addition instructions.

Field Inversion. We use Fermat's theorem, $x^{-1} \equiv x^{p-2} \pmod{p}$, to compute inversion in $\mathbb{F}_p$ in constant time. We use the same addition chain as [5,27], consisting of 254 squares and 11 multiplications, but we reduce the number of temporary field variables required from 10 to only 5.

4   Arithmetic Modulo Ed25519 Group Order

EdDSA-Ed25519 signature scheme requires addition and multiplication modulo the Ed25519 group order (N). We implemented reduction modulo N in C using a constant time version of the Barret algorithm obtained by unrolling the final

---

[3] For example, it is not supposed that field squaring and multiplication exhibits the same leakage patterns.

subtraction loop into two copies of its body (the maximum number of iterations) and using conditional moves implemented in constant time.We precomputed the reciprocal of the modulus, $R = \lfloor b^{2n}/N \rfloor = \lfloor 256^{64}/N \rfloor$, a parameter of the Barret algorithm, and stored it in program memory. The multiplication calls the 256-bit multiplier and then reduces fully. The addition also reduces fully and is implemented in assembly.

5   Scalar Multiplication

The most computationally expensive operation in ECC is the scalar multiplication (ECSM), also known as point multiplication (by a scalar). Protocols usually involve three cases: fixed base point (kG), where G is a fixed point (usually the subgroup generator) and k is a scalar; variable base point (kP), where P is a point not known in advance; and the double scalar multiplication ($kP + sG$), where P is variable and G is fixed.

Several algorithms are available for variable, fixed and double-base scalar multiplication on Curve25519 and Ed25519. The major criteria we used for the selection of ECSM algorithms were high regularity [30], followed by performance. In the case of fixed-base and double-base ECSM, the size of the table of precomputed points was also an important criteria, in view of the small Flash memory space on ATmega328P. We also wanted to explore the performance of SPA-safe ECSM algorithms that, to the best of our knowledge, were not yet implemented in AVR microcontrollers, such as the FLS fixed-base ECSM algorithm [20,8].

5.1   Extended Twisted Edwards Coordinates

The most efficient formulas for point arithmetic on twisted Edwards curves were proposed by Hisil et al [25], representing points in the extended twisted Edwards coordinates: a point $P = (x, y)$ is represented by the quadruple $(X : Y : T : Z)$, such that $x = X/Z$, $y = Y/Z$, $xy = T/Z$ and $Z \neq 0$. The auxiliary coordinate T augments homogeneous projective coordinates $(X : Y : Z)$ with the product of x and y, and has the property $T = XY/Z$. The group identity element is represented by $(0 : 1 : 0 : 1)$, the negative of an element $(X : Y : T : Z)$ is $(-X : Y : -T : Z)$. A point in affine coordinates (x, y) can be converted to extended twisted Edwards coordinates by $X = x$, $Y = y$, $T = xy$ and $Z = 1$. To convert back to affine, T is ignored and an inversion and two multiplications are required: $x = X/Z$ and $y = Y/Z$. Similarly, a point can be converted to homogeneous projective coordinates $(X : Y : Z)$ simply by discarding T.

5.2   Variable-Base Scalar Multiplication

Montgomery Ladder Algorithm. Our implementation uses the formulas introduced by Montgomery [41] for efficient x-coordinate differential point addition and doubling on elliptic curves in the Montgomery form, as do previous implementations of Curve25519-ECDH [7,27]. The so-called Montgomery ladder algorithm comprises a sequence of 255 steps, known as *ladder steps*, each performing one point addition and one point doubling, where a point is represented by projective coordinates $(X : Z)$, where $x = X/Z$ is the respective affine x-coordinate. For a high level description of the algorithm, we refer the reader to [19, §2]. Our implementation conditionally swaps the two point variables, $P1 = (X_1 : Y_1)$ and $P2 = (X_2 : Y_2)$, in constant time, before the point operations in each ladder step. Point addition requires $3M + 2S$ and point doubling requires $2M + 2S + 1M_c$ [4].

Joye's Double-Add Algorithm. Joye's double-add [29] (Algorithm 1) is a variable-base right-to-left scalar multiplication algorithm, with no known SSCA attack, which always repeats the same pattern of effective operations: a point doubling is always followed by a point addition. The first operand (R_{1-b}) in the point addition is the result from the last point doubling, while the second operand is the result from a previous addition, not necessarily the last one. For this reason, we use the following coordinate systems in the point operations:

$$\text{ExtTwistEd} := 2 \cdot \text{HomoProj}$$
$$\text{ExtTwistEd} := \text{ExtTwistEd} + \text{ExtTwistEd}$$

The point doubling algorithm (Algorithm 2 in Appendix B) is based on the dedicated doubling formula from [25, §3.3], is optimized for $a = -1$ (the case for Ed25519) and costs $4M + 4S$. In its implementation, the input point is actually represented in twisted Edwards coordinates, but is then converted to homogeneous coordinates simply by ignoring the T coordinate (see Sect. 5.1). The point addition algorithm (Algorithm 3 in Appendix B) is based in the unified and complete point addition formula from Hisil et al [25, §3.1] and is optimized for the case $a = -1$. It costs $8M + 1M_c$, but as the constant is large in this case, a full multiplication is needed, therefore the effective cost is $9M$. The scalar multiplication cost is thus $255 \cdot (13M + 4S)$.

Goundar *et al*'s Signed Digit Algorithm. In order to prevent SPA-type attacks, Goundar *et al* [24] proposed the use of the *zeroless signed-digit expansion* (ZSD) in the binary left-to-right or right-to-left algorithms. The odd scalar k is recoded on-the-fly with digits in the set $\{-1, 1\}$ (Algorithm 4 in Appendix B). We use extended twisted Edwards coordinates for point addition and doubling. The point addition is actually a readdition, because the second operand, $R_1 = (X_2 : Y_2 : T_2 : Z_2)$, can only be P or $-P$, so we can cache the result of kT_2, $(Y_2 - X_2)$, $(Y_2 + X_2)$ and $2Z_2$, saving a multiplication. Therefore, the scalar multiplication costs $254 \cdot (12M + 4S)$.

5.3   Flash Memory Address Leakage Through Power

When the base point P is fixed, scalar multiplication algorithms can employ (offline) precomputation involving P to speedup the (online) evaluation phase

---

[4] M_c means multiplication by a constant, 121666 in this instance.

of the scalar multiplication. For that end, a table of multiples of the base point is typically precomputed and stored in a non-volatile memory. In the evaluation phase, the points in the table are looked up based on some indexing method, whose index values are dependent on bits of the (secret) scalar.

In the case of AVR, Flash memory is used to store the precomputed point table. The time required to load a word from the Flash to the SRAM is constant, independent of the address referenced. However, different index values correspond to different Flash addresses, with possibly distinct Hamming weights, and therefore potentially distinct power consumption characteristics. We designed an experiment to evaluate whether this kind of leakage occurs and whether the leakage level is sufficient to distinguish between all the possible Hamming weights of the addresses referenced in Flash reads. On AVR, Flash has a different address space than SRAM, and are 16-bit on the ATmega328p.

The experiment consisted of selecting a set of addresses whose Hamming weights are in the set $S_{HW} = \{2, ..., 8\}$. We selected 7 addresses in the range from 0x00A7 to 0x00FF, which have the upper 8 bits zeroed, one for each Hamming weight in S_{HW}. Let S_{addr} be this set[5]. We wrote a fixed byte value (0xDE) to all addresses in this set. We then executed reads from this addresses (LPM instruction) to a (fixed) register (the byte 0x00 is written to this register in advance). For each address Hamming weight in S_{HW}, 100 traces were captured. Each power trace captured consists of the power consumption of a sequence of instructions including the target LPM. The samples corresponding to the LPM instruction were visually identified, and then, for each address Hamming weight, the average of the corresponding traces were computed.

Figure 1a shows the "average traces" for each address Hamming weight, for the sample points corresponding to the LPM instruction. We can see that the voltage values for the sample index 98 are the best single-point distinguishers for the address Hamming weights in the set S_{HW}. Therefore, we select the average and sample standard deviation of voltages at this point to analyze whether this leakage can be exploited to recover the Hamming weights.

Figure 1b shows the average voltage and the 95% confidence interval for each Hamming weight in the set S_{HW}. We cannot classify with strong statistical significance the Hamming weight of a Flash address based only in one voltage sample, because every confidence interval overlaps with at least one other confidence interval[6]. However, the following groups can be distinguished: $\{2\}$, $\{3, 6\}$, $\{4, 7\}$, $\{8, 5\}$. This enables an adversary to detect sets of possible addresses of the points being loaded from Flash to SRAM. In practice, in the context of fixed-base scalar multiplication, during the lookup of a point stored in the precomputed point table an adversary could measure the address leakage from the

---

[5] We selected this range of Flash addresses, because it is available for user programs, but other ranges could be used. The following were the addresses selected: 0x00c0 (hw=2), 0x00e0 (hw=3), 0x00f0 (hw=4), 0x00f8 (hw=5), 0x00fc (hw=6), 0x00fe (hw=7) and 0x00ff (hw=8).

[6] In the case of Hamming weights 4 and 5, the confidence interval for 4 contains the one for 7.

load of each word of each coordinate of the point, and thus could combine the leakage values during the single point lookup to uniquely determine its index.

To counteract this kind of leakage, we implemented a constant time table lookup. For each point table lookup, we read all words in the point table and use bitwise arithmetic such that in the end the words of the coordinates values of the point requested are in the target buffer in SRAM (see Algorithm 6 in Appendix B).

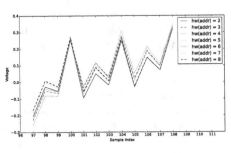

(a) Voltage versus Sample index.

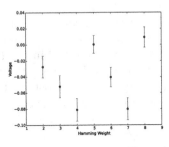

(b) Voltage versus Hamming weight.

Fig. 1. Figure 1a shows the Voltage versus Sample index, for each Flash address Hamming weight from 2 to 8, in the interval of samples/points in the average trace corresponding to the LPM instruction. LPM takes 3 CPU cycles, and the sampling rate is 4 samples per cycle. Figure 1b shows the Voltage versus Hamming weight for the second sample (sample index 98), with 95% confidence interval bars, for LPM instructions referencing Flash addresses with different Hamming weights.

5.4 Fixed-Base ECSM for Ed25519 Key Generation and Signing

Modified LSB-set Algorithm (FLS). We implemented Faz-Hernandez et al's modified LSB-set comb algorithm [20], henceforward named FLS, according to the specification in [8, Alg. 7]. Beyond the curve-related parameters, which have already been fixed by the curve selection, different pairs of values for the number of tables of precomputed points v and the window width w have been selected and experimentally evaluated, to determine their actual performance when protection against Flash memory address leakage is applied, and also to compare the required storage costs. Points are represented in extended twisted Edwards coordinates, both in the working variables and in the precomputed table, and point addition and doubling formulas are the same used for Joye's (Algorithms 3 and 2 in Appendix B). We evaluated the performance with 4 precomputed points (1KB), $(v = 1, w = 3)$ (1 table) and $(v = 2, w = 2)$ (2 tables), and with 8 points (2KB), $(v = 1, w = 4)$ (1 table) and $(v = 2, w = 3)$ (2 tables). We also evaluated the performance impact of the table lookup protection. In the case of two tables, we use a similar technique as that for a single table (Algorithm 6 in Appendix B), to guarantee that all words are read from both tables, but only the desired point is left in the destination variable.

5.5 Projective Coordinate Randomization

In a template SPA [39] attack the adversary first characterizes the power consumption of a sequence of instructions executed on a device similar to the target device, when a fixed pair (key, data) is processed, and repeats the process for several such pairs, resulting in a set of power consumption templates, one for each pair (template building phase). After that, the templates are matched against a single trace captured from the target (template matching phase).

Highly regular scalar multiplication algorithms implemented in constant time are not enough to protect against template SPA attacks, as it was shown in [39,4]. According to Medwed and Oswald [39], the only way to make an implementation resistant to template SPA attacks is to make it resistant against DPA attacks, and they also assert that among Coron's proposed countermeasures for DPA in ECC [16], only randomized projective coordinates can prevent template SPA.

We applied the randomized projective coordinates countermeasure to the projective coordinates $(X : Z)$ in Montgomery Ladder and the extended twisted Edwards coordinates $(X : Y : T : Z)$ in Joye's Double-Add, Goundar's Signed-digit and FLS algorithms. In the case of Montgomery Ladder, we generate random $\lambda \in \mathbb{F}_p \backslash \{0\}$ in the beginning of the algorithm and do $Z_2 \leftarrow \lambda$ and $X_2 \leftarrow u \cdot \lambda$, where u is the x-coordinate of the input point P and $P_2 = (X_2 : Z_2)$ is the second point variable. In the case of Joye's Double-add and Goundar's Signed-digit algorithms, we randomly generate $\lambda \in \mathbb{F}_p \backslash \{0\}$ and do $X' \leftarrow \lambda x$, $Y' \leftarrow \lambda y$, $T' \leftarrow xY'$ and $Z' \leftarrow \lambda$, where $P = (x, y)$ is the input point in affine coordinates and the resultant point $P' = (X' : Y', T', Z')$ is used in place of P in the remainder of the algorithms.

In FLS algorithm, we randomize the coordinates of the first point loaded from the table of precomputed points, $P_0 = (X : Y : T : Z)$, as follows: generate random $\lambda \in \mathbb{F}_p \backslash \{0\}$ and do $X' \leftarrow \lambda X$, $Y' \leftarrow \lambda Y$, $T' \leftarrow \lambda T$ and $Z' \leftarrow \lambda Z$. The resultant point $P_0' = (X' : Y' : T' : Z')$ is used in place of P_0. When this countermeasure is applied, the values of the coordinates of the accumulator point Q are randomized, changing from one execution of the scalar multiplication to the other, because the value of P_0' is assigned to Q in the beginning of evaluation stage [8, Alg. 7]. Furthermore, as an additional measure to protect against template SPA attacks targeting the loading of words stored Flash (i.e., the value of the words itself, rather than their addresses), the extended twisted Edwards coordinates of each point $P_{i,j}$ are randomized before being stored in the table, with a random λ generated for each point, in the same way P_0 was randomized.

6 Hashing and PRNG

SHA-512. The original EdDSA-Ed25519 [6] and the AVRNaCl [27] implementations of EdDSA-Ed25519 have chosen SHA-512 [42] as the hash function, therefore we have also selected it to be able to compare our results to theirs. Our goal is to achieve a small and simple implementation, so we decided to implement in assembly only the low-level functions (add64, and64, or64, xor64, rotr64 and `shr64`), while the higher level ones are implemented in C and optimized for size. The constant `HO` and round constants were kept in program memory.

Hash_DRBG. Random numbers are required for the projective coordinates randomization and for key pair generation on the device, in particular if ephemeral ECDH (ECDHE) is used. For this purpose, we implemented the Hash_DRBG pseudorandom number generator [3] at the 128-bit security level, with SHA-512 as the underlying hash function.[7] The PRNG is seeded during instantiation, and its seed is the output of a derivation function whose inputs are the entropy input and nonce. The nonce is stored in the EEPROM when the device is programmed. The entropy input is also assumed to be stored in the EEPROM, as we do not implement entropy gathering from physical sources.[8]

7 Elliptic Curve Protocols

Elliptic Curve Diffie-Hellman with Curve25519 (ECDH-Curve25519). ECDH-Curve25519 protocol consists of two operations: generate key pair and compute shared secret. The latter consists mainly of a variable-base scalar multiplication, which is implemented using the Montgomery Ladder, and an inversion in $\mathbb{F}_p$. The first requires a scalar multiplication by a fixed base point, also implemented with the Montgomery Ladder.

Edwards Digital Signature Algorithm with Ed25519 (EdDSA-Ed25519-SHA512). Key generation consists of a scalar multiplication by the subgroup generator and a SHA512 hash. The signature generation applies SHA512, a fixed-base scalar multiplication, addition and multiplication modulo the subgroup order, and simple point and scalar encoding operations. The signature verification consists of simple point and scalar decoding operations followed by SHA512 and a double scalar multiplication, where one of the points is fixed (subgroup generator) and the other is variable (the signer public key). The latter is implemented with "Shamir's trick", a special case of Straus's algorithm [49].

8 Benchmarking Results

The source code was compiled with AVR-GCC v4.8.2, the size optimization `-Os` and `-fomit-frame-pointer` options were applied to the C sources, and the program was linked with global linker optimization `-flto`. Table 1 shows the benchmarking results. The signature generation uses the FLS algorithm with

---

[7] Faster approved hash functions, such as SHA-256 or even SHA-1, could be used at this security level, but we decided to just call the SHA-512 function already available to not increase the code size.

[8] One such scheme proposed in the literature is Hlavac et al's [26] method of generating true random numbers on the AVR based on the jitter of the built-in RC oscillator, requiring only an external oscillator. However, the resulting TRNG is slow, being capable of generating only 8 bits of entropy per second.

$(v = 1, w = 4)$ (8 points, 1 table), with and without the table lookup protection and randomized coordinates countermeasures. In the results for the functions protected with the coordinate randomization, the PRNG overhead is not taken into account, i.e., the required number of random bytes are readily available.

The results of our implementation of EdDSA-Ed25519-SHA512 improve the state of the art performance [27], requiring 19 047 706 cycles for signing, an improvement of 17.9%, and 30 776 942 cycles for verification, an improvement of 5.7%. The overhead of the countermeasures table lookup protection and randomized projective coordinates to the FLS algorithm is only 1.0%. Similarly, when these countermeasures are applied on the signature generation function, the overhead is also very small (0.9%). In the case of the compute shared secret function, the overhead of the coordinate randomization is only 0.04%.

Despite having a slower field multiplication than Hutter and Schwabe implementation (6208 cycles) [27], we implemented a dedicated field squaring algorithm in assembly while the authors simply reused the multiplication function for squaring, resulting in faster scalar multiplications for both Curve25519 and Ed25519. Dull et al [19] described an efficient implementation of field multiplication and squaring for AVR using more efficient algorithms, significantly improving the state-of-the-art performance with 13 900 397 cycles for computing a ECDH-Curve25519 shared secret key.

9 Timing and Simple Power Analysis Leakage Evaluation

Side-channel security evaluations of cryptography devices comprise two phases: *measurement* and *analysis*. The output of such an evaluation should be an assertion, indicating whether the device is vulnerable (*Fail*) or not (*Pass*), given the constraints of the evaluation process[9]. The proper measurement of the side-channel traces and its limitations must be properly accounted for, or else the analysis process could be undermined, probably resulting in false positives, or worse, false negatives.

Current evaluation methodologies (e.g. Common Criteria [17]) consist of performing a battery of known side-channel attacks against the device under test (DUT) in an attempt to recover the key. Nonetheless, the rapid evolving set of side-channel attacks proposed in the literature incur both a more demanding level of expertise of test operators and an increase on the evaluation time. Even when all attack attempts have failed, residual side-channel leakages may be available, which may reveal new attack paths for an adversary.

CRI proposed the Test Vector Leakage Assessment (TVLA) testing methodology, to solve the aforementioned issues, which is claimed to be effective, in the sense that it is reproducible and is a reliable indicator of the resistance achieved, and cost effective, meaning that "validating a moderate level of resistance (e.g., FIPS 140 level 3 or 4) should not require an excessive amount of testing time per algorithm or test operator skills" [22]. Their approach differs fundamentally from

---

[9] E.g., accuracy of the testing equipment, technical expertise and available time.

Table 1. Benchmarking results on ATmega328P.

Operation Class	Operation/Algorithm	Msg.(B)	Cycles	Stack(B)
Field Arith.	Field Multiplication	-	7555	-
	Field Squaring	-	5666	-
	Field Inversion	-	2 000 762	-
Group Order Arith.	Barret Reduction	-	43 045	-
	Group Order Addition	-	54 303	-
	Group Order Negation	-	46 773	-
	Group Order Multiplication	-	72 438	-
Variable-base ECSM Curve25519	Montgomery Ladder	-	20 153 658	-
	Montgomery Ladder, rand. coord.	-	20 161 213	-
Variable-base ECSM Ed25519	Joye's Double-Add	-	42 436 422	-
	Joye's Double-Add, rand. coord.	-	42 459 087	-
	Goundar's Signed-digit	-	35 757 016	-
	Goundar's Signed-digit, rand. coord.	-	35 779 681	-
Fixed-base ECSM Ed25519	FLS ($v = 1$, $w = 3$)	-	21 553 188	-
	FLS ($v = 2$, $w = 2$)	-	26 661 293	-
	FLS ($v = 1$, $w = 3$), lookup prot.	-	21 658 857	-
	FLS ($v = 1$, $w = 4$)	-	18 119 234	-
	FLS ($v = 2$, $w = 3$)	-	19 170 150	-
	FLS ($v = 1$, $w = 4$), lookup prot.	-	18 264 710	-
	FLS ($v = 1$, $w = 4$), lookup + rand. coord.	-	18 298 387	-
Double ECSM Ed25519	Shamir's trick	-	28 105 811	-
Hash	SHA-512	64	554 280	-
	SHA-512	1024	4 974 380	-
ECDH-Curve25519	Compute shared secret [27]	-	22 791 579	677
	Compute shared secret [19]	-	13 900 397	494
	Compute shared secret	-	20 254 426	686
	Compute shared secret, rand. coord.	-	20 261 981	743
EdDSA-Ed25519	Signature generation [27]	64	23 216 241	1642
	Signature generation	64	19 047 706	1473
	Signature generation, lookup + rand. coord.	64	19 221 517	1511
	Signature verification [27]	64	32 634 713	1315
	Signature verification	64	30 776 942	1226

the attack-focused evaluation strategies currently employed, taking a black-box and detection-focused strategy [38].

The measurement phase of TVLA is based on the collection of side-channel traces when standardized test vectors are provided as input to the algorithm being tested, and establishes requirements for power measurement equipment and setup, data collection, signal alignment and preprocessing. The analysis phase is based on Welch's t-test, can detect different types of leakages and allows the analyst to identify points in time that deserve further investigation. The testing methodology has so far been applied to AES and RSA implementations[10].

Other methodologies, based on continuous [13] and discrete [12] mutual information have also been proposed. Oswald et al [38] analyzed methodologies [22], [12]

---

[10] For AES, by the methodology authors [22,15] and independently [38]; and for RSA software implementations [50].

and [13], and concluded they have similar statistical power. The recent work of
Schneider and Moradi [48] address how to perform the t-test in [22] at higher orders, and how to extend it to multivariate settings.

9.1 Application of CRI's Methodology to ECC

We apply CRI's methodology to our implementation of ECDH-Curve25519, using Chipwhisperer as the power measurement equipment. Specifically, we select
a set of test vectors (Table 2) to be used for the power measurement phase,
which cover normal and special cases of the field and group arithmetic when
implemented using the chosen algorithms. Table 3 shows categories of special
values used in Sets 4 and 5 for the compute shared secret function.

Table 2. Sets of test vectors for SPA leakage analysis (k is the secret scalar and P is
the point).

Set #	Properties	Rationale
1	constant k, constant P	This is the baseline. The tests compare power consumption from the other sets against it.
2	constant k, varying P	Goal is to detect systematic relationships between power consumption and the P value.
3	varying k, constant P	Goal is to detect systematic relationships between power consumption and the k value.
4	constant k, special P	Edge cases of the algorithms used.
5	special k, constant P	Edge cases of the algorithms used.

Table 3. Categories of special values for n and q in ECDH-Curve25519 compute shared
secret function (q is the encoded point, n is the encoded scalar and l is the subgroup
order).

Cat. #	Properties
1	$q \in \{0, 1, ..., 1023\}$
2	$q \in \{p_{25519} - 1, ..., p_{25519} - 1024\}$
3	$n \in \{0, ..., 1023\}$
4	$n \in \{l - 1, ..., l - 1024\}$
5	q has a low Hamming Weight (≤ 230)
6	q has a high Hamming Weight (≥ 25)

9.2 Measurement Setup and Capture of Power Traces

Time Measurement Setup. In an AVR CPU, as the clock frequency is constant, the elapsed time of an algorithm can be measured by simply counting the
number of cycles it takes to execute. We use timer interrupts which increment a
16-bit and a 8-bit counter, resulting in 24-bit resolution.

Power Measurement Setup. In Chipwhisperer, power consumption traces are captured by the OpenADC board, which features an ADC with a sample rate of 105 MS/s, 10-bit sample resolution, 120 MHz analog bandwidth and 0 to 55 dB gain (software adjustable). The sample buffer capacity is 24k samples. We used the following parameters values in our setup, adhering to the minimum requirements from [22]. ADC frequency is set to 29.5 MHz, which is exactly four times the clock rate provided to the ATMega328P (4 x 7.37 MHz), the analog gain is set to 40 dB. The trigger mode is configured to rising clock edge.

Capture of Power Traces. The first issue we faced to capture power traces using Chipwhisperer was the small size of the samples buffer. In the latest version available of its FPGA bitstream and capture software, the samples buffer is implemented as a FIFO using cells of the small Spartan 6 LX25 FPGA, limiting its size to just 24573 samples, 10 bits each[11]. In our settings, this corresponds to a limit of 6143 cycles (4 samples per cycle) per acquisition operation.

Assuming a Curve25519 variable-base scalar multiplication takes $20M$ cycles, then 3256 acquisitions would be required to cover the whole operation. If such acquisitions are made sequentially, however, samples are lost in the time interval between an acquisition and the next, creating a gap in the trace, because when the buffer is full, its content must be sent to the host computer through serial connection before it could be emptied. To work around this limitation, we captured 6 traces (numbered from 0 to 5) of the full scalar multiplication, each one with gaps. Even and odd-numbered traces have time offsets such that the gaps in even traces don't overlap the gaps in odd traces. We compute the average of the 6 traces, not including the gaps in the average computation, obtaining an *average trace* to be used as a single trace in the analysis phase.

We obtained 200 average traces for each test vector set, for a total of 1000 traces. The complete trace capture process, including averaging, compression and disk storage took around 6 hours. Each uncompressed trace has 80, 614, 632 samples, and occupies 100, 768, 290 bytes. The sample acquisition process begin with a trigger produced by the code running in the AVR, through the assertion of bit 0 of PORTC register, just before the call to the scalar multiplication function. Similarly, the end of the acquisition was triggered by deasserting the same bit after the function returns. As this method provides a very precise synchronization of the start and end times of capture across traces, no trace alignment was needed.

9.3 SPA Leakage Analysis

The leakage analysis phase of our implementation of ECDH-Curve25519 with randomized coordinates countermeasure is identical to CRI's TVLA [50], and is conducted in the following way. Let $\{DS_1, \ldots, DS_5\}$ be the sets of power traces corresponding to the selected test vectors sets. The full test consists of running the (pairwise) tests described in [50] for each of the following pairs of datasets:

---

[11] The board provides a 1GB DDR memory, but it is not supported yet.

$\{(DS_1, DS_2), \ldots, (DS_1, DS_5)\}$. If any of the previous tests fails, then the top-level test fails and the implementation is deemed to have FAILED. Otherwise, it PASSED. We chose the confidence threshold $C = 4.5$, the same value used in CRI's methodology for RSA [50].

10   Side-Channel Analysis Results

Timing Analysis. Timing measurements were obtained for ECDH-Curve25519 compute shared secret function using a superset of the test vectors used in the SPA analysis, which includes additional randomly generated test vectors. For the timing measurements of EdDSA-Ed25519-SHA512 signature generation, we used randomly generated test vectors and those covering corner cases. The results obtained show that the implementations of both functions are constant time, with respect to the private key value.

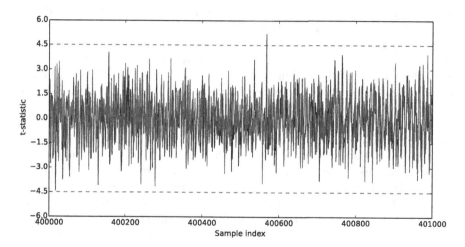

Fig. 2. t-statistic versus sample index for the experiment comparing DS_1 and DS_3, for two independent groups of traces; group A (blue) and group B (red).

SPA Analysis. The leakage analysis methodology was applied to our implementation of ECDH-Curve25519 with randomized coordinates. Figure 2 shows the t-statistic for a small range of sample indices[12] (time instants), for one run of Welch's t-test for group A $(S_{A,1}, S_{A,2})$ of vectors selected from DS_1 and DS_3, and the same test run over the independent group B $(S_{B,1}, S_{B,2})$.[13] The t-statistic for group A is above $C = 4.5$ at one time instant, meaning a possible strong dependence between power consumption and key value at that instant. But, as

---

[12] This time interval was selected because it illustrates a range where the t-statistic values are relatively high, compared to other time instants.

[13] Groups A and B are a partition of test vector sets DS_1 and DS_3: $(S_{A,1} \subset DS_1, \ S_{A,2} \subset DS_3)$ and $(S_{B,1} = DS_1 \setminus S_{A,1}, \ S_{B,2} = DS_3 \setminus S_{A,2})$.

it did not occur at the same time and in the same direction for group B, it is therefore considered a false positive by the methodology and thus discarded. The test results for each pair of test vector sets $\{(DS_1, DS_2), \ldots, (DS_1, DS_5)\}$ showed that at a few time instants the t-statistic value for one of the groups is above 4.5 or below -4.5, but not for both groups at the same time. Therefore, we can conclude that our SPA protected implementation of ECDH-Curve25519 passed the SPA leakage evaluation.

11   Conclusion

We describe an efficient implementation of protocols ECDH-Curve25519 and EdDSA-Ed25519-SHA512 for an AVR 8-bit microcontroller. The implementations prevent timing attacks by using regular algorithms and constant time field arithmetic. SPA and template SPA protection is provided by the use of coordinate randomization and by avoiding secret-address dependent loads from Flash memory. The effectiveness of the SPA countermeasures for ECDH-Curve25519 is evaluated through the application of CRI's TVLA methodology with selected test vectors, using Chipwhisperer.

We identify the following open problems. Consider the operations in this excerpt, which are typically used in constant time code (e.g., CSWAP and CMOV) to avoid branches dependent on secret data: MASK $\leftarrow -b$; $t \leftarrow$ MASK $\wedge$ x. In this example, $b \in \{0, 1\}$ is a secret dependent bit and, therefore MASK $\in \{0, 255\}$, in 8-bit unsigned integer representation. We notice that the difference in Hamming weight between the possible mask values are maximal (7), meaning that if the device leaks the Hamming weight of the (sum) of the AND instruction operands or their Hamming distance, and the adversary knows the value of x, than she may be able to exploit it for a template SPA attack. Also, according to a survey of SCA in ECC [18], some known SCA attacks are not addressed by the countermeasures we used, such as RPA [23] and ZPA [1], and thus deserve an analysis regarding their applicability to Curve25519 and Ed25519. Another further work is to analyze how strong is the leakage of the data read from the Flash and find a simple leakage model that best characterizes it.

References

1. Akishita, T., Takagi, T.: Zero-value point attacks on elliptic curve cryptosystem. In: Boyd, C., Mao, W. (eds.) ISC 2003. LNCS, vol. 2851, pp. 218–233. Springer, Heidelberg (2003)
2. ANSSI. Mécanismes cryptographiques - Règles et recommandations. Technical report, Agence nationale de la sécurité des systèmes d'information (2014)
3. Barke, E., Kelsey, J.: SP 800-90A: Recommendation for Random Number Generation Using Deterministic Random Bit Generators. Technical report, NIST (2012)
4. Batina, L., Chmielewski, L., Papachristodoulou, L., Schwabe, P., Tunstall, M.: Online Template Attacks. In: Meier, W., Mukhopadhyay, D. (eds.) INDOCRYPT 2014. LNCS, vol. 8885, pp. 21–36. Springer, Heidelberg (2014)

5. Bernstein, D.J.: Curve25519: new diffie-hellman speed records. Technical report, University of Illinois at Chicago (2006)
6. Bernstein, D.J., Duif, N., Lange, T., Schwabe, P., Yang, B.-Y.: High-speed high-security signatures. Journal of Cryptographic Engineering 2(2), 77–89 (2012)
7. Bernstein, D.J., Lange, T., Schwabe, P.: The security impact of a new cryptographic library. In: Hevia, A., Neven, G. (eds.) LatinCrypt 2012. LNCS, vol. 7533, pp. 159–176. Springer, Heidelberg (2012)
8. Bos, J., Costello, C., Longa, P., Naehrig, M.: Selecting elliptic curves for cryptography: an efficiency and security analysis. Journal of Cryptographic Engineering, 1–28 (2015)
9. Bos, J.W.: High-performance modular multiplication on the cell processor. In: Hasan, M.A., Helleseth, T. (eds.) WAIFI 2010. LNCS, vol. 6087, pp. 7–24. Springer, Heidelberg (2010)
10. Brent, R.P., Zimmermann, P.: Modern Computer Arithmetic. Cambridge University Press (2010)
11. BSI. Algorithms for Qualified Electronic Signatures. Technical report, Bundesamt für Sicherheit in der Informationstechnik (2014)
12. Chatzikokolakis, K., Chothia, T., Guha, A.: Statistical Measurement of Information Leakage. In: Esparza, J., Majumdar, R. (eds.) TACAS 2010. LNCS, vol. 6015, pp. 390–404. Springer, Heidelberg (2010), http://dx.doi.org/10.1007/978-3-642-12002-2_33, doi:10.1007/978-3-642-12002-2_33
13. Chothia, T., Guha, A.: A statistical test for information leaks using continuous mutual information. In: Proceedings - IEEE Computer Security Foundations Symposium, pp. 177–190 (2011)
14. Chu, D., Großschädl, J., Liu, Z., Müller, V., Zhang, Y.: Twisted Edwards-form elliptic curve cryptography for 8-bit AVR-based sensor nodes. In: Proceedings of the First ACM Workshop on Asia Public-Key Cryptography, pp. 39–44. ACM (2013)
15. Cooper, J., Demulder, E., Goodwill, G., Jaffe, J., Kenworthy, G.: Test Vector Leakage Assessment (TVLA) methodology in practice (Extended Abstract). Technical report, Cryptography Research Inc. (2013)
16. Coron, J.-S.: Resistance against differential power analysis for elliptic curve cryptosystems. In: Koç, Ç.K., Paar, C. (eds.) CHES 1999. LNCS, vol. 1717, pp. 292–302. Springer, Heidelberg (1999)
17. Criteria, C.: Common Criteria v3.1. Technical report, Common Criteria (2014)
18. Danger, J.-L., Guilley, S., Hoogvorst, P., Murdica, C., Naccache, D.: A synthesis of side-channel attacks on elliptic curve cryptography in smart-cards. Journal of Cryptographic Engineering, 1–25 (2013)
19. Düll, M., Haase, B., Hinterwälder, G., Hutter, M., Paar, C., Sánchez, A.H., Schwabe, P.: High-speed curve25519 on 8-bit, 16-bit, and 32-bit microcontrollers. In: Designs, Codes and Cryptography, pp. 1–22 (2015)
20. Faz-Hernández, A., Longa, P., Sánchez, A.H.: Efficient and secure algorithms for GLV-based scalar multiplication and their implementation on GLV-GLS curves. In: Benaloh, J. (ed.) CT-RSA 2014. LNCS, vol. 8366, pp. 1–27. Springer, Heidelberg (2014)
21. Gandolfi, K., Mourtel, C., Olivier, F.: Electromagnetic analysis: Concrete results. In: Koç, Ç.K., Naccache, D., Paar, C. (eds.) CHES 2001. LNCS, vol. 2162, pp. 251–261. Springer, Heidelberg (2001)
22. Goodwill, G., Jun, B., Jaffe, J., Rohatgi, P.: A testing methodology for side channel resistance validation. Technical report, CRI (2011)

23. Goubin, L.: A refined power-analysis attack on elliptic curve cryptosystems. In: Desmedt, Y.G. (ed.) PKC 2003. LNCS, vol. 2567, pp. 199–210. Springer, Heidelberg (2002)
24. Goundar, R., Joye, M., Miyaji, A., Rivain, M., Venelli, A.: Scalar multiplication on weierstraß elliptic curves from co-z arithmetic. Journal of Cryptographic Engineering 1(2), 161–176 (2011)
25. Hisil, H., Wong, K.K.-H., Carter, G., Dawson, E.: Twisted edwards curves revisited. In: Pieprzyk, J. (ed.) ASIACRYPT 2008. LNCS, vol. 5350, pp. 326–343. Springer, Heidelberg (2008)
26. Hlavac, J., Lorencz, R., Hadacek, M.: True random number generation on an Atmel AVR microcontroller. In: 2010 2nd International Conference on Computer Engineering and Technology (ICCET), vol. 2, pp. V2–493–V2–495 (2010)
27. Hutter, M., Schwabe, P.: Nacl on 8-bit avr microcontrollers. In: Youssef, A., Nitaj, A., Hassanien, A.E. (eds.) AFRICACRYPT 2013. LNCS, vol. 7918, pp. 156–172. Springer, Heidelberg (2013)
28. Hutter, M., Schwabe, P.: Multiprecision multiplication on avr revisited. Journal of Cryptographic Engineering, 1–14 (2015)
29. Joye, M.: Highly regular right-to-left algorithms for scalar multiplication. In: Paillier, P., Verbauwhede, I. (eds.) CHES 2007. LNCS, vol. 4727, pp. 135–147. Springer, Heidelberg (2007)
30. Joye, M.: Highly regular m-ary powering ladders. In: Jacobson Jr., M.J., Rijmen, V., Safavi-Naini, R. (eds.) SAC 2009. LNCS, vol. 5867, pp. 350–363. Springer, Heidelberg (2009)
31. Killmann, W., Lange, T., Lochter, M., Thumser, W., Wicke, G.: Minimum Requirements for Evaluating Side-Channel Attack Resistance of Elliptic Curve Implementations. Technical report, BSI (2011)
32. Koblitz, N.: Elliptic curve cryptosystems. Mathematics of Computation 48(177), 203–209 (1987)
33. Kocher, P.C.: Timing attacks on implementations of Diffie-Hellman, RSA, DSS, and other systems. In: Koblitz, N. (ed.) CRYPTO 1996. LNCS, vol. 1109, pp. 104–113. Springer, Heidelberg (1996)
34. Kocher, P.C., Jaffe, J., Jun, B.: Differential Power Analysis. In: Wiener, M. (ed.) CRYPTO 1999. LNCS, vol. 1666, pp. 388–397. Springer, Heidelberg (1999)
35. Liu, Z., Großschädl, J., Wong, D.S.: Low-weight primes for lightweight elliptic curve cryptography on 8-bit AVR processors. In: Lin, D., Xu, S., Yung, M. (eds.) Inscrypt 2013. LNCS, vol. 8567, pp. 217–235. Springer, Heidelberg (2014)
36. Liu, Z., Wenger, E., Großschädl, J.: MoTE-ECC: Energy-scalable elliptic curve cryptography for wireless sensor networks. In: Boureanu, I., Owesarski, P., Vaudenay, S. (eds.) ACNS 2014. LNCS, vol. 8479, pp. 361–379. Springer, Heidelberg (2014)
37. Mangard, S., Oswald, E., Popp, T.: Power analysis attacks: Revealing the secrets of smart cards, vol. 31. Springer (2007)
38. Mather, L., Oswald, E., Bandenburg, J., Wójcik, M.: Does My Device Leak Information? An a priori Statistical Power Analysis of Leakage Detection Tests. In: Sako, K., Sarkar, P. (eds.) ASIACRYPT 2013, Part I. LNCS, vol. 8269, pp. 486–505. Springer, Heidelberg (2013)
39. Medwed, M., Oswald, E.: Template Attacks on ECDSA. In: Chung, K.-I., Sohn, K., Yung, M. (eds.) WISA 2008. LNCS, vol. 5379, pp. 14–27. Springer, Heidelberg (2009)
40. Miller, V.S.: Use of Elliptic Curves in Cryptography. In: Williams, H.C. (ed.) CRYPTO 1985. LNCS, vol. 218, pp. 417–426. Springer, Heidelberg (1986)

41. Montgomery, P.L.: Speeding the pollard and elliptic curve methods of factorization. Mathematics of Computation 48(177), 243–264 (1987)
42. NIST. FIPS 180-2: Secure hash standard (SHS). Technical report, NIST (2001)
43. NIST. FIPS 140-3: Security Requirements for Cryptographic Modules. Technical report, NIST (2009)
44. NIST. SP 800-57 - Recommendation for Key Management. Technical report, National Institute for Standards and Technology (2012)
45. NSA. Fact Sheet Suite B Cryptography. Technical report, National Security Agency (2014)
46. O'Flynn, C., Chen, Z.D.: ChipWhisperer: An Open-Source Platform for Hardware Embedded Security Research. In: Prouff, E. (ed.) COSADE 2014. LNCS, vol. 8622, pp. 243–260. Springer, Heidelberg (2014)
47. Quisquater, J.-J., Samyde, D.: ElectroMagnetic analysis (EMA): Measures and counter-measures for smart cards. In: Attali, S., Jensen, T. (eds.) E-smart 2001. LNCS, vol. 2140, pp. 200–210. Springer, Heidelberg (2001)
48. Schneider, T., Moradi, A.: Leakage Assessment Methodology - a clear roadmap for side-channel evaluations. Cryptology ePrint Archive, Report 2015/207 (2015)
49. Straus, E.G.: Addition chains of vectors (problem 5125). In: American Mathematical Monthly, pp. 806–808 (1964)
50. Witteman, M., Jaffe, J., Rohatgi, P.: Efficient side channel testing for public key algorithms: RSA case study. Technical report, Cryptography Research (2011)

A   ATmega328P Microcontroller and Chipwhisperer

The AVR is a family of 8-bit microcontrollers from Atmel featuring a RISC instruction set. It is a Harvard-based architecture with separate address spaces for data (SRAM), program (Flash) and non-volatile data (EEPROM). The ATmega328P has a 32KB Flash, a 2KB SRAM and a 1KB EEPROM. It has a maximum frequency of 20 MHz, but operates at 7.3728 MHz in Chipwhisperer. The register file contains 32 registers (R0-R31), among which 6 registers serve as pointers for indirect 16-bit addressing and have the following aliases: X (R27:26), Y (R29:R28) and Z (R31:R30). Arithmetic instructions take 1 cycle, with the exception of multiplication instructions, which take 2 cycles. Loads and stores from/to SRAM take 2 cycles. Loads from Flash memory take 3 cycles.

Chipwhisperer [46] is a toolbox consisting of open source hardware and software for side-channel analysis of AVR microcontroller software. It provides features for power and electromagnetic (SEMA and DEMA[14]) side-channel analysis, as well as clock and VCC glitching. On the hardware side, there is a capture board with an ADC and a Xilinx Spartan 6 FPGA, for system control and capture, and a target board with ATmega328P and XMega16A4A microcontrollers. Open source software for trace capture and analysis is also provided.

---

[14] Simple and Differential Electromagnetic Analysis, respectively.

B   Algorithms

Algorithm 1. Joye's double-add right-to-left algorithm [29]

Input: Point $P \in E(\mathbb{F}_p)$ and $k = (k_{n-1}, \ldots, k_1, k_0)_2 \in \mathbb{N}$
Output: $Q = [k] \cdot P$
1: $R_0 \leftarrow P_\infty$, $R_1 \leftarrow P$
2: **for** i from 0 to $n - 1$ **do**
3:   $b \leftarrow k_i$
4:   $R_{1-b} \leftarrow 2R_{1-b} + R_b$
5: **end for**
6: **return** R_0

Algorithm 2. Point doubling in mixed homogeneous and extended twisted Edwards coordinates [25]

Input: $P_1 = (X_1, Y_1, Z_1)$ in homogeneous projective coordinates.
Output: $P_3 = 2P_1 = (X_3, Y_3, T_3, Z_3)$ in extended twisted Edwards coordinates.
1: $A \leftarrow X_1^2$; $B \leftarrow Y_1^2$; $C \leftarrow 2Z_1^2$;
2: $D \leftarrow -A$; $E \leftarrow (X_1 + Y_1)^2 - A - B$; $G \leftarrow D + B$
3: $F \leftarrow G - C$; $H \leftarrow D - B$; $X_3 \leftarrow E \cdot F$
4: $Y3 \leftarrow G \cdot H$; $T_3 \leftarrow E \cdot H$; $Z_3 \leftarrow F \cdot G$

Algorithm 3. Point addition in extended twisted Edwards coordinates [25]

Input: $P_1 = (X_1, Y_1, T_1, Z_1)$ and $P_2 = (X_2, Y_2, T_2, Z_2)$ in extended twisted Edwards coordinates;
   constant $k = -2d$, where $d = -121665/121666$.
Output: $P3 = (X_3, Y_3, T_3, Z_3)$ in extended twisted Edwards coordinates.
1: $A \leftarrow (Y_1 - X_1) \cdot (Y_2 - X_2)$; $B \leftarrow (Y_1 + X_1) \cdot (Y_2 + X_2)$; $C \leftarrow k \cdot T_1 \cdot T_2$;
2: $D \leftarrow 2Z_1Z_2$; $E \leftarrow B - A$; $F \leftarrow D - C$;
3: $G \leftarrow D + C$; $H \leftarrow B + A$; $X_3 \leftarrow E \cdot F$;
4: $Y_3 \leftarrow G \cdot H$; $T_3 \leftarrow E \cdot H$; $Z_3 \leftarrow F \cdot G$;

Algorithm 4. Goundar's signed-digit left-to-right algorithm [24]

Input: Point $P \in E(\mathbb{F}_p)$, $k = (k_{n-1}, \ldots, k_1, k_0)_2 \in \mathbb{N}$ with $k_0 = 1$
Output: $Q = [k] \cdot P$
1: $R_0 \leftarrow P$; $R_1 \leftarrow P$
2: **for** i from $n - 1$ to 1 **do**
3:   $t \leftarrow (-1)^{1+k_i}$
4:   $R_0 \leftarrow 2R_0 + (t)R_1$
5: **end for**
6: **return** R_0

Algorithm 5. Constant-time equality test (CCMP) (AVR assembly code)

Input: Registers R_i and R_t.
Output: register R_d is: 1, if $R_i = R_t$; and 0, otherwise.

```
mov   Rd, Ri
sub   Rd, Rt      ; Z (Zero) flag will be 1, if Rd == Rt; and 0, otherwise.
in    Rd, SREG    ; Rd := SREG, SREG is the status register.
andi  Rd, 0x02    ; isolate Z flag.
lsr   Rd          ; Rd = Z
```

Algorithm 6. Flash table lookup protected against address leakage through power

---

Input: table T with dimensions n x m, where n is the number of points and m is the length in words of a point; and *index* is the index of the point. Here, T[i][j] means the value of the word and also the reading of the said word from Flash by the LPM instruction.
Output: m-word array r containing the words of the requested point, i.e, r = T[index][0..$m-1$].

```
1: for j from 0 to m − 1 do
2:     r[j] ← 0
3: end for
4: for i from 0 to n − 1 do
5:     mask ← CCMP(i, index)−1  /* mask = 0, if i = index. Otherwise, mask = 0xff */
6:     for j from 0 to m − 1 do
7:         r[j] ← r[j] ⊕ (T[i][j] ∧ mask)
8:     end for
9: end for
```

Towards Practical Attribute-Based Signatures

Brinda Hampiholi, Gergely Alpár, Fabian van den Broek, and Bart Jacobs

Institute for Computing and Information Sciences,
Radboud University, Nijmegen, The Netherlands
{brinda,gergely,f.vandenbroek,bart}@cs.ru.nl

Abstract. An attribute-based signature (ABS) is a special digital signature created using a dynamic set of issued attributes. For instance, a doctor can sign a medical statement with his name, medical license number and medical speciality. These attributes can be verified along with the signature by any verifier with the correct public keys of the respective attribute issuers. This functionality not only makes ABS a much more flexible alternative to the standard PKI-based signatures, but also offers the ability to create privacy-preserving signatures. However, none of the ABS constructions presented in the literature is practical or easily realizable. In fact, to the best of our knowledge, there is currently no ABS implementation used in practice anywhere. This is why we put forward a new ABS technique based on the IRMA attribute-based authentication. IRMA already has an efficient and practical smart-card implementation, and an experimental smart-phone implementation too. They are currently used in several pilot projects.

In this paper, we propose an ABS scheme based on the existing IRMA technology, extending the currently available IRMA devices with ABS functionality. We study the practical issues that arise due to the introduction of the signature functionality to an existing attribute-based authentication scheme, and we propose possible cryptographic and infrastructural solutions. We also discuss use cases and implementation aspects.

Keywords: attribute-based signature, attribute-based credential, IRMA, authentication, timestamp, contextual privacy.

1 Introduction

Digital signatures are cryptographic primitives that are used by a person to digitally sign a message, thus declaring that he agrees with the message. The digital signature standard based on asymmetric cryptography requires a signer to sign with his private key and the corresponding public key is used for verifying this signature. The public key of the signer stated in the public-key certificate identifies the signer and links all the messages that he ever signed. This type of digital signature does not allow the signer to make the context or role of the signer explicit, and this limits the cases in which the signer can sign under a particular set of attributes and reveal nothing else about himself.

© Springer International Publishing Switzerland 2015
R.S. Chakraborty et al. (Eds.): SPACE 2015, LNCS 9354, pp. 310–328, 2015.
DOI: 10.1007/978-3-319-24126-5_18

In the case of a medical statement signed by a doctor, the doctor's attributes such as his qualification, speciality and license number (for accountability purpose) are necessary along with his signature. With the current public-key infrastructure (PKI) based signature, a doctor has to reveal his full identity, public-key certificate every time he digitally signs a document. This results in the unnecessary (or undesired) disclosure of excess data about the doctor's identity and all his signatures will always be linkable to him irrespective of the context. This violates the principle of data minimization and harms the privacy of the signer.

Furthermore, a PKI-based signature provides the signer identity but the identity itself does not say much about the individual attributes of the signer that are relevant from the perspective of a signature verifier. Such a signature would just state that *"This message is signed by a signer with common name 'Jack' holding public key 'x' as attested in the corresponding public key certificate signed by CA 'y'."*. Considering the above example, the verifier does not know if the message was indeed signed by a doctor whose speciality is orthopaedics; he just knows that the message was signed by Jack holding public key x. This issue can be solved if the signer could sign under a set of attributes (*e.g. 'doctor', 'orthopaedics'*) specified by the verifier's signature policy.

Attribute-based signatures (ABSs) allow a person to sign under a set of selected authentic/certified attributes based on the context. The signature reveals no more than the fact that a signer, with a specific set of attributes satisfying a certain condition, has attested the message. Here, the signature proves that the attributes hold for him at the time of signing and the signature is generated using a secret key associated with the signer. The signature verification will fail if the message was changed after signing, which ensures the integrity of the signed message. In the case of an ABS, non-repudiation of the signer can be achieved by enforcing the disclosure of signer-identifying attributes in the signature policy (*e.g. the attribute to be revealed may be 'is a doctor with medical license number 12345'*). However, when the disclosed attributes are non-identifying such as *'age $\geq$ 18'* or *'is a doctor'*, the verifier cannot link the signed message to the real identity of the signer solely based on the signature, like for group signatures [1]. Some use cases in which privacy of the signer is essential such as anonymous voting, anonymous petitions *etc.*, can thus also benefit from ABSs.

Role-Based Signature Generation with ABSs. A traditional digital signature seems to offer the same signing functionality as an ABS (to a limited extent), if it dedicates one signing key pair for *each* role under which a signer wishes to sign. It means that the signer who is a doctor, for instance, can generate a key pair, get a medical certification authority sign his public key and use the corresponding private key to sign *as a doctor*. Note, however, that he needs to generate another key pair and get the public key certified from the national government to be able to sign his tax declaration form *as a citizen*. Another example is the Belgian PKI-based national eID card, which allows the cardholders to perform digital signature function but always *as a particular Belgian citizen*. In principle, such a card would require n signing keys for n roles that a cardholder might rightfully assume while signing. This gives rise to complicated key management issues. In contrast, an ABS allows the signer to digitally sign messages or documents under different roles with a *single* signing key. Role-based signatures based on ABSs also make the role of the signer explicit to the verifiers thus, avoiding confusion. Consider the two instances when a notary handles the sale of his client's property and the sale of his own private property. With ABSs, he can sign *as a notary* in the former instance and *as the owner of a property* in the latter instance. The difference in the signer's roles is not apparent to the verifiers when the notary signs both sale documents with PKI-based signatures whereas ABS clearly states the role of the signer in each of his signatures. In sum, ABSs are a generalization of role-based signatures with possibly additional privacy guarantees.

Related Work. Attribute-based signatures (ABSs) have been explicitly introduced by Shaniqng and Yingpei [2] rethinking attribute-based encryption. Maji et al. [3] proposed an ABS scheme in which attributes belonging to a user are represented as a *credential bundle*. They employed a non-interactive proof of knowledge system to prove the knowledge of a credential bundle that satisfies a given access formula. Okamoto et al. [4] propose a decentralized multi-authority ABS which supports non-monotone predicates and prove it to be fully secure in the random-oracle model. Herranz et al. [5] propose constant-size ABS schemes for the case of threshold predicates which can also be extended to admit other, more expressive kinds of monotone predicates. All these schemes employ bilinear pairings for their construction, which makes them complicated and less practical. Anada et al. [6] propose an ABS scheme without pairings in the random-oracle model. Their scheme first obtains a generic attribute-based identification (ABID) from a boolean proof system, combines ABID with a credential bundle scheme, and then applies the Fiat-Shamir paradigm to obtain a generic ABS scheme with attribute privacy.

As we see, there has been a certain amount of research done in the ABS field so far. However, the proposed schemes are very theoretical and focus only on the core cryptography. To the best of our knowledge, none of the above schemes is realized and put into practice. Some of these papers such as [3] mention some use cases which could use their ABS construction. Nevertheless, none of them talks about the implementation of their ABS constructions, nor do they discuss the practicalities in realizing attribute-based signatures.

Contributions. IRMA (I Reveal My Attributes)[1] [7] is an attribute-based authentication technology based on the Idemix [8] specification. A distinguishing feature of IRMA is that it has already an efficient and practical smart card implementation [9]. An important observation is that extending IRMA's authentication mechanism to support attribute-based signatures involves relatively little work. This paper explores the way IRMA can be used for generating practical attribute-based signatures. A similar idea is mentioned in an ABC4Trust[2] deliverable [10] where the authors suggest the possibility of including a application-specific message as an optional input to the credential presentation protocol that

---

[1] https://www.irmacard.org
[2] https://abc4trust.eu/

authenticates and signs the message with the user's private key. However, they do not discuss the way to do it in practice, whereas we focus on the *practical set-up*. Also, we suggest that *attribute-based* signatures provide a viable option to current digital signatures.

An attribute-based signature within IRMA is essentially a non-interactive proof of knowledge of authentic attributes (see Section 3). We use the phrase *IRMA signature* to refer to this particular realisation of an attribute-based signature, as opposed to the general concept of attribute-based signatures. Any device that carries the signer's attributes in IRMA is called an *IRMA token*. An IRMA token can be for instance, a smart card or a mobile phone. In this paper, we propose a practical ABS scheme arising from an existing implementation of the IRMA attribute-based authentication. The idea of merging both authentication and signature on the same token enables fast realization and roll-out of the technology.

2   About IRMA

The IRMA project aims to design and develop attribute-based credentials (ABCs) in practice. It is a partial implementation [9] of the Idemix technology [8,11]. Idemix is an attribute-based credential system, developed at IBM Research in Zürich. IRMA currently has implemented the privacy-enhancing features of ABC such as selective disclosure of attributes using zero-knowledge protocols.

The main idea behind IRMA is that authentic attributes stored on a token can be shown selectively via a zero knowledge proof. The token-holder has to give explicit permission to read a specified set of attributes (*e.g.* age, name) by entering a PIN code known only to him. For instance, an IRMA token can be used to prove the possession of a valid concert ticket or valid credentials to enter an office building by just revealing the 'ticket' or 'is an employee' attribute rather than revealing all the attributes on the token. In such cases there is no need to reveal a uniquely identifying attribute and this attribute-based method prevents linking of different proofs and implicit profiling of the token holder.

Attributes & Credentials. An *attribute* is a characteristic or a qualification of a person. Attributes can either be *identifying* or *non-identifying* properties. For example, 'full name', 'address', 'Social Security Number' are identifying attributes as the person can be uniquely identified by such attributes. Attributes, such as 'student' and 'age over 18' are non-identifying attributes as they do not uniquely identify a person; such properties can belong to other people as well. Collectively, these attributes can constitute the identity of a person.

Attributes are authentic. In the IRMA set-up, several related attributes are grouped into a cryptographic container known as a *credential* [7]. Authorities issue credentials to users following an authentication process. Each credential has an expiry date that denotes the validity of all the attributes contained in that credential. There could be n such credentials on the IRMA token issued by n issuers. However, for reasons of simplicity, in this paper, we consider all attributes to be contained in a single credential.

Cryptographic Background of IRMA. IRMA is based on the Idemix protocol suite [8,11] and Camenisch-Lysyanskaya (CL) signature scheme [12,13]. All the zero-knowledge (ZK) proofs in the Idemix library are implemented as non-interactive ZK proofs using the Fiat-Shamir heuristic [14]. A brief description of Schnorr's schemes and the CL signature are provided in Appendix A and B.

3   IRMA's Selective Disclosure Proofs as Digital Signatures

The concept of revealing only a selection of necessary attributes for completing a transaction is termed as *Selective Disclosure* in Idemix and IRMA. Selective disclosure is a zero-knowledge protocol currently used for authentication purposes. But, as will be shown here, it can also be used by an IRMA token holder for signing under selected attributes. When a selective disclosure (SD) proof is used for signing purposes, it becomes an *IRMA signature*. The key idea is that a *non-interactive zero-knowledge (NIZK) proof* (or so-called signature of knowledge) [14,15] signs a message. See Section A in the appendix for the description of the way a NIZK proof is constructed.

During an IRMA authentication, the verifier sends a nonce to the IRMA token to be included in the SD proof generation. This nonce is strongly bound to the proof and it helps the verifier check the freshness of the proof. It is meant to prevent a user from replaying the same proof to authenticate during different authentication sessions. We adapt this approach in a simple manner: If the hash of a message is used during an SD proof generation instead of the nonce, then the SD proof becomes the user's signature on the message. So, the main functional difference between an SD proof in IRMA authentication and IRMA signatures is the way the *nonce* is defined.

An SD proof acting as a user's signature is written as

$$SD\big((a_i)_{i \in D}; h(msg)\big),$$

where a_i is an attribute within a credential, D is the set of disclosed attributes, and $h(msg)$ is the hash of the message to be signed. Typically, an SD proof that becomes an IRMA signature proves the signer's possession of attributes and of the secret key involved in the proof generation. As this SD proof is a non-interactive zero-knowledge proof, first, the signer commits to a set of attributes and creates a commitment[3]; then he computes a challenge by hashing the commitment and the message to be signed. Conceptually, the challenge computation is denoted as

$$challenge = \mathcal{H}(commitment, h(msg)). \tag{1}$$

We input the hash $h(msg)$ of the message instead of the message itself to the hash function $\mathcal{H}$ that computes the challenge. This double hashing of the input

---

[3] As described in Appendix C, in a selective disclosure proof a commitment comprises an attribute issuer's randomized signature A' and the derived value $\tilde{Z}$.

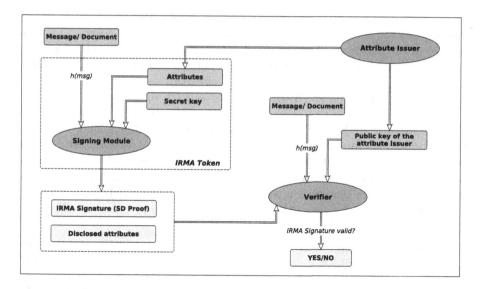

Fig. 1. IRMA signature generation and verification

might seem unnecessary. However, we intend as little change in existing IRMA authentication tokens as possible, and they expect a fixed-length nonce as the input to the selective disclosure proof. The hashes of messages are of fixed length, so they are functionally interchangeable with nonces. Also, computing the hash of a long message can be delegated to an external, more resourceful device from an IRMA token whose computational power and memory are limited. Here $\mathcal{H}$ and h can technically use the same hash algorithm *e.g.* SHA-3. The hash of a message or a document to be signed is denoted by '$h(msg)$' and the hash function to compute challenge in the non-interactive SD proof is denoted by '$\mathcal{H}$' throughout this paper.

3.1 IRMA Signature Scheme

The IRMA signature scheme depicted in Figure 1, consists of four algorithms: *Key Generation, Attribute Issuance, Signature Generation, Signature Verification.*

(1) *Key Generation.* Upon initialisation of an IRMA token, a secret key is generated and stored securely. It is used during attribute issuance, authentication and in signing. Since all these functions require this secret key, they are bound to the token, and hence to the signer.

(2) *Attribute Issuance.* An IRMA token owner can obtain attributes from authorized attribute issuers. An attribute issuer signs the credential containing attributes with its private signing key; the corresponding public key is used by verifiers, both in authentication and in signature verification.

(3) *Signature Generation.* A selection of the signer's attributes on an IRMA token forms the internal input to the signing module on the token. The hash $h(msg)$ of the message to be signed forms the external input. The IRMA token outputs the required attributes and an SD proof ensuring that "the token owner has signed $h(msg)$ and possesses the attributes say, a_1 and a_2 issued by the issuer". A credential[4] on an IRMA token carries a CL signature (see Section B) which is randomized during a selective disclosure. We preserve the randomization of CL signature in IRMA signatures to ensure unlinkability among signature verifications. This randomization happens within the IRMA token. We also use the randomized CL signature to get trusted timestamps for the IRMA signature, as will be discussed in Section 4.1. Using the randomized CL signature, a signer generates an IRMA signature, a selective disclosure proof $SD((a_i)_{i \in D}; h(msg))$ over $h(msg)$. The operations that have to be performed to generate a SD proof are described in Algorithm 1 in Section C.

(4) *Signature Verification.* Any verifier who wants to verify the signature on $h(msg)$ needs to have the public key of the issuer that has issued the relevant attributes to the IRMA token. The verifier calculates the hash of the message and uses it along with the issuer's public key parameters for verification. The verification steps are given in Algorithm 2 in Section C. During this verification, the verifier checks that the message was signed by an IRMA token holder who possesses the required attributes issued by an authorized issuer.

Privacy and Security Assurances Provided by IRMA Signatures. In terms of privacy, there are no public parameters of the IRMA token that act as an identifier of the token or token holder. Thus, it is impossible for the verifier to identify or link signatures to a particular signer if the disclosed attributes are non-identifying. This holds even if the signer signs the same document multiple times. In terms of security, IRMA signatures guarantee integrity and authenticity, more specifically:

- The message is not altered after signing.
- The attributes and the secret key are bound to the issuance and the signature.

3.2   Diversification between SD Proofs Used for Authentication and Signatures

Our goal is to use both the signature and authentication functions with the same set of attributes on the same IRMA token. An SD proof is used either for authentication with a fresh nonce or for signature generation with the hash of a message as input. As we already have an implementation of IRMA SD proofs for authentication, IRMA signatures can be easily realized in practice. Additionally, it is user friendly to have both attribute-based authentication and signature functions on the same token, along with an interactive user interface. We are well aware of the fact that, as the hash of a message and a random nonce

---

[4] A credential is conceptually comparable with a public-key certificate. But unlike a certificate, a credential is randomizable and enables selective disclosure.

look alike, an adversary could possibly send the hash of a message posing as a random nonce during an authentication session and make the user unknowingly sign this hash with the selective disclosure proof. This is a potential attack scenario in which an authentication session is misused to get a signature of the user without the user being aware of it. In this section, we propose a method to diversify signature and authentication protocol runs, in order to prevent the afore-mentioned attack.

Although two secret keys could be used for authentication and signing to separate the two functionalities on the token, all the user credentials would then have to be issued twice on that token as well, corresponding to both secret keys. This is because the secret key is associated with the issuance of every attribute to the IRMA token. Then, using two dedicated keys would be very similar to having authentication and signature functions on two different IRMA tokens. This contradicts our original goal. In order to avoid the duplication of all attributes on the token for authentication and signing purposes, we intend to use the *same secret key* for both purposes.

Domain separation is an efficient means to construct different function instances from a single underlying function. If the underlying function is secure, the derived functions can be considered as independent functions [16]. One can implement domain separation by appending or prepending different constants to the input for each of the function instances. We propose to apply *domain separation* for securely diversifying IRMA authentication and signing instances. We reserve a few bits, called *Dbit*, as the first input to the hash function while computing the challenge (see Line 11 in Algorithm 1) on the signer's end. Mathematically, the *Dbit* value is prepended to the rest of the inputs and indicates if the IRMA token is being used for authentication or for signing. In the current context, we need to separate two domains so we can use a single bit in *Dbit*. This bit will be set to 0 in case of authentication and 1 in case of signatures. We can program the signature generation module such that it takes user consent as the basis while deciding the value of *Dbit*. If the user gives his consent to sign a message *msg*, then the signature generation module (Algorithm 1) sets the *Dbit* to 1 and expects $h(msg)$ as one of the other inputs to the challenge computation. Thus, we rely on a correct token implementation.

The challenge computation during an IRMA signature generation previously denoted by (1) now becomes,

$$c = \mathcal{H}(Dbit = 1, commitment, h(msg)), \qquad (2)$$

where c is the challenge, $\mathcal{H}$ is the hash function used to compute the challenge and $h(msg)$ is the hash function used to hash the message to be signed. If a valid signature is knowingly created by the legitimate signer, then during the verification, a verifier can successfully check its validity by reconstructing the challenge with $Dbit = 1$.

3.3   Brief Security Analysis of IRMA Signatures

In this section, we informally analyze the security of our IRMA signature system by considering the possible ways in which an attacker can undermine the system. We assume that the attacker has access to a polynomially bounded set of IRMA authentication transcripts denoted by AT and signature-message pairs denoted by SM. In the original IRMA authentication scenario, the attacker tries to spoof an authentication using the transcripts from the set AT. This is proven to be impossible in the paper by Camenisch *et al.* [12]. When we introduce IRMA signatures, three more possibilities arise for the attacker to undermine our system:

1. spoof an IRMA authentication by using the signatures from SM;
2. forge a new IRMA signature using the authentication transcripts from AT;
3. forge a new IRMA signature using the signature-message pairs from SM.

Case 1: Using IRMA Signatures to Impersonate a User during Authentication. An attacker attempts to authenticate with one of the IRMA signatures from SM. We show that this is possible if he successfully finds either of the following two collisions. We also mention how we deal with such scenarios.

(i) Collision between the hash of a signed message and an authentication nonce.

$$h(msg) = nonce$$

where $h(msg)$ is the hash of a signed message msg from SM and $nonce$ is a random number sent by the verifier during an authentication session. The attacker can impersonate a user and maliciously authenticate if he finds a collision between the hash of the signed message that he already had and the nonce belonging to an authentication session.

However, because of the domain separation (see Section 3.2), the attacker cannot make the verifier accept this signature as a valid authentication proof.

(ii) Collision between the hash functions used for computing challenge in signature and authentication instances.

$$\mathcal{H}(Dbit = 1, commitment, h(msg)) = \mathcal{H}(Dbit = 0, commitment, nonce)$$

where $\mathcal{H}$ is the hash function used for computing the challenge within an SD proof. The inputs for $\mathcal{H}$ during the signature verification are $Dbit = 1$ and hash of a message $h(msg)$ whereas the inputs are $Dbit = 0$ and $nonce$ for an authentication proof verification. The attack succeeds if the attacker finds a collision between these two $\mathcal{H}$ instances. This is equivalent to having the same challenge results from the hash functions in authentication and signature sessions in spite of different inputs. If the attacker manages to find the above collision then he wins; he can then authenticate with a signature. We note that the attacker's chances of winning in this scenario depends on the collision resistance of the hash function being used in IRMA. If hash functions with no known collision attacks such as SHA-2 or SHA-3 is used then the above attack is highly improbable.

Case 2: Using IRMA Authentication Transcripts to Forge a new IRMA Signature. An attacker eavesdrops on many IRMA authentication sessions and collects authentication transcripts as denoted by AT at the beginning of this section. Then he tries to forge an IRMA signature out of an authentication transcript in the set AT. He is successful if he finds a collision in the two scenarios detailed in Case 1 and the same logic is followed here.

Case 3: Using IRMA Signature-Message Pairs to Forge a New IRMA Signature. As we said before, the attacker possesses IRMA signatures for several messages of a user. In this case, the domain separation bit $Dbit$ is 1 for all signatures that the attacker already has. It is not sufficient if the adversary manages to find a hash collision between a previously signed message and a new message to create a valid signature; the attacker will also have to possess the right attributes of the user on his IRMA token to forge that user's signature. The security assumptions underlying the IRMA technology (same as the assumptions made by Idemix) prevent such forgery attacks. These assumptions are briefly mentioned below.

- As IRMA uses the Camenisch-Lysyanskaya (CL) signature scheme (see Section B for explanation), respective discrete logarithms based proofs prove the possession of valid attributes on the IRMA token.
- Unforgeability of IRMA signatures holds under the strong RSA assumption and the computational Diffie-Hellman assumption.
- In IRMA, a single proof involving all the attributes required by the signing policy, secret key of the IRMA token is considered as a valid signature. So, colluding users cannot combine their attributes associated with their secret keys in a single proof. This guarantees collusion resistance.

So we conclude that the adversary will not succeed in forging a new and valid IRMA signature with the help of given signature-message pairs, even if those pairs are of adversary's choice. Thus, an IRMA signature is *existentially unforgeable* under a chosen-message attack.

4 Infrastructural Concerns for IRMA Signatures

4.1 Timestamps in IRMA Signatures

A practical aspect that becomes important when we migrate from authentication to signature functionality is the actual time of signing. A timestamp on the digital signature attests when the message or the document was signed. It provides a unequivocal proof that the contents of the signed document existed at a point-in-time and have not changed since then.

In the case of IRMA signatures, there are two kinds of dates or timestamps to be considered:

1. date and time at which the signature was generated,
2. expiry dates of the attributes under which the signer has signed $h(msg)$.

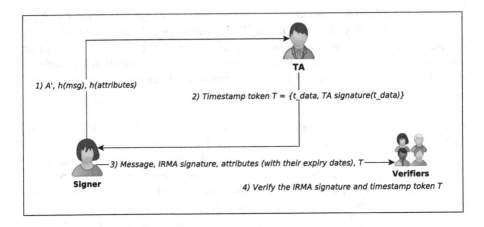

Fig. 2. Timestamping the IRMA signature

To include the time of signing, a signer has two options: The signer can use the local time of his IRMA token (if available) as part of the message to be signed. If a verifier requires a more secure timestamp, the signer can obtain an authorized timestamp signed by a Timestamp Authority (TA). A TA is an entity that is trusted to provide accurate time information.

The selective disclosure proof in IRMA discloses the expiry dates of the attributes involved in the proof by default. These expiry dates are included in the set of disclosed attributes and they can easily be verified by the verifier. Since attributes should be valid when generating an IRMA signature, the expiry dates should be greater than the time included in the timestamp. Therefore, it is recommended to include a validity check at the beginning of an SD proof generation algorithm (see Algorithm 1 in the Appendix).

We propose a timestamping scheme that enables a signer to get a signed timestamp from a TA for an IRMA signature as shown in Figure 2. In our scheme, a signer sends a timestamp request to the TA to get a trusted timestamp. The timestamp request consists of randomized CL signature[5], hash of the message to be signed and hash of the attributes, denoted by A', $h(msg)$ and $h(attributes)$ respectively. This request does not reveal any information about the signer or the message to the TA, hence, it is privacy friendly. TA issues a signed timestamp. Upon receiving the timestamp, the signer inputs the timestamp to the IRMA signature generation. The timestamping scheme is illustrated in Figure 2 and elaborated in the following steps:

1. *Timestamp request.* The signer requests TA for a timestamp by sending $A', h(msg), h(attributes)$.
2. *Timestamp token calculation.* TA does the following:

---

[5] The randomized CL signature is used in both IRMA signature generation and verification (see Algorithms 1 and 2).

- concatenates all the data sent by the signer in the timestamp request with the current timestamp t and digitally signs t_data.
- combines t_data and TA's signature on t_data together into a *timestamp token* T and sends T to the signer.

3. *IRMA signature generation with the timestamp token.* The signer provides the timestamp token T as one of the inputs to the IRMA signature generation algorithm (see Algorithm 1). Now, during the challenge computation, T is hashed along with the diversifier $Dbit$, commitment and $h(msg)$ as,

$$c = \mathcal{H}(Dbit = 1, commitment, h(msg), T). \qquad (3)$$

Finally, the signer sends the IRMA signature on $h(msg)$, T, and the disclosed attributes to the verifier.

4. *IRMA signature with timestamp verification.* Upon receiving the IRMA signature, the verifier verifies
   - the IRMA signature using the attribute issuer's public key and the disclosed attributes,
   - the TA's signature on t_data within the timestamp token T by using the TA's public key,
   - if A', $h(msg)$, *attributes* are the same in the IRMA signature and t_data that is within the timestamp token T.

As we see, an IRMA signature comprises multiple logical layers. Table 1 summarizes the three signatures that have to be verified during an *IRMA signature with timestamp* verification.

Table 1. Abstraction of signature layers involved in IRMA signatures.

Signature	Public key used to verify	Signing party
Attribute-based signature	Disclosed attributes & issuer's signature	Signer
Randomized CL signature	Attribute issuer's public key	Attribute issuer
DSA or RSA signature	TA's public key	TA

Because of the verifications performed in the above step 4 (IRMA signature with timestamp verification), a verifier knows/or has cryptographic assurance of the following properties.

- The IRMA signature was not generated before the time indicated by the TA's timestamp t.
- The signature on the message with the enclosed attributes is bound to this timestamp t.
- The message that is signed has remained unchanged since the time t.

In addition, the implementation guarantees that the signer's attributes used for signing were valid at time t, since this is checked in Algorithm 1.

4.2   Revocation of Credentials in IRMA

The IRMA project has been focused on preserving user-privacy in authentication. The revocation scheme [17] for IRMA authentication that has been proposed by the IRMA design team avoids identifiers in revocation that would enable linking the revocation checks to a single user. This scheme involves a semi-trusted party in the system, a *Revocation Authority (RA)* that is responsible for revoking the credentials. The RA keeps track of the revocation values of revoked credentials.

In the existing IRMA-revocation scheme [17] the time is split into epochs (time intervals) and the RA chooses a generator for each epoch and each verifier. When a credential is revoked the RA makes a global revocation list RL that consists of revocation tokens $R_{i_1..n}$ that are computed from the generators and the individual revocation values of the credential holders. The RA sends this revocation list RL to all the registered verifiers. During an authentication with a revocation check, the verifier sends the IRMA token its specific per-epoch generator, and the token calculates the revocation response R by embedding its token-specific revocation values. This value R is generated along with the selective disclosure proof and made available to the verifier. The verifier can just check $R \in RL$ to know if the credential used in the generation of the selective disclosure proof is revoked or not.

However, in the case of signatures, a signer need not know the verifiers in advance, so, the verifier-specific generators would not work. Also, the per-epoch concept will have to be modified to suit the signature verification scenario. If the signer calculates a revocation token for the current epoch along with the signature, the verifier has to do a revocation check in that epoch. In the case of a delayed verification in a different epoch, the verifier will have to retrieve the revocation token list from the RA corresponding to the epoch in which the signer signed. We realize that the design of a privacy-friendly revocation scheme for digital signatures that ensures complete unlinkability is not trivial. The existing revocation scheme for IRMA authentication has to be adapted to IRMA signatures which is subject to further research.

As a possible solution for revocation, attribute expiry dates can be short and re-issuing of attributes can be made simple. If a security breach or a key compromise is detected then the attribute issuer would just stop re-issuing the attributes to that particular IRMA token.

5   Discussion

We briefly describe a few use cases for attribute-based IRMA signatures, and give an estimate of their performance.

5.1   Use Case Scenarios

Use cases requiring the flexibility offered of *role-based* IRMA signatures.

1. In the introduction we briefly mentioned a medical doctor signing a medical statement about a patient using his own medical license number and specialisation attributes. This can be applied to many professionals signing documents in which their competence is a useful part of the signature. More generally, this leads to what may be called *role-based* signatures.
2. With such role-based signatures one can distinguish professional and personal signatures. For instance, the signature of a notary should be different when he is selling a house professionally or privately. Attribute-based signatures are ideally suited for making such differences explicit, for all verifiers to see.

Use cases for signatures that ensure signer *privacy/anonymity*.

3. *Anonymous voting.* In large scale elections, there are usually two main phases: (i) registration and (ii) vote casting. A crucial difference between these two phases is that the first one should be identifying, whereas the second one should not.

   During the registration phase, a potential voter can authenticate to a voting authority in a properly identifying manner, *e.g.* via his citizen registration number. This identity is needed to check if the person at hand is eligible to vote.

   If the check is successful, then the voting authority can blindly issue a random 'voting ID' attribute (via blind signatures) to his IRMA token. During the election phase, this voter can sign his vote with his IRMA token under his 'voting ID' attribute. The (random) voting IDs of all the voters are stored and if any voter tries to vote for the second time, then the voter ID matches with one of the previously stored voter IDs. This second vote can either be discarded or it can replace the first vote based on the voting authority's policy decision. Thus, we can keep the voters anonymous and also avoid double voting scenario by using IRMA signatures. Here we note that a potential voter can use the same IRMA token for authenticating during registration and for signing anonymously during the vote casting phase.
4. *Anonymous petitions* is another application similar to the anonymous voting that can benefit from IRMA signatures.
5. IRMA signatures can also be used by confidential sources who want to keep themselves unidentified to a journalist to whom they reveal information. But still they can include some relevant attributes in the signatures on their statements, in order to provide credibility.

5.2   Estimating the Efficiency of IRMA Signatures

As we have described in Section 3, a selective disclosure proof can serve both authentication and signing purposes. The applied method depends on the input values given to the proof generation algorithm. Thus, the performance times of an IRMA authentication and an IRMA signature are comparable. We use the performance results obtained and documented in the Idemix chapter of Pim

Vuller's PhD thesis [18] as a starting point for our estimation. Based on these values we assess the execution time of the IRMA signature generation and verification instances. The smart card type used in this calculation is an Infineon SLE78 chip with MULTOS platform (ML3-36K-R1). In IRMA, a typical credential consists of 5 attributes. For estimating the running time of a selective disclosure proof, we consider two cases. Disclosing one attribute takes 1.2 seconds, while disclosing four attributes takes 0.93 seconds. Note that the more attributes are disclosed, the fewer are hidden and the shorter time it takes. Furthermore, we also note that in practice the fifth attribute, the secret key, is never revealed.

Now let us turn from IRMA authentication to *IRMA signatures*. The total time taken for an entire signature generation operation is the sum of a selective disclosure proof and other minor operations like timestamp retrieval, denoted by δ. The value of δ is dependent on the network connection speed as the timestamp request and retrieval takes place online. Therefore, the total execution time for an IRMA signature generation (in the case when only 1 out of 4 attributes from a credential is disclosed) can be estimated as *(1.2 + δ) seconds*.

The signature verification consists of an extra modular exponentiation operation w.r.t. the signature (SD proof) generation. Thus, we expect that the time taken for SD proof verification is a bit more than the time taken for its generation. However, the signature verification terminals (*e.g.* personal computers) are usually computationally more powerful in terms of both time and memory than a smart card. So the time taken to verify an SD proof is mostly in the order of a *few milliseconds*.

We see that IRMA signature generation on smart cards is reasonably efficient in terms of execution time to be put into practice. The execution time could be further decreased if mobile phones are used as IRMA tokens for generating IRMA signatures.

6   Concluding Remarks

We present the first practical and easily realizable form of attribute-based signatures by building on top of the IRMA technology. What we call IRMA signatures are created by extending the existing smart card (and phone) implementation of IRMA authentication. We show how we can securely use authentication and signature functions on a single IRMA token using the same secret key. In addition we elaborate on the infrastructural aspects related to usable digital signatures such as secure timestamping. There is ongoing work in adapting the existing revocation scheme for attribute-based signatures without forgoing any of its privacy and unlinkability guarantees.

In conclusion, IRMA signatures offer much greater functionality and flexibility than traditional PKI-based digital signatures in terms of role-based signing, contextual privacy guarantees to the signers, and ease of comprehending the signature semantics to the verifiers.

References

1. Chaum, D., van Heyst, E.: Group signatures. In: Davies, D.W. (ed.) EUROCRYPT 1991. LNCS, vol. 547, pp. 257–265. Springer, Heidelberg (1991)
2. Shaniqng, G., Yingpei, Z.: Attribute-based signature scheme. In: Information Security and Assurance, ISA 2008, pp. 509–511. IEEE (2008)
3. Maji, H.K., Prabhakaran, M., Rosulek, M.: Attribute-based signatures. In: Kiayias, A. (ed.) CT-RSA 2011. LNCS, vol. 6558, pp. 376–392. Springer, Heidelberg (2011)
4. Okamoto, T., Takashima, K.: Efficient attribute-based signatures for non-monotone predicates in the standard model. In: Catalano, D., Fazio, N., Gennaro, R., Nicolosi, A. (eds.) PKC 2011. LNCS, vol. 6571, pp. 35–52. Springer, Heidelberg (2011)
5. Herranz, J., Laguillaumie, F., Libert, B., Ràfols, C.: Short attribute-based signatures for threshold predicates. In: Dunkelman, O. (ed.) CT-RSA 2012. LNCS, vol. 7178, pp. 51–67. Springer, Heidelberg (2012)
6. Anada, H., Arita, S., Sakurai, K.: Attribute-based signatures without pairings via the fiat-shamir paradigm. In: Proceedings of the 2nd ACM Workshop on ASIA Public-Key Cryptography, pp. 49–58. ACM (2014)
7. Alpár, G., Jacobs, B.: Credential design in attribute-based identity management. In: Bridging distances in Technology and Regulation, 3rd TILTing Perspectives Conference, pp. 189–204 (2013)
8. IBM Research, Security Team. Specification of the Identity Mixer Cryptographic Library, version 2.3.4. Technical report, IBM Research, Zürich (February 2012)
9. Vullers, P., Alpár, G.: Efficient selective disclosure on smart cards using idemix. In: Fischer-Hübner, S., de Leeuw, E., Mitchell, C. (eds.) IDMAN 2013. IFIP AICT, vol. 396, pp. 53–67. Springer, Heidelberg (2013)
10. Camenisch, J., Krontiris, I., Lehmann, A., Neven, G., Paquin, C., Rannenberg, K., Zwingelberg, H.: D2. 1 architecture for attribute-based credential technologies–version 1. ABC4Trust Deliverable D 2 (2011)
11. Camenisch, J., Herreweghen, E.V.: Design and implementation of the idemix anonymous credential system. In: Proceedings of the 9th ACM Conference on Computer and Communications Security, pp. 21–30. ACM (2002)
12. Camenisch, J.L., Lysyanskaya, A.: An Efficient System for Non-transferable Anonymous Credentials with Optional Anonymity Revocation. In: Pfitzmann, B. (ed.) EUROCRYPT 2001. LNCS, vol. 2045, pp. 93–118. Springer, Heidelberg (2001)
13. Camenisch, J.L., Lysyanskaya, A.: A Signature Scheme with Efficient Protocols. In: Cimato, S., Galdi, C., Persiano, G. (eds.) SCN 2002. LNCS, vol. 2576, pp. 268–289. Springer, Heidelberg (2003)
14. Fiat, A., Shamir, A.: How to prove yourself: Practical solutions to identification and signature problems. In: Odlyzko, A.M. (ed.) CRYPTO 1986. LNCS, vol. 263, pp. 186–194. Springer, Heidelberg (1987)
15. Schnorr, C.-P.: Efficient signature generation by smart cards. Journal of Cryptology 4(3), 161–174 (1991)
16. Keccak team. Note on keccak parameters and usage. http://keccak.noekeon.org/NoteOnKeccakParametersAndUsage.pdf (accessed July 6, 2015)
17. Lueks, W., Alpár, G., Hoepman, J.- H., Vullers, P.: Fast revocation of attribute-based credentials for both users and verifiers. In: Federrath, H., Gollmann, D. (eds.) SEC 2015. IFIP AICT, vol. 455, pp. 463–478. Springer, Heidelberg (2015)
18. Vullers, P.: Efficient Implementations of Attribute-based Credentials on Smart Cards. PhD thesis, Radboud University Nijmegen, The Netherlands (2014)

A   Schnorr's Identification Scheme

Schnorr's identification scheme [15] is a simple three-way zero-knowledge proof scheme which proves the knowledge of a discrete logarithm x of a specific number y (mod n):

$$PK\{(x) : y = g^x \pmod{n}\}$$

where PK is the proof of knowledge, x is the discrete logarithm of y and g is the generator belonging to the cyclic group G_q of order q.

In order to prove knowledge of $x = \log_g y$, the prover interacts with the verifier as follows:

1. The prover commits to randomness $r \in [0, q-1]$; therefore, the first message $t = g^r \in G_q$ is also called a commitment.
2. The verifier replies with a challenge $c \in [0, q-1]$ chosen at random. (In practice, c can be chosen from a smaller set – depending on the security parameter –, but here we omit these details.)
3. After receiving c, the prover sends the third and last message (the response) $s = r + cx \pmod{q}$.

The verifier accepts, if $g^s = ty^c$ in G_q.

The security of Schnorr's identification scheme relies on the hardness of the discrete logarithm problem. In the interactive proof, the verifier can be sure in the last step that the prover knows the discrete logarithm of y if it satisfies the correctness condition:

$$g^s = g^{r+cx} = g^r g^{cx} = t(g^x)^c = ty^c.$$

Applying the Fiat–Shamir heuristic [14], one can achieve a non-interactive scheme which reduces the number of rounds of information exchange between the prover and the verifier. This is often used to translate a zero-knowledge protocol into a signature scheme, or to reduce the communication overhead of the interactive protocols. To make a zero-knowledge protocol non-interactive the challenge c is not retrieved from the verifier but computed as

$$c = Hash(msg, t),$$

where msg is the message to be signed and t is the commitment. The Idemix technology uses similar non-interactive proofs of knowledge.

B   Camenisch-Lysyanskaya (CL) Signature

Camenisch *et al.* propose a provably secure signature scheme for issuing a signature on a set of attributes and proving the knowledge of those attributes [13]. The resulting signature from their scheme is termed as *CL signature* and it is used as a building block for IRMA. We briefly explain the structure of a CL signature in this section.

Let us consider the safe primes p and q as the signer's private keys. The signer randomly selects $a, b, c \in QR_n$. Then a, b, c are published as public keys. If a message m is to be signed, a random number v and a prime number e are chosen and the signature is computed as shown below:

$$A \equiv (a^m b^v c)^{e^{-1} \bmod |QR_n|} \pmod{n}.$$

Since we know the values of p and q and they are safe primes, we also know p' and q' and $|QR_n| = p'q'$. The CL signature over the message m is composed as

$$m : \{A, e, v\}$$

In the IRMA context, we can define the Camenisch-Lysyanskaya signature over the messages m as the triplet (A, e, v) such that e is the random prime used as the ephemeral RSA public key for this signature and v is a random number and A is the RSA signature over the message m. The following check is done in order to verify the correctness of the above CL signature:

$$A^e \equiv a^m b^v c \pmod{n}$$

If the verification equation holds, the signature is valid; otherwise, the signature is invalid. The CL signature described here can also be applied over a block of messages. The unforgeability of the CL signature scheme relies on the *Strong-RSA assumption*.

A CL-signature (A, e, v) can be randomized easily. First, one has to select a random value r from a specific, large interval, then, one performs the following computation:.

$$A' := A \cdot b^r \pmod{n}, \qquad v' := v + er.$$

Indeed, (A', e, v') is also a valid signature over message m:

$$A'^e \cdot b^{-v'} \equiv (A \cdot b^r)^e \cdot b^{-v-er} \equiv A^e \cdot b^{er} \cdot b^{-v} \cdot b^{-er} \equiv A^e \cdot b^{-v} \equiv a^m c \pmod{n}.$$

C   IRMA Signature and Verification Algorithms

In this section, we provide the technical details and algorithms used for the IRMA signature generation and verification. As we have described earlier in Section 3.1, a signer signs a message under a set of attributes with his secret key and a verifier uses the attribute issuer's public key to verify this IRMA signature. The public key of the attribute issuer is $(n, S, Z, \{R_i\}_{i \in M})$ where M denotes the set of attribute indices, and hence the maximum number of attributes issued by that issuer. In IRMA selective disclosure, D denotes the set of attributes to be disclosed from the IRMA token to the verifier and H denotes the set of attributes on the token that needs to be hidden from the verifier. Therefore, H and D are disjoint sets of attributes: $H \cup D = M$ and $H \cap D = \emptyset$.

Algorithm 1 describes the operations that have to be performed to generate a proof of knowledge of the secret key and the hidden attributes. The proof

328 B. Hampiholi et al.

Algorithm 1. IRMA signature generation algorithm.

1: **function** IRMA-SIGN($\{a_i\}_{i \in D}, \{a_i\}_{i \in H}, (A', e, v'), h(msg), (n, S, Z, \{R_i\}_{i \in M}), T$)

2:     **for all** $i \in D$ **do**

3:         Verify the validity of each a_i w.r.t. timestamp in T

4:         **if** *invalid* **then** EXIT

5:     $\tilde{e} \leftarrow$ RANDOM( )

6:     $\tilde{v} \leftarrow$ RANDOM( )

7:     $\tilde{Z} \leftarrow A'^{\tilde{e}} \cdot S^{\tilde{v}} \mod n$

8:     **for all** $i \in H$ **do**

9:         $\tilde{a}_i \leftarrow$ RANDOM( )

10:        $\tilde{Z} \leftarrow \tilde{Z} \cdot R_i^{\tilde{a}_i} \mod n$

11:     $c \leftarrow$ HASH($Dbit, A', \tilde{Z}, h(msg), T$)   //compute challenge using commitment, $h(msg)$, timestamp

12:     $\hat{e} \leftarrow \tilde{e} + c \cdot e$

13:     $\hat{v} \leftarrow \tilde{v} + c \cdot v'$

14:     **for all** $i \in H$ **do**

15:        $\hat{a}_i \leftarrow \tilde{a}_i + c \cdot a_i$

       return $(c, A', \hat{e}, \hat{v}, \{\hat{a}_i\}_{i \in H}, T)$

Algorithm 2. IRMA signature verification algorithm.

1: **function** IRMA-VERIFY($(c, A', \hat{e}, \hat{v}, \{\hat{a}_i\}_{i \in H}, \{a_i\}_{i \in D}), h(msg), (n, S, Z, \{R_i\}_{i \in M}, T)$)

2:     $\hat{Z} \leftarrow Z^{-c} \cdot A'^{\hat{e}} \cdot S^{\hat{v}} \mod n$

3:     **for all** $i \in D$ **do**

4:        $\hat{Z} \leftarrow \hat{Z} \cdot R_i^{c \cdot a_i} \mod n$

5:     **for all** $i \in H$ **do**

6:        $\hat{Z} \leftarrow \hat{Z} \cdot R_i^{\hat{a}_i} \mod n$

7:     **if** $c \neq$ HASH($Dbit, A', \hat{Z}, h(msg), T$) **then return** INVALID
    return VALID

---

proves the remaining attributes $\{a_i\}_{i \in H}$, that are hidden during this phase, are known by the signer (i.e. token). In the case of IRMA signature generation, Algorithm 1 takes hash the of message to be signed, denoted by $h(msg)$ and timestamp, denoted by T as inputs while computing the challenge c. The IRMA signature is essentially a selective disclosure proof that is generated over $h(msg)$ and T. This signature can then be verified using the Algorithm 2.

Hierarchical Ring Signatures Revisited – Unconditionally and Perfectly Anonymous Schnorr Version*

Łukasz Krzywiecki, Małgorzata Sulkowska, and Filip Zagórski

Wrocław University of Technology
lukasz.krzywiecki@pwr.wroc.pl

Abstract. We propose a ring signature scheme that creates short signatures for large rings. The scheme allows signers to reuse previously created signatures to enlarge the ring size without expanding the size of signature itself. The relation between signatures is a tree structure in which each signature is a node built upon its predecessors. The set of potential signers of a node grows exponentially with the tree height while the size of the signature may remain even constant. We give the specific example of the scheme built on the top of Schnorr ring signatures. We prove its unconditional anonymity and unforgeability in ROM.

Keywords: short ring signature, anonymity, hierarchical construction, tree.

1 Introduction

Ring signatures are used to sign messages in such a way that the identity of the signer remains hidden in some group of people, called a ring. Intuitively, the bigger the ring is, the better *anonymity* for the signer it provides. Commonly, the anonymity is defined in such a way that the probability of indicating the real signer in the *anonymous* ring equals $1/ring\_size$. However, usually one pays for the better anonymity by the larger size of the resulting ring signature. In many considered models the length of the ring signature is proportional to the cardinality of the set of potential signers. In this paper we focus on the aspect of the dependency of the signature's size and the size of the signature's ring. It seems that in a dynamic scenario where the ring membership changes rapidly the linear size of the ring cannot be omitted, since it is necessary to define the ring by specifying (enumerating) its members. Therefore majority of ring signature constructions are of linear size in the ring cardinality. However, there are situations where several signatures could be issued on behalf of the once previously specified ring, which can be distinguished by a short identifier. For these scenarios ring signature constructions of sub-linear size were proposed in [8] and [5].

---

* This research has been partially supported by Polish National Science Centre contract number DEC-2013/09/D/ST6/03927.

R.S. Chakraborty et al. (Eds.): SPACE 2015, LNCS 9354, pp. 329–346, 2015.
DOI: 10.1007/978-3-319-24126-5_19

Our approach is different. First of all we still want to achieve the sub-linear ring size but similarly we require also small (sub-linear) computational complexity of the signature creation. Moreover we prefer a clear modular construction instead of a dedicated and sometimes difficult to understand monolithic schema. In our method we use previously defined and already proved to be secure cryptographic primitives: regular signatures and ring signatures (they are not of sub-linear size). That approach provides the following advantages: 1) it is easy to analyze and prove security of the resulting scheme; 2) it is easier to implement the scheme using already tested, verified and trusted libraries and modules of software. Therefore we propose the specific example based on Schnorr ring signatures. Our construction is similar to the idea presented in [11]. However, the scheme from [11] is not unconditionally anonymous and does not provide the *perfect anonymity* (users from ring who expose secret keys can prove that they did not sign). Moreover it is provided without the analysis and security discussion and uses different building blocks. We stress that (unlike [11]) our proposition, based on Schnorr ring signatures, does provide unconditional anonymity, i.e., guarantees anonymity even if the secret keys of the ring members are exposed. Our construction is based on a ring signature scheme whose security is proved using *Forking Lemma* [14]. We assume that there is a public repository of signatures, like a bulletin board, available to all the users. The users create and publicize signatures and in this way they steadily create a hierarchy which is a tree built upon previous signatures from the repository. A node in the tree is a ring signature and members of the ring (potential signers) are signers of the direct children of that node. This relation goes recursively to the leaf level nodes. Since each ring signature ensures anonymity, the set of potential signers of a given node includes all the potential signers of leaves of a sub-tree rooted in this node. The additional important feature is that the construction provides a kind of a time-stamping functionality, since parent node signatures have to be created after their descendant nodes. The proposed scheme may be used in various scenarios. Here, we describe its application to implementation of secure anonymous bulletin boards.

Secure Bulletin Board. Secure bulletin boards are authenticated, append-only broadcast channels and are assumed to exist as a primitive by most of remote voter-verifiable cryptographic voting schemes. In order to call a voting system voter verifiable, the following three properties need to be satisfied (i.e., a voter should be able to detect if any of these does not hold): (i) a ballot is cast as intended, (ii) is recorded as cast, (iii) is tallied as recorded.

At some point of a voting process, a voter should verify if a cast ballot is correctly recorded by the voting system (iii), i.e., by comparing the electronic representation of her vote with the record stored on a public bulletin board. The integrity of an election depends on two factors: (a) number of voters who perform this check, (b) reliability of the bulletin board. Implementations of secure bulletin boards need to take into account many threats. One of the biggest threats is a scenario when hackers take control over the bulletin board and are able to: modify already cast ballots, modify new cast ballots, discard already cast ballots, do not accept new ones, add new ballots. Sometimes it is even hard to detect that a given system is under attack [18], [19]. A traditional approach to dealing with data modifications is use of digital signatures – this approach is useful if a PKI is implemented and all voters have their own keys (like in Estonia where all voters have electronic ID-cards). The problem arises when voters cannot sign their ballots and signing is made on the server's side. If hacker gained access to the server, one should assume that the hacker is also capable of obtaining new signatures and thus modifying all new and already cast ballots. So a natural and desired property is to have a distributed way of signing and time-stamping election data. Time-stamping helps with recovering to the state before the attacker gained the control over the system. Distributed signing makes life of a hacker harder – now, in order to successfully modify ballots he should take control over the set of machines that participate in distributed signing election data.

The proposed system of hierarchical ring signatures gives what one needs: (hierarchy) a time-stamping property that does not depend on just trusting a single time-stamping server but rather on the order of events; (ring signatures) ring signatures offer better protection since an attacker cannot tell exactly who is signing (and one can create large enough anonymity set to make attacker work hopeless).

Our Contribution. We propose a construction of a ring signature scheme that: 1) creates a hierarchical structure of the signatures; 2) has a modular architecture and reuse previously defined, secure regular signatures and ring signatures; 3) creates short signatures for large rings; 4) provides small computational complexity of the signature creation; 5) provides a kind of time-stamping functionality for all the node signatures that belong to paths starting from leafs upwards. We propose a specific example scheme built upon regular cryptographic blocks: Schnorr signatures and Schnorr ring signatures. We also prove the security and anonymity of this proposition.

Related Work. The concept of a ring signature was introduced by Rivest et al. in [15]. In [13] ring signatures were combined with deniable authentication into deniable ring authentication scheme. A linkable ring signature scheme was presented in [17] and in [1]; under a strong security model they allow to link signatures signed by the same person. There are identity based ring signature schemes that enable to construct rings for different identity-based master domains (see [20,10,12,7,3,2]). Chen et al. proposed in [6] confessible threshold ring signature scheme, in which the actual creator of a ring signature can prove to be the signer. Bender et al. presented in [4] the summary of the assumptions and the security definitions used in the prior work. They proposed stronger notion of anonymity and unforgeability. Ring schemes of sub-linear size were proposed in [8] and [5] where security is proved without random oracle model.

Comparison with Schemes of Ring Signatures of Sub-linear Size. Scheme from [11]: not unconditionally anonymous, does not provide perfect anonymity (users from ring who expose secret keys can prove that they did not sign); provided without the analysis and security discussion; uses different building blocks (non interactive zero knowledge proof of equality of disc. log.); complexity of the scheme is similar to our proposition; provides the hierarchical construction. Scheme from [8]: security of the proposed efficient implementation is based on Strong RSA assumption; uses different building blocks (dynamic accumulators, ring signatures obtained as from Fiat-Shamir transform applied to the proposed ad-hoc identification scheme); security is proved in ROM; initial time complexity for the new group/ring is proportional to the ring size (subsequently short keys for the established group/ring are used); does not provide hierarchical construction. Scheme from [5]: security is based on subgroup decision assumption, the strong Diffie-Hellman assumption and the assumption that the one-time signature is unforgeable; security is proved without random oracles; uses different building blocks (Boneh and Boyen signatures); time complexity for the signature creation and the size of signature is $\mathcal{O}(\sqrt{n})$ where n is the ring size; does not provide hierarchical construction. From the above mentioned papers, the scheme from [11] is the most similar to our construction. However, our scheme is proved to be unconditionally anonymous (it ensures anonymity even if the secret keys of the ring members are exposed - perfect anonymity) and is proved to be unforgeable in ROM and under Forking Lemma. It is based on Schnorr ring signatures. In terms of creating keys for the new ring it resembles the schemes from [8] and [5] but in our construction those keys are used in a different way; namely to build the tree hierarchy. As a result our scheme creates new ring signatures in constant time and of size $\mathcal{O}(1)$. Signatures are based on previously established rings and the new ring is the sum of previous rings.

Organization of the paper. In Section 2 we state the required assumptions and the definitions of the regular and ring signature schemes. We recall Forking Lemma and the form of a ring signature based on it. Then we provide the overview of our construction based on regular and ring signatures. We discuss its security. In Section 3 we give the detailed description of the specific example of our scheme: we recall the Schnorr ring signature from [9] and propose a specific hierarchical Schnorr ring signature scheme based on methodology from Section 2. We prove its unforgeability and perfect anonymity.

2 Construction Overview

2.1 Preliminaries

We consider a group of n participants. We assume that each user has a pair of secret/public keys (x_i, y_i) $(i = 1, 2, \ldots, n)$ built over an algebraic structure G. All the public keys are known to all the participants. The structure G is constructed by means of the security parameter ξ which is chosen in such a way that it is infeasible to compute x_i from y_i. From now on we assume that all computations are done within that structure. In particular, the cryptographic blocks: hash function $\mathcal{H}$, regular and ring signature schemes given below, are well defined over the parameters of G.

Signature Schemes **REGULAR** and **RING**

Definition 1. *A* REGULAR *signature scheme is defined as a following 4-tuple of procedures:*

- Str – *structure generation – randomized algorithm, takes a security parameter* ξ *and creates an algebraic structure G. We write* $G \leftarrow \mathsf{Str}(\xi)$.
- KeyGen – *key generation – randomized algorithm, takes an algebraic structure G and produces over it a pair* (x, y) *of private/public keys. We write* $(x, y) \leftarrow$ KeyGen(G).
- Sign – *signing procedure – randomized algorithm, takes a message m, the secret key x and returns a signature* σ. *We write* $\sigma \leftarrow \mathsf{Sign}(m, x)$.
- Verify – *signature verification – deterministic algorithm, takes a message m, a signature* σ *for m and the public key y. It returns a bit d (0 or 1) indicating whether the signature* σ *is valid, i.e., whether someone having a public key y has signed m with the corresponding private key x. We write* $d \leftarrow \mathsf{Verify}(m, \sigma, y)$.

Besides the scheme REGULAR the participants use the signature scheme RING, built on the top of their public keys. In the RING scheme the signer may include not only himself but also some other participants in the *ring signature*. The set of all such potential signers (including also the real signer) is called a *ring*. We identify the ring by the set of the public keys $Y = \{y_1, \ldots, y_t\}$ of the participants included in it.

Definition 2. *A* RING *signature scheme is defined as a following 4-tuple of procedures:*

- Str – *structure generation – randomized algorithm, takes a security parameter* ξ *and creates an algebraic structure G. We write* $G \leftarrow \mathsf{Str}(\xi)$.
- KeyGen – *key generation – randomized algorithm, takes an algebraic structure G and produces over it a pair* (x, y) *of private/public keys. We write* $(x, y) \leftarrow$ KeyGen(G).
- RSign – *signing procedure – randomized algorithm, takes a message m, the secret key* x_j *and the set of public keys* $Y = \{y_1, \ldots, y_t\}$, $y_j \in Y$. *It returns a signature* σ. *We write* $\sigma \leftarrow \mathsf{RSign}(m, x_j, Y)$.
- RVerify – *signature verification – deterministic algorithm, takes a message m, a signature* σ *for m and the set of public keys Y. It returns a bit d (0 or 1) indicating whether the signature* σ *is valid, i.e., whether someone having a public key from the set Y has signed m. We write* $d \leftarrow \mathsf{RVerify}(m, \sigma, Y)$.

Throughout this paper we work with the schemes RING and REGULAR that are *correct*. The definitions of correctness for both cases are presented below.

Definition 3. *(*REGULAR *Correctness) Any correctly created signature* σ *is verifiable to "1" via* Verify()*. In other words,*

$$\Pr[G \leftarrow \mathsf{Str}(\xi); (x, y) \leftarrow KeyGen(G); \sigma \leftarrow \mathsf{Sign}(m, x) :$$
$$\mathsf{Verify}(m, \sigma, y) = 1] = 1 \ .$$

Definition 4. *(RING Correctness) Any correctly created signature σ is verifiable to "1" via RVerify(). In other words,*

$$\Pr[G \leftarrow \mathsf{Str}(\xi); Y = \{y_i : (x_i, y_i) \leftarrow KeyGen(G)\};$$
$$j \in \{1, \ldots, |Y|\}; \sigma \leftarrow \mathsf{RSign}(m, x_j, Y) : \mathsf{RVerify}(m, \sigma, Y) = 1] = 1 \ .$$

Moreover we assume that the above schemes are *unforgeable* in the *chosen-message* scenario which means the following. Suppose that a forger's goal is to produce a verifiable signature σ for the message m which was not previously signed in the query stage. We say that the forger succeeds, if it can forge σ for m with a non-negligible probability. Below we state it more formally for both, REGULAR and RING scheme.

Definition 5. *(REGULAR\RING Unforgeability). Suppose that a forger $\mathcal{A}$ is given all the public parameters (including a public key $y \setminus$ a set of public keys Y) and can issue up to q_{max} queries in an adaptive manner to the signing oracle $O_{\mathsf{Sign}}(m_i)$ for signatures of messages m_i of his choice. We say that the scheme REGULAR\RING is unforgeable if the probability, that the forger outputs a pair (m, σ) such that σ is the signature for the message $m \neq m_i$ verifiable to 1 with public key $y \setminus$ public keys from the set Y, is negligible, i.e., is smaller than a negligible function of the security parameter $\epsilon(\xi)$. In other words, scheme REGULAR is unforgeable if*

$$\Pr[G \leftarrow \mathsf{Str}(\xi); (x, y) \leftarrow KeyGen(G); (m, \sigma) \leftarrow \mathcal{A}^{O_{\mathsf{Sign}}(m_i)}(y) :$$
$$\mathsf{Verify}(m, \sigma, y) = 1 \wedge m \notin \{m_i\}] < \epsilon(\xi),$$

scheme RING is unforgeable if

$$\Pr[G \leftarrow \mathsf{Str}(\xi); Y = \{y_i : (x_i, y_i) \leftarrow KeyGen(G)\}; (m, \sigma) \leftarrow \mathcal{A}^{O_{\mathsf{Sign}}(m_i)}(Y) :$$
$$\mathsf{RVerify}(m, \sigma, Y) = 1 \wedge m \notin \{m_i\}] < \epsilon(\xi).$$

Unforgeability of Ring Signatures Under Forking Lemma. *Forking Lemma* [14] is used to prove unforgeability of ring signature schemes in the chosen-message scenario. In order to take advantage of Forking Lemma for attacks in this scenario, the signature scheme should take the form of a tuple (r, h, s), where r depends only on values chosen at random, h is a hash value that depends on the message m to be signed and r, and s depends on r, m and h. Moreover such a signature should be simulatable (in the Random Oracle Model - ROM) without the knowledge of the corresponding secret signing key. According to Forking Lemma, if the forger existed then it could be run, in a reasonable time, to acquire two valid signatures (r, h, s) and (r, h', s'), which subsequently could be used to break some hard problem on which the security of the signature scheme is based. A class of unforgeable ring signatures is introduced in [9]. For a ring of cardinality t a *generic* ring signature (for message m) presented there is based on a tuple $(r_1, \ldots, r_t, h_1, \ldots, h_t, s)$, where $r_1, \ldots, r_t$ $(r_i \neq r_j)$ are the random values, h_i is a hash value of m and r_i, while s is determined by m, $r_1, \ldots, r_t$ and $h_1, \ldots, h_t$. Its unforgeability is proved using Forking Lemma. We use exactly this class of ring signatures as a base of our hierarchical construction proposed in the next section. Note that the size of this signature is proportional to the cardinality of the ring. Additionally, the tuple $h_1, \ldots, h_t$ is not included in the final signature structure since it can be computed from the rest of the parameters (see example in Fig. 5).

Anonymity of Ring Signatures

Definition 6. *(Anonymity). We say that the ring signature is anonymous if the probability that the verifier guesses the identity of the real signer who has computed a ring signature on behalf of a ring of k members is not greater than $1/k$. If the verifier is one of the members of the ring, distinct from the real signer, then the probability that she guesses the identity of the real signer is not greater than $1/(k-1)$.*

While talking about a *perfect anonymity* [4] the verifier is also given the set of corresponding secret keys $\{x_1, \ldots x_k\}$. We stress that the construction presented in this paper is based on the Schnorr Ring Signature Scheme from [9] which ensures the perfect anonymity.

2.2   Hierarchical Ring Signature Scheme

In this section we discuss in general our hierarchical ring signature scheme HI-ERARCH. Its high level description may be found in appendix while the formal and detailed description of a specific hierarchical scheme is presented in Section 3.

Hierarchical Scheme Construction. Recall that we consider a group of n users each of which has a pair of private/public keys (x_i, y_i), $(i = 1, 2, \ldots, n)$. We assume that each of them may use REGULAR and RING signature schemes:

- REGULAR: $(\mathsf{Str}(\xi), \mathsf{KeyGen}(G), \mathsf{Sign}(m, x), \mathsf{Verify}(m, \sigma, y))$,
- RING: $(\mathsf{Str}(\xi), \mathsf{KeyGen}(G), \mathsf{RSign}(m, x_j, Y), \mathsf{RVerify}(m, \sigma, Y))$.

W.l.o.g. we assume that $\mathsf{Str}(\xi)$ and $\mathsf{KeyGen}(G)$ procedures are the same for both schemes. Additionally, we assume that those schemes are correct and unforgeable under Forking Lemma. For definiteness we use the ring signature scheme from [9]. Thus the ring signature can be expressed as a specific tuple (see Section 2.1) and can be simulated in ROM without the knowledge of the secret key. Given schemes REGULAR and RING we construct another ring signature scheme called hierarchical ring signature HIERARCH. It is defined as a 5-tuple of procedures: (Str, KeyGen, NRSign, NRVerify, HierVerify). The HIER-ARCH signing procedure (compare Fig. 6), called NRSign, creates a signature that is treated as a node in the tree. All the resulting signatures of our scheme form a tree structure. NRSign can be regarded as a RING signing procedure $\mathsf{RSign}(m, x_j, Y)$, $|Y| = k$, that produces a tuple $\sigma = (y_{new}, \hat{r}_1, \ldots, \hat{r}_k, s)$, in which the sub-tuple $\hat{r}_1, \ldots, \hat{r}_k$ is computed in a new specific way: a new pair of private/public keys (x_{new}, y_{new}) is created; the private key x_{new} is used to produce a set Σ of a regular signatures $\sigma_1 = \mathsf{Sign}(r_1, x_{new})$, $\ldots, \sigma_k = \mathsf{Sign}(r_k, x_{new})$

over the nonces $r_1, \ldots, r_k$; each pair (r_i, σ_i) is treated as a random $\hat{r}_i$. These are later hashed altogether with the message m, to produce the tuple of hashes $h_1, \ldots, h_k$. The public key y_{new} is included in the resulting signature. Now the tuple $(y_{new}, \hat{r}_1, \ldots, \hat{r}_k, h_1, \ldots, h_k, s)$ embeds the set of regular signatures Σ in the random nonces $\hat{r}_i$. This construction can be regarded as a kind of self certification, in which the set of regular signatures Σ and ring signature σ mutually certify themselves.

The HIERARCH verification procedure (compare Fig. 6) NRVerify verifies the signature created by NRSign. It verifies all signatures σ_i from Σ via regular Verify(r_i, σ_i, y_{new}) and subsequently verifies the ring signature $\sigma=(y_{new}, \hat{r}_1, \ldots, \hat{r}_k, s)$ via RVerify(m, σ, Y). If all the verifications hold the hierarchical signature is accepted. The verifier gets two facts about the creator of the verified hierarchical signature σ: the signer is the holder of a one private key corresponding to one of the public keys from the ring Y, and the signer is the holder of the new pair of private/public keys (x_{new}, y_{new}) (i.e., the ring signature certifies the new public key y_{new} of the ring). Indeed, without both x_j and x_{new} the creation of the correct signature σ is infeasible since the underlying schemes REGULAR and RING are unforgeable. Thus the pair (x_{new}, y_{new}) becomes a new private/public key for the creator of the ring signature σ for the ring Y. Now, if someone verifies positively another signature by means of y_{new} can conclude that the signer should be the same person who created previously the ring signature σ for which keys (x_{new}, y_{new}) were generated.

In Fig. 1 we present the high level description of the HIERARCH scheme construction.

We illustrate the process of the tree structure creation resulting in the hierarchy depicted in Fig. 2. Suppose that two different users u^A and u^B construct two different hierarchical signatures $\sigma_A = (y_{new}^A, ., .)$ and $\sigma_B = (y_{new}^B, ., .)$ for two disjoint rings $A = \{y_1^A, \ldots, y_k^A\}$, $B = \{y_1^B, \ldots, y_k^B\}$. At the leaf level the rings A and B consist of the public keys belonging to the particular users. Now one of the actual σ_A and σ_B creators can build another ring $C = \{y_{new}^A, y_{new}^B\}$ consisting of new public keys generated in the corresponding signatures σ_A and σ_B, and construct another signature $\sigma_C = (y_{new}^C, ., .)$ for the ring C. These scenario can be repeated further with other signatures, e.g. $\sigma_D, \sigma_E, \sigma_F, \sigma_G$, resulting in the tree depicted in Fig. 2.

The verifier of σ_G can conclude the following. The signer of σ_G should know the private key corresponding to one of the public keys from the ring $G = \{y_{new}^C, y_{new}^F\}$, so it is the creator of σ_C or of σ_F. Considering the left sub-tree: the signer of σ_C should know one private key corresponding to one of the public keys from the ring $C = \{y_{new}^A, y_{new}^B\}$, so it is the signer of σ_A or σ_B. Subsequently it is a user of a public key from the ring A or from the ring B. The same reasoning for the right sub-tree (rooted in σ_F) gives: the potential signer of σ_F is a user of a public key from the ring D or from the ring E. Summing up the potential signer of σ_G is a holder of a private key corresponding to one of the public keys from the ring $A \cup B \cup D \cup E$. Note that although the set of potential signers grows with the height of the tree, the size of the node signatures at a given tree level is constant.

- NRSign$(m, x_j, \tilde{Y})$ procedure:
  1. create new key pair $(x_{new}, y_{new}) := $ KeyGen(G),
  2. for a leaf level let $\tilde{Y}$ be the set of public keys of particular users; for a non-leaf levels let $\tilde{Y}$ be the set of public keys coined during the creation of signatures from the lower level,
  3. proceed the computation defined in RSign(m, x_j, Y) for $Y = \tilde{Y}$ till the step of computation of nonces r_i,
  4. after obtaining each random r_i create a signature $\sigma_i := $ Sign(r_i, x_{new}),
  5. treat (r_i, σ_i) as a random $\hat{r}_i$,
  6. use $\hat{r}_i$ instead of r_i in h_i computation, i.e., $h_i := \mathcal{H}(m, \hat{r}_i) = \mathcal{H}(m, r_i, \sigma_i)$,
  7. proceed the computation defined in RSign(m, x_j, Y) for $Y = \tilde{Y}$,
  8. let $\hat{R} = \{\hat{r}_i\} = \{(r_i, \sigma_i)\}$,
  9. include the new public key y_{new} and $\hat{R}$ in the signature tuple.
- NRVerify(m, σ, Y) procedure:
  1. extract y_{new} and $\hat{R} = \{\hat{r}_i\} = \{(r_i, \sigma_i)\}$ from σ,
  2. verify each subsignature σ_i for r_i, i.e., Verify(r_i, σ_i, y_{new}),
  3. follow the steps of RING verification procedure RVerify$(m, \hat{\sigma}, Y)$ for the signature $\hat{\sigma} = (\hat{R}, s)$ computing h_i as $\mathcal{H}(m, \hat{r}_i) = \mathcal{H}(m, r_i, \sigma_i)$,
  4. if all verifications output 1 (OK) then accept the whole signature (output 1) .
- HierVerify(m, σ, Y) procedure:
  1. if σ is a leaf level signature verify NRVerify(m, σ, Y),
  2. if σ is a node signature at a non-leaf level then:
     (a) verify NRVerify(m, σ, Y),
     (b) locate signatures σ_i for each $y_i \in Y$,
     (c) call recursively HierVerify(m, σ_i, Y) for each signature σ_i,
  3. if all verifications output 1 (OK) then output 1.

Fig. 1. High level description of the HIERARCH scheme construction.

In the example from Fig. 2 we assume that cardinalities of rings at the leaf level are equal to k. Thus the set of potential signers for signature σ_C is $A \cup B$ (of cardinality $2k$) and similarly the set of potential signers for signature σ_F is $D \cup E$ (of cardinality $2k$) while the size of both signatures, σ_C and σ_F is proportional to $|C| = |F| = 2$. Also the size of σ_G is proportional to $|G| = 2$ $(G = \{y_{new}^C, y_{new}^F\})$ while the set of potential signers is $A \cup B \cup D \cup E$ of cardinality $4k$ (we assume that A, B, D, E are mutually disjoint). In the HIERARCH scheme we will write $\tilde{Y}$ instead of Y for the set of public keys for which we create a signature. We do so in order to underline that now $\tilde{Y}$ is the set of public keys of particular users only at the leaf level and that at the non-leaf level it is a set of public keys generated in the signatures from the lower level.

Definition 7. *We define a Ring Hierarchy as a tree of signatures created by the procedure* NRSign *in such a way that: 1) at the leaf level the set $\tilde{Y}$ consists only of the public keys of the particular users; 2) at higher levels $\tilde{Y}$ consists only of the public keys generated in the signatures from the lower level.*

Definition 8. *A hierarchical ring signature scheme* HIERARCH *is defined as a following 5-tuple of procedures:*

- Str – *structure generation – randomized algorithm, takes a security parameter ξ and creates an algebraic structure G. We write $G \leftarrow$ Str(ξ).*
- KeyGen – *key generation – randomized algorithm, takes an algebraic structure G and produces over it a pair (x, y) of private/public keys. We write $(x, y) \leftarrow$ KeyGen(G).*
- NRSign – *signing procedure – randomized algorithm, takes a message m, the secret key x_j and the set of public keys $\tilde{Y} = \{y_1, \ldots, y_k\}$. It returns a signature σ. We write $\sigma \leftarrow$ NRSign($m, x_j, \tilde{Y}$).*
- NRVerify – *node signature verification – deterministic algorithm, takes a message m, a signature σ for m and the set of public keys Y. It returns a bit d (0 or 1) indicating whether the signature σ is valid, i.e., whether someone having a public key from the set Y or someone who previously signed one signature from Σ, has signed m. We write $d \leftarrow$ NRVerify(m, σ, Y).*
- HierVerify – *deterministic algorithm, takes a message m, a signature σ for m and the set of public keys Y. It returns a bit d (0 or 1) indicating whether the hierarchy of signatures rooted in σ is valid, i.e., whether someone having a public key in the set Y is the creator of one of the "leaf" signatures of the tree rooted in σ. We write $d \leftarrow$ HierVerify(m, σ, Y).*

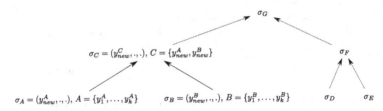

Fig. 2. Hierarchical signature tree.

Correctness, Unforgeability and Anonymity. In this subsection we give the intuitive overview of the correctness, unforgeability and anonymity of the proposed hierarchical scheme. Formal proofs for the specific scheme instance are presented in Section 3.2.

Proposition 1 (Correctness). *Any correctly created Ring Hierarchy tree, i.e., having all nodes created correctly via* NRSign *procedure, is verifiable to 1 via* HierVerify.

Proof. This is a direct conclusion from the assumption that the REGULAR and RING schemes are correct. Indeed, note that every node signature is calculated by means of Sign and RSign procedure, which are verifiable to 1 when they are correctly computed. □

The next proposition (Prop. 2) forbids inserting new *child* nodes below the existing *parent* by users which are not those *parents* creators. This is provided by the unforgeability of the REGULAR scheme. Indeed, if the REGULAR scheme was forgeable then anyone could produce the node signature by producing a new ring including herself, and using her secret key to create ring signature and the forged sub-signatures Σ.

Proposition 2. *Only the creator of the node knows the new secret key x_{new} corresponding to the new public y_{new} used during the node creation.*

Proof. Assume there is an adversary $\mathcal{A}$ that produces a verifiable node signature $\sigma = (\bar{y}_{new}, \dots)$ for some already existing public $\bar{y}_{new}$ for which it does not know corresponding $\bar{x}_{new}$. We can assume that $\mathcal{A}$ is given all other parameters - even all secret keys of the ring members. Then it can be used as a sub-procedure for the adversary algorithm $\mathcal{F}$ which forges REGULAR signatures. Any signature queries from $\mathcal{A}$ can be answered from $\mathcal{F}$ by its oracles. Now if $\mathcal{A}$ produces a valid $\sigma = (\bar{y}_{new}, \dots)$ then any sub-signature from Σ can be returned by $\mathcal{F}$ as a valid existential forgery of REGULAR scheme. $\qquad\square$

Proposition 3 (Unforgeability). *Any node of the Ring Hierarchy is a ring signature unforgeable in the adaptive chosen-message scenario.*

Proof. Take a node signature $\sigma = (y_{new}, \hat{R}, s)$ for message m (recall that during the signature creation we have also computed $h_1, \dots, h_k$; however we do not include them in σ since they can be computed from the rest of parameters). To prove its unforgeability, we follow the proof of unforgeability for the underlying RING signature (which fulfills Forking Lemma assumptions). Therefore it suffices to show that the resulting node signature also fulfills Forking Lemma requirements:

- Here $\hat{R} = \{\hat{r}_i\}$, $\hat{r}_i = (r_i, \sigma_i)$ and $h_i := \mathcal{H}(m, \hat{r}_i) = \mathcal{H}(m, r_i, \sigma_i)$, where σ_i's were created by means of a new key pair (x_{new}, y_{new}). Note that y_{new} and $\hat{r}_i$ depend only on the random values, h_i is a hash value that depends on m and $\hat{r}_i$ and s is determined by m, $\hat{r}_1, \dots, \hat{r}_k$ and $h_1, \dots, h_k$.
- As underlying RING signatures can be simulated without the private key in ROM by programming in advance required oracle answers $\mathcal{H}(m, r_j) := h_j$ for random h_j, the same can be achieved for HIERARCH signatures, by registering in a programmable ROM table all required $\mathcal{H}(m, r_j, \sigma_j) := h_j$ for random h_j.

Thus if the forger for the node signatures existed then it could be run, in a reasonable time, to acquire two valid signatures $(y_{new}, \hat{R}, s)$ and $(y_{new}, \hat{R}, s')$ which subsequently could be used to break the hard problem on which the security of the underlying RING signature scheme is based. Thus the node signature is unforgeable under Forking Lemma. $\qquad\square$

Proposition 4 (Anonymity). *If the RING signature scheme is anonymous, then any node signature in the correctly computed Ring Hierarchy tree is also anonymous (recall that the definition of anonymity was given in Section 2.1).*

Proof. We consider a node signature $\sigma = (y_{new}, \hat{R}, s)$ created by the procedure $\mathsf{NRSign}(m, x_j, \tilde{Y})$. Recall that $\hat{R} = \{(r_i, \sigma_i)\}$. Note that the subsignatures σ_i are created by means of a new key pair (x_{new}, y_{new}) that does not depend on any key pair (x_i, y_i) referring to the leaves of the tree rooted in σ. Indeed the additional (modification) steps that transform $\mathsf{RSign}(m, x_j, Y)$ into $\mathsf{NRSign}(m, x_j, \tilde{Y})$ (Fig. 1) could have been computed by any member of the ring with the same probability, thus do not affect the anonymity of the underlying RING scheme.   □

Suppose that in our tree we have n leaves (not necessarily of the same depth), each associated with a signature σ_{A_i} created by a member from the ring A_i, $1 \leq i \leq n$ (we do not assume that the rings are disjoint). Let σ be any signature from the Ring Hierarchy and let $A_{i_1}, A_{i_2}, \ldots, A_{i_k}$ be the rings associated with the leaves of the tree rooted in σ, $A_\sigma = A_{i_1} \cup A_{i_2} \cup \ldots \cup A_{i_k}$. Then the verifier of σ can conclude that any member of A_σ could create σ. Moreover, the probability that any member of A_σ did it is equal to $1/|A_\sigma|$ (the distribution is uniform on A_σ). If a branch of our tree is cut off at a node π (a successor of σ but not necessarily an immediate one) and $A_{j_1}, A_{j_2}, \ldots, A_{j_s}$ are the rings associated with the leaves of the tree rooted in π, $A_\pi = A_{j_1} \cup A_{j_2} \cup \ldots \cup A_{j_s}$, then the distribution changes. Now it is uniform on $A_\sigma \backslash A_\pi$. The verifier of σ knows that the creator is from the set A_σ but not A_π and the probability that any member of $A_\sigma \backslash A_\pi$ created σ is equal to $1/|A_\sigma \backslash A_\pi|$. The special case of the Ring Hierarchy which is a k-ary balanced tree is discussed below.

Proposition 5. *Let a Ring Hierarchy be a k-ary balanced tree s.t. the sets of public keys from the leaf level are pairwise disjoint and equipotent (k). Then any node signature σ from the level l could have been computed by a holder of any private key corresponding to public keys from leaf level nodes rooted in σ, with the same probability $(1/k)^l$.*
If a subtree of a tree rooted in σ is cut off at level $s < l$ then the probability that σ was created by any holder of any private key corresponding to public keys from remaining leaf level nodes is equal to $1/(k^l - k^s)$.

Proof. This is an immediate conclusion from the construction of the probability tree based on the correctly computed k-ary balanced Ring Hierarchy with anonymous node ring signatures, where probability weight on each link is equal to $1/k$.   □

The proposed construction enables to create short ring signatures with anonymity computed as for the ring of much larger size. For the Ring Hierarchy from Proposition 5 the length of each signature is proportional to k while the set of potential signers grows exponentially to the value k^l for each node signature at the level l. Another advantage is low computational complexity of signing. Typically the number of significant operations required for the creation of ring signatures is proportional to the cardinality of the set of public keys in the ring. Here (for Ring Hierarchy being a k-ary balanced tree) the operational cost is constant since the complexity af a node creation is "spread" into the complexities of previously created nodes from the lower levels. On the other hand the cost of verification is larger than usually, as a node verification requires checking all nodes in the subtree. This, however, can be facilitated by keeping track of step-by-step verification of new signatures that occur in the tree. In fact, in real implementations (signatures bulletin boards), it can be done by the automated process that certifies the verification of whole subtrees.

Timestamping Extension. As the node signatures are built gradually using previously created signatures from lower levels, a kind of straightforward time-stamping functionality based on the hierarchy is provided. If the creator of the signature computes the hash value $\mathcal{H}(\Sigma)$ and concatenates it with the message m before signing (for Σ being the set of previous signatures), it assures that those signatures had to be created earlier than the current node.

3   Construction Based on Schnorr Ring Signatures

In this section we recall the Schnorr ring signature scheme and describe in details the specific hierarchical ring signature scheme based on it. Throughout this section p and q are large primes such that $q|p-1$ and $q > 2^{\xi}$, g is an element of order q in $\mathbb{Z}_p^*$ and $\mathcal{H}()$ is a collision resistant hash function which outputs elements in $\mathbb{Z}_q$. The Schnorr signature scheme (consult [16]) is based on Discrete Logarithm Problem (DLP) and can be implemented in any group G of a prime order, where DLP is hard. We generate a group $G \leftarrow \mathsf{Str}(\xi)$, where security parameter ξ is chosen in such a way that any instance of DLP in G cannot be trivially computed. Let $a \leftarrow_\$ A$ denote that the element a is drawn uniformly at random from the set A. In Fig. 3 we recall the key generation procedure and in Fig. 4 the signature creation and verification procedures.

```
KeyGen(G)
    Input    : G
    Output   : a pair (x, y) of secret/public keys
  1 begin
  2 |    x ←$ {1, ..., q − 1}
  3 |    y := g^x mod p
  4 |    return (x, y)
```

Fig. 3. Key generation.

The algorithm of the Schnorr ring signature construction (proposed in [9]) is recalled in Fig. 5. We omit the key generation procedure as it is the same as in the regular Schnorr signature scheme. The scheme is proved to be unforgeable in a chosen-message scenario under Forking Lemma, and unconditionally anonymous. For proofs refer to [9].

3.1   Hierarchical Schnorr Ring Signature

In this subsection we propose the hierarchical Schnorr ring signature scheme based on the scheme proposed in [9]. The detailed procedures follow the general

a) Sign(m, x)

Input : message m
: private key x
Output : signature $\sigma = (r, s)$
1 begin
2 | $a \leftarrow_\$ \{1, \ldots, q-1\}$
3 | $r := g^a \bmod p$
4 | $h := \mathcal{H}(m, r)$
5 | $s := (a + xh) \bmod q$
6 | return $\sigma = (r, s)$

b) Verify(m, σ, y)

Input : message m
: signature
$\sigma = (r, s)$
: public key y
Output : true or false
1 begin
2 | $h := \mathcal{H}(m, r)$
3 | if $g^s == ry^h \bmod p$
then
4 | | return (true)
5 | else
6 | | return (false)

Fig. 4. a) Schnorr Signature Creation, b) Schnorr Signature Verification.

a) RSign(m, x_j, Y)

Input : message m
: private key x_j
: public keys $Y : y_1, \ldots, y_t$
Output : signature $\sigma = (R, s)$
1 begin
2 | foreach $i \in \{1, \ldots, t\}, i \neq j$ do
3 | | $a_i \leftarrow_\$ \{1, \ldots, q-1\}$, s.t.
| | all a_i's are pairwise different
4 | | $r_i := g^{a_i} \bmod p$
5 | | $h_i := \mathcal{H}(m, r_i)$
6 | $a \leftarrow_\$ \{0, \ldots, q-1\}$
7 | $r_j := g^a \prod_{i \neq j} y_i^{-h_i} \bmod p$
8 | if $r_j = 1$ or $r_j = r_i$ ($i \neq j$) then
9 | | go to step 6
10 | $h_j := \mathcal{H}(m, r_j)$
11 | $s :=$
| $(\sum_{i \neq j} a_i + a + x_j h_j) \bmod q$
12 | $R := \{r_1, \ldots, r_t\}$
13 | return $\sigma = (R, s)$

b) RVerify(m, Y, σ)

Input : message m
: public keys
$Y : y_1, \ldots, y_t$
: signature $\sigma = (R, s)$
: where $R = r_1, \ldots, r_t$
Output : true or false
1 begin
2 | foreach $i \in \{1, \ldots, t\}$ do
3 | | $h_i := \mathcal{H}(m, r_i)$
4 | if $g^s == \prod_i r_i y_i^{h_i} \bmod p$
then
5 | | return (true)
6 | else
7 | | return (false)

Fig. 5. a) Schnorr Ring Sign. Creation, b) Schnorr Ring Sign. Verification.

construction methodology introduced in Section 2.2 in Fig 1. At the leaf level the ring signatures use regular keys (x_i, y_i). At higher levels rings are constructed using the new key pairs (x_{new}, y_{new}) coined ad-hoc. Since these keys could be reused at higher levels, the verification of the signature at a given level has to involve verification of all node signatures on lower levels, as described in HierVerify procedure. The definitions of node ring signature creation (NRSign) and node ring signature verification (NRVerify) procedures are presented in Fig. 6. They are based on the following procedures: Sign and Verify from the Schnorr scheme (Fig. 4), RSign and RVerify from the Schnorr ring scheme (Fig. 5). KeyGen procedure is the same as in the Schnorr scheme (Fig. 3). HierVerify construction described in Fig. 1 is entirely based on the recursive application of NRVerify and Verify thus we do not copy that description here.

a) NRSign$(m, x_j, \tilde{Y})$

Input : message m
: private key x_j
: public keys $\tilde{Y}$: $y_1, \ldots, y_k$
Output : signature $\sigma = (y_{new}, \hat{R}, s)$
1 **begin**
2    $(x_{new}, y_{new}) := \mathsf{KeyGen}(\mathcal{G})$
3   **foreach** $i \in \{1, \ldots, k\}, i \neq j$ **do**
4      $a_i \leftarrow_\$ \{1, \ldots, q-1\}$, s.t. all a_i's are pairwise different
5      $r_i := g^{a_i} \bmod p$
6      $\sigma_i := \mathsf{Sign}(r_i, x_{new})$
7      $h_i := \mathcal{H}(m, r_i, \sigma_i)$
8    $a \leftarrow_\$ \{0, \ldots, q-1\}$
9    $r_j := g^a \prod_{i \neq j} y_i^{-h_i} \bmod p$
10   **if** $r_j = 1$ or $r_j = r_i$ $(i \neq j)$ **then**
11   go to step 8
12    $\sigma_j := \mathsf{Sign}(r_j, x_{new})$
13    $h_j := \mathcal{H}(m, r_j, \sigma_j)$
14    $s := (\sum_{i \neq j} a_i + a + x_j h_j) \bmod q$
15    $\hat{R} := \{(r_1, \sigma_1), \ldots, (r_k, \sigma_k)\}$
16   **return** $\sigma = (y_{new}, \hat{R}, s)$

b) NRVerify(m, σ, Y)

Input : message m
: signature $\sigma = (y_{new}, \hat{R}, s)$
: where
$\hat{R} : \{(r_1, \sigma_1), \ldots, (r_k, \sigma_k)\}$
: public keys $Y = \{y_1, \ldots, y_k\}$
Output : true or false
1 **begin**
2   **foreach** $i \in \{1, \ldots, k\}$ **do**
3      $d_i := \mathsf{Verify}(r_i, \sigma_i, y_{new})$
4    $d := \prod_i d_i$
5   **foreach** $i \in \{1, \ldots, k\}$ **do**
6      $h_i := \mathcal{H}(m, r_i, \sigma_i)$
7   **if** $(g^s == \prod_{1 \leq i \leq k} r_i y_i^{h_i} \bmod p)$ and d **then**
8   **return** (true)
9   **else**
10   **return** (false)

Fig. 6. a) Node Ring Signature Creation, b) Node Ring Sign. Verification.

3.2 Security of the Scheme

In this subsection we prove unforgeability and anonymity of the hierarchical ring signature scheme.

Proposition 6. *The node signatures constructed by the* NRSign *procedure (see Fig. 6) can be simulated in the random oracle model without knowing any of the secret keys of the ring in a polynomial time and with probability distribution indistinguishable from the one of the ring signatures created by a legitimate signer.*

Proof. We follow strictly the methodology described in Section 2.2 applied to the simulation of Schnorr ring signature from [9]. We define the simulation algorithm in Fig. 3.2. It is easy to see that the simulation runs in a polynomial time. Note that in the line 14 we program ROM table (we are in the random oracle model). Thus the returned tuple is a valid hierarchical Schnorr ring signature for the message m. □

Theorem 1. *The scheme HIERARCH (in which signatures are constructed by the* NRSign *procedure, see Fig. 6) is unforgeable (according to Def. 5).*

Proof. We follow the construction of the proof of unforgeability from [9]. The scheme fulfills Forking Lemma requirements:

- it can be represented as a tuple $(y_{new}, \hat{R}, h_1, \ldots, h_k, s)$, where $y_{new}, \hat{r}_i$ depend only on the random values, h_i is a hash value of m and $\hat{r}_i$, and s is determined by $m, \hat{r}_1, \ldots, \hat{r}_k$ and $h_1, \ldots, h_k$;
- it can be simulated in ROM without secret key (see Proposition 6).

```
Input      : message m
           : public keys Ỹ = {y₁, ..., yₖ}
Output     : simulated signature σ = (y_new, R̂, s)
1 begin
2 |   (x_new, y_new) := KeyGen(𝒢)
3 |   j ←$ {1, 2, ..., k}
4 |   foreach i ∈ {1, ..., k}, i ≠ j do
5 |   |   aᵢ ←$ {1, ..., q−1}, s.t. all aᵢ's are pairwise different
6 |   |   rᵢ := g^aᵢ mod p
7 |   |   σᵢ := Sign(rᵢ, x_new)
8 |   |   hᵢ ←$ {0, ..., q−1}
9 |   |   register in ROM table 𝓗(m, rᵢ, σᵢ) := hᵢ
10|   s ←$ {0, ..., q−1}
11|   hⱼ ←$ {0, ..., q−1}
12|   rⱼ := g^(s−∑_{i≠j} aᵢ) ∏_{i≠j} yᵢ^(−hᵢ) mod p
13|   if (rⱼ = 1 or rⱼ = rᵢ for i ≠ j) go to step 10
14|   σⱼ := Sign(rⱼ, x_new)
15|   register in ROM table 𝓗(m, rⱼ, σⱼ) := hⱼ
16|   R̂ := {(r₁, σ₁), ..., (rₖ, σₖ)}
17|   return σ = (y_new, R̂, s)
```

Fig. 7. Node Ring Signature Simulation.

Assume, by contradiction, that the scheme HIERARCH is not unforgeable. We will show that then one can break an instance of a discrete logarithm problem. Suppose that $\mathcal{A}$ is an adversary algorithm that can be used to obtain an existential forgery of the hierarchical Schnorr ring signature presented in Section 3.1. According to Forking Lemma it can be "rewind" to obtain in a polynomial time two different valid signatures with the same random tuple. These subsequently can be used to break an instance of the discrete logarithm problem. Let (p, q, g, y) be the input of this instance in the subgroup $\langle g \rangle$ (recall that $\langle g \rangle$ is of order q) of $\mathbb{Z}_p$. The solution to this problem is the only element x from $\mathbb{Z}_p$ such that $y = g^x \mod p$. We draw at random pairwise different $\alpha_i \in \mathbb{Z}_q^*$ for $1 \leq i \leq k$ and put $y_i = y^{\alpha_i} \mod p$. Then we run the forger $\mathcal{A}$ for the ring of public keys $y_1, \ldots, y_k$ and obtain two different valid signatures for the same random tuple: $(\hat{r}_1, \ldots, \hat{r}_k, h_1, \ldots, h_k, s)$ and $(\hat{r}_1, \ldots, \hat{r}_k, h'_1, \ldots, h'_k, s')$ s.t. $h_j \neq h'_j$ for some j, and $h_i = h'_i$ for all $i \neq j$. Thus we have $g^s = \prod_i r_i \cdot \prod_{i \neq j} y_i^{h_i} \cdot y_j^{h_j}$ and $g^{s'} = \prod_i r_i \cdot \prod_{i \neq j} y_i^{h_i} \cdot y_j^{h'_j}$. So $g^{s-s'} = y_j^{h_j - h'_j} = y^{\alpha_j(h_j - h'_j)}$ and we can compute $\log_g y = (s - s')\alpha_j^{-1}(h_j - h'_j)^{-1} \mod q$. □

Theorem 2. *The node signature of the Ring Hierarchy constructed by* NRSign *procedure (see Fig. 6) is unconditionally anonymous, i.e., it could have been computed by any of the k members of the ring with the same probability.*

Proof. Let $\sigma = (y_{new}, \hat{R}, s)$ be a valid ring signature for a message m for a set of public keys $\{y_1, \ldots, y_k\}$. Recall that $\hat{R} = \{(r_1, \sigma_1), \ldots, (r_k, \sigma_k)\}$. We have for all i: Verify$(r_i, \sigma_i, y_{new}) = 1$, $h_i = \mathcal{H}(m, r_i, \sigma_i)$ and $g^s = \prod_i r_i \cdot \prod_i y_i^{h_i}$. Let u_j be a member of the ring. We have the following.

1. The probability that u_j computes the correct y_{new} (line 2 in Fig. 6) is $1/(q-1)$, and it does not depend on u_j.
2. The probability that u_j computes the correct pairwise different r_i's $(i \neq j)$ of σ is $1/(q-1) \cdot \ldots \cdot 1/(q-k+1)$, it does not depend on u_j.

3. The probability that u_j computes the correct $\sigma_i = \mathsf{Sign}(r_i, x_{new})$ for a given r_i and x_{new} corresponding to y_{new} (line 6 in Fig. 6) is $1/(q-1)$, which is the probability of choosing the right nonce in the Sign procedure (Fig. 4a) corresponding to the first element of the tuple σ_i, and it does not depend on u_j.

4. The probability that u_j chooses exactly the only value $a \in \mathbb{Z}_q$ that leads to the value r_j of σ, different from 1 and different from all r_i's $(i \neq j)$, is $1/(q-k)$, and it does not depend on u_j.

5. The probability that u_j computes the correct $\sigma_j = \mathsf{Sign}(r_j, x_{new})$ for a given r_j and x_{new} corresponding to y_{new} (line 12 in Fig. 6) is $1/(q-1)$, which is the probability of choosing the right nonce in the Sign procedure, and it does not depend on u_j.

Summing up, the probability that u_j generates exactly the ring signature σ does not depend on u_j, so it is the same for each member of the ring.   □

4   Conclusions

We provide the method for obtaining a hierarchy of short ring signatures for large rings. The construction is modular and reuse previously defined cryptographic blocks: regular signatures and ring signatures. As an example we present the specific scheme based on Schnorr regular and ring signatures.

References

1. Au, M.H., Chow, S.S.M., Susilo, W., Tsang, P.P.: Short linkable ring signatures revisited. In: Atzeni, A.S., Lioy, A. (eds.) EuroPKI 2006. LNCS, vol. 4043, pp. 101–115. Springer, Heidelberg (2006)
2. Au, M.H., Liu, J.K., Yuen, T.H., Wong, D.S.: Id-based ring signature scheme secure in the standard model. In: Yoshiura, H., Sakurai, K., Rannenberg, K., Murayama, Y., Kawamura, S.-i. (eds.) IWSEC 2006. LNCS, vol. 4266, pp. 1–16. Springer, Heidelberg (2006)
3. Awasthi, A.K., Lal, S.: Id-based ring signature and proxy ring signature schemes from bilinear pairings. ArXiv Computer Science e-prints (April 2005)
4. Bender, A., Katz, J., Morselli, R.: Ring signatures: Stronger definitions, and constructions without random oracles. In: Halevi, S., Rabin, T. (eds.) TCC 2006. LNCS, vol. 3876, pp. 60–79. Springer, Heidelberg (2006)
5. Chandran, N., Groth, J., Sahai, A.: Ring signatures of sub-linear size without random oracles. In: Arge, L., Cachin, C., Jurdziński, T., Tarlecki, A. (eds.) ICALP 2007. LNCS, vol. 4596, pp. 423–434. Springer, Heidelberg (2007)
6. Chen, Y.-S., Lei, C.-L., Chiu, Y.-P., Huang, C.-Y.: Confessible threshold ring signatures. In: ICSNC, p. 25. IEEE Computer Society (2006)
7. Chow, S.S.M., Yiu, S.-M., Hui, L.C.K.: Efficient identity based ring signature. In: Ioannidis, J., Keromytis, A.D., Yung, M. (eds.) ACNS 2005. LNCS, vol. 3531, pp. 499–512. Springer, Heidelberg (2005)
8. Dodis, Y., Kiayias, A., Nicolosi, A., Shoup, V.: Anonymous identification in ad hoc groups. In: Cachin, C., Camenisch, J.L. (eds.) EUROCRYPT 2004. LNCS, vol. 3027, pp. 609–626. Springer, Heidelberg (2004)

9. Herranz, J., Sáez, G.: Forking lemmas for ring signature schemes. In: Johansson, T., Maitra, S. (eds.) INDOCRYPT 2003. LNCS, vol. 2904, pp. 266–279. Springer, Heidelberg (2003)

10. Herranz, J., Sáez, G.: A provably secure id-based ring signature scheme. Cryptology ePrint Archive, Report 2003/261 (2003), http://eprint.iacr.org/

11. Krzywiecki, L., Kutylowski, M., Lauks, A.: Hierarchical ring signatures. Slides presented at 'Western European Workshop on Research in Cryptology 2009 (2009)

12. Lin, C.-Y., Wu, T.-C.: An identity-based ring signature scheme from bilinear pairings. Cryptology ePrint Archive, Report 2003/117 (2003), http://eprint.iacr.org/

13. Naor, M.: Deniable ring authentication. In: Yung, M. (ed.) CRYPTO 2002. LNCS, vol. 2442, pp. 481–498. Springer, Heidelberg (2002)

14. Pointcheval, D., Stern, J.: Security arguments for digital signatures and blind signatures. J. Cryptology 13(3), 361–396 (2000)

15. Rivest, R.L., Shamir, A., Tauman, Y.: How to Leak a Secret. In: Boyd, C. (ed.) ASIACRYPT 2001. LNCS, vol. 2248, pp. 552–565. Springer, Heidelberg (2001)

16. Schnorr, C.-P.: Efficient signature generation by smart cards. J. Cryptology 4(3), 161–174 (1991)

17. Tsang, P.P., Wei, V.K.: Short linkable ring signatures for e-voting, e-cash and attestation. In: Deng, R.H., Bao, F., Pang, H., Zhou, J. (eds.) ISPEC 2005. LNCS, vol. 3439, pp. 48–60. Springer, Heidelberg (2005)

18. van Dijk, M., Juels, A., Oprea, A., Rivest, R.L.: Flipit: The game of?stealthy takeover? Journal of Cryptology 26(4), 655–713 (2013)

19. Wolchok, S., Wustrow, E., Isabel, D., Halderman, J.A.: Attacking the washington, dc internet voting system. In: FC 2012. LNCS, pp. 114–128. Springer, Heidelberg (2012)

20. Zhang, F., Kim, K.: Id-based blind signature and ring signature from pairings. In: Zheng, Y. (ed.) ASIACRYPT 2002. LNCS, vol. 2501, pp. 533–547. Springer, Heidelberg (2002)

Compact Accumulator Using Lattices

Mahabir Prasad Jhanwar[1,*] and Reihaneh Safavi-Naini[2,**]

[1] CR Rao AIMSCS, UoH Campus, India
[2] Department of Computer Science, University of Calgary, Canada

Abstract. An accumulator is a *succinct* aggregate of a set of values where it is possible to issue *short* membership proofs for each accumulated value. A party in possession of such a membership proof can then demonstrate that the value is included in the set. In this paper, we present the first lattice-based accumulator scheme that issues compact membership proofs. The security of our scheme is based on the hardness of the Short Integer Solution problem.

1 Introduction

Accumulators: An accumulator scheme is a cryptographic authentication primitive for *optimally* verifying set-membership relations. Briefly, given a set X of elements, an accumulator scheme can compute a short representation of X, denoted as Acc_X and called *accumulation value* of X, such that for every element $x \in X$ a short membership *witness* w_x of "x belonging to X" can be generated. The accumulation value Acc_X is published, and everybody can obtain it in an authenticated manner. Later, by exhibiting a *valid* (x, w_x) pair, a prover can convince a verifier that the value x was indeed accumulated into Acc_X. The security of the scheme requires that it be difficult to find a valid value-witness pair (x^*, w_{x^*}) such that $x^* \notin X$. An accumulator is *compact* if it yields accumulation values and witnesses that are of constant size (i.e., independent of the number of elements X contains).

Applications: Accumulators have proven to be a very strong mathematical tool with applications in a variety of privacy preserving technologies. Applications of accumulators include efficient time-stamping [7], anonymous credential systems and group signatures [11,25,26], ring signatures [17], redactable signatures [29], sanitizable signatures [13], P-homomorphic signatures [2], and Zerocoin [24] (an extension of the cryptographic currency Bitcoin), etc.

Evolution: Accumulators were first introduced by Benaloh and de Mare [7], and were later further studied and extended by Baric and Pfitzmann [6]. The security of both constructions was proved under the *strong* RSA assumption.

---

* Part of this research was done while visiting R. C. Bose Center of Cryptology and Security, Indian Statistical Institute, Kolkata.
** Financial support for this research was provided in part by Alberta Innovates - Technology Futures, in the Province of Alberta in Canada.

R.S. Chakraborty et al. (Eds.): SPACE 2015, LNCS 9354, pp. 347–358, 2015.
DOI: 10.1007/978-3-319-24126-5_20

Camenisch and Lysyanskaya [12] augmented the latter work and proposed *dynamic* accumulators, in which elements can be efficiently added to and removed from the set of accumulated values, as well as privacy-preserving membership proofs. Alternative constructions of dynamic accumulators based on bilinear pairings [11, 16, 25], Paillier's trapdoor permutation [30], and vector commitments [15] are also known. Li et al. [20] introduced *universal* accumulators that extend the functionality of accumulators by supporting proofs that a given element is not a member of the set that has been accumulated. The security of their proposed instantiation is based on strong RSA assumption. Camacho et al. [10] and Buldas et al. [9] independently introduced *strong* universal accumulators (also known as *undeniable* accumulators), which do not assume the accumulator manager is trusted. Both constructions were proved secure under the assumption that collision-resistant hash functions exists.

1.1 Our Contribution

In recent years, there has been rapid development in the use of lattices for constructing rich cryptographic schemes (these include digital signatures [8, 14, 19], identity-based encryption [19] and hierarchical IBE [1, 14], non-interactive zero knowledge [28], and even a fully homomorphic cryptosystem [18]). Among other reasons, this is because such schemes have yet to be broken by quantum algorithms, and their security can be based solely on *worst-case* computational assumptions.

In the spirit of lattice-based cryptography, we present the first compact accumulator scheme from lattices and prove that it is secure based on the hardness of the Short Integer Solution (SIS) problem. As the average-case SIS problem was shown to be as hard as certain worst-case lattice problems [3, 19, 23], our scheme owns provable security under worst-case hardness assumption.

1.2 Related Work

Although, there exists no direct lattice-based accumulator scheme, the constructions in [7, 9, 10] give indirect lattice-based instantiations because they only assume collision-resistant hash functions exist. This is true as lattice-based constructions of collision resistant hash functions are known [21, 27], and therefore the security of the resulting schemes can also be reduced to worst-case assumptions on lattices. However, collision resistant hash based accumulator schemes are not *compact*: the size of witness is always logarithmic in the number of values accumulated.

2 Preliminaries

Notation: Let $\lambda \in \mathbb{N}$ be the security parameter and 1^λ its unary representation. We use standard asymptotic notation to describe the order of growth of functions. For any positive real valued functions $f(n)$ and $g(n)$ we write $f = O(g)$

if there exists two constants c_1, c_2 such that $f(n) < c_1 \cdot g(n)$ for all $n \geq c_2$; $f = \Omega(g)$ if $g = O(f)$; $f = \Theta(g)$ if $f = O(g)$ and $g = O(f)$; and $f = o(g)$ if $\lim_{n \to \infty} \frac{f(n)}{g(n)} = 0$. We denote $f = \tilde{O}(g)$ if $f = O(g \cdot \text{poly}(\log g))$. The notation $\tilde{\Theta}$ is defined analogously. We denote $\omega(f(n))$ to denote a function that grows faster than $c \cdot f(n)$ for any $c > 0$. We let $\text{poly}(n)$ denote an unspecified function $f(n) = O(n^c)$ for some constant c. A function $f(n)$ is called negligible, often written as $f(n) = \text{negl}(n)$, if $f = o(\frac{1}{g})$ for any polynomial $g = \text{poly}(n)$. A function of n is called *overwhelming* if it is $1 - \text{negl}(n)$. For a positive integer k, let $[k]$ denote the set $\{1, \ldots, k\}$. We denote the set of integers modulo q by $\mathbb{Z}_q$, and identify it with the set $\{0, \ldots, q-1\}$ in the natural way. Column vectors are named by lower-case bold letters (e.g., $\boldsymbol{b}$) and matrices by upper-case bold letters (e.g., $\boldsymbol{B}$). For a matrix $\boldsymbol{S} \in \mathbb{R}^{m_1 \times m_2}$, we call the norm of $\boldsymbol{S}$ as $||\boldsymbol{S}|| = \max_{1 \leq i \leq m_2} ||\boldsymbol{s}_i||$, where $||\boldsymbol{s}_i||$ denotes the ℓ_2-norm (Euclidean norm) of the column vector $\boldsymbol{s}_i$. We let $\tilde{\boldsymbol{S}} \in \mathbb{R}^{m_1 \times m_2}$ denote the matrix whose columns $\tilde{\boldsymbol{s}}_1, \ldots, \tilde{\boldsymbol{s}}_{m_2}$ represent the Gram-Schmidt orthogonalization of the vectors $\boldsymbol{s}_1, \ldots, \boldsymbol{s}_{m_2}$ taken in the same order. Let $||\tilde{\boldsymbol{S}}||$ denotes the Gram-Schmidt norm of $\boldsymbol{S}$.

2.1 Lattices

Let $\mathbb{R}^m$ be the m-dimensional Euclidean space. A *lattice* $\Lambda \subseteq \mathbb{R}^m$ is a set

$$\Lambda = \left\{ \sum_{i=1}^{k} c_i \boldsymbol{b}_i \mid c_i \in \mathbb{Z} \text{ and } \boldsymbol{b}_1, \ldots, \boldsymbol{b}_k \in \mathbb{R}^m \right\} \tag{1}$$

of all integral combinations of k linearly independent vectors $\boldsymbol{b}_1, \ldots, \boldsymbol{b}_k$ in $\mathbb{R}^m$ $(m \geq k)$ [1]. The integers k and m are called the *rank* and *dimension* of the lattice, respectively. The sequence of vectors $\boldsymbol{b}_1, \ldots, \boldsymbol{b}_k$ is called a *lattice basis* and it is conveniently represented as a matrix $\boldsymbol{B} = [\boldsymbol{b}_1, \ldots, \boldsymbol{b}_k] \in \mathbb{R}^{m \times k}$ having the basis vectors as columns. Using the matrix notation, (1) can be written in a more compact form as $\Lambda = \Lambda(\boldsymbol{B}) = \{\boldsymbol{B}\boldsymbol{c} \mid \boldsymbol{c} \in \mathbb{Z}^k\}$, where $\boldsymbol{B}\boldsymbol{c}$ is the usual matrix-vector multiplication. When $m = k$, the lattice is called *full-rank*. A lattice Λ is called *integer lattice* if $\Lambda \subseteq \mathbb{Z}^m$. In this work, every lattice will be a full-rank lattice.

The *minimum distance* $\lambda_1(\Lambda)$ of a lattice Λ is the length (Euclidean length, i.e., ℓ_2 norm, unless otherwise indicated) of a shortest non-zero lattice vector. More generally, the ith *successive minimum* $\lambda_i(\Lambda)$ is the smallest radius r such that Λ contains i linearly independent vectors of norm at most r. The following are the two standard worst-case approximation problems on lattices: Shortest Vector Problem (SVP_γ) and Shortest Independent Vector Problem (SIVP_γ). In both problems, $\gamma = \gamma(m)$ is the approximation factor as a function of the lattice-dimension.

---

[1] Alternatively, lattices can also be characterized without any reference to any basis. A lattice Λ can be defined as a discrete nonempty subset of $\mathbb{R}^m$ which is closed under subtraction, i.e., if $\boldsymbol{x} \in \Lambda$ and $\boldsymbol{y} \in \Lambda$, then also $\boldsymbol{x} - \boldsymbol{y} \in \Lambda$. Here *discrete* means that there exists a positive real $\lambda > 0$ such that the Euclidean distance between any two lattice vectors is at least λ.

Definition 1 (SVP$_\gamma$). *An input to* SVP$_\gamma$ *is a basis B of a full-rank m-dimensional lattice. The goal is to output a nonzero lattice vector Bx (with $x \in \mathbb{Z}^m \backslash \{0\}$) such that $\|Bx\| \leq \gamma \cdot \|By\|$ for any $y \in \mathbb{Z}^m \backslash \{0\}$.*

Definition 2 (SIVP$_\gamma$). *An input to* SIVP$_\gamma$ *is a basis B of a full-rank m-dimensional lattice. The goal is to output a set of m linearly independent lattice vectors $Bx_1, \ldots, Bx_m \in \Lambda(B)$ such that $max_i\{\|Bx_i\|\} \leq \gamma \cdot \lambda_m(\Lambda(B))$.*

q-ary Lattices. In this work we use q-ary lattices; a special family of full-rank integer lattices. A lattice from this family is most naturally specified not by a basis, but instead by a parity check matrix $A \in \mathbb{Z}_q^{n \times m}$ for some positive integer n and positive integer modulus q. The associated full rank lattice of dimension m is defined as:

$$\Lambda^{\perp}(A) = \{x \in \mathbb{Z}^m \mid Ax = 0 \bmod q\} \tag{2}$$

It is routine to check that $\Lambda^{\perp}(A)$ contains $0 \in \mathbb{Z}^m$ (thus non-empty) and is closed under subtraction, hence it is a lattice. The hardness of these lattices is most naturally parametrized by n (not m, even though m is the dimension of the lattices) and therefore it is standard to consider the parameters $m = m(n)$ and $q = q(n)$ as functions of n. By taking $m = c \cdot n \log q$ for some constant $c \geq 1$, it can be shown that with high probability, the minimum distance $\lambda_1\left(\Lambda^{\perp}(A)\right)$ of $\Lambda^{\perp}(A)$ is at most $\Theta(\sqrt{n \log q})$, where $A \in \mathbb{Z}_q^{n \times m}$ is random.

Ajtai [4], Alwen and Peikert [5], Micciancio and Peikert [22] provided methods to produce a matrix A statistically close to uniform in $\mathbb{Z}_q^{n \times m}$ along with a short basis T_A of lattice $\Lambda^{\perp}(A)$. It is summarized in the following lemma.

Proposition 1 (Short Basis Generation). *There is a PPT algorithm that, on input a security parameter 1^λ, an odd prime $q = \mathsf{poly}(\lambda)$, and two integers $n = \Theta(\lambda)$ and $m \geq 6n \log q$, outputs a matrix $A \in \mathbb{Z}_q^{n \times m}$ statistically close to uniform, and a basis T_A for $\Lambda^{\perp}(A)$ with overwhelming probability such that $\|\tilde{T}_A\| \leq \tilde{\Theta}(\sqrt{m})$.*

We refer to the algorithm of Proposition 1 by $\mathsf{TrapGen}(1^\lambda)$.

<u>Primitive Matrix:</u> We say that a matrix $A \in \mathbb{Z}_q^{n \times m}$ is *primitive* if its columns generate all of $\mathbb{Z}_q^n$, i.e., $A \cdot \mathbb{Z}^m \pmod{q} = \mathbb{Z}_q^n$. It is known that for any fixed constant $C > 1$ and any $m \geq Cn \log q$, a uniformly random $A \in \mathbb{Z}_q^{n \times m}$ is primitive, except with $2^{-\Omega}(n) = \mathsf{negl}(n)$ probability. Therefore, throughout the paper we implicitly assume that such a uniform A is primitive.

Hardness Assumption. The *short integer solution* (SIS) problem was first suggested to be hard on average by Ajtai [3] and later in [23] was formalized as follows. The security of our accumulator scheme is based on the hardness of this problem.

Definition 3 (SIS Problem). *The small integer solution problem* SIS *(in the ℓ_2 norm) is as follows: given an integer q, a matrix $A \in \mathbb{Z}_q^{n \times m}$, and a real β, find an integer vector $e \in \mathbb{Z}^m$ such that $Ae = 0 \bmod q$ and $\|e\| \leq \beta$.*

Clearly, the problem is syntactically equivalent to finding some short nonzero vector in $\Lambda^{\perp}(\boldsymbol{A})$. For functions $q(n), m(n)$, and $\beta(n)$, an *average-case* SIS problem instance is drawn from the probability ensemble over instances $(q(n), \boldsymbol{A}, \beta(n))$ where $\boldsymbol{A} \in \mathbb{Z}_q^{n \times m}$ is uniformly random. This average-case problem was shown to be as hard as certain worst-case lattice problems, first by Ajtai [3], then by Micciancio and Regev [23], and Gentry et al. [19].

Theorem 1. (*[19]*) *For any poly-bounded* m, *any* $\beta = \mathsf{poly}(n)$ *and for any prime* $q \geq \beta \cdot \omega(\sqrt{n \log n})$, *the average-case* $\mathsf{SIS}_{q,m,\beta}$ *is as hard as approximating the Shortest Independent Vector Problem (*SIVP_{γ}*), among others, in the worst-case to within certain* $\gamma = \beta \cdot \tilde{O}(\sqrt{n})$ *factors.*

Discrete Gaussian Distribution over Lattices. For any $s > 0$ the Gaussian function $\rho_{s,\boldsymbol{c}} : \mathbb{R}^m \to \mathbb{R}$ centered at $\boldsymbol{c} \in \mathbb{R}^m$ with parameter s is defined as:

$$\forall \boldsymbol{x} \in \mathbb{R}^m, \ \rho_{s,\boldsymbol{c}}(\boldsymbol{x}) = e^{-\frac{\pi ||\boldsymbol{x} - \boldsymbol{c}||^2}{s^2}}.$$

For any $\boldsymbol{c} \in \mathbb{R}^m$, real $s > 0$, and m-dimensional lattice Λ, define the discrete Gaussian distribution $D_{\Lambda,s,\boldsymbol{c}}$ over Λ (with center $\boldsymbol{c}$ and Gaussian parameter s) as:

$$\forall \boldsymbol{x} \in \mathbb{R}^m, \ D_{\Lambda,s,\boldsymbol{c}}(\boldsymbol{x}) = \frac{\rho_{s,\boldsymbol{c}}(\boldsymbol{x})}{\rho_{s,\boldsymbol{c}}(\Lambda)},$$

where $\rho_{s,\boldsymbol{c}}(\Lambda) = \sum_{\boldsymbol{y} \in \Lambda} \rho_{s,\boldsymbol{c}}(\boldsymbol{y})$.

Micciancio and Regev [23] proved that the norm (ℓ_2 norm) of vectors sampled from the discrete Gaussian distribution is small with high probability. We present this result specialized to q-ary lattices.

Lemma 1. *Let* $\boldsymbol{A} \in \mathbb{Z}_q^{n \times m}$ *be a primitive matrix, and* s *be a Gaussian parameter with* $s \geq \omega(\sqrt{\log m})$. *Then for* m-*dimensional full-rank lattice* $\Lambda^{\perp}(\boldsymbol{A})$, *and* $\boldsymbol{c} \in \mathbb{R}^m$,

$$\Pr_{\boldsymbol{x} \leftarrow D_{\Lambda^{\perp}(\boldsymbol{A}),s,\boldsymbol{c}}} \left[\ ||\boldsymbol{x} - \boldsymbol{c}|| > s\sqrt{m} \ \right] \leq \mathsf{negl}(m).$$

Gentry et al. [19] proved that, given a basis $\boldsymbol{B}$ for a lattice Λ, one can efficiently sample points in Λ with discrete Gaussian distribution for sufficiently large values of s.

Theorem 2. *There is a* PPT *algorithm that, given a basis* $\boldsymbol{B}$ *of an* m-*dimensional lattice* Λ, *a parameter* $s \geq ||\tilde{\boldsymbol{B}}|| \cdot \omega(\sqrt{\log m})$, *and a center* $\boldsymbol{c} \in \mathbb{R}^m$, *outputs a sample from a distribution that is statistically close to* $D_{\Lambda,s,\boldsymbol{c}}$.

We refer to the algorithm of Theorem 2 by $\mathsf{SampleD}(\boldsymbol{B}, s, \boldsymbol{c})$.

We now recall an important lemma from [19] which says that for a vector $\boldsymbol{e}$, chosen from an appropriate discrete Gaussian distribution over $\mathbb{Z}^m$, the vector $\boldsymbol{A}\boldsymbol{e} \bmod q$ corresponds to a nearly-uniform element in $\mathbb{Z}_q^n$.

Lemma 2. *Let* $\boldsymbol{A} \in \mathbb{Z}_q^{n \times m}$ *be primitive. Then for any* $s \geq \omega(\sqrt{\log m})$, *the distribution of* $\boldsymbol{u} = \boldsymbol{A}\boldsymbol{e} \bmod q \in \mathbb{Z}_q^n$ *is statistically close to uniform over* $\mathbb{Z}_q^n$, *where* $\boldsymbol{e}$ *is chosen from* $D_{\mathbb{Z}^m,s,\boldsymbol{0}}$.

The Gaussian Sampling Algorithm: SampleD($\boldsymbol{B}, s, \boldsymbol{c}$)

- Input :
    - a basis $\boldsymbol{B}$ of a lattice $\Lambda \subseteq \mathbb{R}^m$,
    - a positive real parameter $s \geq ||\tilde{\boldsymbol{B}}|| \cdot \omega(\sqrt{\log m})$, and
    - a center vector $\boldsymbol{c} \in \mathbb{R}^n$.
- Output :
    - a fresh random lattice vector $\boldsymbol{x} \in \Lambda$ drawn from a distribution statistically close to $D_{\Lambda, s, \boldsymbol{c}}$.

Basis Delegation. In [14] a deterministic polynomial-time algorithm is given to extend a basis of $\Lambda^\perp(\boldsymbol{A})$ to a basis (without any loss of quality) of an arbitrary higher-dimensional extension $\Lambda^\perp(\boldsymbol{A}||\bar{\boldsymbol{A}})$. We refer to this algorithm by BasisDel.

The Basis Delegation Algorithm: BasisDel($\boldsymbol{T}_{\boldsymbol{A}}, \boldsymbol{A}, \bar{\boldsymbol{A}}$)

- Input :
    - an arbitrary $\boldsymbol{A} \in \mathbb{Z}_q^{n \times m}$ such that $\boldsymbol{A}$ is primitive,
    - an arbitrary basis $\boldsymbol{T}_{\boldsymbol{A}}$ of $\Lambda^\perp(\boldsymbol{A})$, and
    - an arbitrary $\bar{\boldsymbol{A}} \in \mathbb{Z}_q^{n \times \bar{m}}$.
- Output :
    - a basis $\boldsymbol{T}_{\boldsymbol{A}'}$ of $\Lambda^\perp(\boldsymbol{A}' = \boldsymbol{A}||\bar{\boldsymbol{A}}) \subseteq \mathbb{Z}^{m+\bar{m}}$ such that $||\tilde{\boldsymbol{T}}_{\boldsymbol{A}'}|| = ||\tilde{\boldsymbol{T}}_{\boldsymbol{A}}||$.

Cryptographic Accumulators. We now give a formal definition of a cryptographic accumulator scheme.

Definition 4 (Accumulator Scheme). *Let $\mathcal{M}$, $\mathcal{C}$ and $\mathcal{W}$ be three sets (the message set, the set containing accumulated values and the set containing witnesses respectively). An accumulator scheme is a tuple of* PPT *algorithms (*Setup, Accumulate, WitGen, Verify*) with the following functionalities:*

- Setup(1^λ): *Given a security parameter λ, it outputs a public key* pk *and a secret key* sk. *The remaining algorithms take* pk *as an implicit input.*
- Accumulate(X): *If $X \subseteq \mathcal{M}$ then it accumulates all the elements of X into an accumulation value* $\mathsf{Acc}_X \in \mathcal{C}$.
- WitGen($X, x, $sk): *If $x \in X$ and $X \subseteq \mathcal{M}$, then it outputs a membership witness $w_x \in \mathcal{W}$; otherwise it outputs "$\perp$" denoting* Error.
- Verify(x, w_x, c): *For $x \in \mathcal{M}$, $w_x \in \mathcal{W}$ and $c \in \mathcal{C}$ it outputs either "1" denoting* member *or "0" denoting* Error.

The *correctness* of an accumulator scheme requires that correctly accumulated values have valid witnesses with overwhelming probability, i.e., for $x \in \mathcal{M}$, $X \subseteq \mathcal{M}$, the verification algorithm Verify($x, $WitGen($X, x, $sk), Accumulate($X$)) outputs 1 with overwhelming probability if, $x \in X$.

Definition 5 (One-way Security). *An accumulator scheme is one-way secure* [2] *if, for all polynomial time adversaries* $\mathcal{A}$:

$$\Pr[\mathsf{pk} \leftarrow \mathsf{Setup}(1^\lambda); (X^*, x^*, w_{x^*}) \leftarrow \mathcal{A}(\mathsf{pk}) \mid x^* \notin X^* \subseteq \mathcal{M} \text{ and}$$

$$\mathsf{Verify}(x^*, w_{x^*}, c \leftarrow \mathsf{Accumulate}(X^*)) = 1] \leq \mathsf{negl}(\lambda).$$

If an accumulator satisfies this definition, then it is infeasible for an adversary to prove that a value x was accumulated in a accumulation value c when in fact it was not.

3   A Compact Accumulator Scheme

In this section we provide our accumulator scheme from lattices. Next, we discuss the correctness of our scheme. The security analysis of our scheme will be given in § 3.2.

The parameters of our scheme consist of:

- a security parameter 1^λ;
- integers n and q (a prime) with $n = \Theta(\lambda)$ and $q = \mathsf{poly}(n)$;
- a dimension $m \geq 6n \lg q$ and a bound $L = O(\sqrt{m})$;
- a Gaussian parameter $s \geq L \cdot \omega\left(\sqrt{\log(m + m')}\right)$, where $m' = \mathsf{poly}(\lambda) \in \mathbb{N}$;
- a message set $\mathcal{M} = \left\{ \boldsymbol{B}_1, \ldots, \boldsymbol{B}_Q \in \mathbb{Z}_q^{n \times m'} \right\}$, where $Q = \mathsf{poly}(\lambda)$ and $\boldsymbol{B}_i$'s are independently chosen with uniform distribution.

The scheme is defined as follows.

- $\mathsf{Setup}(1^\lambda)$: It uses the algorithm $\mathsf{TrapGen}(1^\lambda)$ from Proposition 1 to generate $(\boldsymbol{A}, \boldsymbol{T_A})$, where $\boldsymbol{A} \in \mathbb{Z}_q^{n \times m}$ is statistically close to uniform and $\boldsymbol{T_A}$ is a short basis of $\Lambda^\perp(\boldsymbol{A})$ with $\|\tilde{\boldsymbol{T}}_{\boldsymbol{A}}\| \leq L$. The public key pk is set to $\boldsymbol{A}$, and the secret key sk is set to $\boldsymbol{T_A}$. In the following, the other algorithms take $\mathsf{pk} = \boldsymbol{A}$ as an implicit input.
- $\mathsf{Accumulate}(X \subset \mathcal{M})$: Without loss of generality, suppose $X = \{\boldsymbol{B}_1, \ldots, \boldsymbol{B}_{Q'}\}$ for some $Q' \in [Q]$. It accumulates the Q' matrices in the set X into a *compact* accumulator value

$$\mathsf{Acc}_X = \left[\sum_{\boldsymbol{B}_i \in X} \boldsymbol{B}_i \right] \in \mathbb{Z}_q^{n \times m'} .$$

- $\mathsf{WitGen}(X, \boldsymbol{B}, \mathsf{sk})$: Let $X = \{\boldsymbol{B}_1, \ldots, \boldsymbol{B}_{Q'}\}$ for some $Q' \in [Q]$. If $\boldsymbol{B} \notin X$, return $\bot$. Otherwise, $\boldsymbol{B} \in X$ and let $\boldsymbol{B} = \boldsymbol{B}_j$ for some $j \in [Q']$. The witness

---

[2] In the literature, the one-way secure accumulators are also known as collision-resistant accumulators.

generation algorithm returns a witness w_B to the fact that B has been accumulated in Acc_X. It first computes the matrix

$$F_B = \left[A \; \| \; \sum_{1 \le i(\ne j) \le Q'} B_i \right] \in \mathbb{Z}_q^{n \times (m+m')}.$$

It then samples a vector $d_B \in \Lambda^\perp(F_B) \subseteq \mathbb{Z}^{(m+m')}$ following the distribution $D_{\Lambda^\perp(F_B),s,0}$. This is done, using $\mathsf{sk} = T_A$, as follows:

$$d_B \leftarrow \mathsf{SampleD} \left(\mathsf{BasisDel} \left(T_A, A, \sum_{1 \le i(\ne j) \le Q'} B_i \right), s, 0 \right).$$

The witness w_B is set to $w_B = d_B$. See Theorem 2 for a description of SampleD, and § 2.1 for BasisDel.

- Verify(B, w_B, Acc_X): For an element $B \in \mathcal{M}$ the verification algorithm proceeds as follows:
  • Compute

$$F_B = [A \| (\mathsf{Acc}_X - B)] \in \mathbb{Z}_q^{n \times (m+m')}$$

  and check if $F_B \cdot w_B = 0 \bmod q$, i.e., if $w_B \in \Lambda^\perp(F_B)$.
  • Finally, check if w_B is small by verifying that $0 < \|w_B\| \le s\sqrt{m+m'}$.
  If all the checks pass, output 1; otherwise, output 0.

3.1   Correctness

It is easy to see by inspection that the accumulator scheme is correct, i.e., the correctly accumulated values have verifying witnesses with overwhelming probability. But for completeness we discuss the correctness of our scheme in detail.

Let $X = \{B_1, \ldots, B_{Q'}\} \subseteq \mathcal{M}$, with corresponding accumulation value $\mathsf{Acc}_X = \sum_{i=1}^{Q'} B_i$. We show that every $B \in X$ admits a verifying witness with respect to Acc_X. Without loss of generality, let $B = B_1$. A valid witness for B_1 is a short vector d_{B_1} in the lattice $\Lambda^\perp(F_{B_1})$ (where $F_{B_1} = \left[A \| \sum_{i=2}^{Q'} B_i \right] \in \mathbb{Z}_q^{n \times (m+m')}$), i.e., $\|d_{B_1}\| \le s\sqrt{(m+m')}$. Lemma 1 says that a sample in $\Lambda^\perp(F_{B_1})$, following $D_{\Lambda^\perp(F_{B_1}),s,0}$, has norm bounded by $s\sqrt{(m+m')}$ if $s \ge \omega\left(\sqrt{\log(m+m')}\right)$. The algorithm of Theorem 2 provides a method to sample from $D_{\Lambda^\perp(F_{B_1}),s,0}$ if it is provided with a basis $T_{F_{B_1}}$ of $\Lambda^\perp(F_{B_1})$, such that $s \ge \|\tilde{T}_{F_{B_1}}\| \cdot \omega\left(\sqrt{\log(m+m')}\right)$. We now see that this is indeed the case.

The witness generation algorithm has access to a short basis T_A of the lattice $\Lambda^\perp(A)$. With $\left(T_A, A, \sum_{i=2}^{Q'} B_i \right)$ as input, the basis delegation algorithm BasisDel of § 2.1 constructs a basis $T_{F_{B_1}}$ of $\Lambda^\perp(F_{B_1})$ such that $\|\tilde{T}_{F_{B_1}}\| = \|\tilde{T}_A\|$. But $\|\tilde{T}_A\| \le L \le \frac{s}{\omega\left(\sqrt{\log(m+m')}\right)}$, and therefore we have $s \ge \|\tilde{T}_{F_{B_1}}\| \cdot \omega\left(\sqrt{\log(m+m')}\right)$.

Hence, the sampled vector $d_{B_1} \leftarrow \mathsf{SampleD}\left(\mathsf{BasisDel}\left(T_A, A, \sum_{i=2}^{Q'} B_i\right), s, 0\right)$ constitute a valid witness for the membership of B_1 in X with respect to Acc_X.

3.2 Security

In the following theorem we reduce the SIS problem to the problem of breaking the security of our accumulator scheme.

Theorem 3. *For parameters* $\lambda, n, q, m, m', L, s,$ *and* $Q,$ *as listed in the scheme, if there is a* PPT *adversary* $\mathcal{A}$ *that breaks the one-way security of our accumulator scheme, with probability* ϵ, *then there is a* PPT *algorithm* $\mathcal{B}$ *that solves the* $\mathsf{SIS}_{q,m,\beta}$ *problem with probability* $\epsilon' \geq \epsilon/3$, *for some polynomial function* $\beta = \mathsf{poly}(\lambda)$; *in particular* $\beta = Qs's(m + m')$, *where* $s' \geq \omega(\sqrt{\log m})$ [3].

Proof: Suppose that there exists such a forger $\mathcal{A}$. We construct a solver $\mathcal{B}$ that simulates an attack environment and uses an invalid element-witness pair ($\mathcal{A}$'s output) to create its solution for SIS problem. The various operations performed by $\mathcal{B}$ are the following.

- **Invocation**
  - $\mathcal{B}$ is invoked on a random instance $(q, A \in \mathbb{Z}_q^{n \times m}, \beta)$ of SIS problem and asked to submit a solution.
- **Simulation**
  - $\mathcal{B}$ sets the public key pk of the accumulator scheme to pk $= A$.
  - It then picks Q short random matrices $R_1, \ldots, R_Q \in \mathbb{Z}^{m \times m'}$ such that $\|R_i\| \leq s'\sqrt{m}$, for some $s' \geq \omega(\sqrt{\log m})$. It can do so, by independently sampling the columns of R_i's from $D_{\mathbb{Z}^m, s', 0}$.
  - It then sets the message space $\mathcal{M}$ to $\{B_1 = AR_1 \bmod q, \ldots, B_Q = AR_Q \bmod q \in \mathbb{Z}_q^{n \times m'}\}$. By Lemma 2 the distribution of $B_i = AR_i$ is statistically close to uniform over $\mathbb{Z}_q^{n \times m}$ when columns of R_i's are chosen from $D_{\mathbb{Z}^m, s', 0}$.
  - Finally, $\mathcal{B}$ gives $(A, \mathcal{M})$ to $\mathcal{A}$.

- **Breaking One-way Security**
  - $\mathcal{A}$ outputs $(X^* = \{B_{i_1}, \ldots, B_{i_k}\} \subseteq \mathcal{M}, B^* = B_\ell \in \mathcal{M}, w_B^* \in \mathbb{Z}^{m+m'})$ such that

$$B^* \notin X^* \text{ and } \mathbf{Verify}\,(B^*, w_B^*, \mathsf{Acc}_{X^*} \leftarrow \mathsf{Acc}(X^*)) = 1.$$

---

[3] To ensure that the SIS instance with norm bound $\beta = Qs's(m + m')$ is hard (worst-case to average-case reduction), the modulus q of the scheme should satisfy $q > \beta \cdot \omega(\sqrt{n \log n})$ (See Theorem 1). In particular, for q we choose the smallest prime bigger than λ^t for the smallest t such that $q > \beta \cdot \omega(\sqrt{n \log n})$. Choosing $n \log n$ for $\omega(\sqrt{n \log n})$, implies $\beta \cdot \omega(\sqrt{n \log n}) = \mathsf{poly}(\lambda)$, as Q, s', s, m, m', n are all bounded above by a $\mathsf{poly}(\lambda)$ size number.

– **Solving SIS Instance**
  • **Verify**$(B^*, w_B^*, \mathrm{Acc}_{X^*}) = 1$ means
  $$w_B^* \in \Lambda^\perp(A || (\mathrm{Acc}_{X^*} - B^*)), \text{ and } 0 < ||w_B^*|| \leq s\sqrt{m + m'}$$

  • Compute $R^* = \sum_{j=1}^k R_{i_j} - R_\ell$. Also, write $w_B^* \in \mathbb{Z}^{m+m'}$ as $\begin{bmatrix} w_B^{*\prime} \\ w_B^{*\prime\prime} \end{bmatrix}$ such that $w_B^{*\prime} \in \mathbb{Z}^m$, $w_B^{*\prime\prime} \in \mathbb{Z}^{m'}$.

  • Finally, $\mathcal{B}$ outputs $e = w_B^{*\prime} + R^* w_B^{*\prime\prime} \in \mathbb{Z}^m$ as solution to SIS instance $(q, A \in \mathbb{Z}_q^{n \times m}, \beta)$.

We now show that e is indeed a valid solution (with probability greater than $2/3$), i.e., $Ae = 0 \bmod q$, $||e|| \leq \beta$, and $e \neq 0$. Clearly $Ae = A(w_B^{*\prime} + R^* w_B^{*\prime\prime}) = Aw_B^{*\prime} + (\sum_{j=1}^k AR_{i_j} - AR_\ell)w_B^{*\prime\prime} = Aw_B^{*\prime} + (\sum_{j=1}^k B_{i_j} - B_\ell)w_B^{*\prime\prime} = [A || (\mathrm{Acc}_{X^*} - B^*)]w_B^* = 0 \bmod q$.
Next, we show that $||e|| \leq \beta$. We have $e = w_B^{*\prime} + R^* w_B^{*\prime\prime}$, where $R^* = \sum_{j=1}^k R_{i_j} - R_\ell$ is a sum of k low norm matrices R_{i_j} minus a low norm matrix R_ℓ ($||R_i|| \leq s'\sqrt{m}$ with overwhelming probability). Therefore we have,

$$||e|| = ||w_B^{*\prime} + (\sum_{j=1}^k R_{i_j} - R_\ell)w_B^{*\prime\prime}||$$

$$\leq ||w_B^{*\prime}|| + ||\sum_{j=1}^k R_{i_j} - R_\ell|| ||w_B^{*\prime\prime}||$$

$$\leq s\sqrt{m + m'}(1 + (k+1)s'\sqrt{m})$$

$$\leq Qs's(m + m').$$

We now complete the proof by showing that $e = w_B^{*\prime} + R^* w_B^{*\prime\prime} \neq 0$. Let us assume $w_B^{*\prime\prime} \neq 0$ (as $w_B^* \neq 0$, $w_B^{*\prime\prime} = 0$ implies $w_B^{*\prime} \neq 0$ and thus $e \neq 0$). As $0 < ||w_B^{*\prime\prime}|| \leq s\sqrt{m + m'} << q$, there must be at least one coordinate of $w_B^{*\prime\prime}$ that is non-zero modulo q. W.l.o.g., let this coordinate be the first one in $w_B^{*\prime\prime}$, and call it z. Let r_1^* be the first column of R^*, and let r_{t1} be the first column of R_t for each t in $\{i_1, \ldots, i_k, \ell\}$. Clearly, $r_1^* = \sum_{j=1}^k r_{i_j 1} - r_{\ell 1}$. We focus on $r_{i_1 1}$. Let $u = z r_{i_1 1}$. Rewrite e as $e = z r_1^* + e' = u + e''$ such that u depends on $r_{i_1 1}$ and e'' does not. Now, the only information about $r_{i_1 1}$ available to $\mathcal{A}$ is contained in the first column of $B_{i_1} = AR_{i_1}$. With even A being known in the worst case, by a simple pigeonhole principle, there are a very large (exponential in $m - n$) number of admissible and equally likely vectors $r_{i_1 1}$, in particular more than $3Q$ of them, that are compatible with the view of $\mathcal{A}$. At most one such value can result in cancellation of e, for if some u caused all coordination of e to cancel, then every other u would fail to do so. Therefore $\Pr[e = 0] \leq 1/3Q$. Since $\mathcal{A}$ can choose B_{i_1} among Q possible values ($Q = |\mathcal{M}|$), it follows that $\mathcal{A}$ can know the value of u with probability at most $1/3$. Hence, $\Pr[e \neq 0] \geq 2/3$.

Therefore, if $\mathcal{A}$ breaks the one-way security of the scheme with probability ϵ, then $\mathcal{B}$ solves the SIS instance with probability $\epsilon' \geq 2\epsilon/3$.

4 Conclusion and Open Problems

We have provided the first lattice-based construction of a one-way accumulator scheme and proved its security from the hardness assumption of the SIS problem (which is itself implied by worst-case lattice assumptions). We leave open the problem of how to extend our basic scheme in order to incorporate dynamic and universal functionalities. Another interesting problem is to extend our scheme such that zero-knowledge proofs of membership can be obtained.

Acknowledgments. The authors would like to thank Dr. Damien Stehlé for very helpful comments and for reviewing parts of this paper. The authors would also like to thank a reviewer of SPACE 2015 for detailed comments.

References

1. Agrawal, S., Boneh, D., Boyen, X.: Efficient lattice (H)IBE in the standard model. In: Gilbert, H. (ed.) EUROCRYPT 2010. LNCS, vol. 6110, pp. 553–572. Springer, Heidelberg (2010), http://crypto.stanford.edu/~dabo/pubs/papers/latticebb.pdf
2. Ahn, J.H., Boneh, D., Camenisch, J., Hohenberger, S., Shelat, A., Waters, B.: Computing on authenticated data. In: Cramer, R. (ed.) TCC 2012. LNCS, vol. 7194, pp. 1–20. Springer, Heidelberg (2012)
3. Ajtai, M.: Generating hard instances of lattice problems (extended abstract). In: STOC, pp. 99–108 (1996)
4. Ajtai, M.: Generating hard instances of the short basis problem. In: Wiedermann, J., Van Emde Boas, P., Nielsen, M. (eds.) ICALP 1999. LNCS, vol. 1644, pp. 1–9. Springer, Heidelberg (1999)
5. Alwen, J., Peikert, C.: Generating shorter bases for hard random lattices. In: STACS. LIPIcs, vol. 3. Schloss Dagstuhl - Leibniz-Zentrum fuer Informatik, Germany (2009)
6. Barić, N., Pfitzmann, B.: Collision-free accumulators and fail-stop signature schemes without trees. In: Fumy, W. (ed.) EUROCRYPT 1997. LNCS, vol. 1233, pp. 480–494. Springer, Heidelberg (1997)
7. Benaloh, J.C., de Mare, M.: One-Way Accumulators: A Decentralized Alternative to Digital Signatures. In: Helleseth, T. (ed.) EUROCRYPT 1993. LNCS, vol. 765, pp. 274–285. Springer, Heidelberg (1994)
8. Boyen, X.: Lattice Mixing and Vanishing Trapdoors: A Framework for Fully Secure Short Signatures and More. In: Nguyen, P.Q., Pointcheval, D. (eds.) PKC 2010. LNCS, vol. 6056, pp. 499–517. Springer, Heidelberg (2010)
9. Buldas, A., Laud, P., Lipmaa, H.: Accountable certificate management using undeniable attestations. In: ACM CCS, pp. 9–17 (2000)
10. Camacho, P., Hevia, A., Kiwi, M., Opazo, R.: Strong accumulators from collision-resistant hashing. International Journal of Information Security 11(5), 349–363 (2012)
11. Camenisch, J., Kohlweiss, M., Soriente, C.: An Accumulator Based on Bilinear Maps and Efficient Revocation for Anonymous Credentials. In: Jarecki, S., Tsudik, G. (eds.) PKC 2009. LNCS, vol. 5443, pp. 481–500. Springer, Heidelberg (2009)

12. Camenisch, J.L., Lysyanskaya, A.: Dynamic accumulators and application to efficient revocation of anonymous credentials. In: Yung, M. (ed.) CRYPTO 2002. LNCS, vol. 2442, pp. 61–76. Springer, Heidelberg (2002)
13. Canard, S., Jambert, A.: On Extended Sanitizable Signature Schemes. In: Pieprzyk, J. (ed.) CT-RSA 2010. LNCS, vol. 5985, pp. 179–194. Springer, Heidelberg (2010)
14. Cash, D., Hofheinz, D., Kiltz, E., Peikert, C.: Bonsai trees, or how to delegate a lattice basis. J. Cryptology 25(4), 601–639 (2012)
15. Catalano, D., Fiore, D.: Vector Commitments and Their Applications. In: Kurosawa, K., Hanaoka, G. (eds.) PKC 2013. LNCS, vol. 7778, pp. 55–72. Springer, Heidelberg (2013)
16. Damgård, I., Triandopoulos, N.: Supporting non-membership proofs with bilinear-map accumulators. IACR Cryptology ePrint Archive, 2008:538 (2008)
17. Dodis, Y., Kiayias, A., Nicolosi, A., Shoup, V.: Anonymous Identification in *Ad Hoc* Groups. In: Cachin, C., Camenisch, J.L. (eds.) EUROCRYPT 2004. LNCS, vol. 3027, pp. 609–626. Springer, Heidelberg (2004)
18. Gentry, C.: Fully homomorphic encryption using ideal lattices. In: STOC, pp. 169–178. ACM (2009)
19. Gentry, C., Peikert, C., Vaikuntanathan, V.: Trapdoors for hard lattices and new cryptographic constructions. In: Dwork, C. (ed.) STOC 2008, pp. 197–206. ACM (2008)
20. Li, J., Li, N., Xue, R.: Universal accumulators with efficient nonmembership proofs. In: Katz, J., Yung, M. (eds.) ACNS 2007. LNCS, vol. 4521, Springer, Heidelberg (2007)
21. Lyubashevsky, V., Micciancio, D.: Generalized compact knapsacks are collision resistant. In: Bugliesi, M., Preneel, B., Sassone, V., Wegener, I. (eds.) ICALP 2006. LNCS, vol. 4052, pp. 144–155. Springer, Heidelberg (2006)
22. Micciancio, D., Peikert, C.: Trapdoors for Lattices: Simpler, Tighter, Faster, Smaller. In: Pointcheval, D., Johansson, T. (eds.) EUROCRYPT 2012. LNCS, vol. 7237, pp. 700–718. Springer, Heidelberg (2012)
23. Micciancio, D., Regev, O.: Worst-case to average-case reductions based on gaussian measures. SIAM J. Comput. 37(1), 267–302 (2007)
24. Miers, I., Garman, C., Green, M., Rubin, A.D.: Zerocoin: Anonymous distributed e-cash from bitcoin. In: IEEE Symposium on Security and Privacy. IEEE Computer Society
25. Nguyen, L.: Accumulators from bilinear pairings and applications. In: Menezes, A. (ed.) CT-RSA 2005. LNCS, vol. 3376, pp. 275–292. Springer, Heidelberg (2005)
26. Nyberg, K.: Fast accumulated hashing. In: Gollmann, D. (ed.) FSE 1996. LNCS, vol. 1039, pp. 83–87. Springer, Heidelberg (1996)
27. Peikert, C., Rosen, A.: Efficient collision-resistant hashing from worst-case assumptions on cyclic lattices. In: Halevi, S., Rabin, T. (eds.) TCC 2006. LNCS, vol. 3876, pp. 145–166. Springer, Heidelberg (2006)
28. Peikert, C., Vaikuntanathan, V.: Noninteractive Statistical Zero-Knowledge Proofs for Lattice Problems. In: Wagner, D. (ed.) CRYPTO 2008. LNCS, vol. 5157, pp. 536–553. Springer, Heidelberg (2008)
29. Pöhls, H.C., Samelin, K.: On updatable redactable signatures. In: Boureanu, I., Owesarski, P., Vaudenay, S. (eds.) ACNS 2014. LNCS, vol. 8479, pp. 457–475. Springer, Heidelberg (2014)
30. Wang, P., Wang, H., Pieprzyk, J.: Improvement of a dynamic accumulator at ICICS 07 and its application in multi-user keyword-based retrieval on encrypted data. In: Qing, S., Imai, H., Wang, G. (eds.) ICICS 2007. LNCS, vol. 4861, pp. 1381–1386. Springer, Heidelberg (2007)

Almost Optimum Secret Sharing with Cheating Detection

Mahabir Prasad Jhanwar[1,*] and Reihaneh Safavi-Naini[2,**]

[1] CR Rao AIMSCS, UoH Campus, India
[2] Department of Computer Science, University of Calgary, Canada

Abstract. A (t, n, δ) secret sharing scheme with cheating detection property (SSCD) is a t-out-of-n threshold secret sharing scheme that has the following additional property; *the probability that any t malicious players can successfully cheat (without being caught) an honest player by opening forged shares and causing the honest player to reconstruct the wrong secret is at most δ.* There are two flavors of security for such schemes known as OKS and CDV. The lower bound on share sizes for an OKS-secure SSCD scheme is known, and concrete schemes in which share sizes are equal to (or almost the same as) the lower bound have been proposed, albeit with some *limitations*. We first present a OKS-secure scheme with share sizes only *one bit longer* than its existing lower bound. Our construction is free from any special requirements. We next present a CDV-secure SSCD scheme, where a stronger form of cheating is allowed. The share size of our CDV-secure scheme is also one bit longer than the existing lower bound.

1 Introduction

Secret sharing is one of the most important primitives in cryptography and in particular distributed systems. Let t, n be positive integers such that $1 \leq t < n$. In a *perfect* t-out-of-n secret sharing scheme [20,2], a dealer $\mathcal{D}$ distributes a secret s to n players, say $P_1, \ldots, P_n$ in such a way that the combined shares of any $t + 1$ or more players can recover the secret s, but no subset of t or less shares can leak any information about the secret s, where the leakage is in information theoretic sense, and without assuming any limit on the computational resources of the adversary. An important efficiency parameter in secret sharing scheme is the size of shares. Let Σ_i be the set of possible shares for P_i, and Σ be the set of possible secrets. It is well known that, for t-out-of-n perfect secret sharing schemes, $|\Sigma_i| \geq |\Sigma|$ [12]. Schemes with $|\Sigma_i| = |\Sigma|$ are called *ideal*. Shamir [20] constructed an ideal (t, n)-threshold secret sharing scheme in which secrets and shares lie in a finite field $\mathbb{F}_q$, where $q > n$, and share generation uses

---

* A major portion of the work was done when the author was a postdoctoral fellow at the Univeristy of Calgary.

** Financial support for this research was provided in part by Alberta Innovates - Technology Futures, in the Province of Alberta in Canada.

R.S. Chakraborty et al. (Eds.): SPACE 2015, LNCS 9354, pp. 359–372, 2015.
DOI: 10.1007/978-3-319-24126-5_21

evaluation of polynomials over $\mathbb{F}_q$. Let $\alpha_1, \ldots, \alpha_n \in \mathbb{F}_q$ be n distinct non-zero field elements known to all players (e.g., if $q > n$ is a prime, we can have $\alpha_j = j$). To share a secret $s \in \mathbb{F}_q$, a *trusted dealer* chooses t random elements $a_1, \ldots, a_t$, independently and randomly with uniform distribution, from $\mathbb{F}_q$. These random elements together with the secret s define a polynomial $f(x) = s + \sum_{i=1}^{t} a_i x^i$ that is used to generate a share $f(\alpha_j)$ for P_j. The correctness and privacy of Shamir secret scheme follow from properties of Lagrange interpolation (see § 2.2).

In its basic form, secret sharing assumes that the corrupted participants are passive (or semi-honest) and follow the protocol during the reconstruction phase. In practice however, one needs to consider stronger adversaries who deviate from the protocol, collude and submit wrong shares. Secret sharing schemes in presence of active adversaries have been considered in different settings and with different requirements. In this paper, we consider secret sharing with cheater detection (SSCD) introduced by Tompa and Woll [21], and focus on threshold schemes. In the following we shall first provide a brief introduction of SSCD schemes, the relevant questions there in, and finally present our contributions.

Informally, an SSCD scheme allows to detect if a set of submitted shares contain incorrect entries. To achieve cheating detection functionality, the reconstruction algorithm is enhanced by a checking mechanism, failing which, the reconstruction outputs a special symbol "$\perp$", indicating that some of the shares presented are incorrect. The two well known security models for SSCD schemes are given by OKS [17] and CDV [5], where the later guarantees stronger security. In the OKS model, t players, say $P_1, \ldots, P_t$, want to cheat a $(t+1)$th player, P_{t+1}, by opening incorrect shares $\mathsf{Sh}'_1, \ldots, \mathsf{Sh}'_t$. The cheaters *succeed if reconstruction does not output $\perp$ and the secret s' that is reconstructed from $\mathsf{Sh}'_1, \ldots, \mathsf{Sh}'_t$ and Sh_{t+1} is different from the shared secret s.* The CDV model has a stronger security requirements. It assumes that the t cheating players *also know the shared secret s* before cheating the $(t+1)$th player. Let δ_{oks} (resp., δ_{cdv}) denote the best probability of successful cheating under OKS (resp., CDV) model and for real numbers $\delta_{\mathsf{oks}}, \delta_{\mathsf{cdv}} > 0$, refer to the schemes as $(t, n, \delta_{\mathsf{oks}})$ OKS-secure and $(t, n, \delta_{\mathsf{cdv}})$ CDV-secure schemes. An SSCD scheme has direct applications to unconditionally secure robust secret sharing [7,6,11,10], secure message transmission [9,13], and cheater identifiable secret sharing [14].

Like basic secret sharing, the most important complexity measure of SSCD schemes is their share size, i.e., the maximum share size of each player. Tompa and Woll [21] have showed that an SSCD scheme *cannot be ideal*. Motivated by the true lower bounds on share sizes, Ogata, Kurosawa, and Stinson [17] showed the following lower bounds on $|\Sigma_i|$ for $(t, n, \delta_{\mathsf{oks}})$ OKS-secure and $(t, n, \delta_{\mathsf{cdv}})$ CDV-secure schemes, respectively:

$$|\Sigma_i| \geq \frac{|\Sigma| - 1}{\delta_{\mathsf{oks}}} + 1; \qquad |\Sigma_i| \geq \frac{|\Sigma| - 1}{\delta_{\mathsf{cdv}}^2} + 1. \qquad (1)$$

One of the most important problems in this area is construction of SSCD schemes in which the share size is equal to (or almost the same as) the lower bounds.

1.1 Our Contributions

We first present an efficient (t, n, δ_{oks}) OKS-secure scheme with share size almost the same as the lower bound. The bit size $\log_2 |\Sigma_i|$ of shares in our scheme is only one bit longer than $\log_2(\frac{|\Sigma|-1}{\delta_{oks}}+1)$, the bit size of lower bound. The scheme is a simple modification of t-out-of-n Shamir secret sharing, and it is obtained by choosing a polynomial whose degree is at most $2t$ (instead of t). We then apply the same technique to obtain an efficient (t, n, δ_{cdv}) CDV-secure scheme. The share size of CDV secure scheme is also one bit longer than the known lower bound. The schemes presented in this paper are proven secure without assuming any limit on the computational resources of the adversary.

1.2 Related Work

An OKS-secure scheme was proposed in [17] (a brief description is given in § 3.3). This is the only known scheme whose share size is exactly equal to the lower bound. However, the scheme imposes the restriction that the *secret be drawn with uniform distribution* from secret space. Later, a few other OKS-secure schemes were presented with share size *almost* the same as the lower bound [3,18,4,10]. However, they also impose restrictions. The OKS-secure scheme of [4] (based on [3,18]) requires *only non-binary fields* for secret space, which is a major restriction (see § 3.3 for a brief description of the scheme). The scheme in [10] (see also § 3.3) requires to publish a *checking* vector on an authenticated public bulleting board. There is no CDV-secure scheme with share size equal to the lower bound. An almost optimum scheme was also proposed in [4].

The cheating probability for all of the above schemes is dictated by the cardinality of the secret space S: $\delta = 1/|\Sigma|$. There are also schemes [15,8] where δ can be chosen such that $\delta \gg 1/|\Sigma|$. This is desirable as it allows flexibility in choosing the security level of the system. The problem of constructing OKS-secure (resp., CDV-secure) SSCD schemes that have share size equal to (or nearly the same) as the lower bound, and allow flexible security level is an interesting open question. In [1,16], secure SSCD schemes are proposed under a stronger cheating model, called CDV', where up to $n-1$ players are allowed to cheat. A closely related cheating model was proposed by Pieprzyk and Zhang in [19] by introducing the concept of cheating-immune secret sharing scheme.

2 Preliminaries

2.1 Notations

For any positive integer n, we let $[n]$ denote the set $\{1, \ldots, n\}$. We write $|S|$ to denote the number of elements in the set S. We write $x \in_R S$ to indicate that x is chosen with respect to the uniform distribution on S. By $x \leftarrow S$, we assume x is chosen with arbitrary distribution. We let $\mathbb{F}_q$ denote a finite field with q elements, and $\mathbb{F}_q[X]$ denote the polynomial ring. For a finite field $\mathbb{F}_q$, we let $\mathbb{F}_q^{\leq t}[X]$ denote the set $\{f \in \mathbb{F}_q[X] \mid \deg f \leq t\}$, where $t \in \mathbb{N} \cup \{0\}$ and $\deg f$ denotes the degree of f. For a positive integer n, let $\mathbb{Z}_n$ denote the ring of integers modulo n.

2.2 Lagrange Interpolation

Let t be a positive integer and $\mathbb{F}$ be a field. Given any $t+1$ pairs of field elements $(x_1, y_1), \ldots, (x_{t+1}, y_{t+1})$ with distinct x_i's, there exists a *unique* polynomial $f(x) \in \mathbb{F}[x]$ of degree at most t such that $f(x_i) = y_i$ for $1 \leq i \leq t + 1$. The polynomial can be obtained using the Lagrange interpolation formula as follows,

$$f(x) = y_1 \lambda_{x_1}^A(x) + \cdots + y_{t+1} \lambda_{x_{t+1}}^A(x), \tag{2}$$

where $A = \{x_1, \ldots, x_{t+1}\}$ and $\lambda_{x_i}^A(x)$'s $(1 \leq i \leq t + 1)$ are Lagrange basis polynomials, given by

$$\lambda_{x_i}^A(x) = \frac{\prod_{1 \leq j \leq t+1, j \neq i}(x - x_j)}{\prod_{1 \leq j \leq t+1, j \neq i}(x_i - x_j)} .$$

When the base point set $A = \{x_1, \ldots, x_{t+1}\}$ is clear from the context, we denote the interpolation of f by $f \leftarrow \mathsf{LagInt}(y_1, \ldots, y_{t+1})$, and $\lambda_{x_i}^A(x)$ by simply $\lambda_{x_i}(x)$.

2.3 Secret Sharing with Cheating Detection

Let t, n be positive integers such that $1 \leq t < n$. Informally, a t-out-of-n threshold secret sharing scheme enables a dealer, holding a secret piece of information, to distribute this secret among a set of n players such that, later, a subset of players can reconstruct the secret only if there cardinality is at least $t + 1$. We let Σ denote the domain of secrets, and Σ_i denote the domain of shares of P_i, $1 \leq i \leq n$. Secutity of SSCD has been studied in different models. We consider the two main models, refered to as OKS [17] and CDV [5] . For fix real numbers $\delta_{\mathsf{oks}}, \delta_{\mathsf{cdv}} > 0$, the schemes secure under OKS model (resp. CDV model) are referred to as $(t, n, \delta_{\mathsf{oks}})$ OKS-secure (resp. $(t, n, \delta_{\mathsf{cdv}})$ CDV-secure) schemes.

Definition 1 (Secret Sharing with Cheating Detection). *A t-out-of-n secret sharing with cheating detection (SSCD) property is consist of two interactive protocols, Share and Rec. The share distribution protocol Share involves a dealer $\mathcal{D}$ and n players $P_1, \ldots, P_n$, and the reconstruction protocol Rec involves $P_1, \ldots, P_n$ and a reconstructor $\mathcal{R}$ (a third party). The protocols work as follows:*

- *Share: The dealer $\mathcal{D}$ runs the share distribution algorithm Share. It is a probabilistic algorithm that, on input $s \in \Sigma$ returns a share vector $(\mathsf{Sh}_1, \ldots, \mathsf{Sh}_n) \xleftarrow{\$} \mathsf{Share}(s)$, where each Sh_i is privately given to P_i.*
- *Rec: The secret reconstruction algorithm Rec is run by $\mathcal{R}$. It is a deterministic algorithm that on input the shares $\mathsf{Sh}_{i_1}, \ldots, \mathsf{Sh}_{i_{t+1}}$ of any $t + 1$ players $P_{i_1}, \ldots, P_{i_{t+1}}$ returns a value $s \leftarrow \mathsf{Rec}(\mathsf{Sh}_{i_1}, \ldots, \mathsf{Sh}_{i_{t+1}})$, where $s \in \Sigma \cup \{\perp\}$. The symbol $\perp$ indicates that a cheating has occurred and the algorithm is unable to recover the shared secret.*

Definition 2 (SSCD Security under OKS Model). *Let $\delta_{\mathsf{oks}} > 0$. An SSCD scheme is said to be $(t, n, \delta_{\mathsf{oks}})$ OKS-secure if Share and Rec protocols satisfy the following properties:*

- **Correctness:** *For every authorized set of players $B \subset \{P_1, \ldots, P_n\}$, i.e., $|B| \geq t + 1$, and for every $s \in \Sigma$, we have*

$$\Pr[\mathsf{Rec}(\mathsf{Share}(s)_B) = s] = 1, \tag{3}$$

where $\mathsf{Share}(s)_B$ denotes the restriction of the n length vector $\mathsf{Share}(s) = (\mathsf{Sh}_1, \ldots, \mathsf{Sh}_n)$ to its B-entries, i.e., $\mathsf{Share}(s)_B = \{\mathsf{Sh}_i\}_{P_i \in B}$, and the probability is computed over the random coins of Share.
- **Perfect Privacy:** *For an unauthorized set $A \subset \{P_1, \ldots, P_n\}$, i.e., $|A| \leq t$, for every pair of values $s_1, s_2 \in S$, and for every possible vector of shares $(\mathsf{Sh}_i)_{P_i \in A}$, it holds that*

$$\Pr[\mathsf{Share}(s_1)_A = (\mathsf{Sh}_i)_{P_i \in A}] = \Pr[\mathsf{Share}(s_2)_A = (\mathsf{Sh}_i)_{P_i \in A}], \tag{4}$$

where the probabilities are computed over the random coins of Share.
- **Cheating Detection:** *The cheating detection property of an OKS-secure SSCD is measured by the maximum probability with which any unbounded adversary $\mathcal{A}_{\mathsf{oks}}$, who actively controls the outputs of up to t P_i, can win the following game - $\mathsf{OKSGame}_{\mathsf{SSCD}}^{\mathcal{A}_{\mathsf{oks}}}$.*

$$\boxed{\begin{aligned}
&s \leftarrow S;\ (\mathsf{Sh}_1, \ldots, \mathsf{Sh}_n) \xleftarrow{\$} \mathsf{Share}(s); \\
&(i_1, \ldots, i_t) \leftarrow \mathcal{A}_{\mathsf{oks}}; \\
&(\mathsf{Sh}'_{i_1}, \ldots, \mathsf{Sh}'_{i_t}, i_{t+1}) \leftarrow \mathcal{A}_{\mathsf{oks}}(\mathsf{Sh}_{i_1}, \ldots, \mathsf{Sh}_{i_t}); \\
&s' \leftarrow \mathsf{Rec}(\mathsf{Sh}'_{i_1}, \ldots, \mathsf{Sh}'_{i_t}, \mathsf{Sh}_{i_{t+1}}); \\
&s' \leftarrow \text{Game-Output}\ .
\end{aligned}}$$

Fig. 1. $\mathsf{OKSGame}_{\mathsf{SSCD}}^{\mathcal{A}_{\mathsf{oks}}}$: The Cheating Detection Game

The game is played between the dealer $\mathcal{D}$ and the adversary $\mathcal{A}_{\mathsf{oks}}$. In the game, $\mathcal{D}$ first picks a secret $s \in S$, and computes $(\mathsf{Sh}_1, \ldots, \mathsf{Sh}_n) \xleftarrow{\$} \mathsf{Share}(s)$. Next, $\mathcal{A}_{\mathsf{oks}}$ corrupts up to t players, say $P_{i_1}, \ldots, P_{i_t}$, learns their shares, and sends possibly modified shares $(\mathsf{Sh}'_{i_1}, \ldots, \mathsf{Sh}'_{i_t}) \leftarrow \mathcal{A}_{\mathsf{oks}}(\mathsf{Sh}_{i_1}, \ldots, \mathsf{Sh}_{i_t})$ along with the identity of a $(t+1)$th player, say $P_{i_{t+1}}$, to $\mathcal{R}$. The adversary is said to win if, $\mathsf{Rec}(\mathsf{Sh}'_{i_1}, \ldots, \mathsf{Sh}'_{i_t}, \mathsf{Sh}_{i_{t+1}}) = s'$ and $s' \notin \{s, \perp\}$. We measure $\mathcal{A}_{\mathsf{oks}}$'s success by the real number

$$Adv_{\mathsf{SSCD}}^{\mathcal{A}_{\mathsf{oks}}} = \Pr[s' \notin \{s, \perp\} \mid s' \leftarrow \mathsf{Rec}(\mathsf{Sh}'_{i_1}, \ldots, \mathsf{Sh}'_{i_t}, \mathsf{Sh}_{i_{t+1}})]. \tag{5}$$

The $(t, n, \delta_{\mathsf{oks}})$ security requires that $Adv_{\mathsf{SSCD}}^{\mathcal{A}_{\mathsf{oks}}} \leq \delta_{\mathsf{oks}}$.

Definition 3 (SSCD Security under CDV Model). *The security is strengthened under the* CDV *model for* SSCD *schemes. In the cheating detection game, it is assumed that t corrupted players also know the shared secret s before they attempt to cheat the* $(t+1)$*th player. Formally, an* SSCD *scheme is called* (t, n, δ_{cdv}) CDV-secure *if* Share *and* Rec *protocols satisfy following properties:*

- *The* Correctness *and* Privacy *hold true as defined in Definition 2.*
- ***Cheating Detection:*** *Let* $\mathcal{A}_{cdv}$ *denote the adversary in the* CDV *model. The cheating detection game, denoted by* CDVGame$_{SSCD}^{\mathcal{A}_{cdv}}$*, is the same as the* OKS *cheating detection game, except the extra information* s *available to the adversary, as shown below.*

$$
\begin{array}{l}
s \leftarrow S;\ (\mathsf{Sh}_1,\ldots,\mathsf{Sh}_n) \xleftarrow{\$} \mathsf{Share}(s); \\
(i_1,\ldots,i_t) \leftarrow \mathcal{A}_{cdv}; \\
(\mathsf{Sh}'_{i_1},\ldots,\mathsf{Sh}'_{i_t},i_{t+1}) \leftarrow \mathcal{A}_{cdv}(\mathsf{Sh}_{i_1},\ldots,\mathsf{Sh}_{i_t},s); \\
s' \leftarrow \mathsf{Rec}(\mathsf{Sh}'_{i_1},\ldots,\mathsf{Sh}'_{i_t},\mathsf{Sh}_{i_{t+1}}); \\
s' \leftarrow \mathsf{Game\text{-}Output}\ .
\end{array}
$$

Fig. 2. CDVGame$_{SSCD}^{\mathcal{A}_{cdv}}$: The Cheating Detection Game

The adversary is said to win if, $\mathsf{Rec}(\mathsf{Sh}'_{i_1},\ldots,\mathsf{Sh}'_{i_t},\mathsf{Sh}_{i_{t+1}}) = s'$ *and* $s' \notin \{s, \perp\}$*. The advantage of* $\mathcal{A}_{cdv}$ *is measured by* $Adv_{SSCD}^{\mathcal{A}_{cdv}} = \Pr[s' \notin \{s, \perp\} \mid s' \leftarrow \mathsf{Rec}(\mathsf{Sh}'_{i_1},\ldots,\mathsf{Sh}'_{i_t},\mathsf{Sh}_{i_{t+1}})]$*. The* (t, n, δ_{cdv}) *security requires that* $Adv_{SSCD}^{\mathcal{A}_{cdv}} \leq \delta_{cdv}$.

Known Lower Bounds. The lower bounds on the share sizes of both OKS-secure and CDV-secure schemes were presented by Ogata, Kurosawa and Stinson in [17]. In the following, we recall the bounds.

Theorem 1. *([17]) For any* (t, n, δ_{oks}) OKS-secure SSCD *scheme with the domain of secrets is denoted by* Σ*, the size of the total shares of* P_i *for every* $i \in [n]$ *is lower bounded by*

$$
|\Sigma_i| \geq \frac{|\Sigma| - 1}{\delta_{oks}} + 1. \tag{6}
$$

The lower bound under the CDV model was derived assuming that the secret is uniformly distributed.

Theorem 2. *([17]) For any* (t, n, δ_{cdv}) CDV-secure SSCD *scheme where the domain of secret is* Σ *with uniform distribution, the size of total shares of* P_i *for every* $i \in [n]$ *is lower bounded by*

$$
|\Sigma_i| \geq \frac{|\Sigma| - 1}{\delta_{cdv}^2} + 1 \tag{7}
$$

Although, the schemes proposed in this paper are not *flexible*, we include the following section for completeness.

2.4   Relationship between δ and $|\Sigma|$

The maximum cheating probability δ for existing schemes is largely dictated by the cardinality of secret space Σ and is given by $\delta \approx 1/|\Sigma|$. But from a practical perspective, it is important to choose δ independently. The schemes in [15,8] can choose δ that is arbitrarily larger than $1/|\Sigma|$. On the other hand, when the secret space is small, it is important for the scheme to have $\delta \ll 1/|\Sigma|$. For example, for 20 bit secret size, one may require $\delta = 1/2^{60} \ll 1/2^{20}$.

The construction of a flexible scheme with share size equal to, or nearly the same as, the known lower bound (under OKS/CDV or both models) is an interesting open problem.

3   A $(t, n, \delta_{\mathsf{oks}})$ OKS-secure SSCD Scheme

In this section, we present an $(t, n, \delta_{\mathsf{oks}})$ OKS-secure SSCD scheme with share size nearly the same as the lower bound of Theorem 1. In our scheme, the secrets are drawn from a finite field $\mathbb{F}_q$ and cheating probability is at most $\frac{1}{q}$. The information rate of our scheme is $1/2$.

3.1   The Proposed Scheme Π_{aopt}

Let t and n be positive integers such that $1 \leq t < n$. Choose a finite field $\mathbb{F}_q$ with $q > 2n$. Choose $2n$ distinct points, $\alpha_1, \ldots, \alpha_{2n} \in \mathbb{F}_q$, known to all players. We now present our scheme.

- Share: On input a secret $s \in \mathbb{F}_q$, the share generation algorithm Share outputs a list of shares as follows. The dealer $\mathcal{D}$ randomly picks a polynomial $f \in_R \mathbb{F}_q^{\leq 2t}[x]$ such that $f(0) = s$. For every j in $1 \leq j \leq 2n$, it computes $s_j = f(\alpha_j)$. Finally, for every i in $1 \leq i \leq n$, player P_i gets $\mathsf{Sh}_i = (s_i, s_{n+i})$ as their share:

Share Distribution Algorithm
Secret $s \in \mathbb{F}_q$
$\downarrow f \in \mathbb{F}_q^{\leq 2t}[x]$
$f(\alpha_1), \ldots, f(\alpha_{2n})$
$P_i \leftarrow (f(\alpha_i), f(\alpha_{n+i})), 1 \leq i \leq n$

- Rec: The secret reconstruction algorithm Rec proceeds as follows. Suppose the following $t + 1$ players $P_{i_1}, \ldots, P_{i_{t+1}}$ provided shares (correct or corrupted) $\mathsf{Sh}'_{i_1}, \ldots, \mathsf{Sh}'_{i_{t+1}}$ respectively. The share of P_i is corrupted if $\mathsf{Sh}'_i = (s'_i, s'_{n+i}) \neq (s_i, s_{n+i})$. This means $\mathcal{R}$ has $2t + 2$ points $\{s'_{i_1}, s'_{n+i_1}, \ldots, s'_{i_{t+1}}, s'_{n+i_{t+1}}\}$ such that at most $2t$ of them are possibly modified. To detect a possible cheating $\mathcal{R}$ proceeds as follows.

  • First, it interpolates a unique polynomial $f' \leftarrow \mathsf{LagInt}(s'_{i_1}, s'_{n+i_1}, \ldots, s'_{i_{t+1}}, s'_{n+i_{t+1}})$ (see § 2.2 for Lagrange Interpolation LagInt).

- It then checks if the degree of $f' \stackrel{?}{=} 2t + 1$. If yes, it outputs $\bot$ which indicates that cheating has occurred.
- Otherwise (i.e., when degree of $f' \leq 2t$), $\mathcal{R}$ outputs $f'(0)$ as the reconstructed secret.

3.2 Security

In order to prove the security of Π_{aopt}, we first prove two simple lemmas.

Lemma 1. *Let $\mathbb{F}$ be any finite field and let $\alpha_1, \ldots, \alpha_k \in \mathbb{F}$ be any k distinct points. Let $f = \sum_{i=0}^{k} a_i x^i$ be chosen at random from $\mathbb{F}^{\leq k}[x]$. Then given $f(\alpha_1)$, $\ldots, f(\alpha_k)$, it holds that one of the coefficients $\{a_i\}_{i=0}^{k}$ of f is uniformly distributed over $\mathbb{F}$.*

Proof: Given $f(\alpha_1), \ldots, f(\alpha_k)$ for a random $f \in \mathbb{F}^{\leq k}[x]$, we have the following system of linear equations, where $a_0, a_1, \ldots, a_k$ form the unknowns of the system:

$$\begin{bmatrix} 1 & \alpha_1 & \ldots & \alpha_1^k \\ 1 & \alpha_2 & \ldots & \alpha_2^k \\ \vdots & \vdots & \ddots & \vdots \\ 1 & \alpha_k & \ldots & \alpha_k^k \end{bmatrix} \cdot \begin{bmatrix} a_0 \\ a_1 \\ \vdots \\ a_k \end{bmatrix} = \begin{bmatrix} f(\alpha_1) \\ f(\alpha_2) \\ \vdots \\ f(\alpha_k) \end{bmatrix} \tag{8}$$

Fixing any of the unknowns, e.g. a_1, will transform system (8) in to:

$$\begin{bmatrix} 1 & \alpha_1^2 & \ldots & \alpha_1^k \\ 1 & \alpha_2^2 & \ldots & \alpha_2^k \\ \vdots & \vdots & \ddots & \vdots \\ 1 & \alpha_k^2 & \ldots & \alpha_k^k \end{bmatrix} \cdot \begin{bmatrix} a_0 \\ a_2 \\ \vdots \\ a_k \end{bmatrix} = \begin{bmatrix} f(\alpha_1) - a_1\alpha_1 \\ f(\alpha_2) - a_1\alpha_2 \\ \vdots \\ f(\alpha_k) - a_1\alpha_k \end{bmatrix} \tag{9}$$

Clearly, the resulting system admits a unique solution (for $(a_0, a_2, \ldots, a_k)^T$) as its coefficient matrix is non-singular. Therefore a_1 is uniformly distributed.

Lemma 2. *Let $\mathbb{F}$ be any finite field and let $a_0, \ldots, a_{j-1}, a_{j+1}, \ldots, a_k$ be any k points in $\mathbb{F}$. Let a_j be chosen at random from $\mathbb{F}$. Define $f_{a_j} = \sum_{i=0}^{k} a_i x^i \in \mathbb{F}^{\leq k}[x]$. Then for every $\alpha, \beta \in \mathbb{F}$ with $\alpha \neq 0$, it holds that $\Pr[f_{a_j}(\alpha) = \beta] = \frac{1}{|\mathbb{F}|}$.*

Proof: Let $f_{a_j}(x) = a_0 + \cdots + a_j x^j + \cdots + a_k x^k$. Then $\Pr[f_{a_j}(\alpha) = \beta] = \Pr[a_0 + \cdots + a_j \alpha^j + \cdots + a_k \alpha^k] = \beta$, where the probability is computed over the random choice of $a_j \in \mathbb{F}$. Hence, for a randomly chosen $a_j \in \mathbb{F}$ we have

$$\Pr\left[\sum_{i=0}^{k} a_i \alpha^i = \beta\right] = \Pr\left[a_j \alpha^j = \beta - \sum_{0 \leq i \leq k; i \neq j} a_i \alpha^i\right]$$

$$= \Pr\left[a_j = (\alpha^j)^{-1}\left(\beta - \sum_{0 \leq i \leq k; i \neq j} a_i \alpha^i\right)\right]$$

$$= \frac{1}{|\mathbb{F}|},$$

where the second equality holds since $\alpha \in \mathbb{F}$ and $\alpha \neq 0$ implying that α^j is invertible, and the last equality is due to the fact that a_j is randomly chosen from $\mathbb{F}$. This concludes the proof.

Theorem 3. *The* SSCD *scheme* Π_{aopt} *of* § *3.1 is* $(t, n, \delta_{\text{oks}})$ *OKS-secure with secret space* $\Sigma = \mathbb{F}_q$, *share space* $\Sigma_i = \mathbb{F}_q \times \mathbb{F}_q$ *for every* P_i, *and* $\delta_{\text{oks}} = \frac{1}{q}$.

Proof: The correctness and privacy of Π_{aopt} follows immediately from Shamir secret sharing scheme: any set of $t + 1$ players can reconstruct the secret as they hold $2t + 2$ shares of f, while a set of t players have only $2t$ shares which do not leak any information about the secret as $f \in \mathbb{F}_q^{\leq 2t}[X]$.

We now derive the maximum probability of cheating. For notational clarity, suppose $t + 1$ players $P_1, \ldots, P_{t+1}$ participate in the reconstruction. We further assume that $P_1, \ldots, P_t$ are corrupted and provide shares $\text{Sh}'_1, \ldots, \text{Sh}'_t$ such that $\text{Sh}'_i = (s'_i, s'_{n+i}) \neq (s_i, s_{n+i})$ for at least one $i \in [t]$. The player P_{t+1} who is honest provides the correct share $\text{Sh}_{t+1} = (s_{t+1}, s_{n+t+1})$. The cheating will not be detected if $s'_1, s'_{n+1}, \ldots, s'_t, s'_{n+t}$ and s_{t+1}, s_{n+t+1} lie on a polynomial of degree at most $2t$. The later is true iff s_{n+t+1} lies on the polynomial passing through $s'_1, s'_{n+1}, \ldots, s'_t, s'_{n+t}$ and s_{t+1}. Let $f' = \sum_{i=0}^{2t} b_i x^i$ be the unique polynomial passing through $2t + 1$ points $s'_1, s'_{n+1}, \ldots, s'_t, s'_{n+t}$ and s_{t+1}. As f' is of degree at most $2t$, and the shares of the corrupted players constitute $2t$ points on f', the Lemma 1 implies that at least one coefficient of f' will remain uniform to the corrupted players. Therefore by Lemma 2 it holds that $\Pr[f'(\alpha_{n+t+1}) = s_{n+t+1}] = \frac{1}{q}$. This concludes the proof.

3.3   Efficiency Comparison

Previous Works. In [17] Ogata, Kurosawa and Stinson proposed a $(t, n, \delta_{\text{oks}})$ OKS-secure SSCD scheme achieving the lower bound of Theorem 1. The scheme uses a combinatorial object called *difference set*. In the following we provide a brief description of their scheme. The scheme is denoted by Π_{oks}.

Definition 4. *([17] (N, ℓ, λ) Difference Set) Let $(\Gamma, +)$ be an Abelian (commutative) group of order N. A subset $B \subset \Gamma$ is called an (N, ℓ, λ) difference set if $|B| = \ell$ and the set of non-zero differences $\{d - d' \mid d, d'(d \neq d') \in B\}$ contains each non-zero element of Γ precisely λ times.*

For an (N, ℓ, λ) difference set $B \subset \Gamma$, it is clear that $|\Gamma| = N = \frac{\ell(\ell-1)}{\lambda} + 1$. The Π_{oks} scheme was constructed in [17] using a special (N, ℓ, λ) difference set $B \subset \Gamma$ such that $(\Gamma, +, \cdot)$ is a *field*. It is known that there exists an $(N, \ell, 1)$ difference set $B \subset \mathbb{Z}_N$ if ℓ is a prime power, and therefore the scheme of [17] can be instantiated using $B \subset \mathbb{Z}_N$ if N is also a prime, i.e., $(\mathbb{Z}_N, +, \cdot)$ is a field. It is also known that if $N \equiv 3 \pmod 4$ is a prime power, then there exists an (N, ℓ, λ) difference set B in the field $\mathbb{F}_N$ such that $N = 4k - 1$, $\ell = 2k - 1$, and $\lambda = k - 1$, where k is a positive integer. We now state the main theorem of [17].

Theorem 4. *([17]) Let N be a prime power, and t, n be positive integers such that $1 \le t < n < N$. If there exists an (N, ℓ, λ) difference set B in $(\mathbb{F}_N, +)$, then there exists a $(t, n, \delta_{\text{oks}})$ OKS-secure secret sharing scheme for a uniformly distributed secret over $\Sigma = B$, such that $|\Sigma| = |B| = \ell$, $|\Sigma_i| = |\mathbb{F}_N| = \frac{\ell(\ell-1)}{\lambda} + 1$ for every $i \in [n]$ and $\delta_{\text{oks}} = \frac{\lambda}{\ell}$, i.e., $|\Sigma_i| = \frac{|\Sigma|-1}{\delta_{\text{oks}}} + 1$ for every $i \in [n]$ (meets the lower bound of Theorem 1).*

The Π_{oks} scheme does not work for an arbitrary prime power N; in particular, it also requires that there exists an (N, ℓ, λ) difference set for some $\ell, \lambda \in \mathbb{N}$. The scheme is proven secure only if secret is *chosen with uniform distribution*. The scheme was also compared in [18] to be less computationally efficient.

In [4] Cabello, Padró and Sáez proposed a method (based on [3,18]) that provides cheating detection functionality for any linear secret sharing scheme realizing general access structures. When their method is applied to Shamir secret sharing (for threshold access structure), it yields a $(t, n, \delta_{\text{oks}})$ OKS-secure SSCD with almost optimum share sizes. A brief description of their scheme, denoted by Π_{cps}, is given below. Let $\mathbb{F}_q$ be a finite field with characteristic different from 2, and $q > n$. Let $\alpha_1, \dots, \alpha_n \in \mathbb{F}_q$ be known to all players. For a given secret $s \in \mathbb{F}_q$, the dealer picks at random two polynomials $f_1, f_2 \in \mathbb{F}_q^{\le t}[X]$ such that $f_1(0) = s$ and $f_2(0) = s^2$ respectively. Every player P_i receives the share $\text{Sh}_i = (s_{i1}, s_{i2}) = (f_1(\alpha_i), f_2(\alpha_i))$. During reconstruction, for any $t + 1$ players $P_{i_1}, \dots, P_{i_{t+1}}$, $\mathcal{R}$ computes (s_1, s_2) from their shares, where $s_1 \leftarrow \text{LagInt}(s_{i_11}, \dots, s_{i_{t+1}1})$ and $s_2 \leftarrow \text{LagInt}(s_{i_12}, \dots, s_{i_{t+1}2})$. If $s_2 = s_1^2$, $\mathcal{R}$ outputs $s = s_1$ as the correct value of the shared secret; Otherwise when $s_2 \ne s_1^2$, it outputs $\perp$. Π_{cps} is summarized in the following theorem.

Theorem 5. *([4]) Let $\mathbb{F}_q$ be a finite field with characteristic different from 2, and $q > n$. The SSCD scheme Π_{cps} is $(t, n, \delta_{\text{oks}})$ OKS-secure with secret space $\Sigma = \mathbb{F}_q$, share space $\Sigma_i = \mathbb{F}_q \times \mathbb{F}_q$ for every P_i, and $\delta_{\text{oks}} = \frac{1}{q}$. Clearly the share size $|\Sigma_i| = q^2$ is nearly the same as $\frac{|\Sigma|-1}{\delta_{\text{oks}}} + 1 = q^2 - q + 1$.*

The main drawback of Π_{cps} is that it works for finite fields with characteristic different from 2. This is a serious constraint as binary fields make for a suitable choice in implementation of cryptographic protocols and in particular for resource constrained devices.

Recently, In [10] Jhanwar and Safavi-Naini proposed a $(t, n, \delta_{\text{oks}})$ OKS-secure SSCD scheme with almost optimum share sizes. Let Π_{js} denote this scheme. The scheme works as follows. Consider a finite field $\mathbb{F}_q$ such that $q > n$. Let $\alpha_1, \dots, \alpha_n \in \mathbb{F}_q$ be known to all players. For a given secret $s \in \mathbb{F}_q$, the dealer first picks at random $X(\ne 0), r \in \mathbb{F}_q$ and computes $Y = s + Xr$. It then picks at random two polynomials $f_1, f_2 \in \mathbb{F}_q^{\le t}[X]$ such that $f_1(0) = s$ and $f_2(0) = r$ respectively. Every player P_i receives the share $\text{Sh}_i = (s_i, r_i) = (f_1(\alpha_i), f_2(\alpha_i))$. The tuple (X, Y) is *kept as part of system's public parameters*. During reconstruction, for any $t + 1$ players $P_{i_1}, \dots, P_{i_{t+1}}$, $\mathcal{R}$ computes (s', r') from their shares, where $s' \leftarrow \text{LagInt}(s_{i_1}, \dots, s_{i_{t+1}})$ and $r' \leftarrow \text{LagInt}(r_{i_1}, \dots, r_{i_{t+1}})$. If $Y = s' + Xr'$, the Rec outputs $s = s'$ as the correct value of the shared secret and it outputs $\perp$ if $Y \neq s' + Xr'$. We now state the security theorem of Π_{js}.

Theorem 6. *([10]) Let $\mathbb{F}_q$ be a finite field with $q > n$. The SSCD scheme Π_{js} is (t, n, δ_{oks}) OKS-secure with secret space $\Sigma = \mathbb{F}_q$, share space $\Sigma_i = \mathbb{F}_q \times \mathbb{F}_q$ for every P_i, and $\delta_{oks} = \frac{1}{q}$. Clearly the share size $|\Sigma_i| = q^2$ is nearly the same as $\frac{|\Sigma|-1}{\delta_{oks}} + 1 = q^2 - q + 1$.*

The Π_{js} construction puts $X, Y \in \mathbb{F}_q$ as part of public parameters that are stored on a publicly accessible authenticated bulletin board. In the case when such public bulleting board is not available, the usual way out is to issue public parameters as part of shares to the players. Because X and Y are used in cheating detection, it is necessary to receive them in correct. But this may not be guaranteed, if they are issued as part of shares.

Efficiency of Our Scheme. We first note that our scheme Π_{opt} does not have any special requirements. Unlike the previous schemes [17,4], the secret in our scheme can be from any field. The only requirement is that the field size be $\geq 2n$. The security against cheating detection holds for arbitrary distribution of secret. Suppose $k = \lfloor \log_2 q \rfloor$. The shares in our scheme consist of $\log_2(q^2) = 2k$ bits, which is only one bit longer than $\log_2(\frac{|\Sigma|-1}{\delta} + 1) = \log_2(q(q-1)+1) \geq \log_2 q + \log_2(q-1) \geq 2k - 1$, the size of lower bound.

4   A (t, n, δ_{cdv}) CDV-secure SSCD Scheme

We present a (t, n, δ_{cdv}) CDV-secure SSCD scheme that is constructed using the technique in § 3.1. In CDV model, the reconstruction is against a stronger adversary who, in addition to the t shares, also knows the shared secret. In the share distribution phase of the new scheme, the dealer picks a polynomial f of degree at most $3t + 1$, and gives out 3 distinct points on f to every P_i. The shares of any t players and the additional knowledge of the shared secret give $3t + 1$ points on f, which means f can not be fully reconstructed. But, any $t + 1$ shares give $3t + 3$ points on f, which is one point more than the required $3t + 2$ points. This extra point is used for cheating detection. We now formally describe the scheme.

4.1   The Proposed Scheme $\tilde{\Pi}_{aopt}$

Let t and n are positive integers such that $1 \leq t < n$. Choose a finite field $\mathbb{F}_q$ with $q > 3n$. Choose $3n$ distinct points, $\alpha_1, \ldots, \alpha_{3n} \in \mathbb{F}_q$, known to all players. We now present our scheme.

- Share: On input a secret $s \in \mathbb{F}_q$, the share generation algorithm Share outputs a list of shares as follows. The dealer $\mathcal{D}$ randomly picks a polynomial $f \in_R \mathbb{F}_q^{\leq 3t+1}[x]$ such that $f(0) = s$. For every j in $1 \leq j \leq 3n$, the dealer computes $s_j = f(\alpha_j)$. Finally, for every i in $1 \leq i \leq n$, P_i receives $\mathsf{Sh}_i = (s_i, s_{n+i}, s_{2n+i})$ as her share:

Share Distribution Algorithm
Secret $s \in \mathbb{F}_q$
$\downarrow f \in \mathbb{F}_q^{\leq 3t+1}[x]$
$f(\alpha_1), \ldots, f(\alpha_{3n})$
$P_i \leftarrow (f(\alpha_i), f(\alpha_{n+i}), f(\alpha_{2n+i})), 1 \leq i \leq n$

- Rec: The secret reconstruction algorithm Rec proceeds as follows. Suppose the following $t+1$ players $P_{i_1}, \ldots, P_{i_{t+1}}$ provided shares (correct or corrupted) $\mathsf{Sh}'_{i_1}, \ldots, \mathsf{Sh}'_{i_{t+1}}$ respectively. The share of P_i is corrupted if $\mathsf{Sh}'_i = (s'_i, s'_{n+i}, s'_{2n+i}) \neq (s_i, s_{n+i}, s_{2n+i})$. This means, $\mathcal{R}$ has $3t+3$ points such that at most $3t$ of them are possibly modified. To detect a possible cheating, $\mathcal{R}$ now proceeds as follows.

  - First, it interpolates a unique polynomial $f' \leftarrow \mathsf{LagInt}(\mathsf{Sh}'_{i_1}, \ldots, \mathsf{Sh}'_{i_{t+1}})$ (see § 2.2 for Lagrange Interpolation LagInt).
  - It then checks if the degree of $f' \overset{?}{=} 3t+2$. If yes, it outputs $\perp$ which indicates that cheating has occurred.
  - Otherwise (i.e., when degree of $f' \leq 3t+1$), $\mathcal{R}$ outputs $f'(0)$ as the reconstructed secret.

4.2 Security

Theorem 7. *The* SSCD *scheme* $\tilde{\Pi}_{\mathsf{aopt}}$ *of* § *4.1 is* $(t, n, \delta_{\mathsf{cdv}})$ CDV-*secure with secret space* $\Sigma = \mathbb{F}_q$, *share space* $\Sigma_i = (\mathbb{F}_q)^3$ *for every* P_i, *and* $\delta_{\mathsf{cdv}} = \frac{1}{q}$.

Proof: The correctness and privacy of Π_{aopt} follow immediately from Shamir secret sharing scheme: any t players hold $3t$ shares which do not leak any information about the secret as $f \in \mathbb{F}_q^{\leq 3t+1}[X]$, and any $t+1$ players can reconstruct the secret as they hold $3t+3$ shares of f. We now derive the maximum probability of cheating. Suppose players $P_1, \ldots, P_{t+1}$ provide shares during reconstruction. We further assume that $P_1, \ldots, P_t$ are corrupted, and they know the shared secret s. The shares $\{(s'_i, s'_{n+i}, s'_{2n+i})\}_{i \in [t]}$ of corrupted players, together with s, give $3t+1$ points on f. As degree of f is at most $3t+1$, Lemma 1 and 2 together imply that $3t+3$ points of $\mathsf{Sh}'_1, \ldots, \mathsf{Sh}'_t$ and Sh'_{t+1} lie on a polynomial of degree at most $3t+1$ with probability at most $1/q$.

4.3 Efficiency Comparison

In [4], Cabello, Padró and Sáez proposed a method (based on [3,18]) that provides cheating detection functionality (under CDV model) for any linear secret sharing scheme realizing general access structures. When their method is applied to Shamir secret sharing (for threshold access structure), it yields a $(t, n, \delta_{\mathsf{cdv}})$ CDV-secure SSCD with almost optimum share sizes. A brief description of their scheme, denoted as $\tilde{\Pi}_{\mathsf{cps}}$, is given below. Let us fix a finite field $\mathbb{F}_q$ with $q > n$. Let

$\alpha_1, \ldots, \alpha_n \in \mathbb{F}_q$ be known to all players. For a given secret $s \in \mathbb{F}_q$ it first picks a random $r \in \mathbb{F}_q$. The dealer then picks at random polynomials $f_1, f_2, f_3 \in \mathbb{F}_q^{\leq t}[X]$ such that $f_1(0) = s$, $f_2(0) = r$ and $f_3(0) = rs$ respectively. Every player P_i receives the share $\mathsf{Sh}_i = (s_{i1}, s_{i2}, s_{i3}) = (f_1(\alpha_i), f_2(\alpha_i), f_3(\alpha_i))$. During reconstruction, for any $t+1$ players $P_{i_1}, \ldots, P_{i_{t+1}}$, $\mathcal{R}$ computes (s_1, s_2, s_3) from their shares, where $s_j \leftarrow \mathsf{LagInt}(s_{i_1 j}, \ldots, s_{i_{t+1} j})$, $j \in \{1, 2, 3\}$. If $s_3 = s_1 s_2$, the Rec outputs $s = s_1$ as the correct value of the shared secret; otherwise, i.e., when $s_3 \neq s_1 s_2$, it outputs $\perp$. The scheme $\tilde{\Pi}_{\mathsf{cps}}$ is almost optimum with respect to the lower bound of Theorem 1. $\tilde{\Pi}_{\mathsf{cps}}$ is summarized in the following theorem.

Theorem 8. *([4]) Let $\mathbb{F}_q$ be a finite field with $q > n$. The SSCD scheme $\tilde{\Pi}_{\mathsf{cps}}$ is $(t, n, \delta_{\mathsf{cdv}})$ CDV-secure with secret space $\Sigma = \mathbb{F}_q$, share space $\Sigma_i = (\mathbb{F}_q)^3$ for every P_i, and $\delta_{\mathsf{cdv}} = \frac{1}{q}$. Clearly the share size $|\Sigma_i| = q^3$ is nearly the same as $\frac{|\Sigma|-1}{\delta_{\mathsf{cdv}}^2} + 1 = q^2(q-1) + 1 = q^3 - q^2 + 1$.*

Efficiency of Our Scheme. To the best of our knowledge the schemes $\tilde{\Pi}_{\mathsf{cps}}$ ([4]) and the proposed scheme $\tilde{\Pi}_{\mathsf{aopt}}$ are the only known schemes that are almost optimum with respect to the share size. Suppose $k = \lfloor \log_2 q \rceil$. The shares in our scheme consist of $\log_2(q^3) = 3k$ bits, which is only one bit longer than $\log_2(\frac{|\Sigma|-1}{\delta_{\mathsf{cdv}}^2} + 1) = \log_2(q^2(q-1) + 1) \geq 2\log_2 q + \log_2(q-1) \geq 3k - 1$, the size of the lower bound.

5   Concluding Remarks

We presented a simple method for adding cheating detection to Shamir secret sharing scheme. We used the same approach for both security models of cheating detection. The resulting schemes have almost optimum share sizes. Unlike existing schemes, our constructions do not impose any special requirement on parameters. It is interesting to see if our technique can be generalized to work for any linear secret sharing scheme. It is also interesting to find its applicability for robust secret sharing and secure message transmission that are based on Shamir secret sharing.

Acknowledgments. The authors would like to thank a reviewer of SPACE 2015 for detailed comments.

References

1. Araki, T.: Efficient (k,n) threshold secret sharing schemes secure against cheating from $n - 1$ cheaters. In: Pieprzyk, J., Ghodosi, H., Dawson, E. (eds.) ACISP 2007. LNCS, vol. 4586, pp. 133–142. Springer, Heidelberg (2007)
2. Blakley, G.: Safeguarding cryptographic keys. AFIPS National Computer Conference 48, 313–317 (1979)

3. Cabello, S., Padró, C., Sáez, G.: Secret sharing schemes with detection of cheaters for a general access structure. In: Ciobanu, G., Păun, G. (eds.) FCT 1999. LNCS, vol. 1684, pp. 185–194. Springer, Heidelberg (1999)
4. Cabello, S., Padró, C., Sáez, G.: Secret sharing schemes with detection of cheaters for a general access structure. Des. Codes Cryptography 25(2), 175–188 (2002)
5. Carpentieri, M., De Santis, A., Vaccaro, U.: Size of shares and probability of cheating in threshold schemes. In: Helleseth, T. (ed.) EUROCRYPT 1993. LNCS, vol. 765, pp. 118–125. Springer, Heidelberg (1994)
6. Cevallos, A., Fehr, S., Ostrovsky, R., Rabani, Y.: Unconditionally-secure robust secret sharing with compact shares. In: Pointcheval, D., Johansson, T. (eds.) EUROCRYPT 2012. LNCS, vol. 7237, pp. 195–208. Springer, Heidelberg (2012)
7. Cramer, R., Damgård, I., Fehr, S.: On the cost of reconstructing a secret, or VSS with optimal reconstruction phase. In: Kilian, J. (ed.) CRYPTO 2001. LNCS, vol. 2139, pp. 503–523. Springer, Heidelberg (2001)
8. Cramer, R., Dodis, Y., Fehr, S., Padró, C., Wichs, D.: Detection of algebraic manipulation with applications to robust secret sharing and fuzzy extractors. In: Smart, N.P. (ed.) EUROCRYPT 2008. LNCS, vol. 4965, pp. 471–488. Springer, Heidelberg (2008)
9. Dolev, D., Dwork, C., Waarts, O., Yung, M.: Perfectly secure message transmission. In: FOCS 1990, pp. 36–45. IEEE Computer Society (1990)
10. Jhanwar, M.P., Safavi-Naini, R.: On the Share Efficiency of Robust Secret Sharing and Secret Sharing with Cheating Detection. In: Paul, G., Vaudenay, S. (eds.) INDOCRYPT 2013. LNCS, vol. 8250, pp. 179–196. Springer, Heidelberg (2013)
11. Jhanwar, M.P., Safavi-Naini, R.: Unconditionally-secure ideal robust secret sharing schemes for threshold and multilevel access structure. J. Mathematical Cryptology 7(4), 279–296 (2013)
12. Karnin, E.D., Greene, J.W., Hellman, M.E.: On secret sharing systems. IEEE Transactions on Information Theory 29(1), 35–41 (1983)
13. Kurosawa, K., Suzuki, K.: Almost secure (1-round, n-channel) message transmission scheme. IEICE Transactions 92-A(1), 105–112 (2009)
14. Obana, S.: Almost optimum t-cheater identifiable secret sharing schemes. In: Paterson, K.G. (ed.) EUROCRYPT 2011. LNCS, vol. 6632, pp. 284–302. Springer, Heidelberg (2011)
15. Obana, S., Araki, T.: Almost optimum secret sharing schemes secure against cheating for arbitrary secret distribution. In: Lai, X., Chen, K. (eds.) ASIACRYPT 2006. LNCS, vol. 4284, pp. 364–379. Springer, Heidelberg (2006)
16. Ogata, W., Eguchi, H.: Cheating detectable threshold scheme against most powerful cheaters for long secrets. Des. Codes Cryptography 71(3), 527–539 (2014)
17. Ogata, W., Kurosawa, K., Stinson, D.R.: Optimum secret sharing scheme secure against cheating. SIAM J. Discrete Math. 20(1), 79–95 (2006)
18. Padró, C., Sáez, G., Villar, J.L.: Detection of cheaters in vector space secret sharing schemes. Des. Codes Cryptography 16(1), 75–85 (1999)
19. Pieprzyk, J., Zhang, X.-M.: On cheating immune secret sharing. Discrete Mathematics & Theoretical Computer Science 6(2), 253–264 (2004)
20. Shamir, A.: How to share a secret. Communications of the ACM 22(11), 612–613 (1979)
21. Tompa, M., Woll, H.: How to share a secret with cheaters. J. Cryptology 1(2), 133–138 (1988)

Author Index

Printed in the United States
By Bookmasters